KV-169-305

THE NEW
ILLUSTRATED
ENCYCLOPEDIA OF
KNOWLEDGE

The new

ENCYCLOPEDIA OF

illustrated

KNOWLEDGE

Compiled under the supervision of J. O'Dell, Ph. D.

Illustrated by Cecile Curtis

SPRING BOOKS · LONDON

Published 1966 by
SPRING BOOKS
Drury House • Russell Street • London WC2

Printed in Czechoslovakia
by Tisk, Brno
T 1446

Preface

This encyclopedia is the first of a trilogy that has been designed specially for the needs of people at home and in schools and offices who require a quick, accurate source of information on a wide range of subjects. In this volume, devoted to general knowledge, are over 3,400 entries about people, places, events, history, philosophy, politics, religion, science, art and sport. Each entry is concise, up-to-date and comprehensive, and all are presented in strict alphabetical order for ease of reference. There are over 100 line drawings, of which 26 are detailed and carefully labelled diagrams, and over 200 photographs which were specially selected to illustrate the 14 main categories under which the majority of entries occur.

In preparation are two companion volumes:

The New Illustrated Encyclopedia of History

and

The New Illustrated Encyclopedia of The Bible

Each will deal comprehensively and authoritatively with its subject and will be an invaluable work of reference.

Illustrations

AACHEN (Fr. Aix-la-Chapelle), a city in North Rhine-Westphalia, West Germany, near the Belgian and Dutch borders. Pop. (1960) 167,593. A spa of long standing, it is also a road and rail junction and has automobile, textile and electrical industries. The cathedral was begun by Charlemagne and contains his remains; from his time until 1562, 28 Holy Roman emperors were crowned in the cathedral or in the Coronation Hall of the Rathaus, built in 1300 on the foundations of the old Carolingian palace. Two peace treaties were signed at Aachen: in 1668 between France and Spain whereby France received part of Flanders; and in 1748, terminating the War of the Austrian Succession. At a third conference, after the final defeat of Napoleon, the Allies agreed to withdraw their troops from France.

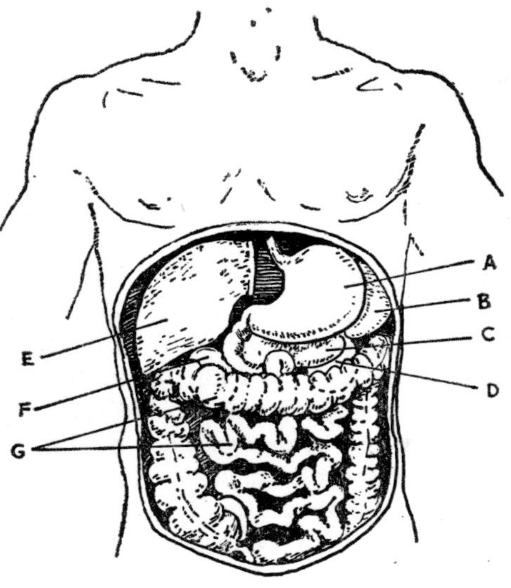

Abdomen
A. Stomach B. Spleen C. Pancreas D. Left kidney E. Liver F. Right kidney G. Intestines

ABBOT, George (1562—1633), Calvinist archbishop of Canterbury (1611—1627) and one of the translators of the New Testament in the King James's (Authorised) version of the Bible. Charles I deprived him of authority because of his refusal to give the king's prerogative precedence over law.

ABDOMEN, in man, the lower section of the trunk of the body, i.e. the body cavity below the diaphragm. This contains the liver, kidneys, pancreas, spleen, stomach and intestines and, in the female, the reproductive organs. The cavity is lined by the peritoneum, the inflammation of which is known as peritonitis.

ABEL, Sir Frederick Augustus (1827—1902), British chemist, who, with Sir James Dewar, invented cordite; he also made an instrument for determining flash-point of fuel oils.

ABÉLARD, Peter (1079—1142), French philosopher and theologian. Despite a tragic love affair with his pupil, Héloïse, whose father instigated his castration, he continued to lecture in Paris. The Church persecuted him for his rationalistic interpretation of the Trinitarian dogma. In his *Sic et Non* (Yes and No), which discussed differences of opinion among the Church Fathers, he developed a method of dialectic later widely accepted by Scholastic philosophers. The letters which passed between Abélard and Héloïse have been published.

ABERDEEN, George Hamilton Gordon, 4th Earl of (1784—1860), British statesman. As ambassador to Austria, he ensured Austrian support against Napoleon in 1813. He served in numerous posts under Wellington and Peel, and with the latter supported Catholic emancipation and the repeal of the Corn Laws. Prime Minister during the Crimean War, he resigned because of criticism of its mismanagement.

ABERDEEN, a city and port in East Scotland. Pop. (1961) 298,503. It is a large manufacturing centre with shipyards, iron foundries and factories for machinery and textiles, including jute. A fishing and commercial centre also, it has important cultural institutions including a magnificent university founded in 1494 and St Machar's Cathedral, which dates from 1136. Numerous granite quarries on its outskirts, which supply the building material for most of its houses, account for its name of 'The Granite City'. Aberdeen was incorporated in 1179.

ABOLITIONIST, a militant advocate of the abolition of Negro slavery in the United States, between 1830 and 1863. By means of the written and spoken word, the abolitionists fought for the immediate liberation of the slaves; some, like John Brown, resorting to the use of force.

ABORTION, technically the expulsion of the foetus before the 28th week of pregnancy, is in common usage a term reserved for induced abortion. In many countries this is a criminal offence unless performed to safeguard the mother's life. Abortion from accidental or pathological causes is known as a miscarriage; birth before full term as premature labour.

ABRAHAM (Abram), the Old Testament patriarch from whom both the Jewish people and many Arabian tribes trace their ancestry. Leaving his birthplace in Ur of the Chaldees *c.* 2000 B.C., he went to Palestine under God's command. According to tradition, he is the founder of monotheism, the belief in a single God.

ACADEMY, a garden in ancient Athens where Plato taught for 50 years and in which his followers met for nine centuries. The name is now applied to learned societies and, in the United States, designates a special secondary school.

ACHILLES, Greek hero of the Trojan War in Greek mythology. His mother, having learnt that he was fated to die at Troy, immersed him in the River Styx to make him invulnerable. However, the heel by which she held him was not protected by the charm of the waters and he was mortally wounded in it by Paris, at Troy.

ACIDS, chemical substances which neutralise alkalis to form salts, have a sour taste and turn blue litmus red. All acids contain hydrogen; dissolved in water they yield hydrogen ions (positively charged hydrogen atoms). Acids found in plant or animal substances are called organic acids. In industry the three mineral acids, sulphuric, hydrochloric and nitric, are of especial importance.

ACOUSTICS, the science of sound and of the conditions under which it is produced, transmitted and heard. The shape and size of a room, as well as the materials used in its construction and furnishings, affect its acoustics. The disturbing reflection and reverberation of sound may be diminished by the use of absorbent surfaces.

ACROPOLIS, the fortified rock or hill round which several ancient Greek cities were built. The most famous is the artificially enlarged hill which rises abruptly 150 ft above Athens; there stand the remains of the Doric Parthenon, a temple of Athene built in the 5th century B.C. In 1816 Lord Elgin bought fragments of the frieze and pediment figures from this temple, which are now in the British Museum. Other buildings on the Acropolis are the Erechtheum with its Caryatides, and the elaborate entrance, the Propylaea.

ADAM, the first man; according to Genesis the progenitor of all mankind. He was expelled from the Garden of Eden together with his wife, Eve, for having eaten from the Tree of Knowledge of Good and Evil. A similar legend existed in Babylonia. In later Jewish legend Adam was as big as the earth, and his first wife was Lilith. To the Manichaeans Adam was the son of Satan.

ADAM, Robert (1728—92), Scottish architect and furniture designer. His use of columns, and the decorative motifs of ancient Greece and Rome, created a style still bearing his name. With his brothers William, James and John, he designed Adelphi (Brothers) Terrace and Landsdowne House in London, and Register House in Edinburgh. His country houses include Harewood House, Kedleston Hall, Osterley Park House and Syon House, all fine examples of his style.

ADAMS, a family of early American statesmen. Samuel (1722—1803) was a leading spirit in the American Revolution and a signatory of the Declaration of Independence. His second cousin, John (1735—1826), was the second president of the United States and its first minister in London. His presidential years (1797—1801) were stormy. He founded the U.S. navy and its naval policy. His son, John Quincy (1767—1848), was the sixth president of the U.S. (1825—29). He served on a number of diplomatic missions, including missions to Britain and Russia. As Secretary of State he had a hand in the Monroe Doctrine, and acquired Florida for the U.S. from Spain.

ADANA, a city in southeast Turkey on the Seyhan River. Pop. (1960) 230,024. It is a trading centre in wool, cotton, corn and sesame. There are cotton mills and tobacco factories.

ADAPTATION, the ability of living organisms to adjust to environmental conditions. Those able to survive through structural specialisation transmit their variations to subsequent generations.

ADDIS ABABA, capital of Ethiopia. Pop. (1956) 400,000. Founded by Menelik II in 1887, on a plateau 8,000 ft above sea-level, it is near one of the sources of the Blue Nile. A commercial centre, it is connected by rail to Jibuti (486 miles) in French Somaliland.

ADDISON, Joseph (1672—1719), English essayist, poet and politician. After holding a number of government posts, he was elected to Parliament in 1708 where he served until his death. During this period he wrote a tragedy, *Cato*, which won fame. He is known chiefly for his essays published in Steele's *Tatler* and his own *Spectator*, the latter designed to appeal to a new middle class of readers, especially women.

ADEN, British Crown Colony and Protectorate, southwest Arabia. Pop. (1956) 152,000; area 75 sq. miles. The colony includes the island of Perim and the town of Aden, which has a good harbour. The town has a large oil refinery and is a commercial centre for adjacent Yemen and the African coast. The Protectorate (pop. 1959, 650,000; area 112,000 sq. miles) consists of the territories and dependencies of Arab chiefs. In 1963 Aden acceded to the South Arabian Federation, Britain retaining sovereignty over Aden.

ADENAUER, Konrad (1876—), West German statesman. In the years immediately following the Second World War, Adenauer organised the Christian Democratic Union and played a leading role in the establishment of the Federal Republic of Germany. He was elected Chancellor in 1949 and retained his position in subsequent elections (1953, 1957, 1961). He retired in 1963. During his tenure of office, West Germany made an amazing recovery from a war-ravaged state to become again one of the leading economic and industrial powers in Europe.

ADENOIDS, lymphatic tissue at the back of the nose and throat which, when infected, may become swollen and obstruct breathing through the nose, as well as causing catarrh and a characteristically vacant expression. The tonsils and adenoids serve the purpose of keeping out infectious germs, and their removal in infancy, once almost routine, is now less common; treatment with drugs when they become infected being the substitute. In adult life the adenoids tend to disappear.

ADLER, Alfred (1870—1937), Austrian psychiatrist, who joined Sigmund Freud's circle in 1902, but left it in 1911, rejecting Freud's emphasis on sex. He believed that a feeling of inferiority is the prime cause of personality aberrations. His school of Individual Psychology held that a striving to overcompensate for real or imaginary deficiencies leads to maladjustment.

ADMIRALTY ISLANDS, a group of 40 islands of the Bismarck Archipelago northeast of New Guinea, under Australian administration as a United Nations trust. Pop. (1958) 17,000; area *c.* 800 sq. miles. The chief island is Manus which contains the principal town Lorengau. The islands produce copra and pearls.

ADOLESCENCE, the period in the individual, marking the transition from childhood to maturity. It is accompanied by physical changes and is characterised by a striving for independence and new social adjustments.

ADRIATIC SEA, an arm of the Mediterranean between Italy, Yugoslavia and Albania. It is *c.* 500 miles long from the Gulf of Venice down to the Straits of Otranto, and ranges in width from 58—140 miles. The principal ports in the west are Venice, Ancona, Bari and Brindisi; in the east, Trieste, Rijeka (Fiume) and Durrës (Durazzo, in Albania).

AEGEAN CIVILISATION, the cultures of pre-Hellenic Greece in the Aegean region, particularly in Minoan Crete and at Mycenae on the Greek mainland. The Minoans may have reached Crete *c.* 4000 B.C., possibly from Asia Minor; from 1800 B.C. the great palaces, e.g. Knossos, were built, and Crete became a great empire based on overseas trade. The arts, showing Egyptian and Libyan influences,

Aegean Civilisation gem engraving (pre 2000 B.C.)

flourished, particularly fresco painting, gem engraving and pottery. Around 1400 B.C. Knossos and the other Cretan palaces were all destroyed, either by earthquake or by Achaean invaders from the north who had established themselves at Mycenae. Thereafter the Mycenaeans dominated the Aegean; their civilisation derived largely from the Cretan, but the political relationship between the two is still conjectural, especially since the discovery of pre-1400 inscriptions at Knossos which were written apparently in Greek (Linear Script B). In 1200 B.C. Dorians destroyed the civilisation of Mycenae.

AEGEAN SEA, an arm of the Mediterranean between Greece and Turkey. About 400 miles long and 200 miles wide, it has a very irregular shore line and is dotted with islands. The Dardanelles, Sea of Marmora and the Bosporus connect it with the Black Sea.

AERODYNAMICS, the science that studies the forces acting on bodies in motion in air, especially conditions affecting the flight of heavier-than-air craft, i.e. the mechanics of flight. Among the problems to be studied are the limitations set by the length of runway available in take-off and landing, and the design of airscrew, control surfaces (elevator, ailerons, rudder etc.), high-lift landing flaps, drag-brakes etc. The stability in flight of a projected new design is tested by experiments with scale models in wind tunnels, in which the effects of alterations to the area, shape or angle of incidence in wings or tail-plane are studied. The problems of streamlining, i.e. of minimising drag, friction and therefore heat, assume particular importance in aircraft designed to fly at supersonic speed; for these, strong, but thin wings of solid metal may be necessary.

AEROPLANE, a heavier-than-air craft (aircraft is a general term that includes airships, gliders etc.). Leonardo da Vinci (1452—1519) designed an aeroplane and Lilienthal's experiments with manned gliders were successful in 1891; but it was not until December 17, 1903 that Orville Wright achieved at Kitty Hawk, North Carolina, U.S.A., the first manned flight in a motor-powered heavier-than-air machine. In an aircraft he had designed with his brother Wilbur, he flew 59 secs. at 30 m.p.h. In 1909 Blériot flew the English Channel in 37 minutes. In 1919 the Atlantic was flown (Lindbergh completed the first solo flight in 1927), and in 1924 the first round-the-world flight was made by members of the U.S.A. Air Service. The first turbojet (German) flew in 1939 and the sound barrier was broken in 1947. A non-stop round-the-world flight-refuelled venture succeeded in 1949. In 1956 a British pilot exceeded 1,000 m.p.h.

Biplanes were normal until after the First World War, and a few triplanes were also flown, but monoplanes are now almost universal and, as speeds have increased, swept-back and delta wings have come into use.

Essential controls are elevators on the trailing edges of the horizontal tail-plane and the ailerons (for banking) on the outer section of the wings; these are both worked by the control column or wheel. The rudder on the vertical fin is controlled by a rudder bar. In high-speed craft the controls are power-assisted. The heavy traffic at big airports led to the invention of various aircraft approach aids. An early system (Instrument Landing System) used a radio beam from the ground to the aircraft indicating the runway; this was often combined with G.C.A. (Ground-Controlled Approach) in which an airport official watches the approaching aircraft on a radar screen and 'talks it down' by radio-telephone. The automatic pilot, a gyro-driven device to keep a plane on a given course, can also be coupled with I.L.S. See also Aerodynamics; Air Warfare; Glider; Helicopter; Hovercraft; Jet-Propulsion.

AESCHYLUS (525—456 B.C.), Greek tragic poet, whose plays are the earliest that have survived. Of his 90 plays only seven have come down to us; they include *The Persians*, *The Seven against Thebes*, *Prometheus Bound* and the trilogy known as the *Oresteia*, which treats the murder of Agamemnon by Clytaemnestra and its results. His main theme is hubris, the human arrogance that calls down retribution from the gods.

AESOP, the possibly legendary Phrygian slave of the 6th century B.C. who lived at the court of Croesus and to whom are attributed numerous fables of animal life, each with a moral. Some of them are undoubtedly of much earlier date. The fables are known to us only in a late translation, in the Greek language, of the 2nd century A.D.

AESTHETICS, the science of sense-perception and beauty. It tries to define the nature of beauty and how it may be perceived and expressed. Plato, Aristotle, St Thomas Aquinas, Kant and Hegel are particularly important amongst the many philosophers who have examined the concept of beauty.

AFGHANISTAN, Moslem kingdom in west central Asia. Pop. (1957) 13,000,000; area 253,000 sq. miles. Consisting mostly of a high plateau traversed by the steep mountain ranges of the Hindu Kush, Afghanistan has throughout history provided a highway to India through the Khyber Pass. In the fertile valleys and plains, cereals, fruits and vegetables are grown. There are few navigable rivers. The standard of living of the population — mostly nomads and peasants — is very low. Westernisation is resisted on religious grounds. Afghanistan's untapped natural wealth includes gold, lead, copper and oil. Grazig is next in importance to agriculture and the fat-tail sheep is indispensable for food and clothing. Karakul lamb-skins are exported. Horses are important. The climate is mostly dry, hot in daytime and cool at night with a range of 0°—100°F. between winter and summer. Rainfall usually occurs between October and April. The principal languages are Persian and Pushtu. Before achieving independence in 1921, it was virtually ruled by Britain which fought three wars (1838—80) to preserve it as a buffer state between India and Russia. The King, Mohammed Zahir Shah, has been trying to raise his country's standards by educational and economic measures. The capital is Kabul (pop. 310,000) and other principal cities are Kandahar (195,000) and Herat (150,000).

AFRICA, the second largest land division, is entirely surrounded by water.

Pop. (1960) 244,000,000; area 11,684,000 sq. miles. The peoples and languages of Africa are as diverse as its topographical and climatic conditions: to indicate the range it is sufficient to mention the Atlas Mountains in the north, the Sahara, the Rift Valley lakes, the jungle forests of equatorial Africa, the plateaux of the south, the Kalahari Desert, the islands (Madagascar is the largest). Even a single country, such as Nigeria, presents a wide variety of climate and terrain. Africa's principal rivers are the Nile, Congo, Niger and Zambesi. Mt Kilimanjaro (19,324 ft) is the highest mountain. Except for tigers, there are all kinds of big game animals, especially in East Africa. Natural resources include diamonds, gold, uranium, manganese and copper, as well as the oil and natural gas of the Sahara. The chief export crops are cocoa, oil palm products, cotton, groundnuts and sisal, together with varied hardwoods. While North Africa was one of the earliest centres of culture, the rest of the continent was virtually unknown to the West until the middle of the 15th century, when Portuguese navigators established trading centres along the coasts. Dutchmen, Danes, Englishmen and Frenchmen followed to trade with West Africa in gold, ivory and slaves. Extensive European colonisation and exploitation, however, did not begin until the 18th and 19th centuries when explorers such as James Bruce, Mungo Park, John Speke, David Livingstone, Sir Henry Stanley, Alexandre Serpa Pinto, Sir Richard Burton, Barth and many others brought back reports of fabulous wealth. The scramble for empire assumed wild proportions in the mid-19th century with the Netherlands, Britain, France, Belgium, Germany, Italy and Spain grabbing what the Portuguese did not own. Following the defeat of Germany in the First World War, progress towards political independence began. Since 1946 the free nations of Egypt, Ethiopia, Liberia and South Africa have been joined by Algeria, Cameroon, the Central African Republic, Chad, Congo (formerly French), Federal Congo Republic (formerly Belgian), Dahomey, Gabon, Gambia, Ghana, Guinea, Ivory Coast, Kenya, Libya, Malagasy Republic, Malawi (formerly Nyasaland), Mali, Mauritania, Morocco, Niger, Nigeria, Rwanda and Burundi, Senegal, Sierra Leone, Somalia, Sudan, Tanzania (formerly Tanganyika and Zanzibar), Togo, Tunisia, Upper Volta, Zambia (formerly Northern Rhodesia). Since Belgian withdrawal from the Congo it has oscillated between anarchy and civil war. Since the dissolution of the Central African Federation the situation in Southern Rhodesia has been politically uncertain. The Republic of South Africa, with its stringent segregation (apartheid) of the Bantu and the limitation of political and civil rights for non-whites, has come under sharp criticism in the United Nations Assembly.

AFRIKANERS, the Boers or inhabitants of South Africa who are of Dutch (or, to a lesser extent, German and Huguenot) ancestry, and speak Afrikaans, a simplified form of Dutch. They comprise over half the white population, and mostly belong to the Dutch Reformed Church. From 1836 the *Boer Voortrekkers* made the Great Trek from the Cape to the northern interior, away from British interference, and from that time relations between them and British settlers have not been good. Today the Afrikaners dominate the ruling Nationalist party which is responsible for the policy of *apartheid* (q.v.). They are sometimes erroneously called Afrikanders, which is the name of a local breed of cattle.

AGINCOURT (Azincourt), a village in northeast France where, in 1415, English archers under Henry V, armed with the longbow, defeated a far larger army of heavily armoured French knights. The French lost some 10,000 dead, the English a few hundred only.

AGRICULTURE, the tilling of the soil, e.g. preparing, sowing, planting, reaping and, if necessary, irrigating it. Related activities include the rearing of livestock, fruit farming, forestry and the processing of foods at home. Agriculture forms the basis of all civilisation. When early man began to engage in it, he gave up his nomadic existence and settled down. The forms of agriculture are varied, depending on such factors as climate, soil, availability of land, nearness to market and degree of mechanisation.

AGNOSTIC, one who holds no belief in religious matters, and maintains that there is no evidence to prove or disprove the existence of God or the immortality of the soul.

AIR WARFARE. Captive observation balloons were used in the Napoleonic Wars. The Austrians attacked Venice with pilotless bomb-carrying balloons in 1849. Britain and Germany built reconnaissance airships before 1914. Aircraft took part in military manoeuvres in Britain in 1910; the next year an air battalion of the Royal Engineers was formed and in 1912 the Royal Flying Corps was inaugurated (to become the R.A.F. in 1918). At the beginning of the First World War aircraft were used mainly on reconnaissance, but on October 8, 1914 a Royal Naval Air Service pilot dropped small bombs on the Zeppelin sheds at Düsseldorf with good effect, and on Christmas Day Germans bombed Dover and British seaplanes raided Cuxhaven. In fighter planes the Germans were first with a machine gun that fired through the propeller; when both sides had this, the era of intensely individualistic 'dog-fights' began; they were succeeded by the tactics of the German Richthofen 'Circus' which fought as a team. Zeppelins proved far too vulnerable for bombing raids. German aircraft raids had more success and Allied aircraft bombed Rhineland towns and even as far away as Stuttgart. Aircraft carriers were used in 1918 and their bombers torpedoed ships and bombed shore targets. Propaganda leaflets were also dropped on Germany.

Between the wars air transport for troops was developed. In the Second World War night-fighters were used to defend London, 'pathfinders' pin-pointed targets with flares for mass raids and aircraft dropped agents, equipment and propaganda behind enemy lines. The Germans had great success in 1940 with Stuka dive-bombers operating just ahead of armoured columns. The Japanese introduced the Kamikaze or suicide bomber, which was crashed on to ships, doing great damage. The Germans used radio to find targets, and the war ended with the radio-controlled V1 flying bomb and the V2 rockets launched against London from occupied France, Belgium and Holland; and atomic bombs over Japan. The U.S. Air Force concentrated on daylight precision bombing, the British on mass raids at night, using radar devices which facilitated the identification of invisible targets. A radar network ringed Britain and improved predictors guided anti-aircraft fire. Helicopters and napalm bombs were used in the Korean War. Since then the stand-off bomb has been developed, rocket-powered and guided, launched from aircraft distant from the target.

ALABAMA, U.S. Gulf state. Pop. (1960) 3,266,740; area 51,609 sq. miles. There are low hills in the northeast and the south is a fertile coastal plain. Apart from the iron and steel industry in the

This wine cask was found in the ruins of the palace of Knossos, Crete. *c.* 1500 B.C.

Photo: Greek National Tourist Office

A beautifully decorated Greek vase from Attica, 7th century B.C.

Photo: Saint-Raymond Museum, Toulouse

A *krater*, a bowl in which wine and water were mixed, depicting a fight between Hercules and Antaeus. Greek, 6th century B.C.

Photo: Photographic Archives, Paris

Bronze was an alloy frequently used by the Romans. This tripod comes from Herculaneum. *c.* 100 B.C.

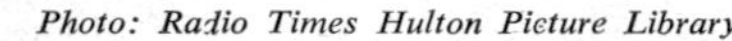

Photo: Radio Times Hulton Picture Library

A majolica dish from Faenza, Italy. Majolica, tin-enamelled ware with painted designs, became fashionable in the 15th century.

Photo: Victoria & Albert Museum

A fine example of Chinese Ming porcelain: a 14th century A.D. incense burner.

Photo: Victoria & Albert Museum

Birmingham region, based on near-by coal and iron ore, the state is predominantly agricultural; the chief crops are cotton, maize, groundnuts and oats. The first permanent settlement was founded at Mobile in 1711. Alabama became the 22nd state of the U.S. in 1819. A slave-owning state, it was a member of the Confederacy. The capital is Montgomery (pop. 134,397). Other principal cities are Birmingham (340,887) and Mobile (202,779). One-third of the population is Negro.

ALASKA, the largest U.S. state, lies at the northwest extremity of North America. Pop. (1960) 226,167; area 571,065 sq. miles. Mountainous and arctic, it contains the highest peak in North America, Mt McKinley (20,320 ft). Its principal product is canned salmon; its mineral resources include gold, silver and coal and the timber potential is great. Wild life abounds but the fur trade has dwindled. Discovered by Bering in 1741, the first settlement was established on Kodiak Island in 1784. Until 1867, when it was sold to the U.S. for $ 7,200,000, it was a Russian possession. Gold was discovered in 1897 in the Yukon valley. Alaska became a U.S. state in 1959. The capital is Juneau (pop. 6797). Other principal towns are Anchorage (44,237) and Fairbanks (13,311). The last is linked by the Alaskan Highway to Dawson Creek (1523 miles) in British Columbia; the Highway was built by the U.S. Army in 1942 and is maintained, over most of its length, by Canada. Military, naval and air bases were built in Alaska during the Second World War.

ALBANIA, a People's Republic (since 1946) in southeast Europe in the Balkan Peninsula. Pop. (1959) 1,556,000; area 10,629 sq. miles. Except for a fertile coastal strip and the basin around Koritsa, Albania is mountainous. Communications are poor. The principal rivers are the Drin, Vijose and Shkumb. Partly exploited mineral wealth consists of copper, bitumen, petroleum and chrome. Agriculture and stock raising are the chief occupations. A colony of the Greeks, it was ruled in turn by Macedonians, Romans, Byzantines, Serbs, Bulgars, and then fell, on the death of Skanderbeg, to the Ottoman Turks, who ruled it from the 15th century until it became independent in 1912, only to be annexed by Italy from 1939 to 1945. Most of the population (65 %) is Moslem. The capital is Tirana (pop. 80,000), of which Durrës (Durazzo) is the port.

ALBERT, Prince Francis Augustus Charles Emmanuel (1819—61), Consort of Queen Victoria, second son of the Duke of Saxe-Coburg-Gotha and father of Edward VII. He married Queen Victoria, his first cousin, in 1840. He was admired for his tact, public spirit, interest in scientific development and the arts; the Great Exhibition of 1851 was inspired by him.

ALBERTA, a Canadian province. Pop. (1959) 1,243,000; area 255,285 sq. miles. The southern part is prairie, the central section is partly wooded and the north has large forests. The Jasper and other national parks are situated in the foothills of the Rocky Mountains to the west. There are many lakes. Graincrops are extensively grown. Alberta has rich coal deposits, petroleum and natural gas. Fur trappers first came to the region in the latter part of the 18th century. It became part of Canada in 1870. The capital is Edmonton (pop. 260,733). Other principal cities are Calgary (218,418), Lethbridge (32,780) and Medicine Hat (21,740).

ALBIGENSES, a religious sect which appeared in southern France in the 11th century; it was one of the western Manichaean sects, collectively known as the Cathari. They divided themselves into believers *(credentes)* and initiates *(perfecti)*, the latter being celibate, pacifist and vegetarian. The Albigenses were ruthlessly put down and almost exterminated when a crusade was declared against them in 1205; in the struggle a brilliant Provençal civilisation was destroyed.

ALCHEMY, the medieval search for the 'philosopher's stone' which would transmute base metals into gold, and for the elixir of life (the secret of eternal life); it obsessed the minds of many learned men from the 12th to the 17th centuries, but laid the foundations of modern chemistry.

ALCOHOL, an organic compound containing one or more hydroxyl (—OH) groups replacing hydrogen atoms. The term generally refers to ethyl or grain alcohol derived from fruits or grains, which has stimulating and intoxicating effects. Alcohol is used extensively in medicine and industry. Industrial alcohol is always denatured or methylated, i.e. rendered unfit to drink, and therefore not liable to taxation.

ALEUTIAN ISLANDS, a chain of four groups of about 150 sparsely inhabited islands curving 1200 miles from south-west Alaska, the U.S. state of which they form part, almost to the Kamchatka peninsula in Siberia. Pop. (1960) 5745; area 6391 sq. miles. They are mountainous, with a number of active volcanoes. Unalaska, the largest island, contains the two principal settlements of Unalaska and Dutch Harbor, a naval base.

ALEXANDER, the name of three kings of Scotland. Alexander I (1078—1124) quelled an insurrection early in his reign. He upheld the supremacy of the Scottish church. Alexander II (1198—1249) exchanged lands in England with Henry III. Alexander III (1241—1285) acquired the Western Isles and the Isle of Man from Norway. His death marked the end for a long time of friendly relations between England and Scotland.

ALEXANDER THE GREAT (356–323 B.C.), King of Macedon, conqueror of the cradles of Western civilisation. Largely educated by Aristotle, he made himself ruler of Greece after ascending the throne in 336. He then defeated the Persians, conquered most of Asia Minor and overran Syria, Palestine and Lower Egypt, founding the city of Alexandria. In 331 he finally defeated Darius at Arbela (Gaugamela). Pushing on through what is now Afghanistan and across the Hindu Kush, he conquered the Punjab and returned to Babylon, where he died of a fever. His adoption of Oriental manners and his belief in the fusion of the Persian and Macedonian peoples into one, led to a mutiny which he suppressed. Although his empire disintegrated after his death, the Greek culture he brought to it profoundly affected the course of history.

ALEXANDRIA, the chief port of Egypt, on the Mediterranean. Pop. (1959) 1,416,000. It is a commercial and industrial centre manufacturing chemicals and foodstuffs. Founded by Alexander the Great in 332 B.C., it was the capital of Egypt during the Ptolemaic period (304—30 B.C.), when it became a centre of Hellenistic art, science and learning. It retained its commercial and cultural importance under Roman rule and was a centre of Christianity under the Byzantines. The famous library founded *c.* 284 B.C. was burnt when Julius Caesar besieged the city; it was said to have been replaced and destroyed twice more, the last time by the Arabs when they took Alexandria in 641. Thereafter, the city's decline was rapid.

ALFRED THE GREAT (849—900), King of Wessex (871—99). He continued the wars of Aethelwulf, his father, and his brothers against the Danes, eventually defeating them; assuring the Anglo-Saxon character of England. The Danish leader and his followers were baptised and agreed to retire into the Danelaw, where they continued masters of north-east England. Alfred strengthened the army and navy and revived learning among clergy and laymen. Importing scholars from abroad, he himself set an example by learning Latin and translating Latin works into Anglo-Saxon. The compilation of the *Anglo-Saxon Chronicle* was begun on Alfred's initiative, and contains an account of his wars against the Danes.

ALGAE, simple flowerless plants containing chlorophyll, among the lowest forms of plant life and varying in size from green pond scums to seaweed hundreds of feet long. Algae are almost all water plants and can manufacture their own food. They are subdivided into Brown and Red (some of which are edible) and Green algae, and diatoms, which are found as plankton.

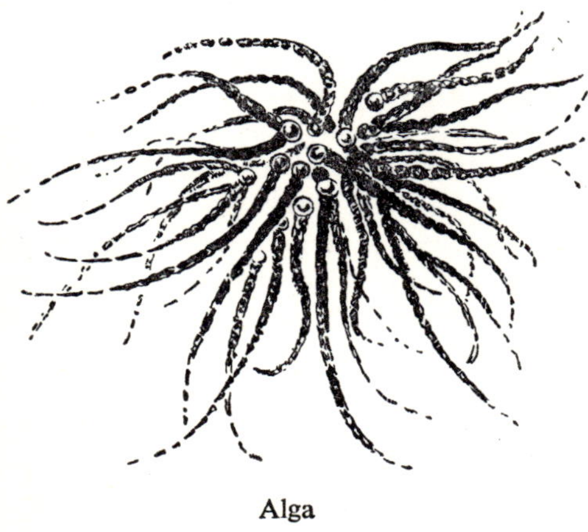

Alga

ALGEBRA, a form of mathematics employing symbols representing numbers in order to make more generalised, results possible. The basic tools are formulae and equations. Algebra was introduced to the West by the Arabs, but it had been developed centuries earlier in Egypt, India and China.

$$f(x) = (5y_1 + 6y_2)^2 - (3y_1 + 10y_2)^2;$$
$$= 16y_1^2 - 64y_2^2$$

Algebraic equation

ALGERIA, a republic in North Africa, on the Mediterranean. Pop. (1960) 9,529,726; area 919,600 sq. miles. From north to south it consists of the mountains and valleys of the Tell Atlas, parallel to the coast, the High Plateaux, and the Saharan Atlas and desert regions of the south. The principal crops are cereal, potatoes, artichokes, beans, peas and tomatoes, grown mostly in the north. Tobacco, the vine, dates, oranges, olives and other fruits are cultivated. There is some timber, and livestock breeding and fishing are important. Algeria has deposits of iron, phosphates, coal, zinc, lead, barytes and petroleum. Highly developed under the Romans in ancient times, it subsequently regressed considerably. In 1518 it came under Turkish control and was for 300 years the headquarters of the Barbary pirates. The French occupied Algiers in 1830 and completed their conquest of the entire country in 1901. French colonists settled in the country and gave much of it a European aspect. In 1954, a revolt of the Moslems — who constituted about 85 % of the population — broke out and resulted in seven years of bloody warfare. In March 1962 a cease-fire agreement was signed. Although the French settlers continued their opposition to the granting of independence to Algeria and their terroristic attacks against both the Moslem population and the French authorities responsible for the transition period, Algeria became independent the following July, but voted to maintain co-operative relations with France. Algeria joined the Arab League in 1962. The capital is Algiers (pop. 1959 750,000). Other important cities are Oran (pop. 1954, 274,722) and Constantine (11,315). The abundant oil and natural gas of the Sahara region are of the highest importance.

ALHAMBRA, a Moorish palace and fortress in Granada, Spain. Built between 1248 and 1354, it is the most perfect specimen of Moorish architecture in the country. The walls and ceilings of the buildings, constructed around open courtyards, are decorated with arabesque, Arabic writing and geometric tracery.

Geometric tracery. Alhambra Palace, Granada, Spain

ALKALI, a soluble member of the chemical group known as bases (q.v.), and a hydroxide of such metals as sodium, potassium and lithium. It liquefies in air and is soluble in water, turning red litmus blue. Alkali solutions neutralise acids, forming a salt and water. Examples are household ammonia, caustic soda, caustic potash and slaked lime. Alkalis are of particular importance to the glass, soap, paper and rayon industries.

ALLEGORY, a narrative, painting or sculpture which has a deeper meaning than the obvious signification (e.g. *The Pilgrim's Progress*). A parable is an allegory, but by usage the latter term has come to refer to a less didactic, more detailed narrative.

ALLENBY, Edmund, 1st Viscount (1861—1936), British soldier. After serving in Bechuanaland and Zululand, he fought in the Boer War. In the First World War he distinguished himself in the cavalry and commanded the expeditionary force which drove the Turks from Palestine. During 1919—25 he was High Commissioner in Egypt.

ALLERGY, an extreme sensitivity to substances (usually proteins) ordinarily harmless, resulting in inflammation. It may be a reaction to a food, drug, plant or animal product such as feathers. It is caused by an inability to produce antibodies in specific cases, and this usually stems from a hereditary predisposition or emotional sensitivity. Examples are hay fever, caused by sensitivity to certain kinds of pollen, and some cases of asthma.

ALLOY, a mixture of two or more metallic elements or of metals and non-metals. It exhibits the general characteristics of a metal. An alloy may combine the best features of its components or may take on entirely new properties, e.g. a little tungsten alloyed with steel produces an exceedingly hard metal used in making cutting tools. Among the commoner alloys are brass (copper and zinc) and pewter (tin and lead). If an alloy contains mercury it is called an amalgam.

ALPHA PARTICLES, a combination of two positively charged protons and two neutrons, as in the nucleus of helium, emitted at high velocities from the nuclei of certain radioactive elements. Streams of these (alpha rays) ionise gases, produce fluorescence on a fluorescent screen, and are so easily absorbed by matter that they can be stopped by a sheet of tissue paper. A substance which emits alpha particles does not, with rare exceptions, emit beta particles, and vice versa.

ALPHABET (from alpha and beta, the first two letters of the Greek alphabet), a series of letters representing graphically the sounds of speech. The earliest alphabets consisted of stylized pictures representing ideas, objects or syllables, called pictographs. A further step was the use of the pictograph to represent a sound or its most conspicuous element. The system of using a single symbol to stand for an individual sound is believed to have originated in the Sinai peninsula. The first purely phonetic alphabet was used by the Phoenicians, from whom it passed with modifications to the Greeks. The latter adapted certain characters to represent vowels lacking in the original Semitic script. Further developments took place in Italy, whence all modern West European alphabets derive.

ALPS, the chief mountain range in Europe. Covering much of Switzerland, Austria, parts of northern Italy, southern Germany and southeastern France, they swing in a great half-circle from the Mediterranean to the Adriatic. They are cut by many passes, the most important being the Brenner and St Bernard passes. Tunnels have been cut through the smaller mountains and, in 1962, under Mont Blanc. The Rhine, Rhône and Po rivers are fed by Alpine waters. The beautiful valleys are dotted with lakes and famous resorts. The highest peaks are Mont Blanc (15,782 ft), Monte Rosa (15,151), the Weisshorn (14,803) and the Matterhorn (14,780).

ALSACE, a region and former province of eastern France bordering on Germany on the Rhine river. A fertile agricultural area, it is famous for its wines. Its chief city is Strasbourg (pop. 200,900). It changed hands many times before it was lost to Germany with Lorraine in 1871; it was restored to France in 1919, and again lost (1940—44) in the Second World War. It was restored again in 1945.

ALUMINIUM, the most abundant metal on earth, but one found only in combination with other elements, from which its separation is often impracticable. The chief source is bauxite, which is widely distributed. Aluminium forms light, strong alloys with other metals, and is of particular importance in aircraft construction.

AMAZON, in Greek legend, a tribe of female warriors whose kingdom bordered on the Black Sea; their right breasts were cut off so that they could use the bow. Men were excluded from their country, the women going elsewhere to mate.

AMAZON River, a river in northern Brazil, the second largest river in the world. Rising in the Andes Mountains in Peru, it flows eastward for 3900 miles to enter the Atlantic above Belem. Its drainage basin comprises about 2,700,000 sq. miles. It traverses thick jungle country where more than 200 tributaries empty into it. Ocean vessels can sail 1000 miles upstream to Manaus and smaller ships can proceed for another 1000 miles. Discovered by Vicente Pinzon in 1500, it was first navigated by Francisco de Orellana in 1540—41.

AMENHOTEP III (Amenophis), Egyptian pharaoh of the 18th dynasty (*c.* 1405—1370 B.C.). He ruled from Thebes an empire extending from Mesopotamia to Ethiopia, and his reign was renowned for an advanced style of architecture and sculpture, of which only the ruins at Thebes still remain.

AMERICAN INDEPENDENCE, War of (1775—83). Originally a protest by the thirteen American colonies against the British colonial policy of taxation without representation, the subsequent conflict eventually culminated in their independence. Open hostility broke out in a skirmish at Lexington (April 1775) and the battle of Bunker Hill (June), and in 1776 the colonies issued the Declaration of Independence (July 4). The colonial army under the command of George Washington suffered initial military setbacks, but with the aid of its French, Spanish and Dutch allies succeeded in forcing the British forces under Cornwallis to surr nder at Yorktown (1781). In 1783 a treaty of peace was signed in Versailles.

AMERICAN LITERATURE. Early American literature was an offshoot of British, the main difference being in emphasis and approach. The 17th-century authors were concerned chiefly with history, travel or theology. Writers of the 18th century included the theologian Jonathan Edwards, the philosopher Benjamin Franklin and political writers such as Thomas Paine. The first poet to write on local themes was Philip Freneau. Royall Tyler wrote the first American comedy and William Hill Brown the first novel. Washington Irving (1783—1859) was the first American writer to achieve recognition in Europe, with his romantic tales of early America. James Fenimore Cooper (1789—1851) wrote of a recent heroic past and Herman Melville (1819—91) produced one of the world's masterpieces in *Moby Dick*. To this period belong America's first outstanding poet, William Cullen Bryant (1794—1878) and the poet prophet of American democracy, Walt Whitman (1819—92). Edgar Allan Poe (1809—49) wrote haunting poetry, and short stories unique for their moods of horror, including *The Murders in the Rue Morgue*, usually regarded as the first detective story. Abolitionism inspired such writers as William Lloyd Garrison, the poet Whittier and the novelist, Harriet Beecher Stowe (*Uncle Tom's Cabin*, 1825). Ralph Waldo Emerson was the poet and essayist of the pre-Civil War period, a period notable also for the writer and philosopher Henry David Thoreau, author of *Walden*, and the poets Henry Wadsworth Longfellow and James Russell Lowell, the latter also a critic. Oliver Wendell Holmes, poet and novelist, is remembered also for his wit. Nathaniel Hawthorne, the first American novelist of outstanding importance, wrote chiefly of Puritan New England. A turn to realism and regional writing marked the post-Civil War period, flavoured by the humour and irony of Mark Twain (1835—1910). Bret Harte, Edward Eggleston and Hamlin Garland were spokesmen of the new West; while William Dean Howells and Sarah Orne Jewett described New England; Thomas Nelson Page, George Washington Cable and Ellen Glasgow the South; James Whitcomb Riley and Booth Tarkington the Middle West; Jack London Canada; and Henry James (q.v.: 1843—1916) wrote of the American in Europe. Edith Wharton (1862—1937), Willa Cather (1876—1947) and Stephen Crane (1871—1900) dealt with psychological problems. O. Henry (William Sydney Porter) was the master of the short story with a surprise ending. The 19th-century American drama imitated the sentimentality of its European counterpart. After the First World War American literature passed through periods of attacking social evils, racialism and narrow nationalism. Greater freedom of expression, an increasing preoccupation with history, and expanding conceptions of the world brought a new spirit to American literature: Upton Sinclair exposed economic evils, and John Steinbeck and Erskine Caldwell portrayed the underprivileged. Sinclair Lewis (1885—1951) pinned down the Middle West Philistine in *Babbitt* and *Main Street*. William Faulkner (1897—1962) in a series of brilliant works minutely studied the deliquescence of Southern society. Ernest Hemingway developed a new style of tough, crisp dialogue and produced an unforgettable picture of the Spanish Civil War in *For Whom the Bell Tolls*. Theodore Dreiser's novels were serious studies of modern social problems and James Branch Cabell in his *Jurgen* (1919) startled America with his novel approach to sex. The Jazz Age of the 1920s the Depression years of the 1930s were described by F. Scott Fitzgerald, Christopher Morley and John P. Marquand. James Gould Cozzens, Norman Mailer and Irwin Shaw have written important novels about the Second World War. John Dos Passos developed a staccato, impressionistic narrative technique. Sherwood Anderson and, in more recent times, Truman Capote and Eudora Welty have written regional novels of significance. Thomas Wolfe produced a series of long semi-autobiographical novels; Katherine Anne Porter has written distinguished novels and critical essays. Humorists have included Ring Lardner, Dorothy Parker, S. J. Perelman, Leonard Ross and the unique James Thurber and Damon Runyon. Eugene O'Neill was the first great American dramatist. Important plays have also been written by Maxwell Anderson, Thornton Wilder, Arthur Miller, Tennessee Williams, Lillian Hellman and S. N. Behrman. In addition to the work of T. S. Eliot, Ezra Pound and Robert Frost (qq.v.), contributions to American poetry have been made by Edgar Lee Masters, Vachel Lindsay, Carl Sandburg, Wallace Stevens, William Carlos Williams, Hart Crane, E. E. Cummings, Marianne Moore, Archibald MacLeish, John Crowe Ransom and Theodore Roethke. Newer notable poets are Robert Lowell, John Ciardi, and Muriel Ruckeyser. Van Wyck Brooks and Edmund Wilson have made their names as critics and literary historians.

AMOEBA, a microscopic single cell animal found in water, soil and on the bodies of other animals. It has no mouth but assimilates food through extensions of its body which flow out around the food organism and enclose it. It reproduces asexually: amoeba rounds up into a spherical mass and constricts until two separate amoebas are produced, each containing a nucleus. It is one of the most primitive forms of animal life.

AMSTERDAM, the constitutional capital of the Netherlands, on the Amstel River and North Sea Canal. Pop. (1960) 869,602. It is a commercial and financial city whose industries include diamond-cutting, shipyards, tanneries, chemicals, breweries, foodstuffs and tobacco. The port is approached by three canals, the width of which restrict the size of shipping that can use the extensive harbours. It is a cultural and educational centre and an international market for paintings and objects of art. Amsterdam was a leading European commercial centre in the 17th century.

AMU DARYA (Oxus), see River.

AMUNDSEN, Roald (1872—1928), Norwegian polar explorer. He navigated the North-West Passage and fixed the position of the north magnetic Pole. In 1911

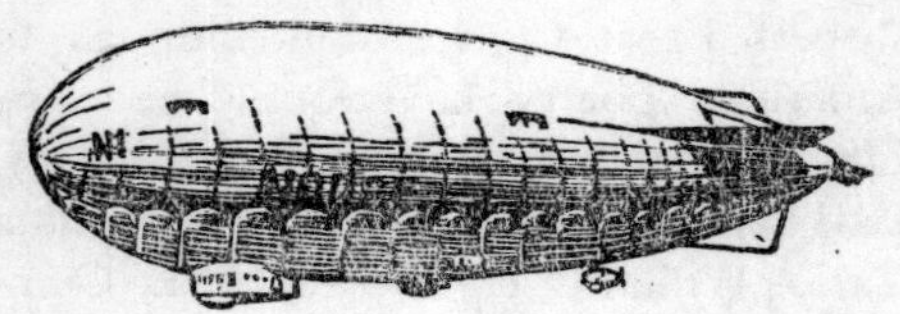

Airship in which Amundsen and Nobile flew over North Pole

he was first to reach the South Pole, a month before Captain Scott. With General Nobile he travelled by airship over the North Pole in 1926, and was killed when trying to rescue Nobile on his second expedition to the Pole.

AMUR, see River.

ANABAPTISTS, a 16th-century Protestant sect so named by their enemies because they held that only adult baptism is valid. Active in central Europe during the Reformation, they believed in the responsibility of each individual solely to God, and in the absolute brotherhood of Christ.

ANAESTHESIA, the loss of feeling or sensation. It is induced temporarily to make a patient insensitive to pain during surgical treatment. In general anaesthesia the patient is totally unconscious. A local anaesthetic leaves the patient conscious but induces loss of all sense of feeling in a part of the body.

ANARCHISM, a political theory advocating the abolition of the state, regarded as a source of oppression, inequality and injustice, and the introduction of flexible voluntary organisations that could be adjusted to meet new needs of society as they arose. Mikhail Bakunin (1814—76) introduced terrorism and revolution into anarchist ideology; Prince Kropotkin (1842—1921) advocated a gentler form of anarchism. Anarchism as a political movement no longer exists.

ANATOMY, the science of the form and structure of living organisms. A knowledge of anatomy is obtained by dissecting the organisms and by studying the size, position, function and relationship of parts as well as the whole.

ANAXAGORAS (*c.* **500—428** B.C.), Greek philosopher of Thrace. Paving the way for atomic theory, he held that all things have been formed by Nous (Mind, Intelligence) from their minutely fragmented state in Chaos, implying, unlike his forerunners, that there is a purpose in life. He taught Euripides, Pericles (whose eloquence saved Anaxagoras after he had been arrested for opposing the polytheistic religion of the day), and possibly Socrates.

ANCESTOR WORSHIP, the belief that dead ancestors continue to take an active part in the affairs of their living descendants. Prayers or religious rites may be addressed to them, and ill fortune attributed to their anger.

ANDALUSIA, a region of southern Spain facing Africa, famous for its sherry. Citrus fruit is grown and cattle raised in the south. Andalusia is ringed by mountains and is rich in minerals, e.g. copper at Rio Tinto, and lead. The Moorish conquest has left its mark on architecture, language and song. The principal towns are Málaga, Granada and Córdova.

ANDAMAN ISLANDS, a group of islands in the Bay of Bengal. Pop. (1961, with the Nicobar Islands but excluding the aborigines, who have never been counted) 63,438; area 3215 sq. miles. The inhabitants are mostly Negrito Stone Age aborigines and settlers from the mainland. Together with the Nicobar Islands to the south they constitute a territory of the Republic of India. Copra, timber, rubber and coffee are exported. There is a fine harbour at Port Blair, the capital. From 1858 to 1942 some of the islands were used by the Government of India as a penal settlement.

ANDERSEN, Hans Christian (1805—75), Danish author who, born into the least propitious of family circles, left for Copenhagen at the age of 14 and became, after initial difficulties, one of the world's most famous writers of fairy tales, the first instalment of which was published in 1835. He also wrote sketches, travel books and novels: and it was a novel, *The Improvisatore,* that gave him his first success.

ANDES MOUNTAINS, a mountain range of South America, extending in two approximately parallel chains along its entire western coast. The mountains rise abruptly out of the Pacific and extend for 4500 miles from the Isthmus of Panama in the north to Cape Horn in the south. There are numerous volcanoes, including Cotopaxi, the world's highest active volcano (19,334 ft). The range has many glaciers, especially in southern Chile. The highest peak in the western hemisphere, Aconcagua (23,091 ft), is in Argentina near the Chilean border. There are abundant and varied mineral deposits, e.g. gold, silver, platinum, tin and mercury. The only rail routes across the Andes start from Santiago and Antofagasta.

ANDORRA, a republic in the Pyrenees mountains. Pop. (1960) 6500; area 191 sq. miles. Semi-independent, it has been under the joint suzerainty of France and the Spanish bishops of Urgel since 1278. It is cut by gorges and defiles. The Catholic Catalan-speaking inhabitants reside mostly in six villages. Sheep-grazing is the chief occupation. The capital is Andorra-la-Vieja.

ANDREA DEL SARTO (1486—1531), Florentine painter. A master of colour and texture, his frescoes, in the High Renaissance style, include *The Birth of the Virgin* and *Madonna del Sacco.* Among his paintings are *Madonna delle Arpie, The Sacrifice of Abraham* and several of the Holy Family. He was ruined by his wife's extravagance, and is the subject of a poem by Browning.

ANGEL, a supernatural being commonly conceived as an emissary of God. In later Christian belief there were hierarchies of angels: the Seraphim and Cherubim, the Principalities and Powers, etc. The chief archangels are traditionally given as Michael, Gabriel and Raphael. In Milton's *Paradise Lost* the Devil (as Lucifer) is the leader of the fallen angels who rebelled against God.

ANGELICO FRA, (1387—1455), Italian painter. Born in Tuscany, he entered the Dominican order in 1408. He executed paintings for his order in Fiesole, Cortona and Florence, and was summoned to Rome by the Pope in *c.* 1446. A saintly and ascetic man, he painted only religious pictures, among the finest of which are the frescoes in San Marco, Florence, and the *Coronation of the Virgin,* Uffizi Gallery, Florence. The tranquil beauty of his compositions, together with his mastery of colour, establishes him as one of the greatest Quattrocento painters.

ANGELL, Sir Norman (1874—), British economist, journalist and author. He achieved prominence with his pacifist work, *The Great Illusion* (1910) which showed prophetically that in modern conditions victory in war brings as little profit as defeat. He was a Labour member of Parliament (1929—31) and was awarded the Nobel Peace Prize for 1933.

ANGKOR, an ancient city in northwest Cambodia. Built in the 9th century A.D. as the capital of the Khmers, it later had a population of a million people; it was captured by the Siamese in 1431 and then abandoned. Discovered in 1860 under a thick jungle growth, the impressive ruins of temples, palaces and public buildings are covered with bas-reliefs.

Relief from Angkor-Vat, Cambodia

ANGLICAN, a term applied to the Church of England (q.v.).

ANGLING, fishing for sport, takes three main forms: coarse fishing for freshwater fish, fly-fishing for salmon or trout, and sea fishing, from boat or waterside. In coarse fishing, ground-bait is thrown into the water and the hook is baited with worms or bread paste. Coarse fish include roach, perch, pike, chub, tench, dace and grayling. In fly-fishing, the fly is artificial, constructed with considerable care for trout, but salmon will take anything bright. The fly is cast on the surface (dry fly) for trout, or below (wet fly) for salmon. Salmon and trout may also be caught by trolling spinners of bright metal. One form of sea fishing is big-game fishing for tunny, barracuda, shark, swordfish etc., all of which are capable of fighting for hours.

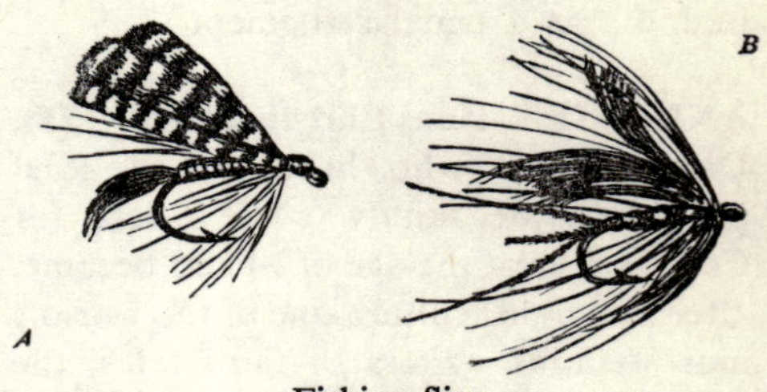

Fishing flies
A. Wet fly B. Dry fly

ANGLO-SAXONS, Germanic settlers of Britain in the 5th and 6th centuries A.D. who subsequently formed an important element in the British nation. The Jutes from the lower Rhine took possession of Kent, the Isle of Wight and the coast of Hampshire, introducing a culture more akin to that of the Franks than the Angles and Saxons. The Saxons, pirates from the Schleswig-Holstein area, settled chiefly in the coastal areas of Wessex, Essex and Sussex, and also in Middlesex. The Angles came from Jutland to East and Middle Anglia and to Northumbria. The seven Anglo-Saxon kingdoms formed the Heptarchy in the 8th century.

ANGOLA (Portuguese West Africa), a Portuguese colony in southwest Africa. Pop. (1960) 4,550,000; area 481,351 sq. miles. Primarily an agricultural country, it has excellent grazing land. It is rich in diamonds and has large deposits of copper and lignite. Palm oil, coffee and maize are exported. The Portuguese first explored and settled the coastal region 1482—85. The port of Lobito is an outlet, by the Benguela Railway, for the mines of Katanga and the Rhodesian Copper Belt. The capital is Luanda (pop. 1960 190,000).

ANHWEI, an inland province in east

central China. Pop. (1953) 30,343,637; area 54,319 sq. miles. The Yangtze River separates the province into a plain in the north and mountainous, fertile areas in the south. Rice, cotton, silk and tea are produced. The capital is Hofei (pop. 1956 220,000).

ANIMISM, the belief, in primitive societies, which attributes consciousness to objects of all kinds; these are conceived of as possessing a soul and even divine attributes. The term was used by E. B. Tylor *(Primitive Culture)* who considered it to be the first step in the development of a religion.

ANKARA (Angora), the capital since 1924 of Turkey. Pop. (1960) 646,151. The modern city was built on an ancient Phrygian and Roman site in the heart of Turkey. Summers are hot and dry, winters cold. There are metallurgical, chemical and textile industries. Kemal Atatürk's Mausoleum is noteworthy.

ANNE (1665—1714), queen of Great Britain and Ireland, and the last of the Stuarts. The daughter of James II, she succeeded William III to the throne in 1702. In 1683 she married Prince George of Denmark. Her court seethed with intrigue regarding the succession, for none of her seventeen children survived even to adolescence; in these intrigues the Queen was much influenced by the Duke of Marlborough and dominated by his formidable wife, Sarah, until they fell from favour in 1710 and were replaced by a Tory clique. The War of the Spanish Succession occupied all but the last year of Anne's reign, which also saw the union of England and Scotland (1707). Parliament continued to increase its powers during this time, and political parties became more sharply defined. Prominent men of letters such as Pope, Swift, Defoe and Addison contributed to a cultural awakening that has been called the Augustan Age of England; the Queen Anne style of domestic architecture was also distinctive.

ANNE BOLEYN, see Boleyn, Anne.

ANNE, St, according to Christian tradition the mother of the Virgin Mary. Women in childbirth sometimes invoke her. Her feast day is July 26.

ANSELM, St (1033—1109), churchman, theologian and philosopher; born in Piedmont, he became Archbishop of Canterbury in 1093. Noted for courage, piety and sincerity, he reluctantly insisted on the church's obligations and loyalty to the pope and its independence of the king. He won a long struggle with William II and Henry I, particularly over the right of investiture. His feast day is April 21.

ANT, an insect belonging to the order of Hymenoptera which lives in colonies. There are up to 4000 species of ants, varying in length from 1/50 to 1 inch. Ants are found in all parts of the world. The body is divided into three parts — head, thorax and abdomen. Ant colonies comprise three castes — the males, the

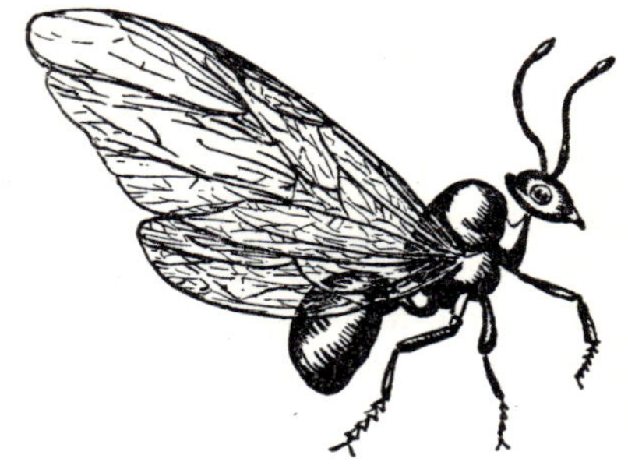

Ant (male)

queens or fertile females, and the workers (and, in some species, soldiers) or infertile, wingless females — each of which has a specific role to perform. The females have stings through which they eject formic acid. Winged individuals of both sexes emerge from the nest at certain seasons, often on the same day over a wide area, for the nuptial flight, after which the males die and the Queens shed their wings. White ants (termites) belong to a different order.

ANTARCTICA, the south polar continent. Area 6,000,000 sq. miles. The roughly circular land-mass is ringed by a rim of tall mountains, the highest of which is Thorvald Nilson (15,400 ft). Temperatures of 70°—80°F. below zero have been recorded in winter. A sheet of ice, at least 2,000 ft thick, covers the central plateau. Strong winds reach a velocity of 150 miles per hour. There are no land animals, but gulls, petrels and penguins abound. Seals and whales live in the surrounding waters of the Antarctic Ocean. The first man to reach the Antarctic ice-pack was Captain James Cook in 1774 and the first to sight land a sealer, William Smith, in 1819. Important expeditions were made by Lt Charles Wilkes (1840), Admiral Dumont d'Urville (1840), James Ross (1841) and Otto Nordenskjold (1903). Captain Scott reached the South Pole a month after the Norwegian Roald Amundsen (1911). Ernest Shackleton located the south magnetic Pole. Sir Hubert Wilkins first flew over the Arctic Circle (1928); Admiral Byrd (1929) was the first to fly over the South Pole. Considerable research was carried out during the International Geophysical Year (1957—58), when Vivian Fuchs led a British party in tractors across the continent (1500 miles) in 99 days, operating in conjunction with a New Zealand party led by Sir Edmund Hillary. Argentina, Australia, Britain, Chile, France, New Zealand, Norway, U.S.S.R. and the U.S. claim certain areas.

ANTHROPOLOGY, the study of man's development, physically, culturally, socially and racially; it includes ethnology and linguistics. Physical anthropology is concerned with man's biological, physiological and mental nature. Social anthropology is the study of the structure of human societies, in the U.S.A. included in the wider term cultural anthropology, the study of man's adjustment to his environment.

ANTIBIOTIC, a substance produced by a micro-organism and capable of killing another micro-organism or inhibiting its growth. Penicillin and streptomycin (important in tuberculosis) are examples. Antibiotics are most effective in curing diseases caused by bacteria, which may however develop strains resistant to them.

ANTIGUA, the seat of government of the Leeward Islands in the Caribbean. Pop. (1958) 56,777; area 108 sq. miles. Its chief products are sugar and cotton. The chief town is St Johns (pop. 12,500). Discovered by Columbus in 1493, it was settled by the British in 1632.

ANTILLES, the islands of the West Indies in the Caribbean, except the Bahamas. The Greater Antilles include Cuba, Jamaica, Hispaniola and Puerto Rico. The Windward and Leeward Islands, Martinique, St Thomas, Trinidad and Tobago, the Virgin Islands and Barbados are in the Lesser Antilles, although geologically Barbados, Trinidad and Tobago are part of South America.

ANTIOCH (Antakya), the ancient capital of Syria, was in 1939 transferred with the sanjak of Alexandretta to Turkey, to form the district of Hatay. Founded by Seleucus in 300 B.C., it later became, in the time of Peter and Paul, a centre of Christianity. Pop. (1960) 45,848.

ANTONINE WALL, a turf rampart built in A.D. 143 by the emperor Antoninus Pius 37 miles across Scotland between the firths of Clyde and of Forth, as a protection against invaders from the north.

ANTONY, Mark (Marcus Antonius) (83—30 B.C.), Roman statesman and soldier. After distinguished service in the cavalry, he became joint consul with Caesar in 44. He delivered the funeral oration that caused Julius Caesar's assassins to flee from Rome. After his defeat by Octavian (Caesar's heir) in 43, Antony eventually joined him and Lepidus to form a triumvirate which defeated the assassins Brutus and Cassius at Philippi (42) and dominated the Roman world. Antony's infatuation for Cleopatra, Queen of Egypt, however, led to civil war, his defeat at Actium by Octavian and his suicide.

ANTWERP (Anvers), the principal seaport of Belgium, on the Scheldt, 58 miles from the sea. Pop. (1959) 261,666. Antwerp is one of the major ports of Europe, and is linked by important canals to parts of the Rhineland and northeast France. It is also a busy commercial and industrial city, famous for its diamond cutting, shipbuilding, distilling and textile industries.

APARTHEID (apartness, separation), the official policy since 1948 of the South African government. It aims at the separation of the white and black population by settling the Africans in tribal reserves, forbids miscegenation, and imposes *baaskap* (white supremacy). The policy was condemned by the U.N. and led to South Africa's withdrawal from the British Commonwealth in 1961.

APENNINES, the chief mountain system of Italy, extending southeast for about 800 miles from the Ligurian Alps near Savon to the Strait of Messina. The highest peak is Gran Sasso d'Italia (9583 ft), and Vesuvius is an active volcano.

APHRODITE (Lat. Venus), in Greek mythology the goddess of love, beauty and fertility, derived from Astarte (q.v.). To the Greeks she was the daughter of Zeus, wife of Hephaestus and lover of Ares. Aphrodite, whose name means 'sprung from the foam', was the mother of Eros (Cupid) and was often represented as being attended by the Graces and the Seasons (Horae).

APOCALYPSE, revelation of the future, particularly the Day of Judgment and secrets of the heavens, hell and the end of the world, a term applied particularly to the last book of the Bible, but also used of passages of this type in Isaiah, Daniel etc. The Four Horsemen of the Apocalypse are Pestilence, Famine, War and Death.

APOCRYPHA, the fourteen non-canonical books of the Old Testament, written in Greek in the 1st and 2nd centuries B.C. and not appearing in the Hebrew version though found in the Septuagint and Vulgate. Among them are Tobit, The Wisdom of Solomon, Susanna and Bel and the Dragon. They were accepted by the Roman Church at the Council of Trent in 1546 as canonical and sacred. In the Anglican Church they may be read for example and instruction but not for the establishment of doctrine. The term Apocrypha of the New Testament is applied to numerous unauthenticated writings of the early Christian era, e.g. the Epistle of Clement.

APOLLO, one of the most important and powerful gods in Greek and Roman mythology. He was the many-sided god of prophecy (as at Delphi), purity (as Phoebus), spring, music, healing and archery, as well as of shepherds and their flocks. He could also punish harshly. Apollo was represented as the Greek ideal of manly youth and beauty. Later he replaced Helios as sun-god.

APOSTLE, the Greek term for messenger or envoy, used to identify the twelve disciples of Jesus who were with him while he spread his doctrine and continued to teach it after the Crucifixion, Judas Iscariot being replaced by Matthias. The title was also given to Paul and other missionary pioneers.

APPALACHIAN MOUNTAINS, the chief mountain system of northeastern North America, extending 1500 miles southwest from the St Lawrence Valley in Quebec Province, Canada, to the Gulf (of Mexico) Coastal plain in Alabama, U.S.A. They are still well forested but, except for the anthracite of Pennsylvania, poor in minerals. They were for long a barrier to expansion to the west.

APPIAN WAY, a Roman highway begun in 312 B.C. When completed, it ran from Rome via Capua to Brindisi for a total distance of 350 miles.

Pattern of stones of the type used in the construction of the Appian Way

APULEIUS, Lucius (2nd century A.D.), Roman writer and philosopher of North Africa. His satirical novel, the *Golden Ass*, includes the tale of Cupid and Psyche. This and his *Apologia* (a defence against the charge of getting his wife by witchcraft) form an unusual source of information on the life of the period.

AQUEDUCT, an artificial channel or trough to convey water, chiefly for urban districts. Aqueducts reached a high point of development in the Roman empire, and the ruins of many survive, e.g. the Pont du Gard near Nîmes and that at Segovia. The French 17th-century engineer Vauban began, but never completed, the magnificent aqueduct of Maintenon to carry water to Versailles. Where ancient aqueducts utilised the power of gravity to bring the water to its destination, modern pipelines convey it by pumps.

Roman Pont du Gard aqueduct at Nîmes, France

AQUINAS, St Thomas (*c.* 1225—74), Italian scholastic philosopher and theologian. His system (known as Thomism) has become the official theology of the Roman Catholic Church. The most important of his numerous works is the *Summa Theologiae* summarising all religious knowledge and demonstrating that faith and reason are not antagonistic. He felt that his predecessors had been too much influenced by Platonic and Neo-Platonic intellectualism and devoted himself to rehabilitating the metaphysical theses of Aristotle. His feast day is March 7.

ARABIA, a nearly rectangular peninsula in southwest Asia. Pop. (1960) 8,000,000; area 1,200,000 sq. miles. One-third sterile desert, the rest is a plateau with little rainfall, no perennial rivers and no forests. About 80% of the inhabitants are engaged in primitive agriculture (dates, coffee, grains). Saudi Arabi, Kuwait and Bahrain have rich oil deposits. Islam, the only religion, originated there in the 7th century. The holy cities of Mecca and Medina are located near the west coast. From the 17th century to 1918 the Turks maintained nominal control over most of Arabia. Ibn Saud gained control of the largest part by 1924 (see Saudi Arabia). Other political divisons are Yemen (where the density of population is highest), Kuwait, Aden Colony and Protectorate, the sultanates of Bahrain (an island) and Oman and Muscat, and the sheikhdoms of Qatar and Trucial Oman. Slavery is common in Saudi Arabia.

ARABIAN NIGHTS, a collection of tales supposed to have been told by Queen Sheherezade to Sultan Shahriar for 1001 nights, interrupted each night just before the climax for the purpose of holding his attention and preventing him from killing her. The stories tell of the times of Haroun al-Rashid, Caliph of Baghdad (786—809) but may be adapted from older Hindu and Persian tales.

ARABIAN SEA, a northwestern extension of the Indian Ocean between Africa and India, bordering on the coasts of Pakistan, Iran, Oman and Aden.

ARAB LEAGUE, a loose association of Arab states formed in 1945 to promote cultural, economic and military co-operation among members. Egyptian influence, at first strong, later lessened. Opposition to Israel is the League's only unifying factor. The original members, Egypt, Iraq, Saudi Arabia, Syria, Lebanon, Jordan and Yemen, were later joined by Libya (1953), the Sudan (1956), Tunisia and Morocco (1958), Kuwait (1961) and Algeria (1962).

ARAGON, an ancient kingdom in northeastern Spain, now the provinces of Huesca, Zaragoza and Teruel. Area 18,294 sq. miles. It is a mountainous, inhospitable country. Becoming a kingdom in 1035, it was united with Catalonia in the 12th century and with Castile in 1479 after the marriage of Ferdinand and Isabella, to form the nucleus of the kingdom of Spain.

ARAL SEA, an inland sea between the Kazakhstand and Uzbekistan S.S.R.s of the U.S.S.R. in central Asia. Area 26,165 sq. miles. Fed by the Amu Darya and Syr Darya rivers, it has no outlet. It is the fourth largest inland body of water in the world.

ARAM, a Biblical name for the geographical area which is now Syria and Iraq and for the ancient Semitic people who inhabited it. The Aramaic language, related to the Syriac and Chaldee languages, became the common tongue of the entire region and of Palestine and was the vernacular spoken by Jesus, the use of Hebrew being kept up only by the Rabbinic schools.

ARARAT, a mountain (16,945 ft) of Turkish Armenia near the Turko-Russo-Iran frontiers, traditionally the resting-place of Noah's Ark, the remains of which were still being pointed out to travellers up to the 19th century.

ARBITRATION, a method of settling disputes between contending parties by requesting and undertaking to abide by the decision of a third disinterested person or body. Much used in labour disputes, it was formally acknowledged at the first Hague Peace Conference in 1899 as a means of settling international issues, but had been successfully employed earlier, e.g. in the Alabama Arbitration of 1872 between Great Britain and the U.S.A.

ARCH, an upward-curving structural form spanning pillars or openings, the component wedge-shaped blocks (voussoirs) of which maintain its shape and strength by mutual pressure. A block, called the keystone, fits into the top centre and supports the entire structure. The principle of the arch was known in ancient times but arches were seldom used until the Roman Empire. The Roman, Byzantine and Romanesque arches were semicircular, the Gothic arch pointed; in England the pointed arch was again flattened to form the four-centred Tudor arch.

ARCHAEOLOGY, the scientific study of relics shedding light on the life of ancient man. Buried cities, mounds and caves are investigated for remains which enable the scientist to reach conclusions regarding every aspect of the culture of ancient peoples. Implements, pottery remains and timber are examined and analysed, and the use of carbon-14 and fluorine tests makes it possible to date bone and some other substances with considerable accuracy. Excavations from 1842 onwards have revealed valuable facts about the civilisations of Sumer, Assyria, Babylon, Egypt, Troy, Crete, Mycenae, Mexico and Peru, the Indus Valley etc. Among the first discoveries made were the Rosetta Stone (1799), key to Egyptian hieroglyphs, Darius's trilingual Rock of Behistun (1835) and Tutankhamun's tomb (1923).

ARCHERY, the skilful use of bow and arrow, originally for hunting and warfare and, now, chiefly for sport, in which competitors shoot 'ends' of six arrows each at a 4-ft target placed at distances up to 100 yd or more.

ARCHIMEDES (*c.* 287—212 B.C.), an outstanding Greek mathematician, physicist, engineer and inventor. The most celebrated scientific thinker of the ancient world, he discovered basic principles in geometry, physics, mechanics and hydrostatics indispensable to the subsequent development of these sciences. He invented a screw, used to raise water, and many devices which delayed the fall of Syracuse, where he was killed when it was taken by the Romans.

Archimedean screw

ARCHITECTURE, the application of principles of science combined with those of aesthetics to the building craft in order to create a structure possessing unity of beauty and function. Architecture is closely tied up with man's environment and reflects his life and times. The earliest examples of architecture, dating from about 4000 B.C., were found in the Mesopotamian and Egyptian areas. The materials available—stone or mud bricks — determined the

'Europe' on horseback, Meissen porcelain *c.* 1745.

Photo: Victoria & Albert Museum

De Morgan tiles, characterised by brilliant blue and green glazes, were widely used during the Victorian era.

Photo: Victoria & Albert Museum

English 18th century pottery: a jasperware teapot by Josiah Wedgewood (q.v.).

Photo: Victoria & Albert Museum

An Assyrian bas-relief depicting King Assurbanipal and attendants out hunting. 668 B.C.
Photo: British Museum

The *Ten Girls* mosaic pavement, Roman, 3rd century A.D., from Sicily.
Photo: Gabinetto, Syraceuse

form of the buildings. Greek architecture, with its horizontal beams resting on tapering columns, is derived from timber construction. It is to the Greeks that we owe the three great Orders of Architecture — Doric, Ionic and Corinthian — taken over by the Romans. Byzantine is a modification of Roman architecture initiated by Constantine in the 4th century, and characterised by the use of the dome. Another offspring of the Roman style is the Romanesque (in England called Norman or Anglo-Saxon), using semi-circular arches and vaults. This style gave way to the pointed arch of Gothic architecture (from *c.* 1200), which developed increased lightness and elaboration of ornament. Renaissance architecture, a new interpretation of classical standards, beginning in Italy in the 15th century reached England a century later, influencing Tudor, Elizabethan, Jacobean, Palladian, Georgian and Regency building. There was a marked reaction to this in the Roman Catholic countries of southern Europe, in the extremely ornate forms of Baroque (17th) and Rococo (18th century), which spread later to Germany and France. Modern architecture has been dominated by experiments with the new material and techniques that have become available, and by a new interest in planning towns, or parts of them, as a whole. The major innovators have perhaps been Le Corbusier and Frank Lloyd Wright.

ARCTIC, the region centred around the earth's geographic North Pole. Most of it is covered by the Arctic Ocean, the middle of which is a permanently frozen area of pack-ice, 10 – 13 ft thick. Temperatures vary from a record of −85°F. in the interior of Greenland to a summer high of 90°F. The land area includes parts of Alaska, Canada, Greenland, Scandinavia and the U.S.S.R. There is abundant animal and bird life. The principal inhabitants are Eskimos, Lapps and Mongoloid tribes of northern Siberia. Mineral wealth includes gold, coal, platinum, copper, nickel and cobalt. The area is important for the defence of the western hemisphere and as an airline route. Following early attempts of the Vikings to explore the region, activities were renewed in the 16th and 19th centuries, first to seek a passage to the northwest or northeast and later for scientific purposes. James Ross discovered the north magnetic Pole (1831). Robert McClure discovered the North-West Passage in 1850 and 50 years later Roald Amundsen took a ship through from east to west. Fridtjof Nansen collected much valuable information in 1893—96. Robert Peary reached the Pole in 1909. Since the beginning of the 20th century Vilhjalmur Stefansson and others have amassed a wealth of data of all kinds on the Arctic regions. The U.S. and U.S.S.R. lead in the establishment of scientific stations. The American nuclear submarine Nautilus sailed under the ice-cap of the North Pole in 1958.

AREOPAGUS, until 461 B.C. the supreme governing council in Athens, named after a hill near the Acropolis where its members met. From this hill St Paul addressed the Athenians.

ARES (Roman Mars), Greek god of war, and son of Zeus and Hera. He delighted in war and was therefore very unpopular with the gods (this reflecting the Greek attitude to purposeless war). Hephaestus took pleasure in trapping him in a net when he was lying with Aphrodite.

ARGENTINA, a federal republic in South America. Pop. (1960) 20,956,000; area 1,072,477 sq. miles. The highest ranges of the Andes border it on the west. In the south, considering the latitude, temperatures are singularly mild. The hub of the country is the fertile plain in the east central part. The north is sub-tropical. Two-thirds of the population live in large cities and are chiefly engaged in industries dependent on agricultural production (meat, grain). Argentina's principal exports are meat, cereals, oilseeds and wool. The River Plate was discovered in 1515 and Buenos Aires founded by the Spanish in 1536. It has known much unrest since it became an independent nation in 1816. Due to immigration, it is the only country in South America with a population almost entirely of European descent (75 % being of Spanish and Italian origin). From 1946 to 1955, Juan Perón exercised a dictatorship over the country. The capital, chief port and commercial, industrial, communications and cultural centre is Buenos Aires (pop. 3,845,279). Other principal cities are Rosario (585,000), Córdoba (520,000), La Plata (350,000) and Tucuman (250,000).

ARGONAUTS, in Greek mythology, heroes who sailed with Jason from Thessaly to Colchis on the Black Sea in the ship Argo to secure the Golden Fleece, in which, with the help of the King's daughter, Medea, Jason succeeded.

ARGYLLSHIRE, a maritime county of western Scotland. Pop. (1959) 57,000; area 3165 sq. miles. The second largest county in Scotland, it is mountainous and has many lochs. Oban is a tourist centre, and Glencoe, a glen famous for its wild beauty and the scene of the massacre in 1692 of members of the Macdonald clan, lies to the north.

ARIANISM, a heresy which maintained that Christ is less divine than God. Condemned by the Council of Nicaea (325), it was for a while the orthodox belief of the Roman empire. It had died out by the end of the 4th century, except among the Goths and other Teutonic tribes, where it lingered on for another two centuries. Disbelief in the divinity of Christ was revived by the Unitarians.

ARISTARCHUS OF SAMOS (*c.* 310—250 B.C.), Greek astronomer and mathematician of the Alexandrian school. He was the first to maintain that the sun is stationary and that the earth revolves around it while rotating on its axis. He also held that the stars were immeasurably more distant than the sun.

ARISTOCRACY, originally meaning government by an élite for the benefit of the many, has come to denote the rule of a privileged nobility.

ARISTOPHANES (*c.* 448—388 B.C.), Athenian writer of comedies. Freely satirising every aspect of individual, social and political relations, he gleefully ridiculed pretentiousness and melodrama. Of the 54 comedies attributed to him only 11 survive. His choruses include some of the best examples of Greek lyric poetry; his wit and fluent mastery of elaborate metres were unmatched.

ARISTOTLE (384—322 B.C.), Greek philosopher and scientist, and founder of the technique of organised research and classification. He studied under Plato and, after a period as tutor to the future Alexander the Great, set up the Peripatetic School (335) at Athens in the Lyceum garden, where he taught for twelve years. In his works, mostly surviving in the form of lecture notes, he seeks to define the fundamental principles of each science. The foundation of knowledge, he held, is logic; the basis of all reasoning is the syllogism.

Man's true end is happiness, attained by pursuit of the golden mean. Every object is a union of Form (or law of organisation) and Matter; change is a process by which what is potential becomes actual. Entelechy is the manifestation of realised Form. Four causes combine to produce an object: the material, formal, efficient and final causes. God is the ultimate source of all change, the Prime Mover, pure Form or Actuality, perfect, eternal. Soul differentiates the inanimate from the animate and manifests itself in three degrees: the vegetative in plants, the instinctive in animals, the rational in man. In his *Poetics* Aristotle deals with tragedy, which by raising pity and fear purges the mind of these passions (katharsis). Through St Thomas Aquinas, Aristotle's philosophy became the basis of Roman Catholic doctrine.

ARIZONA, a southwestern state of the U.S.A. Pop. (1960) 1,302,161; area 113,909 sq. miles. The northeast is a high plateau. Mountain ranges extend from northwest to southeast. The Grand Canyon, over 200 miles long, was cut by the Colorado River; below it the Boulder (or Hoover) Dam was built in 1936 on the Nevada border. Arizona is the leading copper-producing state in the U.S. and also has gold, lead, zinc and other minerals. Cotton, cereals and citrus are produced, and livestock raised. The state has *c.* 27,000 sq. miles of Indian reservations. Jesuit missionaries made the first settlements. Governed first by Spain and then by Mexico, Arizona was ceded to the U.S.A. in 1848. In 1912 it was the 48th state to enter the Union. The capital is Phoenix (pop. 439,170). Other chief cities are Tucson (212,892) and Mesa (33,772).

ARKANSAS, a south central state of the U.S.A. Pop. (1960) 1,786,272; area 53,104 sq. miles. Arkansas is almost equally divided between highlands in the north and lowlands in the south. The Mississippi is its eastern boundary, and the state is bisected by its chief tributary, the Arkansas. Cotton, maize, soya beans, timber and livestock are raised. Rich in bauxite, Arkansas also has coal, petroleum and natural gas. It was first explored by the Spaniards and then by the French. Large-scale settlements were established during the cotton boom of 1818 — 15 years after it became a U.S. territory. Arkansas became a state in 1836. It was a member of the Confederacy. The capital is Little Rock (pop. 107,813). Other chief cities are North Little Rock (58,032), Fort Smith (52,991), Pine Bluff (44,037) and Hot Springs (28,337).

ARKHANGELSK (Archangel), seaport and capital of the Arkhangelsk region of the R.S.F.S.R., U.S.S.R. Pop. (1959) 256,000. At the mouth of the Dvina River on the White Sea, it is ice-free from June to September.

ARKWRIGHT, Sir Richard (1732—92), English inventor and textile manufacturer. Starting life as a barber, he invented in 1769 a cotton spinning frame superior to Hargreaves's spinning jenny in that it could produce yarn compact enough for warp threads. In 1771 he established the first spinning mill worked by water-power and became the founder of the factory system which marked the Industrial Revolution.

ARMADA, Spanish, the fleet sent by Philip II of Spain in 1588 to take over Protestant England, which had been awarded him by the Pope. Consisting of 126 vessels with about 30,000 men, it was defeated by 70 to 80 smaller English ships commanded by Lord Howard of Effingham, under whom

Drake, Hawkins and Frobisher were serving. Howard attacked the lumbering galleons as they sailed up the English Channel, and off Gravelines. Many more ships were wrecked by heavy August storms as they sailed home via the Orkneys, and only 54 ships reached port.

ARMENIA, a mountainous region in southwest Asia. At one time it embraced an independent kingdom extending from the Black Sea to the Caspian and south to the borders of present-day Iraq and Syria, including territory now in the U.S.S.R., Iran and eastern Turkey. A Persian satrapy for two centuries before it was conquered by Alexander the Great (331 B.C.), Armenia achieved the height of its power under Tigranes (*c.* 94—56 B.C.). Christianity was introduced in the 4th century and its spread caused the tribulations suffered under Moslem rule. A history of ceaseless war continued as the country fell into the hands, successively, of Mongols, Persians, Turks and Russians. Russia annexed part of the region in 1828 and wanted the rest; thereafter Armenia became a pawn in the game of Anglo-Russian rivalry, Britain favouring Armenian nationalism, fear of which led to the massacres of 1894—6 under Abdul the Damned. In 1908 the Young Turks at first granted major concessions to the Armenians, but under the stress of the First World War deported them wholesale to Syria and Mesopotamia, and many more were massacred. The area now included in the Armenian Soviet Socialist Republic of the U.S.S.R. (pop. 1959 1,763,000; area 11,580 sq. miles) is that taken by Russia in 1828. It produces copper, cotton, wool and wine. Its capital is Yerevan (509,000). Echmiadzin is the seat of the Catholics of the Armenian Church.

ARMOUR, a device to make wearer or user less vulnerable in combat. Protective body covering developed from a helmet, cuirass, greaves and a shield in the ancient world. Mail (or chain mail) of interlinked metal rings was known to the Romans and earlier, and came into common use in the West during the Crusades, but in the 14th century was superseded by plate armour. Eventually only the cuirass, gauntlets and helmet

Armour—14th century

were retained, and by 1800 these also had been abandoned. The helmet was reintroduced early in the 20th century, and bullet-proof waistcoats were worn by gangsters and dictators; flak suits and nylon vests came into use in the Korean War. The armour plating of warships, occasionally recorded in earlier times, was seen to be essential when the Russians used explosive shells in the Crimean War. The armoured car developed into the tank, which first went into action in 1916. The latest devices are for protection against nuclear radiation.

ARMSTRONG, William George, 1st Baron (1810—1900), English engineer. The greatest of his inventions was the rifled, breech-loading field-gun which revolutionised artillery in the Crimean War.

ARMY, a body of trained men organised for offensive or defensive warfare on land. First to organise an army was ancient Egypt whose military might eventually swept up into Asia Minor and down to Ethiopia. The Assyrians employed archers and spearmen on horseback and in chariots. The phalanx was developed by the Greeks and the Romans stressed discipline and flexible organisation in small units. Cavalry was the dominant military arm of the Middle Ages when feudal levies and knights were mobilised by the lord of the manor. English yeomen fought under leaders of their own choice. The 14th-century Turkish janissaries were the first standing army. In the 14th and 15th centuries English archers and Swiss freemen with sword and halberd put an end to the effectiveness of knights in armour. The development of firearms led to the increased use of professional soldiers or mercenaries. Conscription, which began with the French Revolution, was not introduced in Britain and the U.S.A. until the First World War. New weapons — aircraft, tanks and rockets — completely changed the use and organisation of armies in the two World Wars, and the introduction of 'tactical nuclears' caused further re-thinking thereafter.

ARNOLD, Matthew (1822—88), English poet and critic, son of the famous headmaster of Rugby School. His seminal views on literature and society were at least as important as his poetry, high though it ranks. He attacked Philistinism and pleaded for 'Hellenism', 'the pursuit of sweetness and light' as against what he termed 'Hebraism'. He was preoccupied with the moral and social significance of literature and drew a sharp distinction between the great and the merely good. Culture he defined as acquaintance with the best that has been known or said in the world, and criticism as a disinterested endeavour to propagate this. Religion was 'morality tinged with emotion'.

ART, the manifestation of man's creative powers for aesthetic purposes. The term implies execution based on systematic methods and rules with the artist's expression of feeling and emotion, or the production of beauty as the end-result. The fine arts of architecture, sculpture and painting may have little or no utilitarian value but appeal directly to the aesthetic sense. Music and poetry are not considered to be fine arts, possibly as being too abstract for that rather artificial category. Decorative art begins when something has been added to embellish an object after the purpose for which it was created has been fulfilled, e.g. wood-carving or landscape gardening.

ARTAXERXES II (died 358 B.C.), Persian king (*c.* 405—358 B.C.), succeeded his father Darius II after suppressing a revolt of his brother, Cyrus the Younger, and established Persian control over the Greek city-states.

ARTEMIS (Roman Diana), the Greek virgin goddess of hunting, sister of Apollo. She was also goddess of chastity, presided over childbirth, and in Ephesus was worshipped as the mother-goddess (Great is Diana of the Ephesians). Later she became identified with the Moon (Selene).

ARTHUR (*c.* 6th century A.D.), a Celtic ruler believed to have resisted the settlement of the pagan Saxons in southern Britain. A mass of legends exist about his court at Camelot (variously identified as Caerleon, Monmouth etc.) where his chivalrous knights met with him around the Round Table. Mortally wounded in battle, he was carried away to the isle of Avalon from which he will return to save his people. In another version, he is buried at Glastonbury. His name is first linked with the legend of the Holy Grail in the romances of the 12th-century French poet, Chrétien de Troyes, who also introduced the story of Lancelot's love for Arthur's queen, Guinevere.

ARTIFICIAL RESPIRATION, a means of restoring breathing when it has stopped in such cases as drowning, suffocation, shock, or heart failure. It is done by producing a change of air in the lungs by expanding and compressing the chest and keeping the passageway to them open.

ARTILLERY, heavy guns and the mounts, equipment, transport and personnel that service them. The term does not apply to naval guns and the small supporting cannon and mortars issued to infantry units. The two branches of artillery are field and anti-aircraft. The weapons are classified as guns, howitzers, mortars and rocket launchers, and divided into light, medium and heavy categories. Guided missiles and tactical nuclear weapons of great destructive power and considerable range have replaced some conventional artillery pieces.

ARTSYBASHEV, Mikhail Petrovich (1878—1927), Russian novelist and dramatist. He achieved fame for his novel *Sanine* attacking conventional restraints in matters of sex.

ARYAN, an older term for Indo-European (q.v.). It is no longer used except in connection with the 'Aryan Myth', the long-disproved theory propounded by Max Müller of a master-race from which all Indian and European peoples spring. This theory was taken up by Houston Chamberlain as a basis for anti-Semitism, and borrowed from him by the Nazi movement.

ASBESTOS, a silicate mineral composed of fibres which may be spun and woven into fabrics or sheets which are fireproof and heat-resistant; it is also compounded with portland cement to form asbestos-cement.

ASCETICISM, the mortification of physical needs and self-denial for religious, moral and ethical reasons. It is believed to purify the soul and lead to closer communion with God. To this belief may be traced the ideas of penance, vigil, fasting, celibacy, monasticism, the hermit life and Puritanism, as well as such crude manifestations as flagellation and the excesses of fakirs.

ASIA, the continent of the Eastern Hemisphere, constituting the world's largest land surface and including, properly, Russia east of the Ural Mountains. Excluding U.S.S.R., Pop. (1960) 1,665,000,000; area 17,559,000 sq. miles. Vast lowlands in the north give way to grasslands covering one-third of the continent. Central Asia is an enormous, dry, high plateau west of which lie the Pamirs, Hindu Kush and Himalayas, with the world's loftiest mountains (Everest 29,028 ft; Godwin Austen, or K.2., 28,250 ft; Kanchenjunga 28,140 ft). Eastern Asia comprises both mountains and lowlands, with most of the populations concentrated in the river valleys. Important rivers are the Ob (3200 miles long). Yangtze Kiang (3100 miles), Amur (2900 miles), Lena (2800 miles), Yenisei (2800 miles), Hwang Ho (2700 miles), Mekong (2500 miles) and the Tigris-Euphrates (the Tigris being 1200 miles; the Euphrates 1700 miles). The peninsulas of Asia's east coast continue seaward in chains of volcanic islands. The huge subcontinent of India in the south contains some of the most fertile land in Asia along the banks of its rivers (Indus, Ganges, Brahmaputra, etc.). Asia's resources consist chiefly of petroleum (in the Middle East), iron (India), coal (China), precious stones (Burma), rubber and tin (Malaysia and Indonesia). Over-population, especially in the Indian peninsula, Japan, Indonesia and the Yangtze delta, has brought the standard of living of much of the population down to subsistence level, despite the fertility of the river lowlands. Asia is the home of the world's leading religions and the cradle of the civilisations of Mesopotamia, the Indus Valley and China. Racially, the inhabitants are Semitic or Indo-European in the west and Mongoloid in the east. Although familiar with the cultures of southwest Asia, Europe knew little of the lands of central and eastern Asia until Alexander the Great reached India in the 4th century B.C. The most extensive empire was that of the Mongols which, though shortlived, reached in the 13th century from the Danube and Arabia to China. Contact between Asia and the West was renewed in the late Middle Ages through missionaries and merchants, among them Marco Polo. The discovery of a sea route round the Cape of Good Hope in 1478 led to the establishment of trading posts and then to European domination (Portuguese, Dutch, British, French, Spanish, Russian) in India, Burma, Indo-China, Malaysia, Indonesia and the Philippines. At the end of the 19th century signs of rebellion appeared. The First World War, and even more so the Second, resulted in political social and economic upheavals and the formation of partly or wholly independent states. In addition to the newly independent countries of India, Pakistan, Ceylon, Burma, Cambodia, Laos, Vietnam, Indonesia and Malaysia, Asia's states include Afghanistan, Bhutan, China, Formosa, Iran, Iraq, Israel, Japan, Korea, Kuwait, Lebanon, Mongolia, Nepal, the Philippines, Saudi Arabia, Syria, Thailand, Turkey and Yemen.

ASIA MINOR, a peninsula in the extreme western part of Asia which is occupied by Turkey (q.v.). In ancient times it included the Ionian Greek towns of Miletus, Ephesus, Smyrna and Halicarnassus, and was divided in the Roman period into various kingdoms, e.g. Lydia in the west, Pamphylia and Cilicia in the south, Bithynia, Paphlagonia and Pontus in the north, and Phrygia, Galatia and Cappadocia in the centre. The area was one of the richest parts of the Roman, and later of the Byzantine, Empire. From the 14th century the Turks began to dominate the area, which became the eastern bulwark of the Ottoman Empire and, in the 20th century, its core.

ASPHALT, a bituminous substance occurring naturally in Trinidad, California and elsewhere; the name is also given to a residue in petroleum distillation, and to a mixture of asphalt, limestone and granite chippings used in road-making.

ASQUITH, Herbert Henry, 1st Earl of Oxford and Asquith (1852—1928), British Liberal statesman. Elected to Parliament in 1886, he constantly advocated Home Rule for Ireland. He was Home Secretary (1892—95) in Gladstone's government and Chancellor of the Exchequer (1905—08) in Campbell-Bannerman's government. The first provision for old-age pensions and unemployment insurance was introduced after he became Prime Minister in 1908. His government fell in 1916 because of its conduct of the war.

ASSASSIN, a member of a secret order of the Ismaili sect of Shiite Moslems which spread terror throughout Persia, Iraq, Egypt and Syria in the 11th and 12th centuries. 'The Old Man of the Mountain', operating from a castle in the Elburz mountains, not merely promised his men paradise but gave them a foretaste of it, under the influence of hashish (hence the name), before they set out on a campaign of selective assassination of the sect's oppressors. Their victims included two caliphs and a shah. A branch (the Khojas) survived Mongol attack, and the Aga Khan is their Imam today. The name has come to mean a person who murders a public figure for political reasons.

ASSYRIA, an ancient kingdom of the upper Tigris valley, with its capital at Nineveh. In 1275 B.C. the Assyrians, beginning a ruthless but very chequered career of revenge against the Hittites and Babylonians who had plagued them for 1500 years, conquered Babylon. In 1140 Tighlath-Pileser I founded the Assyrian Empire and dominated West Asia. Tiglath-Pileser III (745—727) invaded Babylonia, Palestine, Syria and Media, and Sennacherib destroyed Babylon in 691. For a time in the 7th century Assyria held Egypt; then Babylonia revolted; in 612 Nineveh was destroyed by Chaldaeans and Medes, and Assyria was absorbed into Media and Persia. The Assyrians have left as monuments the palaces of Nimrud, Nineveh and Dur-Sarrukin, decorated with hunting and martial themes executed in bas-relief, and Assurbanipal's library of 20,000 clay tablets, now in the British Museum.

ASTARTE, Semitic mother-goddess and deity of fertility and love, Ishtar of Assyria and Babylonia and Ashtoreth of the Bible. She was first among the Phoenician gods. Her worship was accompanied by orgiastic rites. Her lover Tammuz (Adonis), a vegetation deity, died each year and was rescued from the underworld by Astarte. The Greeks adopted her as Aphrodite.

ASTHMA, a disorder of the bronchial tubes making breathing difficult. It may be due to chronic bronchitis or an allergy caused by some substance in the environment. Frequently there are emotional causes.

ASTIGMATISM, visual defect in which the image is distorted or blurred. It is due to an irregularity in the curved surface of the cornea or lens of the eyes which throws parts of an object out of focus. It can be corrected by glasses.

ASTOR, Nancy, Viscountess (1879—1964) American-born wife of Viscount Astor of Cliveden, she was the first woman to sit in the British Parliament, as a Unionist-Conservative member, from 1919 to 1945.

ASTROLOGY, a pseudo-science based on the belief that the heavenly bodies, especially the planets and stars near the exliptic, exercise a decisive influence on the nature and fate of man and on world events. Astrologers claim to be able by casting a horoscope to divine the character, potentialities and possible future of a person by the positions of the stars at his birth or even at conception. The only data required are the place and date of birth, and the inescapable presumption is that everyone born in the same town on the same day ought to have approximately the same character and career.

ASTRONAUTICS, see Space Flight.

ASTRONOMY, the science of heavenly bodies. It is concerned with their position distance, movements, composition, structure, history and future development. In the middle of the 16th century Copernicus revolutionised astronomy with his theory that the planets and even the earth revolve around the sun. Invention of the telescope early in the 17th century enabled Galileo to strengthen the Copernican position, but the view that the sun was the centre of the universe had to be abandoned when Herschel (1738—1822) proved that the sun also was in motion; later he studied the Milky Way and decided, incorrectly, that the sun was at the centre of our galaxy. Halley discovered the periodicity of comets. The first measurement of the distance of a star was made in 1838. It is now known that our galaxy, with a diameter of *c.* 100,000 light-years and 100,000 million stars, is but one of many millions of galaxies (sometimes called spiral or extragalactic nebulae, or island universes). The 200 in. Mount Palomar telescope in California can penetrate space to a distance of 2000 million light-years. Radio astronomy studies extraterrestrial matter by the radio waves it emits or reflects back to earth. Cosmogony is concerned with theories of the origin and evolution of the universe, a sphere in which controversy reigns.

ASTROPHYSICS, the science of the chemical composition and physical properties of heavenly bodies, based on spectrum analysis of their light or interferometric investigation of their diameters.

ASWAN, a town in Upper Egypt just below the First Cataract of the Nile about 550 miles south of Cairo, built on the site of ancient Syene. The existing dam and reservoir, built to control floods and provide irrigation, are being expanded to irrigate an additional 1,300,000 acres and to provide hydroelectricity. The submersion or removal of the temples of Abu Simbel is entailed.

ATATÜRK, Kemal (1881—1938), Turkish statesman and soldier. As Mustapha Kemal, he served both in the Italo-Turkish War (1911—12) and in the Second Balkan War (1913), and commanded the successful Turkish defence of the Dardanelles during the First World War. After the war he organised the Nationalist Party, and — after driving the Greeks out of Asia Minor — brought about the downfall of the sultan Cate (1922). Atatürk was elected the first president of the Turkish Republic (1923), and introduced a vigorous programme for its modernisation. Moslem law, schools and dress were abolished, a European alphabet introduced, and women emancipated.

ATHABASKA, see River.

ATHANASIUS, St (*c.* 295—373), theologian and uncompromising adversary of Arianism. Bishop of Alexandria, he was exiled by Emperor Constantine for refusing to admit Airus to communion. The Athanasian creed dates from some centuries later and was so called because Athanasius had become the legendary defender of orthodox views on the Trinity, especially at the Council of Nicaea.

ATHEIST, one who disbelieves in the existence of God.

ATHELSTAN (*c.* 894—940), grandson of Alfred, King of Wessex and Mercia. He annexed Northumbria, subdued the kings of Scotland, Wales and Cumbria, and became King of Britain in 925. In one of the most desperate battles fought on British soil he defeated a coalition of Welsh, Scots and Danes in the Battle of Brunanburh (937) at Bourne, Lincolnshire.

ATHENE (Roman Minerva), a Greek virgin goddess, patroness of Athens, and the embodiment of wisdom and strength. She was born fully armed from the head of Zeus. The Parthenon (maiden temple) on the Acropolis at Athens was her greatest shrine. She was also the goddess of war, and of arts and crafts.

ATHENS, the capital of Greece. Pop. (1961 Greater Athens, including the port of Piraeus and the suburbs) 1,850,000. It was the most important city of ancient Greece, and it was there that a fully democratic political system first evolved. After its leadership in the Persian Wars (490—479) Athens formed the Delian League, which embraced all the Aegean islands and the Greeks of Asia Minor. In 454 the League's treasury was transferred from the sacred island of Delos to Athens, and tribute from members was regularly exacted, rebel cities such as Samos and Mitylene severely punished and the tribute used in part for the embellishment of Athens, notably for the Parthenon, Propylaea and other buildings erected on the Acropolis in the time of Pericles (495—425). With a population of *c.* 200,000, Athens reached the peak of her development and was the cultural centre of all Greece; Socrates, Plato and Aristotle lived and taught there. But these hubristic acts of imperialism brought their retribution. Sparta rebelled and defeated Athens in the Peloponnesian War (431—404). In 338 Philip of Macedon became master of Greece and the centre of Hellenic civilisation passed to Alexandria. In Roman times Athens enjoyed comparative peace; Hadrian (A.D. 117—38) established a new city in the eastern part of the town. From the 3rd century a progressive decline began, so that Athens had become a small town with magnificent ruins when it was proclaimed the capital of the newly established kingdom of Greece in 1833.

ATLANTIC CHARTER, a joint declaration of American and British aims in a democratic world made by British Prime Minister Winston Churchill and the U.S. President Franklin D. Roosevelt in the early stages of the Second World War, 1941, at sea off the coast of Newfoundland. It became the basis of the U.N. Charter.

ATLANTIC OCEAN, the second largest ocean, is about 9000 miles from north to south and from 1600 to 4500 miles wide, with an overall area of about 31,840,000 sq. miles. Its bed consists of a sloping plateau with an average depth of 13,000 ft, rising up in a narrow ridge whose highest elevation is the volcanic peaks of the Azores. The deepest sounding was taken in the Milwaukee Depth (30,246 ft) northeast of Puerto Rico. The Gulf (of Mexico) Stream follows the east coast of U.S.A. and turns east to warm the seas off northwest Europe. The Sargasso Sea is an area between the Azores and the West Indies containing large patches of floating, self-reproducing seaweed. The busiest shipping lanes in the world are in the North Atlantic.

ATLANTIS, a mythical island west of the Straits of Gibraltar. According to Greek legend, recounted by Plato, its inhabitants had achieved a high degree of civilisation but were swallowed up by the sea because of impiety.

ATLAS MOUNTAINS, a system of non-volcanic mountains in northwest Africa extending for about 1500 miles from the Atlantic Ocean to the Mediterranean Sea east of Tunisia. Jebel Toubkal in Morocco is 13,665 ft high.

ATMOSPHERE, a mass of air surrounding the earth, consisting of three layers:

the nearest to the ground is the troposphere (6—10 miles in height); above it is the stratosphere, where the temperature ceases to fall with height, flying conditions are normally excellent and there is almost no cloud; above the 40-mile level is the ionosphere, consisting of strongly electrified rarefied air with sufficient free electrons to reflect all but ultra-short radio waves back to earth. The upper part of the ionosphere (G-layer) is 250—300 miles above sea-level. Above the ionosphere are the Van Allen belts, at heights up to 37,000 miles, of intense ionising radiation and with particles of extremely high energy; it is here that the aurorae occur. At sea-level the atmosphere consists chiefly of nitrogen, oxygen, water vapour, argon, carbon dioxide, hydrogen and many minor gases. Atmospheric pressure at sea level is 14.7 lb. per square inch, corresponding to a barometric height of 30 in.; this drops to $\frac{1}{3}$ in. at a height of 18 miles.

ATOM, the smallest particle of a chemical element capable of combining with other atoms to form a chemical compound. Once believed to be indivisible, the atom is now known to consist of a nucleus formed of neutrons (q.v.), bearing no electric charge, and of positively charged protons. Negatively charged electrons are regarded as revolving in concentric orbits round the nucleus in sufficient number to balance the positive charge of the nucleus. Thus, an atom is mostly empty space. The electric charge of the nucleus balanced by a corresponding number of electrons determines the nature of the element. For example, the helium nucleus has only two electrons revolving in orbit; that of copper has 29 electrons, revolving in five orbits, with one electron in the outermost orbit. It is the number of electrons in the outer orbit that decides what family in the periodical table an element belongs to, and which elements will combine; for all electrons are identical and interchangeable and, under certain conditions, atoms borrow electrons from each other. The atomic weight of an element is the weight of an atom of the element compared with that of a hydrogen atom. The atomic number of an element is the number of positive charges on the nucleus. Isotopes are forms of the same element with the same atomic number and similar properties, but with differing atomic weights because they have different numbers of neutrons. The mass number of an atom or its nucleus is the total number of protons and neutrons in the nucleus. Thus, the atomic number of uranium is 92 and the first of its three isotopes contain 146 neutrons, giving it a mass number of 238. The bombarding of atoms by high-speed particles, e.g. protons, neutrons or alpha particles, results in the transmutation of one element into another. When an atom is thus split, tremendous amounts of energy are released (see Atomic Energy).

ATOMIC BOMB, an aerial bomb which derives its explosive force from the fission of the nuclei of heavy elements such as uranium-235 and plutonium-239 atoms into lighter elements as they absorb neutrons (see Atomic Energy). The fission process is uncontrolled and the energy released in the chain reaction is tremendous. The heat, wind and radiation produced by the explosion possess immense destructive power. The chief source of destruction is the shock wave which spreads out from the centre of the explosion. A bomb exploded at an elevation of 2000 ft may develop a pressure more than 100,000 times atmospheric pressure and produce a temperature above a million degrees. The surrounding air is heated to incandescence and rises rapidly, looking like a ball of fire. As it cools, this ball becomes a bubble of gases which begin to condense, forming the characteristic mushroom-shaped cloud following in the wake of an atomic bomb explosion. Radioactive fission products (fallout) descend to earth in the form of tiny particles which may constitute a serious danger to health and affect the organisms of future generations. The first atomic bomb was dropped on Hiroshima, Japan, on August 6, 1945, seriously damaging or completely destroying an area of more than 4 sq. miles. (See also Hydrogen Bomb.)

ATOMIC ENERGY, the energy produced by the fission or splitting of the nuclei of certain kinds of uranium or plutonium atoms (see Atom). The mass of the atom is converted into energy in a chain-reaction involving the absorption of neutrons. Each nucleus undergoing fission releases one or more neutrons inducing further fission, thus setting up a self-sustaining chain reaction. The nuclei split into fragments which fly apart with tremendous speed, releasing enormous kinetic energy transferred to all surrounding material. Nuclear fission produces tremendous amounts of heat which is used to produce high-pressure steam for turbines driving electric generators. Thus, the energy released in the fission of one out of every hundred atoms in a single pound of uranium is equivalent to that released in the burning of 100 tons of coal. The controlled chain-reaction and heat transfer are carried out in a nuclear reactor. Fast reactors use the neutrons at the speeds produced in fission, slow reactors incorporate a moderator such as graphite. Reactors are used as a source of neutrons, to produce plutonium for atomic bombs or for other reactors, and to generate electric power. In Scotland the fast reactor at Dounreay was the first in the world to produce electricity on a commercial scale, in 1962; in this year also two British nuclear power stations, at Berkeley (Glos.) and Bradwell (Essex), began to feed electricity into the national grid, and were to be followed by six others; but there is doubt about economic disadvantages. Atomic energy is used to power submarines and other ships.

ATOMIC PILE, see Nuclear Reactor.

ATTICA, peninsula in southeast Greece jutting into the Aegean Sea. Since the 5th century B.C. its chief city has been Athens. Its coastline, which encouraged seafaring, was one reason for its predominance.

ATTILA (*c.* 406—453), King of the Huns in the Danube basin, known as the 'Scourge of God' for the destruction and slaughter he left in his path. His kingdom extended from the Caspian Sea to the Rhine, covering most of southern and central Europe. He was defeated at Châlons in 451 by an army of Romans and Visigoths, and persuaded by the Pope, Leo the Great, to withdraw from Italy. His empire did not survive him, except in the name Hungary.

ATTLEE, Clement Richard, 1st Earl (1883—), British Prime Minister in the Labour Governments of 1945—50 and 1950—51. Leader of the Labour Party from 1935 till his retirement in 1955, he was Deputy Prime Minister in Winston Churchill's National Government during the Second World War. His government introduced extensive social services and nationalisation; and during his premiership India and Pakistan attained dominion status.

AUCKLAND, largest city in New Zealand, on North Island. Pop. (1959) 413,100. An important port, it exports dairy products, wool and timber. Industries include shipbuilding, canneries, sugar refining, brick making and ammunition plants. There are several beautiful parks, two cathedrals and institutions of higher learning. Auckland Harbour Bridge is a huge road bridge spanning the Waitemata River. It is 3520 ft long and has a clearance of 142 ft above high-water. The city was founded in 1840, and was the first capital.

AUGUSTINE, St (354—430), Church father and bishop of Hippo, At first an adherent of Manichaeism, he was attracted to Christianity by St Ambrose. He wrote profusely, including exegeses, letters and sermons, which made an enduring impression on medieval Christian teaching; his works include the *Confessions* and *The City of God.* He owed much to Neo-Platonism, and his philosophical outlook tended to mysticism.

AUGUSTINE OF CANTERBURY, St (d. *c.* 604), a prior in Rome and one of the most trusted servants of Pope Gregory I, who chose him to convert the English peoples to Christianity. Landing in Thanet in 597, he first converted King Ethelbert of Kent. He was the first Archbishop of Canterbury.

AUGUSTINIANS, a Roman Catholic religious order of mendicant friars founded in the 11th century which follows the rules established by St Augustine of Hippo. The leading contemporary groups are the Augustinian Hermits, the Recollects of St Augustine and the Discalced Augustinian Hermits; the order was strong in England at the time of the dissolution of the monasteries. Austin Friars is the name of an Augustinian monastery founded in London in 1253.

AUGUSTUS (63 B.C.—A.D. 14), the founder of the Roman empire, chief heir of Julius Caesar and a grandson of Caesar's sister. He became complete master of the Roman domains after defeating Mark Antony at Actium in 31 B.C. In 29 B.C. Octavian, as he then was, took the name of Augustus and the title of *princeps civitatis*, first citizen of the state, but preserved as far as possible the symbols of the republic. During his peaceful reign the arts and commerce flourished, Rome became an impressive city, and public administration was improved. After his death, he was worshipped as a god.

AURELIUS, Marcus, see Marcus Aurelius.

AUSCHWITZ (now Oswiecim), a town in Poland. Pop. (1960) 31,000. It was the site of a huge Nazi German concentration and extermination camp in 1940—45. The total number of victims is estimated at 4,000,000.

AUSTEN, Jane (1775—1817), English novelist. She seems to have begun her main novels in 1796, but it was not until 1811 that the first, *Sense and Sensibility*, was published, to be followed by *Pride and Prejudice*, *Mansfield Park* and *Emma*. *Northanger Abbey* (written in 1798) and *Persuasion* appeared posthumously in 1818. In all her novels, she restricted herself to the well-to-do rural society which she knew, surveying it with an observant and ironic eye. The largely undramatic events recounted in her cool and elegant prose come vividly to life from her exact portrayal of character against the background of naturally developing situations.

AUSTRALIA, Commonwealth of, the smallest continent, the largest island in the world. Pop. (1960) 10,281,000 plus 50,000 aborigines; area 2,974,581 sq. miles. Most of Australia is a plateau, the highest peak being just over 7000 ft;

the west is mainly desert. The climate varies from sub-tropical to temperate. In the north tropical rains fall from December to March; in the coastal areas of the southeast and southwest there is a pleasant Mediterranean climate. The Murray (1600 miles) and Darling drain the southeast plains. The lakes are saline. Fortunately for the country's merino sheep industry, there is abundant subterranean water in the Great Artesian Basin, which covers a fifth of the continent, including most of Queensland and parts of South Australia and New South Wales. In most desert areas no irrigation is possible. The Great Barrier Reef runs for 1250 miles parallel with the Queensland coast, the longest coral reef in the world. Vegetation and animal life are unique; Australia is the last home of the marsupials. The main crop is wheat, which is exported. Oats, barley and sugar-cane are also important. Australia produces nearly one-third of the world's wool. Minerals are of great importance and include silver, lead and zinc at Broken Hill, gold at Kalgoorlie, uranium, copper, coal and iron ore, providing material for the expanding industrial economy of Sydney and Newcastle. The population is heavily concentrated in the six ports and state capitals. The few aborigines survive from very primitive nomadic tribes who knew neither metals nor agriculture. The first to explore any part of the Australian continent was Captain Cook in 1770. From 1788 to 1840 the British Government sent convicts to the penal colonies of Botany Bay (Sydney) and Tasmania. However, from 1809 a free population had also been growing. In 1901 the six states of New South Wales, Victoria, Queensland, South Australia, Western Australia and Tasmania were federated into the Commonwealth of Australia. The two Internal Territories — Northern Territory and the Australian Capital Territory — who also joined the Commonwealth in 1901, do not have full voting rights: they are administrated from Canberra and have one member each in the House of Representatives. New Guinea (including Papua) and various groups of islands are administered by Australia. After the Second World War, in which it suffered direct attacks by the Japanese, the Commonwealth established closer ties with the U.S.A., although still firmly linked to Britain. The social services of Australia are very progressive. Since 1945 over a million immigrants have entered the country. The capital is Canberra (pop. 43,973). The principal cities are Sydney (2,054,800), Melbourne (1,777,700), Brisbane (567,000), Adelaide (562,500) and Perth (389,000).

AUSTRIA, a republic of Central Europe. Pop. (1960) 7,050,000; area 32,375 sq. miles. The main features of the country are the Danube valley of the north and the Alpine south, with the lake district of the Salzkammergut east of Salzburg. Tyrol and the Dolomites are shared with Italy. The highest Alpine peak is the Grossglockner (12,440 ft). The country is too mountainous to be self-sufficient in agriculture; the Alps are used for pastoral farming. There is abundant timber and water-power, an oilfield north of Vienna, and anthracite. Heavy industry has been developed in Styria and at Linz, aluminium is produced at Salzburg and Vienna produces clothing and luxury goods; but the tourist attractions of Vienna, Innsbruck, the Salzburg festival and the Alps are the country's economic salvation. Nearly a quarter of the population lives in Vienna (1,669,546). Other important cities are Graz (226,453), Linz (184,865), Salzburg (102,927) and Innsbruck (92,055). In 1282 the German king, Rudolf of Hapsburg, won the duchies of Austria and Styria; Tyrol was added to the Hapsburg lands in 1363, Hungary (with Croatia) and Bohemia in 1526 and Bosnia in 1878. The Hapsburg duke of Austria was from 1439 to 1740 always also the Holy Roman Emperor. Thereafter, with the accession of Maria Theresa, the Hapsburg-Lorraine branch provided emperors until the title was changed in 1806 to Emperor of Austria. The Hapsburgs continued to rule in Austria until Charles was exiled in 1918. It was the murder at Sarajevo of Franz Ferdinand, heir to the Austrian throne, on June 28, 1914, that precipitated the First World War, as a result of which Austria was separated from Hungary and shorn of all its dominions. Thus, lacking both markets and sources of supply, and even an outlet to the sea, Austria had difficulty in maintaining its economic independence. In 1938 it was absorbed by the Nazis and it was not until 1955 that it regained full freedom.

AUSTRIA-HUNGARY, a dual monarchy comprising a federation of Austria and Hungary from 1867–1918. Pop. (before 1914) 51,390,223; area 261,242 sq. miles. With separate parliaments, the countries had common ministers for foreign affairs, the army and finance.

AUSTRIAN SUCCESSION, War of the (1741—48), a product of Hohenzollern-Bourbon rivalry, precipitated by Frederick the Great's seizure of Silesia in 1740 when, under the terms of the Pragmatic Sanction (q.v.), Maria Theresa succeeded to the Hapsburg dominions. France, breaking a promise to respect the Sanction, decided to support Frederick (thereby in due course both losing Canada and India, and establishing Hohenzollern supremacy in Germany); and England, already at war with Spain, came to Maria Theresa's aid. Walpole, who opposed this policy, foreseeing a Jacobite rising, fell from office. After a fluctuating and bitter struggle the powers signed in 1748, and without enthusiasm, the peace of Aix-la-Chapelle by which Frederick retained Silesia and the *status quo* was otherwise, on the whole, restored.

AUTOMATION, the use of automatic control in manufacturing or in handling a mass of routine data, is not a new development; it is only the speed and ingenuity with which it is being applied to a wider range of operations that is new. Devices used include the computer (q.v.) and transfer mechanism that passes a work-piece automatically from one machine to another. Control engineering is the design of automatic devices applying the principle of feedback (q.v.) either to servo systems (see Servomechanism), which control position, speed etc., or to process control, in which a predetermined condition, e.g. of temperature pressure, waterlevel, is maintained.

The spread of automation leads to the replacement of semi-skilled labour by skilled technicians, and thus necessitates a rising standard of technical education, but although it may cause local displacement of labour it need not involve an overall redundancy. Automation is economic only if used on a large scale, and thus leads to larger factory units, and reduction in the costs of the product. It has made most progress in oil refineries, the chemical industry and the mass-production of automobiles.

AUTOMOBILE. The genesis of the modern automobile begins with a 16th-century vehicle propelled by coiled springs, Cugnot's steam carriage of 1770, Lenoir's wagon of 1862, powered by a gas engine, the first petrol engines of Daimler and Otto Benz (in the 1880s), and the invention of the pneumatic tyre, by R. W. Thomson in 1845, and independently by J. B. Dunlop in 1888. The problems of differential gear to enable vehicles to corner, and of the clutch, had engaged attention from early days. In 1895, a Daimler car won the Paris—Bordeaux race averaging 14.9 m.p.h. over 735 miles. Electric cars were not a success, but steam cars continued to hold their own against competition from petrol cars until after the turn of the century, and steam vans, e.g. the commercial vehicle made by Thorneycrofts, lasted till the 1930s. The first petrol-driven lorry had appeared in 1902, and in the 1930s heavy-oil compression-ignition precursors of the diesel-engine were introduced. By the mid-1920s giant tyres were making possible large motor-coaches and multi-wheel heavy lorries.

High costs made mass production inevitable. This was pioneered by Henry Ford with his Model T (1909) and, in Great Britain after the First World War, by the Morris-Cowley and the Austin-20. Rolls-Royce took an early lead in the luxury car market, the first six-cylinder 50 h.p. Silver Ghost having been produced in 1907. Popular rear-engined cars came in after the Second World War with the German Volkswagen, and the Citroën and Fiat versions. The gas-turbine car is now awaited.

AUXINS, growth hormones (see Endocrinology), which affect the rate of growth of plants and their metabolism (q.v.), found in plants and also in fungi, bacteria, human saliva and urine. They can be used by gardeners and farmers to stimulate or (in excess) retard growth of roots, leaves, buds, seeds etc., and for selective weed-killers.

AYUBKHAN, Mohammed (1907—), Pakistan statesman. He entered the Indian Army from Sandhurst, fought in Burma during the Second World War, and was promoted to be the first Commander-in-Chief of Pakistani forces in 1951. In 1958 he became President and head of a non-party government.

AZERBAIJAN, a province of north-west Iran and also a constituent Transcaucasian republic of the U.S.S.R. Iranian Azerbaijan is mountainous but the valleys are fertile. Pop. 3,200,000; area *c.* 41,150 sq. miles; the principal city is Tabriz. The Azerbaijan S.S.R. is highly industrialised and rich in oil. Pop. (1959) 3,700,000; area 33,200 sq. miles. The capital is Baku (pop. 968,000), on the Caspian, from which oil is shipped to other Caspian ports and also pumped by pipeline to the Black Sea port of Batumi in Georgia. The people are Turkish-speaking Moslems of Indo-Iranian stock.

AZIKIWE, Nnamdi (1904—), Nigerian politician. Educated at a number of American universities, where he acquired several degrees, he was editor of the *West African Pilot* from 1937—47, a member of the Legislative Council (1948—51), Premier of Eastern Nigeria (1954—59), Governor-General and, in 1963, President of Nigeria.

AZORES, islands in the North Atlantic, 1000 miles west of Portugal, to which they belong. Pop. 319,000; area 912 sq. miles. The Principal islands are São Miguel, Terceira and Pico. Fruits and grains are raised. The capital and chief seaport is Ponta Delgada (pop. 25,000).

AZOV, Sea of, a shallow northern arm of the Black Sea, to which it is connected by the Strait of Kerch. Its area is *c.* 14,000 sq. miles. The River Don flows into it.

AZTECS, an American Indian nation who conquered the Toltecs of the Mexican Valley, where they built their capital Tenochtitlan (now Mexico City) in Lake Texcoca in 1325, and which they dominated at the time of the Spanish conquest in 1519. They excelled in political, military and social organisation, and in agriculture, but their art was in keeping with their barbarous and sanguinary religion, based on human sacrifice.

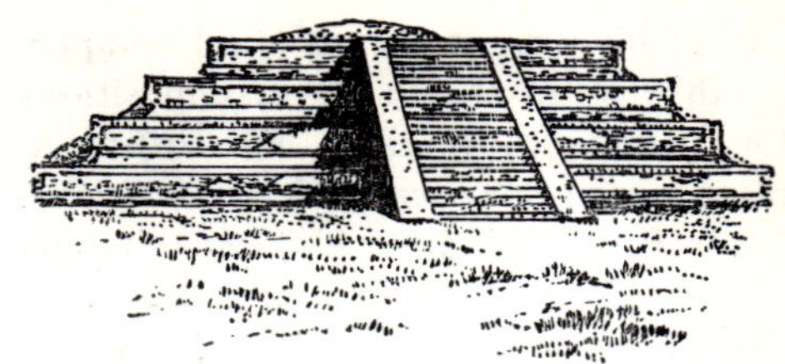
Aztec architecture. Base of a pyramid

B

BABYLON, the ancient capital of Babylonia. It rose to importance in the reign of Hammurabi, who made it his capital in *c.* 1780 B.C. Until the end of the 3rd century B.C., it was one of the most important cities in the Orient. The Tower of Babel was probably the first ziggurat (templetower), built just outside Babylon. A later building with trees growing on the upper terraces led to stories of the Hanging Gardens of Babylon.

BABYLONIA, the home of the Sumerian and succeeding civilisations, between the Euphrates and Tigris in lower Mesopotamia. The Sumerians, who were possibly there as early as 4000 B.C. eventually merged with the Semitic Accadians who arrived *c.* 2750 and under Sargon I (*c.* 2400) founded the first empire in western Asia. During this period cuneiform writing had been developed. The Amorites, also Semites, were the next to rule Babylonia, and attained prominence particularly under Hammurabi (*c.* 1770), whose legal code has survived. In 1275 B.C. Babylon was conquered by Assyria, and its greatness was in abeyance until the Chaldaeans revived it in the 6th century B.C., when Nebuchadnezzar rebuilt the city.

BACH, Johann Sebastian (1685—1750), German composer. His six Brandenburg concertos and the four suites for orchestra are among his greatest instrumental compositions. He wrote 295 church cantatas, five masses, four Passions, six motets and many secular cantatas. He brought counterpoint to highest perfection in the fugue, and was one of the earliest to see the potentialities of the 'well-tempered clavier' (i.e. with equal temperament, tuned so that acoustic differences are spread over all the keys and all sound tolerable). The surface clarity and simplicity of his work subtly conceal complex depths of mystery. His compositions for the organ would alone suffice to place him in the front rank of musicians. Two of his sons, Karl Phillipp Emanuel (1714—1788) and Johann Christian, also made notable contributions to music.

BACON, Francis Baron Verulam, Viscount St Albans (1561—1626), English politican, writer and philosopher. As an adviser of James I, he was convicted of accepting bribes (1621) and withdrew from political life. He devoted the rest of his life to science and literature, advocating an inductive method in science and philosophy. Although he himself made no outstanding contribution to science, his unique approach greatly influenced subsequent generations. His *Essays*, written as advice for a monarch, are full of subtle metaphor and illuminating phrase, but their inspiration runs no higher than expediency and the pursuit of material advantage.

BACON, Roger (*c.* 1214—94), English scientist and Franciscan philosopher. An outspoken opponent of the scholastic philosophers and advocate of active experimentation in place of passive speculative thought, he was commissioned by Pope Clement IV to write a general treatise on the sciences (*Opus majus*, *c.* 1266). He wrote on mathematics, geography and alchemy.

BACTERIA, microscopic one-celled organisms of the plant kingdom. They have three main forms, spherical *cocci*, rod-shaped *bacilli*, and spiral *spirilla* Bacteria multiply rapidly by splitting. Some cause disease, while others are useful to man in preserving and flavouring foods and in fertilising the soil.

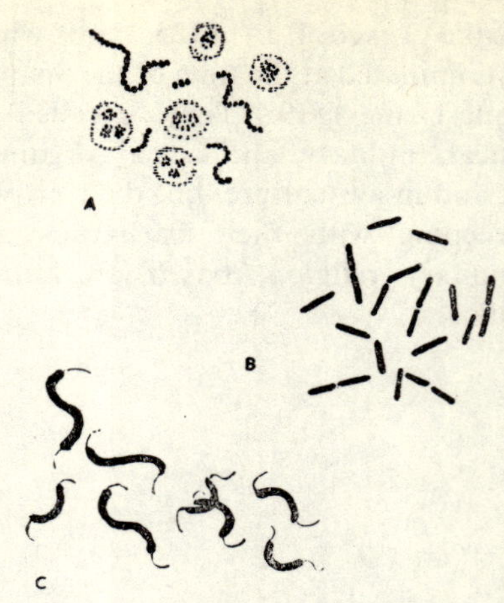

Bacteria
A. Spherical cocci B. Rod-shaped bacilli
C. Spiral spirilla

BADEN-POWELL, Robert S., 1st Baron (1857—1941), British soldier and founder of the Boy Scout movement in 1908. He distinguished himself in the Boer War, holding out in besieged Mafeking for 215 days against superior numbers.

BADMINTON, an indoor, usually winter, game of the lawn-tennis type played with long rackets and feathered shuttles over a net. It takes its name from the Duke of Beaufort's house in Gloucestershire, where the game originated in the 1860s from the children's game of battledore and shuttlecock.

BAER, Karl Ernst von (1792—1876), Estonian biologist. The founder of the science of embryology, he discovered the mammalian ovum and the notochord, one of the characteristics of the chordates.

BAGEHOT, Walter (1826—77), English economist, critic and journalist. His most important works are *Physics and Politic* and *The English Constitution*. He edited *The Economist* magazine from 1860 until his death.

BAGHDAD, capital of Iraq, on the Tigris. Founded in the 8th century A.D., it was the capital of the Abbasid caliphate for nearly five centuries, except for brief interruptions. In the reign of Haroun-al-Rashid, it was noted for its splendour and cultural life. Pop. (1957) 355,958. Its manufactures consist of silks and other textiles, leather goods, and articles of copper and brass.

BAHAISM, an eclectic religion founded in 1863 by Baha-Ullah in Persia. The basic precept of Bahaism is that all religions have an essential unity, their various revelations being manifestations of the same Divine Being. There are groups in Europe and the United States.

BAHAMAS, British archipelago of some 20 inhabited islands in the Caribbean. Pop. (1960) 106,677; area 4404 sq. miles. The principal island is New Providence, containing the capital Nassau (pop. 50,405). Sponges, crayfish and salt are exported. Columbus's earliest landfall in the New World was one of these islands — it has not been established which. The Bahamas were occupied first by the Spanish and then, in 1629, by the English. In 1940 land for a naval base was leased for 99 years to the United States.

BAHRAIN ISLANDS, an archipelago off the east coast of Arabia, forming a Sheikhdom under British protection. Pop. (1959) 143,213; area 213 sq. miles. There are large oil deposits, an oil refinery and a pearling industry. The capital is Manama (pop. 61,837).

BAIN, Alexander (1818—1903), Scottish psychologist and educationist. Founder of the world's first psychological journal, *Mind*, he was the author of *The Senses and the Intellect* and *The Emotions and the Will*.

BAIRD, John Logie (1888—1946), Scottish physicist and television pioneer. His television system was first demonstrated (1926) and used for public transmissions in Germany and England (1929), but in 1936 the B.B.C. gave preference to the alternative Marconi-E.M.I. system. In spite of this bitter disappointment Baird continued to work on stereoscopic, colour and large-screen television.

BAKELITE, the first synthetic phenolic resin, a plastic, consisting of phenol and formaldehyde, of great strength. A non-conductor of electricity, it is insoluble in most chemicals and resists temperatures up to 300°c. It was named after L. H. Baekeland, the American chemist who first developed it in 1907.

BALACLAVA, Battle of (1854), an indecisive engagement in which the British repelled a Russian attack on the port of Balaclava at the beginning of the Crimean War; it is immortalised by Tennyson's poem *The Charge of the Light Brigade*.

BALBOA, Vasco Nuñez de (*c.* 1475—1517), Spanish adventurer, explorer and leader of the expedition which crossed the Isthmus of Panama and discovered the Pacific Ocean. He was charged with treason and executed before he could carry out his plan to conquer Peru.

BALDER, in Scandinavian mythology, god of light. Immune to harm from everything but the mistletoe, he was killed by a mistletoe dart thrown by the blind Hodur, at the instigation of the evil Loki.

BALDNESS, the loss of hair from the scalp. It results from destruction of the hair follicles and cannot be remedied. Baldness occurs mostly in men as they grow older. Its occurrence and cause are believed to be hereditary. A variety called *alopecia areata* results from nervous stress and is usually temporary; but the recovery of the hair can in no way be aided or speeded by treatment.

BALDWIN I (1058—1118), King of Jerusalem (1110—18). He succeeded his brother, Godfrey of Bouillon, as Defender of the Holy Sepulchre, and then assumed the title of King. His reign was energetic and saw the expansion of the Crusader Kingdom.

BALDWIN, Stanley, 1st Earl, of Bewley (1867—1947). British statesman who achieved prominence in 1922 when he moved the Carlton Club resolution, by which the Conservatives withdrew from the Lloyd George Coalition Government. He subsequently became Chancellor of the Exchequer and negotiated the American War Debt Settlement. He succeeded Bonar Law as Premier in 1923 although he failed to secure a majority in the 1924 General Election. The Labour Government lasted only a few months and he again became Premier (1924—9) during which time the General Strike occurred.

BALEARIC ISLANDS, an archipelago and Spanish province in the western Mediterranean. Pop. (1959) 441,842; area 1936 sq. miles. Majorca (q.v.) is the largest island; Minorca (q.v.) and Ibiza are also of importance.

BALFOUR, Arthur James, 1st Earl of (1848—1930), British statesman and philosopher. A Conservative, he became Prime Minister in 1902 but resigned when his party was split on the tariff reform issue. He served under Asquith as First Lord of the Admiralty in 1915. As Foreign Secretary (1916—19) he issued the Balfour Declaration pledging British support for a Jewish national home in Palestine. He subsequently represented Britain at various international conferences. His chief philosophic work was *Theism and Humanism* (1914).

BALI, an island in Indonesia immediately east of Java. Pop. 1,200,000; area 2250 sq. miles. The Balinese, notably handsome and of fine physique, are akin to the Javanese racially, but in religion have been Hindu since the 10th century. They are devoted to religious drama, music and dance. They are highly skilled craftsmen and tillers of the fertile volcanic soil, and thus their standard of living is high. The island is administered with neighbouring Lombok. The capital is Singaradja.

BALIOL, John de (1249—1315), King of Scotland, of Norman ancestry. His weak claim to the throne was supported by Edward I of England, against whom he subsequently revolted and he was forced to abdicate. His mother founded Balliol College, Oxford, when his father died in 1269.

BALKAN PENINSULA, a peninsula of southeast Europe south of the lower Danube and the Sava. The Balkan countries are Rumania, Bulgaria, Yugoslavia, Albania, Greece and Turkey-in-Europe. A stepping-stone from Asia to Europe, and lacking any great agricultural or mineral resources, the Balkans have become, through their stormy history, a by-word for political fragmentation, strife and retarded development.

BALKAN WARS (1912—13), two wars, the first of which was fought by the allied forces of Bulgaria, Serbia, Greece and Montenegro against Turkey, and ended in the enlargement of Bulgaria at the expense of Macedonia and Thrace, and the recognition of an independent Albania. After the capitulation of Turkey in May 1913 the allies quarrelled over the division of spoils and Bulgaria was crushed by its former allies, aided by Rumania and Turkey. In addition to losing its recent gains in Macedonia and Thrace, Bulgaria was forced to cede Southern Dobruja to Rumania; in consequence the central powers were able to enlist Bulgaria on their side in the First World War.

BALL, John (d. 1381), English priest. Illegally preaching the doctrines of John Wycliffe, he later became a leader in Wat Tyler's Peasants' Revolt (1381) and was captured and executed.

BALLAD, a narrative folk-poem in straight verse. Ballads are produced by the people and transmitted from generation to generation, often sung and accompanied by dancing. English ballads are particularly rich, the most outstanding being the Robin Hood cycle and the North Country and Scottish Border ballads. Some ballads are found widely distributed, e.g. 'Lord Randal' found from Scandinavia to southern Italy; and United States ballads, e.g. 'Frankie and Johnny' have become well known in Europe.

BALLET, a composite art form in which, as equal partners, dance, music, wordless mime and décor combine to tell a story or suggest an atmosphere; the performers are rigorously trained in an exacting and rigid convention of steps and poses based on the five basic positions of the feet, from which all movements begin and at which they all must end. The convention of dancing on the points (toes) was introduced in the early 18th century. In its modern form ballet owes its revival to Russian influence, through the impresario Diaghilev, the choreographers Fokine, Nijinsky, Massine, the dancers Pavlova, Anton Dolin. In Britain Dame Ninette de Valois founded the Sadler's Wells (later to become the Royal) Ballet, where Dame Margot Fonteyn was trained and another famous English dancer, Alicia Markova, appeared.

BALLISTICS, the science of projectiles expelled from firearms as they travel along the barrel, through the air and through the target. It is used in crime-detection to determine what weapon discharged a particular bullet.

BALLOON, a lighter-than-air craft containing one or more compartments filled with a lifting gas. Balloons consist of a bag inflated by a gas such as hydrogen or the more common, non-flammable, helium. Dirigible balloons are elongated in shape and driven by motors; they may be rigid, semi-rigid or non-rigid. The first balloon to carry a man was a hot-air balloon invented by the Montgolfier brothers in 1783. Incendiary bullets rendered observation balloons of little use in war, but in 1939—45 barrage balloons were successful in keeping bombers too high for accurate bombing. In peacetime balloons are used up to 100,000 ft to collect meteorological data, and in 1957 an American doctor ascended to this height.

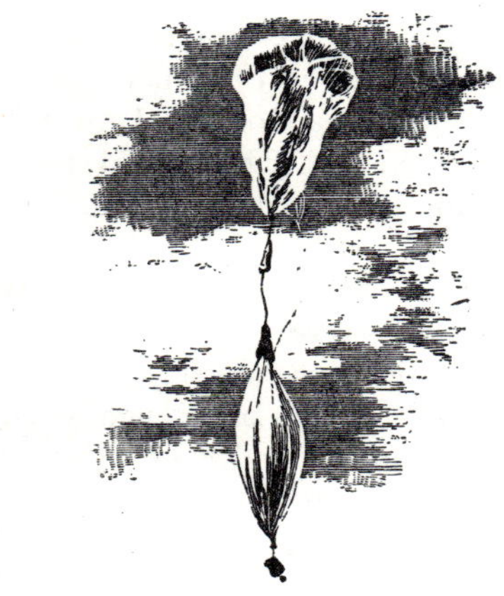

Balloon for collection of meteorological data

BALMORAL CASTLE, a royal residence in western Aberdeenshire, Scotland, on the River Dee. Prince Albert purchased it in 1852 and bequeathed it to his wife, Queen Victoria.

BALTIC, see Sea.

BALTIMORE, largest city in Maryland, U.S.A. Pop. (1960) 939,024. An international port on the Chesapeake Bay, it is also an important industrial and communications centre. Its industries include heavy transport equipment, engineering, petroleum refining, chemicals foodstuffs, canning, textiles and sawmill products. The city has numerous monuments and institutions of higher learning, including the Johns Hopkins University. It was founded in 1729. In 1904 a great fire ravaged the business section.

BALZAC, Honoré de (1799—1850), French novelist. Wrote 40 novels, constituting two-thirds of his projected total history of all aspects of French society after the Revolution, entitled *La Comédie humaine*. *César Birotteau*, *La Cousin Bette* and *Le Cousin Pons* are set in bourgeois Paris, *Le Curé de Tours* in the provinces. The most representatively Balzacian are perhaps *Les Illusions perdues* and its sequel *Splendeurs et misères des courtisanes*. Balzac wrote with acute insight and immense liveliness in styles (for he used many) that are vigorous and apt rather than elegant.

BANDA, Hastings (1902—), Nyasaland politician. Educated at the High School, Ohio, and B.Phil., Chicago University (1931), he studied medicine in Tennessee until 1937 and then took a diploma in medicine at Edinburgh University. He worked in a Tyneside mission during the Second World War and set up in practice in Willesden, London, after the war. After the formation of the Federation of Rhodesia and Nyasaland, he practised in Kumasi, Gold Coast, until his return to Nyasaland in 1958. Elected President of the Nyasaland African Congress, he was in prison from 1959—60. He then became President of the Malawi Congress Party and in 1963 Nyasaland's first Prime Minister.

BANGKOK, capital of Thailand, on the Menam (Chao Phraya) River. Pop. (1957) 1,204,894. Most of the inhabitants (a high proportion of them are Chinese or Malayan) live in boats on the numerous *klongs* or canals. Bangkok is 20 miles from the sea and, for large ships, was rendered inaccessible by a sand-bar; a new harbour now takes vessels up to 28-ft draught at high water. There are rice and teak mills, and much timber is floated down the river to Bangkok.

BANK, a business establishment specialising in services involving money. It accepts deposits on which it pays a fixed rate of interest and extends credit of all kinds. Banks also maintain facilities for the safekeeping of valuables and make it possible for depositors to pay by cheque. The nationalised Bank of England issues legal tender notes and serves as the banker of the government and of other banks.

BANKRUPTCY, the legal status of insolvency providing for the equitable division of the assets of a debtor who is wholly or partially unable to meet his obligations. If there is no claim of intent to defraud, the debtor is then discharged from all liabilities, and is free to make a fresh start.

BANNOCKBURN, a village near Stirling, Scotland, where King Robert the Bruce defeated the numerically superior

English troops of Edward II in 1314.

BANNS OF MARRIAGE, the announcement of intention to wed made on three Sundays in a place of divine worship. It is a summons to anyone who might wish to oppose the marriage to state his objections or remain silent forever.

BANTING, Sir Frederick Grant (1891—1941), Canadian physician and co-discoverer of insulin. He was awarded the 1923 Nobel Prize for his contribution to physiology and medicine.

BANTU, a term originally applied to African languages spoken south of a line drawn across the continent from the Cameroons to Kenya, and by extension to the people speaking them. Some prominent Bantu groups are the Zulu, Matabele, Swazi, Mashona, Baganda, Kikuyu. Hottentots, Bushmen and Masai are not Bantu. The term is an invented name meaning 'people'. These peoples appear not to be aborigines but to have come from the north.

BAPTISM, a Christian sacrament originating from the Jewish custom of baptising proselytes (but not Jews); John the Baptist preached the baptism of total immersion in the Jordan, to which Jesus submitted. Jesus did not himself baptise but told his disciples to do so (Matt. 28.19). In the Roman Catholic Church it used to be held necessary for salvation, as washing away original sin, but Protestants do not hold salvation to depend of necessity on baptism.

BAPTISTS, a Protestant religious denomination founded in Amsterdam (*c.* 1606) by John Smyth and Thomas Helwys, dissenters who had fled from England. Baptists are so called because of their belief in the sacrament of baptism by immersion only.

BARBADOS, an island in the West Indies. Pop. (1959) 237,000; area 166 sq. miles. The main products are sugar, molasses and rum and sea-island cotton is grown. The principal town is Bridgetown (pop. 19,000).

BARBAROSSA, see Frederick I.

BARBIROLLI, Sir John (1899—), British conductor of French and Italian parentage, associated with the Hallé Orchestra in Manchester since 1943. He conducted the New York Philharmonic from 1937—42.

BARBIZON SCHOOL, a group of French painters associated with the village of Barbizon near Paris, which concentrated on painting nature in the open air. It included Corot, Millet, Charles-François Daubigny. Jules Dupré and Théodore Rousseau.

BARBUSSE, Henri (1873—1935), French novelist. His principal work was *Le Feu*, describing the brutalities of war from the point of view of the ordinary soldier. He was attracted by Communist ideals, and died in Moscow.

BARCELONA, sea port and capital of Catalonia, Spain, on the Mediterranean. Pop. (1960) 1,503,062. A leading commercial and industrial centre, it produces textiles, chemicals, clothing, machinery, foodstuffs and glass. The old Citadel town has many historic buildings, including a university (founded in 1430). Barcelona was first settled by the Carthaginian Hamilcar Barca, after whom it is named.

BARENTS, Willem (d. 1597), Dutch Arctic explorer. He discovered Spitsbergen while searching for a northeast passage along the north coast of Europe; the Barents Sea is named after him.

BARIUM, see Elements.

BARLEY, a cereal grown throughout the world. Botanically a grass, it is one of the world's oldest grains. It is used for human consumption and also for feeding livestock, and for malting in the brewing of beer and the manufacture of alcohol for whisky.

BARNARDO, Thomas John (1845—1905), British physician and social reformer. He devoted his life to aiding waifs, establishing homes for them throughout England. He also organised their emigration to Canada.

BARNACLE, a small, hard-shelled marine animal which attaches itself to moving objects in the sea, including the bottoms of ships (goose barnacle), and to rocks, breakwaters, etc. (acorn barnacle).

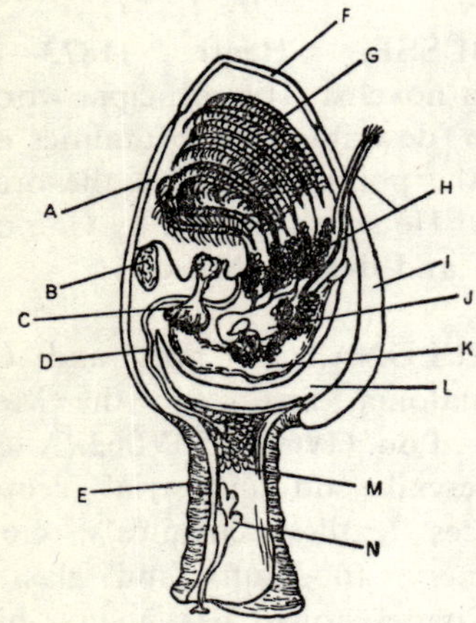

Barnacle
A. Scutum B. Adductor muscle C. Digestive caeca D. Oviduct E. Stalk F. Tergum G. Thoracic limbs H. Male reproductive organs I. Carina J. Seminal vesicle K. Stomach L. Mantle cavity M. Ovary N. Cement gland

BARNUM, Phineas Taylor (1810—91), American showman. After achieving fame with the attractions he exhibited in the American Museum in New York, he entered the circus business and eventually, with James A. Bailey, directed 'The Greatest Show on Earth'.

BAROMETER, an instrument for determining atmospheric pressure, and altitude. The mercurial barometer consists of a column of mercury in an upright glass tube placed in an open vessel. The height of the mercury fluctuates according to changes in air pressure. Aneroid barometers consist of a metal box, from which all air has been removed, and a sensitive diaphragm. A falling barometer, indicating lowered atmospheric pressure, is a storm warning. Meteorologists express the readings in millibars, units of pressure, instead of inches of length of the mercury column: 1000 millibars (mb) = 29.53 ins.

BAROQUE, the name (originally a derogatory nickname) for an art style of dramatic and exuberant character, and especially for the architectural style of Roman Catholic countries of southern Europe from the 16th to 18th centuries. The use of ornament was lavish, sometimes excessive. Rubens and Bernini were early practitioners. The style was the precursor of Rococo.

BARRIE, Sir James, (1860—1937), Scottish author and playwright. In his novels he led the Kailyard or tartan-and-whimsy school, with sentimental pictures of Scottish rural life that ensured a great but evanescent popularity for *The Little Minister* and *A Window in Thrums*. The same qualities mark some of his other plays, such as *Dear Brutus*, *The Boy David* etc., and only *Peter Pan* lives on to delight the young.

BARRYMORE, a family of American actors headed by Maurice Barrymore (Herbert Blythe; 1847—1905) who began his career in England. His wife Georgiana

Drew (1856—93), his sons John (1882—1942) and Lionel (1878—1954), and his daughter Ethel (1879—1959) all achieved fame, the last three in motion pictures as well as on the stage.

Detail of baroque architecture

BARTHOLOMEW'S EVE, Massacre of St (Aug. 24, 1572), the massacre of Huguenots by order of Charles IX, who had been persuaded by the Queen Mother, Catherine de' Medici, that there was a Protestant plot against him. Catherine did not hesitate to use the Guise family, whom she hated, to further her designs. It was decided to use the opportunity provided by the wedding of the Protestant Henry of Navarre (later Henry IV) to the King's sister, Margaret of Valois, which would bring most of the leading Huguenots to Paris. The first victim was Admiral Coligny, whose influence over Charles was the cause of Catherine's mad jealousy. The massacres spread all over France and lasted until October. There is insufficient evidence to give even an approximate number of the victims, but figures varying from 2000 to 70,000 have been mentioned. Henry of Navarre saved his life by a prudent and temporary recantation.

BARTÓK, Béla (1881—1945). Hungarian composer and pianist. He collected folk-music in Hungary and the Balkans which strongly influenced his own compositions. In 1940 he emigrated to the United States, where he died.

BARTOLOMMEO, Fra (1475—1517), Florentine artist. He fell under the influence of Savonarola, following whose death at the stake he burnt his work and entered a Dominican monastery. A portrait of Savonarola and other work has, however, survived from this period. After some years he resumed painting, executing work for his order, such as '*The Vision of St Bernard*' (Accademia, Florence).

BASE, a chemical substance which, when combined with an acid, produces a salt and water. In water solutions it forms negatively charged particles called hydroxyl ions. Soluble bases are termed alkalis.

BASEBALL, the American national game. It is played by teams of nine players. The pitcher delivers the ball at great speed, the batter tries to hit it with his round bat; should he succeed and the ball not be caught, he tries to run round the infield, a square enclosed by the three bases and the home plate, without being 'put out'. If he gets back to the home plate he scores a point for his team.

BASIL, St (*c.* 330—379), Church father. A fearless opponent of Arianism, he drew up the rules which still guide the monks of the Greek Orthodox Church.

BASILICA, originally a Roman public hall or court of justice, with a central nave flanked by aisles. Early Christians used the same ground plan in building their churches, which thus came to be called basilicas.

BASKERVILLE, John (1706—75), English printer and typefounder. He printed the Bible, the Book of Common Prayer and Latin classics.

BASKETBALL, outdoor and indoor game played by opposing teams of five players each. A ball about 30 in. in circumference is used. Each team attempts to throw it into the opposing team's basket (which is suspended from a back-board at the end of the court), in order to score a point.

BASLE, the third largest city in Switzerland (pop. 205,800), it stands on the Rhine near the German border and is an important centre of the textile and chemical industries.

BASQUES, a people of undetermined origin living on the mountain slopes of southwest France and northern Spain. They speak a language which has no affinities with any other language. There are about 700,000 Basques, of whom 500,000 live in Spain. Ignatius Loyola and Francis Xavier were Basques.

BASTILLE, a 14th-century prison in Paris where persons were imprisoned without trial on the royal authority of a *lettre de cachet*. Although they could take their own servants and furniture, and ask friends to dinner, the prison became a symbol of tyranny, and so was stormed by the revolutionaries in 1789. The attack, which brought down the *ancien régime*, succeeded on that still-observed Fourteenth of July in rescuing the inmates: four forgers, two lunatics and an *aristo* incarcerated at his family's request.

BASUTOLAND, a High Commission Territory and a British enclave in the Republic of South Africa. Pop. (1961) 897,845 (nearly all Africans); area 11,716 sq. miles. The capital is Maseru. Grains are its main crop; wool and mohair are exported. Under the South Africa Act (1910) it was provided that Basutoland should not be united with South Africa without the consent of its inhabitants.

BATH, English county borough and spa in Somerset on the Avon River. Pop. (1961) 80,856. The medicinal waters were known in Roman times and in the 18th century led to Bath's becoming the greatest resort of fashion in the country, embellished with Georgian buildings built by 'Wood of Bath' and his son, John Wood the Younger, notably the stately Circus and noble Royal Crescent.

BATH, Order of the, a British knightly order revived by King George I in 1725, but said to have been founded in 1399 by Henry IV.

BATHYSCAPHE; Bathysphere, diving apparatus for observing and photographing at great depths below the surface of the sea. The bathyscaphe is a deep-sea boat equipped with all kinds of apparatus and controlled by two men. The bathysphere is a spherical chamber lowered by a strong cable. In 1953 Professor Piccard reached a depth of 10,000 ft in his bathyscaphe.

BATTENBERG, ancient German family name revived in favour of the grandchildren of a Duke of Hesse, one of whom was the father of Queen Ena of Spain and the 1st Marquess of Carisbrooke. Another was Prince Louis of Battenberg (1854—1921), who became a naturalised British subject in 1868 and was appointed First Sea Lord in 1912. Public prejudice led to his resignation at the beginning of the First World War. In 1917 he took the name of Mountbatten and was created 1st

Marquess of Milford Haven. He married Queen Victoria's daughter, Princess Alice, by whom he had four children, the youngest of whom was Earl Mountbatten of Burma (q.v.) who, in 1955, was also made First Sea Lord. Another of the children was Princess Alice, mother of the Duke of Edinburgh.

BATTERY, electric, a device for producing an electric current through chemical action. A dry-cell or primary battery, involving the interaction of zinc, carbon and ammonium chloride, exhausts itself and cannot be recharged. Secondary or storage batteries (accumulators) can be restored by recharging. There are two main types of accumulator, the lead-acid and the alkaline (nickel-iron or nickel cadmium); the latter does not deteriorate through disuse.

BATTLESHIP, a heavily armoured warship mounting powerful guns, once regarded as the main source of a fleet's strength, but now displaced by the aircraft carrier. The last British battleship, H.M.S. Vanguard (44,500 tons), completed in 1946, mounted eight 15-in. guns. U.S.S. Iowa (57,450 tons) had nine 16-in. guns. Battleships were equipped with extensive batteries of anti-aircraft guns, but they remained too vulnerable in conditions of modern warfare.

BAUDELAIRE, Charles (1821—67), French poet and critic. He published only one book of poems, *Les Fleurs du mal* (1857). A prey to anguish after the remarriage of his mother, to whom he was inordinately attached, and to despair from a deep conviction of sin, he was able to evoke magical beauty even from the contemplation of the sordidities of modern life, in resonant alexandrines full of startling imagery and bizarre juxtapositions of words. He is generally regarded as a precursor of the Symbolists, and his critical works have had great influence. He also translated much of Edgar Allen Poe, whom he deeply admired. Dissipation and debt ruined his health, and his last two years were spent in hospitals.

BAVARIA, (Bayern), administrative division in the south of West Germany. Pop. (1961) 9,514,000; area 27,112 sq. miles. Much of it is mountainous; the main crops are wheat, potatoes and sugar-beet. Originally occupied by Celtic tribes, the area was ruled by dukes of the Wittelsbach line from 1180 to 1918. The capital is Munich (pop. 1,101,400).

BAYEUX TAPESTRY, ancient embroidery preserved at Bayeux, France. It depicts the invasion and conquest of England by William the Conqueror in 1066 and, in the margins, incidents from Aesop's fables, grotesque animals and sporting scenes. It probably dates from the early 12th century.

BAYREUTH, a town in southern Germany, famed for its annual musical festival at which the works of Richard Wagner — its founder — are performed.

BEACHY HEAD, a headland near Eastbourne in Sussex, England, on the English Channel. Its white chalk cliffs, which mark the end of the South Downs, rise almost vertically to a height of 575 ft.

BEACONSFIELD, Earl of, see Disraeli, Benjamin.

BEAR, a large, heavily built, fur-bearing mammal of which there are seven main kinds, widely distributed over Europe, Asia and America. The eyes and ears are small and the tail very short. Although they are carnivorous, their teeth are small and adapted to a vegetarian diet; the white polar bear is mainly aquatic and feeds on fish and cetaceans. Bears are plantigrade (i.e. walk on the soles of their feet). Species living in cold climates hibernate, but remain warm-blooded during this period. The Brown bear became extinct in England about the 11th century. Silver grizzly bears are found in the western states of America.

BEATIFICATION, an act of the Pope by which he declares a deceased person to be in heaven and entitled to be called blessed (*beatus*), and grants him a form of homage which is the first step towards canonisation.

BEATTY, David, 1st Earl (1871—1936), British Admiral of the Fleet and First Sea Lord (1919—27). He commanded the battlecruiser squadron at the outbreak of the First World War. His force sank four German ships in Heligoland Bight and he commanded the advance fleet in the indecisive Battle of Jutland in 1916.

BEAVERBROOK, Maxwell Aitken, 1st Baron (1879—1964), British newspaper publisher and politican. Coming to England from his native Canada in 1907, he became a member of Parliament and was made a peer in 1917. Serving as Minister of Information in the First World War, he later bought the London *Sunday Express*, *Evening Standard* and *Daily Express*, which he used to advance his views on Empire Free Trade. In 1940—42 he was Minister for Aircraft Production and Minister of Supply. He began a series of political memoirs with *Men and Power*, 1917—18 (1956).

BECHUANALAND, a High Commission Territory under British protection in southern Africa. Pop. (1960) 327,305; area *c.* 275,000 sq. miles (including the Kalahari desert). The capital is Serowe, but the country is administered from Mafeking. Most of the population, including the Bamangwato, are Bantu. Rearing of cattle is the chief occupation.

BECKET, St Thomas (1118—70), Archbishop of Canterbury; became involved in serious controversy with Henry II over the rights of the clergy; when he continued intransigent, the King lost his temper and cried out: 'Is there none that will rid me of this low-born priest?' Some knights who heard this murdered Becket in his cathedral. He was canonised in 1172.

BECKETT, Samuel (1906—), Anglo-Irish playwright who settled in France early in his career. A characteristic work is *Waiting for Godot* (1955), in which, with the minimum of characterisation and incident, he poses the deepest questions of existence.

BECQUEREL, Antoine Henri (1852—1908), French physicist. He discovered that certain uranium salts emitted radiation (then called Becquerel rays); in 1903 he shared the Nobel Prize for physics with Pierre and Marie Curie for his work on spontaneous radioactivity. He was the first to suggest using radium for treating cancer. His other work was on phosphorescence, light and magnetism.

BEDE, The Venerable (*c.* 673—735), English monk and historian. Working at Jarrow, where he became abbot, he wrote a number of scientific and exegetical works of no great interest today. His importance lies in his histories, the greatest of which was the *Ecclesiastical History of the English Nation*, notable for style, accurate chronology and careful use of sources. Another major work was his *Life of St Cuthbert*. He influenced the revival of learning at York and, indirectly through Alcuin, in Europe.

BEDFORDSHIRE, a county in south-central England. Pop. (1961) 380,704; area 473 sq. miles. Mostly flat, it is devoted to farming. Wheat is the main crop. The county town is Bedford; the largest town is Luton (pop. 131,505), with its automobile industry.

BEDLAM, the popular name for the Hospital of St Mary of Bethlehem, Bedlam being a corruption of Bethlehem. At first a priory, it became a mental hospital late in the 14th century. The name came to be used of any mental hospital and, since their inmates were through ignorance infamously treated, of any riotous uproar.

BEECHAM, Sir Thomas (1879—1961), English conductor. Capable of playing every musical instrument, he did much to further music in England. He was associated with six orchestras, including the London Philharmonic, introduced Russian ballet and opera, and helped new musicians. In 1945 he became conductor of the Royal Philharmonic Orchestra. He was especially noted for his interpretations of Mozart, Richard Strauss and Delius.

BEER, a fermented drink usually made from malted barley and other cereals, with hops added for the characteristic flavour. From the 15th century onwards, beer was the name given to ale to which hops were added, but the name ale is still given to many beers, e.g. bitter ale, a medium-strength draught beer; mild ale, a low-strength draught beer; pale ale, a bottled strongly hopped beer similar to bitter; brown ale, a beer of the same strength as this but using darker malt and sugar; and light ale, a bottled lager-coloured beer.

BEES, insects of the order Hymenoptera, of which the honey-bee is the most important to man. It gathers plant pollen and nectar and stores honey in honeycombs made of the wax it secretes for the purpose. By "dancing" at the entrance to the hive the honey-bee can indicate the direction and distance of food supplies. The occupants of the hive are divided into queens, infertile females (workers) and male drones. Bee-keeping is an occupation that dates back to ancient times. Bees of various kinds are found all over the world, some solitary, some living in colonies, but all rendering service to man by the pollination of flowers.

Honey Bee

BEETHOVEN, Ludwig van (1770—1827), German composer. Beginning to study music at the age of five, he published his first compositions aged 13. For a short time he studied with Haydn and Mozart in Vienna. Troubled by his two younger brothers and beset by ill-health, he was an unhappy and resentful man. In his late twenties he began to go deaf, and by 1819 he had completely lost his hearing. His work falls into three periods — the first, when he was close to Haydn and Mozart; the second (1802—12), when he wrote the great music for which he is most widely known; and, after five years of inactivity, the last ten years of his life, during which he rose to even greater heights, as in his last five string quartets. In works as diverse as the Fifth and Ninth (Choral) symphonies, the *Emperor* concerto, the violin sonata, the Archduke trio, the *Appassionata*, *Pathétique* and *Moonlight* sonatas, the *Mass in D*, the last string quartets, and his only opera *Fidelio*, Beethoven showed himself the greatest composer the world has known.

BEHAVIOURISM, a school of psychology which derives from lectures given by J. B. Watson (q.v.) from 1908 onwards. It regards the derivation of psychological theory from introspection as basically unsound and substitutes the study of overt behaviour. Much use is made of the conditioned reflex (q.v.), all behaviour being explained as conditioned responses built up on the innate emotions of fear, anger and love. Watson's work has had great influence on other psychologists, although many of his subsidiary theories were too extreme to win general acceptance.

BEHN, Aphra (1640—89), English dramatist, novelist and poet. She was the first British professional woman writer. For three years she was a spy in Antwerp. Her best-known novel, *Oronooko*, draws on her childhood experiences in Surinam and deals with the theme of slavery.

BELFAST, capital of Northern Ireland, on the Lagan River. Pop. (1961) 416,094. A leading seaport and commercial and industrial centre, it has important shipyards. The chief industries are linen, food canning and processing, textiles, jute, footwear, tobacco, machinery, metal goods, chemicals and aircraft. There are institutions of higher learning. The Parliamentary centre is at Stormont on the outskirts of the city.

BELGIUM, a kingdom in Western Europe. Pop. (1960) 9,110,000; area 11,775 sq. miles. The northern and central parts consist of plains, whereas the Ardennes highlands make up most of the south. The main river is the Scheldt. The country grows mostly cereals, vegetables and potatoes and sugar-beet for industrial use. Ghent is the chief textile centre. Extensive coal deposits support heavy industry at Antwerp and along the Meuse and Sambre. Belgium is highly industrialised. The Teutonic Flemings of the north speak Flemish (Dutch), and the Celtic Walloons in the south, French. The country was conquered by Julius Caesar in 57—50 B.C. In the Middle Ages Belgian towns such as Ghent and Ypres acquired prominence as important textile centres, and Bruges was a great port. Part of Burgundy, and later of Spain under Philip II, Belgium came into the possession of the Austrian branch of the Hapsburgs in 1713. A part of post-revolutionary France until 1814, the Belgians belonged to the Kingdom of the Netherlands until they revolted and established their independence in 1830. Occupied by Germany in both World Wars, Belgium is a member of N.A.T.O. The capital is Brussels (pop. 1,000,744). Other large cities are Antwerp (261,666), Ghent (160,669) and Liège (156,599).

BELGRADE (Beograd), capital of Yugoslavia and of Serbia, at the junction of the Danube and the Sava rivers. Pop. (1959) 542,000. Of strategic importance since the Middle Ages, it has changed hands many times since the 12th century. It is a commercial and cultural centre. Few old buildings survived the destruction of the Second World War. Industries include tobacco, woollen goods, chemicals, engineering products and aircraft.

BELISARIUS (*c.* 505—65), Byzantine general under Justinian I. Although often mistrusted by the emperor, he suppressed a revolt against him and won victories over the Ostrogoths in Italy, the Vandals in North Africa and the Bulgars attacking Constantinople.

BELL, Alexander Graham (1847—1922),

Scottish-born American inventor. His teaching of the deaf led him to invent a device which became in 1876 the first telephone. Bell's telephone patent was disputed, but the U.S. Supreme Court upheld his claim. He worked with Edison on early forms of gramophones, and with Curtis in 1908 on aeroplanes.

BELLINI, Giovanni (*c.* 1430—1516), Venetian painter. The most illustrious of a family of painters, he executed magnificent altarpieces. A founder of the Venetian school of Renaissance painting, he taught many famous artists. His best-known works include *Christ's Agony in the Garden* and *The Doge Leonardo Loredano,* both in the National Gallery, London.

BELLOC, Hilaire (1870—1953), English author, historian, and member of Parliament. He wrote essays, light verse and controversial articles on history, and was author of 153 books on diverse subjects. Pope Pius XI decorated him for his service to Catholicism as a writer. He was a close friend of G. K. Chesterton.

BELLOWS, a device for expelling a blast of air by compressing a flexible container, chiefly for increasing the intensity of a flame.

BELORUSSIA (White Russia), a constituent republic of the U.S.S.R. in eastern Europe. Pop. (1959) 8,060,000; area 81,090 sq. miles. It is a sparsely populated land, much of it marsh, including the Pripet marshes. The inhabitants speak their own dialect of Russian. There are only three towns of any size. The capital is Minsk (509,000).

BELTS, THE, two Danish straits: the Great Belt (37 miles long) which separates Fyn Island from Zealand Island, and the Little Belt (30 miles long), separating Fyn Island from Jutland.

BEN BELLA, Mohammed (1916—), Algerian leader. During the Second World War he served with the French forces in Italy. In 1948 he started an underground revolutionary movement and was imprisoned in 1952, but escaped a few days later to found the National Liberation Front (F.L.N.). Released from a further term of imprisonment in March 1962, he became the first Prime Minister of Algeria in the following September. Overtrown in 1965.

BENDETTI, Vincent (1817—1900), a French diplomat who, while ambassador in Berlin, demanded from King William I of Prussia a guarantee that no Hohenzollern prince should ever be a candidate for the Spanish throne. Bismarck exploited this incident to precipitate the outbreak of the Franco-Prussian War in 1870.

BENEDICT, St (*c.* 480—543), Italian monk and founder of the Benedictine Order at Monte Cassino (*c.* 529). He is generally regarded as the father of Western monasticism; his *Rules for Monks,* though not sanctioned by the Pope until 595, was the model used by all later orders.

BENEDICTINE ORDER, the Catholic religious order founded (*c.* 529) by St Benedict. Education and teaching being its principal task, it was particularly influential in the spread of civilisation in Western Europe. The English province of the order includes the abbeys of Downside and Ampleforth.

BENEDICTION, a solemn invocation of divine blessing. The Roman Catholic church has a number of Benedictions and a Benediction service, whereas in Protestant churches the Benediction usually denotes only the closing prayer at the end of worship.

BENEFIT OF CLERGY, a prerogative of the clergy in the Middle Ages to be tried in an ecclesiastical, rather than a secular, court; at one time it was extended to all who could read aloud in court 'like a clergyman'. In England (it was never recognised in Scotland) the privilege, already much whittled down, was abolished by two statutes of 1779 and 1827.

BENELUX, a convenient short name for Belgium, the Netherlands and Luxembourg, which formed an economic union in 1944, later incorporated in the Common Market.

BENEŠ, Eduard (1884—1948), Czechoslovak statesman. A member of Thomas Masaryk's party, he worked hard for Czech independence during the First World War. From 1918—35 he was Minister for Foreign Affairs in the new republic. He then served as President, resigning after the Munich Conference in 1938. In 1940—45 he was president of the government-in-exile in England, and subsequently of the restored government in Prague. In 1948 he resigned after the Communist assumption of control.

BENGAL, a former state of India. West Bengal is now a state of the republic of India, and the eastern portion, together with the Sylhet district, formerly in Assam, comprises East Pakistan. West Bengal, pop. (1961) 34,967,634, area 33,928 sq. miles, includes Cooch Behar. The capital is Calcutta (2,926,498). East Pakistan, pop. (1961) 50,844,000, area 54,501 sq. miles. Capital Dacca (500,000). The chief port is Chittagong.

BEN-GURION, David (1886—), Israeli statesman. Polish-born. Emigrated to Palestine 1906 and held offices in the General Federation of Jewish Labour and in the Jewish Agency. He assumed leadership of the Mapai (Labour) Party in 1930 and, with the establishment (1948) of the independent State of Israel, became the country's first prime minister. He retired in 1953 but was returned to office by the 1955 elections, and again retired in 1963.

BENNET, Arnold (1867—1931), English novelist and playwright. His novels depict the bleak life in the 'Five Towns'—the industrial district known as the Potteries. *The Old Wives' Tale*, *Clayhanger*, *Hilda Lessways* and *Riceyman Steps* are his outstanding works and he also published his *Journals* covering the period 1896—1930.

BENTHAM, Jeremy (1748—1832), English reformer and Utilitarian philosopher. He was largely responsible for the far-reaching judicial reforms in England during the 19th century, his major work being *Introduction to the Principles of Morals and Legislation* (1789). It was he who propounded the basic principle of Utilitarianism, namely that 'the greatest happiness of the greatest number is the foundation of morals and legislation'. From 1808 he worked in close collaboration with J. S. Mill.

BENZENE (benzol), a colourless liquid with a pleasant odour, of great importance to industry. It is a solvent for fats, resins and waxes and forms compounds used in the manufacture of drugs, explosives, insecticides, synthetic dyes and plastics. Benzene is highly inflammable; it has anti-knock properties when mixed with petrol.

BEOWULF, earliest English epic poem, dating back to the 8th century. The manuscript in the British Museum is in

Modern theatre has evolved directly from the plays of early Greek writers, as in many ways have the places in which they are performed: *above*, the theatre of Herodus Atticus in Athens.

Photo: Greek National Tourist Office

Early English theatre: a stage design by Inigo Jones (q.v.) for *Oberon, The Fairy Prince*.

Photo: Devonshire Collection, Chatsworth. Reproduced by permission of the Trustees of the Chatsworth Settlement

Edwardian England was famous for its music halls, from which modern variety shows developed on both sides of the Atlantic.

Photo: Radio Times Hulton Picture Library

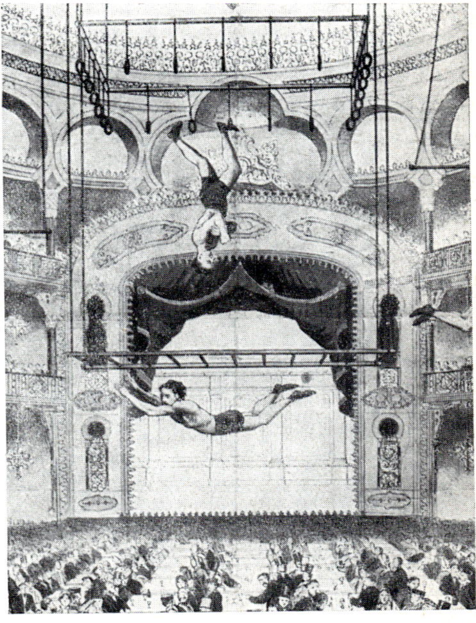

One of the most modern theatres in England, the Chichester Festival Theatre opened in 1962, has reverted to the open stage design of the early Greek theatre.

Photo: Reg Wilson

In Europe, printing from moveable type was invented in the early 15th Century. One of the earliest examples, dating from 1456, is the Gutenberg Bible—otherwise known as the Mazarin Bible—a page of which is shown here.

Photo: British Museum

The Diamond Sutra, one of the earliest known examples of Chinese engraved block printing, dating from A.D. 868.

Photo: British Museum

the West Saxon language. The story is about Beowulf and his adventures in tracking down and killing Grendel, a monster in human form, and in fighting a dragon, which finally kills him.

BERBERS, North African non-Arab people speaking a Hamitic language related to ancient Egyptian. Many speak Arabic. Although the Berbers are nominally Moslems, they observe their own customs which give women more rights. Except for the nomadic Tuaregs of the western Sahara, they are mostly agriculturists. The Barbary States were the Turkish regencies of Morocco, Algeria, Tunisia and Libya from the 16th to the 19th centuries, whence the Barbary pirates operated, often under European renegades, up to 1830.

BERGERAC, Cyrano de (1619—55), French writer. He wrote satires, comedies and the first science fiction (voyages to the sun and moon). Offensive references to his large nose involved him in numerous duels and misadventures. He is the subject of a play by Rostand, whose hero bears little resemblance to the historical Cyrano.

BERGSON, Henri (1859—1941), French philosopher and winner of the Nobel prize for literature (1927). His most celebrated work is *Creative Evolution* (1907). He held that all evolution and progress are due to the workings of the *élan vital* or life force; and that to attain philosophic truth we must use not Reason but Instinct.

BERIA, Lavrenti (1899—1953), chief of the Soviet secret police (N.K.V.D.). A personal friend of Stalin, he became a member of the Central Committee of the Communist Party in 1934 and subsequently headed various secret-police and espionage organisations in the U.S.S.R. He bore the military rank of marshal. After Stalin's death, he ranked in power second to Malenkov, until executed for treason.

BERI-BERI, a deficiency disease due primarily to the lack of vitamin B_1, or thiamine, in the diet. It is widespread among people eating polished rice.

BERING, Vitus Jonassen (1681—1741), Danish explorer. He headed a Russian expedition to northeastern Siberia, travelling overland from St Petersburg to Kamchatka and charting the Siberian coastline. In 1741 he sailed almost to Alaska (which he sighted) across the strait which was subsequently named after him.

BERKSHIRE, a county in the south of England. Pop. (1961) 503,357; area 723 sq. miles. It is gently rolling country, rising in the centre to the Berkshire Downs. Oats, wheat, vegetables and fruits are the main crops. Dairy-farming and pigbreeding are important. There is some industry in the county town of Reading.

BERLIN, former capital of Germany, on the Spree River. West Berlin (pop. 2,203,631) is politically attached to the German Federal Republic. East Berlin (pop. 1,084,010) in the U.S.S.R. sector is the capital of the German Democratic Republic. Berlin became the capital of Prussia in 1701. Soviet troops took the city in 1945. Very little of the pre-war city survived. It is entirely surrounded by East German territory.

BERLIN, Congress of, a meeting of European powers held in Berlin in 1878 under the presidency of Bismarck to consider the Treaty of San Stefano which Russia had forced on a defeated

Turkey, depriving her of most of her European territories. Britain, represented by Disraeli, feared expanding Russian power and forced the Czar's government to participate, under threat of war. The powers stripped Russia of most of her gains in the Balkans. Britain received Cyprus, and was the only power satisfied by the treaty.

BERLIN DECREE, an order issued by Napoleon in 1806 proclaiming a blockade of the British Isles, in retaliation for the British blockade of France.

BERLIOZ, Hector (1803—69), French composer and music critic. An outstanding figure in the French Romantic movement, he was the creator of the dramatic symphony and of the 'motto' theme from which Wagner's *leitmotiv* derived. All his compositions were on a large scale and he excelled in orchestration and instrumentation. His notable works include *Requiem*, the dramatic symphonies *Romeo and Juliet* and *Harold in Italy*, and the dramatic cantata *The Damnation of Faust*.

BERMUDA, a group of British islands lying to the southeast of the U.S.A. Pop. (1961) 45,491; area 21 sq. miles. Twenty of the 360 islands are inhabited. Their climate and scenery make them a favourite winter resort for Americans. The chief town is Hamilton (pop. 3000). There are British and American air and naval bases.

BERNADOTTE, Jean Baptiste Jules (1764—1844), French king of Sweden and Norway as Charles XIV. After having distinguished himself as a marshal in Napoleon's armies, he was elected crown prince of Sweden in the hope that this would induce the French emperor to help the Swedes recover Finland from Russia. However, two years later, in 1812, he joined Britain and Russia against France. He was proclaimed king in 1818.

BERNARD OF CLAIRVAUX, St (1090—1153), French Cistercian scholar, Abbot of Clairvaux, and an influential personality in church politics, who secured support for Innocent II as Pope. He reformed monastic life, and left numerous writings, including letters, mystical treatises and sermons.

BERNE, the capital of Switzerland (pop. 166,100). It has a famous university and important textile and engineering industries.

BERNHARDT, Sarah (1844—1923), French actress, considered the most outstanding of her time. She was a member of the Comédie Française and appeared on the stage in numerous countries. An emotional and magnetic personality, gifted with a wonderful voice, the 'divine Sarah's' major successes were in the title role of Racine's *Phèdre* and as *La Dame aux camelias*.

BERTHELOT, Marcellin (1827—1907), French chemist and politician. He was a pioneer in physical chemistry and the first to produce synthetic organic compounds, e.g. fats and sugars.

BERTILLON SYSTEM, an early method of identifying criminals, later replaced by finger-printing. It consisted of body measurements and a general physical description.

BERYLLIUM, see Elements.

BESSARABIA, a region of steppes in southwest Europe, formerly Rumanian. After the Second World War, it was divided between the Ukrainian and Moldavian Soviet republics. It was on the invasion route into Europe. Grain and livestock are the chief products.

BESSEMER, Sir Henry (1813—98), British engineer and inventor. His inventions include the Bessemer process which revolutionised steel production, making it possible to produce tons of steel in a few minutes. It converts pig-iron into steel by oxidising the impurities in iron.

BETA PARTICLES, fast-moving electrons or positrons emitted by radioactive substances. Streams of these (beta rays) have greater penetrating power than alpha rays, and are sometimes emitted at any speed up to very nearly that of light. Beta emission changes the ratio of neutrons to protons without altering the total number of particles in the nucleus.

BETHLEHEM, a hill town in Jordan. Pop. 20,000. The birthplace of Christ, it lies six miles south of Jerusalem and is the scene of pilgrimages at Christmas and Easter.

BEVAN, Aneurin (1897—1960), British Labour leader. A member of Parliament from 1929, he was Minister of Health in 1945—51 and Minister of Labour for a short time in 1951. As Minister of Health he introduced the National Health Service.

BEVERIDGE, William Henry, 1st Baron (1897—1963), English economist and sociologist. He was originator of a plan providing for comprehensive state social insurance and full employment, and thus of the Welfare State.

BEVIN, Ernest (1881—1951), British Labour leader. A key figure in the trade union movement, he was Minister of Labour from 1940—45 in Winston Churchill's government. From 1945—51 he served as Foreign Secretary.

BHAGAVAD-GITA, ('The Song of the Blessed One'), a mystical dramatic poem written in Sanskrit by an unknown author in the 1st or 2nd century A.D. which sets forth the Hindu precept that through faith and devotion all may obtain salvation.

BHUTAN, a Buddhist kingdom in the eastern Himalaya. Pop. 700,000; area 18,000 sq. miles. The chief crops of this mountainous country are rice, maize and millet. The capital is Punakha. A motor road linking it with India was constructed in 1960—62.

BIBLE (from the Gk *ta biblia*, 'the books'), the sacred scriptures of the Christian religion, comprising the Old and New Testaments and Apocrypha (q.v.). The Old Testament, nearly all of it written in Hebrew, was compiled by many hands between *c.* 850 and 300 B.C. but included oral traditions of earlier date. Until the discovery of the Dead Sea Scrolls (q.v.) the earliest manuscript in Hebrew dated only from A.D. 895. The earliest translations were the Alexandrine Greek Septuagint (*c.* 250—100 B.C.) and St Jerome's Latin Vulgate of A.D. 342—420; the latter is the version accepted as authentic by the Roman Catholic church, and was translated into English in the Rheims-Douay version of 1582—1610. The first complete English Bible was the Coverdale edition of 1535.

The Old Testament is divided by the Jews into the Law, the Prophets and the Sacred Writings (Hagiographa). It is convenient to divide it into the books from Genesis to Numbers, edited under the influence of the Priestly tradition of the 5th century B.C., with its emphasis on the Jewish idea of the Chosen People;

Deuteronomy to Kings, the history of the Jews from the Exodus; the four prophetic histories (Joshua, Judges, Samuel and Kings); the major prophets (Isaiah, Jeremiah, Ezekiel, Daniel); the twelve minor prophets; and the miscellaneous writings (Psalms, Proverbs, Job etc.). Many of the books are written by different hands at different periods, e.g. there are two contradictory accounts of the Creation in Genesis, and Isaiah was the work of at least three persons, probably of the 8th, 6th and 5th centuries B.C. respectively. The dates in the margins of older editions of the Old Testament were the work of Archbishop (of Armagh) Ussher (1650), who was responsible for deciding that the Creation took place in 4004 B.C.

The New Testament written in Greek, begins with the three Synoptic Gospels, which record the acts and sayings of Jesus. The earliest was written down by St Mark at the dictation of St Peter *c.* A.D. 60. Matthew and Luke were written a little later and were based partly on Mark. The fourth Gospel is that of St John. Then come the Acts of the Apostles, which recount the expansion of the Church through the missions of Peter, Paul and Stephen. There are also various epistles to churches, mostly written by St Paul; and the Book of Revelation. The earliest texts are Greek papyri of the 2nd and 3rd centuries, the Codex Vaticanus and Codex Sinaiticus of the 4th century, and the Vulgate.

In caves near the Dead Sea, manuscripts have been found from 1947 onwards which are a thousand years older than the earliest Hebrew text previously known. These Dead Sea Scrolls now cover the whole of the Old Testament except for Esther, and most of them appear to have been written B.C.

Various attempts have been made to produce versions of the Bible in more modern language with ancient errors and obscurities corrected. Among these are the versions of Moffat (1913), Ronald Knox (1955), the American Revised Version (1952) and the British New English Bible (1961 onwards).

BICYCLE. A rider astride a hobby-horse is depicted in a stained-glass window dated 1642, in Stoke Poges Church, Bucks. The first bicycle using foot-treadles, driving-rods and handlebars, was made in 1839 by Kirkpatrick Macmillan, a Scottish blacksmith. Half a century later the front wheel of the 'Penny-farthing' had grown to 5 ft in diameter for greater speed, and women and short men had taken to riding tricycles. James Starley first manufactured the modern safety bicycle (the Rover) with wheels of equal size and a sprocket chain-drive, in 1885. This innovation inaugurated a boom in cycling, with tandem bicycles much in evidence. The free-wheel was introduced in 1894 and the Sturmey-Archer three-speed hub in 1901.

BIHAR, a state of the Indian Union in northeast India. Pop. (1961) 46,457,042; area 67,164 sq. miles. The principal crops are rice, maize and wheat. Coal and iron are mined. The capital is Patna (362,817).

BILE, a liver secretion stored temporarily in the gall bladder which aids in the digestion and absorption of fats. An alkaline yellowish or greenish fluid, it is discharged into the upper part of the small intestine (duodenum). If the flow is obstructed, digestive disturbances or jaundice may result.

BILL OF RIGHTS, an enactment passed by the British Parliament in 1689 on the accession of William III and Mary II to the throne after the abdication of James II in 1688. Stating the civil and political rights of the people, it restricted royal power, granted supremacy to Parliament and ensured against a Roman Catholic ever becoming an English sovereign. The American Bill of Rights consists of the first ten amendments to the Constitution guaranteeing the rights and liberties of the individual.

BILL OF SALE, an agreement in writing transferring the ownership but not the possession of goods by way of security for the payment of money. Full details must be given and the document registered. The lender cannot sell the goods except in specified circumstances, e.g. non-payment of interest. There are also other, less common, forms of bills of sale.

BILLIARDS, a game played with three ivory balls on a rectangular table with raised edges and covered with dark green cloth. The balls are struck with a tapered cue. In Britain the table has six pockets. Snooker is played with 15 red balls, 6 balls of other colours and a striking ball (white). The object is to pocket all the balls in accordance with certain rules, the red balls scoring one point each and the others from two to seven points. There are many other varieties of billiards, including games on pocketless tables.

BIMETALLISM, a monetary system based on the free coinage of two metals, usually gold and silver, at a fixed ratio. It was tried in France and a few other countries in the 19th century at a ratio of 1 oz. of gold to 15½ oz. of silver, but could not survive the Franco-Prussian War of 1870 when Germany demanded huge payments from France in gold.

BINYON, Laurence (1869—1943), English poet and art critic. An authority on art in the Far East, he held important posts in the British Museum. He wrote much poetry and many books on art.

BIOGRAPHY, is the history of an individual. Biographies appear among all early civilisations and were written primarily to support a point of view or teach a moral lesson. An autobiography is an account of the author's own life. An early example of English biography was William Roper's *Life of Sir Thomas More* published in 1626. James Boswell's *Life of Johnson* (1791) is the first attempt to present a complete portrait of the subject. Modern biographers aspire to an objective presentation of the subject, often applying psychoanalytical ideas in interpreting personality. Famous early autobiographies include those of St Augustine, Benvenuto Cellini (1500—71) and Rousseau (1770).

BIOLOGY, the study of living organisms, has two main divisions: plant (botany) and animal biology (zoology). Living things undergo continuous physical and chemical change, involving nutrition, growth, respiration, excretion etc.; they respond to external stimuli and to changes in environment, and reproduce. There are numerous subsidiary sciences which study development (embryology), form (morphology), structure and function of tissues (histology), the cell (cytology), heredity (genetics), fossils (palaeontology), relationship to environment (ecology), the chemistry of living organisms (biochemistry), their classification into order, genus, species, etc. (taxonomy) and the broader aspects of such classification (systematics). Evolution is the theory that living and extinct plants and animals were formed from a common ancestry by processes of change and selection. Biochemistry covers widely varied fields of research that combine physics and biology, e.g. the study of nerves and muscles. There are numerous other specialised studies, e.g. bacteriology, microbiology.

BIRD, a feathered, warm-blooded, vertebrate animal whose skeleton and fore-limbs are adapted for flying. Birds lay hard-shelled eggs from which offsprings emerge after an incubation period. They have an acute sense of vision, and night-feeding birds have good hearing. Their bills, body structure and feet are adapted to their habitat, which may be water, desert, arctic snow or high mountain. Not all birds can fly. The speed of flight varies from 20—100 m.p.h. While some birds eat anything, many live on seeds, plants and insects. Eagles and hawks prey on small animals. Birds may fly great distances to reach the climate and food they need in order to survive. The means by which birds migrate annually over huge stretches of featureless ocean (e.g. waders and ducks from the Aleutian Islands to Hawaii, over 2,000 miles), and return to the same locality on almost the same day each year, are still not understood.

BIRKENHEAD, a county borough in Cheshire, England, on the Mersey River. Pop. (1961) 141,683. A seaport and industrial centre, it has important shipyards and heavy steel industries. Other manufactures include clothing, wood and glass products and foodstuffs.

BIRMINGHAM, county borough of Warwickshire, England, and the second largest city in Britain. Pop. (1964) 1,115,651. It was an iron-working town from the 12th century, with coal and iron in the vicinity. The Industrial Revolution and a network of roads, railways and canals made Birmingham the centre of one of the most important industrial conurbations in the world, producing a wide range of goods manufactured from metal (including precious metals) and glass. Wolverhampton, West Bromwich, Bilston and Smethwick all lie to the northwest in the adjoining Black Country.

BIRTH CONTROL, the prevention of conception for the purpose of limiting births. This includes the use of mechanical and chemical means and the limitation of sexual intercourse. A pill taken by mouth has been proved to be effective. Birth control, although strongly opposed by the Roman Catholic and other churches, is widespread in the Western world.

BISHOP, a high order of clergy in the Roman Catholic Church, ranking next below a cardinal; the highest order in the Anglican and Greek churches, the higher ranks of which are called archbishop, primate, metropolitan and patriarch. Bishops usually exercise jurisdiction in a specified area or diocese. Archbishops have jurisdiction over other bishops. The Archbishop of Canterbury is Primate of All England, while the Archbishop of York is Primate of England. The doctrine of Apostolic succession, that bishops have been consecrated in an unbroken line from the Apostles, is a fundamental tenet of the Roman Catholic Church, but has never been formally accepted by the Anglican Church, and is rejected by many Protestant sects.

BISMARCK, Prince Otto von (1815—98), German statesman. Embarking on a policy of unifying Germany under Prussian leadership, he carried out military reforms after becoming prime minister and foreign minister of Prussia in 1862. After taking Schleswig-Holstein from Denmark with Austria's help he defeated his erstwhile ally, giving Prussia the dominant position in Europe which it henceforth held. Through annexation and treaties, he formed alliances with the other German states. On a trumped-up excuse he then forced France into war, defeated it in 1870—71, and subsequently became Chancellor of a united Germany under Wilhelm I. He succeeded in keeping France politically isolated, and acquired a colonial empire for his country. His downfall came in 1890 when Wilhelm II ascended the throne. On the domestic front he clashed with the Roman Catholic Church and introduced social legislation.

BISMARK ARCHIPELAGO, a group of more than 100 islands northeast of New Guinea administered by Australia as a Trust Territory. Pop. (1958) 156,677; area 1115 sq. miles.

BISMUTH, see Elements.

BIZET, Georges (1838—75), French operatic composer whose most famous work is *Carmen*. He also wrote piano music, songs and orchestral music. His incidental music for *L'Arlésienne* is widely known.

BJØRNSON, Bjørnstjerne (1832—1910), Norwegian poet, dramatist, novelist and political leader. His works deal with peasant life and social reform. In 1903 he was awarded the Nobel Prize for literature. One of his poems was chosen as the Norwegian national anthem.

BLACKBURN, a county borough of Lancashire, England. Pop. (1961) 106,114. A leading cotton-weaving centre, it has engineering works, machine shops, iron foundries, coal mines and breweries.

BLACK HOLE OF CALCUTTA, a dungeon about 18 feet square in which the nawab of Bengal, Siraj-ud-Daula, confined 146 British prisoners in 1756. The next morning only 23 were still alive.

BLACKMORE, RICHARD Doddridge (1825—1900), British novelist. He wrote several volumes of mediocre poetry and achieved fame with his romantic novel about 17th century England, *Lorna Doone*.

BLACKPOOL, a county borough in Lancashire, England, on the Irish Sea. Pop. (1961) 152,133. A popular seaside resort, it is famous for its illuminations and the Eiffel-like Tower.

BLACKSTONE, Sir William (1723—80), English jurist. A lecturer at Oxford and a legal scholar, his fame rests on one work, *Commentaries on the Laws of England*, an admirably clear exposition of the whole field of English law, published at a time when this was urgently needed.

BLACK WATCH (Royal Highland Regiment), a famous Scottish infantry regiment. It was first organised in 1668 to preserve peace in the Scottish High lands. At first the 43rd, it was incorporated in the British army in 1751 as the 42nd Foot.

BLAKE, William (1757—1827), English poet, mystic and artist, renowned for his engravings and water-colour paintings. His poems include *Songs of Innocence* and *Songs of Experience*. His long 'prophetic' poems portray mythological figures of changing significance and are a complex attack on nationalism, governmental tyranny and legalism. He printed and illustrated almost all his own works.

BLARNEY STONE, a nearly inaccessible stone at the top of an old castle wall in Blarney, County Cork, in the Irish

Republic. Those who kiss it are supposed to acquire unusual powers of persuasion and eloquence.

BLASCO-IBÁÑEZ, Vicente (1867—1928), Spanish Liberal novelist. Among other works he wrote *The Four Horsemen of the Apocalypse*, a war novel which gained him considerable fame, and which was produced as a film by the American Director, Rex Ingram.

BLAST FURNACE, a tall circular structure for extracting metals, chiefly iron, from their ores. A blast of air forced in through the bottom supports the combustion of coke. This in turn forms carbon monoxide, serving to remove the oxygen from the metal oxide ore. The molten metal (e.g. pig-iron) is run off at the bottom in a continuous process.

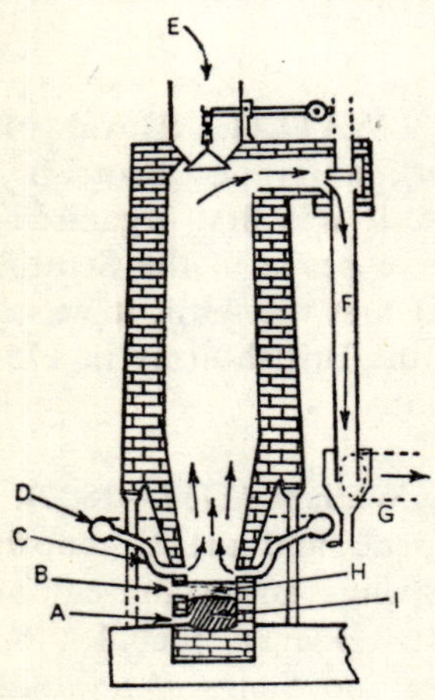

Blast furnace
A. Iron withdrawn here B. Slag hole C. Tuyeres D. Air blast E. Charge here F. Downcomer G. Dust box H. Slag I. Molten iron

BLEEDING, loss of blood, either accidental or intentional. A sudden loss of more than 30% of the body's blood is usually fatal. Arterial bleeding is characterised by the bright red colour of the blood, which comes in spurts. Venous blood is a dark colour and flows continuously. Bleeding, by the application of leeches, cutting a vein or 'cupping' (extraction by suction), was at one time a favourite remedy for a variety of conditions.

BLÉRIOT, Louis (1872—1936), French airman who played an important role in the development of the monoplane and was the first to fly the English Channel in 1909.

BLINDNESS, varying degrees of loss of vision, arises from degenerative changes in the path between the cornea of the eye and the brain centre for sight. The causes may be mental or they may be due to a pathological condition of any of the organs concerned with vision. Special aids for the blind include books in braille, talking-book records and guide-dogs. Night-blindness is caused by dietary deficiencies.

BLITZKRIEG ('lightning war'), a technique of warfare developed by German strategists after World War I. Surprise, speed and the effective use of air power, artillery, tanks, paratroops and motorised divisions are its main features.

BLOCH, Ernest (1880—1959), American composer of Swiss birth. The founder and director of the Cleveland Institute of Music and director of the San Francisco Conservatory of Music, he won several awards for his compositions. His work, much of which has a distinctly Jewish flavour, includes a lyric drama, symphonies, chamber music and a concerto grosso.

BLOOD, a circulating body fluid carrying substances needed by the body tissues and removing their waste products. The blood also transfers heat throughout the body and carries hormones and antibodies. It consists of an almost colourless fluid called plasma, red cells carrying oxygen and carbon dioxide between the lungs and the tissues, white cells which fight infection, and platelets important in blood clotting. There are various blood types which must normally be matched when giving a blood transfusion, although there is one type which can be given universally.

BLÜCHER, Gebhard Leberecht von (1742—1819), Prussian general. He won several victories over Napoleon and played an important part in turning the tide at Waterloo in 1815, after a defeat at Ligny.

BLUE RIDGE, a mountain range in eastern U.S.A. extending for 600 miles from south Pennsylvania to north Georgia. Mt Mitchell (6684 ft) is the highest peak in North America east of the Mississippi.

BLUM, Léon (1872—1950), French political leader and writer. He wrote books and articles before turning his interest to politics. A Socialist from 1902, he helped to form the Popular Front in 1934 and was Premier 1936—37 and, briefly, during 1946—47. He was in a German concentration camp during the Second World War.

BOADICEA (Boudicca; d. A.D. 62), Queen of the Iceni, an ancient British tribe inhabiting what is now Norfolk and Suffolk. She led an unsuccessful revolt against the Romans using sharp implements like scythes lashed to her soldiers' chariots, following which she poisoned herself.

BOAT, a small undecked sea or river vessel which can be launched from a beach. Motive power is provided by oars, poles, sails, paddles or engines. Beginning with early dug-out canoes constructed from hollow logs, and coracles made of hides stretched over a wicker frame, boats have varied in size and shape to conform to the purpose for which they were made.

BOCCACCIO, Giovanni (1313—75), Italian writer, poet and scholar. After a number of romances and poetical works, he wrote his greatest book, the *Decameron*, consisting of a hundred tales of great wit and piquancy. He was a friend of Petrarch and an admirer of Dante.

BODLEIAN LIBRARY, the library at Oxford University, the second largest in England. Founded originally by Duke Humphrey in 1327, it was the first public library in Europe. It is now named after Sir Thomas Bodley (1545—1613) who devoted himself to restoring it after the purges of Edward VI and refounded it in 1598. The library receives a copy of every book published in the U.K.

BOER WAR (1899—1902), a war between Britain and the Boers (Afrikaners, Europeans of Dutch descent) in South Africa, caused by the unyielding attitude towards the Uitlanders (English settlers) by President Kruger of the Transvaal, which led to the Jameson raid (q.v.). At the beginning of the war the British forces, under General Roberts, met with a series of defeats at Spion Kop and elsewhere, and it was not until May 1900 that Mafeking, Kimberley and Ladysmith were all relieved after many months of siege. The Boers then formed commandos which carried on guerrilla warfare under Botha and de Wet, but these tactics were defeated by Kitchener's line of blockhouses constructed across the country. By the Treaty of Vereeniging Britain annexed the Orange Free State and Transvaal.

BOGOTA, capital of Colombia. Pop. (1962) 1,329,230. Situated on a plateau of the Andes, 8700 ft above sea-level, it has, in spite of difficulty of access, retained cultural and religious ascendancy over the republic — it is known as the Athens of America — and is also of commercial importance.

BOHEMIA, a region and former province in western Czechoslovakia. Pop. (1947, before it was abolished as a province) 5,627,181; area 20,101 sq. miles. It consists of mountains enclosing a plateau. Livestock and lumbering are the main occupations in the forested areas of the plateau. In the northern valleys sugar-beet, potatoes, cereals, flax, vegetables, fruit and grapes are produced. Hops and barley support a large brewing industry at Pilsen, which is also the home of the Skoda (now Lenin) armament factories. There are large deposits of coal and iron. There is also a large variety of other minerals, including pitchblende. The region has much heavy industry, and textiles and chemicals are likewise important. A flourishing, advanced, independent kingdom during the Middle Ages, it came under Hapsburg rule early in the 16th century and remained Austrian until 1918. The chief city is Prague.

BOLEYN, Anne (1507—36), second wife of Henry VIII of England and mother of Elizabeth I. For her sake Henry's marriage with his first wife, Catherine of Aragon, was annulled. The King tired of her and, when she bore a daughter instead of a son, brought charges of incest and adultery against her. She was found guilty and beheaded. No evidence survives on which to assess her guilt.

BOLIVAR, Simon (1783—1830), the liberator of the northern region of South America from Spanish rule. He freed Venezuela, Colombia, Ecuador and Peru, and helped to found Bolivia. He became president of the Greater Colombia Republic, into which these countries were formed, but he resigned just before he died and the republic peacefully broke up.

BOLIVIA, a republic in the west central area of South America. Pop. (1960) 3,462,000; area 514,155 sq. miles. Landlocked, Bolivia consists of a plateau (altitude: 12,000 ft) enclosed by two chains of the Andes to the west, and a low alluvial plain to the east. The country has large deposits of tin, lead, zinc and petroleum. It is the second largest exporter of rubber in South America. Quinine, hides and cattle are its other chief products and agriculture is undeveloped. For external trade Bolivia has to rely on two trans-Andean railways to the Chilean ports of Arica and Antufagosta. Part of the ancient Inca empire, Bolivia's Indian population was reduced to slavery by the Spaniards. The country became independent in 1825. Since then its history has been marked by political instability and wars with all five of its neighbours which have cost it nearly 500,000 sq. miles of territory. The capital is La Paz (pop. 347,394). Other important cities are Cochabamba (90,037) and Oruro (81,553).

BOLSHEVISM, Russian revolutionary Socialism based on the main tenets of Marxism and proletarian dictatorship. Led by Lenin, the Bolsheviks (majority members) parted company with the democratic group of Russian Socialists, the Mensheviks (minority members), in 1903. In November 1917 Bolsheviks won control of the revolutionary government established in March and laid the foundations of the Soviet regime. The party then changed its name from Bolshevik to Communist.

BOLTON (Bolton-le-Moors), a county borough of Lancashire, England. Pop. (1961) 160,887. It is an important textile centre. Other industries include metal products, textile machinery, leather, chemicals and electrical equipment.

BOMBAY, a seaport on the west coast of India, capital of Maharashtra state. Pop. (1961) 4,146,491. The city has textile, oil-refining, metal and chemical industries. Bombay state was divided into the states of Maharashtra and Gujarat in 1960.

BOND, an obligation to pay a fixed sum of money on a specific date and a fixed rate of interest on the face amount. They are usually issued by corporations, governments or municipalities against money loaned.

BONIFACE, St (*c.* 680—755), English missionary to the Germans who is said to have felled the sacred oak at Geismar and destroyed other objects of heathen worship, thus proving their impotency against Christianity. He was martyred in Frisia.

BONIFACE VIII, Pope from 1294 to 1303. His unsuccessful attempts to increase papal temporal power continually brought him into conflict with Philip IV of France, who eventually had him accused of heresy and arrested; Boniface died shortly after this.

BONNER, Edmund (*c.* 1495—1569), Bishop of London who supported Henry VIII against the Pope. On Henry's death he was imprisoned for his opposition to Protestantism. Later, when Mary restored him to office, he persecuted Protestants until he was sent to prison by Elizabeth I in 1560.

BOOK, a collection of printed or written pages bound between covers. In ancient times books were made of bark, papyrus, skins or parchment. The Assyrians wrote on clay tablets. The Chinese in the 9th century printed books from blocks. The first book printed in Europe from movable type was a Latin Bible published by Johannes Gutenberg in Mainz, Germany, about 1455. Books printed before 1501 are called incunabula. Early books had no title page; the name of the printer or publisher, the place of publication, and the date of issue sometimes appeared in the closing paragraph or colophon. The first book printed in English was a history of Troy, printed at Bruges, Flanders, in 1474 by William Caxton. Three years later Caxton brought out *Dictes and Sayings of the Philosophers*, the first book printed in England. With printing, the reign of Latin as an international language ended and the assault on lay illiteracy began.

BOOK OF THE DEAD, the, Ancient Egyptian collection of prayers, incantations and hymns buried together with the dead in order to deliver the soul from the trials and torments of the nether-world.

BOOTH, William (1829—1912), founder and first general of the Salvation Army. At first a Methodist lay preacher, he later settled in London and addressed evangelistic meetings in Whitechapel. In 1878 with his wife, Mary, he founded the Salvation Army to carry out evangelistic and social work in the slums of the East End of London and elsewhere.

BORGIA, Cesare (1475—1507), a feared and ruthless political intriguer. Though ostensibly in the service of the Holy See, he — together with his father (Pope Alexander VI) — almost succeeded in establishing the Borgia family as an independent power in Italy. He was imprisoned soon after his father's death, and escaped to die in battle.

BORGIA, Lucrezia (1480—1519), daughter of Pope Alexander VI. Her father and brother Cesare arranged a series of marriages for her to further their political aims. The second of these husbands, to whom Lucrezia was devoted, was murdered by Cesare. She maintained a brilliant court which attracted many Renaissance figures. No evidence has been found to substantiate popular stories of her part in various poisonings and of her incestuous relations; indeed, after her marriage to the Duke of Ferrara she gave herself to good works and proved an excellent wife and mother, whose praises were sung by Ariosto.

BORNEO, the largest island of the Malay Archipelago. The northern part comprises Sabah (formerly North Borneo) and Sarawak, members of the Federation of Malaysia, and the British-protected sultanate of Brunei. Pop. (1960) 1,282,681; area 78,684 sq. miles. The remainder, Kalimantan, is part of Indonesia; pop. (1959) 3,900,000; area 208,286 sq. miles. Sparsely populated and only partially explored equatorial forests cover most of the interior, which in the north is mountainous; the south consists of marshy plains. There are oilfields (Brunei and Kalimantan), rubber and coal deposits.

BORODIN, Alexander (1834—87), Russian composer. Trained as a physician and chemist, he wrote two symphonies, the opera *Prince Igor*, two string quartets, and songs, set to his own poems, which are considered outstanding.

BORON, see Elements.

BOSNIA AND HERZEGOVINA, a federated republic of Yugoslavia, formerly part of Austria-Hungary. Pop. (1962) 3,500,000; area 19,768 sq. miles. Mountainous and forested, the region is primarily agricultural. The capital is Sarajevo (pop. 176,000).

BOSPORUS, a strait in northwest Turkey, separating Asia Minor from southeast Europe. Seventeen miles long, it connects the Black Sea with the Sea of Marmora.

BOSTON, capital and largest city in Massachusetts, U.S.A., Pop. (1960) 697,197. A historic city with an 'old town' of narrow streets and a cultural centre, Boston has long been an important international port, the growth of which has been inhibited by poor east-west landward communications. Trade has played a large part in the city's development and it is a leading market for fish, wool and leather. Its industries are extremely diversified, producing textiles, shoes, foodstuffs, electrical appliances, machinery, rubber goods and petroleum products. Boston is also a printing and publishing centre and is important in the financial world. Greater Boston, with a population of 2¼ million, has numerous museums and educational institutions, including Harvard University, Massachusetts Institute of Technology, Boston University, Boston College, Northeastern University, Suffolk University, Tufts University, and seven colleges. Founded by Puritans in 1630, the city played a decisive role in the early history of North America and contains numerous historical relics. In 1773 the 'Boston Tea Party' occurred, precipitating the American War of Independence — the movement for separation from England. American writers Emerson,

Poe, Dean Howells and Longfellow, lived in Boston.

BOSWELL, James (1740—95), Scottish writer. His plans to practise law were side tracked by an early interest in literature. An intimate friendship with Samuel Johnson resulted in a well-rounded portrait of the great lexicographer and writer in a two-volume biography which brought him immediate recognition. His own journals reveal, with great frankness, a not altogether attractive personality.

BOTANY, the branch of biology (q.v.) comprising the scientific study of plant life. Interest in it was stimulated by the fact that plants constitute an essential part of man's diet and play a vital role in medicine. Botany studies the form, structure and function of plants and determines their classification, their relation to their surroundings and other plants, their usefulness and their distribution. The binominal nomenclature for classifying plants by genus and species was an important step forward in botanical science.

BOTHA, Louis (1862—1919), South African Boer military and political leader. He commanded the Transvaal troops in the Boer War. In 1907 he became the first prime minister of Transvaal and, in 1910, of the Union of South Africa. Botha suppressed De Wet's brief uprising by the Boers at the outbreak of the First World War and subsequently conquered German South West Africa.

BOTHWELL, James Hepburn, 4th Earl of (1536—78), third husband of Mary Queen of Scots. After a mock trial in which he was charged with the murder of Mary's second husband, Lord Darnley, he married the Queen. The Scottish nobles offered to submit to Mary if she gave him up and she agreed. Bothwell fled to Denmark where he was well treated until Mary's downfall. He was later imprisoned and died insane.

BOTOLPH, St (7th century), English monk and founder (654) of a monastery in Boston (shortened form of Botolphstown), Lincolnshire, where he instituted the Benedictine rule.

BOTTICELLI, Sandro (1444—1510), Florentine Renaissance painter. A master of colour and especially of line, he painted both pagan and, from *c.* 1498, religious compositions in the same sensuous style. He is noted for his illustrations to Dante's *Inferno.* Botticelli participated in decorating the Sistine Chapel. His works include a series of Madonnas, *Birth of Venus*, and *Primavera (Spring).*

BOUNTY, Mutiny on the, a mutiny led by Fletcher Christian of H.M.S. Bounty against William Bligh in December 1787 in the Pacific Ocean. Bligh, charged with tyranny and set adrift in an open boat with 18 men, reached Timor with 12 of the others after travelling 3600 miles. Some of the mutineers founded a colony on Pitcairn Island and their descendants still live there; others were caught and hanged.

BOURBON, a royal family which ruled France from 1589—1792, and from 1814—30, and branched off to provide rulers of Spain, the two Sicilies, Lucca and Parma. The founder was Robert of Clermont (d. 1317), the youngest son of the Capetian king, Louis IX.

BOURGUIBA, Habib (1903—), Tunisian statesman. A lawyer and political journalist, he became the first secretary-general of the Neo-Destour party in 1934. Arrested in 1938, he was later deported to Vichy France and released by the Nazis in 1942, after which he travelled widely, returning to Tunisia in 1955, to become Premier in 1956 and President in 1957.

BOURNEMOUTH, a coastal town and county borough of Hampshire, on the English Channel. Pop. (1961) 153,965. It is a leading holiday resort in a pine-sheltered valley with fine beaches. It has 700 acres of parks and gardens.

BOWLS, an old game played on a green, in which the object is to place bowls (woods), with a bias and weighing up to 3½ lbs, as near as possible to the small white target ball (jack).

BOXER REBELLION, an uprising against foreign and missionary influence in China which broke out in 1899. It was led by a section of militia known as 'Righteous Harmonious Fists' (hence the name Boxer), who believed themselves immune to bullets. After the murder of the German ambassador and the burning of several foreign legations in Peking, foreign (including Japanese) residents and a number of Chinese Christians took refuge in the British legation where they fought off numerous attacks. An international force rescued them two months later and remained to loot Peking.

BOXING, a sport which developed from prize-fighting with the bare fists. Gloves were introduced by gentlemen pugilists in the 18th century, but it was not until rules were drawn up by the Marquis of Queensberry in 1867 that the sport became respectable. From 1884 amateur boxing was controlled by the Amateur Boxing Association, and the Boxing Board of Control was formed in 1929 for professional boxing. Contests consist of not more than fifteen rounds of, usually, three minutes, with one-minute intervals. A win is either on points or by a knock-out, when the opponent fails to resume after a ten-second count. The classes and their maximum weights are: flyweight 8 stone, bantamweight 8 stone 6 lbs, featherweight 9 stone, lightweight 9 stone 9 lbs, welter weight 10 stone 7 lbs, middleweight 11 stone 6 lbs, cruiser or light-heavyweight 12 stone 7 lbs, heavyweight, no restriction. In amateur boxing these weights are slightly different and two additional classes, light-welter-weight 10 stone, and light-middle-weight 11 stone, are added.

BOY SCOUTS, an international organisation for boys founded in 1908 by Sir Robert Baden-Powell. It promotes mental, moral and physical development. The organisation is non-military and makes no distinctions on racial, religious or political grounds. It stresses civic responsibility, nature lore, sports and creative activities. The movement has spread to countries the world over.

Boy Scout badge

BOYLE, Robert (1627—91), British chemist and physicist. Together with Robert Hooke he performed numerous experiments on the pneumatic properties of air, and designed an early thermometer. The first to distinguish between a chemical element and a compound, he formulated Boyle's law, which states that the volume of a gas varies inversely as the pressure upon it, providing that the temperature is constant.

BRADFORD, a town and county borough of the West Riding of Yorkshire, England, on a tributary of the Aire River. Pop. (1961) 295,768. A centre of woollen and worsted manufacture, it also produces other textiles, chemicals, textile machinery, automobiles and electrical equipment. There is a considerable German element in the population and a widespread interest in music; Bradford was thus an appropriate birthplace for the composer Delius.

BRAGG, Sir William Henry (1862—1942), British physicist. Together with his son, Sir William Lawrence Bragg, he developed the X-ray spectrograph for studying the arrangement of atoms in crystals of various kinds. Father and son shared the 1915 Nobel Prize in physics for this. Both also formulated the Bragg rule for the reflection of X-rays from a crystal.

BRAHE, Tycho (1546—1601), Danish astronomer. He perfected instruments for more accurate observation of the heavens. On the basis of his observations, Kepler later formulated his laws of planetary motion. Brahe believed that only the other known planets and not the earth revolved around the sun.

BRAHMANISM, the religious system founded by the Brahmans, the highest caste of the Hindu society. Brahmanism represents a transition from the ancient Vedic religion to Hinduism.

BRAHMAPUTRA, see River.

BRAHMS, Johannes (1833—97), German composer. Playing a number of instruments as a small child, he first performed his own piano compositions at the age of 14. He composed four celebrated symphonies, two piano concertos, a violin concerto, a double concerto for violin and cello, choral work *(A German Requiem)*, songs, and chamber music. His interest in Hungarian music led him to create a number of Hungarian dances. Brahms is regarded as the culmination of German musical Romanticism.

BRAILLE, Louis (1809—52), French educator of the blind. Himself blind from the age of three, he invented a system consisting of combinations of six raised dots for teaching the blind to read and write.

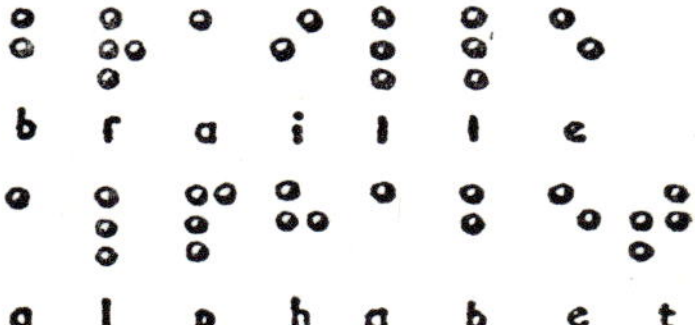

Letters of the Braille alphabet

BRAIN, a mass of tissue in the cranium which serves as the centre of the nervous system. It consists of three principal parts. The largest portion is the cerebrum, partially consisting of two convoluted hemispheres covered with a layer of grey matter. This is the seat of man's personality, will, perception, voluntary muscular activity and the intellectual capacities that mark him off from the lower animals. Behind and underneath it is the cerebellum, or little brain, which co-ordinates the motor activity of the organism. Still lower down is the medulla oblongata which is the enlarged upper end of the spinal column. It contains the centres controlling breathing, the heart and reflex actions. The brain is not only the centre of all of man's mental processes but, by controlling the heart beat, breathing and other vital functions, it is the centre of life itself.

BRANGWYN, Sir Frank (1867—1956), British painter and etcher. He painted numerous works reflecting his life at sea and his visits to the Orient. His works include easel and mural paintings, etchings, designs for stained glass, metalwork and tapestry.

BRAQUE, Georges (1882—1963), French painter and sculptor. At first a member of the Fauvistes, he worked with Picasso on the development of Cubism (1904—14) and from 1917 produced semi-abstract still-lifes and figure compositions.

BRATISLAVA, a city in southern Czechoslovakia. Pop. (1959) 256,046. An important river port on the Danube, it is the economic and cultural centre of Slovakia. It has engineering, chemical and textile industries. It is linked to the U.S.S.R. by an oil pipeline.

BRAZIL, a federal republic in the east of South America. Pop. (1960) 70,528,625; area 3,288,063 sq. miles. The north consists mostly of equatorial, jungle-covered plains dominated by the Amazon and other rivers. The south is nearly all plateau, including the Mato Grosso, except for the narrow belt of coastal lowland. An agricultural country, Brazil ranks first in the production of livestock, coffee and castor beans. Oranges, cocoa, sugar, maize, rice and tobacco are also leading products. The staple Indian food is cassava. The country is rich in rubber, brazil-nuts and maté, and has extensive but little exploited deposits of high-grade quartz, industrial diamonds, chrome, mica, zirconium, manganese and gold, and perhaps half the world's reserves of iron ore. There is a large textile industry. The only South American country deriving its culture and language from Portugal, it was discovered by Pedro Alvarez Cabral in 1500. In 1882 it declared its independence of Portugal and Pedro I became emperor. A republic was established in 1889. The new capital is Brasilia (pop. 120,000). Other principal cities are São Paulo (3,315,553), Rio de Janeiro (3,307,163), Recife (788,580) and Salvador (655,735).

BREAD, principal article of food of much of the world's population, made from grain flour mixed with water and then baked. In the early 17th century yeast was first used in England for baking raised bread. The grains used, ingredients added for flavour, and the size and shape vary throughout the world. Enriched bread contains additions of vitamins and minerals to compensate for those lost in the milling process.

BRECHT, Bertold (1898—1956), German playwright, born in Bavaria. His first success was with the ironic *Threepenny Opera* (1928), based on Gay's ***Beggar's Opera***. From 1930 his plays became vehicles for Communist ideology, and in 1933 he had to leave Germany; he settled in the U.S.A., returning to Germany and living in East Berlin from 1949. Brecht believed that the audience should not be caught up in a play emotionally and, in Aristotle's phrase, purged through fear and pity; it should remain detached and be made to think for itself. To this end he developed the 'epic' form of play, consisting of a loosely linked series of scenes. By his 'alienation effect' he tried to make the familiar suddenly appear strange, to heighten the response of the audience to his message.

BREMEN, a city of West Germany, on the Weser River. Pop. (1960) 563,300. A major freight and passenger port and communications centre, it exports iron and wood products, glass, buildings materials and woollen goods. Industries include shipbuilding, automobiles, chemi-

Early book illustrations were reproduced from hand-made woodcuts. The two examples shown here are from *The Printer*, a German book published in 1568, and *Book of Falconrie*, published in 1575.

Photos: Victoria & Albert Museum

Modern newspaper printing machines. When running, such machines are capable of printing 40,000 copies an hour.

Photos: Cambridge News and Daily Mirror

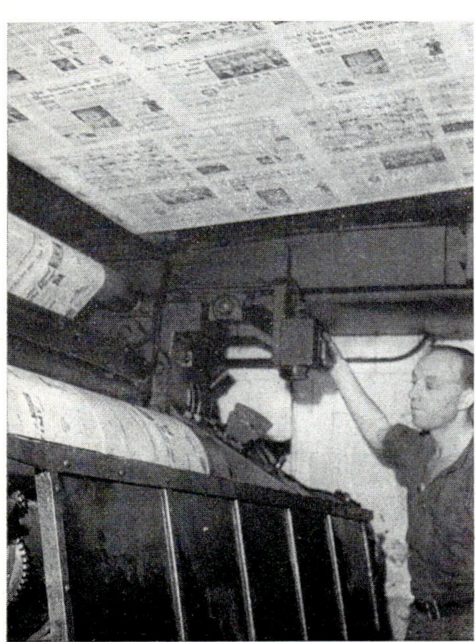

One of the earliest types of building constructed by man: a model of a Neolithic Longhouse.
Photo: British Museum (Natural History)

The Ancient Greeks, followed by the Romans, made tremendous advances in building techniques. It is to the Greeks that we owe the three great Orders of Architecture—Doric, Ionic and Corinthian. Shown here is a corner of the Ionic temple known as the Erechtheion. Inaugurated 421 B.C.
Photo: The Mansell Collection

Built between A.D. 532-36 by the Byzantine emperor Justinian I (q.v.), the basilica of St Sophia at Istanbul is one of the most glorious and original buildings that have ever been erected.
Photo: Paul Popper Ltd

Another example of Byzantine architecture is shown in this picture of the magnificent façade of St Mark's Cathedral, Venice. Built between 1042-85. *Photo: Paul Hamlyn Library*

Durham Cathedral, built 1093, is one of the later yet most important of the Romanesque cathedrals. Its Norman nave is perhaps the finest example known. *Photo: F. H. Crossley*

The Italian Gothic period produced solid-looking yet ornate buildings in which the development towards Baroque is evident. Shown here is the Santa Maria Novella, Florence, built *c.* 1456. *Photo: Larousse*

Baroque extravaganza is typified in the Zwinger palace, Dresden, built 1711-22 for the rulers of Saxony. *Photo: Marburg Picture Archives*

'Scenic' works, such as the Trevi Fountain, were part of the architectural revival experienced in Rome in the early 18th century. Built 1732-62, it is the work of Nicola Salvi. *Photo: Paul Hamlyn Library*

cals, machinery, foodstuffs, tobacco, petroleum refining and textiles. Bremen has some historic buildings. It was a leading member of the Hanseatic League.

BREVIARY, the short prayer book of the Roman Catholic Church containing the Divine Office, i.e. the canonical services of each day. All priests must recite the whole of the breviary services allotted for each day. The word means 'abridgement'.

BREWSTER, Sir David (1781—1868), Scottish physicist, educationalist and writer. He made important studies of double refraction and the polarisation of light. The British government adopted his recommendation to use the dioptric system of lighthouse illumination. Brewster invented the kaleidoscope and was one of the founders of the British Association for the Advancement of Science.

BRIAND, Aristide (1862—1932), French statesman. Premier 11 times, he served as Minister for Foreign Affairs in several governments. In the decade preceding his death he was a strong force for international peace. In 1930 he advocated a United States of Europe. He shared the Nobel Prize for peace in 1926 for his part in the Locarno Pact of 1925.

BRIDGE, a structure of ropes, brick, concrete, stone, wood or metal to enable men or vehicles to cross water, valley, road or railway. Bridges are either fixed — permanently anchored in position on piers or abutments — or movable. In the latter type some part can be moved to enable water-borne traffic to pass; it may be opened upward from the end, on a pivot swinging in the middle, or by lifting the central segment. Fixed bridges may be continuous from pier to pier, cantilever or suspension. Bridges supported on boats are called pontoon bridges. Bridges have been in use since prehistoric times; the Clapper Bridge on Dartmoor, made of 16 ft stone slabs laid on stone piers, was constructed about 2000 years ago. The Romans developed the art of bridge-building as their empire expanded. The railway and automobile gave modern bridge-building a special impetus. The world's longest single-span suspension bridge is the 1¼ mile Golden Gate bridge across San Francisco harbour, California; the span over clear water is 4200 ft, and the road is 250 ft above water-level. The Firth of Forth road bridge was completed in 1965, the largest single-span bridge in Europe. Other notable bridges of recent years are the Volta River bridge in Ghana and the Auckland Harbour bridge, New Zealand. The Transbay Bridge from Oakland to San Francisco (8½ miles long) is a series of bridges divided by an island tunnel section, with a suspended span on one side of 2310 ft and a cantilever span on the other of 1400 ft.

BRIDGET, St (or Brigid; *c.* 451—525), the patron saint of Leinster, Ireland. Daughter of a prince and his bondwoman, she founded the monastery at Kildare.

BRIGHTON, a county borough in Sussex, on the English Channel. Pop. (1964) 162,757. It is one of the largest and most popular British holiday resorts, with a sea-front seven miles long; owing to fast and frequent non-stop trains it has even become one of London's dormitories. Brighthelmstone, as it then was, owes its rise to a quack who persuaded countless patients that their health depended not only on bathing there, but on drinking its sea-water by the pint. From 1782 Brighton was taken up by the Prince Regent, who built the oriental Royal Pavilion (designed by Nash) there, and made the place fashionable. As a consequence there is much good Regency architecture to be seen. The heart of the old town is 'The Lanes', a warren of narrow passages now given over to antique shops. Roedean, a girls' school, is near by.

BRISBANE, capital of Queensland, Australia, 10 miles up the Brisbane River. Pop. (1961) 620,121. A communications and cultural centre, it is a major seaport. In the midst of a farming, dairying and mining region, it manufactures textiles, munitions, sawmill products and foodstuffs. There are shipyards and railway repair shops.

BRISTOL, county borough and seaport on the borders of Gloucestershire and Somersetshire, England, six miles up the Avon. Pop. (1961) 436,440. It is the major commercial and industrial centre of southwest England. Industries include shipbuilding, automobiles, aircraft, tobacco, chocolate and petroleum products. It has been a major seaport since the 12th century, and has many historic buildings. Large ships berth at Avonmouth.

BRITISH COLUMBIA, Canadian Pacific coast province. Pop. (1961)1, 629,082; area 355,855 sq. miles. Consisting of two mountain chains enclosing a plateau, the province has numerous forests and is well-drained. Its chief products are lumber, silver, zinc, lead, gold, copper, coal and salmon. Dairy products, fruits and vegetables are also produced. Discovered by Juan de Faca in 1592 and visited by Vancouver in 1792, British Columbia was at first disputed between Britain and Spain. In 1871 it became a province of Canada. The capital is Victoria (pop. 1961 154,152), the largest city (790,165) being Vancouver.

BRITISH COMMONWEALTH OF NATIONS, an association of countries united by common allegiance to the British Crown, or by the recognition of the sovereign of Great Britain as the head of the Commonwealth. It comprises 15* sovereign independent states — the United Kingdom, Canada, Australia, New Zealand, Cyprus, India, Pakistan, Ceylon, Ghana, the Federation of Malaysia, Nigeria, Sierra Leone, Tanzania Uganda, Singapore, together with a number of dependencies of varying status. The latter include Zambia and Southern Rhodesia, colonies, protectorates, protected states and trust territories.

BRITISH GUIANA, British colony on the northern coast of South America. Pop. (1960) 560,620; area 83,000 sq. miles. Hot and humid, with mountains in the south, British Guiana produces chiefly sugar-cane and rice, also bauxite and gold. It has rich tropical forests. The capital is Georgetown (pop. 120,000).

BRITISH HONDURAS, British colony in central America on the Caribbean Sea. Pop. (1960) 90,343; area 8866 sq. miles. Its main product is timber. The capital is Belize (pop. 32,824).

BRITISH ISLES, archipelago off the northwest coast of Europe. Geographically it consists of Great Britain and Ireland and some 5000 smaller islands and islets. Its area is 121,633 sq. miles.

BRITISH MUSEUM, the national museum of Britain, in London. It contains extensive collections of printed books, manuscripts, prints, drawings, antiquities, coins and medals. Its treasures include numerous illuminated manuscripts, two original copies of the Magna Carta, the Rosetta Stone which provided

* currently increasing in numbers

the key to Egyptian hieroglyphics and the Elgin Marbles taken from the Parthenon in Athens. There are more than 6,000,000 volumes in the library, where a copy of every item published anywhere on British territory must be deposited. The British Museum was opened in 1759 in Montagu House and subsequent additions have made it necessary to expand its premises continually. The Natural History Museum at South Kensington is part of the British Museum.

BRITTANY, a region of northwest France. It was subdued by the Romans in 51 B.C. In the 5th century A.D. Celtic tribes from Britain settled in the region, and the Breton language closely resembles Welsh and Cornish. In 1171, Geoffrey, son of Henry II of England, became ruler of the duchy. It was annexed to France in 1532.

BRITTEN, Benjamin (1913—), British composer. Born at Lowestoft, Suffolk, he is chiefly known for his War Requiem, his operas *Peter Grimes*, *Billy Budd* and *Albert Herring*, but has written all kinds of compositions, including *The Young Person's Guide to the Orchestra*. He founded the Aldeburgh Music Festival, in Suffolk.

BRNO, a city in southern Czechoslovakia, at the junction of two rivers. Pop. (1959) 312,330. It was formerly the capital of Moravia and has old buildings, institutions of higher learning and museums. Its principal manufactures are heavy steel equipment of all kinds, including armaments, tractors and factory machinery, woollen textiles, chemicals, paper and shoes. It was Napoleon's headquarters in 1805.

BROMIDE, a widely used bromine salt with sedative properties. It alleviates anxiety and nervousness and has a quietening effect in certain illnesses. Sodium and potassium bromides are used in photography.

BROMINE, see Elements.

BRONTË, a literary family of three daughters of an Irish clergyman who lived together at Haworth Parsonage between a graveyard and the Yorkshire moorland. Charlotte (1816—55) joined her other sisters in publishing a book of poems anonymously, and then turned to novel-writing. Her *Jane Eyre* (1847) was an immediate success. She alone lived to marry, but died in childbirth. Emily (1818—48) wrote a few great poems and one great, and from such a source, astonishing novel, *Wuthering Heights* (1848). Anne (1820—49) based one of her two novels on the life of her drunken brother Branwell (1817—48).

BRONZE AGE, the period in the development of civilisation between the New Stone Age and the Iron Age in which bronze (an alloy of copper and tin) was the principal metal. It dates from *c.* 2500 to 1000 B.C. in the Middle East and somewhat later in Europe. The inhabitants of Britain began using bronze *c.* 2000 B.C. The use of bronze led to a cultural revolution of great importance. Trade increased and peoples learned from one another. The invention of the wheel marked the beginning of rapid technical development. Draught animals and the plough came into use, and towns grew as centres of craftsmanship and commerce.

BROOKLYN, the largest and most populous of New York City's five boroughs, lying at the western end of Long Island. Pop. (1960) 2,627,319. Connected to Manhattan by three bridges and four tunnels, it has shipyards, docks (there are 33 miles of waterfront) and a wide variety of industries. The leading manufactures are chemicals, paints and varnishes, drugs, machinery, foodstuffs, furniture, household supplies, and foundry and machine-shop products. There are several institutions of higher learning.

BROWN, John (1800—59), American abolitionist. At first seeking to effect the abolition of slavery by education, he later became convinced that it could only be done by force. From the murder of pro-slavery men in Kansas and the armed liberation of slaves, his activities increased in violence to the extent of capturing a U.S. arsenal at Harper's Ferry, West Virginia, in 1859, when two of his sons were killed. He was subsequently taken prisoner by U.S. troops, tried for treason and murder, and hanged. While some northern abolitionists considered him a patriot, others strongly joined the South in condemning him. The bitterness he engendered was a factor in the Civil War. He is the John Brown of the ballad, whose 'body lies a-mouldering in the grave'.

BROWNING, Elizabeth Barrett (1806—61), English poetess. Suffering from ill-health most of her life, she married the poet, Robert Browning, before the latter achieved fame. In view of her domineering father's disapproval of the marriage, they went to live in Italy. Her best-known works are *Sonnets from the Portuguese*, inspired by her own feelings for Robert Browning, *Casa Guidi Windows*, and *Aurora Leigh*, a long sociological romance in verse.

BROWNING, Robert (1812—89), English poet. He published his first volume of verse at the age of 22. After his marriage to Elizabeth Barrett in 1846, he went to live in Italy. His poetry achieved recognition slowly because of its obscurity and his concern with psychological details. His style may be blunt, colloquial and bellicose, but he wrote lines which stick like burrs in the memory. Among his outstanding poems were the dramatic monologues (a form he invented) *Soliloquy of the Spanish Cloister* and *Rabbi ben Ezra*, *Mr Sludge the Medium*, inspired by his wife's credulity in such matters, and *Bishop Blougram's Apology*. His *tour de force* was the immensely long *The Ring and the Book*, a 17th century murder story told in turn by each of the characters and by the judges.

BRUCE, Robert (1274—1329), King of Scotland. A Scottish nationalist, he was crowned king at Scone in 1306. Defeated by the English, he fled to Ireland, whence he returned to gain a series of victories over them, culminating in a triumph over Edward II at Bannockburn in 1314. In 1328, he became king of an independent Scotland. He died of leprosy.

BRUCE, Stanley Melbourne, 1st Viscount (1883—), Australian statesman. Born in Melbourne, he practised as a lawyer in England, and served with distinction in the First World War. He sat in the Australian Parliament from 1918—29 and 1931—33, was Prime Minister of a National-Country Party coalition (1923—29), High Commissioner in London (1933—45) and a member of the War Cabinet (1942—45). He played a prominent part in the League of Nations and was president of the World Food Council.

BRUEGHEL, the name of a family of Flemish painters. Pieter (*c.* 1525—69) was the greatest of them. He painted crowded scenes of peasant life of great vivacity and often grotesque satirical humour *(The Peasant Dance, Village Wedding)*, reminiscent of Bosch. His son Pieter (*c.* 1564—1638), called 'Hell'

Brueghel (from the subject-matter of many of his works), painted religious pictures. Another son, Jan (1568—1625), known as 'Velvet' Brueghel because of the smoothness of his painting, made detailed studies of flowers and other still-life subjects, and also painted landscape. Rubens collaborated with him.

BRUNEI, British protected sultanate in north Borneo. Pop. (1960) 83,869; area 2226 sq. miles. It has rich oil deposits.

BRUNO, Giordano (1548—1600), Italian philosopher, Dominican monk and martyr. He was forced to flee from Rome because of his opposition to the Catholic church and established religion. While in England in 1583—85, he wrote *Expulsion of the Triumphant Beast*, an allegory containing the essence of his heresies. He subsequently lectured in Germany, France and Switzerland. Arrested by the Inquisition in Italy in 1592, he was burned at the stake.

BRUSSELS, capital of Belgium. Pop. (1960) 1,000,774, including suburbs. An inland port, the city is divided by the Senne River. A commercial and cultural centre with many historic buildings, Brussels also has varied industries. Founded in the 7th century, it has been the capital of the duchy of Burgundy, the Austrian Netherlands and the Netherlands. Brussels is the headquarters of the European Economic Community.

BRUTUS, Marcus Junius (85—42 B.C.), one of the Roman conspirators who murdered Julius Caesar. Although he had fought against Caesar in 49 B.C. during the civil war, Caesar pardoned him and appointed him governor of Cisalpine Gaul. Cassius persuaded him to join the plot against Caesar in 44. After the assassination, he fled with Cassius and took possession of Macedonia. Mark Antony and Augustus defeated them at Philippi and Brutus then committed suicide.

BUCHAREST, capital of Rumania. Pop. (1960) 1,291,251. Situated on the Dambovita River, the city is the industrial as well as cultural centre of Rumania. There is an old town with narrow streets and old churches. The industrial suburbs have developed since the Second World War.

BUCKINGHAMSHIRE, a county in the south of central England. Pop. (1961) 486,183; area 749 sq. miles. Hilly in the north, it consists of a clay plain in the south. Agriculture is the leading industry and livestock breeding and dairy farming are important. There are numerous historical relics. The county has fine beech woods, source of a timber and furniture industry. The county town is Aylesbury.

BUDAPEST, capital of Hungary. Pop. (1960) 1,807,299. Formed by the union of Buda and Pest on either bank of the Danube, the city is an industrial, commercial and cultural centre. The site of the Roman town Aquincum, it became a Magyar city in the 10th century. Destroyed by the Tartars (1241), and occupied by the Turks (1541—1686) and the Austrians (1866), it became the capital of Hungary under the Dual Monarchy in 1867. Buda is the older town, built on a series of steep hills, and contains the Royal Palace; Pest, on a plain, was reduced to ruins by the Turks and little of it dates back earlier than the 18th century.

BUDDHA (*c.* 563—483 B.C.), Indian religious leader and philosopher, founder of the Buddhist religion. After, as the legend puts it, he had seen one day an old man, a sick man and a corpse, he decided to forsake a life of ease and devote himself to a search for the true significance of life and death. At first he experimented with a rigorous asceticism, but found it no help, and it was only after he had abandoned this way that enlightenment (Buddha means 'the enlightened one') came to him under the Bo-tree (a fig-tree allied to the Banyan tree) at Gaya (in southern Bihar). He spent the next 43 years preaching, and died of dysentery at the age of 80 near his birthplace in Nepal.

Statue of Buddha

BUDDHISM, the religion which grew out of the teachings of Buddha against a background of Hindu religious belief, is based on the Four Sublime Truths: pain exists; is caused by selfish desire (attachment); can be eliminated; but only by following the Eightfold Way. This Way comprises: right doctrine, right purpose, right speech, right behaviour, right humility, right purity, right thought, right concentration; it leads to release *(nirvana)* from the cycle of reincarnation through the enlightenment that overcomes ignorance. *Nirvana* is the merging of the individuality in the universal life. Renunciation is the key to release, and by the law of *karma* a person's actions in one life decide his fate in his next life.

After a schism in the 2nd century A.D. two main divisions appeared: the Hinayana ('lesser vehicle'), the older form, which stresses individual sainthood, immediate experience and intuition, and is the religion of Ceylon, Burma and Thailand; and Mahayana (great vehicle), which preaches universal salvation by a Bodhisattva, an enlightened being who abandons *Nirvana* to save others. The latter form is found in China, Japan and, in the very different guise of Lamaism (q.v.), in Tibet. A Japanese sect which has attracted attention in the West in recent years is Zen Buddhism (q.v.).

Buddha himself committed nothing to writing; the sacred texts were written down in the 1st century B.C. from oral traditions dating from *c.* 500 B.C.

BUENOS AIRES, capital of Argentina. Pop. (1960) 3,845,279. A port on the Rio de la Plata, and the largest city in South America, Buenos Aires is the administrative, commercial, industrial and cultural centre of Argentina. Meat-packing and wheat-milling are the chief industries. Founded in 1580, it suffered from attacks by Indians in its early years. In 1776 it became the capital of the newly-founded vice-royalty of the Rio de la Plata. The city was virtually rebuilt in the 20th century, and so has no slums.

BUFFALO, a city in western New York State, U.S.A. Pop. (1960) 532,759. A port on Lake Erie, it is a commercial, industrial and communications centre. Grain, iron ore, coal, limestone, lumber and livestock are shipped. Buffalo produces tinned meat, chemicals, rubber products, automobiles, machinery, textiles, aircraft and electrical equipment, and has important oil refineries.

BULGARIA, People's Republic (since 1946) in southeast Europe in the Balkan Peninsula. Pop. (1960) 7,870,000; area 42,796 sq. miles. From north to south, Bulgaria consists of the Danubian tableland, the Balkan Range, and the rich plain of the Maritsa River flanked on the southwest by the Rhodope Mountains. Chiefly agricultural, the country raises cereals, cotton, tobacco, sugarbeet and grapes; rose oil is a speciality. Bulgaria's minerals are iron, lead, copper, manganese, and petroleum. Of Turkish origin, the Bulgars established themselves in the area from the 6th—8th centuries. They adopted Christianity and a Slavonic dialect and twice (893, 1280) conquered most of the Balkan Peninsula. From 1396—1878 Bulgaria was a Turkish province. It became Germany's ally in both World Wars. Most of the population is still Greek Orthodox. The capital is Sofia. Pop. (1956) 725,756. Other important cities are Plovdiv (162,518) and Varna (199,769).

BUNYAN, John (1628—1688), English writer and dissenting preacher. Twice imprisoned for his opposition to the religious conformity enforced by the reigning Stuarts, he wrote during his latter imprisonment a celebrated work, *The Pilgrim's Progress*, an allegorical account of a soul, beset by trials, searching for salvation. He also wrote a remarkable autobiography *Grace Abounding to the Chief of Sinners.*

BURKE, Edmund (1729—97), Anglo-Irish statesman, orator and political writer. He founded the Annual Register in 1759. At the same time he began taking an active part in politics. In 1776, Burke became a Whig member of Parliament where he acquired considerable influence by his eloquence. He held that a member of Parliament should represent all his constituents and not merely his supporters. Although in office only twice, and although a Whig, he laid the foundation of conservative thought in Britain. He was deeply concerned about four great issues — the curbing of royal authority, conciliation with the American colonies, affairs in India, and the dangers of the French Revolution, which he was one of the few Whigs to oppose.

BURMA, a republic in southeast Asia. Pop. (1960) 20,662,000; area 261,789 sq. miles. Mountains in the northwest, a central basin down which the Irrawaddy river flows to a delta, and a plateau in the east drained by the Salween, are the country's main topographical features, together with a long narrow tongue of land down to the Malay peninsula. Rice, rubber, cotton and tropical woods (particularly teak) are the main products. Minerals include rubies, sapphires and petroleum (a mineral oil). Under British rule from 1826, it was occupied by Japan 1942—45. It became an independent union of states in 1948.

BURMA ROAD, a vital supply route in southeast Asia during the Second World War, extending through difficult mountainous terrain from the Burmese railhead at Lashio to Kunming, China. Opened late in 1938, it was the principal means of contact with China after the Japanese cut off the Chinese seaports and the road from Indo-China in 1939.

BURNEY, Fanny (Madame D'Arblay; 1752—1840), English novelist. Her first work, *Evelina*, or *The History of a Young Lady's Entrance into the World*, was an immediate success. Of her subsequent novels, only *Cecilia* is of literary interest. Her *Diary and Letters* covering the period from 1778 to her death, give a vivid picture of her times. Her father, Dr. Burney, was a fashionable music master.

BURNS AND SCALDS, burns are injuries caused by dry heat; scalds are caused by wet heat. In increasing degree of severity, burns are classified as first degree characterised by a reddening of the skin; second degree with the formation of blisters; and third degree involving serious damage to the deeper layers of skin. A simple ointment or paste of baking soda may be applied to small, superficial burns. Second and third degree burns involving more than one-third of the body's surface are dangerous to life.

BURNS, Robert (1759—96), Scotland's greatest poet. Born on a farm, his life was marked by poverty and hard work. After a day of back-breaking toil in the fields, he wrote poetry in the stable loft where he slept. On the publication of his first work *Poems, Chiefly in Scottish Dialect* he was persuaded to abandon his plan to emigrate to Jamaica, Between working as excise man and farming, he wrote poems of genuine emotion about mankind's problems. His greatest is *Tam o' Shanter*. Burns contributed more than 300 Scottish folk-songs to various collections, frequently writing his own lyrics to popular Scottish melodies.

BURTON, Sir Richard (1821—90), English explorer, linguist, writer and diplomat. A master of more than 35 languages and dialects, he was one of the first Englishmen to enter Mecca, which he did disguised as a Moslem. He wrote vivid scholarly accounts of his observations in India and Africa. He was the first to explore Somaliland and the districts of the great lakes of Africa. His crowning achievement was a translation of *The Arabian Nights* from the Persian.

BURUNDI, an independent kingdom in Central Africa. Pop. (1962) 2,213,000; area 10,747 sq. miles. It is a mountainous, predominantly agricultural and cattle-breeding country, which exports coffee. Until 1962 it was called Urundi and was part of the U.N. Trust Territory of Ruanda-Urundi, under Belgian administration since 1919, and previously German. The capital is Usumbura.

BUSTAMENTE, Sir Alexander (1884—), Jamaican politician. The son of an Irishman and a mulatto mother, he entered politics in 1934, joining the party of his cousin Norman Manley, but forming his own party in 1943. He was appointed Chief Minister in 1953 and pressed for Jamaica's secession from the West Indies Federation. In 1962 he became Labour Prime Minister of Jamaica.

BUTLER, Samuel (1835—1902), English author. He shocked his parents by refusing ordination in the church, and became a sheep-farmer in New Zealand. Although primarily interested in art and music, he began writing articles and sketches. His *Erewhon* and *Erewhon Revisited* are utopian satires. *The Way of All Flesh* describes the impact of the Victorian environment on what resembles his own boyhood. A famous *jeu d'esprit* was a book in which he contended that the Homer who wrote the *Odyssey* was a woman.

BYBLOS, (Biblical Gebel) an ancient city on the Mediterranean in what is now Lebanon. A major Phoenician port, it was important under the Persians and Alexander the Great. The site has interesting archaeological relics dating from 3000 B.C.

BYRD, Richard Evelyn (1888—1957), American naval officer, airman and polar explorer. Having made important contributions to the development of aerial navigation after the First World War, he explored the Arctic regions from the air in 1925. He made the first successful flights to the North pole (1926) and South pole (1929). From his base at Little America in the Antarctic, Byrd carried out valuable exploration and scientific work. He discovered new mountain ranges, a peninsula, islands and large new areas of coastline. Byrd was one of the first to point out the military importance of Antarctica. During the Second World War he served at Washington and with the Pacific fleet.

BYRON, George Gordon, 6th Baron (1788—1824), English poet. His first successful book was the first two cantos of *Childe Harold*, an exotic, sentimental poem based on his own travels. He followed this with more verse tales in the Romantic style: *The Giaour*, *The Bride of Abydos*, and *The Corsair*. In 1816 he settled in Italy, where he wrote some of his best works, *The Prisoner of Chillon*, *Manfred*, *Mazeppa* and the unfinished *Don Juan*, his longest and last great poem. In 1823 he sailed for Greece to devote himself to the cause of Greek independence but died there of malaria soon after his arrival.

BYZANTINE ART, the formal, stylised art of the Byzantine Empire, fully developed under Justinian (6th century) and continuing to flourish until the fall of Constantinople (1453). It drew its inspiration from Greece, Rome, Syria, Egypt, Islam and elsewhere, and Byzantine architecture is found all over the eastern Mediterranean, the Balkans and Asia Minor. The chief characteristics are found in the churches (see Orthodox Eastern Church), which have a dome, or cluster of domes, and the interior walls and ceilings covered with mosaics and frescoes. The icon (a picture of Christ or a saint, mostly painted on wood panels), jewellery, Oriental metalwork and sumptuous textiles are other features. Justinian's church of St Sophia, Istanbul (537), the mosaics of S. Vitale, Ravenna, and St Mark's, Venice (10th century), are the finest examples of Byzantine art.

BYZANTINE EMPIRE (Eastern Empire), eastern division of the Roman Empire originating when the Roman Emperor Constantine the Great founded near ancient Byzantium a second capital (named after him in 330). From the time of Constantine's death there were usually separate emperors of the west and east, until, with the collapse of the Western Empire in the 6th century, the Byzantine emperors alone were left to keep alive for another nine centuries the traditions of Roman administration, Greek language and literature, and Christianity. Constantine had adopted Christianity, which eventually became the state religion, with the emperor regarded as God's vice-regent on earth. In the 9th century increasing disagreements between the patriarchs of Constantinople and the popes of the Western Church culminated in the Great Schism of 1054 (see Orthodox Eastern Church).

From the first Byzantium had to fight off attacks, successively from Goths, Vandals, Avars, Persians, Bulgarians and Arabs. The peak of artistic achievement was reached under Justinian (527—65), and of political expansion under a Macedonian dynasty (867—1057), which reconquered territory up to the Danube and the Euphrates. The Seljuk Turk victory at Manzikert in Asia Minor in 1071 marked the beginning of a decline, and the empire, further weakened by Latin Crusaders of the Fourth Crusade who took Constantinople in 1204, finally fell to the Ottoman Turks, in the reign of Constantine XI, in 1453.

C

CABINET, in Britain an inner group of ministers of the crown who advise the Prime Minister, are dependent on the support of the House of Commons, have seats in parliament, and accept collective responsibility for governmental actions and policy; they form a close link between executive and legislature by which the latter can control the former without impeding its efficiency. The Cabinet grew in importance under Robert Walpole (1676—1745), the first Prime Minister, its evolution from a committee of the Privy Council being aided by George I's ignorance of the English language and consequent absence from the committee's deliberations.

Certain ministerial offices automatically carry Cabinet rank, but the Cabinet's composition is varied from time to time and often includes some 'ministers without portfolio', consultants free from the burden of running a department. Members are appointed by the Prime Minister, and must resign if they cannot accept a Cabinet decision. The party in opposition usually forms a Shadow Cabinet of members ready for office if their party comes into power.

The U.S. Cabinet is essentially different, since its members are appointed by the President and are not members of Congress; there is no Prime Minister.

CABOT, John (1450—98), Italian explorer in the service of England. Encouraged by Henry VII to seek a North-West Passage to the Orient, he sailed westward in 1497 and discovered the mainland of North America, sailing from Newfoundland to Virginia. His son Sebastian (1476—1557), a famous cartographer, explored the coast of Brazil, and sailed up the River Paraguay. He also made a voyage to Hudson Bay and, as governor of the Merchant Adventurers' Company, supervised Chancellor's voyage to Muscovy.

CADMIUM, see Elements.

CAESAR, Gaius Julius (*c.* 102—44 B.C.), Roman statesman, orator, writer and general. An adherent of the anti-Senate popular party, Caesar had to flee from Rome when Sulla crushed this party (82), but upon Sulla's death (78) he returned and advanced rapidly: from magistrate (68), pontifex maximus (chief priest of Rome) (63), to praetor (62). In 60 B.C., together with Crassus and Pompey, he formed the First Triumvirate. From 58 to 50, he led the Roman forces against the Germanic tribes in Gaul and invaded England, in campaigns which are described in his *Commentaries.* In 49, hostilities between Caesar and Pompey came to a head; Caesar crossed the Rubicon river to march on Rome and civil war began. After a long series of engagements extending from Spain to Egypt, Caesar emerged victorious (45). In 44 he assumed perpetual dictatorship but was assassinated by a group of conspirators led by Cassius. The last of the great republicans of Rome, he destroyed the republic; but its end was perhaps inevitable. In the short time available to him he had effected many important reforms; building, colonising, extending Roman citizenship, planning the draining of the Pontine marshes, preparing a digest of the law, occupied his last few months.

CAESAREAN SECTION, the delivery of a child by an incision made in the mother's abdomen and uterus. It is resorted to when normal birth may endanger the mother or child. The name derives from the Roman *lex Caesarea* which required that this operation should be performed on women who died pregnant.

CAESIUM, see Elements.

CAINE, Sir Henry Hall (1853—1931), English novelist. Some of his works deal with life on the Isle of Man. His novels include *The Deemster*, *The Bondman* and *The Eternal City*.

CAIRO, capital of Egypt. Pop. (1959) 3,035,000. Situated at the head of the Nile delta, it is an administrative, communications, commercial and industrial centre. There are numerous mosques, at one of which is the medieval Moslem university of El Azhar. The present city was built in 969 on the site of towns of great antiquity. To the southwest are the Sphinx and the Great Pyramid.

CALCIUM, see Elements.

CALCUTTA, capital of the state of West Bengal, India, lies on the Hooghly River, a stream of the Ganges delta. Pop. (1961) 2,926,498. Its port and rail, road and river connections have made it one of the greatest commercial centres of Asia. Calcutta is joined by a great bridge to Howrah (514,090) on the opposite bank. The industrial area, where jute is of most importance, and where also iron foundries, chemical works, paper mills and rice mills are found, extends 25 miles up river, and the metropolitan area has a total population of 5,500,195, many of whom live in extreme poverty and squalor.

CALDERÓN DE LA BARCA, Pedro (1600—81), one of the two great Spanish dramatists. In many of his 200 plays, influenced by his Jesuit and university training, he examined the effects of the application of a rigid code of honour to a particular situation. His style is precise and simple, but he lacked invention and insight into human nature. His best work is contained in his *autos sacramentales* (allegorical plays for the feast of Corpus Christi), which combined poetry, ballet, music and drama in a Baroque setting. In some of these he dramatised the dogmas of the Fall, Incarnation and Redemption.

CALENDAR, the system of reckoning time according to an arrangement of fixed periods. Calendars are based on the rotation of the earth on its axis in a 24-hour period; the movement of the moon around the earth in a 29½-day period; and the movement of the earth around the sun in 365¼ days. Hours are divisions of a day; weeks are divisions of a year. In 45 B.C. Julius Caesar introduced a system for eliminating the confusion caused by the existing Roman calendar in which there were discrepancies between the solar and lunar systems of reckoning. In the Julian calendar there is an error of one day in every 128 years. To correct this, Pope Gregory XIII abolished the Julian calendar in March 1582 and introduced a new system (the Gregorian calendar) in which there is an error of only one day in every 3,000 years. Britain adopted the Gregorian calendar in 1752. U.N.O. is dealing with several proposals for calendar reform to eliminate some of the defects of the Gregorian system, but they are opposed by church groups.

CALIFORNIA, U.S. Pacific coast state. Pop. (1960) 15,717,204; area 158,693 sq. miles. From east to west the state's main regions are the Sierra Nevada Mountains (Mt Whitney 14,495 ft), the Great Central Valley and the Coast Ranges. Death Valley in the southeast is 282 ft below sea level. California's climate ranges from the temperate to the semi-tropical. It raises cereals and fruit, including citrus. The state produces large quantities of timber and fish. It is the third largest producer of oil in the U.S.A. Gold, silver, gypsum, mercury and tungsten are found in large quantities. Industry includes aircraft, machinery and electronic equipment. The film industry of Hollywood is of declining importance. First settled in 1769, California was part of Mexico until 1846. It became an American state in 1850. The capital is Sacramento (pop. 191,667). Other important cities are Los Angeles (2,479,015), San Francisco (742,855), San Diego (573,224) and Oakland (367,548). Lower California (pop. 1957, 538,400; area 55,654 sq. miles) is part of Mexico.

CALIPHATE, the term designating the leadership of Islam, the office held by the successors (Ar. *Khalifah*) of Mahommed. The first caliph was Abu Bakr; the caliphate became hereditary and passed in turn to the Umayyads (661), the Abbasids (750) and finally to the Ottoman Turks (1517), who retained this office until its abolition in 1924.

CALORIE, a unit of heat. The gram-calorie or small calorie is the amount of heat required to raise the temperature of a gram of water by 1°c. The kilogram (or large) calorie equals 1000 gram-calories, and is used in dietetics as the unit for measuring the energy content of foods.

CALVARY, the name of the hill outside Jerusalem where according to tradition Christ was crucified, is derived from the Vulgate Latin rendering *calvaria* of the Aramaic word *golgotha*, 'skull'. The hill was probably so called either because its shape resembles a skull or because it was habitually used for public executions. Calvary also means a representation of the Crucifixion.

CALVIN, John (1509—64), Protestant reformer and theologian. Born at Noyon in Picardy, France, and destined for an ecclesiastical career, he broke with the Catholic Church and embraced Protestantism (*c.* 1532). He fled from Paris to Basel where he wrote his monumental work, *Institutes of the Christian Religion*, and later moved to Geneva, of which he became the administrator. Calvin was the dominating influence in French, Dutch and Scottish Protestantism, and English Puritanism, and his teachings left their mark on subsequent generations. Calvinism is distinguished by its characteristically harsh dogma of Predestination, i.e. souls are irrevocably predestined by God for salvation or damnation. See Reformation; Reformed Church.

CALYPSO, a form of ballad originating from Trinidad, usually accompanied by drumming on steel. It is an improvisation on a topic of current interest sung in colloquial English, politics and sex being common themes. The melodies reveal African, Spanish and French influences.

CAMBODIA, an independent kingdom in southeast Asia. Pop. (1958) 5,040,000; area 67,550 sq. miles. A largely forested plain enclosed by mountains and the

Mekong River, the country grows chiefly rice and rubber. The capital is Phnom-Penh (500,000).

CAMBRIDGESHIRE, a county in eastern England. Pop. (1961) 189,913; area 505 sq. miles. The northern portion is known as the Isle of Ely and is a separate administrative unit; pop. 89,112; area 372 sq. miles. Ely is lowland, mostly reclaimed marsh; the county town is March. Cambridgeshire is one of the chief grain producing counties; fruit and market-garden produce are also important. The county town is the university town of Cambridge, where the oldest foundations are Peterhouse (1284) and Clare (1326) and the newest Churchill (1959). There are also two women's colleges, Girton (1869) and Newnham (1871). The Cavendish Laboratory has a world-wide reputation for research in physics.

CAMELOT, the legendary site in England of King Arthur's court, palace and Round Table; it has been variously identified with Caerleon, Winchester, Monmouth and Queens Camel (in Somerset).

CAMEROUN, Federal Republic of, an independent state in West Africa, on the Gulf of Guinea. Pop. (1961) 4,907,000; area 143,500 sq. miles. Originally a German colony, it became Trust Territory, with the eastern portion administered by the French and the western by the British, from Nigeria. The former attained independence in 1960 and the latter voted in 1961 to federate with it. The Cameroon Mountain (13,350 ft) in the southwest is the 'Chariot of the Gods' seen during the Carthaginian Hanno's voyage in 500 B.C. The principal products are bananas, rubber, hides, palm produce, cocoa and coffee. The federal capital is Yaoundé (55,000), linked by rail to the principal port, Douala (120,000).

CAMOËNS (Camões), Luis de (1524—80), Portuguese poet. His greatest work is the epic *Os Lusiadas*, dealing with Vasco da Gama's discovery of the sea route to India, but essentially a glorification of the Portuguese nation. He also wrote lyric poetry.

CAMPAIGN FOR NUCLEAR DISARMAMENT (C.N.D.) was formed to persuade the British government to renounce the use and production of nuclear weapons; to stop patrol flights of aircraft carrying nuclear weapons; and to stop the establishment of missile bases in Britain.

CAMPBELL-BANNERMAN, Sir Henry (1836—1908), English statesman, leader of the Liberal party (1899) and Prime Minister from 1905—8. He was largely responsible for settlement of the South African problem after the Boer War.

CAMPION, Thomas (1567—1620), English poet and musician. A physician by profession, he wrote a number of songs, both words and music. His best-known poems include *Cherry Ripe* and *Come, Cheerful Day*.

CAMUS, Albert (1913—1960), French author. He wrote essays, plays and novels. His best works are *The Stranger (The Outsider)*, *The Plague* and *Myth of Sisyphus*. He was awarded the Nobel Prize for literature in 1957. Although rejecting the existentialism of Jean Paul Sartre, he wrote in an existentialist vein.

CANADA, Dominion of, an independent confederation in North America, and a member of the British Commonwealth. Pop. (1961) 18,238,247; area 3,851,809 sq. miles. From east to west the country consists of the mountainous Appalachian region of the southeast; the vast Laurentian plateau, stretching as far as the Arctic Ocean; the St Lawrence lowlands in the south central portion; the Great Plains; and the Pacific coastal ranges, including the Rocky Mountains (Mt Logan 19,850 ft). Canada has countless lakes and its numerous rivers are important sources of hydro-electric power. The St Lawrence River (1900 miles long) became, in 1959, a major seaway. One-third of Canada is coniferous forest, and timber, with its subsidiary industries, particularly pulp and paper, is the chief source of wealth. The main crops are wheat (a leading export), and oats. Mineral resources are extremely rich and varied, the most important being oil and nickel; asbestos, silver, copper, gold and uranium provide valuable exports. Fishing is a major industry and there is still a considerable trade in furs. Apart from sawmilling and other timber-based activities, meat-packing and metallurgical industries are the most important.

In 1534 Jacques Cartier took possession of Canada for France. While French explorers penetrated as far as the western prairies, the British established the Hudson's Bay Company in 1670 for fur trading. In 1763, when Canada came under British control after a military victory, most of the population was still French. Immigration increased the number of British colonists but nearly a quarter of the population is of French ancestry. The right of Canada to self-government was recognised in 1849. In 1867 the Dominion of Canada was formed; it has ten provinces — Alberta, British Columbia, Manitoba, New Brunswick, Newfoundland, Nova Scotia, Ontario, Prince Edward Island, Quebec and Saskatchewan — and two territories — the Northwest Territories and Yukon. The capital is Ottawa (pop. 429,750). Other principal cities are Montreal (2,109,509), Toronto (1,824,481), Vancouver (790,165), Winnipeg (475,989) and Hamilton (395,189); the figures given are for metropolitan areas.

CANARY ISLANDS, a Spanish archipelago in the Atlantic Ocean, 60 miles west of North-West Africa. Pop. (1959) 908,718; area 4685 sq. miles. The main islands are Tenerife (cap. Santa Cruz), Gran Canaria (cap. Las Palmas) and Palma. Tropical fruits are grown, particularly bananas, and wine produced.

CANCER, a malignant growth formed by the disorganised multiplication of the cells of the cellular tissue which covers many surfaces within the body. Cancerous cells progressively destroy and replace adjacent normal tissue. They also spread via the blood and lymph channels to other parts of the body. The disease is extremely widespread, with certain people more susceptible to specific kinds than others, and certain occupations and environments more conducive to the disease. There appears to be no one cause; recent researches point to smoking as one cause of lung cancer and diesel fumes are also under suspicion. In all instances there appears to be a precipitating agent which may be a chronic irritation of some sort; and possibly psychological factors are important. The effective control of cancer depends upon early diagnosis and immediate treatment, either by surgery or irradiation, or both.

CANDLEMAS, a feast commemorating the Purification of the Virgin Mary, observed by the Roman Catholic Church on February 2; so called because, since the 11th century, candles are blessed and distributed on this occasion. In Scotland Candlemas is also a term (quarter) day.

CANNING, George (1770—1827), English statesman who was the mastermind behind the capture of the Danish fleet (1807) during the war against Napoleon. His recognition (1823) of the independence of the Spanish colonies in America established the basis for the Monroe Doctrine, and he supported liberal movements in Greece and elsewhere in Europe.

CANON, a term applied by the Christian Church to the collection of books approved and recognised as belonging to the Holy Bible. There are several discrepancies between the Roman Catholic and Protestant canons, the former containing books (the Apocrypha) not included in the latter.

CANONISATION, the act by which the Roman Catholic, and Eastern Orthodox churches bestow the title of saint on a deceased person, whose name is subsequently recorded in the *Canon Sanctorum* (list of saints). In the former Church a court may be instituted not less than 50 years after the candidate's death, to examine the claims made on his or her behalf. The titles 'Venerable' and 'Blessed' are stages on the path to formal canonisation.

CANTERBURY, a city in Kent, England. Pop. (1961) 30,376. It has a famous cathedral founded by St Augustine in 597, which contains the shrine of St Thomas à Becket, for many centuries a place of pilgrimage, immortalised in Chaucer's *Canterbury Tales*. Canterbury is the ecclesiastical capital of England, although the Archbishop of Canterbury resides at Lambeth Palace, London.

CANTON, a seaport of southern China, in Kwangung Province. Pop. (1958) 1,840,000. Situated on the Pearl River in the densely populated Canton delta, Canton is an important commercial centre at the end of a railway from Peking, with industrial suburbs making textiles, paper, machinery and cement.

CANUTE (Cnut; 995—1036), King of England. The son of Sweyn, King of Denmark, who had driven Ethelred the Unready into exile, he inherited England on his father's death in 1014 but was opposed by Ethelred's son, Edmund Ironside who, after further fighting, agreed to partition the country between them. Edmund, however, was murdered shortly afterwards, and Canute became King of England. He also became King of Denmark in 1018 and of Norway in 1030. He reconciled the Danes and Anglo-Saxons, married Ethelred's widow, and allied himself with the Church. His strong and prudent rule brought peace and prosperity. He died at Shaftesbury.

CAPE BRETON ISLAND, an island off Nova Scotia, Canada. Pop. (1951) 157,696; area 3120 sq. miles. Hilly, with a rugged coast, the island produces timber, fish and coal.

CAPE OF GOOD HOPE (Cape Province) in the south of Republic of South Africa. Pop. (1951) 4,417,330, including 935,674 whites; area 277,137 sq. miles. Grapes, wheat and livestock are raised. The capital is Cape Town (q.v.).

CAPE TOWN, the legislative capital of the Republic of South Africa. Pop. (1960) 745,942. An important seaport and communications centre, it is also a leading fishing port. Clothing is the chief industry. As a commercial centre Cape Town has yielded place to Johannesburg.

CAPE VERDE ISLANDS, Portuguese islands in the Atlantic Ocean, 350 miles west of Cape Verde, West Africa. Pop.

(1959) 190,000; area 1557 sq. miles. The chief occupation is agriculture. Praia is the capital. São Vicente is a coaling station on the trade route to South America.

CAPET, Hugh (*c.* 938—96), elected King of France from 987—96 and founder of the Capetian dynasty which, with its Valois and Bourbon branches, was to rule France for the next 800 years. Louis XVI was sent to the guillotine as Louis Capet.

CAPITALISM, the economic system based on the private ownership of resources and goods, the production of goods for profit, the use of money, the opportunity to increase income by competing in a free market, and the possibility of securing credit. Both labour and capital have freedom of action and movement. Capitalism began to flourish during the Industrial Revolution of the 18th century. The growth of large-scale financial, industrial and commercial enterprises is directly attributable to the freedom of individual enterprise characteristic of capitalism. The disadvantages of a capitalist economy, such as periodic unemployment, restrictive trade practices, misleading advertising and gross inequality of income, have to be set off against the advantages of personal liberty, minimum government intervention, freedom of choice of employment, and the absence of standardisation of design and quality of consumer goods.

CAPRI, a rocky island in the Bay of Naples. Pop. 8050; area 5⅜ sq. miles. It is a famous tourist resort. The Blue Grotto is a limestone cave just above sea-level. Tiberius retired there in his last years.

CAPUCHINS, a branch of the Franciscan Order founded (*c.* 1528) by Matteo da Bassi, who advocated a return to the rigid observances of St Francis. The name comes from the shape of their hoods *(capuches)*.

CARACALLA, Marcus Aurelius (186—217), Roman Emperor from 211—17, murdered his brother and co-regent, Geta (212), in order to become sole Emperor of Rome. He conducted victorious campaigns against the Germanic tribes (213—14) and was assassinated at Carrhae while campaigning against the Parthians. The Edict of Caracalla granted Roman citizenship to all free-born members of the Roman Empire.

CARACAS, capital of Venezuela, on the Guaire River. Pop. (1959) 711,673. It is a cultural, commercial and industrial centre owing its growth to the discovery of oil, and a market for the coffee, cocoa, sugar-cane and vegetables of the surrounding region. Industries include automobiles, textiles, sawmill-products, leather goods, foodstuffs, chemicals and paper. Caracas lies only 20 minutes by road from Venezuela; the chief port is La Guaira.

CARAVAGGIO, Michelangelo Merisi da (1573—1610), one of the great revolutionaries in Italian art. He was in opposition to the reigning Mannerist painters and embarked on a path of stark realism using the clothing and attitudes of common people for religious models. After many rejections his style became popular and spread through Europe, particularly among the artists of Spain and the Netherlands.

CARBOHYDRATES, a group of organic compounds composed of carbon, hydrogen and oxygen. They include sugars, starches and cellulose, which form the chief foodstuffs of animals; in plants starch is the principal stored food and

The Royal Pavilion at Brighton, rebuilt by John Nash in 1815, is incredibly exotic, being part Moslem, part Indian. Cast iron was freely used in its construction. Described as Picturesque, it is an entirely different form of architecture from the Neo-classic façades John Nash was erecting in London's Regent Street and Regent's Park at the same time. Also shown is his York Gate, Regent's Park.

Photos: A. F. Kersting

The early 19th century produced many public buildings described as classical revivals. Clearly influenced by the Ancient Greek Parthenon, this is the Assemblée Nationale in Paris.

Photo: French Government Tourist Office

The Albert Memorial in London, which was started in 1863 and took ten years to complete, is an example of the High Victorian style.
Photo: Paul Hamlyn Library

Designed by Frank Lloyd Wright and built 1943-59, the spiral Guggenheim Museum in New York is the last major work carried out during the architect's lifetime.
Photo: United States Information Service

In the interior of Brazil a great modern and architecturally exciting capital city, Brasilia, is being carved out of the jungle. Here is the magnificent Palace of Dawn.
Photo: Brazilian Commercial and Information Service

cellulose the chief structural part. Carbohydrates are built up by the action of photosynthesis (q.v.) from carbon dioxide and water. They break down again by slow oxidisation, releasing energy used by the organism, into their constituent parts, a process called the carbon food cycle.

CARBON, a non-metallic chemical element. It is ubiquitous, appearing as carbon dioxide in air, as hydrocarbons in coal and petroleum, as carbonates in limestone, etc., and as the essential constituent of all organic matter. The chemistry of carbon compounds is known as organic chemistry. Carbon has two crystalline forms, diamond and graphite; other forms are charcoal, coke, lampblack. See also Elements.

CARBON MONOXIDE, a poisonous, invisible, tasteless, odourless gas present in ordinary coal gas, oil-burner fumes and car exhaust fumes. When inhaled it combines readily with the haemoglobin in the blood, thus decreasing the amount available for carrying oxygen to the tissues.

CARBONARI (charcoal burners), a secret revolutionary society in Italy during the early part of the 19th century, which opposed foreign and reactionarv rule.

CARDIFF, a seaport and county borough of Glamorgan, and since 1955 the official capital of Wales. Pop. (1961) 256,270. The port ships coal and, to a lesser extent, iron and tinplate. There are steel-works, shipyards and chemical industries. In the well-planned civic centre stand the National Museum of Wales and the university buildings. The 11th century (restored) castle overlooks the main shopping streets.

CARDINAL, a counsellor of the Pope, member of the Sacred College and, next to the Pope himself, the highest dignitary in the hierarchy of the Roman Church. Cardinals are appointed by the Pope, and upon his death a new Pope is elected by them, in conclave, from among their own body.

CARIBBEAN, see Sea.

CARILLON, a set of bells arranged on a chromatic scale and capable of producing music with a range of two or more octaves when struck manually or mechanically.

CARINTHIA, a mountainous province in southern Austria. Pop. (1951) 474,764; area 3681 sq. miles. It has large mineral deposits. The capital is Klagenfurt.

CARLSBAD CAVERNS, a series of connected caverns in New Mexico, U.S.A. There are several levels extending for over 4000 ft. Unusual formations of stalactites and stalagmites are an attraction to tourists.

CARLYLE, Thomas (1795—1881), Scottish essayist and historian. Unable to apply himself to any definite employment, he retired to a farm where he wrote his first important book, *Sartor Resartus*, a spiritual autobiography and criticism of modern life. In his subsequent works he attacked the evils of industrialism, democracy and laissez-faire economics. Carlyle believed that history was shaped by outstanding individuals. His works include *The French Revolution*, *Chartism*, *Heroes and Hero-Worship*, and the *Heroic in History*, and biographies of *Oliver Cromwell* and *Frederick the Great*.

CARMARTHENSHIRE, a county in south Wales. Pop. (1961) 167,736; area 920 sq. miles. It is hilly and has coal and anthracite mines. The production of milk predominates in agriculture. The county town is Carmarthen (13,249).

CARMELITES, originally (12th century) a colony of hermits on Mt Carmel in Palestine, it received papal recognition (1226) as a mendicant order of the Roman Catholic Church. It was later reformed by St Teresa as the discalced (bare-footed) Carmelites in 1562.

CARNEGIE, Andrew (1835—1919), American industrialist and philanthropist. Born in Scotland, he emigrated (1848) to the United States where he began as a cotton factory hand at $1.20 a week. He amassed a fortune in the iron and steel industry, retired in 1901 and devoted himself to philanthropy.

CARNOT, Lazare (1753—1823), French military strategist and mathematician, who organised the armies of the revolution (1793—95). As Minister of War from 1800 he showed efficiency in the direction of the Italian and Rhineland campaigns. He then retired to write a work on fortifications, but again saw service in 1814 in the defence of Antwerp. He was Minister of the Interior during the Hundred Days.

CAROL, a term which has come to denote a festive song, particularly one sung at Christmas.

CAROLINE ISLANDS, a Micronesian archipelago in the west Pacific Ocean. Pop. (1954) 39,304; area 460 sq. miles. First a German colony and then Japanese mandated territory, the islands and atolls, which number some 900, are now administered as a Trust Territory by the U.S.A. The chief export is copra.

CAROLINGIANS, a Frankish dynasty which replaced the Merovingians (751) and ruled various European kingdoms for about 250 years. Beginning with Pepin II, grandson of Pepin I and Arnulf of Metz, the Carolingians reached their zenith under Charles Martel and Charlemagne (from whom they take their name), but the dynasty began to disintegrate when the empire was partitioned (843) among Charlemagne's three grandsons. The Capets succeeded the Carolingians in France in 987 and the last of the dynasty was Otto, King of Lotharingia (1012).

Among the achievements of this vigorous line was the spread of Christianity to Germany and Frisia, the expulsion of the Arabs from Gaul by Martel (Poitiers, 732), and of the Avars from Hungary by Charlemagne, and the creation of a Papal state in Italy.

CARPATHIAN MOUNTAINS, a range in eastern and central Europe curving in a semicircle for 805 miles through Czechoslovakia, Poland, Hungary, the Ukraine and Rumania to the Yugoslav border. The highest peak is Mt Gerlachovka (8743 ft) in the High Tatra group in Czechoslovakia. Minerals include gold, silver, mercury, copper, iron and salt.

CARPENTARIA, Gulf of, on the north coast of Australia, is 370 miles long from north to south and extends about 300 miles from east to west, from Cape York to Cape Arnhem.

CARROLL, Lewis (1832—98), pen-name of the Rev. Charles Dodgson, English writer and mathematician, renowned as the author of children's books, including *Alice's Adventures in Wonderland* (1865) and *Through the Looking Glass* (1872). He also wrote on mathematics and logic.

CARSON, Sir Edward, later Baron (1854—1935), Irish politician and lawyer who devoted himself, as leader of the Ulster Unionists in Parliament, to saving Protestant Ulster from domination by the Catholic majority of Ireland. His efforts were crowned by the establishment of Northern Ireland (1920) as a separate government under the British Crown.

CARTHAGE, an ancient city in north-east Tunisia. Founded in 814 B.C. by the Phoenicians, it was for several centuries a dominant power in the region and Rome's most serious rival. The third Punic War (see Punic Wars) ended in the total destruction of the city by Rome in 146 B.C. A Roman foundation on the site became the chief city of Roman Africa, but after the Arab conquest in A.D. 698 it declined rapidly.

CARTHUSIANS, a Roman Catholic monastic order, known for its extreme austerity, founded by St Bruno (1084) at La Chartreuse near Grenoble, France. The monks, living isolated in their cells, rarely meet. Their Rule, 'never reformed because never deformed', has survived many vicissitudes and expulsions. The Chartreuse liqueurs are no longer distilled by the monks, but at the village of Voiron close by.

CARUSO, Enrico (1873—1921), Italian operatic tenor, the greatest of the 20th century. His repertoire included 43 operas. His first great success was as Alfredo in *Traviata*. He excelled particularly in *Rigoletto*.

CASABLANCA, the chief seaport and city of Morocco. Pop. (1960) 965,227. Casablanca has one of the largest artificial harbours in the world. Around the ancient Arab quarter a modern and expanding city has been built which retains a Moorish flavour. There are fertiliser, cement and other factories. In January 1943 President Roosevelt and Winston Churchill conferred together at Casablanca and adopted the controversial 'unconditional surrender' formula.

CASABLANCA GROUP, a group of African states formed in 1961, consisting of the U.A.R., Ghana, Guinea, Mali, Morocco and Algeria, who advocate a militant Pan-Africanism.

CASANOVA DE SEINGALT, Giovanni Giacomo (1725—98), Italian adventurer and author. Expelled from a seminary for his amorous escapades, he embarked upon a life of wandering and deception. Living by his wits, he practised numerous and varied professions in the major capitals of Europe and was an intimate of some of the leading personalities of his day. His 12 volumes of memoirs deal mostly with his *amours* and are an interesting picture of the life and manners of his period.

CASEMENT, Sir Roger (1864—1916), Irish patriot who, in attempting to gain support for an Irish revolution, worked with the Germans in the First World War, and was executed in London for treason. After much controversy his remains were returned to Dublin in February 1965.

CASSANDRA, daughter of Priam, King of Troy. Though she was endowed with the gift of prophecy, it was her fate that none would listen to her advice. She was murdered by Clytaemnestra.

CASSATT, Mary (1845—1926), American painter and engraver, studied under Degas and achieved fame as a member of the Impressionist school.

CASTE, the term applied to the exclusive social classes and divisions of Hindu society. Originally there were only five castes: the Brahmans, or priests; the rulers and soldiers; tradesmen and merchants; craftsmen and peasants; and the untouchables. Today, however, there are approximately 2,400 different castes. Caste membership is hereditary and it is not normally possible to ascend the scale of the caste-hierarchy. Attempts by Indian leaders to break the caste system, and particularly the obsession with 'pollution' by contact with members of lower castes, have as yet had little success.

CASTILE, an ancient kingdom of north central Spain. It is now divided into Old Castile in the north and New Castile in the south. Castile became an independent kingdom in the 11th century and was united with Aragon (q.v.) in 1479.

CASTLEREAGH, Robert Stewart, Viscount (1769—1822), British statesman. He supported Catholic Emancipation and helped Pitt to achieve the union of England and Ireland (1800). The Walcheren disaster led to a duel between Castlereagh and his more liberal rival Canning, the latter being slightly wounded. Wellington's successes in the Peninsular War were based on Castlereagh's vigorous policy as Foreign Secretary. His wise diplomacy at the Congress of Vienna and subsequent European conferences did much to ensure stability in the post-Napoleonic era, but he was much hated at home, where his oligarchic outlook was already outmoded, and his name was associated with the repressive Six Acts, restricting public meetings, and the massacre of Peterloo. In 1821 he succeeded to his father's title of Marquess of Londonderry, but the following year committed suicide.

CAT, a member of a family of carnivores, is distinquished by sharp retractable claws and by certain specialities of the teeth. The most familiar member is the domestic cat; the lion and tiger are larger members. In ancient Egypt cats were worshipped, and throughout medieval Europe they were associated with witchcraft.

CATACOMBS, subterranean burial chambers used by Christians from the 1st century, who buried their dead in niches cut in the rock. They became places of pilgrimage and, in times of persecution, of refuge. The best-known examples are at Rome but there are many in other parts of Europe, particularly Syracuse, mostly constructed in the 3rd and 4th centuries.

Catacomb of St Callistus, Rome

CATALONIA, an ancient region of Spain, lying between the Ebro and the Pyrenees. Pop. 3,595,0C0; area 12,427 sq. miles. Catalonia is mountainous with fertile valleys, and produces wheat, wine, flax, hemp, vegetables, fruit and timber. It is the most important industrial area of Spain and Barcelona (1,503,312), its capital, is Spain's chief port and industrial centre, specialising in textiles. The Catalans are racially distinct from the Spanish and speak a Romance language akin to Provençal. Catalan literature flourished from the 13th to 15th centuries and was revived in the 1830s. Although politically Catalonia became part of Aragon as early as 1137, it has always sought, and sometimes briefly achieved, independence; it enjoyed a measure of autonomy in 1931—36, but is now partitioned into four provinces.

CATALYST, a substance which alters (usually to increase) the rate at which a chemical reaction takes place, but itself remains chemically unaffected by the reaction. A small amount of catalyst may produce a vast increase in the rate. The process is called catalysis. In biology, enzymes and chlorophyll act as catalysts.

CATECHISM, instruction in religious dogma by means of question and answer. The term has come to denote a book of such instruction.

CATHEDRAL, a church in which a diocesan bishop has his throne or *cathedra* (Gk. seat, throne). During the Middle Ages the cathedral served not only as a religious but also as a civic place of assembly. In England, before the Dissolution of Monasteries they were either secular, served by canons (e.g. York), or monastic, served by monks (e.g. Canterbury). After the Dissolution several new cathedrals were established in formely monastic churches (e.g. Gloucester). Of the 20th century cathedrals the most important are the Roman Catholic and Anglican cathedrals at Liverpool, the rebuilt Coventry Cathedral, and that at Guildford.

CATHERINE II (The Great; 1729—96), Empress of Russia, was the daughter of a Prussian general invited to Russia by the Empress Elizabeth, whose nephew she married in 1745. Six years later this vicious weakling became emperor as Peter III, but was deposed after six months and murdered. Catherine, who had become notorious for her *amours*, was proclaimed empress. She attempted to carry out ambitious reforms, but was foiled by the great Russian families. During her reign serfdom was intensified, Poland was partitioned and territory was wrested from Sweden and Turkey. Catherine was a great patroness of learning and the arts, and corresponded with Voltaire and others of the European intelligentsia.

CATHERINE DE' MEDICI (1519—89), Queen of France, daughter of Lorenzo II de' Medici, wife of Henry II and mother of three kings of France — Francis II, Charles IX and Henry III. Her later conduct stemmed from the humiliations of her first 40 years — her apparent inability to produce an heir, her husband's open liaison with Diane de Poitiers, the contempt of her daughter-in-law, Mary Queen of Scots, whose mother was a Guise, and the hatred that existed between her sons. After the death of Francis II in 1560 Catherine came into power as regent for the young Charles IX. At first, out of hatred for the Catholic Guises, she intrigued with the Huguenots; but suspecting that Charles was being unduly influenced by the Huguenot Coligny, she turned against them and was largely responsible for the Massacre of St Bartholomew (1572). Politically a failure, it can at least be said of her that she was a true Medici in her patronage of the arts.

CATHERINE OF ARAGON (1485—1536), Queen of England, daughter of Ferdinand and Isabella of Spain, and first wife of Henry VIII, who, as there was no male issue, had the marriage annulled (1533) so that he could marry Anne Boleyn.

CATHOLIC EMANCIPATION, the freeing of Roman Catholics from civil and legal restrictions by a series of Acts from 1780, and in particular the emancipation of Irish Catholics after the Act of Union (1800), when they were still debarred from election to the House of Commons. In 1823 Daniel O'Connell formed the Catholic Association and eventually, under pressure, Wellington and Peel introduced the Catholic Emancipation Act (1829) permitting Catholics to sit in parliament and to hold all but a very few offices of state.

CATO the Elder (234—149 B.C.), Roman statesman and soldier who advocated a return to the austere, simple life of early Rome, and constantly warned the Romans that Carthage must be destroyed. He was the author of a text-book on farming, a history of Rome and an encyclopedia.

CAUCASUS MOUNTAINS, a mountain chain in southern European U.S.S.R., extending for about 950 miles between the Black and Caspian seas, and forming a natural boundary between Europe and Asia. Mt Elbruz (18,463 ft) is Europe's highest peak.

CAVELL, Edith (1865—1915), English nurse who, working as a nurse in Brussels during the First World War, helped Allied soldiers escape over the Dutch border. She was arrested by the Germans and executed as a spy.

CAVENDISH, Henry (1731—1810), English physicist and chemist. Having discovered hydrogen and nitric acid, he was the first to isolate argon. His electrical researches anticipated many later discoveries. He made the first accurate determination of the weight of the earth.

CAWNPORE (Kanpur), the largest city in Uttar Pradesh, on the Ganges, northern India. Pop. (1961) 947,793. The principal industrial centre of northern India, Cawnpore produces aircraft, textiles and leather goods.

CAXTON, William (*c.* 1422—91), English typographer who introduced printing into England. He learned the art of printing on the Continent but returned to England in 1476 where he then practised.

CECIL of Chelwood, 1st Viscount (1864—1958), English statesman. As Lord Robert Cecil, he was a member of the cabinet in the First World War; he later wrote *A Way of Peace* and helped draft the covenant of the League of Nations. In 1937, he was awarded the Nobel Peace prize.

CELEBES (Sulawesi), Indonesian island and province. Pop. (1959) 6,600,000; area 73,160 sq. miles. Mountainous and thickly forested, it produces copra and spices. The principal city is Makassar (357,400).

CELESTINE V (1215—96), Pope and saint. Elected (1294) Pope as a compromise candidate, his innocence and naivety soon made him a puppet of Charles II of Naples. Realising this, he abdicated within the year and withdrew to a life of praying and fasting.

CELLINI, Benvenuto (1500—71), Florentine sculptor, goldsmith, musician and writer. Extremely versatile and talented, he engaged in dangerous escapades, including murder. He executed notable works in gold and bronze. *Perseus with the Head of Medusa* is one of his greatest sculptures and the salt cellar in the Vienna Museum is a famous example of his gold and silver work. His egocentric *Autobiography* is not always credible but gives a fascinating if disconcerting picture of the vicissitudes of a craftsman's life in those times.

CELLULOSE, an organic compound comprising most of the cell-wall of plants. It is abundant in cotton and flax and is found in wood and cereal straws. Chemical celluloses are used in the manufacture of gun-cotton, plastics, rayon, celluloid, cellophane and cellulose finishes.

CEMENT, a fine white or grey powder made from silica, lime and aluminium heated at high temperatures. The various ingredients fuse to form a clinker which is ground. Mixed with water, it hardens to form a rock-like mass. For the first 30 days it becomes rapidly stronger, and the process of gaining in strength continues for about two years. Cement mixed with sand, gravel and water forms concrete which may be reinforced by inserted steel rods or beams, or prestressed, i.e. kept in permanent compression by highly stressed groups of steel wires, giving a concrete of much greater strength.

CENTRAL AFRICAN REPUBLIC, a republic in equatorial Africa. Pop. (1961) 1,227,000; area 190,000 sq. miles. The country is nearly all park savannah in the north with increasingly dense forests towards the south. Cotton, coffee, diamonds and timber are exported. Formerly the French territory of Ubangi-Shari, it became independent in 1960. The capital is Bangui.

CENTRAL AMERICA, the area lying between Mexico and South America. It includes British Honduras, Guatemala, Honduras, El Salvador, Nicaragua, Costa Rica and Panama. Pop. 56,000,000. Mostly mountainous, Central America has numerous islands off both coasts. The climate ranges from temperate in the highlands to hot and humid in the coastal regions. Coffee and bananas are grown. Formerly part of the Maya and Aztec empires, Central America was discovered by Columbus (1502) and subsequently subjugated by Spain.

CENTRAL HEATING, in the indirect warm-air system, air is drawn by fan over a heat exchanger fed from the domestic hot-water boiler, and circulated round the building by ducts and outlet grilles. In the direct system air is taken from a central point and drawn over surfaces directly heated by gas or oil burners; the air is then distributed by fan. Radiators can be heated by gravity circulation through large-bore pipes, the water being heated by the domestic boiler; alternatively hot water can be pumped through small-bore pipes, which are less unsightly. Underfloor heating by hot-water pipes or by electric coils is an alternative; in the latter method electricity can be used in the cheaper off-peak periods. All these methods have advantages and disadvantages, which have to be balanced against the particular circumstances in each case; there is the smell of oil, the labour of stoking a boiler, the intermittent noise of pumps and fans, and the relative cost of fuels. Various automatic appliances are on the market to keep the heating at a set temperature, and to switch the system on and off at set hours. Costs can be cut by attention to the insulation of the roof, and by fitting double windows, etc. With many systems it may be found that the heat provided is inadequate in really cold weather, and that electric fires, etc., have to be used to top it up. The cost of installation is above all affected by whether the house is already built and in occupation; if it is, underfloor heating may be very expensive to install.

CENTRAL TREATY ORGANISATION (Cento), a pact of mutual defence signed by Turkey and Iraq in 1955 and joined by the U.K., Pakistan and Iran; the U.S.A. is an associated member. Iraq withdrew in 1959. The headquarters are at Ankara.

CEREALS, important food plants of the grass family, bearing dry fruits or grains. They include wheat, rice, corn, barley, rye and oats. Cereals are good sources of minerals and B-vitamins.

CERIUM, see Elements.

CERVANTES, Miguel (1547—1616), Spanish dramatist, poet and novelist. He served in the Spanish Army (1570—5), was captured by pirates (1575) and ransomed (1580). Returning to Spain he served as a public official, but soon fell into disfavour. His most celebrated work is *Don Quixote* (first part, 1604; second part, 1615), which has been translated into most languages. Often regarded as the earliest novel, it contrasts the idealistic knight and his materialistic squire, Sancho Panza.

CEYLON, an island state off southeast India, and a member of the British Commonwealth. Pop. (1959) 9,612,000; area 25,332 sq. miles. Mountainous in the south, the island is mostly flat, with a hot humid climate. The main crops are tea, coconuts and rubber. An Indian became the first king of the Sinhalese in the 6th century B.C. There were several Indian invasions of the kingdom until the 19th century, when the British assumed control. Ceylon became a fully self-governing dominion in 1948. The population is 65% Buddhist. A further 20% are Hindu Tamils from south India who vigorously demand autonomy. The capital is Colombo (pop. 1953 423,481).

CÉZANNE, Paul (1839—1906), French painter. A highly original painter, he soon encountered considerable opposition in official art circles, although encouraged by the Impressionists. From 1879 he spent most of his time in seclusion at Aix-en-Provence, where he was born. He had his first public exhibition in 1906. Brilliant colours and a striving for depth characterise his painting. His work includes *The Brothers*, *Landscape with Viaduct*, and *The Card Players*. Although unregarded during his lifetime he is now recognised as being, with Gauguin and Van Gogh, one of the three great post-Impressionist painters.

CHAD, a land-locked republic in equatorial Africa. Pop. (1961) 2,675,000; area 495,794 sq. miles. Northern Chad is desert with some high mountains; the south is mostly grassland. The country is almost exclusively agricultural, but produces some cotton and livestock for export. Formerly a French territory, Chad became independent in 1960. The capital is Fort Lamy (70,000).

CHADWICK, Sir James (1891—), British physicist. A major figure in atomic research, he discovered the neutron in 1932 (see Atom). Chadwick was awarded the Nobel prize in physics and served as a part-time member of the U.K. Atomic Energy Authority. He was also adviser to the U.N. Commission on Atomic Energy. In 1948 he was appointed Master of Gonville and Caius College, Cambridge.

CHALIAPIN, Fyodor (1873—1938), Russian bass. Possessor of an exceptionally fine voice, he was also a talented actor; his performances of *Mefistofele*, *Boris Godunov* and *Ivan the Terrible* were particularly noteworthy.

CHALK, a white, or yellowish, soft variety of limestone consisting of nearly pure calcium carbonate, formed by accumulations of shells and minute marine animals on the bed of shallow seas. There are extensive chalk deposits in England, especially the white cliffs of Dover. Chalk has numerous uses in the manufacture of building materials, in farming and for burning in kilns to produce lime. French chalk, used for polishing, is a kind of talc.

CHAMBER MUSIC, music intended for small, private halls, composed especially for a limited ensemble of instruments. Usually one instrument of each kind is used. The predominant form of chamber music is the string quartet.

CHAMBERLAIN, Arthur Neville (1869—1940), English political leader. He was elected Conservative member of parliament in 1918 and served as Prime Minister from 1937—40. His name is associated with the policy of appeasement. He acquiesced in Mussolini's conquest of Ethiopia, provided the Italian dictator withdrew from Spain, and to the dismemberment of Czechoslovakia in 1938, at Hitler's demand, during the Munich Conference. After the fiasco of the Norway campaign, in the face of growing dissatisfaction with his leadership, he resigned in May 1940 and died shortly afterwards.

CHANNEL ISLANDS, a group of islands in the English Channel, off the northwest coast of France. Pop. (1961) 110,503; area 75 sq. miles. The largest islands are Jersey (45 sq. miles), Guernsey (24 sq. miles), Alderney and Sark. Fruit, vegetables, flowers and Jersey and Guernsey dairy cattle are raised for export. Tourism is of major importance. St Helier (Jersey) and St Peter Port (Guernsey) are the chief towns. The islands were part of the Duchy of Normandy and have belonged to the British Crown since the Conquest; they have their own elected governing bodies and levy their own taxes. There is still a large Norman-French element, speaking a French *patois.*

CHAPLIN, Charles Spencer (1889—), film actor and producer, born in England. He achieved a world-wide reputation as a comedian in a series of American films permeated by an undercurrent of social consciousness and satire. His most famous films are *The Kid*, *Shoulder Arms*, *The Gold Rush*, *Modern Times*, *The Great Dictator* and *Monsieur Verdoux*.

CHARLEMAGNE (742—814), King of the Franks and Emperor. He waged a long war (772—804) against the Saxons, finally conquering and Christianising them. In 773, as an ally of Pope Adrian I, he made war on the Lombards, subdued them (774) and made himself their king. He campaigned unsuccessfully against the Arabs in Spain (778), conquered Bavaria (788) and the Asiatic Avars (791—96). In 800 Pope Leo III crowned him as Emperor of the Romans in Rome. His patronage of the arts and sciences helped to revitalise Western civilisation.

CHARLES I (1600—49), King of Great Britain and Ireland from 1625, and son of James I, early in his reign incurred the displeasure of his people by his marriage to the Catholic Henrietta Maria and his reliance on Buckingham. His unpopularity increased when, after he had dissolved successive parliaments which refused him adequate financial supplies, he resorted to the levying of ship money and other unauthorised taxes. In 1628 Charles was forced to accept the Petition of Right which demanded the abolition of arbitrary taxation and imprisonment, but he then dissolved parliament and ruled without it for 11 years. His support of Strafford and of the High Church Archbishop Laud, whose prayer book he tried to force on Presbyterian Scotland,

and the Star Chamber's persecution of Puritans, deepened the breach between king and parliament. When Charles made his disastrous attempt in January 1642 to arrest the Five Members of the Long Parliament (q.v.) on the floor of the House, the Civil War (q.v.) became inevitable. It ended in Charles's defeat at Naseby (1645), and his surrender to the Scots, who handed him to the parliamentarians in 1647. His intrigues led to a Scottish invasion crushed by Cromwell (1648), and after Pride's Purge had cleared the House of royalist support, the Army and the Rump Parliament combined to have the king tried for treason and beheaded.

CHARLES II (1630—85), King of Great Britain and Ireland, second son of Charles I, fled to the Continent after Naseby. On his father's death he returned to Scotland where he was crowned king at Scone on January 1, 1651. In September he led a Scottish army into England but was defeated at Worcester and smuggled across to France. Monk negotiated his restoration to the throne in 1660. For the first seven years of his reign, which saw the Plague, the Fire of London and the Dutch fleet in the Medway, he left government largely to the bigot Clarendon, but turned against him and used the disasters of the Dutch Wars as a pretext for his banishment. He then entrusted the administration to the Cabal, a commission of five ministers — Clifford, Arlington, Buckingham, Ashley (Shaftesbury) and Lauderdale — representing both Catholics and Dissenters, and including a freethinker in Ashley.

In 1670 Charles signed the secret Treaty of Dover, under which Louis XIV promised subsidies and, if necessary, troops in return for English support against the Dutch and Charles's promise to restore Catholicism. He followed this up with the Declaration of Indulgence (1672) to Catholics and Dissenters alike, but, forced by the expense of the Dutch war to resort to parliament for funds, he had to accept their demand for its repeal a year later and its replacement by a Test Act excluding Catholics from office.

This drove the two Catholics from the Cabal, and a third member, Shaftesbury, having learnt the terms of the Treaty of Dover, formed an opposition party, the Country party or Whigs, who used the panic caused by Titus Oates's revelation in 1678 of a non-existent Popish Plot to get the king to accept an Exclusion Bill excluding the Catholic James, Duke of York, from the succession in favour of Charles's natural son, Monmouth. By 1681 Charles had vanquished the Whigs, and for the rest of his reign he ruled without a Parliament, subsidised by Louis.

Charles's children, none legitimate, included Monmouth, by Lucy Walters, Charles Lennox, Duke of Richmond, by the Duchess of Portsmouth, and the Duke of St Albans, by Nell Gwynne.

CHARLES V (1500—58), Holy Roman Emperor and King of Spain. Succeeding his grandfather, Ferdinand V, in Spain (1516) and inheriting the territories of the Hapsburgs from Maximilian I (1519), Charles became the most powerful ruler in Europe; he was crowned emperor in 1520. He waged almost unceasing war against Francis I of France, who feared domination by the Hapsburg power, and against attacks by the Ottoman Turks and their allies, the Moors.

Charles was unsuccessful in his efforts to reach a settlement with Luther who, at the Diet of Worms (1521), had defied Pope and Emperor. He had to crush the popular and Lutheran Peasants' Revolt (1524) in southwest Germany. Eventually the Protestants, in alliance with France, were able to obtain most of their demands.

The Religious Peace of Augsburg (1555) legalised Protestantism; it also divided Germany into Catholic and Protestant states according to the religion of the reigning prince, and led to the Thirty Years War. A sick and disappointed man, Charles abdicated, to spend his last three years in a Spanish monastery.

CHARLES XII (1682—1718), King of Sweden. A military leader, he compelled the Danes to make peace with him and in 1703 defeated the Russians and Poles. In 1709 he was routed by a large Russian force at Poltava and barely escaped to Turkey. His efforts to secure Turkish aid against Russia failed. He was killed during his second invasion of Norway.

CHARLES XIV, King of Sweden, see Bernadotte, Jean Baptiste Jules.

CHARLES Martel (*c.* 689—741), Frankish ruler. An illegitimate son of Pepin II he ruled Austrasia from 717 as mayor of the palace under a Merovingian king, and the whole Frankish kingdom from 731. He saved Gaul from Arab rule by his defeat of Abdurrahman at Tours and Poitiers (732). Charles Martel was the first of the great Carolingians (q.v.).

CHÂTEAU THIERRY, town in northern France. The scene of numerous battles in French history, it was twice occupied (1914 and 1918) by the Germans during fierce fighting in the First World War.

CHATEAUBRIAND, François René, Vicomte de (1768—1848), French writer and diplomat. His varied work was based on the belief that the truest beauty and poetry are to be found in Christianity (*La Génie du Christianisme*, *Atala* and *René*). He wrote travel books about America and Palestine, an autobiography (*Mémoires d'outre-tombe)*, and an epic about life among the Red Indians. With a deep feeling for nature went a gift for making the past live and a complete mastery of word-music; he was a precursor of the Romantic movement in literature. Exiled by the Revolution, he was given an appointment by Napoleon and various diplomatic posts by Louis XVIII, whom he helped to the throne.

CHATHAM, William Pitt, 1st Earl of (1708—78), English statesman. A critic of Walpole, Carteret and Newcastle and much disliked by both George II and George III, Pitt's career was naturally chequered. He was able to demonstrate his probity when he broke with tradition by refusing to make a fortune out of the office of Paymaster-General to the Forces (1746), and displayed his efficiency and diplomatic skill in the conduct of the Seven Years War (1756—63) which won Canada and India for Britain. Dogged by ill-health and the opposition of George III, he resigned office in 1768, but returned 10 years later to make a vigorous speech in the House on America, during which he was seized with apoplexy, dying shortly afterwards.

One of the finest parliamentary orators, the 'Great Commoner' championed civil liberties and parliamentary reform, and strongly opposed the measures taken against the American colonies, while refusing to countenance 'the dismemberment of this ancient empire' by the grant to them of full independence.

CHAUCER, Geoffrey (1340—1400), English poet. Through the patronage of John of Gaunt, who married his wife's sister, Chaucer was appointed to a succession of important posts and was able to travel extensively in France and Italy, whence he drew much of his inspiration, the plots of his stories and, from Italy, his characteristic ten-syllable line, then new to England. The Prologue to the *Canterbury Tales*, the work by which he is best known, portrays a party of pilgrims joking and quarrelling on their way to Canterbury and whiling away the journey with their tales. These, numbering 23, are mostly based on Boccaccio or French verse romances, and contain much gentle irony and shrewd comment on the foibles of the time. The whole work represents the highest achievement in English poetry up to that time, and indeed for many generations afterwards. His numerous other works include *Troilus and Criseyde*, *Legend of Good Women*, *The Book of the Duchess*, various translations and even a treatise on the astrolabe.

CHAUTAUQUA, a religious and cultural movement founded by Rev. John Vincent and Lewis Miller at Chautauqua, New York in 1874, which attained great popularity immediately preceding the First World War.

CHEKHOV, Anton (1860—1904), Russian dramatist and short story writer. His plays and stories of Russian life reveal penetrating insight into character and mood, and into the isolation and loneliness of the individual. Of Chekhov's plays, *The Cherry Orchard*, *The Sea Gull* and *Three Sisters* are the best known and most frequently staged.

CHEKIANG, a maritime province of China, on the East China Sea. Pop. (1953) 22,865,747; area 39,486 sq. miles. Although mountainous, this smallest of the provinces of China is densely populated. The climate is sub-tropical. Silk, cotton, hemp and timber are produced. The capital is Hangchow (pop. 700,000).

CHEMISTRY, the study of the elements and their compounds, and the laws of their combination and change under varying conditions. Modern chemistry, derived from alchemy (q.v.), may be said to begin with Robert Boyle (1627—91) who put forward an atomic theory to replace that of the alchemical elements. In the 18th century Priestley and Lavoisier exploded the theory that 'phlogiston' was present in anything combustible. Priestley discovered oxygen and Cavendish the composition of water. Dalton (1766—1844) was responsible for the atomic theory from which modern chemistry developed. In 1811 the shorthand system in which chemical formulae are written was introduced. In 1869 Mendeleyev's Periodic Table grouped elements according to atomic weight.

Matter is composed of minute particles (molecules), always in motion, which are in turn composed of atoms (q.v.). Molecules containing atoms of the same kind are elements; those containing different kinds are compounds. The separation of compounds into their components is analysis, and the reverse process of building them up is synthesis. A combination of elements unaccompanied by a change of molecular structure is a mixture. Compounds are produced by chemical action which alters the arrangement of atoms in the molecule, e.g. by heat, light or moisture. The same chemical compound always contains the same elements combined in the same proportion by weight. All matter can exist in three states, gas, liquid or solid. Matter is also classified by chemists into metals, which are opaque and have lustre and conduct heat and electricity, and non-metals which do not have these properties.

Organic chemistry studies carbon compounds; inorganic chemistry studies all the elements and their compounds (except carbon compounds). Other branches are analytical chemistry, biochemistry, and physical chemistry, the study of the structure of matter and all the general laws governing their behaviour.

CHESAPEAKE BAY, an inlet of the Atlantic Ocean in Maryland, U.S.A. It is about 200 miles long from north to south.

CHESHIRE, a county in western England on the Irish Sea. Pop. (1961) 1,367,860; area 1056 sq. miles. A famous farming area, it is noted for its dairy products. Livestock raising is important. Industries consist mainly of textiles, chemicals, shipbuilding and soap manufacture. It has many old timbered houses. The county town is Chester (59,283), and Birkenhead the chief port.

CHESS, a highly skilled and very ancient game played with 16 pieces a side (eight of them pawns) on a board of 64 squares. The permissible moves of

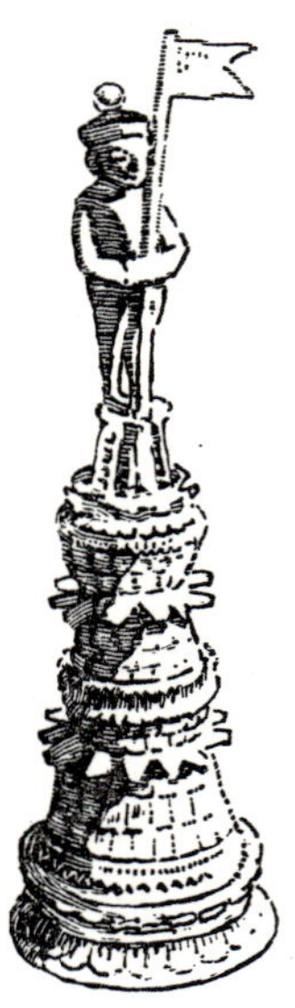

Indian chess piece (18th century Castle)

each piece are restricted, e.g. a bishop can move only diagonally, a castle only parallel with the sides of the board. The object of the game is to checkmate the opponent's king by manoeuvring it into a situation where it cannot move out of check, i.e. out of the line of an attacking piece; the game ends in a draw if the king is unable to move except into check and there are no other pieces which can be moved (stalemate) or if neither side can win. The game requires concentration and the visual memory and imagination to see several moves ahead; a short-term sacrifice of a valuable piece (or pieces) may ensure a long-term win.

CHESTERFIELD, Philip Stanhope, 4th Earl of (1694—1773), English writer. Although he engaged in politics, his fame rests largely on the well-written, witty but worldly-wise *Letters to His Son.* He also wrote *Letters to His Godson* and anonymous letters to the press denouncing the government of George II.

CHESTERTON, Gilbert Keith (1874—1936), English writer. Versatile, witty and a master of paradox, he wrote numerous books and essays on social, political and religious issues. He was the author of the *Father Brown* detective stories, criticism, biographies, an autobiography and a series of fantastic novels *(The Man who was Thursday*, *The Napoleon of Notting Hill).* His first two works were books of verse which he illustrated. He was a convert to Roman Catholicism and strongly defended his new faith.

CHEVIOT HILLS, a range of rolling grassy hills on the border of England and Scotland. Extending northeast-southwest for 35 miles, they afford grazing for sheep. The highest point is The Cheviot (2676 ft) in Northumberland.

CHIANG KAI-SHEK (1887—), Chinese military and political leader. Head of the government (1928—31) and leader of the resistance against the Japanese from 1937—45, he withdrew to Formosa with the Nationalist government after the Communist conquest of the mainland (1949). In 1950 he resumed the presidency of the Nationalist government.

CHICAGO, capital of Illinois. U.S.A. Pop. (1960) 3,550,404. On Lake Michigan, Chicago is the shipping centre and market for the farms, mines and timberlands of the Middle West. It is the largest railway centre in the U.S.A. and is the second largest city in population. Chicago is a leading steel-producing city. Refrigerated rail transport enabled it to develop its enormous meat-packing and ancillary industries; other industries include foods, chemicals, printing, petroleum and coal products. The largest education and culture centre in the Middle-West, Chicago is also the headquarters of commercial and financial enterprises, and has numerous mail-order houses.

CHILE, a republic in South America. Pop. (1960) 7,627,000; area 285,133 sq. miles. Narrow and mountainous, one-third of Chile consists of the Andes range. The Atacama Desert, rich in minerals, lies in the north. Its central area is a 700-mile long, thickly populated valley, with hot summers and mild rainy winters. The forested south is cold, cloudy, and windy. The chief agricultural products are field crops and grapes. Stockraising is the most important industry. Chile's wealth consists chiefly of minerals. It has large reserves of copper and nitrates. There are deposits of gold, silver, iron, cobalt, zinc, molybdenum, tungsten and manganese. Chile supplies about two-thirds of the world's iodine. The new steel mills at Huachipato have given a great fillip to local industry. Spaniards began to colonise the region in the mid-16th century. In 1818, Chile achieved independence. In a war with Bolivia and Peru, in 1879—83, Chile won important areas from both countries. The capital is Santiago (pop. 1958 830,897). Other principal cities are Valparaiso (271,431), Concepcion (163,798) and Viña del Mar (105,779).

CHINA, People's republic in Asia. Pop. (1960) 670,000,000; area 4,300,000 sq. miles. Most of the country is mountainous especially in the north and west. There are extensive plains in the lower regions of the Hwang Ho (2700 miles long) and the Yangtze (3100 miles) rivers respectively in the north and centre. The Si Kiang (1650 miles) is an important river in the south, mostly navigable. All rivers flow eastward. More than three-quarters of the population is engaged in agriculture. The important crops are wheat and maize in the north, rice and sugar-cane in the south. Tea, silk, tobacco, jute and hemp are also produced. Much teak is grown and tung for tung-oil. Coal, gold, iron, copper, lead, zinc, silver, tungsten, mercury, antimony and tin are mined. There are very large reserves of coal, iron and petroleum. Textile, food processing, iron and steel, and electrical industries are rapidly developing. An attempt is being made to spread industry more evenly over the country. Hitherto there has been a great concentration of heavy industry, developed during Japanese occupation, in Manchuria (Anshan), and of textile industries at Shanghai. The newer industrial areas now being developed include Paotow (Inner Mongolia), Lanchow, Sian and Tauyian, and the conurbation of Wuhan. By 2000 B.C. the Chinese had achieved an advanced stage of civilisation. The golden age of Chinese history was during the T'ang dynasty (A.D. 618—907). Foreign activities were closely restricted but, during the 19th century, a number of European powers obtained numerous concessions from the weak central government. The Manchu dynasty which had ruled China since 1644 was overthrown in 1912 and a republic under Sun Yat-sen established. Civil war clouded Chinese history during the republic. In 1931 the Japanese overran Manchuria and later attempted to take most of China. Following the Japanese defeat in 1945, People's forces gradually gained control of the entire country and established in 1949 a Soviet-type government in all of China, except the island of Formosa. The capital is Peking (pop. 1958 5,420,000). The largest cities are Shanghai (7,100,000), Tientsin (3,230,000), Shenyang (2,561,000), Wuhan (2,150,000) and Chungking (2,120,000). At least six other cities in the republic have over a million inhabitants.

CHINESE REVOLUTION (1912—49), began with the abdication of the last of the Manchu emperors in 1912 after a revolution started by Sun Yat-sen (q.v.), who founded the Kuomintang Nationalist party. Chiang Kai-shek (q.v.) succeeded him in 1925, unified China as far as the Great Wall, and then tried to suppress his Communist left wing. The Communists, under Mao Tse-tung (q.v.), made the Long March (6000 miles) in 1935 to Yenan, where they established a Communist régime well out of Chiang's reach. Later Chiang had to form a common front with the Communists against the Japanese, who had occupied Manchuria in 1931 and invaded China in 1937. After the Second World War, which Chiang entered following the attack on Pearl Harbor, civil war again broke out, Chiang was defeated and set up the National Government in the island of Formosa (1949). Mao Tse-tung based the Communist Revolution on the peasantry, there being no proletariat in the Marxist sense, and embarked on a campaign of land reform, rapid industrialisation and friendship with Russia. See Commune, Chinese.

CHIPPENDALE, Thomas (1718—79), English cabinet-maker. His book *The Gentleman and Cabinet-Maker's Director* brought him immediate fame as a furniture designer. Solidity, harmony and elaborate ornamental features distinguish Chippendale furniture. Dark mahogany was his favourite wood.

CHLORINE, see Elements.

CHLOROFORM, a volatile, colourless liquid used as an anaesthetic and a solvent for organic compounds. As an anaesthetic, it works rapidly but taken in excess is fatal. It has a harmful effect on the heart, blood vessels and liver.

CHLOROPHYLL, see Photosynthesis.

CHOPIN, Frédéric (1810—49), Polish pianist and composer. At the age of 20 he made a grand tour of Europe which ended triumphantly in Paris, where he settled and made many friends, including Liszt, Schumann, and the authoress George Sand. His best known works are melodious and original compositions for the piano.

CHOU EN-LAI (1898—   ), Chinese statesman. He took a prominent part in Chinese Communist activities from 1922, and was with Mao Tse-tung on the Long March (see Chinese Revolution). He became the first Communist Chinese Prime Minister after Chiang Kai-shek's defeat in 1949, and still holds that post; he was also Foreign Minister until 1958.

CHRIST, a title, derived from the Greek *Christos* — the equivalent of the Hebrew Messiah (the anointed) — which was given by early Christians to Jesus of Nazareth. In modern usage it is used as a proper name for Jesus, i.e. 'Jesus Christ', or simply 'Christ'.

CHRISTADELPHIANS (Brethren of Christ), a religious sect founded in the U.S.A. *c.* 1848 by an Englishman, John Thomas (1805—71) of Brooklyn, who preached a return to the faith of the Early Church. They believe that only they will rise from the dead when Christ returns to earth after Armageddon.

CHRISTIAN BROTHERS, an organisation of Roman Catholic lay brothers, founded at Rheims in 1679 by Jean Baptiste de la Salle, whose primary goal was the education of boys.

CHRISTIANITY, the religion of the followers of Jesus of Nazareth. Christianity grew out of Judaism, its mother-religion, and incorporated many of the religious tenets of the latter. Unique to the Christian faith is the belief in Jesus as the Christ (Messiah), the Son of God, through whom God gave His ultimate revelation to mankind. The life and teachings of Jesus and his disciples are recorded in the New Testament, and are accepted by Christians as divinely inspired. After an initial period of persecution, Christianity was recognised as a legal religion by Constantine (313) and quickly spread throughout the whole of the Roman Empire. Today, Christianity has the largest number of adherents of any religion in the world.

CHRISTIAN SCIENCE, a religious system established in the U.S.A. in 1866 by Mary Baker Eddy (1821—1910). The underlying concept of Christian Science is that God is Mind or Spirit and, therefore, since matter and evil do not exist in the Mind (of God), they are unreal and do not exist at all. Doctors and drugs are irrelevant, spiritual healing being the only cure for what is in effect an illusion. The sacred text of the sect is Mrs Eddy's *Science and Health with Key to the Scriptures*. The movement is wealthy and has Temples of Christ Scientist in many countries; it also publishes a widely read newspaper, the *Christian Science Monitor*.

CHRISTMAS, derived from 'The Christ Mass', a religious festival celebrated by Christians in commemoration of the birth of Jesus. It is observed on December 25 by the Western churches and on January 6 by the Eastern. The choice of date, in the 4th century, may have been due to a desire to replace and displace pagan festivals celebrating the winter solstice. Many customs, originally pagan, have been incorporated and re-interpreted in the Christmas festivities, e.g. the Christmas tree and Yule log, the giving of presents and the decoration of houses with mistletoe and holly.

CHRISTMAS ISLAND, (1) an island in the Indian Ocean about 850 miles southeast of Singapore belonging to Australia; pop. (1960) 2919; area 62 sq. miles. It has phosphate deposits. (2) an atoll in the Western Pacific in the Line Islands group; area 222 sq. miles. It has been used by Britain and the United States for nuclear bomb tests.

CHROMIUM, see Elements.

CHROMOSOME, a minute body in the nucleus of every living cell which

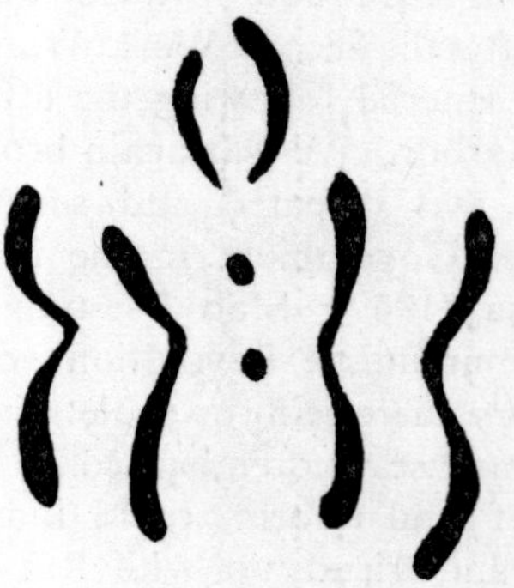

Chromosome

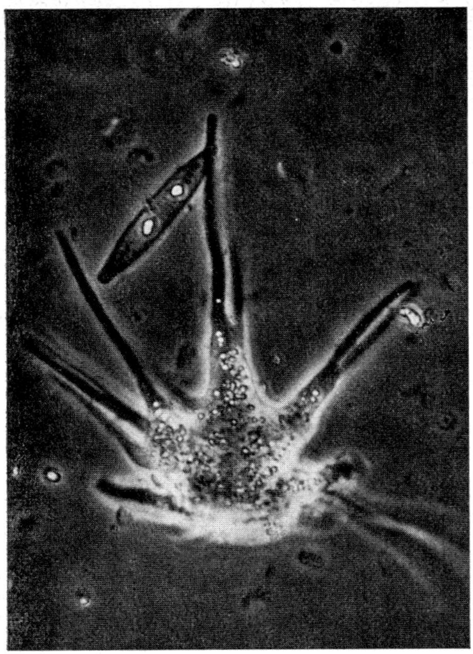

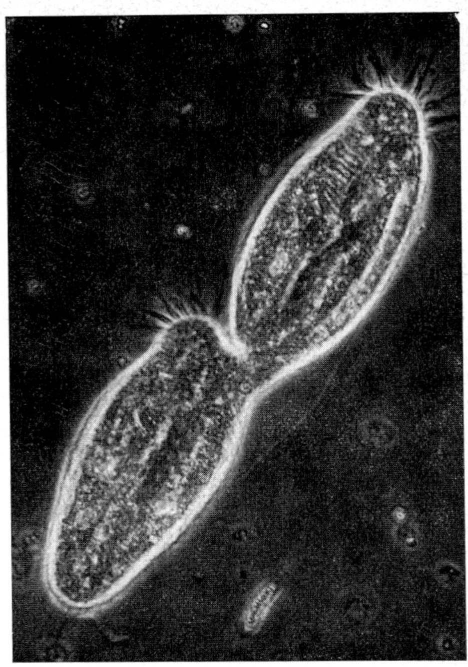

The simplest form of life on earth: the single-cell microscopic amoeba (q.v.). The second photograph clearly shows how amoeba reproduces by dividing into two parts. *Photos: Lennart Nilsson*

Still primitive but multi-cellular is the microscopic vorticella. Anchored by its stalk, vorticella is capable of movements limited to contraction and extension of this stalk. *Photo: Lennart Nilsson*

Microscopic tunicatas are simple animals with a brain, seen as a bright spot in the centre of each 'tube', and a beating heart. They live underwater and their food consists of plankton organisms. *Photo: Lennart Nilsson*

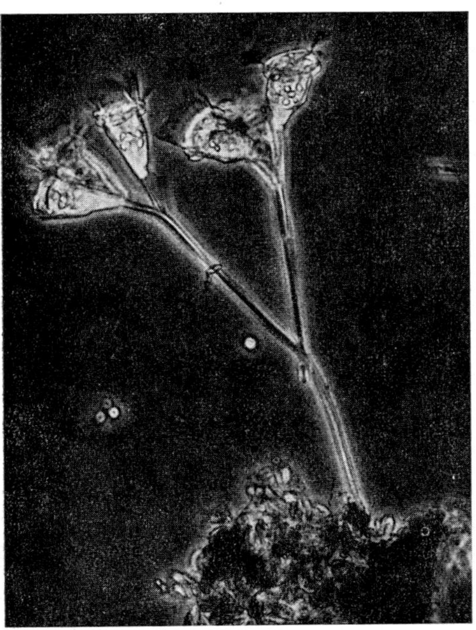

Sponges are the simplest multi-cellular invertebrates (q.v.). The body consists of a loose collection of cells supported by a framework of fibres, but there is little inter-cellular co-ordination.

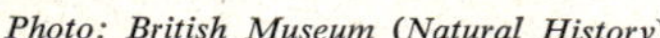

Photo: British Museum (Natural History)

Butterflies are undoubtedly the most colourful members of the insect family. This exotic specimen, Parnassius Mnemsyne, comes from equatorial regions and has a wingspan of 42 centimetres. *Photo: Camera Press*

Despite their diminutive size, ants lead a highly civilized community existence. The smallest ants are given the important task of caring for the newly-laid eggs. *Photo: Lennart Nilsson*

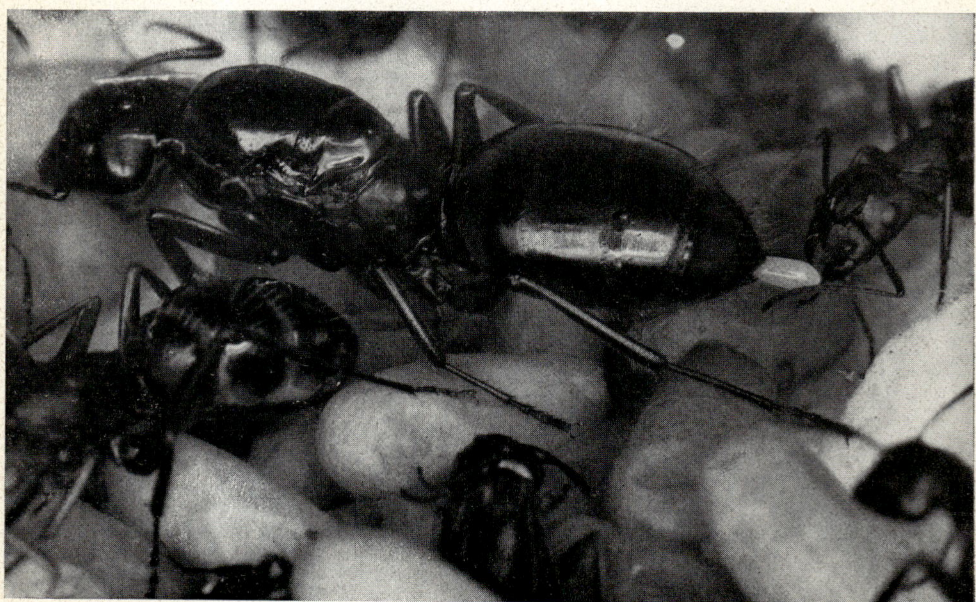

carries the genes, or transmitters of hereditary characteristics, from one generation to another. Chromosomes are usually constant in number, size, shape and arrangement in all the cells of the same individual and in all the individuals of the same species. They consist mainly of proteins combined with nucleic acid (q.v.). When a cell divides into two, the same pattern is reproduced in both new cells. Human cells have 24 pairs of chromosomes.

CHUNGKING, a city in Szechwan, south central China. Pop. (1958) 2,120,000. On the Yangtze River, it is an important industrial centre with metallurgical and textile manufactures. It was the capital of wartime China 1938—45.

CHURCH, the entire body of Christian believers; or one particular denomination as distinct from others; or the edifice used for Christian worship.

CHURCH OF ENGLAND, the officially recognised episcopal church in England. The power of the Roman Catholic Church, which had been established in the 6th and 7th centuries, was first limited in the 13th. In 1351, Edward III proclaimed the English church a national institution, although Rome continued to exercise great power over it. The struggle between civil authority and the Catholic Church reached its climax in the reign of Henry VIII when Parliament passed the Reformation Acts (1531) terminating papal control and establishing the supremacy of the English king. There was a brief and bloody restoration of Catholicism under Mary Tudor, but the accession of Elizabeth I to the throne in 1558 firmly re-established the state church. Under Cromwell, Puritanism dominated the church. The attempts of James II (1633—1701) to introduce Catholic doctrine again failed. The doctrines of the Church of England are those set forth in the Book of Common Prayer, the Catechism, the Homilies and the Thirty-nine Articles, in which basic tenets are Original Sin and the Justification by Faith. The Church has not formally rejected the doctrine of Apostolic Succession and accepts the Apostolic, Nicene and Athanasian creeds. Supreme authority in all matters pertaining to the Church rests with Parliament, with the sanction of the Crown. The Church is divided into two archbishoprics. The Archbishop of Canterbury is the Primate of All England and the Archbishop of York has the title of Primate of England. The three principal orders among the clergy are bishops, priests and deacons. See also Methodism.

CHURCH OF SCOTLAND, the state church of Scotland, Presbyterian in form. In 1557, largely under the influence of John Knox, the 'First Covenant' was signed in Scotland. Roman Catholic jurisdiction was abolished as well as the Mass. The Reformed Church then adopted a new confession of faith which formed the basis for the establishment of a Presbyterian system of church government and a Calvinistic church doctrine. Presbyterianism was opposed by the Crown, which favoured episcopacy, but in 1690 Presbyterianism won official recognition as an ally of the Crown, and has remained the state church of Scotland.

CHURCHILL, Sir Winston (1874—1965), British statesman and author. Entering the army in 1895 he saw action in India and the Sudan, and while serving as a newspaper correspondent in the Boer War (1899) was captured but made a daring escape. Elected to parliament in 1900, he served as Under-Secretary for the Colonies (1905—8) and Home Secretary (1910—11). In the First World

War he resigned office as First Lord of the Admiralty when he saw that the Gallipoli campaign which he had launched was not being prosecuted with sufficient vigour, and went to serve in France. He returned in 1917 as Minister of Munitions and held other posts under Lloyd George. As Chancellor of the Exchequer under Baldwin, he restored the gold standard and introduced imperial preference. His criticism of Conservative policy on India and foreign affairs kept him out of office and his forebodings about the rearmament of Nazi Germany were unpopular in the appeasement period. At the outbreak of war, however, he was immediately recalled to office as First Lord, and on May 10, 1940, he succeeded Chamberlain as Prime Minister. He prosecuted the war with the utmost energy and initiative and his oratory sustained the nation's morale after Dunkirk and during the Battle of Britain. Among his more courageous and difficult decisions were the sending of reinforcements to North Africa when they could least be spared, his persistence in sending arms to Russia, and the changes of staff that led to the appearance of Alexander and Montgomery in the Middle East.

Defeated with his party at the polls in 1945, he returned in 1951 as Prime Minister, resigning in 1955. His Nobel prize for literature (1953) was well earned by his histories of the two World Wars and the biographies of his father, Lord Randolph, and of his ancestor, the first Duke of Marlborough. His election (1948) as Honorary Academician Extraordinary of the Royal Academy was justified by the real merit of his paintings.

CICERO, Marcus Tullius (106—43 B.C.), Roman author, orator, and statesman. He took a prominent part in the political life of Rome and rose to position of consul, in 63 B.C. His prompt and courageous action in crushing the conspiracy of Catiline, who sought to overthrow the republic, earned him the enmity of Julius Caesar and subsequent exile. On his return, he took to writing. In the civil war of 49, he joined Pompey against Caesar. After Caesar's assassination, Cicero returned to Rome, delivered his two *Philippics* against Mark Antony and became the acknowledged leader of the republican party. When Antony and Octavian formed a triumvirate with Lepidus, Cicero was one of the victims of the proscription that followed. His extant works include 58 speeches, three philosophical works and his valuable and revealing *Letters*, Ciceronian Latin became the standard language of scholars for the next 1500 years.

CINCINNATI, a city in Ohio, U.S.A. Pop. (1960) 502,550. On the Ohio River, it has diversified industries, mainly machine tools, clothing and soap. It is also a communications centre.

CINEMA Industry. In 1894, Thomas Edison perfected his kinetoscope through which one person could view apparently moving pictures on a strip of celluloid film. A year later another American, Thomas Armat, discovered the principle of the modern projector. In 1902 the Frenchman Georges Méliès produced *A Trip to the Moon*, and a year later Edwin S. Porter laid the foundations of the motion picture industry with *The Great Train Robbery*. The first indication of the financial potentialities of the cinema was the enormous success of the D. W. Griffith epics, *The Birth of a Nation* (1915) and *Intolerance* (1916), and of the Chaplin comedies and crude serials such as *The Exploits of Elaine*. The post-war period saw more serious work by Eisenstein in Russia and von Stroheim in Germany, and the comedies of René Clair and the Marx Brothers. Sound came in 1927 and had displaced the silent film by 1930. There followed colour film and, in an effort to combat the pull of television after the Second World War, stereoscopic, stereophonic, wide-screen and other devices. In the meantime the newsreel had been developed, and the documentary, in which Flaherty and the G.P.O. Film Unit excelled; Disney perfected the animated film. After the war America produced huge fast-moving 'musicals', and much sensitive work came from Italy, Sweden, Japan and Greece. The British excelled in light-hearted, very English, comedy.

CINQUE PORTS, ancient ports of southeast England whose duty it was to supply and man warships for the king. The earliest, before the Conquest, were Sandwich, Dover, Fordwich and Romney, and by the 12th century they included also Hastings and Hythe; later Winchelsea and Rye and many others were added. The Lord Warden, now honorary, has his official residence at Walmer Castle near Deal.

CIRCUMCISION, an operation to remove the foreskin which covers the end of the penis. Circumcision is practised as a religious rite by various groups, including the Jews and Moslems. In the New Testament the term 'uncircumcised' came to mean not Jewish and hence heathen, unregenerate.

CISALPINE REPUBLIC, a former state in northern Italy. It was created by Napoleon on either bank of the Po River in 1797 and abolished in 1799.

CIVIL WAR, American (1861—65), a conflict between the southern states, who wished to secede from the Union, and the northern states who maintained that the Union was indissoluble. Upon the election of Abraham Lincoln, 11 southern states (Alabama, Arkansas, North and South Carolina, Florida, Georgia, Lousiana, Mississippi, Tennessee, Texas and Virginia), fearing that the Republican president would attempt to abolish slavery, seceded from the Union and formed (1861) the 'Confederate States of America' with Jefferson Davis as president. When Lincoln attempted to provision Federal forces at Fort Sumter, Confederate soldiers opened fire (April 12, 1861) and thus political strife spread into civil war.

From the very beginning the South was in a hopeless position — 23 Union states against the 11 members of the Confederacy. The North had three fighting men to every one of the South's, and 92% of the nation's industry was in Union hands. The Federalist Navy could thus play an important role by effecting an ever-tightening blockade of the southern ports.

The fighting developed on two fronts. In the east, each army attempted to capture the enemy's capital while defending its own. In the west, Union forces tried to drive a wedge between the Confederate States and so isolate them from the west coast. The Confederates won a whole series of battles on the eastern front (Bull Run, 1861; Second Battle of Bull Run, 1862; Fredericksburg, 1862; Chancellorsville, 1863) but were unable to press home their advantage. In 1863 Robert E. Lee took the offensive with the Confederate troops, advancing as far as Gettysburg, Pa., where he was unable to break the Union lines. This battle proved to be the turning-point of the war. In the meanwhile Ulysses Grant, leading the Union forces in the west, brought the Mississippi under Federal control. On January 1, 1863, Lincoln issued the famous Emancipation

Proclamation, which abolished slavery and freed the slaves.

In March 1864, Grant was made commander of the Union armies and the end was in sight. Sherman marched through Georgia, captured Atlanta (September 1864), and pushed through to the sea at Savannah. Grant began hammering away at Lee, and though Lee retreated skilfully, inflicting heavy losses on the Union forces, his supply lines were cut and his army boxed in. On April 9, 1865, Lee surrendered to Grant at Appomattox Court House and the war was over. Casualties on both sides were very heavy, and the war left an aftermath of extreme bitterness; to this day American domestic policy is under its shadow.

CIVIL WAR, English (1642—51), the conflict between Charles I and the parliamentarians (Roundheads) who were opposed to the king's high-handed rule and intolerant religious policy. War broke out in 1642 and at first the royalist forces (Cavaliers) seemed to have the advantage, without being able to win a decisive victory, partly because parliament controlled the navy and the chief ports. By the end of 1643 two-thirds of the country was in royalist hands and parliament hurriedly made an alliance with the Scots. At the battle of Marston Moor (1644) Cromwell's military genius enabled the parliamentarians to crush the royalist northern army under Rupert. This battle proved to be the turning point of the war. In another decisive victory at Naseby (1645) Cromwell's New Model Army destroyed royalist hopes. On May 5, 1646, Charles surrendered to the Scots, but continued to intrigue between parliament, the army and the Scots. In 1647 the army, fearing that parliament would restore the crown, took Charles into custody. In 1648 insurrection broke out in Wales, Kent and Essex on the side of the king, and the Scots invaded England. Cromwell put down the rebellion and routed the Scottish army at Preston. Charles, by his constant intriguing, had sealed his own fate and was executed by the 'Rump Parliament.' There still remained the task of settling with Scotland and Ireland, but by mid-1650 Cromwell had subdued all Ireland, and his victory over Prince Charles (Charles II) and the Scots at the 'crowning mercy' of Worcester (1651) marked the end of the civil war.

CLARENDON, Edward Hyde, 1st Earl of (1609—74), English statesman and historian. A supporter of Charles I, he followed his son (later Charles II) into exile in 1646, becoming his Lord High Chancellor after the Restoration. The sale of Dunkirk to the French and his failure in the Dutch War were pretexts for his dismissal in 1667, and he fled to France. His three-volume *History of the Rebellion and Civil War in England* is a valuable record of the period. Under Charles II he was responsible for the Clarendon Code, a series of measures by which he sought to restore the Anglican Church to its former position.

CLAUDE LORRAINE (1600—82), French landscape painter. Born, as Claude Gelée, near Nancy, he lived in Rome for most of his life. Influenced by Poussin, he painted poetic landscapes with luminous skies, trees in the foreground, and romanticised architecture and figures; he also painted quayside scenes, such as the *Embarkation of the Queen of Sheba*.

CLAUDIUS (10 B.C.—A.D. 54), Roman emperor. Becoming emperor in 41, he introduced many reforms and carried through extensive building activities.

Under Claudius, Britain, Mauretania, Judaea and Thrace were added to the empire and an efficient civil service was formed. A childhood attack of infantile paralysis impaired his physique for life. He married four times; one wife was Messalina, executed for treason. The fourth wife, his niece Agrippina, is thought to have poisoned him in order to secure the succession of Nero, her son by Domitius Ahenobarbus.

CLAUSEWITZ, Karl von (1780—1831), Prussian officer and military theorist. He participated in all the Prussian wars and fought on the Russian side when Napoleon marched on Moscow. His book *On War* is still an important textbook on military strategy and tactics.

CLEMENCEAU, George (1841—1929), French statesman and writer. A leader of the left in the Chamber of Deputies, he was strongly republican and anti-clerical. He founded the newspaper *La Justice* and edited *L'Aurore*; he wrote essays, a novel and two plays. Nicknamed 'The Tiger' for his part in the overthrow of six cabinets, he was active in the defence of Alfred Dreyfus. He was twice prime minister (1906—09, 1917—19), the second time playing a major role in the defeat of Germany and the post-war settlement.

CLEMENT I (A.D. 90), reputed to have been the third Pope. An epistle of his to the church at Corinth was for a short time included in the New Testament.

CLEOPATRA (*c.* 68—30 B.C.), Ptolemaic Queen of Egypt. Julius Caesar restored her to the throne from which she had been driven by usurpers, and fell in love with her. She bore him a son, Caesarion, later Ptolemy XIV. She lived for a while in Rome until Caesar's death and later became the mistress of Mark Antony, to whom she bore twins. Defeated at Actium by Octavian (Augustus), Antony's brother-in-law, and threatened with capture, she killed herself by letting an asp bite her, after Antony had killed himself, believing her dead.

CLEOPATRA'S NEEDLES, two granite obelisks originally erected in Heliopolis, Egypt, in about 1475 B.C. by Tuthmosis III, and transported to Alexandria in 14 B.C. Ismail Pasha sent them as gifts to Britain and the U.S. The one in London is 68½ ft high and stands on the Thames Embankment. The other in Central Park, New York City, is 69½ ft in height.

CLEVELAND, largest city in Ohio, U.S.A., on Lake Erie. Pop. (1960) 876,050. Important for its iron and steel industries, it is also a centre for communications and has large oil refineries.

CLIMATE, the weather elements characteristic of a given region. These elements are temperature, precipitation, humidity, cloudiness, winds and air pressure. Variations in climate from one place to another are determined by latitude, the relative positions of land and water areas, ocean currents, altitude, mountains, prevailing winds and atmospheric storms. The interiors of large land-masses tend to have a large range of temperature and low rainfall (continental climate), while proximity to oceans gives a milder climate with heavier rainfall (oceanic climate). The Mediterranean has given its name to another type of climate, marked by summer drought and cool season rainfall. Köppen classified climatic zones into tropical rain, dry (desert or steppe), warm temperate rainy, cool snow-forest, and polar. The tropics lie between 23½° N. and S., the polar regions are those in latitudes higher than $66\frac{1}{2}°$.

The trade winds near the equator blow steadily from northeast and southeast, converging on the doldrums near the equator, where rainfall is heavy, elsewhere winds tend to be westerly. The monsoons, a marked feature in India particularly, blow from the sea in summer and from the land in winter.

The range of temperature between winter and summer is of major importance, and the average number of frost-free days conditions types of vegetation, including crops. From 1850 average world temperatures steadily increased, but this trend seems to have become less marked recently.

CLIVE, Robert, Baron Clive of Plassey (1725—74), British soldier and statesman, who laid the foundations of British rule in India. Clive destroyed French power there, first by defeating them militarily and later by replacing their ally, Suraj ud-Daulah, on the throne of Bengal with a pro-British ruler. He captured Calcutta, avenging the incident of the Black Hole. As Governor General of Bengal, Clive introduced administrative reforms and acquired additional territory. He was accused of corruption but acquitted, and died, probably by his own hand.

CLOCK, a device for measuring elapsed time or indicating the time of day. It replaced the sun-dials and water- and sand-clocks of the ancients. Henry de Vick made the first mechanical clock for Charles v of France in 1360. It was weight-driven and contained all the fundamentals of a mechanical clock: a series of gears, a source of constant motive power, an escape wheel and a governor. Later, coiled iron springs replaced the weights. The grandfather clock first appeared *c.* 1660. Electric clocks, first invented in 1843, are synchronised with the number of cycles per second of the current.

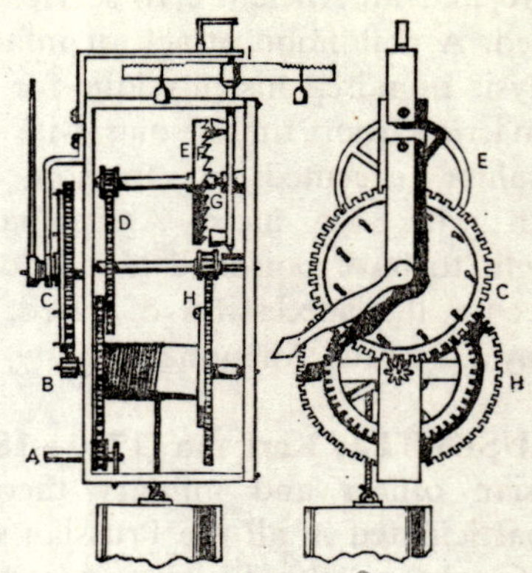

14th century clock

A. Axle B. Small gear or pinion C. Hour hand wheel D. Pallet E. Escape wheel F. Pallet G. Axle or verge H. First or great wheel I. Weighted regulating bar

CLOISTER, a place of retreat (from the Latin, meaning 'a place shut in') for monks or nuns. The term is also applied to an arcade or colonnade around an open court or garden, generally placed on the south, and warmer, side of a cathedral, etc.

CLOUD, a collection of condensed water-vapour, or ice crystals, suspended in the air. Clouds are formed when air currents lower the temperature to a point where the air can contain no additional moisture. There are three general types of clouds: cirrus clouds are feathery formations in the upper air at over 15,000 ft; cumulus clouds are masses at intermediate heights down to 3000 ft; stratus clouds are low, fog-like masses. Nimbostratus is the low thick cloud of rainy weather, and cumulonimbus the anvil-headed heap cloud, 10,000—30,000 ft in vertical depth, which brings showers and often thunderstorms. There are intermediate forms.

CLOWN, the jester or buffoon, originally

attached to a royal entourage, now relegated to the circus. There are three basic types of circus clowns: acrobats, slap-stick comedians wearing bizarre make-up, and the forlorn outcast.

CLYDE, see River.

CLYDE, Colin Campbell, 1st Baron (1792—1863), English general. He distinguished himself in the Peninsular and Crimean wars, and played a leading part in suppressing the Indian Mutiny in 1857.

CNOSSOS, see Knossos.

COAL, a combustible solid of plant origin consisting mainly of carbon, hydrogen and nitrogen. It is an important fuel and occurs in seams, or beds, with layers of other minerals between. Coal was formed by the decomposition of vegetable matter which sank to the bottoms of swamps. The weight of successive layers caused the mass to solidify into various forms of coal. The final or top layer forms peat, the lowest and hardest layer being anthracite. Peat has a carbon content of 29.9%, bituminous coal 66%, anthracite 93.8%.

COAL TAR, a sticky mixture of organic substances obtained from the destructive distillation of coal. These substances provide the raw materials for the manufacture of pharmaceuticals, dyes, explosives, plastics, insecticides, varnishes, wood preservatives and water-proofing materials.

COALITION, a temporary association of two or more states or political parties. On the national level it is resorted to in order to form a Cabinet when no one party has a parliamentary majority. Coalition governments are also formed in times of great emergency in order to strengthen national unity, as was the case in Britain during the two World Wars. On the international scene, coalitions, such as those formed against Napoleon, are less binding than an alliance.

COBALT, see Elements; Nuclear Weapons.

COBDEN, Richard (1804—65), English politician. An advocate of free trade, he opposed war and the holding of colonies. He served for many years in parliament, and fought tirelessly against the monopoly of the aristocracy. He was a founder of the Anti-Corn-Law League.

COCHIN CHINA, see Vietnam.

COCKCROFT, Sir John Douglas (1897—), English nuclear physicist. For his work in splitting the lithium and other atoms, he, together with E. T. S. Walton, was awarded the Nobel prize for physics in 1951. He was director of the Atomic Energy Research Establishment at Harwell (1946—58) and a research member of the U.K. Atomic Energy Authority (1958—59), and is now Master of the new Churchill College, Cambridge.

COCTEAU, Jean (1889—1963), French writer. He produced several volumes of verse before he was 30 and kept up a tremendous output of varied works throughout his life: poetry *(Plain-chant, Le Potomack)*; plays (*La Machine infernale, Les Parents terribles*, the latter appearing later in a film version); novels *(Les Enfants terribles, Thomas l'imposteur)*; autobiography *(Opium, La Difficulté d'être*, 1947); ballets *(Le Boeuf sur le toit*, 1920); films *(La Belle et la bête*; *Orphée*, first written for the stage, and dealing with a favourite theme, romantic love and death). He also painted, decorated a chapel, and wrote works of criticism.

CODE NAPOLÉON (Code Civil), the unified body of law established by Napoleon in 1804. It deals with personal status, property, and obligations, and relies on precedents and commentaries. Napoleon imposed it on all countries under his domination and it continues to exert a strong influence on the legal systems of most countries, with the notable exception of Great Britain.

COFFEE, a beverage prepared from roasted coffee beans which has a stimulating effect. The plant originated in Arabia and requires a semi-tropical climate. Its use was introduced into England in the 16th century. About one-half of the world's supply comes from Brazil.

COIN, a piece of metal used as money which bears the authority of a sovereign ruler or state guaranteeing its value. It is generally in the form of a disc of gold, silver, nickel alloy, bronze or copper. The edges of gold and silver coins are often milled to discourage the removal of particles of the metal.

COKE, Sir Edward (1552—1634), English jurist. Winning the post of Attorney-General over his hated rival, Francis Bacon, he wielded great influence during the reigns of Elizabeth I, James I and Charles I. He strictly upheld English Common Law against all other bodies of legal interpretation. Coke was the first Lord Chief Justice of England. His four-volume *Institutes* is a summary of statutes and historical precedents.

COLD WAR, clash of interests between two blocs of nations led by the U.S.A. and U.S.S.R. following the Second World War. Each side believed itself threatened and employed economic blockade, propaganda, military and financial aid, subversion and local outbreaks in order to weaken its rival.

COLERIDGE, Samuel Taylor (1772—1834), English poet, philosopher and critic. Although his literary criticism and his introduction into England of German literature and Kantian philosophy mark him as a great thinker, he is noted chiefly for a few poems, especially *The Ancient Mariner*, *Kubla Khan* and *Christabel*. He laid the foundation for Shakespearean critical studies and wrote works on philosophy, religion and politics. *Aids to Reflection* and *Of the Constitution of Church and State* are his most important works on religion and society, *Biographia Literaria* is the best of his critical works, and *Table Talk* is also essential to an understanding of Coleridge.

COLLECTIVE BARGAINING, a procedure by which employers' associations and trade unions negotiate in order to reach collective agreements on pay and conditions of work. Permanent joint industrial councils, meeting periodically, make it easier to reach such agreements, and these are often applied to their employees by employers who were not parties to the negotiations.

COLLINS, Michael (1880—1922), Irish patriot. An active participant in the Dublin Easter Rebellion of 1916, he became a prominent leader of the Sinn Fein movement two years later. He led the guerrilla warfare which followed and was one of the signatories of the treaty setting up the Irish Free State. He was murdered by Republican partisans shortly afterwards.

COLOGNE (Köln), a city in North Rhine-Westphalia, Western Germany, on the Rhine. Pop. (1960) 801,100. The largest city and commercial centre of the lower Rhineland, Cologne is a busy river port and a focal point of road and rail communications. A cultural centre in the Middle Ages, it became an important member of the Hanseatic League in 1201. One of the few medieval buildings to survive the air-raids of the Second World War is the magnificent cathedral, with its treasures.

COLOMBIA, a republic in South America. Pop. (1962) 14,768,590, area 439,997 sq. miles. Bordering on both the Pacific and Atlantic oceans, Colombia consists mostly of mountains in the west and jungle-covered plain in the east. Its main products are coffee and bananas. Colombia is rich in minerals which include gold, platinum, emeralds, uranium, copper, lead, mercury, manganese, coal and petroleum. Santa Marta was founded by the Spanish in 1525 and Bogotá in 1538. In the 18th century Colombia became part of the viceroyalty of New Granada, which included Peru, Ecuador and Venezuela. After the dissolution of Bolivar's Greater Colombia, the republic of New Granada was formed in 1831 and renamed Colombia in 1861. Panama seceded in 1903. For centuries the main trade artery was the River Magdalena, but a railway to the Atlantic coast has now been built to supersede it. The capital is Bogotá (pop. 1,329,230). Other large cities are Medellin, (690,700), Cali (693,120) and Baranquilla (431,250).

COLOMBO, capital of Ceylon. Pop. (1953) 423,481. It is the chief port and commercial centre of the island. It was founded in 543 B.C.

COLOMBO PLAN, an organisation, formed in July 1951 and continuing until 1971, for mutual help by credits and technical assistance to countries of southeast Asia. The original members were Australia, Canada, Ceylon, India, Pakistan, New Zealand and the U.K. (the 'providing countries'), the countries of Malaysia and Indo-China, Burma, Nepal, Indonesia, Japan, the Philippines and Thailand (the 'receiving countries'). The U.S.A. is an associated member. Each country is free to revise its programme.

COLORADO, a western state of U.S.A. Pop. (1960) 1,753,947; area 104,247 sq. miles. It consists of a plateau in the west, the Rocky Mountains in the centre and the Great Plains in the east. The principal farm products are wheat, sugar-beet, maize, barley and potatoes. Colorado has a highly developed irrigation system. Livestock is raised. Minerals include coal, molybdenum, gold, silver, zinc and lead, copper, petroleum, natural gas and uranium. The steel industry is important. French and Spanish explorers were in the region in the early 18th century, but the first permanent settlement was not established until 1858. Colorado became a state in 1876. The capital is Denver (pop. 493,887). Other principal cities are Pueblo (91,181) and Colorado Springs (70,194). See also under River.

COLOSSEUM, the name given to the largest Roman amphitheatre in Rome. Begun by Vespasian (72 A.D.) and inaugurated by Titus (80), it accommodated 50,000 seated spectators and had standing room for an additional 20,000. Gladiatorial displays and mimic naval battles were staged here.

COLOSSUS, the name given to a statue of gigantic size. The bronze statue straddling the harbour at Rhodes, representing the sun-god Helios and 100 ft high was one of the seven wonders of the ancient world. It was demolished by an earthquake in 224 B.C., some 50 years after it was erected.

COLOUR, an impression made on the eye by light. If light, which consists of electromagnetic radiations of various wavelengths, is refracted through a prism it can be spread out into a spectrum each colour of which corresponds to a particular wavelength. These colours range from the longer-wave red through orange, yellow, green and blue to violet at the shorter-wave end. The colour of an object depends on which wavelengths are absorbed by it and which are reflected, and this in turn depends on the molecular structure of the object's surface. Thus, an object that has absorbed the shorter wavelengths appears red; if it has absorbed all wavelengths it appears black; if it reflects all of them it appears white.

The primary colours are red, yellow and blue; they combine to form white.

Insensitivity of the eye to certain wavelengths is the cause of colour blindness, the commonest form of which is a confusion of yellow and green.

COLUMBIA, see River.

COLUMBIUM, see Elements.

COLUMBUS, capital of Ohio, U.S.A. Pop. (1960) 471,316. At the confluence of two rivers, it is a communications and industrial centre. The iron and steel industry is the most important, and mining machinery is manufactured.

COLUMBUS, Christopher (1451—1506), discoverer of America. In 1492 he obtained three ships from King Ferdinand and Queen Isabella of Spain and sailed westward on August 3 to seek the 'Indies' — India, China and Japan. On October 12, he sighted Watling Island in the Bahamas. Later, he discovered the islands of Cuba and Hispaniola. On two successive voyages he discovered additional islands in the Caribbean Sea, reaching the coast of South America at the mouth of the Orinoco on the third trip. At Haiti he found the colonists he had settled there in revolt, and a new governor sent out from Spain had him put in chains and shipped home. There the king released and compensated him and he set out on his fourth and last voyage, during which he sailed along the coast from Honduras to Panama. He returned to Spain a sick man, to die in comparative poverty, still thinking he had discovered India.

COMBUSTION, the chemical combination of oxygen with a substance accompanied by the production of heat. There may also be considerable light. The material must be combustible and the temperature high enough to allow the combination to take place. For combustion to continue, there should be an adequate supply of the material and of oxygen, and enough heat must be liberated to maintain a high temperature. In lighting a match, friction raises the temperature of the compound at the tip to kindling point and combustion ensues.

COMÉDIE FRANÇAISE, the French state theatre, in Paris. Founded in 1680, the organisation still functions according to the principles laid down by Molière. There are no stars; and roles are assigned by common agreement. The troupe selects its own plays and profits are shared by the members. The repertoire is primarily classical. It now maintains a second company at the Odéon.

COMEDY, in drama, is essentially a play with a happy ending. It deals with the foibles and follies of mankind. It can take many forms, from the biting political satire of Aristophanes, through the elegantly cynical and immoral comedy of manners of the Restoration period in England, to farce and burlesque. Tragi-comedy may introduce a romantic or tragic element, but still ends happily.

COMET, a nebulous heavenly body travelling in orbit around the sun. It consists of a luminous rounded head which may be thousands of miles in diameter. Some comets have tenuous tails formed by gas and fine dust streaming out of the head. The tail always points away from the sun because of the pressure exerted on it by solar radiation. Some comets return periodically. They have no known effect on the earth or on other planets. Halley (1656—1742) was the first to predict the return of a comet. Halley's comet has a period of about 76 years and is due to return in 1986.

COMMITTEE OF 100, an organisation with the same aims as the Campaign for Nuclear Disarmament (q.v.) but more militant in its methods, e.g. sit-down protests at airfields.

COMMON LAW, that part of English law, other than Equity (q.v.), that is not embodied in legislation (Statute law). In case of conflict, Equity and Statute law overrule Common Law.

Common Law goes back a thousand years and is based on maxims and customs derived from immemorial usage. It is sometimes called unwritten law, and this it was until, early in its history, the practice grew of recording, in increasing detail, the decisions of the courts. From that time it is more appropriately referred to as case law, judge-made law, i.e. the law of judicial precedent.

The guiding rule is that, in deciding a case, courts must follow the principles laid down in previous decisions in similar cases; if none exists, they may lay down new principles, which then become part of the Common Law; if there are new circumstances, existing principles may be modified to fit them. Common Law, so called because it is common to the whole realm, thus operates, more flexibly and promptly than a codified law, to keep the law in tune with the times to the extent that that has not already been done by Statute law; it also comes into operation when some point of Statute law needs further interpretation.

COMMON MARKET (European Economic Community, E.E.C., 'The Six'), formed in 1958 as a result of the Treaty of Rome (1957), is an organisation for the integration of the economies of its six members, France, West Germany, Belgium, the Netherlands, Luxembourg and Italy. It has effected reductions in internal tariffs and has made some progress in the more difficult task of agreeing on a common external tariff on imports from outside the Community and formulating a common agricultural policy. Britain's application to become a member was rejected in 1963 under pressure from President de Gaulle. Under the Treaty the Community has the further aim of 'closer relationship between its member states', but no progress has been made towards political union. Brussels is the headquarters.

COMMUNE, Chinese, a feature unique to Communist China, is a large unit of rural administration based on groups of co-operative farms. It provides roads, houses, clothing, schools, health centres, nurseries where working mothers can leave their children, and communal restaurants, where for the first time in Chinese history the peasant is assured of three meals a day. The commune also administers rural industry.

COMMUNE of Paris. (1) The revolutionary government of Paris set up after the storming of the Bastille in 1789. In 1792, inspired by the Jacobins, it intimidated the National Assembly and, under Marat, carried out the September Massacres, thus inaugurating the Reign of Terror. It fell with the death of Robespierre, in 1794.

(2) The first Socialist government in history, though it lasted only a few weeks. It was elected in March 1871 to protest at the National Assembly's readiness to agree to the terms of the victorious Prussians, especially the surrender of Alsace-Lorraine. It attempted to seize control of Paris and civil war raged for some weeks until government troops marched in from Versailles and put down the revolt with extreme brutality; over 17,000 people were executed.

COMMUNISM, the revolutionary movement based on the *Communist Manifesto* (1848) written by Marx and Engels, as interpreted by the Russian Bolsheviks, in particular by Lenin (Marxist-Leninism) and, for a period, by Stalin (Stalinism). The philosophical basis of Marxism is dialectical materialism (see Dialectic). Marxism emphasises the economic basis of history; it links the successive phases of slavery, feudalism and capitalism with the changing relations between producers and the owners of the means of production. It holds that each phase was higher than the last, was inevitable and, after an initial period of progress, stagnated and degenerated, capitalism now being in a state of decline. The view is not so much that the supersession of capitalism is desirable as that it is inevitable, and that the workers, as natural heirs, must be prepared for its disappearance.

First, in the Marxian view, there is a transitional period (called Socialism) in which, under the dictatorship of the proletariat, all the means of production are transferred to state ownership. Differentiation between hand and brain worker remains, and there is some private property. The slogan of this period is: 'From each according to his ability; to each according to his work'.

This phase will give way to a higher phase, true Communism, unattained as yet in any country. In this the state will wither away, all property will belong to the community, which will be classless, and the slogan will be: 'From each according to his ability; to each according to his needs'.

Communism was first applied in Russia, in 1917. An early rift was caused by Trotskyism, the view that internal progress in Russia must be subordinated to the demands of international revolution. Although Trotsky was expelled, attempts to foment world revolution did not end; the Third International (later called Comintern), led by Lenin, was formed for this purpose; it was replaced by the less militant Cominform, itself dissolved in 1956. A second division then appeared between leftist deviationists, who urged too rapid an advance towards full Communism, and rightist deviationists, who urged concessions to the immediate needs of the people that would unduly retard that advance. A third heresy was revisionism, the denial of the absolute right of the Party to lay down policy.

In Russia the mistake was made of trying to go too fast too ruthlessly. In the face of bitter opposition by the peasants, who resented their subordination to the interests of the urban workers, the New Economic Policy (1921—27) was introduced, which partially restored private enterprise. Stalin (1929—35) started a second revolution of ruthless collectivisation of farms and planned industrial development. This enabled

Russia to face Hitler, but Stalin's régime of the police state and the 'liquidation' or 'purge' not only of critics but of loyal supporters who, as soon as they showed ability, became to Stalin's insanely suspicious mind potential rivals, hampered all progress. Since he died as recently as 1953 there has been insufficient opportunity to judge how Communism may develop under sane leadership.

China became Communist in 1950 and its leaders introduced a new feature, the commune (see Commune, Chinese); they have also become increasingly militant and critical of what they regard as Russian appeasement of the capitalist countries.

COMORO ISLANDS, a French possession in the Indian Ocean, about 300 miles northwest of Madagascar. Pop. 181,288; area 832 sq. miles. Vanilla, copra, cacao and sugar-cane are produced. The capital is Dzaoudzi.

COMPASS, a device for indicating direction. Most common is the magnetic type with a free-swinging needle, utilising the principle that a magnet will align itself with the earth's magnetic lines of force, which extend approximately in a north-south direction. In Western Europe it has been in use from the 12th century.

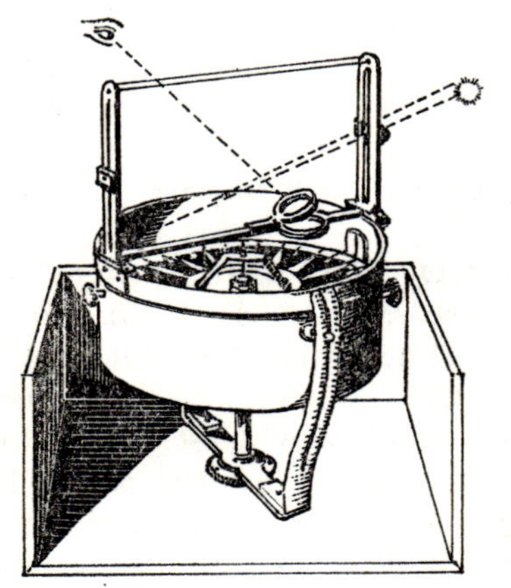

An early compass. The Azimuth compass

COMPIÈGNE, a town in northeast France. Formerly a country retreat of French rulers, it was the site of Joan of Arc's capture. Germany surrendered to the Allies there in 1918, and France to Hitler in 1940.

COMPTON, Arthur Holly (1892—), American physicist. He made important discoveries in the fields of X-rays and cosmic rays. During the Second World War, he organised and directed the project which developed self-sustaining nuclear chain-reaction and methods for producing plutonium. He shared the 1927 Nobel prize in physics with C. T. R. Wilson.

COMPUTER, an electronic machine which makes a series of arithmetical calculations each stage of which is determined by the results of the previous calculation; it can automatically introduce earlier results at a later stage as if it possessed memory. Programming is the process of setting the controls of the computer so that it will do the work required of it. A digital computer is one that uses conventional arithmetical digits.

COMTE, Auguste (1798—1857), French philosopher. He founded Positivism (q.v.) and laid the basis for modern sociology. In his six-volume work, *Cours de philosophie positive*, he sought to establish a new religion centred on the essential good in humanity.

CONCORDAT, an agreement between a secular government and the Pope for the regulation of ecclesiastical affairs within the state. The Concordat of Worms (1122), between Pope Calixtus II and Henry V of Germany, settled the issue of the investiture of church officials. The Concordat between Pope Pius VII and Napoleon (1801) provided for the re-establishment of the Catholic Church in France after the Revolution.

CONDITIONED REFLEX, in psychology, a form of learning in which a response is produced by a stimulus which previously did not produce that response. For example, every time a dog is fed he salivates (an instinctive, unconditioned reflex); if a bell is rung every time he is fed he learns to associate the bell with food, and will salivate at the sound of the bell even when he can see no food and knows that it is not his feeding time (a conditioned reflex). Learning and habit formation is considered by Behaviourists (see Behaviourism) to be explicable in terms of conditioned reflexes, though the later and more general view is that the conditioned reflex is only one of several forms of learning. See Pavlov.

CONDOTTIERI, leaders of groups of mercenary soldiers in Italy, especially in the 14th and 15th centuries. They sold their services to the highest bidder, often changing sides for better payment.

CONFEDERATE STATES OF AMERICA, the 11 Southern states of the U.S.A. which seceded from the Union in 1860—61 over the question of slavery and formed a separate government. They ceased to exist in 1865 after their defeat in the Civil War (q.v.). Their capital was Richmond, Virginia.

CONFUCIUS (*c.* 551—479 B.C.), the greatest Chinese philosopher. He established standards of ethics which still dominate Chinese life. Although he founded schools, and sought to introduce reforms during the period when he served as a public official, he exerted no influence until after his death. In addition to his ethical teaching, he made the first attempt to write a systematic Chinese history. Most of his teachings have been transmitted in the *Analects*, compiled by his disciples after his death. He believed that man is essentially good; and taught loyalty, obedience and abhorrence of violence.

CONGO, Federal Republic of the, a federated republic in Central Africa, formerly a Belgian possession. Pop. (1961) 14,150,000; area 905,400 sq. miles. The country is a depression in the African plateau enclosed by uplands which are highest in the east. It is almost entirely within the drainage basin of the 3,000 mile long Congo River. The climate is hot and humid. The north is dense jungle and the south savannah. Wild-life is abundant and diversified. Fats and oils, timber, cotton, coffee, rubber, tea and cocoa are the chief products in addition to vast mineral wealth which includes copper, diamonds, gold, silver, tin, cobalt, uranium, radium, germanium, zinc and iron. Founded by King Leopold II, who exploited it unscrupulously, the Belgian Congo remained a primitive country. Independence in 1960 brought in its wake civil war and chaos, further complicated by the secession of the rich Katanga province. U.N. troops were flown in, and order finally restored two years later. The capital is Leopoldville (pop. 1958 390,000). Other principal cities are Elisabethville (182,000) and Stanleyville (80,000). See also River.

CONGO REPUBLIC, a republic in West Africa (since 1960), formerly a French territory. Pop. (1961) 795,000; area 132,047 sq. miles. There is savannah in the south and dense forests in the equatorial region. Timber, palm-oil products and a little tobacco are exported. Some lead is mined. The capital is Brazzaville (pop. 100,000).

CONGREGATIONALISM, a system of church government which advocates the autonomy of the individual congregations. The first Congregationalists were the Brownists, formed in 1582 in a period of persecution, many of whom emigrated to Massachusetts. In the 17th century they were called Independents (i.e. independent of the king and of bishops). Cromwell and many of the Ironsides were Independents. The Evangelical Revival swelled the ranks of Congregationalism. In 1831 a national union was formed as a purely advisory body. Missionary work was carried out by the London Missionary Society (1795), to which Livingstone belonged. Congregationalists accept the Bible as the supreme authority, but do not believe in uniformity of doctrine.

CONGRESS, U.S., the legislative branch of the U.S. government as defined by Article 1 of the Constitution. Congress consists of two houses: the House of Representatives, composed of varying numbers of members each serving a two-year term, apportioned among the states according to population; and the Senate, composed of two senators from each state, serving six-year terms of office. This arrangement ensures that the President must always be ready to compromise with the Opposition since he cannot rely on having majority support in either House.

CONNACHT (Connaught), a western province of the Irish Republic on the Atlantic Ocean. Pop. (1961) 419,221; area 6863 sq. miles. Mountainous in the west, it has poor soil and there is much emigration. It was an independent kingdom until the 13th century. It now consists of the counties of Galway, Leitrim, Mayo, Roscommon and Sligo.

CONNECTICUT, a state of New England, U.S.A. Pop. (1960) 2,535,234; area 5009 sq. miles. The central region is lowland and is enclosed by highlands. Tobacco and fruits are grown, and poultry raised. Metal products of all kinds are produced. First settled in 1637, it was the first political unit in the world to adopt a written constitution (1639). It was one of the 13 original states of the Union. The capital is Hartford, the insurance capital of the U.S.A. (pop. 162,178). Other cities are New Haven (152,048), the seat of Yale University, and Waterbury (107,130).

CONRAD, Joseph (1857—1924), Polish-born English writer. After serving in both the French and British merchant navies, he devoted himself to writing and became a master of English prose. Most of his short stories and novels were at first based on his knowledge of the sea. His books include *The Nigger of the Narcissus*, *Typhoon*, *Lord Jim* and *Nostromo*, his masterpiece.

CONSCIOUSNESS, awareness of one's surroundings with varying degrees and vividness of perception. The intensity of this response is determined both by the nature of the stimulus and the personality of the individual. In the early stages of learning (e.g. to ride a bicycle) there is strong conscious awareness of what one is doing, but this progressively diminishes as skill is attained until finally there appears to be no conscious awareness at all.

CONSERVATIVE PARTY, a British political group whose philosophy is based on the acceptance of existing institutions and the rejection of revolutionary change. Tradition is regarded as an important stabilising force in orderly, evolutionary development. Individuals are held to vary in their characters and abilities from birth. The leading spokesmen for conservatism were Robert Peel and Benjamin Disraeli, under whose direction the party achieved its greatest success during the 19th century. The question of tariff reform split the party in 1906 and it remained in opposition until 1915. Supported chiefly by agricultural interests at first, it later became identified with commercial and financial interests. From 1918—64, the Conservatives were either in power or dominated coalition governments, except for periods of Labour control in 1923—24, 1929—31 and 1945—51. In the elections of 1951, 1955 and 1959, they progressively increased their parliamentary strength (49.4% of the votes in 1959).

CONSTABLE, John (1776—1837), English landscape painter. Son of a miller who owned the mills he painted, he restricted himself entirely to painting the simple beauty of the English landscape, a field in which he reigns supreme. His greatest works include *The Hay Wain*, *The Leaping Horse* and *The Cornfield*.

CONSTANTINE THE GREAT (*c.* 272—337), Roman emperor. Proclaimed Caesar in 306, he had first to defeat Maxentius (312) and then Licinius to become (324) ruler of the entire empire. Before his victorious battle with Maxentius a cross is said to have appeared to him in a vision, and he took it as his standard. He made Christianity the State religion, and used it in an effort to consolidate his empire. In 330 he built Constantinople and made it the capital of his empire. Constantine was responsible for many reforms including the separation of civil from military administration; he was also the convener of the Council of Nicaea.

CONSTELLATION, a group of stars forming a coincidental pattern in the sky. The ancients named the constellations after gods, animals, and heroes. Modern astronomers recognise the existence of 88 such groupings.

CONSTITUTION OF THE UNITED STATES, the written document which is the supreme law of the U.S.A. in regulating relations between the government and the people. It consists of seven articles providing for a republican form of government and defining the nature and powers of the legislative, executive, and judicial branches into which it is divided. It has 23 amendments, of which the first 10 are known as the Bill of Rights. After having been ratified by 11 of the 13 states, it went into effect in 1788.

CONTRACT, in general, is an agreement between parties, expressed in words or implied by conduct, whereby one party promises to do something, or to refrain from doing something, in return for a consideration (a *quid pro quo*) offered by the other party. To be legally enforceable, a contract must be for a lawful purpose and unambiguous; both parties must be agreed on its intention, and legally capable of making the contract; and it must be accompanied by a consideration, expressed or implied. Thus, if A promises to give B £5 next Wednesday, B cannot legally enforce the promise, since there is no consideration and therefore no contract; but if A accompanies the promise with a stipulation (e.g. that B prunes his apple-trees), then there is a contract. A deed is a written contract, sealed, signed and delivered; it reinforces a contract because it provides clear evidence of what was agreed. When there is a deed a consideration is not necessary. In transfers of ownership of freehold and leasehold property, and in the grant of a tenancy for more than three years, a deed is

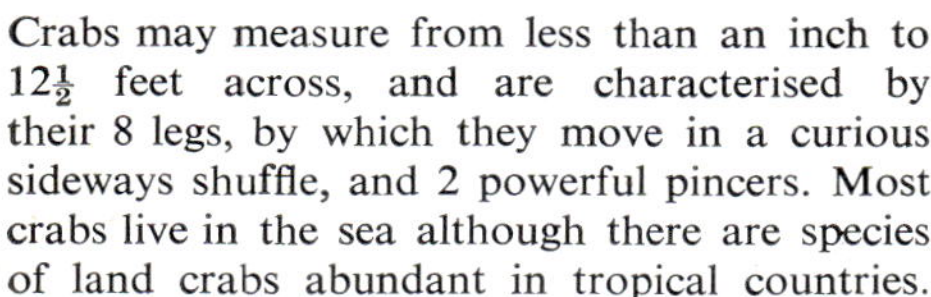

Crabs may measure from less than an inch to $12\frac{1}{2}$ feet across, and are characterised by their 8 legs, by which they move in a curious sideways shuffle, and 2 powerful pincers. Most crabs live in the sea although there are species of land crabs abundant in tropical countries.
Photo: British Museum (Natural History)

Spiders range from minute creatures to those capable of catching small birds or mice (illustrated here). Of particular interest is the fact that spiders produce a fine thread from within the abdomen with which they construct different types of web for the purpose of catching the flying insects on which the majority feed.
Photo: British Museum (Natural History)

Locusts are flying insects which cause devastating destruction to all forms of plant. Millions fly together stripping every leaf, flower and bud off every plant in their path. Locusts occur over a wide area of the earth's surface.
Photo: Werner Braun

The frog is a vertebrate (q.v.) amphibian: tadpoles develop from the eggs, which are laid in water. Gradually the tadpole's tail and gills diminish as its legs and lungs develop. It then becomes a land animal, returning to water only to mate.
Photo: John Gajda

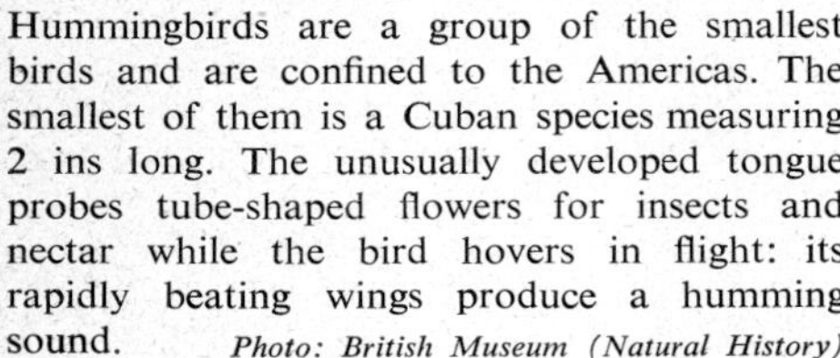

Hummingbirds are a group of the smallest birds and are confined to the Americas. The smallest of them is a Cuban species measuring 2 ins long. The unusually developed tongue probes tube-shaped flowers for insects and nectar while the bird hovers in flight: its rapidly beating wings produce a humming sound. *Photo: British Museum (Natural History)*

Birds of prey, such as this osprey, catch and eat small animals and occasionally small birds. They are characterised by powerful claw-like feet and sharp, curved beak.

Photo: Teuvo Suominen

Reptiles (q.v.) are the oldest class of animals still living. This marine iguana is a large (up to 6 ft) lizard from the Galapagos Islands. It swims strongly and lives entirely on seaweed. Other iguanas eat leaves and fruit and sometimes even small birds and mammals. They are covered with small scales, as can be seen in the photograph. *Photo: Paul Popper Ltd*

required by law. There are contracts in which agreement is not essential, e.g. a statute may impose a contractual obligation on a citizen without his consent and despite his dissent.

CONVERSION, in its religious sense denotes a 'turning to' God, though the term is also applied to a change from one religion to another — particularly to Christianity.

COOK ISLANDS, an island group in the South Pacific belonging to New Zealand. Pop. (1959) 17,654; area 89 sq. miles. Bananas, oranges and copra are produced. The largest island is Rarotonga.

COOK, James (1728—79), English navigator. Between 1768 and his death, in Hawaii, he twice circumnavigated the globe, and after his death his ships completed a third circumnavigation. The greatest of English navigators, he was the first European to sail round New Zealand, to discover the east coast of Australia, to cross the Antarctic Circle and to chart the coast of northwestern America; he also mapped the Pacific and proved that there was no 'southern continent' there. From his ships the scurvy which had plagued all previous voyages of discovery was banished. He was murdered on a beach at Hawaii while investigating the theft of a ship's cutter. His own unedited journals of his three voyages were not published until the Hakluyt Society undertook this task, publishing the first volume in 1955.

COOKERY, the art of preparing tasty, attractive and nourishing food by the use of heat. The development of canned, dehydrated and frozen foods, coupled with the introduction of new techniques for supplying heat, the widespread use of refrigeration, the pressure cooker, which reduces the time of cooking, and increasing knowledge of dietetics, have revolutionised cookery in the 20th century. Meats of animals, fish and poultry hold a prominent place in man's diet. They are prepared by roasting, broiling, frying, braising or stewing. Eggs and dairy products are basic to any menu. Fruits and vegetables are indispensable and should be prepared with a minimum loss of food value. Cereal grains constitute a staple item in world-wide diets.

COOPER, James Fenimore (1789—1851), American author. He wrote romantic adventure stories of early American life. His works include *The Pathfinder*, *The Last of the Mohicans*, and *The Deerslayer*.

CO-OPERATIVE, an economic enterprise which is owned by those who use its services. The first co-operative was established (1844) in Rochdale, England, by 28 weavers, the Rochdale Pioneers. In 1846, 54 English retail co-operatives organised the Co-operative Wholesale Society which now has over 11 million members. Consumer co-operatives account for about 15% of all English retail and wholesale trade. Among the many types of co-operative found the world over are those for agricultural credit, marketing and export, for the purchase of seed and fertilisers, and producers' co-operatives founded on a basis of co-partnership among the employees. The movement owes its inspiration to Robert Owen, and its guiding principle is 'All for each and each for all'.

COPENHAGEN, capital of Denmark, Pop. (1960) 1,243,000. A seaport on the Öresund strait between Denmark and southern Sweden, it is a major industrial, communications and cultural centre. The city was chartered in 1254.

COPERNICUS, Nicolaus (1473—1543), Polish astronomer. He revolutionised thinking and laid the foundation of modern astronomy with his conception of the universe. This was that the planets, including the earth, revolved around the sun, the stars are infinitely distant and the Universe spherical. His great work was *De Revolutionibus Orbium Coelestium*, published as he lay dying, and greeted with ridicule.

COPPER, see Elements.

CORAL, a marine animal with a calcareous skeleton. The body (polyp) is cylindrical, with a mouth at the top. Corals reproduce themselves either by budding or sexually. Most species live in warm, shallow sea-water. Some newly-born polyps swim around freely until they attach themselves and secrete their skeletons. The bodies of polyps are connected with each other through extensions of their epidermis. As new polyps are produced, the lower individuals die and new layers are formed on the old skeletons. The working of ornamental coral is an Italian industry; the pink forms are preferred. There are three types of coral reef: the fringing reef on a shore; the barrier reef off-shore forming a lagoon, usually with a navigable entrance; and the coral island or atoll, often horse-shoe shaped, enclosing a lagoon.

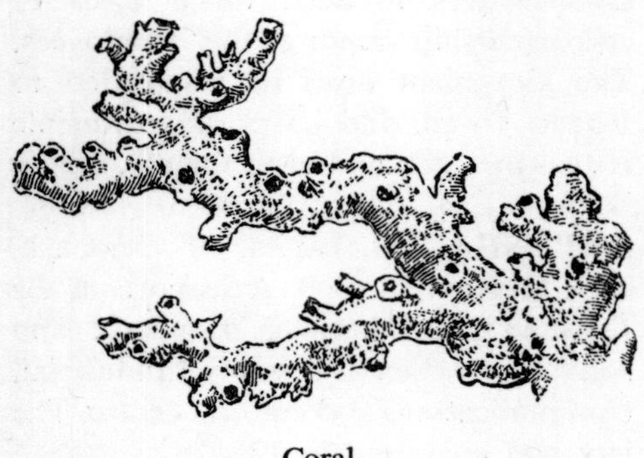

Coral

CORDOBA, a city of Andalusia, Spain. Pop (1959) 181,166. On the Guadalquivir River, Cordoba is an important commercial, communications and industrial centre. It is also the market for a rich agricultural region. Captured by the Moors in 711, it became a centre of learning and wealth by the 10th century. Moorish remains include a great mosque which was later converted into a cathedral.

CORINTH, a town in Greece on the narrow isthmus separating Greece from the Peloponnese, has been important in Greek history ever since ancient times. Rivalling Athens in wealth and power, Corinth founded numerous colonies. St Paul visited Corinth and addressed two epistles to the Church there. The town was destroyed by the Romans in 146 B.C. and was later re-founded by Julius Caesar and renamed Achaea. The Corinth canal, 3½ miles long, was opened in 1893.

CORK, the largest county in the Irish Republic, in the southern province of Munster. Pop. (1961) 330,106; area 2890 sq. miles. Cork is generally mountainous, with lowlands near the coast and in the east. The principal occupation is farming. The county town is Cork (115,000), the harbour of which, Cobh, is a port of call for transatlantic liners.

CORN LAWS, restrictions and duties imposed by the English government on the import and export of grain, especially wheat. In force from 1436 to 1849, they were intended to curb speculation and encourage production. They caused considerable hardship, however, by raising the price of wheat. This led to strong opposition from the Anti-Corn-Law League, formed in Manchester by Cobden and Bright in 1837, as a result of which Peel reduced them in 1846 and they became merely nominal three years later. The price of wheat did not fall, however, nor was domestic agriculture injured, as had been feared.

CORNEILLE, Pierre (1606—84), French dramatist. He created French drama, both comedy and heroic tragedy. He chose kings and heroes for his subjects, showing them striving to retain their personal integrity in clashes between duty and love; the passions are finally conquered by the will, in contrast to Racine's conflicts, in which the passions triumph. *Le Cid*, a tragedy which also has comic elements, was an immediate success. His other works include *Horace*, *Cinna*, *Polyeucte* and the comedy *Le Menteur*.

CORNWALL, a county in southwest England, a peninsula in the Atlantic Ocean. Pop. (1961) 341,746; area 1357 sq. miles. It is mostly moorland interrupted by wide valleys and has a rugged coastline. The minerals include tin, copper and kaolin. The warm climate permits the growing of early vegetables and flowers, and attracts a large influx of tourists. Fishing and dairy-farming are other occupations. There are many archaeological remains. The Cornish language, akin to Welsh and Breton, ceased to be spoken about 1800. The county town is Bodmin.

CORONATION, the ceremony by which a sovereign is formally invested with the powers of the crown. It consists of taking the oath, anointing with oil, investiture, crowning, enthronement and homage. It is accompanied by much pomp and pageantry to endow the occasion with deep and enduring significance. Since 1066, English sovereigns have been crowned in Westminster Abbey. The coronation of Elizabeth II in 1953 followed the rites prescribed in 1307 in *Liber Regalis*.

COROT, Jean Baptiste (1796—1875), French painter. His early landscapes were much admired; he then turned, after visiting Italy, to classical pictures, and his later work was less successful.

CORSICA (Corse), an island in the Mediterranean, a department of France. Pop. (1960) 247,000; area 3367 sq. miles. Generally mountainous, it subsists chiefly on agriculture. Occupied by various Mediterranean peoples since the 6th century B.C., it became French in 1768. The capital is Ajaccio, where Napoleon was born.

COSMIC RAYS, highly penetrative atomic particles (mostly protons, but also alpha particles) of unknown origin, bombarding the earth from outer space. Entering the atmosphere, they collide with atomic nuclei which starts a chain-reaction of collisions subjecting the earth to a radiation shower. Much space research is devoted to their study.

COSSACKS ('wanderers'), a section of the Russian population of mixed race, originally Slav refugees, including escaped serfs, who joined the Turkish nomads of the southern steppes, adopted their way of life, and intermarried. Their organisation was democratic and they held land communally. With the Tartars they harried the Russian and Polish states and, becoming famous as mounted warriors, were engaged in increasing numbers to guard the Russian frontiers. By the 19th century they numbered about three million, divided into 11 groups; the largest settled along the Don, but others spread to the Urals and Siberia. Under imperial rule they had to serve in the army for 20 years, beginning at the age of 18, in return for the grant of larger holdings of land than other peasants. Cossacks were specially skilled in horsemanship.

COSTA RICA, a republic in Central America. Pop. 1,173,000; area 19,656 sq. miles. Mostly highland, with several mountain ranges, the country raises coffee, bananas, cocoa and cabinet woods. Discovered by Columbus in 1502, it became independent of Spain in 1821. From 1824—38 it was part of the Confederation of Central America. The capital is San José (pop. 100,000).

COTOPAXI, the highest active volcano in the world (19,613 ft), in the Andes near Quito, Ecuador. Permanently snow-capped and usually above the clouds, it has caused considerable damage.

COTTON, a plant producing soft natural fibres used in the manufacture of yarns and fabrics. The pods (bolls) are full of seeds, to which the fibres are attached. Varieties with the longest fibres (long-staple) are the most valuable, especially Egyptian and Sea Island cotton (once grown on islands off the coast of Georgia, U.S.A., now in the West Indies). The chief producers are the southern states of the U.S.A., Egypt, China, Russia and India. Boll-weevil and cotton stainer are crop pests. Before being baled the cotton is ginned, i.e. the fibres are separated from the seed.

The chief by-products are cotton-seed oil, refined and used in making soap and margarine; linters, the short stiff fibres remaining on the seed after ginning, used in making paper, rayon, cellulose plastics, celluloid and guncotton; and residues used for animal feed and fertiliser.

COUNCIL OF EUROPE, formed in 1949 as a Parliament of Western Europe. The members are Britain, France, the Benelux countries, Denmark, Norway, Sweden, the Irish Republic, Italy, West Germany, Turkey, Greece, Iceland, Austria, Cyprus and Switzerland. Strasbourg is the headquarters.

COUNTER-REFORMATION, a term covering the reactions of the Papacy to Protestant secessions. The Jesuit Order was appointed to be the spearhead of the movement. The Council of Trent (1545—64) reaffirmed the dogmas to which the Lutherans had taken chief exception, but tried to put down some of the abuses that they had criticised, e.g. simony and the selling of indulgences. The Inquisition suppressed heresy in Catholic countries with vigour. A series of wars were fomented to halt Protestant expansion and reclaim Protestant countries. The first object was achieved, but the only gain for Rome was Hussite Bohemia. The Spanish Armada (1588) against England ended in disaster; the French Wars of Religion ended in the Edict of Nantes granting full religious freedom to the Huguenots; and the Thirty Years War (1618—48) was hardly more successful.

COUNTY, in Britain a territorial division derived from the old shire. Counties are administered by county councils, but a territorial county may be divided into two or more parts for administrative purposes (e.g. Yorkshire is subdivided into North, East and West Ridings), and county boroughs are excluded from their jurisdiction. A county council, which is elected, is responsible for the county constabulary, roads, education, health and the collection of vehicle taxes, etc. The lord-lieutenant, originally the Crown's representative responsible for the maintenance of law and order in a county, has now duties which are mainly honorific; he is the head of the county magistracy.

COURT, a tribunal for punishing offences against the state and settling disputes between individuals. Under the English system, the proceedings are open to the public and the courts do not go out of their way to administer justice or enforce the law but deal with issues brought before them. Their decisions may change the law by establishing precedents. Courts are classified in accordance with the character and scope of their jurisdiction. A court of first instance hears the original case, while an appellate court reviews the judgments submitted from a lower tribunal. In England, the Supreme Court of Judicature is divided into two parts: the High Court of Justice, generally having only original jurisdiction; and the Court of Appeal. The former consists of the Chancery Division (wills, trusts, bankruptcy, mortgages); the Queen's Bench Division (the administration of common law); and the Probate, Divorce and Admiralty Division. The House of Lords is the supreme court of appeal. In civil cases, the courts of first instance are the county courts and the Queen's Bench at the Assizes and, in London and Middlesex, the High Court of London. Criminal cases are tried in the High Court sitting at Assizes, the Central Criminal Court in London, the Courts of Quarter Sessions, and the Courts of Petty Sessions. Appeals are heard in the Court of Criminal Appeal and the House of Lords (except for Scottish cases).

COVENTRY, a city and county borough of Warwickshire, England. Pop. (1961) 305,060. An important industrial centre for the manufacture of automobiles, aircraft, machine tools, metallurgical products and textiles, it suffered severely from German bombings in 1940 when many of its ancient monuments were badly damaged. A new cathedral was consecrated in 1962, built at the side of the shell of the old cathedral which was almost totally destroyed.

COVERDALE, Miles (*c.* 1488—1568), English reformer. He made the first complete translation of the Bible into English. Coverdale made valuable contributions to the 'Great Bible' published in 1539, and to the first *Book of Common Prayer.*

COWARD, Noël (1899—), English playwright, actor, composer and writer. A prolific and versatile playwright, he had early successes with *Vortex* and *Hay Fever*, the revue *This Year of Grace* and the operetta *Bitter Sweet.* His most successful films were *In Which We Serve, Brief Encounter* and *Blithe Spirit.*

COWPER, William (1731—1800), English poet. A prey to repeated bouts of intense melancholia, he was for most of his life a semi-recluse. He collaborated with the converted slave-trader, the Rev. John Newton, in the Olney Hymns (he wrote *God moves in a mysterious way*), and under his influence attacked slavery in *The Task.* But he could also write the light-hearted *John Gilpin* and the patriotic *The Loss of the Royal George.* In many of his works and in his letters he gives a delightful picture of English home life.

CRAMP, a painful contraction of muscle fibres, causing the muscles to feel hard and knotty. Muscles used excessively are often affected. Pressure or brisk rubbing may afford some relief. Swimmers experiencing cramp in the arm or leg should float on the back and knead the affected limb.

CRANE, Stephen (1871—1900), U.S. writer. The first American to write naturalistic novels, he is noted for *Maggie: A Girl of the Streets* and *The*

Red Badge of Courage. He also wrote poems and short stories, including the classic *The Open Boat.*

CRANMER, Thomas (1489—1556), English archbishop and religious reformer. Henry VIII appointed him Archbishop of Canterbury after he had declared the king's marriage to Catherine of Aragon void. Cranmer urged the severing of all relations with the Roman Catholic Church and became a leader in the newly-established Anglican Church. He held that the sovereign had the right to determine the state religion. After the death of young Edward VI, he supported Jane Grey as successor to the throne, and when Catholic Mary Tudor became queen he was deposed and burned at the stake as a heretic. He was responsible for the issue of the Prayer Books of 1549 and 1552, to which he contributed.

CRASSUS, Marcus Licinius (115—53 B.C.), Roman consul. The richest man in Rome, he became praetor and later crushed the Spartacus revolt. In 60 B.C. he formed an uneasy alliance with Caesar and Pompey (the first Triumvirate), to which he contributed much money but little loyalty. He was given the governorship of Syria which, in his greed, he looted very thoroughly before crossing the Euphrates to lose almost the whole of his army and his own life at the hands of the Parthians in the battle of Carrhae.

CRÉCY, Battle of (1346), the battle in northern France fought between the English under Edward III against a far superior French force under Philip VI. It ended in a complete victory for the English. In this engagement the Black Prince won his spurs. It was the first battle in which artillery (King Edward's 'bombards') was used in the field.

CREMATION, the disposal of dead bodies by burning them to ashes. Except in Egypt, China and Judaea, it was common in antiquity. The practice declined in Western Europe with the spread of Christianity. An argument used to support cremation today claims that cemeteries constitute a threat to health, especially during epidemics; but this theory is rejected by the medical profession. The growth of population coupled with high land values in and near towns has probably been a more powerful factor in the enormous increase in cremations in comparison with burials in Western Europe and America since the beginning of the 20th century. The body is burned under intense heat, leaving 4—6 lb. of residue.

CRETE, a Greek island in the Mediterranean. Pop. (1951) 463,459; area 3,235 sq. miles. Consisting of rugged mountains, it is chiefly agricultural, exporting citrus and wines. The Minoan Palace of Knossos, near Herakleion (Iraklion, Candia), dates from 4000 B.C. (see Aegean Civilisation). The capital is Canea (Khania; pop. 127,624), where there is a museum of Minoan relics.

CRICKET, the English national summer game, first became an organised game with the founding of the Hambledon Club, Hampshire, in 1750. The Marylebone Cricket Club (M.C.C.) was started in 1787 at Thomas Lord's first ground, and moved to the present site in St John's Wood, London, in 1814, where it became the controlling authority of the game. The essence of the game is the defence by the batsman of his wicket (once two stumps and a bail, now three with two bails), with a bat which (unlike the baseball bat) has a flat surface, from attack by the bowler who bowls (overarm since 1865) a ball weighing approximately 5½ oz. over a pitch 22 yds long. After the ball has been hit, the two batsmen may exchange wickets, scoring a run each time they cross and reach the opposite popping crease before the ball is returned to 'break' the wicket; the batsman may also score four or six runs by hitting the ball to or over the boundary. A batsman may be bowled, caught, run out, declared lbw. (leg before wicket), etc. The half of the field on the bat side of the batsman is the off side, the other half the leg or on side; thus the off becomes the leg side when a left-handed batsman is playing. Fielders (there are 11 men to a team) are placed by the bowler and the catpain to suit the circumstances, the main positions being (from behind the batsman in a semicircle): on the off side, slip, third man, gully, point (level with the batsman), cover, mid off, long off; and on the leg side, long leg, short leg, square leg (level with the batsman), (silly) mid on, long on, with the wicket-keeper behind the wicket.

The popularity of the game is very localised, interest being largely restricted to the countries which play Test Matches against each other; England (not Scotland or Ireland), Australia, New Zealand, South Africa (but not Canada), India, Pakistan and the West Indies. The first Test Match was England v. Australia in 1877. Among the great cricketers in the history of the game were Dr W. G. Grace (1848—1915), who scored 126 centuries and took 2,876 wickets; Sir Jack Hobbs (1882—1964), who made 197 centuries; K. S. Ranjitsinhji, one of the most stylish batsmen; and Sir Donald Bradman (b. 1908) of Australia, who scored 452 runs at Sydney in 1930.

CRIMEA, a peninsula in the Black Sea Region of the Ukrainian S.S.R. Pop. (1959) 1,201,000; area 9952 sq. miles. Mountains in the centre are enclosed by plains in the north and south. The narrow southern plain is dotted with resorts. Greek colonies flourished there in the 6th century B.C. The Russians annexed it in 1783. In 1853—56, the Crimean War was fought on its southern shore.

CRIMEAN WAR (1853—56), a war waged between the allied forces of Britain, France, Turkey and Sardinia against Russia. Disputes over the protection of the holy sites in Palestine (then Turkish), and Russia's claim to protect Christians in the Turkish territories of the Balkans, furnished the pretext. Russia's real aim was to acquire a port on the Mediterranean. France, where Napoleon III had ambitions for personal glory, and Britain, misled by Russophobe despatches from Stratford de Redcliffe, declared war on Russia in 1854. The battles of Alma, Balaclava and Inkerman were fought in 1854 in the Crimea, where the port of Sebastopol was besieged for a year. When it fell in September 1855 the fighting ceased, and peace was made the following year. The war, which was badly mishandled throughout, found the British troops quite unequipped to stand a winter campaign in the Crimea. Florence Nightingale led a body of volunteer nurses to do what they could in the shocking conditions obtaining, and she was afterwards given the task of reorganising the medical services.

CRIPPS, Sir Stafford (1889—1952), British politician. He was Solicitor-General in Ramsay MacDonald's Labour government (1930—31). For advocating collaboration with extreme left-wing parties, he was expelled from the Labour Party in 1936. In 1940—42 Cripps was ambassador to the U.S.S.R. He was President of the Board of Trade in Attlee's cabinet in 1945—47, and Minister of Economic Affairs and Chancellor of the Exchequer in 1947—50. In the latter capacity his steps to balance the budget included a rigorous austerity policy and a programme for increasing exports and securing loans abroad.

CROATIA, a federal unit of Yugoslavia, on the Adriatic Sea. Pop. (1962) 4,299,000; area 21,840 sq. miles. Mostly mountainous, it has considerable mineral resources. Croatia is essentially agricultural. Until 1918 it was part of Hungary. The capital is Zagreb (470,000). Other important cities are Split and Rijeka-Susak (Fiume).

CROCE, Benedetto (1866—1952), Italian philosopher. He was founder and editor of the review *La Critica* and published his views in the four-volume *Philosophy of the Spirit*. Minister of Education in 1920—21, he was forced out of public life by Mussolini and mention of his name was forbidden until the fall of Fascism in 1943. He held that the only objective world is the mind's subjective awareness and that history reflects man's search for truth.

CROESUS (d. 546 B.C.), King of Lydia. Extending his rule over most of western Asia Minor, he became unusually rich and a patron of the arts. His empire was finally destroyed by Cyrus of Persia.

CRO-MAGNON MAN, a race living in south and central Europe, perhaps between 70,000 and 30,000 B.C. in the Palaeolithic or Old Stone Age. These people were cave dwellers and possessed a high degree of artistic development. Their culture was far superior to that of Neanderthal man who preceded them.

CROMWELL, Oliver (1599—1658), English military and political leader. Serving in the parliamentary forces against Charles I and his Royalist army, Cromwell organised his own cavalry troop called the 'Ironsides.' Through his military victories he gradually advanced to become supreme commander of the army. When the Presbyterian Parliament seemed about to return Charles to the throne, Cromwell's army — which was Independent—ousted the subversive members, and the 'Rump Parliament' put Charles to death. After putting down revolts in Ireland and Scotland, he defeated Charles II at Worcester. At home he dissolved two parliaments (the Rump and Barebones) and became Lord Protector in 1654; a period of military dictatorship followed (the rule of the major-generals) and then another parliament, which offered him the Crown, was dissolved. Abroad he raised his country's prestige by advantageous settlements with France, Spain and Holland, gaining Jamaica and Dunkirk. Though ruling as a virtual dictator, he proved a wise ruler, of political ability.

CROOKES, Sir William (1832—1919), English chemist and physicist. He discovered thallium and invented the radiometer and the cathode-ray tube. Crookes also developed a new method of spectrum analysis. He wrote a book on diamonds, was an authority on sanitation and interested himself in psychical research.

CROWN, circular head-dress representing achievement or royalty. Since ancient times, wreaths and crowns have been worn by persons of unusual accomplishments, by priests and by brides. The official crown of England is the crown of St Edward. It was made in 1661 for the coronation of Charles II and is a replica of the one destroyed in Cromwell's time. British sovereigns also wear a second crown, the imperial state crown worn on state occasions. Queen Elizabeth II was crowned on June 2, 1953, with the crown of St Edward, which was shortly afterwards replaced with the state crown made in 1838 for Queen Victoria. It is this latter crown which the Queen wears on state occasions. The state crown and the crown jewels are normally kept in the Tower of London.

St Edward's Crown

CROWN COLONY, a British territorial possession with little or no self-government. Such colonies are governed by the Crown either because they are regarded as not being ready for self-government or because of their strategic importance. Their governmental structure varies.

CRUIKSHANK, George (1792—1878), English caricaturist and illustrator. His first work consisted of etchings possessed of a sinister grotesque quality. Later he turned to painting. He had a gift for depicting facial expressions and achieved distinction with his illustrations to *Oliver Twist* by Charles Dickens. He was a regular contributor to most contemporary journals.

CRUSADES, military expeditions undertaken by the Christians of Europe from the 11th—13th centuries to recover the Holy Land from the Moslems. Under the auspices of Pope Urban II, the first Crusade (1096—99) captured the Holy City and established the Kingdom of Jerusalem. The Second Crusade (1147—49) attempted to regain territory lost to the Moslems, but ended in failure. In 1187 Saladin, at the head of a united Arab army, completely vanquished the Crusaders and took possession of Jerusalem. A Third Crusade was started, but was ineffective as its leaders quarrelled and withdrew their forces. The Fourth Crusade (1202—4) never reached Moslem territory, being diverted by Venetian intrigue to the sack of Constantinople; a Latin Empire was set up there under Baldwin of Flanders. Several subsequent crusades were also started but were unable to regain control.

CUBA, an island republic in the Caribbean Sea. Pop. (1960) 6,743,000; area 44,206 sq. miles. Except for mountains in the west, centre and southeast, Cuba is mostly flat. Its principal products are sugar and tobacco. There are iron ore deposits. Discovered by Columbus in 1492, it was a Spanish colony until 1898, when it was governed by the U.S.A. for four years. In 1959 the dictatorship of Fulgencio Batista was replaced by that of Fidel Castro, whose government is characterised by social and agrarian reforms and pro-Soviet sympathies. The capital is Havana (pop. 1953 785,455). Other principal cities are Marianao (219,278), Santiago de Cuba (163,237) and Camagüey (110,388).

CUBISM, a form of modern art inspired by Cézanne and Negro sculpture and developed by Braque and Picasso from 1904—14, in which the subject was broken up into geometric planes which were organised in a pictorial composition presenting several aspects of the same object simultaneously.

CUMBERLAND, a county in northwest England. Pop. (1961) 294,162; area

1516 sq. miles. Consisting of lowlands in the coastal areas and in the northwest, it is mainly mountainous (Scafell Pike, 3,210 ft, the highest in England). It has coal and other minerals. Farming is the leading occupation. Carlisle (pop. 1961 71,112) is the county town. Much of the Lake District lies within its boundaries.

CUNARD, Sir Samuel (1787—1865), Canadian businessman and shipowner. In 1840 he organised the British and North American Royal Mail Steam Packet Company, the first regular steamship service between America and Europe. This was superseded by the Cunard Line which, following a merger, became the Cunard-White Star Line in 1934.

CUNEIFORM, a system of writing, dating from *c.* 4000 B.C., consisting of varying combinations of wedge-shaped strokes impressed on clay. It was used by the Sumerians and later by the Assyrians and Babylonians. Among other ancient peoples to employ this script were the Elamites and Hittites. The forms of cuneiform writing developed from pictographic to phonetic systems.

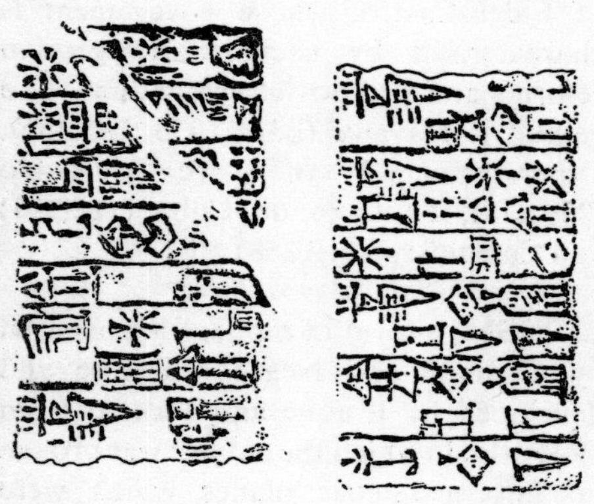

Sumerian cuneiform writing (2400 B.C.)

CUNNINGHAM, Sir Alan Gordon (1887—), a British general in the Second World War. He directed the Ethiopian campaign (1940—41) and subsequently commanded the Eighth Army in North Africa. He was the last High Commissioner for Palestine and Transjordan, carrying out the British evacuation in 1948. He is a brother of Admiral Lord Cunningham.

CUNNINGHAM, Andrew Browne, 1st Viscount of Hyndhope (1883—), British admiral. He distinguished himself at Gallipoli in the First World War, commanded the Mediterranean fleet from 1939—42, and was Allied naval commander in the North African invasion. From 1943—46 he was First Sea Lord and Chief of the Naval Staff.

CURAÇAO, an island in the Carribbean Sea, in the Netherlands Antilles. Pop. (1959) 126,103; area 210 sq. miles. Its main occupation is oil refining. The capital is Willemstad.

CURIE, Marie Sklodowska (1867—1934) and Pierre (1859—1906), French physicists and co-discoverers of radium. They shared the Nobel prize in physics for 1903. After processing eight tons of pitchblende ore, they succeeded in isolating a gram of pure radium salts. Marie Curie was awarded a second Nobel prize (in chemistry) in 1911, for isolating pure metallic radium.

CURZON of Kedleston, 1st Marquis (1859—1925), English statesman. He was viceroy and governor-general of India (1898—1905), where he aroused nationalist opposition. During the First World War, he was Lord Privy Seal and President of the Council; he then became foreign secretary (1919—24). At the Paris Peace Conference in 1919 he suggested a boundary (the Curzon Line) for settling the question of Poland's eastern frontier, which, at first rejected, was adopted in 1945. He had every expectation of succeeding Bonar Law as

Premier in 1923 but was passed over in favour of Baldwin, a blow which he bore with outward stoicism.

CUVIER, Georges Léopold, Baron (1769—1832). French naturalist. He devised a system for classifying the animal kingdom according to structural types and published a 20-volume work on zoology. Cuvier laid the foundations of comparative anatomy, and established palaeontology as a separate science.

CYANIDES, salt of hydrocyanic acid. The most important are compounds of potassium, sodium and calcium. Sodium cyanide is used to extract gold and silver from their ores. Most cyanides are deadly poisons.

CYBERNETICS (Greek *kubernetes,* **'helmsman'),** the theory of the control mechanisms of automation (q.v.) and the information theory of communication (i.e. the problems of transmitting information, whether in telecommunications, programming computers or in human society), as applied to the study of the mechanism and behaviour of the human brain. It has been found that analogies can be drawn between human beings and machines in these fields.

CYCLADES, a group of about 220 islands, and a Greek province in the Aegean Sea, west of the Dodecanese. Pop. (1951) 121,256; area 1023 sq. miles. Citrus, figs, olives and grapes are grown. The capital is Ermoupolis on the isle of Siros.

CYPRUS, an island republic in the eastern Mediterranean, a member of the British Commonwealth. Pop. (1960) 563,000 (more than three-quarters Greek; the rest mostly Turks); area 3572 sq. miles. Its chief products are citrus fruits, copper and iron. The site of ancient Phoenician and Greek colonies, it was later ruled by Venice until 1571, when it became a Turkish possession until ceded to Britain in 1878. A revolt to support demands for self-determination, or union with Greece *(enosis)*, ended in 1959, when independence was promised and granted in 1960.

CYRANO DE BERGERAC, Savinien de, see Bergerac, Cyrano de

CYRUS THE GREAT (*c.* 600—529 B.C.), King of Persia from 550 B.C. and founder of the Persian empire. After uniting Media with Persia, he conquered Lydia, gaining control of most of Asia Minor. His final conquest was Babylon, where he permitted the Jews to return to Jerusalem and rebuild their temple.

CZECHOSLOVAKIA, People's republic in central Europe, comprising the former regions of Bohemia, Slovakia, Moravia and Silesia. Pop. (1960) 13,649,000; area 49,381 sq. miles. Mountainous in the northwest and east, it has fertile lowlands drained by the Labe (Elbe) and Danube rivers. The main crops are grains, potatoes, sugar-beet and hops. The country is thickly wooded. Mineral deposits include coal, iron, copper, lead and uranium. There are important armaments, iron and steel, glass, pottery and textile industries. After 300 years of Austrian rule, the Czechs and Slovaks established an independent republic in 1918. In 1938 Germany annexed the Sudetenland region in the west. Poland and Hungary also occupied border areas and Germany soon assumed control of the rest of the country. The capital is Prague (Praha). Pop. (1959) 987,865. Other leading cities are Brno (312,330), Bratislava (256,046) and Ostrava (231,698).

D

DACCA, capital of East Pakistan, on the Burhi Ganga River. Pop. (1958) 600,000. A commercial centre, it produces textiles, jute, chemicals and electrical goods.

DAGESTAN, an autonomous S.S.R., R.S.F.S.R., in the Caucasus region of the U.S.S.R. Pop. (1959) 1,063,300; area 13,124 sq. miles. It is mostly very mountainous except for a narrow strip along the Caspian Sea. There are extensive deposits of petroleum, natural gas and sulphur. The capital is Makhachkala.

DAHOMEY, a republic in West Africa. Pop. (1961) 1,934,000; area 44,696 sq. miles. The coastal regions are low, rising further inland. Palm oil and cotton are produced in the hot, moist climate. A French possession from 1893, it became independent in 1960. The capital is Porto Novo.

DAIREN (Ta-Lien), a seaport in northeast China, on the Liaotung Peninsula, now linked with Port Arthur (q.v.) and called Lüta. Pop. (1952) 1,054,000. A leading export centre, it has metallurgical, food and textile industries.

DAKAR, capital of Senegal. Pop. (1960) 300,000. A major West African seaport, Dakar is a communications and commercial centre, the international airport being used by airlines to South America. Dakar was formerly the capital of French West Africa.

DALI, Salvador (1904—   ), a Spanish painter and the most controversial and bizarre of contemporary Surrealists. In his works, objects are juxtaposed to totally unrelated subjects and distorted. His technique is one of perfection of detail.

DALLAS, a city in northeast Texas, U.S.A. Pop. (1960) 672,684. On the Trinity River and surrounded by oilfields, it has oil refineries and is a leading commercial, communications and industrial centre. It manufactures aircraft, chemicals, electrical equipment and machinery. It has a large cotton market and is a centre of banking and insurance.

DALMATIA, a region on the Adriatic coast of Yugoslavia in Southern Croatia. Pop. 665,000; area 4916 sq. miles. There are many islands off the coast. Much of it is a treeless limestone plateau (karst). The ancient towns of Dubrovnik and Split attract a large tourist trade. The coastal area was in Venetian hands during the 16th—18th centuries, when it fell to Austria. The hinterland was in turn under Croatian, Serbian, Bosnian and Hungarian rule.

DALTON, John (1766—1844), English chemist and mathematician. His investigations of gases led him to formulate an atomic theory for the structure of matter to explain the laws of chemical combination. He published the first table of relative atomic weights, and also described colour-blindness, being himself colour-blind.

DAMASCUS, capital of Syria. Pop. (1957) 475,399. A centre of fine craftsmanship and commerce, it has an uninterrupted history going back to the 14th century B.C. Since it was sacked by the Assyrians in 733 B.C. it has been occupied by the forces of Alexander the Great, the Arabs, Egyptians, Mongols, Turks, British and French. The 'Street that is called Straight' is associated with St Paul. The Umayyads built the Great Mosque in the 7th century. Damascene sword blades and damask linen originated in Damascus, now more famous for crystallised fruit, skilled goldsmiths' work and other handicrafts. The port is Beirut, 57 miles to the northwest.

DAMOCLES, a Greek courtier at the court of Dionysius I of Syracuse. Having extolled the happiness of the tyrant, Damocles was invited by Dionysius to sample this happiness by partaking of royal banquet, with a sword suspended above his head by a single horse-hair.

DANCE, an organised response of the body to rhythm. As an expression of human emotions and basic instincts, it may be considered the earliest of the arts. It has been practised as a sacred ritual, a magic ceremonial and as a social pastime. With the rise of Christianity it was frowned upon but still remained in a disguised form. There was a revival of dancing in Europe in the 14th century. Folk-dancing reflecting native traditions grew up in many countries. Inspired by the dance-drama, ballet developed elaborate techniques of its own. Mass media of communications are today largely responsible for successive waves of new dances being immediately learned by people throughout the world.

D'ANNUNZIO, Gabriele (1836—1938), Italian poet, novelist and political figure. A distinguished airman in the First World War, in 1919 he occupied Fiume for more than a year with a private army during the dispute between Italy and Yugoslavia over the city. Both Italy and the League of Nations condemned his action. He later became an ardent supporter of Mussolini.

DANTE ALIGHIERI (1265—1321), Italian poet and author of the immortal *Divine Comedy*. Entering the political life (1295) of his native city Florence, he was elected to the highest municipal office (1300). In 1302, while on a mission to Rome, his party was overthrown and he himself exiled. The remainder of his life he spent travelling and writing. He fell in love with Beatrice (Bice Portinari) at the age of nine, but she married another and died young. It was as a memorial to her that he wrote the *Divine Comedy*, a history of his own spiritual pilgrimage, in which he describes a journey he made through Hell and Purgatory, under the guidance of Virgil (who symbolises human reason) and through Paradise with Beatrice (who represents divine revelation). The work is allegorical, with three levels of interpretation: moral, political and religious.

DANTON, Georges (1759—94), a leading figure in the French Revolution. A man of great intellectual ability and a patriot, he was made Minister of Justice in 1793. In this capacity he condoned the September Massacres, in which, however, he had taken no part; and he voted for the king's execution. One of the original members of the Committee of Public Safety, and its president for a brief period, he led the party of the Montagnard which ousted the more moderate Girondins from the National Convention. He twice rallied his countrymen to expel the Prussians and to carry the revolution abroad but when, in view of the successes of the armies and the Revolution, he declared that the continuation of the Reign of Terror was no longer necessary, he was supplanted by a jealous Robespierre and sent to the guillotine as a counter-revolutionary.

DANUBE, see River.

DARDANELLES (Hellespont), the straits linking the Aegean Sea with the Sea of Marmora and separating Turkey in Europe from Turkey in Asia. It is 40 miles long. In April 1915 a force of British, Australian, New Zealand and French troops landed at Gallipoli, but were stoutly resisted by the Turks under Mustapha Kemal (Kemal Atatürk) and the German Liman von Sanders. The Allied forces were withdrawn at the end of the year, with great loss in men and ships. The campaign was instigated by Winston Churchill as First Sea Lord, in order to open the straits to Russian ships; Constantinople was the objective. The force sent was too small and inadequately supported; a premature naval bombardment alerted the Turks. Disgusted with the half-hearted manner in which his plan had been implemented, Churchill resigned and was unfairly blamed for the failure. Much diplomatic energy after the war was expended on efforts to make the straits a demilitarised international seaway, but the issue was never satisfactorily settled.

DARIUS I (*c.* 550—485 B.C.), King of Persia. After establishing supremacy in his own kingdom, he subdued Thrace and Macedonia, and drove the Scythians from the region of the Danube; he did not live to attain his ultimate goal, the conquest of Greece, his army being defeated by the Greeks at Marathon (490). He had an account of his reign inscribed in cuneiform writing in three languages on the Behistun rock which was first translated in 1846.

DARLING, see River.

DARMSTADT, a city in Hessen, West Germany. Pop. (1960) 134,898. It is a railway junction and industrial centre.

DARNLEY, Henry Stewart, Lord (1545—67), a Scottish nobleman, second husband of Mary Queen of Scots, by whom he had a son, later James I. He became suspicious and jealous of Mary's Italian secretary, Rizzio, and murdered him in her presence. Although she appeared to condone this, Darnley was murdered by a group led by the Earl of Bothwell, possibly with her connivance; Bothwell married her three months later, before she was dethroned.

DARWIN, Charles (1809—82), English naturalist. In the course of a voyage round the world, recorded in his *Journal of a Naturalist* (or *The Voyage of the 'Beagle'*; 1842), he noted the marked variations in the shape of the beak in groups of what appeared to be one species of finch, isolated from each other over a very long period of time on islands of the Galapagos Archipelago, and realised that the beak had undergone modification to suit the differing types of food available to them. On this and much other evidence of the kind he gradually built up his theory that species arise through modification and that, in the general struggle for existence, modifications that are favourable lead to survival and those that are unfavourable may lead to extinction. Later A. R. Wallace reached similar conclusions and together they published a preliminary work on the subject. In 1859 Darwin published his *On the Origin of Species by means of Natural Selection*. He concluded further that the more complex forms of life, such as Man, must have evolved from simpler forms, and published his views in *The Descent of Man* (1871). Modest and retiring, he never defended his theories, which came under vigorous attack both by scientists and the churches, though he found an able champion in Huxley. He wrote numerous other works, on botany, zoology and geology. See Evolution.

DAUDET, Alphonse (1840—97), French novelist. His best and most famous works were two of his earliest books, *Lettres de mon moulin*, a collection of Provençal stories, and *Tartarin de Tarascon*, in which he caricatured his fellow Provençals with such verve as to offend them. He also wrote a play, *L'Arlésienne*, which Bizet set to music. A vein of sentimentality runs through much of his work.

DAVID (*c.* 1000 B.C.), the first king of a united Israel. He dispelled King Saul's melancholy by playing the harp and slew the giant Goliath with his sling. His greatest friend was Saul's son, Jonathan, and he married Saul's daughter. However, he fell from grace and retired to the cave (hill fortress) of Adullam on the border, where he lived with a small band of outlaws who levied protection-money from their neighbours. After the death of Saul and Jonathan he became king, conquered Jerusalem from the Jebusites and set up the Ark there, making it his capital. He smote the Philistines and united all the tribes 'from Dan to Beersheba'. Falling in love with Bathsheba, he sent her husband Uriah into the forefront of the battle, where he was killed; for this he was rebuked by the prophet Nathan. He quelled a rebellion by his favourite son, Absalom, who was killed. The Jews regarded him as the ideal hero and expected the Messiah to be of his line. It is unlikely that he wrote any of the Psalms attributed to him.

DAVID I (1084—1153), King of Scotland. Succeeding to the throne in 1124, he encouraged trade, consolidated the feudal system and built numerous monasteries. All his attempts to invade England (1135, 1138, 1140) failed. He supported his niece Matilda in her struggle with Stephen over the English throne.

DAVID II (1324—71), King of Scotland. He succeeded to the throne in 1329 and was sent to France as a child. In 1341 he returned to Scotland. A series of unsuccessful raids into England to help the French king culminated in his capture in 1346. He was released 11 years later upon the payment of a ransom.

DA VINCI, Leonardo, see Leonardo da Vinci.

DAVIS, Jefferson (1808—89), U.S. statesman and President of the Confederate States of America (1861). As a member of the U.S. Senate for Mississippi, he defended slavery, the right of secession and the priority of states' rights. After the defeat of the Confederacy, he was captured and held prisoner for two years, but released without trial.

DAVY, Sir Humphry (1778—1829), English chemist and physicist. He suggested the use of nitrous oxide (laughing gas) as an anaesthetic, produced potassium and sodium by electrolysis and discovered chlorine. Davy invented a universally used miner's safety lamp, which he refused to patent.

DAY, the time required for the earth to complete a single rotation on its axis. An astronomic or sidereal day is measured by the apparent movement of the

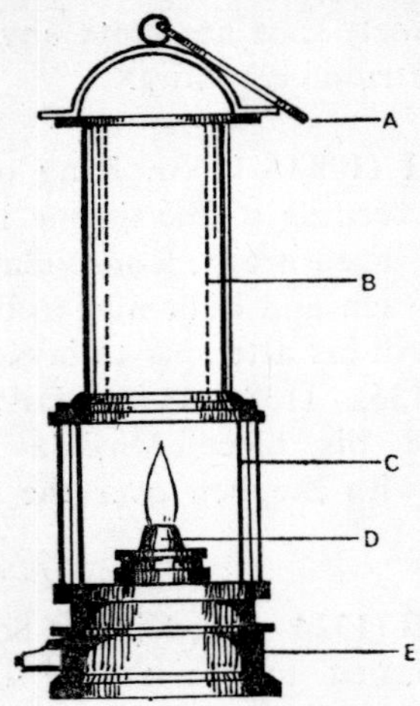

Sir Humphry Davy's miner's safety lamp
A. Handle B. Wire gauze cylinder (double layer at top) C. Glass D. Wick E. Oil vessel

stars; its length is 23 hours, 56 minutes, 4 seconds. A solar day, based on the apparent movement of the sun, varies with the tilt and speed of the earth's motion and its distance to the sun. Due to the fact that the sun is somewhat further east among the stars after each rotation of the earth, the solar day is about 4 minutes longer than the sidereal day. In order to facilitate time-keeping, a theoretical or mean solar day of 24 hours was introduced. This is subdivided into mean solar minutes and seconds. The duration of daylight varies with the altitude, latitude and season of the year.

DAYTON, a city in Ohio, U.S.A. Pop. (1960) 262,332. It is a centre for aeronautical research and aircraft manufacture as well as mechanical equipment, being especially famous for its cash registers.

DEAD SEA SCROLLS, a large collection of Hebrew and Aramaic manuscripts, dating back to *c.* 150 B.C., found from 1947 onwards in caves in the Dead Sea region of Palestine. They include texts of all but one of the books of the Old Testament, a thousand years older than any previously known.

DEAFNESS, apart from that caused by the accumulation of wax, which can be syringed out, can be classified into two main types. In middle-ear deafness, due to obstruction or defect of the conductive apparatus, high-pitched letters such as s and f, and whispering, are relatively well heard, and lower tones, such as r, are poorly heard; bone conduction (tested by placing a tuning fork on the mastoid bone just behind the ear) is better than air conduction; and a hearing aid is likely to be a great help. In nerve deafness, due to a defect of the perceptive apparatus, the tests have the reverse results — s and f and whispering are poorly heard, air conduction is better, and a hearing aid is less likely to help; lip reading may be more useful. There is also hysterical or psychological deafness.

Deafness is rarely hereditary and is usually caused by injury, deformity or disease, e.g. catarrh of the middle ear, or otosclerosis, an infection of the bone around the inner ear of unknown cause or cure. The ear infection may be the aftermath of a variety of diseases, e.g. adenoids in the young, or due to a bomb explosion, or working in conditions of continuous loud noise. Great progress has been made in the education of the deaf and of deaf-mutes. Tinnitus, noises in the ear, is very common and may be traced to a number of causes, but in a surprising number of cases it is of neurotic origin.

DEATH, the cessation of all vital bodily functions. The heart action and respiration cease and muscle tone disappears. Shortly afterwards, the body begins to cool, the muscles stiffen and blood settles in certain parts of some tissues. The final stage is the process in which body

Other heavily armoured reptiles are the American Alligators, which grow to 12 ft. They live on the banks of rivers and spend much time in the water. Their food consists of almost anything they can catch and overpower. They reproduce by laying eggs. *Photo: Ken Lambert*

Pike, pictured here, are the most voracious of fresh water fish (q.v.); large specimens will seize rats or water-voles. They may weigh up to 50 lb, and generally lead a rather sedentary existence. *Photo: Ken Lambert*

The kangaroo is a mammal (q.v.) of the Marsupial Order, i.e. the female carries her young in a pouch for a period after its birth. Marsupials are among the very oldest mammals, and are prevalent in Australasia where they were separated from the sweeping evolutionary changes taking place elsewhere on earth.

Photo: Radio Times Hulton Picture Library

The Primate group are the most highly developed mammals and include man, the apes, monkeys, tarsiers and lemurs. As can be seen in this photograph of an orang-outang from Sumatra, in primates the brain is far larger and more complex than in other mammals, and the hands and feet are specially adapted for climbing and manipulating. The female gives birth to live young that develop within her body.

Photo: Camera Press

Another mammal dating from prehistoric times and still living today is the armour-plated rhinoceros. Despite its cumbersome appearance and massive size (up to 5 ft 8 in at the shoulder) it is capable of running at 40 m.p.h. Rhinoceroses are vegetarian in diet and largely nocturnal. They have small intelligence and are extremely dangerous.

Photo: Helen Fischer

tissues putrefy and break down. Individual tissues and cells may continue to live for some time after death has set in. In the last century, better methods of sanitation, and the control of disease and malnutrition, have lowered the death rate. The principal causes of death now are, in descending order of frequency, heart disease, cancer, arterial disease of the brain, and accidents. In Britain deaths must be notified to the registrar within five days, and a medical certificate produced. Violent death and death from unknown causes must be investigated by a coroner.

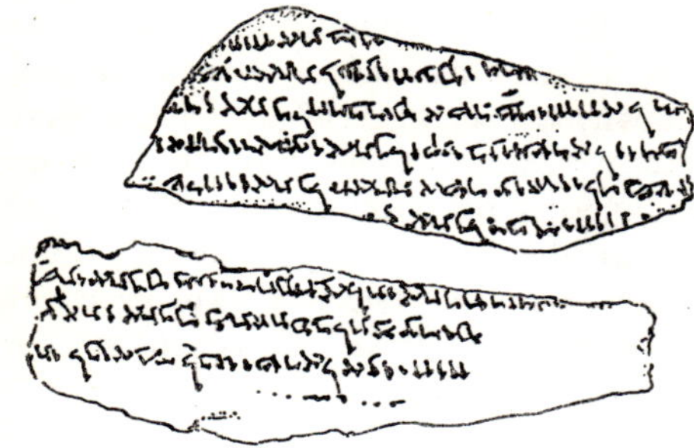

Dead Sea Scroll (fragment of Exodus) (see previous page)

DEBUSSY, Claude (1862—1918), French composer. His originality won him the Grand Prix de Rome in 1884 for the cantata *L'Enfant prodigue.* Poetry, as in *L'Après-midi d'un faune,* exerted considerable influence on his music, which reflects the strong impact of sensory impressions. He mainly composed for the piano. His major work is the opera *Pelléas et Mélisande.*

DECALOGUE (Gk *deka*, ten, and *logos*, word), the Ten Commandments, attributed to Moses, and found in Exodus xx and also in Deuteronomy v.

DECLARATION OF INDEPENDENCE, the document adopted on July 4, 1776, by the Continental Congress representing the 13 American colonies which declared themselves independent of Britain. It justified separation from the mother country on the basis of wrongs inflicted by the British king and Parliament. July 4 is a national holiday in the U.S.A. The Declaration, drafted by Thomas Jefferson, contains the famous passage: "We hold these truths to be self-evident, that all men are created equal, that they are endowed by their Creator with certain unalienable rights, that among these are Life, Liberty and the pursuit of Happiness. That to secure these rights, Governments are instituted among Men, deriving their just powers from the consent of the governed."

DEFENCE MECHANISM, the unconscious behaviour that enables an individual to avoid becoming aware of matters that threaten his self-esteem, arouse anxiety or shame, or are otherwise unpleasant.

DEFOE, Daniel (1660—1731), English political writer and novelist. He published pamphlets dealing with social and political problems of his time, spending a term in prison for *The Shortest Way with Dissenters.* At times he served both the Tories and Whigs, shifting his allegiance to conform to the affiliation of the ministry in power. His literary career proper began when he was nearly 60, with the famous *Robinson Crusoe.* Other notable works include *Moll Flanders, The Journal of the Plague Year* and *A Tour Through the Whole Island of Great Britain.*

DE FOREST, Lee (1873—), U.S. inventor. He invented some 300 devices connected with radio, sound films and television. His most important invention was a three-electrode vacuum tube which made possible transcontinental telephony.

DEISM, a rationalistic philosophy that flourished in England during the 17th and 18th centuries. Its proponents believed in one God, creator of the universe but detached from the world and making no revelation. They regarded the Bible as a collection of fabulous books, and were opposed, sometimes bitterly, to all revealed religion, and particularly to Christianity.

DELAWARE, Atlantic coast state of U.S.A. Pop. (1960) 446,292; area 2057 sq. miles. Most of the state is lowland. Its industries, mainly concentrated on Wilmington, include chemicals, nylon, shipbuilding, cars, aircraft and canning. Maize, wheat and poultry are the chief farm products. Fruits and vegetables are grown. First settled in 1638, Delaware is one of the original 13 states of the U.S. The capital is Dover (pop. 7250). Wilmington is the largest city (pop. 95,827).

DELHI, the capital of the Republic of India and, since 1956, a Union Territory. Pop. (1961) 2,700,000; area 578 sq. miles. At the head of the navigable Jumna river and on the traditional invasion route into India from the northwest, it was from the 12th—19th centuries the Mogul capital; the ruins of their buildings still remain, and the Red Fort encloses the Shah Jahan (or Imperial) Palace (1638—48), below which is the Great Mosque. Lutyens and Baker designed the buildings for near-by New Delhi, the capital of British India from 1912. There is an expanding industrial area, and the bazaars still sell the finest products of Indian craftsmanship, gold and silverware, gems and shawls.

DELIUS, Frederick (1862—1934), an English composer of German descent whose output includes many choral *(The Magic Fountain, A Village Romeo and Juliet)* and orchestral *(Brigg Fair, On Hearing the first Cuckoo in Spring)* works of exceptional poignancy.

DELPHI, the ancient Greek site of a famous oracle, lies 2000 ft above sea-level, overlooking the vale of Amphissa and the Gulf of Corinth, and beneath Mount Parnassus. There are the remains of the Temple of Apollo, often destroyed by earthquake but always rebuilt, the Sacred Way lined by State Treasuries and votive offerings, a well-preserved Theatre of Dionysus, and the stadium where competitors ran till they dropped, the survivor being the winner. The exact site where the prophetess sat on a golden tripod chewing laurel leaves is not known; her incoherent utterances were interpreted by priests into the famous ambiguous prophecies (e.g. 'If you go to war you will destroy an army' — but which army?). There is an excellent museum, the pride of which is the *Bronze Charioteer.*

DEMETER (Roman Ceres), the Greek corn-goddess, sister of Zeus, by whom she had a daughter, Persephone, who was carried off into the underworld by Hades. The Eleusinian Mysteries were celebrated in honour of both mother and daughter.

DEMOCRACY, a form of government in which the people exercise ultimate control through representatives elected by them. The wishes of the majority, expressed in universal, secret, equal elections in which at least two parties participate, determine the laws and circumstances of the population. Basic concepts in a democracy are civil liberties and recognition of the dignity of the individual.

DEMOCRATIC PARTY, one of the two major political parties in the U.S.A.

It has in the past stood for states' rights, social liberalism and reform, and active international co-operation. It has strong conservative elements in the South and in rural areas. In this century Woodrow Wilson and Franklin Roosevelt have been the great Democratic leaders. The latter put through the New Deal and the establishment of the Tennessee Valley Authority (q.v.).

DEMONOLOGY, belief in the existence of superhuman beings who interfere in human affairs to cause harm. It is to be found in most religions. There are cults in which demons are regarded as having supreme power and requiring to be propitiated. In Britain the raising of demons was an offence punishable by death from the reign of James I until George II repealed this law.

DEMOSTHENES (*c.* 383—322 B.C.), Athenian statesman and orator. His most famous speech is *On the Crown* (330), a defence of his own political career. Most of his orations stem from his opposition to the encroachments of Philip of Macedon (in the *Philippics*). His policy led to a disastrous war, and he took his own life to escape capture by the Macedonians.

DENMARK, a constitutional monarchy in Scandinavia. Pop. (1960) 4,590,000; area 16,576 sq. miles. Consisting of the Jutland Peninsula and Zealand (Sjaelland), Fünen, Bornholm and other islands in the Baltic, it is nearly all lowland. There are many lakes and short rivers. Barley and other grains are the chief crops, and much livestock is raised, the principal exports being bacon and butter. The largest industries are shipbuilding, marine engineering, textiles and the manufacture of diesel engines. At the end of the 12th century Denmark was a dominant power in northern Europe. In 1815 it lost Norway to Sweden. Bismarck attacked Denmark in 1864 and deprived it of territory (Schleswig-Holstein) which was partially restored after the First World War. Denmark was occupied by Germany from 1940—45. The capital is Copenhagen (pop. 1955 960,319). Other important cities are Aarhus (118,205) and Odense (109,136).

DENTISTRY, the treatment and care of the teeth, includes the prevention, diagnosis and treatment of disorders of the teeth and gums and the replacement of missing teeth. From a branch of medicine, dentistry developed in the last century to a science and art in its own right. The use of X-rays, local anaesthetics, metal fillings, plastics for artificial teeth and high-speed drilling machines have increased the effectiveness of modern dental treatment. An important branch of dentistry is orthodontics, the correction of malformations of the jaw and teeth in the young.

DENVER, capital of Colorado, U.S.A. Pop. (1960) 493,887. One mile above sea-level at the foot of the Rocky Mountains, Denver enjoys an equable climate which has made it an important health resort. In first became important in the 1870s when gold was found in this area. There are oil refineries, canning and smelting works, and tyres and mining machinery are made. Denver is a mining and financial centre.

DE QUINCEY, Thomas (1785—1859), English writer and essayist. While a student at Oxford (1803—8) he became an opium addict; he described his experiences in *The Confessions of an English Opium-Eater* (1821), which established his literary reputation. For 20 years he lived in Wordsworth's old cottage at Grasmere, in the Lake

District, and he was a friend of the 'Lake poets', Wordsworth, Coleridge and Southey.

DERBY, the county town of Derbyshire, central England. Pop. (1961) 132,325. It manufactures railway locomotives and rolling stock, aircraft and car engines, machine tools, Crown Derby china, and has a wide range of other important industries. The first English silk mill was established here in 1717.

DERBYSHIRE, a county in central England. Pop. (1961) 877,548; area 1041 sq. miles. Much of the north and west is a National Park, containing the Peak District at the southern end of the Pennine Chain. The eastern parts are highly industrialised, with coal-fields and an iron and steel industry. The county town is Derby; Chesterfield is famous for its twisted spire. The county contains many famous houses, Chatsworth, home of the Dukes of Devonshire, Harwick Hall, built by 'Bess of Hardwick' (1591—7) and Haddon Hall, the most complete and authentic example in England of a medieval, manorial home, in beautiful surroundings with charming terraced gardens.

DESCARTES, René (1596—1650), French philosopher and scientist. An outstanding mathematician, he is better remembered as a philosopher. Rejecting the scholasticism of his day, he built his (Cartesian) philosophical system on the basis of his now famous axiom *cogito, ergo sum* (I think, therefore I am). His importance lies in his bold break with tradition. The first rationalist, prepared to explain the whole universe in purely mechanical terms, his insistence that the worlds of mind and matter were completely independent, and unable to affect each other directly, may have led him into difficulties; but he had sown the seeds of doubt that were to grow into the scientific outlook of later generations.

DES MOINES, capital of Iowa, U.S.A. Pop. (1960) 208,982. The business centre of a corn-raising area, it is the head-quarters of insurance companies and publishing firms, and has a big meat-packing industry.

DESTROYER, a speedy, light warship armed with guns of small and medium calibre and equipped for firing torpedoes, it has proved an effective defence against submarines. Electronic listening devices and a large complement of anti-aircraft guns further enhance its function as a convoy escort. Destroyers are also used for laying mines, night raids, patrol duties and reconnaissance. The average destroyer now has a displacement of between 2000 and 4000 tons.

DETERGENT, a synthetic cleansing agent usually derived from petroleum. Most detergents are sulphonated alcohols and sodium alkyl sulphates. They dissolve in both fat and water, producing a suspension of oil, grease or dirt in the water, which is then washed out. They are equally effective in hard or soft water. Detergents were introduced *c.* 1930.

DETERMINISM, the philosophical and theological doctrine that Free Will (q.v.) does not exist. A man's actions are the inescapable result of physical laws, heredity, environment, etc. If man is free he is an exception to the rest of creation, which is governed by law. Hobbes and Spinoza were Determinists; Descartes held that the mind is free, the body completely determined. The theory of evolution and the findings of psychoanalysts are thought to support Determinism, which is also reflected in such doctrines as *karma* (see Hinduism) and Predestination (q.v.).

DETROIT, a city in Michigan, U.S.A. Pop. (1960) 1,670,144. On the Detroit River, bordering on Canada, and served by the Great Lakes waterway, it is one of the most important industrial, commercial, shipping and distributing centres in the country. Detroit has the largest motor-car industry in the world and makes aircraft, tanks and artificial diamonds; it is also a major grain market. It has many institutions of higher learning. First settled by the French, it was the centre of French power in the west until captured by the British in 1760.

DEUTERIUM, the heavy isotope of hydrogen. Also known as heavy hydrogen, it produces heavy water when oxidised. The presence of a neutron in its nucleus makes deuterium valuable for transmuting elements, producing artificial radioactive substances and releasing atomic energy. It is used in the hydrogen bomb.

DE VALERA, Eamon (1882—), Irish national leader and statesman. Born in New York of a Spanish father and an Irish mother, he was brought to Ireland as an infant, and there he taught mathematics. For his part in the Easter Rebellion in 1916 he was sentenced to death but was reprieved and became president of Sinn Fein. He was rearrested in 1918 but made a daring escape from Lincoln gaol and returned to the United States. In 1920 he returned to Ireland to direct the struggle against British rule. He rejected the 1921 settlement for an Irish Free State, and in the ensuing Civil War was arrested by the Free State government. In 1926 he founded a new party, Fianna Fail (soldiers of destiny) which came into power in 1932 and elected him Premier. He abolished the oath of allegiance to the British Crown, declared an All-Ireland Republic, and renamed his country Eire. In 1938 he came to an agreement on most outstanding points with the British Government. His party was defeated in 1948, but he was again Prime Minister from 1951 to 1954 and from 1957 to 1959, when he was elected President of the Republic.

DEVONSHIRE, maritime county in southwest England. Pop. (1961) 822,906; area 2611 sq. miles. Dartmoor occupies much of the centre and part of Exmoor lies to the northeast. The English and Bristol Channel coasts are lined with seaside resorts, of which Torquay is the largest, and the tourist industry is all-important. Plymouth is a seaport and neighbouring Devonport has a naval dockyard. The county is famous for its cream and cider, and its fertile red soil and warm climate produce rich crops of orchard fruits and vegetables. There is little industry; pottery is made from locally mined clay. The centres of the county town, Exeter, and of Plymouth were almost completely rebuilt after devastating air-raids during the Second World War. There is a Naval College at Dartmouth.

DEW, moisture formed on the surface of the ground by the condensation of water vapour in the air or the soil. In the daytime it evaporates quickly, but the chilly night air condenses it on the cool surface of the earth. Below 32°F. it turns to frost. There is little dew on a cloudy day or when strong winds are blowing.

DEWAR, Sir James (1842—1923), British chemist and physicist. In addition to studies in spectroscopy and the low-temperature liquefaction of gases, he was the first to produce liquid and solid hydrogen. He invented the thermos bottle and, together with Sir Frederick Abel, cordite.

DEWEY, John (1859—1952), American philosopher, educationalist and psychologist. During his teaching career at the universities of Minnesota, Michigan, Chicago and Columbia he became a major influence in American education. A Pragmatist and associate of William James, he considered that educational methods must be modified to suit a democratic and industrial society.

DIABETES, a disease in which there are unusually large quantities of sugar in the blood. In the body there is a substance, insulin, which makes it possible for it to utilise starch and sugar. When the pancreas does not produce sufficient insulin, the body cannot make use of its sugar intake, which accumulates in the blood. On the one hand the body receives no benefit from the sugar taken in and, on the other, it becomes poisoned by excess sugar in the blood. Balanced insulin injections serve to remedy the condition.

DIAGHILEV, Sergei (1872—1929), Russian ballet impresario. He founded the Russian Ballet, which achieved unusual distinction with its world-famed dancers. Those whose talents he promoted were the dancers Pavlova, Nijinsky and Massine, the choreographer Fokine, the composer Stravinsky and the painter Bakst.

DIALECTIC, originally the method of question and answer used by Socrates in thinking out philosophical problems, leading to the formulation of positive thesis and negative antithesis, the contradictions of which are eventually reconciled in a transcending, unifying synthesis of the two. This method was applied by Hegel (q.v.) to the philosophy of history, where he saw civilisations as embodying opposed ideas which, usually after war, are synthesised in a new civilisation which reigns supreme until another challenger appears. Karl Marx in his Dialectical Materialism adopted the method while rejecting the basic assumptions; he held that cultures and the process of history are determined by the conflict of material forces in an inescapable sequence, e.g. feudalism leads inevitably to capitalism which yields just as inevitably to socialism.

DIAMOND, the hardest and purest form of carbon, valued as a precious stone. The hardest known mineral, it cannot be dissolved or fused and has a brilliant lustre. The index of refraction is three times that of glass, the resultant strong dispersion of light producing the characteristic 'fire'. Black and impure diamonds are used in industry for drilling and cutting. There are important diamond fields in India, Brazil and various parts of Africa. The weight of a diamond is expressed in carats, 142 carats equalling 1 oz. The largest rough diamond found was the Cullinan (1905) in South Africa, weighing 3025 carats. The production of diamonds is restricted to keep up the

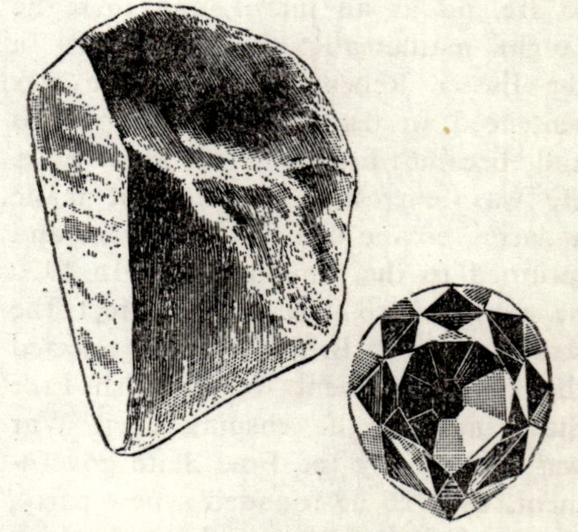

Diamond ('Cullinan', the world's largest). Uncut, and one of the stones cut from it

price. Synthetic diamonds good enough for industrial use have been made by the General Electric Company under very high pressures and temperatures.

DICKENS, Charles (1812—70), English novelist. Son of a navy pay-clerk who was put in the Marshalsea debtors' prison, he had to work in a blacking factory at the age of 12. At 15 he became a lawyer's clerk and later he reported parliament for the press. These events are all brought into his novels, and he seems to have been haunted by early memories of prison life and of life in a debt-ridden household.

His career as a novelist began almost by accident when sketches intended to illustrate some sporting prints developed into the *Pickwick Papers*, which won him immediate fame. Even in this early and light-hearted work he had begun to expose abuses in legal procedure, and the poor law was the target of his next novel, *Oliver Twist*, commenced before Pickwick was finished. All his early works were published in monthly parts, and this accounts for the loose, episodic construction which he was in later years to tighten up. In 1842 he visited the United States, and satirised the inhabitants in *Martin Chuzzlewit. David Copperfield* was to some extent autobiographical.

A new, sterner and more disciplined Dickens began to appear in *Dombey and Son* (1846—48), followed by *Bleak House, Little Dorrit* and, one of his best works, *Great Expectations.* His final novel, *Edwin Drood*, a mystery story written under the inspiration of his friend Wilkie Collins, was left unfinished. Dickens also edited and published various periodicals, and in his later years made much money by giving dramatic readings from his works. From the beginning Dickens showed a genius for creating vivid eccentric minor characters; his heroes are less successful and his heroines, no doubt tailored to contemporary tastes, are barely tolerable today. The targets of his satire were numerous and very varied: the law, officialdom, business morals, schools, hospital nurses and many others. If the melodrama and sentimentality of many passages are no longer to our taste, it has to be remembered that Dickens was writing for a public which almost went into mourning when Little Nell died. But in Mr Micawber, Sam Weller, Sarah Gamp and her non-existent friend Mrs Harris, Spenlow and Jorkins and a hundred others, he created immortal characters.

DICOTYLEDONS comprise the largest group of angiosperms, the flowering plants, and include trees, shrubs and herbs. The leaves are net-veined and the root system complex, with many branch roots. The floral parts are usually in fives or multiples of five and the stems are again complex and may be woody.

DICTIONARY, a book consisting of an alphabetical list of words with their meanings, or equivalents in another language. Pronunciation, etymology and specimens of usage may be added to the definition of each word. Among famous dictionaries of the English language are Dr Johnson's idiosyncratic work, published in 1755, Noah Webster's dictionary published in the U.S.A. in 1828, and the New English Dictionary ('Oxford Dictionary') of 1884—1928.

DIEFENBAKER, John George (1895—), Canadian politician. He became leader of the Progressive Conservative party in 1956, and Prime Minister (1957—63).

DIET, the customary daily food intake of an individual. To be balanced it must include proper proportions of such energy-producing substances as proteins, fats and carbohydrates, together with water, vitamins and minerals.

DIGESTION, a series of processes which make it possible for food to be assimilated and utilised by the body. Beginning in the mouth, it breaks down complex compounds into simpler soluble compounds. Digestion takes place chiefly in the stomach and is completed in the small intestine.

DIJON, capital of the department Côte-d'Or, eastern France. Pop. (1954) 112,844. An important railway junction, it is the centre of the Burgundy wine trade. Its industries include automobiles and precision tools. It was the capital of Burgundy.

Dinosaur (Triceratops)

DINOSAUR, the popular name of two separate orders of extinct reptiles which walked the earth 170,000,000—60,000,000 years ago. They ranged in length from 3—90 ft and weighed as much as 50 tons. Changes in topography and climate may have been responsible for their disappearance.

DIOCLETIAN (245—313), Emperor of Rome from 284—305, instigated many reforms, concluded a peace with the Persians and established an absolute monarchy. The Edict of Diocletian (301) attempted to fix maximum prices and wages, but was unsuccessful.

DIOGENES (412—323 B.C.), Greek Cynic philosopher. He practised rigid asceticism.

DIONYSUS (Greek and Roman Bacchus), the Greek god of intoxication, vinous and mystic. Originally a rural god, represented as followed by frenzied bands of satyrs and Bacchantes (Maenads), who believed themselves to be one with their god, his greatness was celebrated in the festival of the Bacchanalia. He carried the thyrsus, a wand wreathed with ivy and crowned with a fir-cone. He was also the god of tragic art.

DISARMAMENT, the reduction and limitation of armaments through international agreement. It is intimately bound up with the problem of security against aggression. All disarmament talks after the Second World War reached a deadlock because of Russia's refusal to allow inspection in her territory.

DISCIPLES, the 12 chosen followers of Jesus. They were: the brothers Andrew and Simon Peter; Philip; Simon (the Zealot); Thomas; Matthew (Levi); Judas (called Jude or Thaddeus); James and John, called Boanerges, the sons of Zebedee; Bartholomew; James, the son of Alphaeus; and Judas Iscariot, who betrayed Jesus. After the suicide of Judas Iscariot, Matthias was chosen to replace him. The 12 disciples are sometimes regarded as representing the 12 tribes of Israel.

DISINFECTION, the destruction of micro-organisms causing communicable diseases. Everything which has come in contact with or issued from the diseased person should be disinfected either by burning, soaking in a suitable solution or sterilising by steam under pressure.

DISRAELI, Benjamin, 1st Earl of Beaconsfield (1804—81), English statesman and writer. Disraeli's first novel (*Vivian Grey*, 1826) won him recognition as a writer, but his interests turned to politics. In 1837 he entered parliament and became (1847) leader of the Conservative opposition in the House of Commons. He served as Chancellor of the Exchequer (1852, 1858—9, 1866) and Prime Minister (1868, 1874—80). Under his leadership, England obtained the controlling interest in the Suez Canal (1875) and Queen Victoria was made Empress of India (1876). He propagated his views on Tory democracy in his novels *Sybil* and *Coningsby*.

DISSOLUTION OF MONASTERIES (1536—9), the suppression of monastic orders in England and the confiscation of their properties by Henry VIII and Thomas Cromwell at the Reformation. There were some 650 monasteries, mostly Benedictine or Cistercian, some very small. Henry, being bankrupt, sold most of the properties to laymen, who turned some buildings into manor houses (e.g. Battle Abbey) and demolished others to provide materials for new houses, selling the land to speculators; others became cathedrals and churches. Many historically valuable manuscripts were lost through destruction of the monastery libraries.

DISTILLATION, heating a liquid or solid and condensing some of the vapours produced. The process is used in purifying water, producing petroleum derivatives and concentrating alcohol. The separation of liquids with different boiling points, used in the chemical industry, particularly in obtaining the various petroleum products from crude oil, is called fractional distillation, each separate distillate being termed a fraction.

DISTRICT OF COLUMBIA (D.C.), a Federal district in the United States since 1790, containing the national capital, Washington. Pop. (1960) 763,956; area 69 sq. miles.

DIVORCE, the total dissolution of a valid marriage for a cause which has arisen subsequent to the legalisation of the marriage bond. Owing to the sacramental character of marriage established by the Roman Catholic church, divorce was for a long time forbidden to Christians and is still not permitted in a number of Catholic countries. Most non-Catholic countries accept the view that marriage is a civil institution and that divorce is therefore a matter for civil regulation. Until the middle of the 19th century only an Act of Parliament could pronounce a divorce in Britain. Since then this power has been vested in the courts of all non-Catholic countries of Europe and the U.S.A. Grounds for divorce differ considerably and their scope is from time to time extended. Women's greater economic independence is one of the main contributing factors to the increasing incidence of divorce.

DJAKARTA, capital of Indonesia. Pop. (1958) 2,081,200. On the island of Java, it is a communications and distributing centre with an important port. It has a university and its industries include textiles, food-processing, rubber goods, shipbuilding and foundries. It was formerly called Batavia.

DNIEPER, see River.

DOBRUJA, a region in Rumania and

Bulgaria, between the Black Sea and the Danube. Area 8969 sq. miles. Its main port is Constanta, Rumania.

DODECANESE, Greek islands, forming the largest group in the Aegean Sea. Pop. (1951) 121,480; area 1,055 sq. miles. The principal products are wines, olive oil, sponges, tobacco, and honey. Having been successively under Greek, Roman, Byzantine, Turkish and Italian rule, the islands were restored to Greece after the Second World War. Rhodes, on the island of Rhodes, is the capital. Although the name means '12 islands' the term was, from 1912, extended to include Rhodes and Castelorizon, making a total of 14 of these. Cos, Leros and Patmos follow Rhodes in importance.

DOG, an intelligent and devoted animal, of the same family as wolves, coyotes and jackals, which has long been domesticated. Originally carnivorous, dogs now eat a variety of foods. Dogs have been associated with man since prehistoric times. They are useful in countless ways, including hunting, shepherding, pulling carts and sledges, defending man from attack, tracking, and leading the blind.

DOGGER BANK, a sandbank in the North Sea, half way between England and Denmark. It is an internationalised fishing ground.

DOGMA, a formal statement of doctrine established by authority and accepted on faith. As used in the religious sense, it is a truth originally revealed by God. The Roman Catholic Church maintains that there has been no new revelation of dogma since Christ. Some Protestant churches have either rejected or re-defined old dogmas.

DOLL, a small human or animal figure, commonly used as a toy. In ancient times magical powers were ascribed to dolls and originally they were used only by adults. They came into use in many European countries to portray religious scenes. Materials for making dolls have ranged from terra-cotta in ancient Greece to wax, bisque, china, rubber, paper and plastics, employed to give modern figures a life-like appearance.

DOLMEN, a structure consisting of a flattish stone supported by two or more upright stones. Dolmens were erected during the later Stone Age and Bronze Age over graves. The term has replaced the earlier name, cromlech.

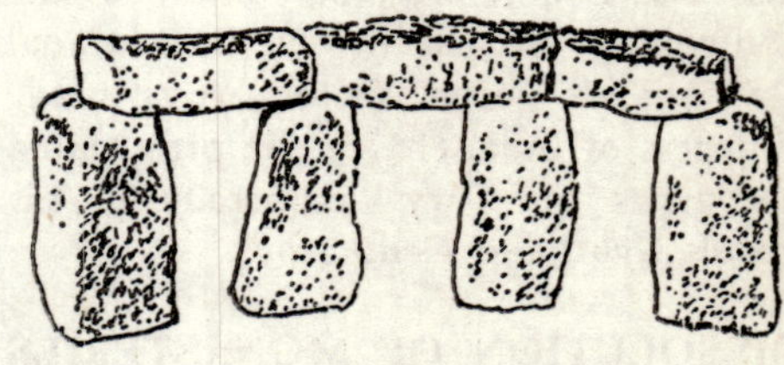

Dolmen

DOMESDAY BOOK, a record of the survey of a considerable part of England made for William the Conqueror in 1085—87 to show the fiscal state of the kingdom for purposes of taxation and assessing manpower. It contains information regarding ownership, area and state of cultivation of lands for various classes of the population.

DOMINIC, St (1170—1221), Spanish missionary and founder of the Dominican Order. During his preaching crusade against the Albigenses he conceived the idea of an order of preaching friars to combat heresy.

DOMINICA, a British colony in the Windward Islands, West Indies. Pop. (1958) 66,645; area 305 sq. miles. Copra, cocoa and bananas are produced.

DOMINICAN REPUBLIC, a republic in the West Indies, in the eastern two-thirds of the island of Hispaniola, in the Caribbean Sea. Pop. (1960) 2,994,000; area 19,332 sq. miles. The central portion is heavily forested, and there are four mountain ranges (Mt Tina 10,417 ft). Most of the population live in the northern plain. Primarily agricultural, the country produces sugar, coffee and cocoa. The capital is Santo Domingo the oldest city of the Americas (1946) 350,847. Discovered by Columbus in 1492, it became independent of Spain in 1821. It seceded from Haiti in 1844, and again came under Spanish rule from 1861—1865. From 1916 to 1922 it was under U.S. military occupation. In 1961 Rafael Trujillo was assassinated after 31 years of dictatorial rule.

DOMINICANS, a Catholic religious order founded in 1215 by St Dominic. Primarily a missionary order, with emphasis on teaching and preaching, it was influential in shaping the religious and secular thought of the Middle Ages. The order has provided many popes and cardinals; St Thomas Aquinas was a Dominican. The friars wore a black cloak, hence the name Black Friars. In Paris the headquarters were in the Rue St Jacques, to which they owe their French nickname 'Jacobins'.

DON, see River.

DONEGAL, a county in the northwest of the Irish Republic. Pop. (1961) 113,815; area 1865 sq. miles. Mostly mountainous, it has an indented coast and many offshore islands. Grazing, fishing and quarrying are the main occupations. Agriculture is limited. Donegal tweeds are famous.

DONETS BASIN (Donbas), a coal-producing region of the U.S.S.R., north of the Black Sea. It is a centre of heavy industry.

DONIZETTI, Gaetano (1797—1848), Italian operatic composer. He wrote some 70 operas, the most famous being *Lucia di Lammermoor*, *The Daughter of the Regiment* and *Don Pasquale*. Influenced by his contemporaries, Bellini and Rossini, he was a master of the melodious aria.

DONNE, John (1573—1631), English poet and preacher. He studied law and, after a period of profligate living in London, sailed with Essex to Cadiz, where he witnessed the defeat of the Spanish fleet. Brought up a Roman Catholic he turned Anglican, and entered the service of the Lord Keeper of the Seal, whose daughter he secretly married. When this was discovered, he was dismissed and lived in poverty for several years. In 1615 he took orders and became chaplain to the king, and Dean of St Paul's. His passionate eloquence made him the foremost preacher of his time. His poetry, neglected for the most part until the 1930s, is now held in the highest esteem. Its content, ranging from amorous lyrics to religious meditation, is as various as its style, and united only in its intense passion and complexity. The fusion of theology, philosophy and science with the other elements of his verse led to his being styled a 'metaphysical poet'.

DORÉ, Gustave (1832—83), French painter and illustrator of books. He made his name among his contemporaries with fantastic, sometimes grotesque, illustrations for the works of Balzac, Cervantes, Dante and Rabelais, among many others. He also illustrated an edition of the Bible, and painted some huge canvases of Biblical subjects. His works were popular in England and America.

DORSET, a county in southwest England, on the English Channel. Pop. (1961) 309,176; area 988 sq. miles. It has Purbeck marble and Portland stone quarries, and china and clay pits. The old towns of Sherborne and Shaftesbury, Corfe Castle and the prehistoric Maiden Castle, the scenic beauties of Lulworth Cove, the seaside resorts of Lyme Regis and Swanage, the unspoilt beauty of much of this farming county, and the fact that it is Hardy's Wessex, all serve to attract tourists. The county town is Dorchester.

DORTMUND, a city in North Rhine-Westphalia, West Germany, Pop. (1960) 637,105. In the Ruhr coalfield on the Ems Canal, it is an important industrial and commercial centre, producing coal, iron and steel products, and chemicals.

DOSTOIEVSKY, Fyodor (1821—81), Russian novelist. The son of a doctor who was murdered in 1839, and after a childhood troubled by the epilepsy that was to plague him all his life, Dostoievsky began his career as an army engineer, but soon turned to literature. His first novel, *Poor Folk* (1846), was an immediate success, but in 1849 he was arrested as a revolutionary and was actually facing a firing-squad when his death sentence was commuted to penal servitude in Siberia. This searing experience led to *The House of the Dead* (1861). His next work was *Crime and Punishment*, in which the hero Raskolnikov, feeling himself to be 'above good and evil', commits a motiveless murder to prove to himself that he can step outside the bounds of orthodox morality; he then confesses to the crime. At this stage Dostoievsky fled to Europe to escape his creditors. He never, however, succumbed to European influence; a slavophil, he regarded Russia as a country with a mission to replace the 'fake' Christianity of Europe with its own true Christianity. In *The Idiot* he contrasts intuitive intelligence and logical reasoning. His last and greatest novel, *The Brothers Karamazov*, treats all his favourite themes with consummate skill. Most Russian of all the Russian novelists, Dostoievsky wrote with deep insight of the problems of urban life seen through the eyes of the criminal, the underdog and the insane, and the struggle in the minds of his characters, torn between atheism and religion, reflects the conflict in his own.

DOUGLAS-HOME, Sir Alexander (1903—), British Conservative politician. He entered the House of Commons in 1931 and succeeded as 14th Earl of Home in 1951. He was made Minister of State, Scottish Office, in 1951, Secretary of State for Commonwealth Relations in 1955, and Foreign Secretary in 1960. On Macmillan's resignation in 1963, Lord Home renounced his title and succeeded him as Prime Minister until the general election in 1964.

DOUKHOBORS, see Dukhobors.

DOWN, a maritime county in Northern Ireland. Pop. (1961) 267,013; area 957 sq. miles. Much of the county is hilly and the Mountains of Mourne (Slieve Donard 2796 ft) 'sweep down to the sea' above the seaside resort of Newcastle. The area around Belfast is industrialised. Granite is quarried and linen manufactured. The county town is Downpatrick.

DOWNS, The, chalk ridges in southeast England. There are two ranges, North and South Downs, enclosing the fertile Weald and providing pasture for sheep, the Southdown breed being famous. In face of the necessities of war much downland was ploughed up. 'Downs' is a derivative of the French 'dune'.

DOXOLOGY, a short liturgical form of praise to God. The Greater Doxology is an expansion of the hymn of the angels in Luke ii. 14, whereas the Lesser Doxology (the *Gloria Patri*, or 'Glory be to God, etc.') has no direct scriptural basis but is a result of the Arian controversy.

DOYLE, Sir Arthur Conan (1859—1930), English novelist. He was the creator of the famous fictional detective, Sherlock Holmes. He also wrote historical novels and a book on spiritualism.

DRAKE, Sir Francis (*c.* 1540—96), English admiral and navigator. His most notable voyage was that in the Golden Hind; setting sail in December 1577 he rounded Cape Horn, sailed up the coast as far as California and then across the Pacific, returning home in September 1578, the first circumnavigation by an Englishman. During the voyage he plundered many Spanish ships, and for this the queen knighted him. In a raid on Cadiz in 1587 he 'singed the King of Spain's beard' by burning 33 ships in the harbour, thus delaying the Spanish Armada for a year. He fought well in engagements with the Armada in the English Channel, but was less successful in a counter-attack off the coasts of Portugal and Spain. He died on another voyage to the West Indies.

DRAMA, the representation of human activities and character by action on a stage before an audience. As a form of literature, the drama delineates human emotion and conflict, stresses certain values, and seeks to inculcate a point of view. Originally a religious ritual calculated to influence the gods or to celebrate their actions, it had its beginnings in ancient Greece in the tragedies of Aeschylus, Sophocles and Euripides, and the comedies of Aristophanes. In Christian Europe, first the miracle plays and later the morality plays preceded the emergence of dramas based on the ancient classics and the world of chivalry. The Elizabethan period in England was marked by an efflorescence of the drama with the appearance of Shakespeare, Marlowe, Ben Jonson, John Webster and John Ford. In France, Corneille, Racine and Molière brought the drama to a new peak of development. In later centuries Ibsen in Norway, Strindberg in Sweden, Pushkin, Chekhov and Turgenev in Russia, Schiller and Hauptmann in Germany, and Pirandello in Italy influenced the 20th century dramatists, Wilde, Shaw, Galsworthy, O'Casey T. S. Eliot, Brecht, Ionesco, Giraudoux and Anouilh. Important American playwrights include O'Neill, Maxwell Anderson, Tennessee Williams and Arthur Miller.

DRAVIDIAN, the name given to a group of non-Indo-Aryan peoples who now live mainly in southern India and northern Ceylon, with remnants in the hills of central India and Baluchistan. They appear to have entered India from the northwest in very early times and to have been driven south by the subsequent Aryan invaders. They speak languages which are held to be akin to Finnish and allied languages of Europe and Asia. The main races are the Tamils (Madras and Ceylon), Malayalam (Travancore-Cochin), Telugu (Andhra and Hyderabad) and Kanarese (Mysore, Bombay). Dravidian languages are written with circular characters, originally devised to avoid splitting the palm-leaves on which they were written. Tamil literature dates back to the 2nd or 3rd century A.D. The Indian aborigines whom the Dravidians conquered adopted the languages of their conquerors but can still be distinguished from the true Dravidians, who are of slighter build and browner skin than Aryan Indians.

DREAMS, images and experiences, often incoherent, which appear during sleep or a diminution of consciousness. All types of sensation are reproduced and the dreamer may be completely unaware that he is asleep. While the ancients believed that dreams foretold the future, modern psychology regards them as throwing light on the past and the personality of the dreamer. Dreams may express suppressed personal conflicts, hidden wishes, and apparently insoluble problems in a disguised or symbolic form. Recent research has established that periods of dreaming occur at fairly regular intervals during each night's sleep, and that they appear to be necessary to mental health. J. W. Dunne evolved a theory of time on the basis of the fact that some people dream of future events of which they could have no knowledge.

DREISER, Theodore (1871—1945), American novelist. An exponent of realism with penetrating insight into varied aspects of American life, he wrote *Sister Carrie*, *Jennie Gerhardt*, *The Financier* and his chief work, *An American Tragedy*.

DRESDEN, a city in Saxony on the Elbe, East Germany. Pop. (1960) 493,515. It has chemical, textile and light industries. The capital of Saxony until 1945, it was a centre of artistic and intellectual activity. The first European porcelain was made at Meissen, 20 miles away, from *c.* 1710; by convention the term 'Meissen' is restricted to the (finer) products of the 18th century, later work being called Dresden porcelain. The Meissen factory is still in production. There is a wide range of light industry, and general breweries.

DREYFUS, Alfred (1859—1935), a French army officer of Jewish extraction convicted of treason on flimsy evidence and sentenced to life imprisonment on Devil's Island. Anti-Semitic feeling was largely responsible for his conviction. The case divided France into two bitterly opposed camps. In 1906 Dreyfus was completely exonerated and reinstated in the army, in which he served as lieutenant-colonel in the First World War.

DRUG, a substance useful in the treatment of disease. It may be of plant, animal or mineral origin, or synthetic, and its action is usually predictable. A drug acts specifically against definite manifestations. Some stimulate, while others act as sedatives. Certain drugs are poisonous when taken in excess or under specific circumstances. Mental and physical dependence on a narcotic or stimulant may lead to varying stages and kinds of addiction. The use of synthetic drugs began in the 19th century with Ehrlich's arsenical compounds; other landmarks were the discovery of anti-malarial drugs more effective than quinine, of the sulphonamides (q.v.), and of penicillin and other antibiotics (q.v.). The pharmaceutical industry has expanded enormously in recent years, and extensive trials are essential to ensure that new drugs, of which there is a steady flow, have no unforeseen and disastrous side-effects such as thalidomide had on the pregnant, causing deformed births. Premature newspaper publicity for exaggerated claims of a drug's effectiveness is another modern problem.

DRYDEN, John (1631—1700), English poet, dramatist and critic. Dryden was the first writer of modern English prose, and a master of the hard-hitting heroic couplet. In his best-known poem, *Absalom and Achitophel* (1681), he attacked the Earl of Shaftesbury and his Whigs. In the same year he wrote *Religio Laici*, advocating a middle course in matters of religion, but on the accession of James II he was converted to Roman Catholicism, which he defended in *The Hind and the Panther* (1685); this conversion was to cost him his laureateship after the Revolution of 1688. Dryden's best work is his verse; his plays have no great merit, but the *Essay on Dramatic Poesy* established his reputation as a critic.

DRY ICE, the common name for solid carbon dioxide which is manufactured in compressed cakes for refrigeration purposes. It is a dense, snow-like substance with a temperature of —78·5 °C or lower. A block of 10 cu. in. weighs 45 lb. Dry ice is used in shipping perishable products, primarilly foodstuffs, over long distances.

DU BARRY, Marie Jeanne Bécu, Countess (1746—93), mistress of Louis xv of France. She exercised considerable influence at court. After a brief trip to England to pawn her jewels, she was guillotined by the Revolutionary Tribunal.

DU CHAILLU, Paul Belloni (1835—1903), French traveller and author. He spent many years travelling in equatorial West Africa, discovering rare birds and animals and studying the habits of the gorilla, and of the pygmies and other native tribes.

DUBLIN (Baile Atha Cliath), capital of the Irish Republic. Pop. (1961) 535,488. Situated on the River Liffey, it is the republic's chief port, and has a subsidiary port seven miles away at Dun Laoghaire (formerly Kingstown), which is also a seaside resort. The main features of Dublin are the wide streets and squares, with elegant Georgian buildings, some of which have been well maintained; the large Phoenix Park and St Stephen's Green; the university, still known as Trinity College, and the Guinness factory where stout is brewed. Dublin was the scene of the Easter Rebellion of 1916, in which the General Post Office and many other buildings were burnt out. The castle, symbol of alien rule, dates mostly from the 17th century.

DUCTLESS GLANDS, see Endocrinology.

DUKHOBORS (Doukhobors), a Russian sect founded about 1740. They deny the Holy Ghost, consider the Bible of minor importance, and hold land in common. Because of their pacifism they were persecuted by the government and in 1899 large groups emigrated to Canada. Their objection to taxes and the registration of births and deaths is a source of friction between them and the Canadian authorities. They have been disfranchised in British Columbia because they burned schoolhouses and paraded in the nude as a protest against the government.

DULUTH, a city and port at the westernmost point of Lake Superior, in Minnesota, U.S.A. Pop. (1960) 106,884. It is a great shipping port for the plentiful iron ore and wheat of Minnesota, and forms a conurbation with Superior, in neighbouring Wisconsin.

DUMAS, Alexandre, The Elder (1802—1870), French novelist and dramatist. He wrote nearly 300 works. His most famous works are *The Count of Monte Cristo*, *The Three Musketeers* and *The Black Tulip*. His drama, *Antony*, was the first attempt to write a social play.

DUMAS, Alexandre, The Younger (1824—95), French dramatist and novelist and natural son of the elder Dumas.

His most famous work is *La Dame aux camélias*, which typifies the social consciousness of all his writings. Most of his efforts were directed to drama and include *Le Demi-monde*, *Le Fils naturel* and *Monsieur Alphonse*.

DU MAURIER, George (1834—96), English artist and novelist. The son of a naturalised French refugee, he became a regular contributor to Punch, and illustrated works by Thackeray, Hardy, James and Meredith. He is the author of *Peter Ibbetson*, *Trilby* and *The Martian* His son, Sir Gerald (1873—1934) acted in a stage version of *Trilby*. His granddaughter, Daphne (1907—), wrote the successful novels *Jamaica Inn* and *Rebecca* and also a life of her father, *Gerald, a Portrait*.

DUMFRIESSHIRE, a border county in southwest Scotland. Pop. (1961) 88,423; area 1068 sq. miles. On Solway Firth, it is hilly in the north. Agriculture, livestock raising and dairy farming are the chief occupations. The county town is Dumfries. Gretna Green is on the border.

DUNDEE, a city in Angus, Scotland, on the Firth of Tay, beside the Tay Bridge. Pop. (1961) 182,959. An important seaport, it is the headquarters of a sealing and whaling fleet. In addition to shipbuilding and allied industries, it has important jute and linen mills; marmalade is a famous speciality.

DUNEDIN, a city of Otago, South Island, New Zealand. Pop. (1961) 105,053 It produces woollen goods and chemicals. As a seaport it has lost ground to Christchurch. Dunedin is the Celtic name of Edinburgh, and many of the inhabitants retain a Scottish accent.

DUNKIRK (Dunkerque), a seaport town in northern France, on the Straits of Dover. It was the scene of a large-scale evacuation of Allied troops to England in the final phase of the Battle of Flanders in 1940. Dunkirk was sold to France by Charles II.

DUNSTAN, St (*c.* 909—988), English prelate. He was abbot of Glastonbury, bishop of Worcester and London, and Archbishop of Canterbury. In addition to strengthening the power of the clergy, he wielded great political influence. His feast-day is May 19.

DUODECIMAL SYSTEM, the system of reckoning based on the number 12. Its advantage over the decimal system is that 12 can be divided into 2, 3, 4 and 6 equal parts.

DURBAN (Port Natal), a city in Natal province, Republic of South Africa, on the Indian Ocean. Pop. (1960) 655,370. It is a leading commercial port and resort town, and also has oil refineries and other industries.

DÜRER, Albrecht (1471—1528), German painter and engraver. The greatest German medieval artist, he executed copperplate engravings, woodcuts, drawings and oil and water-colour paintings. His famous works include *Feast of the Rosary*, *The Great Passion*, *Melancholia*, *The Adoration of the Magi* and *The Knight, Death and the Devil*.

DURHAM, a maritime county of northeast England. Pop. (1961) 1,517,039; area 1015 sq. miles. Consisting of the elevated Pennine moorland in the west and the lowlands in the south and west, it has coal and iron mines and deposits of minerals and building stone. Grains are grown and cattle bred. There is shipbuilding and other heavy industry, and an important chemical industry at

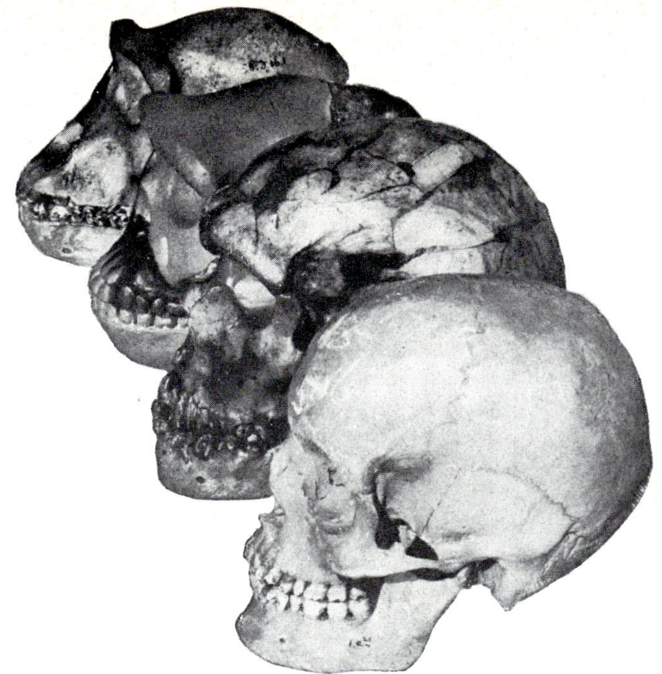

Comparisons of brain development showing skulls of gorilla, Java man, Neanderthal man and modern man. *Photo: British Museum (Natural History)*

Grasses make up a large proportion of monocotyledonous (q.v.) plants (q.v.). In the first photograph, of a common ryegrass, the parallel-veined and straight stems can clearly be seen. The second photograph shows the ultimate development in the grass family.
Photos: The Grassland Research Institute and India House

Perhaps the most unusual, beautiful and sought-after monocotyledonous flower is the orchid, of which two varieties that clearly show the characteristics of the group are shown here.

Photos: Georges Viollon and Camera Press

Close-up of a dicotyledonous (q.v.) blossom: a pink Oriental Poppy. *Photo: Lennart Nilsson*

Billingham. The county town is Durham, which has a cathedral, a university and Anglo-Saxon relics.

DURHAM, John George Lambton, 1st Earl of (1792—1840), English statesman. A leading parliamentary supporter of the Reform Bill of 1832, he was subsequently Governor-General of Canada and drew up a report, which marked a turning-point in the relations between Britain and her colonies, in which he recommended the union of Upper and Lower Canada, and the formation of an executive council responsible to a legislative assembly.

DÜSSELDORF, a city in North Rhine-Westphalia, West Germany, on the Rhine. Pop. (1960) 691,740. A commercial, cultural and financial centre, it has a busy port, and is a leading iron and steel town. It has a famous Academy of Fine Arts. The birthplace of Heine; Brahms, Schumann and Goethe all lived in Düsseldorf.

DUTCH GUIANA, see Surinam.

DUTCH WARS, a convenient name for three 17th-century naval wars between England and Holland, fought in a struggle for world commercial supremacy. The first (1652—54) was caused by Cromwell's Navigation Act of 1651, whereby goods from Asia, America and Africa could be brought to England in English ships only. At the head of the two greatest fleets in the world, Blake and Marten van Tromp met in four battles. In the final engagement, the first battle of the Texel, van Tromp was killed, the Dutch were defeated by Monk, and the war ended with the English in the ascendant.

In the second (1664—67) Charles II declared war on Holland, and the French went to their aid. The English defeated a combined fleet in the West Indies, but De Ruyter appeared in the Medway, and disaster was only just staved off by Albemarle. In the Treaty of Breda England gained New Holland, the colonies that had separated Virginia from New England, and renamed New Amsterdam New York; in exchange the Dutch gained Surinam in Guiana and other territories in Malaya.

The third war (1672—74) was declared by Charles under the terms of the secret Treaty of Dover, by which he had pledged himself, in return for money, to help France overrun Holland. The Dutch recaptured New York for a time, and indecisive battles were fought off Southwold and the Texel against De Ruyter and Cornelis van Tromp, who raised the blockade of Holland. Charles then left France to fight alone.

DVINA, see River.

DVOŘÁK, Anton (1841—1904), Czech composer. His music exhibits the influence of Bohemian folk melodies and the work of Richard Wagner. He wrote nine symphonies, the most famous of which are the Fourth and the Fifth *(From the New World).* His work includes chamber music, piano pieces, a violin concerto, operas and a *Te Deum.*

DYE, a substance which colours materials, especially fabrics. Dyes are found in plants, animals or minerals. Modern dyes are manufactured synthetically, especially from coal tar. Some dyes act directly, while others require the use of a dye fastener or mordant.

E

EAR, the organ of hearing. In man it consists of a skin-covered cartilaginous mass outside the head, which collects sound, and from which a canal leads inside to the ear-drum, behind which lies the air-filled middle ear. Beyond this is the inner ear, consisting chiefly of the snail-shaped cochlea, which transforms sound vibrations set up in the eardrum into nerve-impulses carried to the brain by the acoustic nerve, and there perceived as sound.

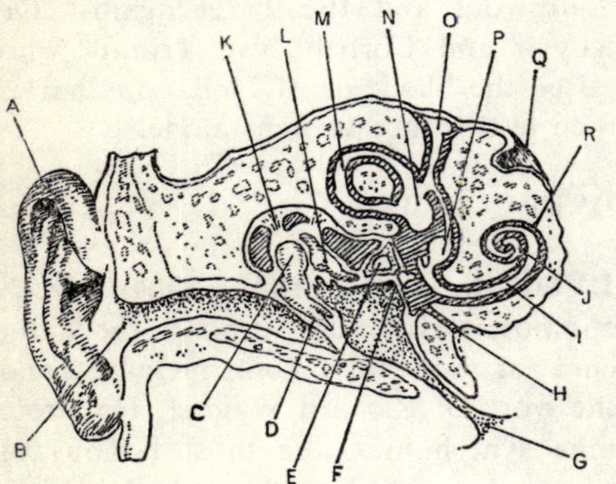

Human ear
A. Auricle B. External auditory meatus C. Malleus D. Tympanic membrane E. Stapes F. Fenestra cochleae G. Auditory tube H. Aqueduct of cochlea I. Cochlear duct J. Scala vestibuli K. Ligament L. Incus M. Semicircular duct N. Utricle O. Endolymphatic duct and sac P. Saccule Q. Internal auditory meatus R. Scala tympani

EARTH, the third planet from the sun in our solar system. The fifth largest in size, it is about 93,000,000 miles away from the sun. It revolves in an elliptical orbit at an average speed of 18½ miles per second. The rotation of the earth on its axis results in the time interval perceived as a day. The plane of the earth's equator tilts 23½° from the plane of its orbit, thus bringing about the formation of climatic zones and seasons. The earth's rotation has slightly flattened it at the poles. The earth's diameter is about 7926 miles and its circumference, 24,902 miles. Its central core extends more than half-way to the surface and is believed to consist of iron or nickel or both, either fluid or solid. The temperature increases with depth at the rate of about 20°F. per 1,000 ft. The surface of the earth is irregular, otherwise it would be covered entirely by water, which now comprises three-quarters of its area. The outer crust of the earth is about 20—30 miles in depth. Changes in it are due to storms, tides, earthquakes and volcanoes. The earth is believed to have been formed by a mass of whirling hot gases being flung off the sun and becoming first molten and then solid, about two thousand million years ago.

EARTHQUAKE, a violent disturbance of the earth's crust due to subterranean causes. Most earthquakes result from the slipping of huge areas of rock surface. Others are caused by volcanic eruptions. Violent shocks are usually preceded and followed by slight tremors. The preliminary tremors are caused by rapidly-travelling, longitudinal and transverse waves. The violent shock is brought about by the surface waves. Earthquake tremors are recorded by the seismograph. Some regions are more prone to seismic activity than others. Major earthquakes on record include those at Shensi, China

(1556, 830,000 killed), Calcutta (1737, 300,000), Lisbon (1755, 60,000), San Francisco (1906, 1500), Tokyo and Yokohama (1923, 142,807) and Agadir (1960, 12,000).

EAST ANGLIA, a 6th-century Anglo-Saxon kingdom in eastern England. It comprised the modern counties of Norfolk and Suffolk.

EASTER, the Christian festival commemorating the resurrection of Jesus. Easter is celebrated by the Western Church on the first Sunday following the first full moon after the spring equinox. The word 'Easter' is derived from the name of the goddess of spring, Eostre. Easter can fall on any of 35 days, and the proposal that it should be celebrated on the Sunday after the second Saturday in April each year failed for lack of public support.

EASTER ISLAND, an island in the southeastern Pacific Ocean belonging to Chile. Pop. *c.* 250; area 64 sq. miles. The island was discovered in 1722. The Norwegian ethnologist, Thor Heyerdahl in his book *Aku-Aku* records his theory that is was occupied by people from Peru *c.* A.D. 400, who were later joined by Polynesians; the two racial strata are distinguishable today and were noticed by early explorers. Heyerdahl's expedition were able to solve the problem of how the huge stone statues, up to 33 ft high, were transported and raised.

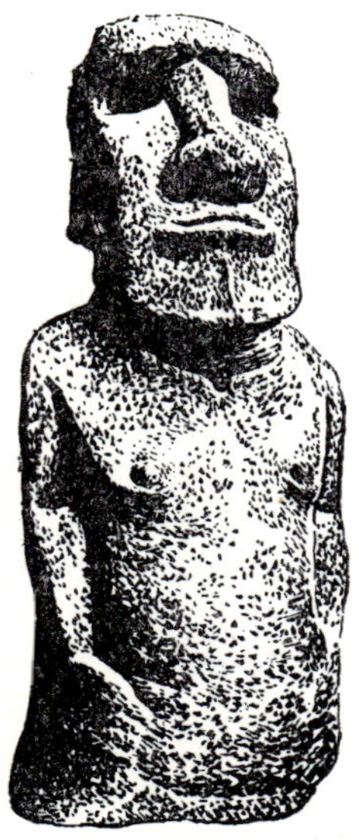

Easter Island stone statue

EASTMAN, George (1854—1932), American inventor and industrialist. He invented roll-film and a light portable camera called the Kodak. Eastman built a world industrial enterprise on his photographic developments and devoted over £60,000,000 to philanthropy, mostly to educational institutions.

ECLIPSE, the obscuration of a heavenly body by another coming between it and the observer. An eclipse of the sun occurs when the moon passes between it and the earth. In an eclipse of the moon, the earth comes between the moon and the sun. There are eclipses of varying degrees. In a total solar eclipse, the moon appears as a black disc on the face of the sun with only its corona visible. When a total eclipse of the moon occurs, the surface of the moon is darkened to a dull coppery colour. The next total eclipse of the sun will be visible in the British Isles on August 11, 1999. (Illus. overleaf).

ECONOMICS, the study of the general principles that govern the production and distribution of things of value, and of the social phenomena which arise from these activities. Among the more important subjects with which economics has to deal are: rents, wages and prices; price control; inflation; free trade, tariffs and quotas; competition, monopoly and restrictive practices; state and municipal enterprise and nationalisation; economic planning and laissez-faire; co-operatives;

money and the mechanism of exchange; balance of trade between countries; distribution of wealth between employers, employees and investors; unemployment and full employment; slump and boom; mass production, automation and redundancy.

The basic problems were formulated in Adam Smith's *Wealth of Nations* (1776). Ricardo held that the movement of wages and rents was governed by unalterable laws; J. S. Mill was the apostle of laissez-faire; J. M. Keynes advocated economic planning and the control of credit and currency to prevent recurrent crises. See also Communism.

Moon eclipsing the sun

ECUADOR, a republic in the northwest of South America. Pop. (1960) 4,298,000; area 104,506 sq. miles, excluding a large area of Amazonian territory which, under an arbitration award of 1842, went to Peru. From west to east the country consists of a hilly coastal strip, the Andes (Chimborazo, 20,600 ft), and humid jungles. The Andean region contains lofty volcanoes which often erupt. Ecuador has some gold, silver and petroleum and produces cocoa, bananas and coffee. It is the world's chief source of balsa wood and is rich in other valuable timber. The Spaniards conquered the region in 1532. From 1822—30 it was a member of the confederation of Colombia. There have been frequent dictatorships, and constant boundary disputes with Peru. The capital is Quito, pop. 1959 267,700. The principal city and chief port is Guayaquil (295,791).

EDDY, Mary Baker (1821—1910), the founder of Christian Science (q.v.) who discovered its healing power while recovering from a serious injury.

EDEN, Sir Anthony, 1st Earl of Avon (1897—), English politician. He entered parliament as a Conservative member in 1923, becoming Foreign Secretary in 1935 but resigning three years later because of his opposition to Chamberlain's appeasement policy. He again served as Foreign Secretary, in 1940—45, working closely with the U.S.A. and U.S.S.R. and helping to lay the foundation of the United Nations. In 1951 he returned to the post of Foreign Secretary, later becoming Deputy Prime Minister, and finally Prime Minister (1955). The Suez controversy a year later involved him in serious difficulties. He resigned in 1957. His memoirs, *Full Circle*, were published in 1960.

EDEN, Garden of, the garden of paradise described in Genesis ii. v. 8. Adam and Eve were banished from Eden for eating the forbidden fruit of the tree of knowledge.

EDINBURGH, capital of Scotland, on the Firth of Forth. Pop. (1961) 468,378. A centre of education, the city is also noted for its historical remains. It has a few industries including publishing, printing, foods and chemicals. Its northern suburb is the port of Leith. The city goes back to the 7th century A.D. The official capital of Scotland since 1437, it became the intellectual and literary capital in the latter half of the 18th century. The annual International Festival of Music and Drama was inaugurated in 1947. Holyrood Palace (15th—16th centuries) is joined by the Royal Mile to the Castle, which contains

Scotland's oldest building, St Margaret's Chapel. The University was founded in 1582, and its medical faculty has a high reputation. The old ten-storey buildings, which once housed the aristocracy, and the wynds (narrow alleys) contrast with the wide thoroughfare of Princes Street and the large, dignified squares, one designed by the Adam brothers, of the 'new' town.

EDINBURGH, Prince Philip, Duke of (1921—), consort of Queen Elizabeth II of Great Britain, whom he married in 1947. The great-great-grandson of Queen Victoria and the son of Prince Andrew of Greece, he was Prince Philip of Greece and of Denmark until 1947 when he became a British subject. He served in the Royal Navy during the Second World War, and was present at the battle of Cape Matapan. See Battenberg.

EDISON, Thomas Alva (1834—1931), American inventor. A persevering experimenter, he first devised improvements for the telegraph and tape-machine. His inventions include the phonograph, the incandescent electric lamp, a system for distributing electric current, and the carbon telephone transmitter. He played an important part in developing motion pictures, electric vehicles and synthetic chemical compounds. Edison held more than 1200 U.S. patents.

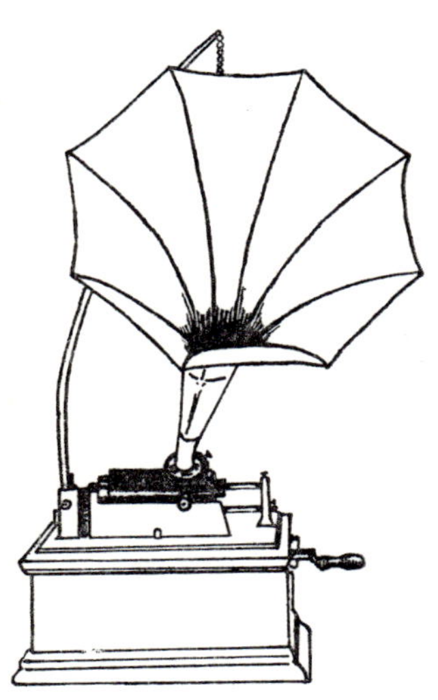

Edison's phonograph

EDMONTON, capital of Alberta, Canada. Pop. (1961) 337,568. At the head of navigation on the North Saskatchewan River, it is the starting point of the Alaska Highway and the gateway to the Canadian Northwest. Situated in a rich agricultural and coal mining area, it produces metal goods and dairy products and refines petroleum.

EDMUND, St (*c.* 1170—1240), English churchman. Famous as a religious teacher, he was designated by the Pope to preach the Sixth Crusade. He became Archbishop of Canterbury in 1234. A defender of the powers of English bishops, he became involved in a controversy with Henry III and Pope Gregory IX.

EDMUND II (Ironside; *c.* 981—1016), King of the English. He was accepted as ruler only by London, the rest of the country acknowledging Canute as king. Failing to gain possession of all England, he divided the country with Canute, receiving Wessex, East Anglia, Essex and London.

EDWARD (The Black Prince) (1330—76), eldest son of Edward III, proved himself a skilled and valiant warrior in the early campaigns of the Hundred Years War, capturing King John II of France at the battle of Poitiers (1356). He was made ruler (1363) over the English possessions in southern France, where a revolt broke out in 1369 which he tried unsuccessfully to suppress. Having contracted a fatal disease, he returned to England (1371) where he died.

EDWARD THE CONFESSOR (1004—66), King of England 1042—66. After the death of King Hardicanute, he was elected to the throne largely through the influence of the powerful Earl of Essex, Godwin. Edward proved to be a weak and ineffective king, devoutly religious, whose reign paved the way for the Norman conquest of England.

EDWARD THE ELDER (d. 924), English king, succeeded his father, Alfred the Great, in 899. He spent the greater part of his reign warring against the Danes and re-won most of England south of the Humber.

EDWARD THE MARTYR (d. 978), King of the English. Crowned in 975, he was murdered in 978, probably at the instigation of his stepmother, who wanted the throne for her own son, Ethelred.

EDWARD I (1239—1307), King of England 1272—1307. Son of Henry III, he was renowned as a lawgiver, instigating many legal and administrative reforms. He put down rebellions in Wales (1277, 1282—83) and incorporated it into England (1284). In 1295 he established an English administration in Scotland, but died in the campaign against Robert Bruce, who led the Scottish insurgents.

EDWARD II (1284—1327), King of England 1307—27. Soon after his accession to the throne, he came under the influence of Piers Gaveston who was intensely disliked by the barons of the kingdom. In 1312 the barons executed Gaveston and Edward's authority was further weakened by his defeat at Bannockburn at the hands of the Scots (1314). Isabella, Edward's wife, intrigued with her lover Roger de Mortimer and with the help of the barons imprisoned Edward (1326). He was compelled to abdicate in 1327 and was murdered five months later.

EDWARD III (1312—77), King of England from 1327—77. He ascended the throne after the murder of his father Edward II, put Mortimer to death (1330) and banished the queen-mother Isabella. In 1337 he went to war with the French over his rights to the French crown (the beginning of the Hundred Years' War). Together with his son, Edward the Black Prince, he had initial success, but in a subsequent war with the French king, Charles V, Edward lost almost all his possessions in France.

EDWARD IV (1442—83), King of England from 1461—83. Fighting for the House of York he defeated the Lancastrians under the weak and foolish Henry VI and made the king prisoner. In 1461 Edward was proclaimed king, but aroused the wrath of his followers by marrying (1464) Elizabeth Grey, from the House of Lancaster. Warwick the Kingmaker, who had put him on the throne, now turned against him, and restored Henry VI to the throne. After defeating the Kingmaker at Barnet and Henry's wife, Margaret of Anjou, at Tewkesbury, Edward regained his throne and had Henry murdered.

EDWARD V (1470—83), King of England. He succeeded his father Edward IV, in April 1483, but his uncle and protector Richard III, usurped the throne and is reported to have had him and his brother Richard put to death in the Tower of London.

EDWARD VI (1537—53), King of England from 1547—53. Ailing from birth, Edward himself had little say in the government as he was under the regency of his uncle Edward Seymour (Duke of Somerset), who was later replaced by John Dudley (Duke of Northumberland). During Edward's reign the Reformation made great advances in England, and the Prayer Book was published. The Duke of Northumberland managed to persuade him as he lay dying to nominate Lady Jane Grey as his successor in preference to his sisters Mary and Elizabeth.

EDWARD VII (1841—1910), King of Great Britain and Ireland. Eldest son of Victoria and Albert, he ascended the throne on January 22, 1901. In 1862 he married Alexandra, daughter of Christian IX of Denmark. Edward travelled extensively, visiting the U.S., Canada, Egypt, Palestine and India. His liking for France and his dislike of his nephew, the Kaiser, fitted in with governmental policy.

EDWARD VIII (1894—), King of England from Jan. 20 to Dec. 10, 1936. Edward ascended the throne in 1936 following the death of his father George V. His intended marriage with an American divorcee, Mrs. Simpson, met with opposition and Edward was forced to abdicate. He was succeeded by his brother, George VI, who conferred on him the title of the Duke of Windsor.

EGYPT (United Arab Republic), a republic in northeast Africa. Pop. (1961) 26,059,000; area 386,198 sq. miles. Most of the country is desert. The inhabited portion (13,600 sq. miles) consists of the Nile valley and its delta on the Mediterranean in the north. The annual rise of the Nile and irrigation make it possible to grow cotton, sugar-cane, rice, cereals and vegetables. Manganese, phosphates and petroleum are important products.

Upper and Lower Egypt were united *c.* 3100 B.C. by Menes, the founder of Memphis and the First Dynasty of the Old Kingdom (3100—2240 B.C.). Already at this early period hieroglyphic writing and most of the characteristic features of Egyptian rule and art are found. The Old Kingdom was the era of the great pyramid builders. After a period of confusion there was, in the Middle Kingdom (2050—1730), a revival of prosperity and artistic activity. Nubia was conquered and contact made with the East through Syria. The Kingdom then fell into the hands of foreign invaders of unknown origin, who provided the Hyksos kings that ruled Egypt down to 1580, when they were expelled. Under the New Kingdom (1580—663) Egyptian power had by 1480 reached to lands beyond the Euphrates. Prosperity returned, as evidenced by the tomb of Tutankhamen. An important figure of this age was the religious revolutionary Akhenaten, whose reforms and capital at Tell el-Amarna were short-lived. The empire collapsed *c.* 1200, and fell to the Assyrians in 663 B.C. Persia conquered Egypt in 525, and it fell to Alexander the Great in 332. The Ptolemies ruled the country until, on Cleopatra's death, it became a Roman province in 30 B.C. From A.D. 640—1517 it was controlled by various Arab dynasties until its annexation to the Ottoman Empire. Egypt, nominally Turkish, came under British protection from 1882—1922, when it became a kingdom, after the rise of a nationalist movement, the Wafd, under Zaghlul Pasha. The second and last king, Farouk, was deposed in 1952 by a military junta. From 1958—61, Egypt merged with Syria and Yemen to form the United Arab Republic, but Syria seceded in 1961. In 1948 and 1956, Egypt was involved in war with Israel. Nationalisation of the Suez Canal led to an unsuccessful Anglo-French attempt in 1956 to restore Western control of the Canal. The capital is Cairo (pop. 1959

3,035,000). Other large cities are Alexandria (1,416,000) and Port Said (226,000).

EHRLICH, Paul (1854—1915), German physiologist. The first to use chemicals for curing disease, he discovered the arsenical compounds salvarsan and neosalvarsan, of great value in the treatment of syphilis, and did much work at Frankfurt on cancer research. He received the 1908 Nobel Prize for physiology and medicine.

EINDHOVEN, a city in North Brabant, Netherlands. Pop. (1960) 166, 032. A communications centre, it also produces electrical and radio equipment and some textiles.

EINSTEIN, Albert (1879—1955), a mathematical physicist of German-Jewish extraction. Born in Bavaria, he went to Italy at the age of 15 and then to Switzerland, of which he became a naturalised citizen. After professorships at Zurich, Prague and Berlin, he became an American citizen in 1941, having moved to the United States after the Nazis had expelled him from his Berlin post. His formulation of the theory of relativity revolutionised modern science. He published his first theory of relativity in 1905 and his general theory in 1913. Einstein also made outstanding contributions to the quantum theory and carried out important investigations in thermodynamics, the Brownian movement and photochemistry. In 1939 he suggested the possibility of producing an atomic bomb to U.S. President Franklin D. Roosevelt. He was awarded the Nobel Prize for physics in 1921.

EISENHOWER, Dwight David (1890—), U.S. military commander and 34th President. Supreme commander of Allied forces in North Africa 1942—43, he subsequently controlled all Allied troops in Europe until the end of the Second World War. From 1945—48 he was U.S. Army Chief of Staff. In 1950—52 he was supreme commander of N.A.T.O. forces in Europe. As a candidate of the Republican party, he served as President from 1953 to 1960 when he retired.

ELBA, an Italian island in the Mediterranean, six miles off the west coast of Italy. Pop. 29,000; area 86 sq. miles. Napoleon I was exiled to this mountainous island in 1814. It has iron mines.

ELEANOR OF AQUITAINE (1122—1204), Queen of Henry II of England. Her marriage to Henry gave the English extensive areas in southern France and set off 300 years of warfare between the two countries. The mother of two English kings, Richard I and John, she participated in her sons' revolt against their father and was imprisoned until Henry's death in 1189, when she became regent for five years during Richard's participation in the Third Crusade.

ELECTRICITY, a form of energy manifested in a large variety of magnetic, chemical, thermal, visual and mechanical phenomena. Electrically-charged bodies either repel or attract each other, depending on the nature of the charge. Similar charges repel each other, while unlike charges attract. Bodies can be charged in this way by rubbing. The nature of a charge depends on the structure of the body's component atoms, in which positive and negative charges are normally balanced. Electrons charge an atom negatively. When they exceed the positive protons the atom is negatively charged, and when they are less the atom is positively charged. When charged particles such as electrons and protons are set in motion, an electric current results. Some metals, e.g. copper, permit a more rapid flow of electrons and are said to be good conductors. A current may be generated either by a chemical process such as immersing copper and zinc strips in diluted sulphuric acid, or by rotating a coil of wire in a magnetic field (dynamo). If a conductor offers considerable resistance to the flow of a current, heat results. If the heat is sufficiently intense, and the conductor strong enough to withstand the high temperature, light is produced. Running an electric current through a wire or iron rod establishes a magnetic field at both ends. This fact, and the utilisation of the principle that opposite magnetic poles attract and like-charged poles repel, made possible the development of the electric motor. Running a current through certain solutions conducting electricity (electrolysis) breaks down chemical compounds and makes it possible to separate and refine a number of metals and to electroplate others.

ELECTROMAGNETIC WAVES, a wide range of wave motions, consisting of a magnetic field accompanied by an electric field at right-angles to it, travelling at the speed of light (186,000 miles per second), and not requiring any known medium for their propagation. In order of increasing wavelength they are: gamma rays, X-rays, ultra-violet rays, visible light, infra-red (heat) rays, and radio (Hertzian) waves. They may be regarded as electromagnetic disturbances in transit. This was the accepted view until it was discovered, during experiments carried out between 1900—20, that in radiant heat and in photo-electric effect, light behaves like a stream of particles and not like waves, for there is a point below which the energy of electromagnetic waves cannot be further subdivided. On the other hand, it was found in 1927 that electrons, protons, etc., can behave as waves. The irreducible amount of energy involved whenever light interacts with anything was found to depend on the wavelength. This quantum (see Quantum Theory) is called a photon and regarded in theory as one of the fundamental particles, while every fundamental particle is regarded as a manifestation of electromagnetic waves, although it is convenient to continue to call them particles. Their behaviour is predicted and described by certain equations, and it is of minor importance whether they are really particles or waves. Thus, at this frontier, physics merges into higher mathematics.

ELECTRON, a fundamental particle with a negative electrical charge, and about 1/1840th of the mass of a proton or neutron. Electrons are regarded as moving round the nucleus of an atom in orbit or, where there are many of them, in concentric orbits (or shells). Radium and uranium, for example, have seven shells. The number of electrons, which is equal to the number of protons in the nucleus, is called the atomic number and is used to classify the elements. The number of electrons in the outermost shell determines the valency (q.v.) of an atom. The study of the behaviour of electrons in the atom is atomic physics.

Electrons are also found in motion away from atoms; e.g. a cathode ray is a stream of electrons, and so, usually, are beta rays, which are emitted from the nucleus in certain circumstances (see Isotope). Electrons are expelled from solids by light, heat, electric fields, etc.

ELECTRONICS, the branch of electrical engineering concerned with the movement of a stream of electrons (see Atom) through a vacuum or a gas or in a semiconductor, and the devices operated in this fashion. It covers a wide range of uses from the simple radio valve to instruments for telemetering data collected by space satellites. The latest development is the transistor, which substitutes a solid for a vacuum or gas.

ELEMENTS, substances which cannot be broken down into other substances by normal chemical action. The nature of an element is determined by the structure of its atom (see Atom). There are 92 elements in nature and 11 more have been created artificially by nuclear fission. Elements are designated by their atomic weight (in relation to oxygen fixed at 16) and atomic number (the number of protons in the nucleus of each atom). A number of elements have the same atomic number but differ in atomic weight. The atomic number determines an element's position in the periodic table, in which elements are grouped by families possessing similar properties (see Chemistry).

Name	*Symbol*	*Atomic number*	*Atomic weight*	*Special use*	*Special properties*
Actinium	Ac	89	227.05	—	Radioactive
Aluminium	Al	13	26.97	Kitchenware; construction	Light, malleable, ductile, good conductor
Americium	Am	95	241.00	—	Radioactive; transuranic
Antimony	Sb	51	121.76	Printing type; bearings	Brittle, expands as solidifies
Argon	A	18	39.944	Electric bulbs	Inactive gas
Arsenic	As	33	74.91	Insecticides	Crystalline solid
Astatine	At	85	210.00	—	—
Barium	Ba	56	137.36	Pigments	Soft metal; salts
Berkelium	Bk	97	243.00	—	Transuranic
Beryllium	Be	4	9.02	Alloys	Lightest rigid metal
Bismuth	Bi	83	209.00	Fusible alloys	Low melting point
Boron	B	5	10.82	Medical compounds	Powder
Bromine	Br	35	79.916	Important compounds	Poisonous liquid
Cadmium	Cd	48	112.41	Alloys	Lustrous metal
Caesium	Cs	55	132.91	Electronics	Unstable
Calcium	Ca	20	40.08	Important compounds	Alkali earth; malleable, ductile
Californium	Cf	98	244	—	Transuranic
Carbon	C	6	12.01	Fuel; industry; important compounds	Solid
Cerium	Ce	58	140.13	Alloys	Pyrophoric; rare earth
Chlorine	Cl	17	35.457	Industry	Poisonous gas
Chromium	Cr	24	52.01	Steel alloys	Hard metal
Cobalt	Co	27	58.94	Alloys	Hard metal
Copper	Cu	29	63.57	Machinery; utensils	Malleable, ductile; good conductor
Curium	Cm	96	242.00	—	Radioactive; transuranic
Dysprosium	Dy	66	162.46	—	Rare earth
Einsteinium	E	99	255	—	—
Erbium	Er	68	167.2	—	Rare earth
Europium	Eu	63	152.00	—	Rare earth
Fermium	Fm	100	255	—	Transuranic
Fluorine	F	9	19.00	Compounds; fuel	Poison gas
Francium	Fr	87	223.00	—	Alkali metal
Gadolinium	Gd	64	156.90	—	Rare earth
Gallium	Ga	31	69.72	—	Hard metal
Germanium	Ge	32	72.60	Electronics	Rare metal
Gold	Au	79	197.2	Coinage; alloys	Malleable, ductile
Hafnium	Hf	72	178.6	—	—

Name	*Symbol*	*Atomic number*	*Atomic weight*	*Special use*	*Special properties*
Helium	He	2	4.003	Balloons	Light gas
Holmium	Ho	67	164.94	—	Rare earth
Hydrogen	H	1	1.008	Compounds; acids; fuel gases	Lightest element
Indium	In	49	114.76	Bearings	Ductile
Iodine	I	53	126.92	Antiseptic	Solid
Iridium	Ir	77	193.1	Alloy	Hard metal
Iron	Fe	26	55.84	Most important metal	Metal of varying strength
Krypton	Kr	36	83.7	Airport lights	Inert gas
Lanthanum	La	57	138.92	Optical glass	Rare earth
Lawrencium	—	103	—	—	—
Lead	Pb	82	207.21	Alloys; pipes	Soft metal
Lithium	Li	3	6.940	Fireworks	Lightest metal
Lutetium	Lu	71	174.99	—	Rare earth
Magnesium	Mg	12	24.32	Industry; medicine	Light metal
Manganese	Mn	25	54.93	Alloys	Hard metal
Mendeleevium	Mv	101	256	—	—
Mercury	Hg	80	200.61	Instruments	Liquid metal
Molybdenum	Mo	42	95.95	Steel alloys	Metal
Neodymium	Nd	60	144.27	Ceramics	Rare earth metal
Neon	Ne	10	20.183	Red light	Inert gas
Neptunium	Np	93	239	—	Transuranic
Nickel	Ni	28	58.69	Alloys	Non-rusting metal
Niobium	Nb	41	92.91	—	—
Nitrogen	N	7	14.008	Industry	—
Nobelium	No	102	253	—	—
Osmium	Os	76	190.2	Electric Light filaments	Hard metal
Oxygen	O	8	16.000	Welding	Vital gas
Palladium	Pd	46	106.7	Alloys	Heavy metal
Phosphorus	P	15	30.98	Phosphates	Inflammable
Platinum	Pt	78	195.23	Industry	Strong metal
Plutonium	Pu	94	239	—	Transuranic
Polonium	Po	84	210	—	Highly radioactive
Potassium	K	19	39.096	Compounds	Inflammable
Praseodymium	Pr	59	140.92	Ceramics	Rare earth
Promethium	Pm	61	147	—	Rare earth
Protactinium	Pa	91	231	—	—
Radium	Ra	88	226.05	Medicine	Radioactive
Radon	Rn	86	222	Medicine	Radioactive gas
Rhenium	Re	75	186.31	Catalyst	Rare earth
Rhodium	Rh	45	102.91	Platinum alloy	Heavy metal
Rubidium	Rb	37	85.48	—	Inflammable
Ruthenium	Ru	44	101.7	—	Rare heavy metal
Samarium	Sm	62	150.43	—	Rare earth
Scandium	Sc	21	45.10	—	Rare metal
Selenium	Se	34	78.96	Physics; chemistry	Powder
Silicon	Si	14	28.06	Iron alloys; transistors	Powder
Silver	Ag	47	107.880	Coinage; tableware; alloys	Malleable, ductile; best conductor
Sodium	Na	11	22.997	Important salts	Inflammable, light metal
Strontium	Sr	38	87.63	Salts	Light metal
Sulphur	S	16	32.06	Industry	Component of many minerals
Tantalum	Ta	73	180.88	Electronics	Absorbs gases
Technetium	Tc	43	99	—	—

Name	*Symbol*	*Atomic number*	*Atomic weight*	*Special use*	*Special properties*
Tellurium	Te	52	127.61	Alloys	Non-tarnish
Terbium	Tb	65	159.2	—	Rare earth
Thallium	Tl	81	204.39	Vermin poison	Soft metal
Thorium	Th	90	232.12	Atomic energy	Radioactive
Thulium	Tm	69	169.4	—	Rare earth
Tin	Sn	50	118.70	Alloys; plating	Malleable, flexible
Titanium	Ti	22	47.90	Anti-rust; strong alloy	Metal
Tungsten	W	74	183.92	Strong alloy	Acid-resistant
Uranium	U	92	238.07	Atomic energy	Radioactive, source of radium
Vanadium	V	23	50.95	Alloy	Metal
Wolfram	See Tungsten				
Xenon	Xe	54	131.3	—	Inert gas
Ytterbium	Yb	70	173.04	—	Rare earth
Yttrium	Y	39	88.92	—	Rare earth
Zinc	Zn	30	65.38	Industry; anti-rust	Malleable
Zirconium	Zr	40	91.22	Ceramics	Metallic powder

ELGAR, Sir Edward (1857—1934), English composer and Master of the King's Musick, 1924—34. His most important composition was the *Dream of Gerontius*. Elgar's other works include an oratorio, the *Enigma Variations*, the tone-poem *Falstaff*, a violin concerto, two symphonies and the *Pomp and Circumstance* marches.

ELIOT, George (Marian Evans; 1819—1880), English novelist. Her most famous works are *Adam Bede*, *The Mill on the Floss*, *Silas Marner* and *Middlemarch*. The combination in her novels of wide-ranging erudition, quiet humour and deep insight make her one of England's greatest novelists.

ELIOT, Thomas Stearns (1888—1965), English poet and critic, of American birth, who came to England in 1914. He first gained fame with his poem about the intellectual sterility of the period following the First World War, *The Waste Land*. His other major poetic works are *Ash Wednesday* and *Four Quartets*. His verse plays, including *Murder in the Cathedral*, *The Cocktail Party* and *The Confidential Clerk*, were very successful. Through his critical works, Eliot has exercised an immense influence over his contemporaries. He received the Nobel Prize for literature in 1948.

ELISABETHVILLE, the capital of the former Katanga province of the Congo Federal Republic. Pop. (1960) 185,000. It is the mining capital of the Congolese Copperbelt where, in addition to copper, cobalt, uranium and radium are mined. Situated well over a thousand miles from the nearest port, it has a choice of three rail outlets to the sea, to Beira, Lobito and Cape Town, in East, West and South Africa respectively.

ELIZABETH I (1533—1603), Queen of England and Ireland from 1558, and daughter of Henry VIII and Anne Boleyn. After her mother had been beheaded, she, together with her half-sister Mary, was declared illegitimate. Elizabeth lived a secluded life of study, but this did not prevent her from being thrown into the Tower by Mary in 1554, on suspicion of being implicated in Wyatt's rebellion. She survived, however, to take over from her sister a country which had lost all its overseas possessions and was at a low ebb. She refused Philip II's offer of marriage, restored Protestantism, and issued the Thirty-Nine Articles. Under the guidance of Sir William Cecil (Lord Burghley) she helped the Low Countries against Spain and the Huguenots against their Catholic King. She made Mary Queen of Scots, married to Francis II of France, drop her claim to the English throne and later imprisoned her (1568) until her execution in 1587, which Elizabeth is thought to have opposed. Philip then launched his Armada, which was defeated by Lord Howard of Effingham and his distinguished band of sea-captains, Drake, Raleigh, Hawkins and Frobisher. In 1559 Elizabeth had publicly declared that she would never marry, and she used the resultant situation to play off one royal suitor against another, and to amuse herself with a string of favourites, chief of whom were Robert Dudley, Earl of Leicester, and Robert Devereux, Earl of Essex (who was executed in 1601). The Elizabethan age saw a remarkable national resurgence, not least of all in literature, which Shakespeare, Marlowe, Spenser and Sir Philip Sidney raised to new heights.

ELIZABETH II (1926—), Queen of Great Britain. In 1947 she married Prince Philip, Duke of Edinburgh, and they have four children: Prince Charles (heir apparent to the throne, b. 1948), Princess Anne (b. 1950), Prince Andrew (b. 1960) and Prince Edward (b. 1964). She ascended the throne in 1952 on the death of her father George VI.

EL PASO, a city in western Texas, on the Rio Grande which forms the border with Mexico. Pop. (1960) 276,687. It is a port of entry from Mexico, and the centre of a copper mining area, cattle range and rich agricultural region. There is a large Mexican population living in Spanish-style homes; the tourist industry is important.

EL SALVADOR, a Central American republic on the Pacific coast. Pop. (1960) 2,613,000; area 7722 sq. miles. A country of mountains and high plateaux, it is predominantly agricultural and produces coffee, cotton, rice and balsam. Most of the people are mestizos. The region was conquered by Spain in 1525. After the dissolution of the Central American Federation, of which it had been a member, in 1839, El Salvador became independent. The capital is San Salvador (pop. 1959 221,708).

ELY, ISLE OF, see Cambridgeshire.

EMBROIDERY, once the needle was invented, provided the stimulation to pass the limits of utility and to indulge in decoration. The art of using silks and wools of brilliant hues to create design on cloth was practised in Greek and Roman times in much the same way as it is today. Earliest known examples come from Egypt of the 15th century B.C. England was renowned for its embroidery, and the embroideries of Elizabethan times show much beauty in design.

EMERSON, Ralph Waldo (1803—82), American philosopher, essayist and poet. One of the founders of the transcendentalist school of philosophy, he first won attention with his tractate, *Nature.* He made two trips to England and published *English Traits.* His works include *Representative Men, The Conduct of Life* and *Sovereignty of Ethics.*

EMMET, Robert (1778—1803), Irish patriot. With exiled Irishmen on the Continent, he plotted a rebellion in Ireland with Napoleon's help. His attempts to seize Dublin Castle failed and he was executed.

EMPEDOCLES (*c.* **500—430** B.C.), Greek philosopher. His theory that the world consists of four elements, earth, air, fire and water, is expressed in his poetic works. These elements are brought together by Love and separated by Strife. He was also the first to propound a theory of four 'humours' to account for differences in human temperament. Only fragments of his work remain, but many legends grew up about his miracles and final apotheosis; he is also said to have thrown himself into Mt Etna.

EMPIRICISM, the philosophical theory which emphasises the role of experience as against that of reasoning in the learning process, adopting a commonsense approach to the problems of philosophy. The leading Empiricists were Locke, Berkeley and Hume.

ENDOCRINOLOGY, the study of the endocrine (or ductless) glands and the hormones they secrete. The hormones (Gk stimulators), are chemical messengers secreted directly into the bloodstream and circulating to all parts of the body, acting as co-ordinators of the whole bodily mechanism, and thus supplementing the functions of the nervous system. A slight departure from the normal amount of any of the numerous hormones secreted by the mentally and physically healthy may have serious effects. Hormones may operate directly, or through their action on other endocrine glands. They control growth, the metabolism of carbohydrates, proteins and fats, the salt balance in the body, its fluid content, sexual development, etc.

The most important is the pituitary, situated above the roof of the mouth, which controls all the other glands; it seems to link the chemistry of the body with the nervous system and the emotions (see Psychosomatic Medicine). It has two lobes, of which the anterior is by far the more influential. Overactivity causes overgrowth and underactivity may lead to dwarfism, fat, timidity and lassitude. The thyroid lies astride the windpipe and secretes iodine. Excess causes a quickened pulse, restlessness and insomnia, and can also lead to exophthalmic goitre. Thyroid activity is increased by anxiety and overexcitement, but tends to decrease with age, producing a characteristic forgetfulness, sensitivity to cold and dulling of the mind. The parathyroids lie behing the thyroid and control calcium, which builds bones and acts as a sedative, a deficiency leading to fear and depression. The pancreas secretes insulin, which affects the carbohydrate metabolism, and is so important in diabetes. The adrenals lie on top of each kidney. The outer part (cortex) controls the salt level, the inner (medulla) produces adrenalin which constricts the blood vessels and prepares the body for 'fight or flight'. The sex glands or gonads (ovaries and testes), in addition to being concerned with all forms of sexual development, hold the balance between aggression, initiative and cowardice. Little is known about the functions of the pineal gland and the thymus, which may not be endocrine.

ENERGY, the power to do work. Mechanical energy is the product of a force moving through a specified distance. Energy is either kinetic, i.e. due to motion; or potential, i.e. stored in a system at rest, such as a coiled spring or an object raised to a height. The sources of energy may be electrical, mechanical, chemical, thermal or atomic. All forms of energy may be transformed into one another. According to the theory of relativity, energy and mass are also sometimes interchangeable.

ENGLAND, the largest territorial division of the island of Great Britain, the heart of the United Kingdom. Pop. (1961) 43,874,661; area 43,487 sq. miles. The granite Cheviot Hills mark the northern border of the country. The Pennine Chain of hills extends southward through the centre of northern England, to meet the Midland Plateau at the Trent River. West of the Pennines, separated by the Eden valley, are the Cumbrian Mountains of the Lake District. The Cotswold Hills are in the southwest, between the lower Severn and the upper Thames valleys. East Anglia is flat, and there are moorlands in Devon, Somerset and Yorkshire.

The main features of English agriculture are livestock farming (sheep and cattle) in the west and arable (wheat and barley predominating) in the lowlands, with many specialities such as fruit in Hereford, the Vale of Evesham and Kent (which also grows hops), potatoes and bulbs in the Fens and Lancashire, and spring flowers and vegetables in Cornwall and the Scillies.

The early industrialisation of England was based on coal, now mined chiefly in Yorkshire, Durham and the East Midlands, and iron-ore, from Scunthorpe (Lincs.) and Corby (Northants.), and to a lesser extent Cumberland and north Lancashire. The only other mineral of particular importance is china clay, from Devon and Cornwall. Industrial conurbations are found on Tyneside (Newcastle, shipbuilding); Teeside (iron and steel); the West Riding of Yorkshire (high-grade steel at Sheffield and Rotherham, woollens at Bradford, clothing at Leeds); the Midlands (vehicles and machine tools at Coventry, steel tubes at Chesterfield, pottery in north Staffordshire, footwear at Leicester and Northampton, knitwear at Leicester, Mansfield and Northampton, brewing at Burton, steel at Corby and Scunthorpe); cotton industries in Lancashire; and London, which manufactures a very wide range of goods. Aircraft are made near Gloucester and elsewhere. The main ports are Liverpool (for North America), Newcastle (for Scandinavia and the Baltic), Bristol (for the West Indies) and London. The chemical industry is widespread; one centre is in Durham. Shipping, fishing and tourism are other important industries.

The capital is London (pop. 1961; administrative county, 3,195,114; Greater London, 8,171,902). Other leading cities include: Birmingham (1,105,651), Liverpool (747,490), Manchester (661,041) and Leeds (510,597).

Julius Caesar landed in England in 55—54 B.C. The Romans ruled England from the 1st century B.C. to the 5th A.D. In the north they constructed a series of forts against the Picts in Caledonia (Scotland). Roman influence did not penetrate deeply and did not eliminate the Celtic language. In the 5th century, the Angles, Saxons and Jutes, tribes from northern Germany, overran the area and forced the aboriginal Britons to migrate westward, northward and to the northwest coast of Gaul (France). The Anglo-Saxons established a number of kingdoms, traditionally believed to have been seven (Northumbria, Mercia, East Anglia, Essex, Kent, Sussex and Wessex). In about 600, the Christianisation of England began. The English peasants were unable to ward off the attacks of Danish Vikings who first invaded England in 787. By 878 the Danes ruled nearly all the kingdoms. Alfred, King of Wessex (871—99), defeated them, leaving them with the eastern portion of the island. The foundations of a new political organisation were laid during his reign. In 1013 the Danes conquered England and their king, Canute, proclaimed himself ruler of the entire country (1014—35). In

1042 the Anglo-Saxon dynasty under Edward the Confessor was restored to the throne. In 1066 William Duke of Normandy invaded England and brought Norman-French law and customs to the country. The Normans introduced the French language and a feudal society. In 1154 Henry II of the Plantaganet dynasty, a great-grandson of William the Conqueror, ascended the throne. He had acquired large feudal principalities in France through marriage and inheritance. The dynasty's affairs in France involved England in wars with France for 300 years. Henry II's son, Richard I (the Lion-Hearted), participated in the Third Crusade, and spent most of his reign away from England. In 1215 the nobles forced his brother and successor, John, to sign the Magna Carta which specified that they were not to be taxed without their consent and provided for their participation in the enactment of laws. The great barons began to take part in the King's Council and in 1265 the lesser nobles and the towns were represented, thus laying the basis of the future parliament. In 1202 John lost his estates in France and was left with territory in England only. This furthered the crystallisation of a national English consciousness. In 1282 Edward I conquered Wales and from that time the heir to the throne of England has been called the Prince of Wales. His son, Edward II, was defeated by the Scots at Bannockburn. In the reign of Edward III, who demanded the crown of France, the Hundred Years' War (1338—1453) between England and France broke out. This devastating war won England large parts of France by the battles of Crécy (1346) and Poitiers (1356) in the middle of the 14th century and, at the beginning of the 15th century, the crown of France. It ended, however, in an English defeat, leaving them with only the city of Calais on the Continent, and that reverted to France in 1558. The fact that the Papacy had established its seat at Avignon in France, and its dependence on the French king was among the many causes that aroused English opposition to the Catholic church. The Lollards, led by an Oxford theologian, John Wycliffe, rejected the Pope's authority and prepared the way for the Protestant Reformation in England. A dispute between the royal houses of Lancaster (whose emblem was a red rose) and York (a white rose) led to the Wars of the Roses (1455—1485) from which Henry Tudor (Henry VII) emerged victorious as the founder of a new dynasty. The Tudors ruled England (until 1603) with firmness, without formally offending parliament. It was during the reign of Henry VII that John Cabot was granted royal permission to set out on a voyage of exploration and in 1497 he reached North America. Henry VIII (1509—47) freed the English church from Papal authority and, in 1534, parliament by the Act of Supremacy proclaimed the king head of the Anglican Church and transferred to him the properties of the monasteries. His daughter, Queen Mary, ruthlessly endeavoured to restore the Catholic faith. Her sister, Elizabeth I (1558—1603), established Anglicanism as the English state religion. The English defeat of the Spanish Armada in 1588 laid the foundation for England's rule of the seas. English trade expanded, and commercial companies with monopolistic privileges came into being. The most important was the East India Company which ultimately secured India for the Crown. In the Elizabethan period, England became a world power and literature and the arts flourished. For subsequent history see Great Britain.

ENGLISH CHANNEL, the sea separating England and France. It is 21 miles

Water plants include some of the most beautiful, especially when seen against the rich green of the large leaves. Shown here is a water lily and a lotus blossom.

Photos: Les Williams and Datta B. Khopher

The fruits (q.v.) of flowering plants come in a tremendous variety of forms. Apples, pictured here, are accessory fruits.

Photo: Camstock

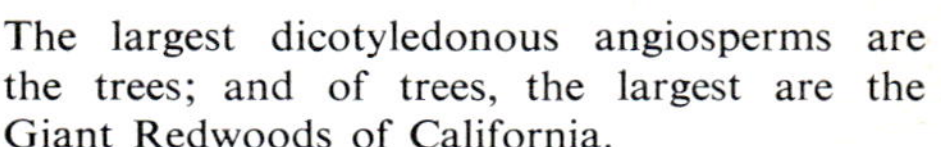

The largest dicotyledonous angiosperms are the trees; and of trees, the largest are the Giant Redwoods of California.

Photo: United States Information Service

Many plants have defence mechanisms designed to protect them. The stinging nettle's 'stings', shown in this close-up, are an effective deterrent to any animal that might damage the plant by coming too close. *Photo: Lennart Nilsson*

Thousands of plants serve man in thousands of ways. An example is the rubber tree from which latex, the basis of rubber, is made. *Photo: Horace Bristol*

wide at its narrowest (Dover to Cape Gris-Nez) and 280 miles long. The Seine River enters it from France. It contains the Channel Islands.

ENGLISH LANGUAGE, the language spoken in the British Isles, Australia, New Zealand, much of Canada and the Republic of South Africa, numerous parts of the British Commonwealth, and in the U.S.A. It is the language of 290,000,000 people. Important as an auxiliary language, it is studied throughout the world. Essentially derived from Low German, it was brought to Great Britain by the Angles, Saxons and Jutes who invaded the island in the 5th and subsequent centuries. It developed four main dialects, the Northumbrian, Mercian, Kentish and West Saxon (or Wessex), and the last of these eventually came to dominate the rest; dialects, and especially dialectal differences of pronunciation, are still a marked feature of the language. Its enrichment by the Norman Conquest led to the wealth of synonyms which is another major feature. English bears a closer resemblance to Dutch, Flemish and Frisian than to High German and the Scandinavian tongues. It has borrowed from many languages and reveals, in particular, French, Latin and Greek influences. Its development may be divided into three periods: Anglo-Saxon or Old English until about 1150; Middle English, up to about 1450; and Modern English. Old English and Modern English are almost two different languages. Since the spelling has changed more slowly than the pronunciation, English orthography is confusing.

ENGLISH LITERATURE, which for the non-specialist may be regarded as commencing with the *Canterbury Tales* (*c.* 1380), had been developing for seven centuries before Chaucer's day; and from that period both epics, e.g. *Beowulf*, dealing with the pre-Christian legends brought over by the Anglo-Saxon invaders, and religious poems survive. The first native English works are Caedmon's *Paraphrase of the Scriptures* and Cynewulf's *The Dream of the Rood*. Inaugurated by King Alfred, who had translated various religious works from the Latin, the *Anglo-Saxon Chronicle* was compiled by successive generations of monks from *c.* 890 to *c.* 1066, and gives a history of England from mythical times down to the Conquest. The Norman-French refashioned the language of England but did little for its literature. A contemporary of Chaucer, William Langland, wrote his popular and moralistic *Piers Plowman* in alliterative verse, which was a return to the favourite Old English verse-form. The Morality plays, in which allegorical figures illustrate the struggle of virtue and vice, belong to the 15th and 16th centuries, as do the best ballads, especially the border ballads on which Walter Scott drew.

The first major prose work is Malory's *Morte d'Arthur* (1485), mostly adapted from French medieval prose romances; while Spenser's *Faerie Queene* (1590—96) is the last of the medieval verse romances, an elaborate allegory in Spenserian stanzas of nine lines, the last an alexandrine 'that like a wounded snake drags its slow length along'. In the Golden Age of English literature ushered in by the Renaissance and the Reformation, the intoxicating rhetoric of the young Marlowe's plays has naturally tended to be overshadowed by the works of his great contemporary, Shakespeare; but his plays merit a high place. Other main features of Elizabethan drama were the 'revenge' tragedies of Kyd and Webster, the realistic comedies of Dekker and the savage, even morose, wit of Ben Jonson's comedies.

English Literature

The impact of the new learning on the old is seen in the complex poetry of the metaphysical school (1590—1650), and also in Milton; while lyric poetry reached perfection in Andrew Marvell and in Herrick, the chief of the 'Cavalier' poets. Prose works of the 16th and 17th centuries include Francis Bacon's *Essays* and philosophical treatises, Robert Burton's *Anatomy of Melancholy* and Sir Thomas Browne's *Urn Burial* and *Religio Medici.*

In the year of the Restoration (1660) Samuel Pepys began his diary and at about the same time Bunyan began, in prison, his autobiography, which was followed in 1678 by *The Pilgrim's Progress.* More typical of the post-Restoration Augustan age, in which a classical simplicity of language was the aim, were the satirical verse and prose of Dryden, Pope and Swift, the brittle, amoral comedies of Congreve, Wycherley and Farquhar, and the elegant essays of Addison and Steele, written for the new prosperous middle class. Dr Johnson, Gibbon and Hume were other great figures of the age.

Defoe established the English novel with his publication in 1719, when he was already 59, of his first fictional work, *Robinson Crusoe.* The form quickly developed in the hands of the prolix Richardson and his much greater rival, Fielding, into that typical of the English novel for the next 150 years. The unclassifiable *Tristram Shandy,* into which Sterne packed wit, bawdy and learning, the rollicking picaresque novels of Smollett and Goldsmith's kindly *Vicar of Wakefield,* show the range and variety of the early novelists.

Blake, together with the Lake Poets (Wordsworth, Coleridge and Southey), writing under the influence of the French Revolution, ushered in the Romantic movement which was to dominate English poetry until Browning broke with the tradition; Keats, Shelley, Byron and Tennyson formed a later generation of Romantics, all but Tennyson being largely disregarded during their lifetimes except on the Continent. Jane Austen opened the 19th century with novels of a new distinction and delicacy; Walter Scott, whose artistic stature is a matter of dispute, wrote romantic reconstructions of history in his Waverley novels; Trollope concentrated on fierce strife in the cathedral close. Emily Brontë is a lonely figure in this company, writing one novel, *Wuthering Heights,* which fits into no category. Social comment was the keynote of the next generation of novelists: on high life by Thackeray, on Midland rural life by George Eliot, and on low life by Dickens. Carlyle's search for heroes took him from *Frederick the Great* to the *French Revolution.* Matthew Arnold and Ruskin smote the British Philistines, and William Morris attempted to improve their taste. Meredith and Hardy wrote verse and novels, the latter creating a self-contained world in his Wessex novels. The expatriate American, Henry James, wrote of his own kind, the expatriate Pole, Conrad, of the sea and Malaysia, and the Irishman, George Moore, introduced the Zolaesque realist novel. Arnold Bennett described the Five Towns (the Potteries) and Wells dealt exuberantly with past, present and future. D. H. Lawrence, in trying to plumb the darkest recesses of the unconscious mind, revealed, almost incidentally, an unmatched gift for vivid descriptive writing. W. B. Yeats led his followers through the Celtic Twilight to a mythological Irish past in poems of great beauty, and J. M. Synge made music of Irish peasant talk. Another Irishman, G. B. Shaw, tore relentlessly away at the remaining veils of Victorian hypocrisy and muddled thinking. The later generation of poets, over whom T. S. Eliot towered, included

Auden and Spender. The heartless short story was exploited with skill by Somerset Maugham, and humour was supplied by the earlier Evelyn Waugh and P. G. Wodehouse.

ENGRAVING, the use of designs cut, drawn or etched on wood, stone or metal, for reproduction by printing. The chief forms are relief and intaglio engraving and lithography. Of the forms of relief engraving the woodcut is the commonest, seen to perfection in the work of Thomas Bewick; it is made by cutting away all parts which will appear white in the print.

Intaglio engraving is almost always on copper. A line engraving has V-section lines cut with a sharp graver, the burr or shavings being removed. This method was practised by Dürer. In dry-point a pencil of hard steel replaces the graver, and the burr is left, giving a characteristic effect but limiting the number of copies that can be made. In etching the design is made by a needle on a wax-covered plate, and is bitten into the surface with acid. This and dry-point were processes used by Rembrandt. Whistler revived etching in the later 19th century. In mezzotint, used in 18th-century England to reproduce the works of Reynolds and Gainsborough, the plate surface is roughened all over with a 'rocker' and the burr smoothed to produce the various tones and highlights. Aquatint, particularly effective in reproducing water-colours, is a tone process, lacking the richness of mezzotint, in which acid is applied to etch through a porous ground. It was used by Paul Sandby and Goya, among others.

In lithography the drawing is made on porous limestone with a greasy crayon, and printer's ink is rolled over it, the ink adhering only to the design. It was employed by 19th-century artists (Goya, Daumier, Delacroix) and is a favourite method in commercial art as there is no limit to the number of copies that can be taken.

ENTABLATURE, the part of a structure directly above a column. It is composed of three parts: the architrave, the main beam, consisting of a marble or stone slab resting on the columns; the frieze above it which, in the Doric Order of Architecture, is divided into alternate triglyphs (projecting blocks decorated with three vertical grooves) and plain surfaces (metopes); and the cornice on top.

ENTENTE CORDIALE, the name given to a friendly understanding between Britain and France from 1904 to the First World War. Existing without a formal treaty, it was concluded for the purpose of combating the threat of German expansionism.

ENZYMES, proteins produced by living cells which act as catalysts in chemical changes, each enzyme affecting only a small range of chemical reactions, most of them in only one specific substance; e.g. diastase is the enzyme in malt which converts starch to maltose in brewing. Metabolism (q.v.) is dependent on enzymes. They are easily destroyed by heat and by many chemical substances.

EPIC, a long, narrative poem treating heroic events. Based on folk themes, some took generations to develop. Famous Western epics include Homer's *Iliad* and *Odyssey*, Virgil's *Aeneid*, the Old English *Beowulf*, the French *Chanson de Roland*, the Norse *Volsunga Saga*, and the German *Nibelungenlied.* Dante's *Divina Commedia* and Milton's *Paradise Lost* are epic poems. Most great European epics were written during the 15th and 16th centuries.

EPICTETUS (1st century A.D.), Greek Stoic philosopher. Although his high moral teachings survive only in the notes of a pupil, they exerted considerable influence in his time.

EPICURUS (342—270 B.C.), Greek philosopher. He founded a system, Epicureanism, based on the doctrine that the attainment of happiness is the essence of morality. He defined happiness as the good in life that comes from the peace of mind induced by self-control and simplicity.

EPISCOPAL CHURCH, Protestant, the independent American branch of the Church of England. In 1780 the Rev. William Smith called together the various followers of the Church of England in America with the idea of organising a separate independent group. A general convention was held at Philadelphia (1789) and the Episcopal Church was then established.

EPSTEIN, Sir Jacob (1880—1959), American-born English sculptor. His work aroused considerable controversy because of its break with tradition. It includes *Rima*, *Day* and *Night*, *Madonna and Child*, *Christ in Majesty* and, for Coventry Cathedral, a bronze group depicting *St Michael triumphing over the Devil.* In strong contrast to his monumental carving, he made several realistic portrait busts, of *Einstein*, *Shaw* and *Paul Robeson* among others.

EQUATOR, the greatest circumference of the earth midway between the poles. It amounts to 24,902 miles. At this point, the earth's diameter is 7926 miles.

ERASMUS, Desiderius (1466—1536), Dutch scholar, critic and author. Ordained as a priest in 1492, he attacked the abuses in the Roman Catholic church but refused to follow the radical trends of the Reformation, and crossed swords with Luther. He was recognised as the leading scholar of his age and did more than any man to stimulate the revival of learning.

ERFURT, a city of East Germany, on the Gera River. Pop. (1959) 184,588. An important commercial centre, it manufactures machinery, leather goods, textiles and foodstuffs.

ERITREA, a federal unit of Ethiopia on the southwest shore of the Red Sea. Pop. (1960) 1,300,000; area 45,754 sq. miles. An Italian colony from 1890, it was occupied by British forces during the Second World War and federated with Ethiopia in 1952 by a resolution of the United Nations. Its products include tobacco, cereals and pearls. The capital is Asmara (130,000) and the chief port Massawa.

EROS (Roman Cupid), the son of Aphrodite, represented as a lovely irresponsible boy, flying on golden wings, shooting men and women with his golden arrows. He was sometimes depicted as blindfold. In late legend he was the lover of Psyche.

ESCHATOLOGY, the doctrine of the 'last things' (from the Gk *eschata*). It is most fully developed in the Jewish-Christian tradition in which God is represented as working in and through history. The coming of the Messiah, the resurrection of the dead, divine judgment, a new creation and the establishment of the kingdom of God are all concepts associated with this doctrine.

ESKIMO, Mongolian people of the Arctic regions of Alaska, northern Canada, Greenland and eastern Siberia. They probably spread from Siberia across the Bering Strait. They have broad faces with straight noses and coarse black hair, and live in small groups which hunt together, but often break up into families. Their principal foods comprise seal, walrus and fish. Their most important possessions are the dog sledge and the skin boat (kayak). They live in snow houses (igloos) in winter, and in summer they use structures made of skins stretched over a whalebone framework. In spite of their habitat they are a cheerful, kindly race and fond of song. They are skilled craftsmen with a highly developed artistic sense.

ESSENES, a Jewish sect vowed to a life of strict asceticism, celibacy and prayer, which flourished during the latter period of the Second Temple (*c.* 200 B.C.—A.D. 70). The Dead Sea Scrolls are usually ascribed to this group.

ESSEX, Robert Devereux, 2nd Earl of (1566—1601), English soldier and favourite of Queen Elizabeth I. After distinguished service in Portugal, Normandy and Cadiz, he was appointed Lord-Lieutenant of Ireland. His failure to quell a rebellion there, and a number of personal insults to the queen, led to his falling into disfavour at court. He was tried, condemned to death and executed at the Tower.

ESSEX, a county in southeastern England, on the Thames estuary. Pop. (1961) 2,286,970; area 1528 sq. miles. Low along the coast, it is relatively high and wooded in the north. Stock-raising and agriculture are the principal occupations. There is some heavy industry. The area is rich in antiquities. The county town is Chelmsford. East Ham, West Ham, Leyton and Walthamstow are part of Greater London. Southend-on-Sea (164,976) is a seaside resort and dormitory town. Colchester is famous for its oyster fisheries, which supply many London restaurants.

ESTONIA, a constituent republic of the U.S.S.R., on the Baltic Sea. Pop. (1959) 1,196,000; area 17,610 sq. miles. The country is generally flat with numerous lakes and marshes. Agriculture and livestock-raising are the chief occupations. There are important textile and sawmill industries. Estonia has rich shale deposits. The capital is Tallinn (280,000). From 1721 part of the Russian empire, and independent from 1921—40, it was occupied first by Soviet troops, then by Germany (1941—44).

ETHELBERT (d. 616), King of Kent. He was converted to Christianity by St Augustine of Canterbury. Ethelbert compiled the first written Saxon code of laws.

ETHELRED II (*c.* 968—1016), King of England. Called the 'Unready' (i.e. without counsel), he was unable to prevent the Danes from overrunning his kingdom. He married the daughter of the Duke of Normandy; she became the mother of Edward the Confessor and, after Ethelred's death, married Canute.

ETHIOPIA (Abyssinia), a kingdom in northeast Africa, federated with Eritrea. Pop. (1961) 21,800,000; area 457,267 sq. miles. It consists of a great central plateau with several high mountains, and hot coastal lowlands. Lake Tana, the source of the Blue Nile, is in the north. Grains, vegetables, livestock and coffee are raised. Some gold and other minerals are mined. A vassal of the ancient Pharaohs, Ethiopia dominated Egypt in the 7th century B.C. It adopted Christianity in the 4th century. An Italian attempt to invade the country failed in 1896 but was successful in 1936.

Ethiopia was liberated in 1941. The emperor's power is absolute.

ETRUSCANS, an ancient people of undetermined racial origin who lived in Etruria, central Italy. Until about 500 B.C., they were extremely powerful. They were skilful artists, and exerted considerable influence on the Romans who, however, subjugated them in 283 B.C. Etruscan inscriptions are numerous, but only a few words have been deciphered. It is established that Etruscan is not an Indo-European language.

Etruscan inscription

EUBOEA (Evvoia), a Greek island in the Aegean off the east coast of Greece. Pop. (1951) 163,720; 115 miles long. It is mountainous, with fertile valleys and pine forests. Agriculture and grazing are important. Minerals include a beautiful grade of marble. It was ruled by Athens at one time. The chief town is Chalcis (Khalkis).

EUCHARIST (Holy Communion, Mass), the central Christian sacrament, observed by most sects except the Society of Friends, which consists of a ritual partaking of consecrated bread and wine in remembrance of the Last Supper. It is based on the words 'Do this in remembrance of me' in Luke XXII. 19, which some scholars think may not have been in the original text, and on 1 Corinthians X and XI. By the doctrine of Transubstantiation accepted by the Roman Catholic Church these elements are held to become, by consecration, the actual body and blood of Christ, a doctrine evolved between the 9th and 13th centuries. Luther held a middle view called Consubstantiation, which accepted the Real Presence of Christ at the rite. Calvin taught that the elements remained bread and wine, but that the communicant received Christ's body and blood through these symbols. In the Anglican Church the 28th Article condemns Transubstantiation and affirms that 'the body of Christ is given, taken and eaten in the Supper, only after an heavenly and spiritual manner'. 'Eucharist' comes from the Greek for 'thanksgiving', and refers to the words 'and he took the bread and gave thanks'.

EUCLID (*c.* 300 B.C.), Greek mathematician who founded a school at Alexandria, Egypt. His most famous work was *The Elements* in 13 books, dealing with plane and solid geometry and the properties of numbers. His work has been the basis of geometry text-books ever since.

EUPHRATES, see River.

EURATOM, an organisation formed in 1958 by the six Common Market countries to co-operate in the development of nuclear energy for peaceful purposes. The headquarters is at Brussels.

EURIPIDES (*c.* 480—406 B.C.), Athenian dramatist. The third of the great Greek tragedians, his outlook was very different from that of Aeschylus and Sophocles. He was an innovator who dared to question the ways of the gods with man, and several of his plays are nearer to comedy than tragedy, e.g. *Helen*. Because of his 'impiety' his works were often ill received, and it was not until after his death that his genius was fully appreciated. He is said to have written 92 plays, but only 18 survived. Those most widely known include *Alcestis*,

Medea, the two *Iphigeneia* plays, *The Trojan Women* and *The Bacchae.*

EUROPE, the smallest continent except Australia. Pop. (1959) *c.* 533,000,000; area 3,825,000 sq. miles, including European Russia. The Great European Plain runs from the Low Countries, where it is narrowest, widening through northern Germany and central Europe to form the greater part of European Russia; it is bounded on the south by mountain ranges — Pyrenees, Alps, Carpathians and Caucasus — beyond which lie the three peninsulas of Iberia (Spain and Portugal), Italy and the Balkans, balanced by the Scandinavian peninsula in the north. The Ural Mountains in the U.S.S.R. form the dividing line between Europe and Asia. Offshore lie the islands of Britain and Ireland. The chief rivers are the Rhine and Rhône, the Oder, Elbe, Weser and Danube, the Vistula and, in Russia, the Dnieper, Don and Volga. The main products of agriculture are wheat, oats, barley, sugar-beet and olive oil. Scandinavia and northern Russia provide timber. A belt of coal and iron, with attendant heavy industry, runs right across Europe from central England and the Ruhr to the Donbas in Russia. North and south of this belt industry relies mainly on hydro-electricity, which is abundant. Other minerals are bauxite, copper, lead, zinc, chrome, tungsten, mercury (Italy and Spain), oil (Rumania), uranium (Czechoslovakia) and potash (Saxony).

The population is usually classified into Northern European, Alpine and Mediterranean; the Basques do not fit into these, categories, and the Hungarians, Lapps, Finns and the inhabitants of the three Baltic countries, Estonia, Latvia and Lithuania, speak non-Indo-European languages grouped together under the name Finno-Ugrian.

The centre of early civilisation was the eastern Mediterranean. Recorded history begins with the Greeks, who were superseded by the Roman empire. Christianity began to spread over the continent in the 4th century. The disintegration of Rome was followed by the rise of Charlemagne's empire in the west and Byzantium in the east. The west at first retained the Roman Catholic tradition which inspired the Crusades. With the end of the Middle Ages in the 14th and 15th centuries, nation states appeared, and Europeans began to conquer new worlds across the seas. Spain and France, in turn, became dominant powers and yielded later to England. The Reformation of the 16th century added religious disruption to existing political causes of discord. Russia and Prussia appeared as powerful states and the French Revolution marked a new epoch in the history of Europe. The era of nationalism set in, to be followed by imperial expansion in Africa and Asia. In 1914—18 most of Europe was involved in a war of unprecedented dimensions, followed by the emergence of new states. Democratic government, which had been spreading throughout the continent, was checked by the rise of dictatorships in Italy, Spain and Germany. Nazi Germany, bent on conquest, precipitated the Second World War in 1939. Their defeat in 1945 was followed by the redrawing of national boundaries and the rise of socialist states in eastern Europe. In Western Europe tendencies towards unification were first expressed in the form of economic co-operation and the elimination of trade barriers. The European nations which joined in the North Atlantic Treaty Organisation are the United Kingdom, France, Belgium, Netherlands, Luxembourg, Denmark, Norway, the German Federal Republic, Portugal, Italy, Turkey and Greece. The countries grouped around the U.S.S.R. are Poland, the German Democratic Republic, Czechoslovakia, Hungary, Rumania and Bulgaria. Sweden, Finland, Switzerland, Austria and the Irish Republic are uncommitted states. Spain is a dictatorship.

EUROPEAN COAL AND STEEL COMMUNITY (E.C.S.C.), an organisation formed in 1952 to co-ordinate coal and steel production in the six Common Market countries. Its High Authority has the right to deal direct with coal and steel enterprises of member countries without prior reference to their governments. Luxembourg is the headquarters.

EUROPEAN ECONOMIC COMMUNITY, see Common Market.

EUROPEAN FREE TRADE ASSOCIATION (E.F.T.A., 'The Seven'), an association formed in 1959 after the Common Market (q.v.) had rejected British proposals for a wider free trade area. It consists of Great Britain, Austria, Denmark, Norway, Sweden, Portugal and Switzerland. The objective is the elimination of internal tariffs but with the retention of separate external tariff systems.

EUSEBIUS (*c.* 260—339), historian and Church Father. Appointed bishop of Caesarea, Judaea, he played a leading role in the Council of Nicaea (325). Possessed of great learning, he wrote the *Ecclesiastical History* and *Chronicon*, a history of the world up to his own time.

EVANS, Sir Arthur (1851—1941), English archaeologist. He carried out extensive excavations at Knossos, in Crete, where he discovered the pre-Phoenician script.

EVIDENCE, testimony in a court of law for the purpose of proving or disproving alleged facts. The burden of proof is the responsibility of the party making a positive assertion. The court may presume that certain facts are true, and decides which evidence is admissible. The law requires that witnesses be competent and that they be examined and cross-examined. Witnesses have certain privileges, e.g. not to divulge conversations between lawyer and client. There are also clearly established procedures regarding what is admissible as evidence. Only the best evidence available is acceptable; for example, a carbon copy of a document is not acceptable if the original could have been produced. Hearsay evidence is accepted only in special circumstances.

EVOLUTION, the theory which holds that all forms of life have evolved from previously existing forms over an extended period. Because of the factor of natural selection, suitable adaptations to the environment are perpetuated and enable the species to survive. There is sufficient evidence from the study of fossil remains, comparative anatomy and embryology and from the study of how heredity operates, to prove the soundness of this concept. Darwin (q.v.) thought that the hereditary factors (now called genes) provided by any pair of parents 'blend' when they come together, and since blending would tend to produce uniformity, there must be changes (mutations) in the genes themselves. It is now held that this does not happen, or does not happen frequently enough to achieve the results required, and that variability is due to the combination of unaltered genes in new ways. Lamarck's theory of the inheritance of acquired characteristics caused by change of environment is now similarly discounted. Darwin's theory of natural selection was based on the fact that the offspring of any parents exhibit slight variations, and that those whose variations are best adapted to their environment (itself changing over a long period) will tend to produce more of the best-adapted offspring than the others; their special qualities will thus tend to spread through the population of the neighbourhood, causing it to evolve.

EXCOMMUNICATION, the act of excluding a person from the rites and privileges of the church for the purpose of disciplining the malefactor and protecting the faithful from evil influences. Two forms developed: the greater, which entailed total exclusion from the Christian community, and the lesser, exclusion from the sacraments. Among those excommunicated by the Pope were King John, Henry VIII and Elizabeth I.

EXISTENTIALISM, an anti-intellectualist body of divergent philosophies which stress the need for each of us to think out our own solutions to the fundamental problems of life; we are 'condemned to be free and responsible'. The source of Existentialism is Kierkegaard (q.v.; 1813—55), and his followers were Heidegger, Karl Jaspers, Karl Barth, Unamuno and Martin Buber. They held that life is too short to argue in a detached manner about the unknowable — life, death, God; we must each make a great leap into the unknown and commit ourselves irretrievably, not waiting to be convinced by argument. To Barth, for example, this meant accepting Christ by an act of faith. Existentialist attitudes developed in Germany after World War I.

Through the publicity given to his works, Existentialism is today associated with Sartre (q.v.), but Sartre is not really a philosopher. He calls himself an atheist existentialist, and an attitude so negative is more accurately described as a personal derivative from Existentialism rather than Existentialism, which has no true link with beatnik philosophies of surrender to anti-social despair.

EXPLORATION. The first explorers were ancient peoples in search of food. Later, men ventured into the unknown seeking for treasure, lands to conquer, peoples, to trade with and convert to their religion. The pressure of growing populations and persecution and harassment by other races impelled men to travel far from their homes. Sometimes it was curiosity which lured travellers to places from which they might never return. In the ancient world, Cretans, Phoenicians, Greeks, Romans and, later, Vikings discovered hitherto unknown seas and lands. While Marco Polo travelled eastward, Columbus sailed to the west to discover a new continent. In the 15th and 16th centuries Portuguese, Spanish and English navigators opened up vast new regions in the western hemisphere. Early in the 17th century the Dutch discovered Australia which was explored more than a century later by James Cook. While Englishmen ranged across the northern wastes of Canada, others sought a passage from the Atlantic to the Pacific across the top of Europe and Asia. In 1850—54 Sir Robert McClure was the first to sail from the Pacific to the Atlantic along northern North America. This was the period of great discoveries in Africa and Antarctica. In the past 100 years, expeditions have gone into the jungles of eastern and northeastern South America and New Guinea and across the deserts of central Asia to chart new topographical features and bring back information of unknown animals, plants and peoples. The conquest of the highest mountain peaks, e.g. Mt Everest, presented further challenges. In the middle of the 20th century man turned his attention to the heavenly bodies for new worlds to explore.

EXPLOSIVE, a substance or mixture which burns violently, producing much heat and large quantities of gases. The first such invention was gunpowder. Later discoveries were guncotton, nitroglycerine, dynamite and cordite. Chemical explosives (TNT, picric acid and cyclonite) are being replaced, in some instances, by atomic explosives.

EXPRESSIONISM, a movement in art which holds that the artist should paint objective reality as an expression of his own inner mental life. A person or landscape is not as he actually perceives it but as he interprets it. The movement has its roots in northern Europe and among Slavs and Jews, and the mood is usually one of gloom. Typical of Expressionism are the lonely, fearful subjects in the paintings of the Norwegian, Edvard Munch (1863—1944). Rouault, Marc, Kandinsky, Klee and Kokoschka have been numbered among the Expressionists. In music, the term applies to completely free musical expression; in drama, to a trend among German playwrights after the First World War.

EXTRASENSORY PERCEPTION (E.S.P, Parapsychology), name invented by Dr Rhine of Duke University, North Carolina, as a comprehensive term to cover telepathy, clairvoyance and precognition. These faculties he tries to test objectively with cards bearing symbols. Subjects guess the symbol when it has been seen by the dealer (telepathy), or when it has not been seen by anyone (clairvoyance), or before the cards have been shuffled and dealt (precognition). He also tests the ability of the mind to affect the movements of objects (psychkinesis, P.K.). The faculty behind E.S.P. and P.K. he called the Psi force. Thousands of results are examined statistically to detect percentages of correct guesses that significantly exceed those due to chance. His experimental work was subjected to continual critical comment.

EXTREME UNCTION, the final sacrament in the Roman Catholic and Greek churches, administered when death is imminent. It consists of confession, absolution and anointing with oil.

EYCK, Jan Van (*c.* 1385—1441), Flemish painter. He and his brother, Hubert (*c.* 1366—1426), were both court painters to Philip, duke of Burgundy. He had unusual technical skill in the use of oil-colours and great ability in rendering detail. A famous joint work of the two brothers is the Ghent altarpiece, *The Adoration of the Lamb*. Jan van Eyck's best-known masterpiece is the *Marriage of Giovanni Arnolfini and Giovanna Cerami* (National Gallery, London).

EYE, in man a nearly spherical globe enclosed in a socket (orbit), in which it is moved in concert with its twin by co-ordinated muscular movements. The whole organ is protected by eyelids and eye-lashes. The front of the eye is protected by a mucous membrane (conjunctiva) over a horny, transparent covering (cornea) which is kept in shape by

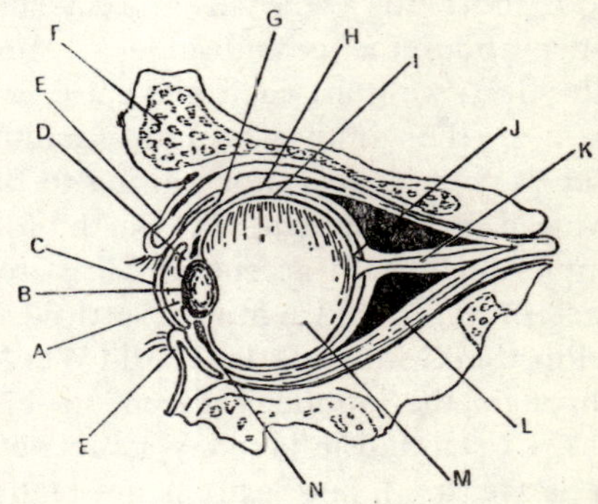

Human eye
A. Aqueous chamber B. Lens C. Cornea D. Iris E. Eyelids F. Frontal bone G. Conjunctiva H. Sclerotic or 'white of the eye' I. Retina J. Blind spot K. Optic nerve L. Muscles moving eye M. Vitreous body N. Ciliary muscles

a fluid (aqueous humour). Behind this is a muscular protective coat (choroid) lined with blood-vessels, in which is the iris, the coloured part of the eye. In the middle of the iris is an opening (pupil); the iris contracts and expands to adjust the pupil to the intensity of the light striking the eye. Immediately behind the pupil is the lens, through which the light is focused on to the sensitive inner lining (retina) at the back of the eye. The whole eyeball is filled with a transparent jelly (vitreous humour). The impressions received by the retina are passed on to the brain through the optic nerve at the back of the eye. Muscles adjust the lens for near or distant sight. Myopia is short sight; presbyopia is the long-sightedness and impairment of vision common in old age; squinting is a defect in the co-ordination of the movements of the eyes. Cataract is opacity of the lens, which can be removed surgically with good results. Glaucoma is due to raised pressure within the eyeball.

FALKLAND ISLANDS, British crown colony in the South Atlantic Ocean, 300 miles east of the Straits of Magellan. Pop. (1959) 2191; area 4618 sq. miles. Sheep grazing and whaling are the chief pursuits. The South Georgia, South Shetlands, South Orkneys and Sandwich Islands and Graham Land are regarded as dependencies.

FAMILY, a basic social unit consisting of parents and their children. Originally a biological unit for the purpose of reproduction and care of the young, it has, as the human race developed, become a medium for transmitting skills, perpetuating social organisation, and preparing children for a full, useful life.

FAMINE, a general scarcity of food, usually caused by failure of crops. Artificial famines arise as the result of inadequacy of transport systems bringing food to large centres, excessive taxes on foodstuffs, failure to sow because of political or social disturbances, blockades, or the deliberate destruction of crops. Recent famines in India and China due to floods, earthquakes, crop failures and inadequate transport have caused considerable loss of life.

FARADAY, Michael (1791—1867), English physicist and chemist. He discovered benzene, liquefied chlorine and other gases, and invented new kinds of optical glass. His greatest discoveries were in the field of electromagnetism. He formulated the laws of electromagnetic induction and of electrolysis, and discovered the rotation of the plane of polarised light by a magnetic field.

FAROE ISLANDS, a group of 21 Danish islands in the North Atlantic, 200 miles northwest of the Shetland Islands. Pop. (1959) 34,000; area 540 sq. miles. The most important occupations are fishing and sheep grazing. Less than 4% of the land area is under cultivation.

FARSIGHTEDNESS, a visual defect which occurs when the rays of light focus behind the retina (see Eye). It may be due either to inadequate refracting power of the eye or congenital shortness of the eyeball from front to back. It causes eyestrain and can be corrected by wearing spectacles.

FASCISM, a political movement started in Italy by Mussolini in 1919, and taking its name from the symbol of power *(fasces)* carried before the magistrates of Ancient Rome, consisting of an axe surrounded by a bundle of rods. Mussolini adopted this symbol, together with the black shirt and the Fascist salute.

After the so-called March on Rome (Mussolini went by train), the Fascists established a one-party dictatorship, forcibly dosed Communists with castor oil and set about restoring Italy's past glories. Trains ran on time, the Pontine Marshes were drained, *autostrade* built, and the idea of the corporative state was given its first trial. The regime proved an unmitigated disaster for Italy. A grandiose scheme to colonise Libya was followed by invasions of Ethiopia and Albania, intervention in the Spanish Civil War, subservience to Hitler and defeat in the World War which the movement had done so much to foment.

The Fascist idea spread to Germany, Spain and South America.

FASHION, a prevalent mode in a given period. It is usually applied to dress but also affects speech, manners, walking, posture, and even the shape of the body. Famous individuals (in later years especially film stars), wars, cultural, religious and social movements, and internationally recognised designers have been the creators or arbiters of fashion. In the interests of planned obsolescence and a quick turnover, dress designers must, like motorcar manufacturers, change the style annually.

FASHODA, a Sudanese village on the Nile which was the source of a diplomatic dispute between Britain and France in 1898—99. A small body of French explorers at the end of a march through Africa planted a French flag there. Kitchener was instructed to demand the party's withdrawal, and the French Foreign Minister, Delcassé, braved his countrymen's wrath and acquiesced.

FATALISM, the doctrine that everything is predetermined by fate and therefore man's efforts are to no avail. See Determinism.

FAULKNER, William (1897—1962), American novelist. His works depict the decadence and racialism of the American South. He wrote several collections of short stories. His novels include *Sartoris*, *Sanctuary*, *Absalom*, *Absalom!*, *Light in August*, and *The Sound and the Fury*. He received the Nobel Prize for literature in 1949. The insight and feeling that he put into his exploration of the intense social conflicts of the Mississippi district where he was born and lived have won him a very high place in American literature.

FAUST, the name of a legendary German doctor who made a pact with the devil to exchange his soul for supernatural powers, youth and supreme knowledge. Marlowe in England and Goethe in Germany are leading writers who transformed the legend into literature, while Berlioz and Gounod used it in opera.

FAUVISTES (wild beasts), a nickname given rather arbitrarily to a group of French painters who happened to exhibit together in 1905 and whose works had in common violent colouring and distortions. Among them were Matisse and Rouault, and later Dufy and Braque. They parted company three years later.

FAWKES, Guy (1570—1606), English conspirator executed for his part in the Gunpowder Plot to blow up the Houses of Parliament and the king on November 5, 1605. Although born of Protestant parents, he had become a Roman Catholic and served in the Spanish army.

FEDERAL BUREAU OF INVESTIGATION (FBI), a branch of the U.S. Department of Justice which investigates the violations of federal laws ranging from theft to treason.

FEEDBACK, in electronics, is the sending back of an electrical signal from one point of a system (e.g. a radio amplifier) to an earlier part in order to control output (e.g. loudness) or in other ways to improve performance. This principle, applied to control engineering (see Automation), is used in mechanical devices which compare some physical quantity with a predetermined quantity and, if there is any difference (i.e. an error), send back a signal to another part of the system which corrects it. An early application was in training a gun-turret on a target; a device compares the direction and elevation of the gun with data fed into it regarding the position of the target and sends back amending 'instructions' to the controlling mechanism until they correspond.

FEMINISM, the concept that women are entitled to the same economic, social, and political rights as men. Prominent in the movement in England were Godwin's daughter, Mary Wollstonecraft Shelley (1797—1851) and Mrs Emmeline Pankhurst (1858—1928), leader of the women's suffrage (q.v.) campaign. The first victory was the passing of the Married Women's Property Act in 1882 which recognised a wife's right to acquire her own separate property.

FENIANS, a secret society founded by Irish-Americans in 1858 with the object of securing Irish independence by force of arms. It had a large following in the U.S.A. and incited rebellions in south and west Ireland, and disturbances in England and Canada.

FENS, The, a lowland region in eastern England west and south of the Wash. The area includes parts of six counties and was once a bay of the North Sea. It was gradually reclaimed, first by the Romans and from the 17th century with Dutch help, many drainage canals being constructed. The Fens provide extremely fertile land, used mainly for growing potatoes and bulbs.

FERDINAND V (1452—1516), the first King of Spain. In 1469 he married his cousin Isabella (1451—1504), who in 1474 succeeded to the throne of Castile, of which they were appointed the joint sovereigns. In 1479 Ferdinand inherited the throne of Aragon, and the two kingdoms were united for the first time. In 1500—03 Ferdinand conquered Naples and Sicily, and later acquired southern Navarre. Through the marriages he arranged for his children he contracted alliances with various neighbours of France which had the effect of isolating that country. During the reign of Ferdinand and Isabella the Moors were expelled from their last remaining kingdom in Spain, Granada (1492), Columbus set sail for America, the Jews were expelled and the horrors of the Inquisition were introduced.

FERMENTATION, a chemical process in which carbohydrates (especially sugars) and certain other organic compounds are decomposed by enzymes (q.v.) found in bacteria, moulds and, in particular, yeasts. It is by this process that milk turns sour, sugar is converted to alcohol, and alcohol to acetic acid (vinegar). The saliva and gastric juices contain enzymes which aid digestion by converting starch to sugar and proteins to peptones.

FERMI, Enrico (1901—54), Italian nuclear physicist. His studies of atomic nuclei led to important discoveries in connection with neutrons and artificial radioactive substances. In 1938 he was awarded the Nobel Prize for physics. In 1939 he emigrated to America, and in 1942 at Chicago University put the world's first nuclear reactor into operation. In his last few years he made great contributions to the study of meson physics.

FERNANDO PO, a Spanish island in the Gulf of Guinea, West Africa. Pop. (1960) 31,347; area 700 sq. miles. Cocoa and palm oil are the main products. The capital is Santa Isabel.

FERRARA, a city in north Italy. Pop. (1959) 147,443. Under the dukes of Este it was a flourishing cultural centre in the 15th and 16th centuries. There is a Romanesque Cathedral (1135), many palaces dating from the 13th to 17th centuries and a university first founded in 1391. The processing of sugar-beet and hemp are the most important of the many industries of Ferrara.

FERTILISATION, the term applied in biology to the union of male and female reproductive cells to produce a new individual. The result is a fertilised egg or zygote from which a new animal or plant develops, taking various characteristics from each parent.

FETISHISM, in primitive religions, the worship of an object believed to possess supernatural powers. In psychology the term is applied to an inordinate emotional attachment to an object, usually an article of clothing or a part of the body. It is usually sexual in nature.

FEUDALISM, the social and economic system which prevailed in Western Europe from the 9th to the 14th centuries. It arose from a need for protection as central authority disintegrated. The basic pattern was the relationship between the lord and his tenants. In return for a piece of a land, or fief, which the lord permitted the tenant to till, the tenant was accorded protection. In return, he performed certain services for the lord, e.g. aid in war. The tenant was the lord's subject. The lord owed allegiance to a hierarchy of higher nobles who were subject to the king, or supreme overlord.

FEZ, a city in Morocco. Pop. (1960) 215,812. The ancient capital of the country, it is the religious and commercial centre of Moslem northwest Africa.

FICHTE, Johann (1762—1814), German philosopher. One of the German Idealist school, he forms a link between Kant and his own successors, Schopenhauer, Hegel and Emerson. In his *Address to the German Nation* he called on the Germans to found an empire of reason in which mind alone would guide human affairs.

FIELDING, Henry (1707—54), English novelist. From 1748 he made a name for himself as the incorruptible principal Justice of the Peace for Middlesex and Westminster, his interest in prison reform and social questions being reflected in his novel *Amelia*. His first novel, *Joseph Andrews* was a parody of Richardson's *Pamela*. *Tom Jones* (1748) was his masterpiece.

FIFE, a maritime peninsula county in east central Scotland. Pop. (1961) 320,541; area 492 sq. miles. Lying between the Firth of Tay and the Firth of Forth, it has numerous small seaside resorts. Industries include linen, linoleum and aluminium. The county town is Cupar. Other places of interest are the naval base of Rosyth, and St Andrews, home of golf and Scotland's oldest university, founded in 1413.

FIFTH COLUMN, a subversive group working within a country in co-operation with the enemy. The term is derived from a boast of the Franco nationalists, when they were marching in four columns on Madrid in the Spanish Civil War of 1936—39, that they had a 'fifth column' working for them within the city.

FIJI, an archipelago of 322 coral islands forming a British colony in the South Pacific. Pop. (1961) 413,872; area 7083 sq. miles. The islands are mostly mountainous, volcanic and densely forested, and only a third of them are inhabited. They export sugar, coconut products, bananas, pineapples, manganese and gold. Discovered by Tasman in 1643, they have been British since 1874. The largest group of the population is Indian, and there are some 5000 Chinese. The capital is Suva on Viti Levu, the largest island (4010 sq. miles); the second largest island is Vanua Levu (2137 sq. miles).

FILM, in photography, a sheet of celluloid or similar material bearing a thin, sensitised coating for making pictures. It is flexible and is manufactured either in rolls or cut sheets.

FINANCE, PUBLIC, the management of the receipts and expenditures of a government or local authority. It includes the raising of revenue by taxation or borrowing; current expenditure on goods and services on behalf of the public (e.g. police) or transferred to the public (e.g. state pensions); capital expenditure (e.g. on housing); the service of the public debt; the financing of nationalised industries if these have to be subsidised; and the use of the budget to control the country's economy. The submission to parliament of an annual budget is the responsibility of the Chancellor of the Exchequer, who has the difficult task of deciding on the relative urgency of the needs of the various departments as shown in their annual estimates for the coming year.

FINGAL'S CAVE, one of several caves of striking beauty on Staffa, one of the Inner Hebrides Islands off northwest Scotland. The entrance, fronting the sea, is supported by gigantic rows of basaltic columns, similar to those of the Giant's Causeway in Northern Ireland.

FINGER-PRINTING, a technique for identifying individuals based on unique unchanging impressions left by the ridge patterns in the finger-tips. The system was adopted by Scotland Yard in 1901.

FINLAND, a republic in northern Europe. Pop. (1961) 4,460,000; area 117,975 sq. miles. Consisting solely of lowland and containing countless lakes, Finland has large forests of high-quality timber. Grains are cultivated and livestock raised. The principal manufactures are wood products, machinery and textiles. Finland belonged to Sweden from 1157—1809, when it finally became Russian after a series of annexations. In 1917 the country achieved independence. Conquered by the U.S.S.R. in 1939—40,

Finland ceded 16,000 sq. miles of territory to the victor. From 1941 to 1944 Finland allied itself to Germany against the U.S.S.R. and yielded further territory at the end of the war. The capital is Helsinki (pop. 1961 468,700). Other principal cities are Turku (138,380) and Tampere (128,898).

FIORD, a narrow inlet of the sea extending far inland, flanked by steep cliffs interspersed with waterfalls. Fiords were formed by glaciers gouging out narrow valleys on their way to the sea.

FISH, a cold-blooded vertebrate living in water, breathing through gills and possessing fins for locomotion. Most fish are covered by scales or plates. There are more than 30,000 known living species. The gills absorb oxygen from the water. Fish reproduce sexually. Their strongest senses are smell and taste. As food, fish are a valuable source of proteins.

FISHER, John (1459—1535), English prelate. He was confessor to Henry VII's mother. Famed for his learning, he became chancellor of Cambridge University in 1504, and shortly afterwards Bishop of Rochester. He was beheaded by Henry VIII, after the Pope had made him a cardinal, for his refusal to acknowledge the king's supremacy and his opposition to the king's divorce from Catherine of Aragon.

FISSION, see Atomic Energy.

FITZGERALD, Edward (1809—83), English poet and translator. He published translations of a number of Persian poets. His crowning achievement was the *Rubáiyát of Omar Khayyám.*

FITZGERALD, F. Scott (1896—1940), American novelist. Born in Minnesota and educated at Princeton, he was one of the first novelists to concentrate the whole of his attention on the aimless and worthless misfits of modern society: Americans in *The Great Gatsby* (1924); expatriate Americans in southern Europe in *Tender is the Night*; Hollywood in *The Last Tycoon*; and himself in *The Crack-up* (1945).

FITZSIMMONS, Robert (Ruby Rob; 1862—1917), English boxer, born in Cornwall, who went first to New Zealand and then to the U.S.A. A hard-hitting pugilist, he was successively world's middleweight, heavy, and light-heavyweight champion.

FIVES, two court games in which the ball is struck with the gloved hand (the 'bunch of fives'). Eton fives is played in an open court with no back wall, and a buttress (pepper) on the left-hand side; Rugby fives are played in a covered-wall court.

FIVE-YEAR PLAN, short-range economic planning, first introduced by the U.S.S.R. in 1928. Each plan established production targets derived from an overall plan for the development of the country, in which the needs of agriculture and industry, urban worker and peasant, capital and consumer goods, were balanced against one another, and manpower was trained for, and directed to, the sector where it was most required. When it was realised that ruthlessness, though prominent under Stalin, was not an essential element of such plans, the idea spread to other countries.

FLAG, a coloured piece of cloth symbolising political authority. It is usually attached to a fixed pole or a portable staff. The national flag of Great Britain, called the Union Flag or Union Jack, was established by royal proclamation

The basic designs of much furniture at present in use has changed little during the course of centuries. Illustrated here is an Egyptian chair dating from *c.* 1500 B.C. The seat is of woven cord—still used today—and the figures on the back are gilded. *Photo: Paul Hamlyn Limited*

A stone relief showing a provincial Roman funeral banquet scene. Notice the high-backed chair for the nursing mother, the draperies, the couch and the lion-supported side table. *Photo: A. C. L., Brussels*

An Etruscan (q.v.) bronze bed taken from a tomb at Cerveteri. The frame is strung with latticed metal straps over which a mattress was laid. *Photo: Alinari*

Vast oak forests covered much of Northern Europe during the Middle Ages and oak timbers were for that reason extensively used in furniture building. This crude oak chest dates from the 17th century.
Photo: Victoria & Albert Museum

At the close of the Middle Ages in England furniture carving was becoming more sophisticated. This oak armchair dates from *c.* 1550.
Photo: Victoria & Albert Museum

This Dutch oak pew end, dating from the 16th century, illustrates the biblical story of the Prodigal Son.
Photo: Victoria & Albert Museum

in 1606. It consists of a combination of the crosses of St George and St Andrew, to which the cross of St Patrick was added at the union with Ireland in 1801. The ancient flag bearing only the red upright cross of St George in a white field survives as a flag of command in the Royal Navy.

FLAGELLANTS, religious groups in Europe which practised scourging as a means of penance and discipline. They appeared at intervals from the 13th to 16th centuries, usually after a period of great tribulation such as the Black Death. Condemned by the Roman Catholic Church in 1261, the practice was finally suppressed by the Inquisition in 1414, when the leader of the latest outbreak was burnt at the stake.

FLANDERS (Vlaanderen), a region in Western Europe on the North Sea, extending from the Scheldt in the Netherlands to the Nord *départment* of France. It is the land of the Flemings, and the Flemish language, a form of Dutch, is still spoken by some of the inhabitants over all this area, which is also identifiable by the distinctive style of Flemish architecture. The name is now officially given, however, only to East and West Flanders, two provinces of Belgium. Flanders was from early times famous for the manufacture of cloth; for geographical reasons, it has frequently been overrun by war. Bruges, Ghent, Brussels and Antwerp were the great cities of Flanders, and there the leading Flemish artists worked, among them Van Eyck, Memlinc, Brueghel and Rubens.

FLAUBERT, Gustave (1821—80), French novelist. He expended much of his energy on the perfection of form appropriate to his varying subjects, each sentence being highly polished. In spite of this, his novels are intensely dramatic, perceptive studies of human failings. *Madame Bovary* (1857) is the acknowledged masterpiece, the misanthropic story of the wife of a country doctor whose infidelities lead to suicide. *Salammbô* is set in ancient Carthage; but he returned in later novels to his obsession with the *bourgeoisie* whom he despised so deeply. He also wrote some perfect examples of the short story, e.g. *Hérodias.*

FLEET STREET, the centre of newspaper publishing in London. It takes its name from a river which used to run from Hampstead to the Thames but is now underground and forms part of the sewage system.

FLEMING, Sir Alexander (1881—1955), British bacteriologist. In 1922 he discovered a substance called lysozyme which can destroy bacteria. This led to his discovery of penicillin six years later. In 1945 he was awarded the Nobel Prize for physiology and medicine, together with H. W. Florey and E. B. Chain.

FLINT, a city in Michigan, U.S.A. Pop. (1960) 196,940. On the Flint River, it is an industrial city producing automobiles, aircraft engines, steel, foods and cotton goods.

FLINTSHIRE, a maritime county in northeast Wales. Pop. (1951) 149,888; area 257 sq. miles. Stock-raising is the principal agricultural occupation. It has textile and chemical industries, and iron and coal mines.

FLOODS. Excessive rainfall, thawing snow or rain falling on melted snow are the commonest causes of rivers overflowing. Tidal waves caused by earthquakes or unusually strong winds also result in floods. Protection against river floods is afforded by deepening the rivers, constructing dykes and channels for confining the waters, and spillways to divert the flow. Other means are erecting dams and reservoirs for storing excess water, and reforestation to diminish the rise of floodwaters.

FLORENCE, a city in north central Italy. Pop. (1959) 424,625. The capital of Tuscany, the home of the Medici, who ruled it from 1421 to 1737, the birthplace of Dante, Botticelli, Michelangelo and Donatello, and for long the home of Leonardo da Vinci, Florence still has many art treasures and fine buildings despite the destruction of the Second World War. All the old bridges over the River Arno, except the Ponte Vecchio with its silversmiths' shops, were blown up by the Germans, and the Uffizi gallery was wrecked, though the Pitti escaped. The 12th century cathedral has a dome by Brunelleschi and a campanile by Giotto; the baptistery has the famous bronze doors of Ghiberti. The university is one of the oldest in Italy.

Today Florence is a communications centre, famous for its straw hats.

FLORES, an island in eastern Indonesia. Pop. 500,000; area 8870 sq. miles. Mountainous, volcanic and densely forested, it supports a population engaged in agriculture, commerce and fishing. The chief town is Larantuka.

FLORIDA, the southernmost state of U.S.A., a peninsula in the southeast. Pop. (1960) 4,951,650; area 58,560 sq. miles. Rarely rising more than 200 ft above sea-level, the state has innumerable small lakes and, in the south, cypress and mangrove swamps. The climate is humid and sub-tropical. Famed as a resort area, Florida produces oranges, grapefruit, tomatoes, tobacco and garden vegetables. Fishing, cattle raising, and industries such as chemicals, metal working and wood products are important. The capital is Tallahassee (pop. 48,174). Other important cities are Miami (291,688), Tampa (274,970) and Jacksonville (201,030). Cape Canaveral (now Cape Kennedy), on the Atlantic coast, is the site from which rockets and satellites are launched.

FLOUR, a finely ground meal of wheat or other grains or of potatoes, beans, peas or groundnuts. When used alone the term is normally applied to wheat flour. Whereas once the grain kernels were crushed by manual labour, they are now ground by giant steel rollers.

FLOWER, the organ of reproduction of a plant. A complete flower has the following parts; a receptacle at the top of a stem which contains the calyx or outermost envelope consisting of individual sepals; the corolla inside the calyx

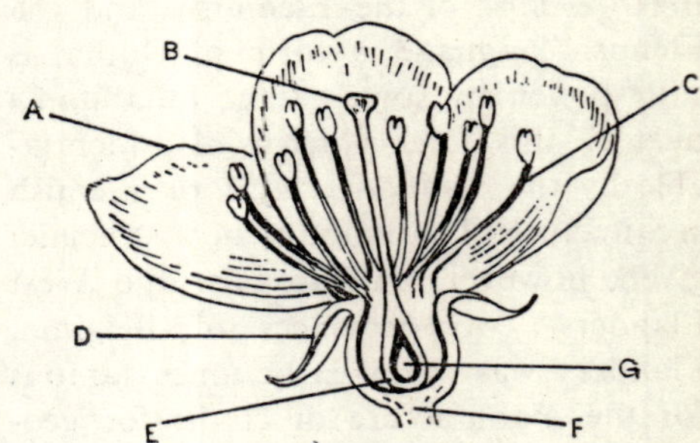

Flower (Cherry)
A. Petal B. Pistil C. Stamen D. Sepal E. Ovary F. Receptacle G. Ovule

made up of individual petals; stamens inside the petals which produce pollen; and pistils inside the stamen in the centre of the flower which produce seeds. The corolla is the colourful scented part which attracts insects who serve to fertilise the flower, as the wind does, by transferring pollen grains to the stigma at the top of the pistil.

FLUORESCENCE, the quality certain substances have of emitting light when exposed to ultra-violet rays or other forms of invisible radiation. Fluorescent light is produced by ultra-violet rays on fluorescent powders of various kinds mixed to produce the exact colour required. The fluorescent screen of a television set is that part of the cathode-ray on which the picture appears. Luminescence is a general term covering both fluorescence and phosphorescence; in the latter, emission of light after absorption of the invisible rays is not instantaneous, as it is in fluorescence.

FLUORINE, see Elements.

FLY, the common name for a large variety of insects with a single pair of wings and a body divided into a movable head, fused thorax and a segmented abdomen. There are over 70,000 species, including the housefly, mosquito, gnat and bot fly. Flies usually lay their eggs near or inside a source of food which may be garbage, excrement, plants or animals. The housefly is a menace because it carries disease germs. Many flies are serious pests to farmer and gardener, while several fatal diseases are fly-borne, e.g. sleeping sickness, carried by the tsetse fly.

Fly

FOCH, Ferdinand (1851—1929), French Field-Marshal and Commander-in-chief of the Allied Armies in the First World War. With Marshal Joffre, in the Battle of the Marne he stopped the German advance on Paris in 1914. In 1915 he directed the Battle of Ypres which saved the Channel ports. Chief of the French general staff in 1917, he became Allied supreme commander the following March, checking the German offensive and turning the tide to end the war.

FOG is caused by a cloud of tiny drops of water at the surface of the earth in a suspension dense enough to impair visibility in varying degrees, and is formed when the ever-present, invisible atmospheric vapour is cooled and condenses. Technically a mist is classified as a fog if visibility drops below 1100 yards, but in common usage the term is reserved for a thicker mist than this; if contaminated by the smoke of industrial areas it is called smog.

FOLK-LORE, customs, beliefs, legends and art-forms reflecting the life and spirit of a people, especially in rural districts. It includes folksongs, tales, and all kinds of activities, superstitions and traditional amusements.

FOOCHOW (Minhow), a seaport and capital of Fukien, east China, on the East China Sea. Pop. (1960) 700,000. It was formerly a treaty port, from which most of China's tea was exported. It also handles lacquer ware and timber, and has steel and chemical industries.

FOOD, see Cookery; Diet.

FOOD AND AGRICULTURE ORGANISATION (F.A.O.), formed by the U.N. in 1945 to promote international action to attain higher levels of nutrition and the conservation of natural resources. It also takes part in Technical Assistance programmes for the development of the poorer countries.

FOOTBALL, AMERICAN, a handling and kicking game developed from Rugby football, using a similar, but smaller, ball, on a ground marked off in five-yard strips. Scoring is by touchdown, goal after touchdown, field goal during play, and the 'safety', where the defenders make a touchdown behind their own line, their opponents scoring two points. The ball becomes dead when its carrier is tackled (a down), and a team must advance ten yards in four downs or surrender the ball.

FOOTBALL, ASSOCIATION (Soccer), a game played in England since the Middle Ages, with origins going back to antiquity, but organised in its present form by the Football Association in 1863. Since then it has spread to most countries of the world, and is particularly popular in Europe (including Russia) and South America. There is an international federation, the F.I.F.A. with headquarters in Switzerland, which runs a World Cup competition every four years; a European Cup is played for annually. The game is played between two teams of 11 men each — five forwards, three half-backs, two backs and a goalkeeper. The object is to kick the ball between the uprights and under the cross-bar of the opponents' goal. The main differences from Rugby Football are that the ball may not be handled except by the goalkeeper, and that it is round.

FOOTBALL, RUGBY, a form of football which differs widely from Association football. It is a handling code, i.e. the ball may be carried, the shape of the ball is oval, players may be brought down by the tackle, a score is made by touching the ball down behind the opponents' line (a try, 3 points), by converting a try (2 points) by a standing kick of the ball between the uprights but over the cross-bar, or by a penalty goal (3 points). A drop-kick is a goal scored in play. The team of 15 comprises eight forwards (who with their opponents form scrums from which the game is re-started), two halves, four three-quarters and a full back. The game traditionally originated with a Rugby schoolboy, William Webb Ellis who, during a game of ordinary football in 1823, broke the rules by picking up the ball and running with it. Rugby Union football is an entirely amateur game. Rugby League football, played mostly in Northern England, was developed by clubs which split from the parent game over the question of compensation for time lost by players in employment. There are 13 to a team and several other points of difference. The game remains primarily amateur, but the larger clubs are mainly professional. Among other countries, rugby is popular in France, New Zealand and South Africa.

FORD, Henry (1863—1947), American industrialist. Founder of the Ford Motor Company in 1903, he introduced new methods of mass production which made him the world's leading automobile manufacturer.

FOREST, a large wooded area. There are three leading types of forest: those in which the predominant trees lose their leaves at the end of each growing season (deciduous, slow-growing and producing hardwoods); those in which the predominant trees are evergreens (coniferous, quick-growing, producing softwoods); and dense equatorial jungles containing a wide variety of trees, vines, and other plants (tropical rain-forest). The first type is found mostly in temperate climates, the second, in cold or mountainous regions. It has long been realised that the forest resources of the world have been, and are still being, used recklessly. Intensive measures have been taken in most countries to remedy this situation by speeding up replacement, by creating forest reserves where no interference with the trees is permitted, and by improved organisation of fire-fighting and the scientific study of tree diseases. The conservation of forests is essential not merely to provide resources for future generations, but to prevent soil erosion and to control floods.

FORMOSA (Taiwan), an island off the coast of China in the China Sea, controlled by the Chinese Nationalist Government. Pop. (1960) 10,611,000; area 13,890 sq. miles. A central mountain range runs parallel to the east coast. The plains in the west are devoted to growing rice, tea, sugar, bananas and pineapples. A little gold, silver, copper and low-grade coal are mined. Oil is produced. Ceded to Japan by China in 1895, the island surrendered to General Chang Kai-shek after the Second World War. The capital is Taipei (pop. 1958 809,169). Other large cities are Kaohsiung (371,225) and Tainan (287,797). The government of this island has, with U.S. support, retained one of the five permanent seats on the Security Council of the United Nations.

FORSTER, Edward Morgan (1879—), English author. His best-known work is *A Passage to India*, dealing with the social barriers between the English and Indians in India. He also wrote *A Room with a View* and *Howards End*.

FORTALEZA, the capital of Ceará state, and a seaport on the northeast coast of Brazil. The port is the principal outlet for the products of the state. Pop. (1960) 300,000. It produces textiles and sugar and exports cotton, hides, rubber and wax.

FORTUNE-TELLING, the foretelling of a person's fate or destiny or of specific future events in a person's life. The materials used are various — the crystal ball, cards (including the ancient tarot pack), tea-leaves, etc. — but the methods appear to be two: either to use predictions of events so common (a dark stranger) or so vague (you will have anxiety about a loved one) that they can hardly fail to come true; or to develop keen observation of deportment, habits of speech, facial expression, etc., and make intelligent use of it. Palmistry claims to be a more exact method, and books are published giving the exact significance of the lines and bumps on the hand; it is reasonable to suppose that the scrutiny of these may be aided by the methods mentioned.

FORT WORTH, a city of north central Texas, U.S.A. Pop. (1960) 356,268. It is the largest cotton market and meat-packing centre of the southwest, and has extensive oil refineries and stockyards. Other industries are the manufacture of oilfield and agricultural machinery and the processing of cotton.

FOSSIL, the mineralised remains of prehistoric plants and animals. They may consist of bones, shells or wood. Impressions of parts of an animal's body or a leaf are found on mineral deposits. Plants are usually preserved in carbonised form. Fossil remains help palaeontologists to reconstruct life on earth millions of years ago.

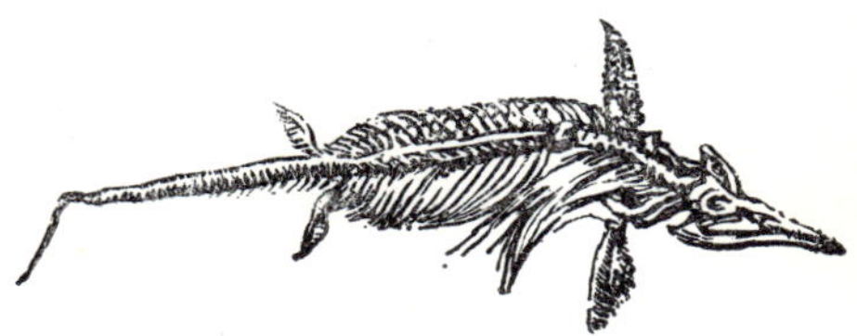

Fossilised skeleton of Ichthyosaurus intermedius (Lower Lias, Somerset)

FOUR FREEDOMS, a formulation of the basic goals of democratic peoples made by U.S. President Franklin D. Roosevelt in January 1941, when the Nazis were everywhere on the offensive. They are freedom of worship, freedom of speech, freedom from want and freedom from fear.

FOURTEEN POINTS, the basis for a peaceful settlement of the First World War formulated in 1918 by U.S. President Woodrow Wilson and later accepted by the other Allied powers. They provided for open diplomacy, freedom of the seas and the removal of trade barriers, reduction of armaments, impartial adjustment of colonial claims, restoration of conquered territory and the establishment of a number of independent states based on the wishes of the native populations, and the establishment of a League of Nations to guarantee peace.

FOX, Charles James (1749—1806), English statesman. An outstanding orator, he was a member of Lord North's cabinet (1770—74) until he opposed George III's marriage bill and his policy towards the American colonies. Foreign secretary in 1782—83, he furthered the cause of Irish independence, favoured the French Revolution, and opposed war with France. He secured the passage of a Libel Act and advocated political freedom for Catholics and Dissenters. The slave trade which he opposed was abolished a year after his death.

FOX, George (1624—91), founder of the Society of Friends, or Quakers. He believed that the presence of Christ in the heart was the only guidance required and that ritual and creeds were unnecessary. Often imprisoned, he visited North America and the Continent to spread his beliefs. The nickname of Quakers was given by Justice Bennett.

FOXE, John (1567—87), English martyrologist. A vigorous opponent of Catholicism, he fled to the Continent when Mary Tudor ascended the throne. He wrote the celebrated *Book of Martyrs*.

FRACTURE, a break in a bone. In a simple fracture, the skin is not punctured. A compound fracture, in which the skin is broken, is more dangerous because it is open to infection. Where bones are not completely calcified, as in children, the bones are not broken completely through and the fracture is known as a green-stick. In a comminuted fracture there are many bone fragments resulting from shattering. A fracture in which the broken ends are jammed together is known as impacted. The use of X-rays has been of immense benefit in diagnosing fractures.

FRANCE, a republic in Western Europe. Pop. (1960) 45,355,000; area 212,922 sq. miles. France consists of lowlands in the north and west, a central plateau west of the Rhône valley, the forest-covered Vosges and Jura Mountains in the east, the Alps along the Swiss and Italian borders, and the Pyrenees on the Spanish border. Mont Blanc (15,782 ft) is the second highest mountain in Europe. By means of the Rhône, Saône, Seine, and linking canals, barges can travel from the English Channel to the Mediterranean. The Rhône flows into the Mediterranean, the Seine into the English Channel, the Loire and the Garonne into the Bay of Biscay. The Rhine is France's eastern border for about 100 miles. The leading agricultural products are grains, potatoes, sugar-beet, wines and fruit. Livestock-raising and dairy-farming are important. Industrial products include textiles, iron and steel, chemicals, automobiles, machinery, aircraft, ships, and luxury and fashion goods. Coal, lignite, iron ore, bauxite and potash are the principal minerals, there is also some petroleum. Fishing and timber products are an integral part of the economy.

Ancient France — known as Gaul — was partly conquered by Caesar. France begins its history with the dissolution of Charlemagne's empire in the 9th century when the Capetian dynasty assumed power in the north central part of the country and gradually expanded its domains. A long struggle with the English for the domination of France ended in a French victory in 1429 which expelled the English from almost the entire country. In 1589 Henry of Navarre succeeded to the throne and settled the religious question which threatened to plunge France into civil war by granting religious freedom to the Protestants (Edict of Nantes). His grandson, Louis XIV (1643—1715) was the most powerful king in Europe and the head of a vast colonial empire. The misgovernment, corruption and oppression of his reign was continued by his successors and led to a revolution in 1789. The military absolutism of Napoleon which followed the French Revolution brought glory, reforms and defeat in its wake. The Congress of Vienna (1815) restored the monarchy which lasted until the revolution of 1848 when the Second Republic was established. Napoleon III, who had been president, proclaimed himself emperor in 1852 and became involved in war with Prussia which ended in a French defeat and the establishment of the Third Republic in 1871. Four years of war with Germany (1914—18) devastated France and left her beset by political instability and economic difficulties. In 1939 France entered a new struggle with Germany and was overrun by the Nazi war-machine a year later. Liberated in 1944, France established the Fourth Republic in 1946. To ensure stable government and solve the difficult problems posed by warfare in Algeria and involved foreign relations, a new constitution setting up the Fifth Republic was adopted in 1958. After the loss of Indo-China, France's pressing problem remained Algeria. Keeping in step with the international trend after the Second World War, France granted independence to most of her former possessions, with whom she maintains close relations within the framework of the French Community. The capital is Paris (pop. 1962 2,811,171). Other large cities are Marseilles (661,492), Lyons (471,270), Toulouse (268,283), Bordeaux (257,946), Nice (244,360), Nantes (222,790) and Strasbourg (200,921).

FRANCE, Anatole (Jacques Anatole Thibault, 1844—1924), French novelist. He wrote ironic novels in pellucid prose, of which the best-known is *Penguin Island*, a history of modern France in the form of a fable. As he grew older he became increasingly critical of religion and moved to the left in politics; irony turned to satire, and sensibility to sensuality. Of his many novels, *The Crime of Sylvestre Bonnard*, *La Rôtisserie de la reine Pédauque* and *Thaïs* are representative; of his other miscellaneous works, his debunking of France's great heroine in *La Vie de Jeanne d'Arc* was particularly unpopular. Anatole France was awarded the Nobel Prize for literature in 1921.

FRANCHISE, originally a special privilege granted to a citizen or a corporation by a governmental authority, has come to mean the right to vote. The degree to which this approaches universality is regarded as the chief index of progress towards full democracy. The normal development is from a franchise based on status and property qualifications to one limited only by sex and age, and finally by age alone. In colonies developing towards independence special problems arise owing to mass illiteracy and sharp differences in average educational standards, especially in multiracial communities, and many ingenious franchise systems have been devised to meet them; but they collapsed one by one before the cry 'one man, one vote'.

In Britain the Reform Act of 1932 admitted the middle class to the franchise, and swept away rotten boroughs (i.e. those where representation was out of all proportion to population). The slogans 'no taxation without representation' and 'votes for women' led to successive enlargements: in 1867 and 1887 Acts of Parliament brought in all adult male householders and lodgers; in 1918 all men over 21 and all women of 30 or more; and in 1928 all people over 21 except peers, lunatics and felons, were given the vote. See Women's Suffrage.

FRANCIS I (1494—1547), King of France from 1515. He recovered Milan and secured the right of choosing French bishops and abbots but was defeated by Charles V in his efforts to be elected Holy Roman emperor. He fought four fruitless wars with Charles, in one of which he was taken prisoner and forced to agree to humiliating terms. In 1546 he made peace with Charles and his ally, Henry VIII of England. Though a patron of arts and literature, Francis was a worthless and cynical monarch, who did not hesitate to foment Protestant risings abroad while persecuting their fellow-religionists at home, as in the massacre of 1545. His chief success was in consolidating the power of the French throne.

FRANCIS JOSEPH I (1830—1916), Emperor of Austria. He ascended the throne of Austria in 1848 and became King of Hungary in 1867, founding the Dual Monarchy of Austria-Hungary. He lost Lombardy to Italy in 1859, helped Prussia rob Denmark of Schleswig-Holstein, and was himself defeated by Prussia at Sadowa (Königgratz, 1866). In 1878 he annexed Bosnia and Herzegovina. The Triple Alliance of Germany, Austria and Italy (1883) led to the First World War, but by that time he had, with old age, long ceased to control the destinies of his country.

FRANCIS OF ASSISI, St (1182—1226), monk and founder of the Franciscan Order. The son of a wealthy merchant, after a wild youth he renounced his inheritance (1206) and devoted himself to helping lepers, beggars and the poor. After a visit to Palestine, he saw a vision and found upon his body the stigmata of the wounds suffered by Jesus during the Crucifixion. By his own example and preaching, he sought to pattern his life after that of the Saviour. See Franciscans.

FRANCIS XAVIER, St (1506—52), Spanish Jesuit missionary. One of the founders of the Society of Jesus, he devoted his life to missionary work in India and Japan. He was canonised in 1622.

FRANCISCANS (Grey Friars), a Roman Catholic mendicant religious order founded (1209) by St Francis of Assisi. They are renowned for their work among the lower social classes, their missionary efforts and their contributions to theology.

FRANCK, César Auguste (1822—90), Flemish-born French composer and organist. His works were mostly of a religious nature. His chromatic style, derived from Liszt and the German Romantics, influenced French music.

His outstanding works are the Symphony in D Minor, the Violin Sonata, the Piano Quintet, Symphonic Variations and *Les Béatitudes*.

FRANCO, Francisco, (1892—), Spanish dictator. In 1936 he led an uprising against the republican government and three years later, victorious with the help of Nazi Germany and Fascist Italy, established a totalitarian form of government.

FRANCO-PRUSSIAN WAR (1870—71). The Prussian Prime Minister, Bismarck, provoked France into declaring war in 1870 by his intrigues to place Prince Leopold, a Hohenzollern relative of the King of Prussia, on the throne of Spain. Assured of the neutrality of the other European powers and the support of the south German states, Bismarck built up an effective war-machine which inflicted a series of defeats on the French, culminating in that of Sedan, and took Emperor Napoleon III prisoner. The peace treaty signed in May 1871 provided for the cession of Alsace and Lorraine to Germany, which, as Bismarck had planned, had become a unified empire four months earlier, and for the payment of an indemnity amounting to £20,000,000.

FRANKFURT-ON-MAIN, a city in Hessen, West Germany. Pop. (1960) 657,735. A banking and industrial centre on the Main River, it was the city where the Holy Roman Emperors were crowned from 1152—1806, and the seat of the German Diet from 1816—66. It was the birthplace of Goethe and of the early Rothschilds. The chemical industry is famous for the production of aniline dyes and drugs.

FRANKLIN, Benjamin (1706—90), U.S. statesman, author and scientist. A successful publisher in Philadelphia, he was active in public affairs and interested in scientific experiment. He was an agent in England for several American colonies, and later helped to draft the Declaration of Independence. Franklin succeeded in negotiating alliances with France for help against England. He proved the electrical nature of lightning and invented the lightning conductor, a stove and a clock.

FRANKLIN, Sir John (1786—1847), English Arctic explorer. He explored northern Canada and served as governor of Tasmania. Franklin died attempting to discover the North-West Passage to the Pacific Ocean.

FRASER, see River.

FRAZER, Sir James George (1854—1941), Scottish anthropologist. His most important work is *The Golden Bough*, a mine of information on ancient religions and customs.

FREDERICK I (Barbarossa; *c.* 1123—90), Holy Roman Emperor from 1152. Although he succeeded in maintaining domination over his vassals at home, he lost Lombardy after a series of revolts. Marriage of his son to the daughter of the King of Sicily later brought about the union of that country with the empire. Leading the Third Crusade, he was drowned in Cilicia, en route to the Holy Land.

FREDERICK II (1194—1250), Holy Roman Emperor and King of Sicily. An admirer of learning and culture, he preferred diplomacy to war. A long struggle with the Papacy led to his excommunication. In 1228 he led a crusade and was crowned King of Jerusalem. In organising his Sicilian kingdom, he laid the foundations of the first modern state. His erudition and versatility earned him the name *Stupor Mundi* given him by Matthew Prior.

FREDERICK II (The Great; 1712—86), King of Prussia. In 1740 he succeeded his father, Frederick William I, who had for many years brutally mistreated him. In a series of wars against Austria, he gained Silesia, winning bloody victories in the Seven Years' War, which he precipitated. In the First Partition of Poland, he annexed large areas to his kingdom. An enlightened despot and able administrator, he was a patron of the arts and sciences and wrote essays in French.

FREEMASONRY, a mutual-aid society for men, taking the form of a secret society with initiation ceremonies, regalia, secret signs and passwords. There is a code of morality and a form of symbolic liturgy. Well-equipped hospitals and charities are maintained. Formed in Britain in the 17th century, it became organised in lodges, on the model of the guilds of stone-masons, whose technical terms have been given symbolic significance by the 'free' (i.e. non-) masons. On the Continent the movement became involved in politics and was banned by the Roman Catholic Church. It is sometimes claimed that inner circles of the Freemasons are the transmitters of some ancient lore, but the main activities noticed by outsiders are the holding of convivial dinners and the giving of mutual assistance.

FREETOWN, capital of Sierra Leone, West Africa. Pop. (1959) 100,000. It has one of the finest natural harbours of West Africa (the second largest in the world) and was much used in the Second World War. It is a coaling station and exports palm oil. Freetown was founded as a home for freed slaves.

FREE WILL, the freedom of man to choose, held to be essential if judgments about the good and evil of men's actions are to have any meaning. Other theological arguments were that if God is good the evil in the world must be man's responsibility; and that the very concept of sin implies guilt, and guilt implies freedom to act otherwise. The Pelagians held that when men act righteously it is of their own free will and God will reward them, a view attacked by St Augustine (see Predestination) and condemned as heretical. Pascal put forward the view that whatever the rational arguments against Free Will, we know from inner experience that we are in fact free. Rousseau stemmed the tide of 18th-century Determinism (q.v.), and Kant pointed out that 'ought' implies 'can'. Modern developments in scientific thought lead to the view that although most things obey physical laws some demonstrably do not, thus offering another loophole for attack on Determinism.

FREIBURG-IM-BREISGAU, a city in Baden-Württemberg, West Germany. Pop. (1960) 138,972. Between the Black Forest and the Rhine, it has one of the finest German cathedrals and a 15th-century university. Industries include metals, textiles and paper.

FRENCH GUIANA (Guyane), a French overseas department on the northeast coast of South America. Pop. (1960) 32,000; area 34,740 sq. miles. The area is rich in timber and gold. Bananas, cocoa, maize, rice and sugar-cane are grown. There was a notorious penal colony on Devil's Island from 1854—1938.

FRENCH POLYNESIA, French overseas territory in the east Pacific. Pop. (1960) 65,000; area 1544 sq. miles.

It consists of the scattered islands of the Windward, Leeward, Tuamotu, and Marquesas groups. The most important products are phosphates and copra. The capital is Papeete on Tahiti.

FRENCH REVOLUTION (1789—99). Among the many factors which converged to bring about the Revolution were the waning prestige of an absolute monarchy, the growing irresponsibility of a supreme aristocracy, the undermining of Church influence by the intelligentsia, vexatious taxation and the survival of feudal dues, the ideas assimilated by Frenchmen who participated in the American War of Independence, and the rise of a prosperous middle class. It was clear that absolute monarchy had already become an anachronism. Louis XVI had inherited a bankrupt France and his pleasure-seeking court opposed all Turgot's and Necker's attempts at reform. On May 5, 1789 Louis was forced to convene, for the first time since 1615, the States-General, an assembly representing the three orders — nobles, clergy and the Third Estate (the commons or *bourgeoisie*). In June the Third Estate broke away from the States-General to form the National Assembly, which took the 'tennis-court oath' not to dissolve itself until it had given the country a constitution.

The king ordered its dissolution, dismissed Necker and called in troops from the provinces. The people of Paris rose in support of the Assembly, stormed the Bastille (q.v.) and formed the National Guard. There were similar uprisings in the provinces, and Louis was forced to withdraw his troops and recall Necker. A Declaration of the Rights of Man was promulgated, and the royal family were brought from Versailles to Paris as virtual prisoners; Louis attempted to escape the next year, but was caught at Varennes and brought back.

In 1791 under a new constitution, formally accepted by the king, a new Legislative Assembly met, dominated by the moderate republican Girondists. French émigré nobles in Austria and elsewhere on the frontiers of France were scheming for a counter-revolution, and it occurred to the Girondists that nothing would be more likely to discredit the king than a foreign war. The king and the Austrian Marie Antoinette, on the other hand, felt that in the disorder of war they might hope to be rescued, especially by the queen's relatives. The extremist Jacobins, however, under Danton, Robespierre and Marat, opposed war, thinking that it might help the king. The Girondists won their point, and France in April 1792 declared war on Austria, and later on Prussia. The first result was a series of defeats, which so angered the Paris mob that they attacked the Tuileries and deposed the king; this was followed by the September Massacres, the first great excess of the Revolution, organised by the Commune (q.v.) and the Jacobins. On September 22 the Legislative Assembly gave place to a National Convention of 749 members chosen by universal suffrage, and its first act was to declare a republic. In January 1793 the Jacobins outvoted the Girondists, and had their way by sending Louis and Marie Antoinette to the guillotine. The Girondins were expelled from the Convention, and the Jacobins, supported by the Commune and the mob, set up the Committee of Public Safety and the Revolutionary Tribunal, thus starting the Reign of Terror (March, 1793—July, 1794) which sent thousands of counter-revolutionaries to the guillotine.

By the following year, thanks to Carnot's brilliant organisation of a 'people's army', France's enemies were on the defensive, and Danton argued that the terror was no longer necessary. Robespierre, regarding this as heresy, had Danton guillotined. He overreached himself, however, by his Prairial Law, which deprived members of the Convention of their immunity from arrest. In Thermidor (July/August 1794) they had Robespierre arrested and, in spite of Commune support for him, executed. In Vendemiaire (September/October) the Convention was replaced by a Directory of five (including Barras and Carnot), which abolished the Commune, disbanded the Jacobin Club and recalled the moderate Girondists.

In the meantime the war abroad went well for France. Prussia, Spain and Holland withdrew from the war, leaving Austria and Britain to fight on alone. In 1796 Bonaparte conquered Lombardy and in 1798 he was in Egypt, dreaming Alexandrine dreams of conquest. Alarmed, Russia re-entered the war, and the French were driven out of Italy. In the *coup d'état* of Brumaire (November 9, 1799) Napoleon overthrew the Directory and ended the Revolution. He was proclaimed First Consul and then Emperor. Peace was made with Austria in 1801, with Britain in 1802.

FREUD, Sigmund (1856—1939), Austrian psychiatrist, founder of psychoanalysis. His investigations in hysteria led him to discover the decisive functions of the unconscious mind. Tracing the formation of an individual's personality from his early psychosexual development, Freud attributed to repression a leading role in the evolution of neurotic behaviour. Although many of his concepts at first met with violent opposition, they continue to exert a strong influence not only in psychology but also in medicine, literature, art, anthropology and sociology. His works include *The Interpretation of Dreams*, *The Psychopathology of Everyday Life* and *A General Introduction to Psychoanalysis.*

FREYBERG, Bernard Cyril, 1st Baron (1889—1963), New Zealand soldier. Born in London and educated at Wellington College, New Zealand, he served in the Dardanelles campaign and won the V.C. in the Battle of the Somme (1916). In 1939 he was appointed Commander-in-Chief New Zealand Forces Overseas, commanded all Allied forces in Crete (1941) and won the third bar to his D.S.O. in Italy in 1945. He was Governor-General of New Zealand (1946—52), then Deputy Constable and Lieutenant-Governor of Windsor Castle.

FRICTION, the resistance engendered when two surfaces slide or roll over one another. More effort is necessary to initiate such motion than to maintain it. Lubricants and bearings minimise the destructive effects of friction.

FRIENDS, SOCIETY OF (Quakers), a Christian sect which grew out of the preaching of George Fox in England during the 17th century. Their basic conviction is that a measure of God's spirit is given to every human being, and that this is sufficient guidance; they do not therefore feel any need for ordained clergy or for sacraments. They have always been champions of liberty, supporting anti-slavery measures, penal reform and freedom of conscience in general. They abhor war, but their pacifism has not prevented their giving distinguished service in both World Wars in the Friends' Ambulance Unit.

FRISIAN ISLANDS, a chain of islands parallel to the coasts of the Netherlands and Germany. The main islands are Texel, Vlieland and Ameland, all of which are Dutch; an eastern group of small islands is German.

FROBISHER, Sir Martin (1535—94), English navigator. Seeking a North-West Passage to the Pacific he discovered the bay now named after him in the southeast of Baffin Island. In search of gold, he twice returned to the same area, and also visited the West Indies. He distinguished himself in battles against the Spanish Armada (1588).

FROEBEL, Friedrich Wilhelm August (1782—1852), German educationist. He established the kindergarten system for the purpose of providing early training in furthering the natural physical and mental development of the child's personality.

FROST, Robert Lee (1874—1963), American poet. He wrote sensitive poetry about his native New England. His works include *North of Boston*, *Mountain Interval*, *A Further Range*, *A Witness Tree* and *New Hampshire*. Considered one of the great modern poets of American democracy, he was awarded the Pulitzer Prize for poetry in 1924, 1931, 1937 and 1943.

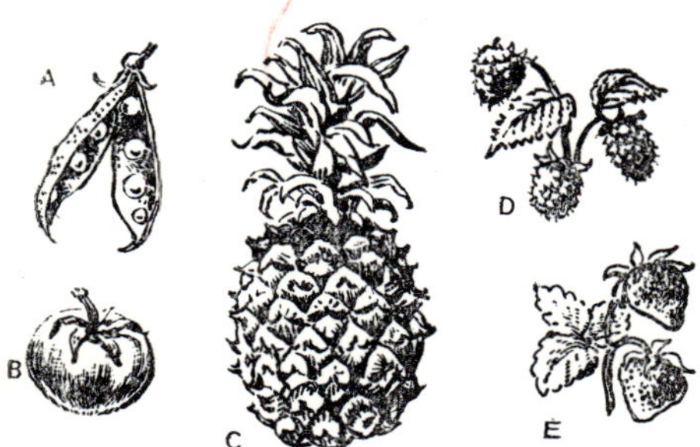

Fruit
A. Pea B. Tomato C. Pineapple D. Raspberries E. Strawberries

FRUIT, the mature ovary, or central reproductive organ, of the pistil of a flower. Most fruits consist of a single such ovary and are either fleshy (tomato, cucumber, cherry, orange) or dry (pea, poppy, mustard). Aggregate fruits consist of a cluster of matured ovaries (raspberry). Multiple or compound fruits are made up of a cluster of matured ovaries which have developed from a number of separate flowers (pineapple). Accessory fruits consist of an ovary, together with other parts of the flower (apple, pear, strawberry).

FUKUOKA, a city of Kyushu, Japan. Pop. (1955) 544,312. It is the largest city of Kyushu and an important port. It has a university, and silk weaving and ceramics industries.

FULTON, Robert (1756—1815), American inventor and engineer. Applying the use of steam to navigation, he constructed the first steamboat. His *Clermont* sailing between New York City and Albany, New York, was the first steamboat plying on a regular service.

FUNDY, Bay of, an arm of the Atlantic Ocean between New Brunswick and Nova Scotia, Canada. It is 145 miles long, and averages 35 miles in width. There is a 50-ft difference in the rise and fall of the tide.

FUNGI, a group of plants lacking chlorophyll. They include moulds, mildews, yeasts, mushrooms and toadstools. Since the lack of chlorophyll makes it impossible for them to manufacture their own

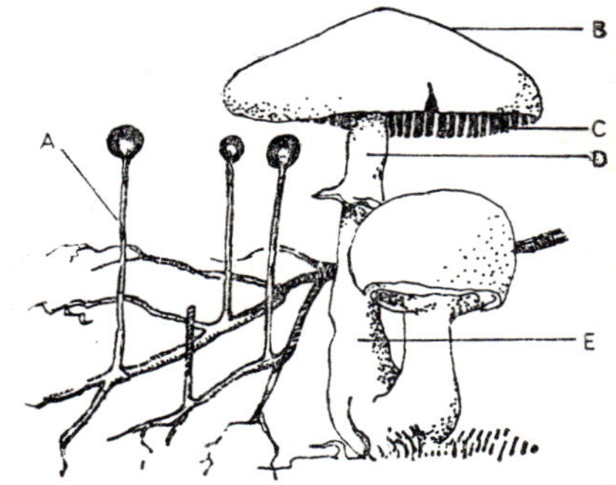

Common Mould and Toadstool
A. Mucor or Pin Mould (highly magnified)
B. Pileus C. Gills D. Vellum E. Stipe

food, they either live upon plant or animal hosts as parasites, or on dead organic matter. They reproduce by forming spores. Fungi grow best in warm, humid climates. They can destroy crops, clothing, foodstuffs and certain aquatic animals. They can also cause disease. On the other hand, some fungi provide penicillin, flavour cheeses, etc., and many species are edible.

FURNESS, a peninsula in north Lancashire, England. It has deposits of haematite iron ore. Barrow-in-Furness has shipbuilding and other industries.

FYN, the second largest island in Denmark. Pop. (1955) 346,578; area 1320 sq. miles. It has beautiful wooded countryside and produces fruit, flax, hemp and grains. The chief city is Odense.

GABON, a republic in West Africa. Pop. (1961) 440,000; area 103,088 sq. miles. The coastal lowland rises to a plateau in the interior. Gabon is covered with tropical forests. By far the most important product is okoumé (Gabon mahogany), which accounts for half the total exports by value; other exports are plywood, veneers, petroleum, cocoa and a little gold. Gabon, formerly part of French Equatorial Africa, became independent in 1960. The capital is Libreville.

GAGARIN, Yuri (1934—), Soviet cosmonaut. The first man to travel in space, he was launched by a multi-stage rocket and made a complete circuit of the globe in 108 minutes on April 12, 1961.

GAINSBOROUGH, Thomas (1727—88), English portrait and landscape painter. He painted more than 600 canvases. His work is realistic and noted for its fine colouring, grace and expressiveness. His paintings include *Cornard Wood*, *The Blue Boy*, *The Painter's Daughters*, *The Market Cart*, and portraits of *George* III, *Clive*, *Sheridan*, *Burke*, *Mrs Siddons* and *Dr Johnson*.

GALAPAGOS, a group of volcanic islands in the Pacific Ocean *c.* 600 miles west of Ecuador, to which they belong. Pop. 1500; area 2868 sq. miles. The group has peculiar plant and animal life, including giant tortoises.

GALAXY, a star system containing millions of stars. Galaxies vary considerably in size and shape and may be separated from one another by millions of light-years. The space between them is nearly devoid of heavenly bodies. The name was originally given to one such system, the Milky Way, of which the solar system forms a small part. The other galaxies, of which there are many millions, were called extra-galactic nebulae.

GALEN (Claudius Galenus; A.D. 131—200), Greek physician. Famed in Rome for his methods of diagnosis and prognosis, he left a large body of works, some of which misled physicians up to the time of the Renaissance because of their erroneous hypotheses; but his physiology, anatomy and descriptions of common complaints show accurate observation.

GALICIA, a region of southeast Poland and southwest Ukrainian S.S.R., north of the Carpathians. A part of Austria before the First World War, it was subsequently awarded to Poland. It was the scene of major battles in both World Wars. Important cities are Lvov, Krakow and Przemysl.

GALILEO (1564—1642), Italian astronomer and physicist, and father of modern experimental science. His discoveries include the law of vibrations of a pendulum; the four satellites of Jupiter; the moon's monthly and annual librations; and sun spots. He invented a hydrostatic balance and by dropping

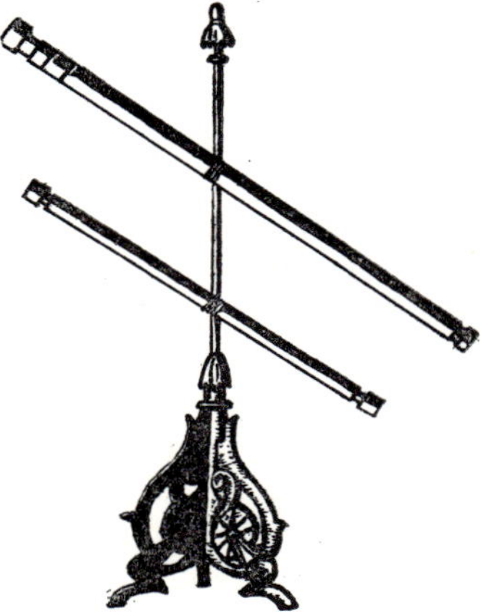

Galileo's telescopes on stand

objects from the Leaning Tower of Pisa proved that all falling bodies descend at the same velocity. On his knees he was forced by the Inquisition to abjure his belief that the earth revolves around the sun, the Copernican theory which he had supported, but which had recently been declared heresy; the story that he muttered '*eppur si muove*' ('nevertheless, it does move') is, unfortunately, pure legend. He made the first astronomical telescope, named after him, with which he made many of his most important observations. It was Galileo's work on which Newton based his laws of motion.

GALLIPOLI (Gelibolu), a town and peninsula dominating the Dardanelles, European Turkey. It was the scene of an unsuccessful landing by Allied troops in 1915 (see Dardanelles).

GALSWORTHY, John, (1867—1933), English novelist and dramatist. He described upper middle-class English family life. His most famous work is embodied in the vast sweep of the *Forsyte Saga* and its sequel *A Modern Comedy*. He also wrote *The Patrician*, and a collection of short stories called *Caravan*. He wrote several successful plays on themes of social conflict, e.g. *Strife, Justice* and *The Skin Game*. In 1923 he was awarded the Nobel Prize for literature, and the Order of Merit in 1929.

GALTON, Sir Francis (1822—1911), English anthropologist and eugenist. From meteorology he passed to studies of heredity. He established a laboratory for the purpose of assembling data on various individual characteristics and traits. Galton believed that the human race could be improved by breeding among superior persons, thus founding the study of eugenics.

GALVANI, Luigi (1737—98), Italian physiologist and anatomist. He discovered galvanic activity in animals.

GALWAY, a maritime county in the western province of Connacht, Irish Republic. Pop. (1961) 149,800; area 2452 sq. miles. Agriculture (field crops; livestock), fishing and quarrying are the principal occupations. Oil and mineral deposits have recently been reported.

Textiles are manufactured. The county has numerous antiquities. The county town and chief port is Galway.

GAMA, Vasco da (*c.* **1469—1524),** Portuguese navigator. Taking with him Bartholomeu Diaz, who had already doubled the Cape of Good Hope, he sailed round the Cape, up the east coast of Africa and across to India where he landed at Calicut, the first European to make the sea voyage to India. On a second voyage he founded a colony at Mozambique and returned to Calicut to revenge a previous massacre with great savagery, returning laden with plunder and having laid the foundations of Portuguese rule in India. Towards the end of his life he was sent out to Goa as viceroy of India, but died within two months of his arrival.

GAMBIA, British colony and protectorate in West Africa. Pop. (1960) 280,000; area 4003 sq. miles. A narrow strip of territory on either bank of the Gambia River, it produces chiefly groundnuts. The capital is Bathurst.

GAMMA RAYS, electromagnetic waves with a wavelength much shorter than light, which carry away excess energy from a nucleus. Having no electric charge they penetrate matter easily. They accompany alpha and beta ray emission. See also Positron.

GANDHI, Mahatma Mohandas Karamchand (1869—1948), Indian political leader, social reformer and saint. An advocate of non-cooperation and passive resistance to British rule, he was imprisoned a number of times for inciting to civil disobedience. A self-imposed fast became one of his principal weapons. From 1893 to 1915 he was in South Africa practising as a barrister, and did much to improve the conditions of the large Indian community there. From 1921 he led the Indian Congress party, and remained politically active until his assassination. He did more than any man to win India's independence, and his ideals are still remembered there, if not always followed.

GANGES, see River.

GARIBALDI, Giuseppe (1807—82), Italian patriot born in Nice of working-class parents. In 1834 he joined Mazzini, but was sentenced to death and escaped to South America, where he led an adventurous life. He returned to Italy in 1848 and commanded the army of the Roman Republic which defended Rome against the French. After a period of exile he again fought in the war of liberation against the Austrians in 1859. When revolt against Bourbon tyranny broke out in Naples and Sicily, he and his famous Thousand Redshirts conquered the Two Sicilies for the new kingdom of Italy. His relations with Cavour had, however, become strained, over the handing-over of his birthplace to the French and the refusal to allow him to destroy the Papal government, and he went into retirement. France, with some reluctance, accepted his assistance in the Franco-Prussian War. For the rest of his life he was an invalid in retirement at Caprera in Sicily.

GAS, a substance capable of unlimited expansion and diffusion. Gas molecules are in constant motion. Gases easily mix with each other, unless a chemical action takes place, and are soluble in water and other solvents to varying degrees. Decreasing the temperature or increasing the pressure diminishes the volume. Most gases can be liquefied at appropriate lowered temperatures, or at corresponding high pressures. Coal gas is extracted from coal and used in lighting and heat-

This Sheraton (q.v.) bookcase and writing desk is a fine example of English 18th century furniture, as is the Adam (q.v.) rosewood and satinwood cabinet inlaid with marble mosaics.

Photos: Victoria & Albert Museum

French 18th century furniture is renowned for its elegance. Shown here is a Louis xv writing table of sycamore and lime wood, inlaid with landscape scenes, flowers and medallion of a female head—it belonged to the Princess Sophia. *Photo: Victoria & Albert Museum*

This beautifully worked Louis xvi carved and gilt wood chair is covered in the finest damask.

Photo: Victoria & Albert Museum

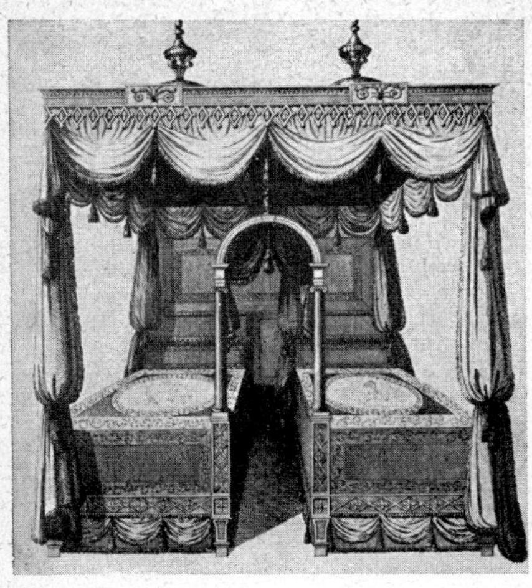

The most exciting modern furniture designs largely originate in Scandinavia. Here is a Danish teakwood chair with leather seat and back. *Photo: Danasco Ltd*

One of Sheraton's more fanciful ideas, 'A Summer Bed in Two Compartments', from one of the volumes of furniture designs he published. *Photo: Victoria & Albert Museum*

William Morris (1834-96) could be called one of the first interior decorators. His furniture, wall-papers carpets, tiles, needlework and tapestries enjoyed a wide popularity during the Victorian era. Shown here is a cabinet with painted panels. *Photo: Victoria & Albert Museum*

A typical Victorian sofa. The back panels are made of papier mâché (q.v.) painted with flowers and inlaid with mother-of-pearl incrustations. *Photo: Victoria & Albert Museum*

ing. Town gas is made for domestic or industrial use. In the U.S.A. gas (short for 'gasolene') also means petrol.

GATT (General Agreement on Tariffs and Trade), an organisation formed at Geneva in 1948 by 23 major trading countries, later joined by others and now responsible for 80% of the world's trade. Its object is to reduce tariffs on a most-favoured-nation basis (i.e. a concession to one country is extended to all members). Many reductions have been made but achievement has fallen short of expectations, and the importance of GATT in Europe has been diminished since the formation of the Common Market and E.F.T.A.

GAUGUIN, Paul (1848—1903), French painter. In 1881 he finally abandoned his family and a business life in order to devote his life to painting. At first working under Impressionist influence, and after a brief period at Arles with Van Gogh, who tried to murder him, he went to the South Seas where he remained, first at Tahiti and for the last few years in the Marquesas. His championship of the islanders got him into frequent trouble with French colonial officials.

Gauguin has been placed among the Post-Impressionists and the Symbolists, and regarded as a precursor of the Fauvists, but he was in fact unclassifiable. He used colour for its own sake, painting red roads and violet grass, in a highly simplified style with large areas of flat colour, almost without modelling, and with strongly rhythmical lines. His last important work was entitled *D'où venons-nous? Que sommes-nous? Où allons-nous?*

GAULLE, Charles de (1890—), French statesman and military leader. After the fall of France in 1940, he escaped to England and formed the National Liberation Committee, commanding the Free French army which continued the war against Germany. From 1944—46 he was provisional President. In 1947 he founded a reform party, the French People's Rally. From 1953—58 he retired from public life, but returned as President when a popular referendum changed the constitution and inaugurated the Fifth Republic based on a strong presidency. De Gaulle sought to restore France to the status of a world power. The solution of the Algerian problem has occupied much of his later years.

GDANSK (Danzig), a city in northern Poland, on the Baltic Sea. Pop. (1960) 286,000. Near the mouth of the Vistula River, it is a major port and shipbuilding centre. Part of Prussia from 1793—1918 and then a Free City, it became the pretext for Hitler's invasion of Poland in 1939. Faced with Nazi threats to absorb the Free City, Poland developed the neighbouring port of Gdynia, the importance of which has diminished since the return of Gdansk to Poland after the Second World War.

GEIGER COUNTER, a device for detecting and counting individual atomic particles. It is used for detecting the presence of radioactivity in atomic projects, and in the wake of atomic bomb explosions. For many purposes it has been superseded by the scintillation counter.

GEISHA, a Japanese female entertainer, hired out for parties. Geishas receive a long period of training, often beginning as early as the seventh year, in deportment, singing, dancing and playing musical instruments. Originally an honourable profession, it has, especially under the influence of military occupation, somewhat degenerated.

GENETICS, the science which deals with heredity and variation among living organisms. Although similar traits are transmitted from one generation to another, no two individuals are exactly alike. The study began with Mendel's experiments in hybridising garden peas. He found the results were due to the part played by dominant and recessive 'factors' — now identified as the genes and chromosomes, which can be combined in different ways, and which, in complex interaction with one another, determine the rate at which various chemical reactions take place.

GENEVA, a city in Switzerland, on Lake Geneva and the Rhône River. Pop. (1960) 174,300. In addition to having libraries, museums and a university, it is the headquarters of the International Red Cross and various U.N. agencies. It manufactures watches, precision instruments and chemicals. The headquarters of the League of Nations, dissolved in 1946, was at Geneva.

GENEVA CONVENTION, an agreement concluded at Geneva in 1864 (revised in 1868 and 1906) providing for the humane treatment of the sick and wounded in wartime, and for those who care for them. A distinctive white flag with a red cross was adopted to identify personnel, their vehicles and installations, and gave its name to the International Red Cross movement. Later additions dealt with the treatment of prisoners and civilians in occupied territory.

GENGHIS KHAN (1162–1227), Mongol emperor. He conquered and efficiently ruled empires extending from the Black Sea to the Pacific Ocean. His well-disciplined armies plundered regions stretching from Russia to India and as far as northeast China.

GENOA, a city in northwest Italy. Pop. (1959) 752,983. A busy western Mediterranean port, it is an important industrial centre, producing ships, automobiles, foodstuffs, textiles and chemicals. There are numerous historical relics, and a university founded in 1471.

GEOGRAPHY, the science dealing with the physical features of the earth's surface and the distribution and activities of its peoples. Physical geography studies the topographic features; economic geography, the relationship of industry, communications, mineral resources, etc., to their geographic background; political geography, the influence of geography on international relations; and historical geography, the geography of times past.

GEOLOGY, the study of the composition, structure, and history of the earth. It interprets the past as it is revealed in rocks. It is concerned with the origin of the earth; the forces which cause its crust to change; the chemical composition of minerals; the arrangement of different layers and kinds of rocks; and the fossil remains of ancient living organisms. The data assembled by geologists is also useful in solving engineering problems and discovering valuable minerals. Rocks are classified into three groups: igneous, crystalline rocks formed by the consolidation of molten rock from the interior of the earth (e.g. granite, basalt, gabbro); sedimentary, deposits of material worn away from older rocks (e.g. sandstone, shale, limestone); metamorphic, transformed from older rocks by intense heat or pressure (e.g. slate, gneiss). From the earliest times to the present, the earth's history is divided into the following eras, each of which marked a new stage of development; they are shown in the accompanying table.

Era	*Period*	*Age (millions of years)*	*Forms of life*
Archaean	Pre-Cambrian	1750	None
Palaeozoic	Cambrian	600	Aquatic invertebrates; no life on land
	Ordovician	500	
	Silurian	400	
	Devonian	350	Primitive plants, fish
	Carboniferous	300	Amphibians, insects, dense forest.
	Permian	220	Mammals, reptiles
Mesozoic	Triassic	190	Birds, dinosaurs
	Jurassic	160	
	Cretaceous	130	
Cainozoic (Tertiary)	Eocene	70	Flowering plants, molluscs
	Oligocene	50	
	Miocene	30	
	Pliocene	15	
Cainozoic (Quaternary)	Pleistocene (Glacial)	1	Stone Age Man
	Recent (Holocene)	—	Modern Man (25,000 years)

GEORGE, St (d. 303), patron saint of England. A devoted adherent of Christianity, he is supposed to have come from Cappadocia. Legend portrays him slaying a dragon in order to rescue the daughter of the King of Libya, Selena, who subsequently adopted Christianity. He was made patron of the Order of the Garter by Edward III.

GEORGE I (1660—1727), King of Great Britain and Elector of Hanover. The first king of the house of Brunswick, he ascended the throne in 1714, on the death of Queen Anne, as a direct descendant of James I. He was unpopular on account of the favouritism he showed Hanover. Because the king spoke little English and was often absent in Hanover, Robert Walpole was able to initiate the cabinet system. During his reign, the Jacobite insurrection was suppressed.

GEORGE II (1683—1760), King of Great Britain and Elector of Hanover. Succeeding his father, George I, in 1727, he witnessed the expansion of British power in North America and India. He had to contend with the second Jacobite rebellion (1745) under the Young Pretender (Bonnie Prince Charlie). He sided with Maria Theresa in the War of the Austrian Succession. In the Seven Years War, which broke out during his reign, Britain was allied with Prussia. His reign was dominated by the Whigs.

GEORGE III (1738—1820), King of Great Britain and Ireland. The grandson of George II, he ascended the throne in 1760. He managed to rid himself of Whig domination and chose his own prime minister, Lord North, who was instrumental in losing the American colonies in 1776. The Seven Years War ended during his reign. From 1793—1815 England was usually at war with France. George III became permanently insane in 1810, and the country was ruled by his son, the Prince Regent.

GEORGE IV (1762—1830), King of Great Britain and Ireland. He served as Prince Regent for nine years before ascending the throne in 1820. His extravagant and profligate way of life made him unpopular. He married Mrs Fitzherbert, but the marriage was declared void; in 1785 he married Caroline of Brunswick, and parliament celebrated the occasion by paying off his debts; he then tried to divorce Caroline. He opposed reform, and especially Catholic Emancipation.

GEORGE V (1865—1936), King of Great Britain and Ireland. The second son of Edward VII, he ascended the throne in 1910. The first ruling monarch to visit his dominions, he travelled to India to be proclaimed Emperor. George V displayed a strong and enduring interest in his people and his country's affairs. He celebrated his silver jubilee in 1935.

GEORGE VI (1895—1952), King of Great Britain and Northern Ireland. The second son of George V, he ascended the throne in 1936 on the abdication of his brother, Edward VIII. Highly respected throughout the Commonwealth, he and his queen visited France, the U.S.A., Canada and the Union of South Africa; as Duke and Duchess of York they had previously visited Australia and New Zealand and opened the new Parliament House at Canberra.

GEORGIA, a constituent republic of the U.S.S.R., on the Black Sea. Pop. (1959) 4,049,000; area 37,570 sq. miles. In its warm climate are grown tea, grapes, tobacco, citrus fruits and grains. Livestock raising is important. There are deposits of manganese, oil, coal and iron. Textiles, foods, and metal equipment are manufactured. The capital is Tbilisi (Tiflis; pop. 694,000). Other important cities are Kutaisi (128,000) and Batoumi (82,000).

GEORGIA, a southeastern state of the U.S.A. Pop. (1960) 3,943,116; area 58,876 sq. miles. Mountainous in the west and north central region, it is flat in the south and southeast. Cotton, tobacco, peaches, pecans, groundnuts and maize are grown. There are deposits of kaolin and fuller's earth. Its forests are rich in resin and turpentine. Settled in 1733, it was one of the original 13 states of the U.S.A. Georgia was a member of the Confederacy (1861—65).

GERMAN DEMOCRATIC REPUBLIC, the socialist state of East Germany, a former U.S.S.R. zone of occupation. Pop. (1959) 16,213,000; area 41,571 sq. miles. Level in the north it becomes a plateau merging with mountain ranges farther south. Grains, potatoes and sugar-beet are raised. Livestock is important. The area has coal, lignite, uranium and potash. There are iron and steel, cement and chemical industries. The capital is East Berlin (pop. 1,071,800). Other important cities are Leipzig (pop. 1960 589,600), Dresden (493,600), Karl-Marx-Stadt (Chemnitz) (286,300), Halle (277,900) and Magdeburg (261,600).

GERMAN FEDERAL REPUBLIC, the Republic of West Germany. Pop. (1961) 53,973,000; area 95,707 sq. miles. The terrain consists of a plain in the north, hills in the central portion and mountains in the south. Administratively it is divided into ten states. Field crops and livestock are the principal agricultural products. Timber and fishing are important. Coal, lignite, iron, copper, potash and petroleum are produced. Industrial products consist of machinery, textiles, vehicles, ships and chemicals. West German industry recovered in a remarkably short time from the effects of the Second World War. The capital is Bonn (pop. 146,216). Other important cities are Hamburg (1,837,000), Munich (1,101,400), Cologne (801,100), Essen (729,500), Düsseldorf (697,900), and Frankfurt-on-Main (675,000). The population of West Berlin is 2,202,200. The highly industrial area of the Saar was incorporated in 1956.

GERMANY, former state in central Europe, divided since 1949 between the German Federal Republic and the German Democratic Republic (qq.v.). It consists of a wide plain in the north, fanning out towards the east. The valley of the Danube, and the basin of the Neckar and the Main, extend across the southern portion. The Oder and Neisse rivers form the eastern boundary; the Rhine valley runs north along the western border. The Bavarian Alps in the south reach a height of 9722 ft in the Zugspitze. Parts of Germany came under Roman rule. The area east of the Rhine, under Lewis the German, formed the basis of Germany after the division of Charlemagne's Frankish empire in 843. Otto the Great created the *Mark* of Austria, conquered Italy and was crowned emperor at Rome in 962. Germany became the foremost power in Europe and for several centuries was virtually identical with the Holy Roman Empire. In the 12th century, there were bitter disputes between the emperor and the Pope. Frederick I (Barbarossa) made peace with the Pope but lost the north Italian cities. Between 1254 and 1273 the feudal lords of Germany were almost independent. Until Maximilian I ascended the throne in 1486, the country was racked by constant internecine warfare. The religious animosity engendered by the Reformation gave rise to the Thirty Years War which devastated Germany. Under Frederick the Great, Prussia assumed leadership in German affairs in the 18th century. After Napoleon's defeat, a confederation of German states came into being which did not become an effective instrument of unity until it was revived in 1867. In 1871 the North German Confederation combined with the South German states to form a united Germany under Wilhelm I, after the defeat of France in the Franco-Prussian War. German science, industry and commerce made immense strides in the subsequent years. Germany's interests soon conflicted with those of Great Britain. Conscious of its vast military and economic power, Germany recklessly precipitated the First World War. The collapse of the German Empire in 1918 was followed by the establishment of a republic which had to grapple with increasing enonomic disruption and social unrest in a country unused to, and even contemptuous of, democratic rule. In 1933 Hitler and his National Socialist Party seized power in Germany and established an ultra-nationalist totalitarian state, based on racialism and the doctrine of German superiority. After abrogating the Versailles Treaty, Hitler annexed Austria and Czechoslovakia. In 1939 he threw his newly-forged military machine against Poland. For three years Germany was victorious on all fronts, overrunning most of Europe, except the British Isles, Switzerland, Spain, Portugal and Sweden. In the autumn of 1942, the tide was turned and in May 1945 Germany surrendered unconditionally. Occupied by the four principal allied powers (France, the United Kingdom, the U.S.A. and the U.S.S.R.), Germany was divided, having lost territory to Poland and to the U.S.S.R.

GESTALT PSYCHOLOGY (German, 'pattern'), a German school of psychology which holds that there is an instinctive tendency in man, and in animals, to find significant patterns in sensations, the whole being more than the sum of the parts, as a tune is more than a collection of notes. These patterns and significant relationships are the main basis of learning and mental activity. Similarly, the personality is an integrated whole and not merely the sum of various traits. Founded by Max Wertheimer, Wolfgang Köhler and Kurt Koffka, this school joined issue with Behaviourism (q.v.) and those who emphasised the importance of learning by trial and error or by association of ideas; it considered that an important feature of the learning process was 'insight', the summing up of a situation as a whole and taking action accordingly. This was demonstrated by experiments with animals placed in situations novel to them.

GESTAPO, the secret state police of Nazi Germany *(Geheime Staatspolizei)*. Founded in 1933, it was first led by Hermann Goering. Combined with the Elite Guard (S.S.) in 1936 under Heinrich Himmler, it was subordinate only to the Security Service *(Sicherheitsdienst)* which held a stranglehold on German civilian and political life until the end of the war.

GHANA, a republic within the British Commonwealth, in West Africa. Pop. (1961) 6,691,000; area 91,843 sq. miles. Incorporating the Gold Coast and Togoland under British trusteeship, it became independent in 1958 and was declared a republic two years later. Ghana consists of coastal lowlands behind which are uplands, once forested but to a large extent now cleared for cocoa farming. Further north is savannah and parkland, with broken hill country in the far north and northwest; the northeast is tsetse-ridden and infertile. Ghana produces cocoa (two-thirds of all exports, and one-third of world supplies), kola-nuts, coffee and copra; timber is very important. Minerals include gold, diamonds and bauxite; the last, and industry generally, will be further developed when the great Volta hydro-electric scheme comes into operation. There is an oil refinery, and aluminium, fertiliser, brewing and other industries. The two universities are at Lagon, a suburb of Accra, and Kumasi. Ghana is served by two large artificial harbours, at Takoradi and Tema (opened 1960). The capital is Accra (pop. 1960 491,060). Other important towns are Kumasi (220,922) and Takoradi (41,000).

GHENT, a city in Belgium, capital of eastern Flanders, at the junction of the Scheldt and Lys rivers. Pop. (1959) 160,669. On a canal to the North Sea, Ghent is a textile-manufacturing centre with many historic buildings. It is famous for its horticultural establishments.

GIBBON, Edward (1737—94), English historian. His monumental *History of the Decline and Fall of the Roman Empire* is a scholarly work written in a stately, elegant style. It aroused hostility because of its critical attitude towards Christianity.

GIBRALTAR, a British naval base and colony on the strait of the same name at the southern tip of Spain. Pop. (1961) 24,502; area 2½ sq. miles. The English, who occupied it in 1704, transformed its rocky promontory into a fortress.

GIBRALTAR, STRAIT OF, a body of water between southern Spain and northern Morocco, connecting the Atlantic Ocean with the Mediterranean Sea. It is 50 miles long and varies in width from 9—23 miles.

GIDE, André (1869—1951), French novelist and essayist. He exerted a profound influence on the intellectual life of his country. His best works are *The Counterfeiters*, *The Immoralist*, and *If It Die*. His *Journals* also rank as a modern classic.

GILBERT, Sir Humphrey (*c.* 1539—83), English navigator and soldier. He served in Ireland and the Netherlands. His first attempt to seek out new lands in North America was thwarted by a clash with the Spaniards. On his second trip he sailed to Newfoundland, establishing the first English colony in North America at St John's (1583), but perished on the return voyage with all his company.

GILBERT, Sir William Schwenck (1836—1911), English librettist. The comic operas he wrote in collaboration with Sullivan made him world-famous. They include *Trial by Jury*, *H.M.S. Pinafore*, *Patience*, *The Pirates of Penzance*, *The Mikado*, *The Gondoliers* and *The Yeomen of the Guard*. Gilbert's brilliantly witty and polished lyrics, though topical, still delight today; it was sad that Sullivan, who had always wanted to devote himself to more serious music, felt compelled to break up the partnership after 20 years in 1891. Gilbert's *Bab Ballads* was a masterpiece of light verse.

GILBERT AND ELLICE ISLANDS, a British colony in the Western Pacific. Pop. (1961) 47,508; area 369 sq. miles. The colony consists chiefly of the Gilbert, Ellice, Phoenix and Line groups, together with the adjacent Ocean Island. Copra and phosphates are exported.

GIOTTO (1266—1337), Italian painter, architect and sculptor. The founder of the Florentine school, he broke away from the stiffness of Byzantine art and became the most influential painter before the Renaissance. His chief surviving works are a series of frescoes at Padua depicting scenes from the life of Christ, and another series at Assisi on the life of St Francis. He designed a mosaic, still to be seen in St Peter's, Rome. There is a much restored portrait of Dante, who praised him in the *Divine Comedy*. The campanile known as Giotto's Tower in Florence, was designed and, in part, built by Giotto.

GISSING, George (1857—1903), English novelist. Concerned mostly with the manifestations of poverty, he was the first modern English writer to write realistically of sex. His most famous work is *New Grub Street*.

GIZA (Gizeh), a town in Lower Egypt, three miles from Cairo, on the Nile. Pop. (1960) 250,000. The ancient pyramids of Cheops and Chephren, the Sphinx and the ruins of Memphis (Sakkara) are near by.

GLACIER, an immense slowly moving mass of compacted ice. Glaciers, descending from heights, shape the surface of the earth, leaving lakes and waterfalls and forming rivers and fiords. As the ice in front of a glacier melts, it forms a moraine of rocks, stone, earth and debris collected in its descent.

Tshierva Glacier. Pontresina, Switzerland

GLADIATORS, professional fighters in ancient Rome. They fought with each other, or with wild animals. A thumb gesture of the spectators decided the fate of a vanquished gladiator. Thumbs down meant death. Some gladiators were low-class freemen fighting for hire, while others were captives, criminals or slaves. Gladiatorial shows were a favourite form of entertainment in Rome until the 5th century A.D.

GLADSTONE, William Ewart (1809—98), British statesman. He began his political career as a Conservative member of parliament in 1833. As President of the Board of Trade under Peel, he became a supporter of free trade. In 1846 he was appointed colonial secretary. As chancellor of the exchequer in Lord Aberdeen's coalition cabinet from 1852—55, and later under Palmerston, he introduced important financial reforms. Having joined the newly-formed Liberal party, he became its leader in 1867. Before becoming Prime Minister for the first time in 1868, he brought about the enactment of resolutions favouring the disestablishment in Ireland of the Church of England. He was Liberal prime minister 1868—74, 1880—85, 1886, and 1892—94. Gladstone was consistently an outspoken advocate of Irish independence but his Home Rule bill of 1886 was defeated when the Liberal Unionists, who included Joseph Chamberlain, voted with the Conservatives against it; his second bill on this subject was rejected by the House of Lords. His legislative achievements include the Education Act of 1870 and the Ballot Act of 1872. An outstanding administrator and financier, he was also a classical scholar and a man of strong religious convictions.

GLAMORGANSHIRE a maritim e county of southeast Wales, on the Bristol Channel. Pop. (1961) 1,227,828; area 813 sq. miles. Possessing rich coalfields and iron deposits, it has copper, tin, iron and lead smelting works. The iron and steel industry has spread to new works at Margam. Agriculture and stock raising are important. The county town is Cardiff.

GLAND, a bodily cell secreting substances from materials extracted from the blood and lymph. In most cases the secretion is a new substance. Glands of external secretion expel their fluids either on the skin (sweat), the mucous membrane of the alimentary canal (saliva) or as milk or sebum, etc. Glands of internal secretion (ductless or endocrine glands) deliver their secretions into the blood stream (e.g. thyroid, adrenal). Some glands, e.g. the pancreas and liver, secrete both internally and externally. See Endocrinology.

GLASGOW, a city in Lanarkshire, west central Scotland, on the Clyde. Pop. (1961) 1,054,913. It is the commercial and industrial centre for all Scotland. Shipbuilding, textiles, and metallurgical products are leading industries. It has few historic buildings except the Cathedral, which dates back to the 13th century and the university (1451), but has many famous cultural institutions.

GLASS, a hard artificial substance of varying transparency manufactured from a mixture of sand (or some form of pure silica), lime or lead oxide, with an alkali (carbonate of soda, sulphate of soda, slaked lime). It softens gradually as the temperature is increased and is easily moulded. It can be welded when red hot. Molten glass can be drawn out into thin threads which are flexible enough to be woven when cool. In manufacturing glass, the proper ingredients in powder form are thoroughly mixed and then fused in open pots and crucibles. The molten mass is then ready for future treatment which may consist of blowing, drawing, casting and pressing. Different kinds of glass are secured by varying the chemical composition of the ingredients. Glass was used in ancient Egypt but it is not clear who invented it.

GLASTONBURY, a town in Somerset, England. It is chiefly famous for its antiquities, which include an 8th-century abbey. Joseph of Arimathaea is said to have brought the Holy Grail there, and to have planted his staff which took root and grew into a thorn-tree.

GLIDER, an aircraft whose only motive power is provided by air currents and the force of gravity. By proper manipulation of the craft in upward currents, the pilot can maintain it in flight for a considerable time. To rise in the air, a glider must move with sufficient speed for suction above its wings and pressure below them to lift it into the air. This can be done by towing, or by some form of catapult. Leonardo da Vinci designed the first glider in the 15th century. Sir George Cayley built several gliders early in the 19th century.

GLIDING, flying in engineless aircraft, developed as a sport after the First World War. Launched from a hill by catapult or towing, the pilot makes use of rising air currents to gain height. Experts have reached heights of 40,000 ft, stayed in flight over 57 hours and covered distances of hundreds of miles. Towed gliders were used in the Second World War for transporting troops.

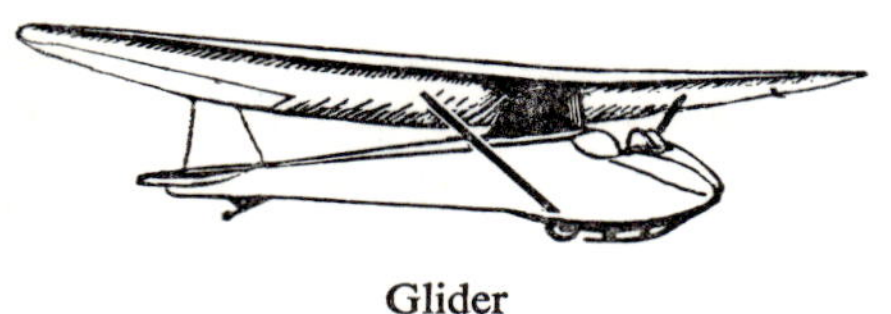

Glider

GLOBE, a sphere used to represent the earth or the heavens. Celestial globes, showing the stars in their relative positions in the heavens, were constructed as early as the 4th century B.C. Illustrations survive of a terrestrial globe thought to have been made as early as the 2nd century B.C.

GLOBE THEATRE, the London playhouse on Bankside, Southwark, where most of Shakespeare's dramas were first

Origina Globe Theatre

presented. Built in 1598, it consisted of a circular pit for standing spectators and three galleries with seats for those paying more. Persons paying the highest fees sat on the stage itself. The Puritans completely destroyed it in 1644.

GLORIOUS REVOLUTION (1688—9), the deposition of James II and the accession of William and Mary to the English throne. At the birth of James's son, Protestants feared the establishment of a Catholic dynasty, and invited William and Mary to rule the country. James fled, and a revolution was accomplished without bloodshed when William landed at Brixham in Torbay. William III, Prince of Orange, was the son of James II's sister, and Mary, who refused to rule without him, was James II's daughter, and a sister of the future Queen Anne.

GLOUCESTERSHIRE, a county in southwest England. Pop. (1961) 1,000,493, area 1257 sq. miles. Consisting of rich valleys in the central portion, it contains the Forest of Dean in the west and the

Cotswold Hills extending from southwest to northeast. Dairy and fruit farming are the main agricultural pursuits. An important industrial region drained by the Severn and Thames rivers, it manufactures heavy machinery, aircraft, textiles, electronic equipment and foodstuffs. There are coal mines. The county town is Gloucester.

GLYCERINE (Glycerol), an alcohol which is the basic ingredient of all fats and oils. It is completely soluble in water and alcohol and is an excellent solvent. Industrial uses include nitroglycerine, pharmaceuticals, perfumes, polishes, plastics, inks, sweets and antifreeze.

GNOSTICISM, a mystical school of thought which flourished in the first centuries A.D. and emphasised the primacy of revelation.

GOBI (Shamo), a large desert in Central Asia, in southern Mongolia and northern China. Its total area is 300,000 sq. miles. Its length is 1500 miles and the average width 600 miles. A railway runs southwards from Ulan Bator across the desert to link with the Chinese system.

GOD, a word of Teutonic origin denoting a deity. In the monotheistic religions the word is applied to the one supreme and absolute being, the creator and preserver of the universe.

GODFREY OF BOUILLON (*c.* 1060—1100), a French knight, one of the leading figures in the First Crusade. He was proclaimed ruler of Jerusalem (1099) and defeated the Egyptians at Ascalon.

GODIVA, Lady (1040—85), a heroine of English legend. She saved the people of Coventry from excessive taxation by accepting the condition of her husband, Leofric, earl of Mercia, that she should ride through the town naked. One man, Peeping Tom, disobeyed orders to stay indoors and was, of course, struck blind.

GOERING, Hermann (1893—1946), German Nazi leader. In the First World War he served in the German Air Force, and in the Second World War he commanded the Luftwaffe. A bullying braggart, he became Hitler's right-hand man, and devised many gorgeous uniforms for himself; a new rank of Reichsmarschall was created for him. However, when it came to organising the whole of the economy of Germany, the limitations of his genius became apparent, and he steadily lost influence with Hitler. He was sentenced to death at Nuremberg, but escaped execution by suicide.

GOETHE, Johann Wolfgang von (1749—1832), Germany's greatest literary genius, with a wider range of interests and achievements than any man since Leonardo da Vinci. Trained as a lawyer, he started to study astrology and mysticism as a young man, and then the literatures of Europe; later he took to the sciences and made important contributions in anatomy, the theory of colour, mathematics and many other subjects. He became the leader of the German *Sturm und Drang* (Storm and Stress) movement of reaction against classical and French standards in literature. His first major work was a play, *Götz von Berlichingen*, which was followed by his famous novel of sentiment, *The Sorrows of Young Werther*. At this stage he settled in Weimar, under the patronage of the Duke of Weimar, visited Italy and met Schiller. His next work included a classical drama, *Iphigeneia*. The novels *Wilhelm Meister* and *Elective Affinities* and the autobiography *Truth and Fiction* were followed by the completion of the second part of his magnum opus, *Faust*, on which he had worked through most of his life.

GOGH, Vincent van (1853—90), Dutch artist. He began to paint in 1880, financed by his brother, at Brussels, Antwerp and Paris, and finally found what he sought in the strong sun and brilliant colours of Provence at Arles. Here he asked Gauguin to join him, tried to murder him, and then cut off his own ear in remorse. He went into an asylum, where he continued to paint masterpieces, but in another fit of insanity shot himself. A leader of the Post-Impressionists, he painted always with passionate vigour and violent colour, throwing the whole of himself into each picture, so that he would fall exhausted when he had finished. His paintings included landscapes of cypresses and fields of waving corn, portraits and self-portraits, and such famous still-lifes as *The Sunflowers* and *The Yellow Chair*.

GOGOL, Nikolai (1809—52), Russian novelist and short-story writer. One of the Russian realists, he wrote *Evenings on a Farm near Dikanka*, *Mirgorod* (including *Taras Bulba*), the celebrated unfinished *Dead Souls*, and the plays *The Inspector General* and *Revizor*. His popular fame is based on his supreme comic and satiric gift, but towards the end of his life he claimed, in a book that made him unpopular in Russia, that his work had aims far more profound than is apparent.

GOLD, see Elements.

GOLDSMITH, Oliver (1730—74), Anglo-Irish novelist, dramatist and poet. His most famous book is the sentimental novel *The Vicar of Wakefield*. Other works of his include the poem *The Deserted Village* and the comedy *She Stoops to Conquer*.

GOLF, the Scottish national game, still controlled from St Andrews where the Royal and Ancient Club was founded in 1754. Played on a course (the original sandy seaside courses were called links) of eighteen holes and a total length of about 6000 yds, with a set of clubs (since the 1930s with steel shafts) and a small ball, the specification of which has been frequently changed, the game consists in getting the ball into the hole in fewer strokes than the opponent(s). Inaccuracy is penalised by the placing of sandy bunkers at strategic points on the fairway, and by the rough ground on either side. To the ability to hit a long drive straight down the fairway has to be added skill in the approach shot to the green and meticulously accurate putting on the level green in the final stage. In match play the scoring is by holes, the game being won when one side is more holes up than there are holes to play (e.g. 3 up and 2 to play, '3 and 2'; 3 and 3 would be dormy). In medal play scoring is by total strokes for the whole round. Bogey is the average number of strokes required for a hole by a good player; par is the number required by a very good (scratch) player; a birdie is one and an eagle two under par. A good player usually returns a score of under 70 for a round. Club members are given a handicap e.g. plus 4 for a very good player, six (i.e. minus 6) for a less expert player.

The game is particularly popular in Scotland, England and the U.S.A. International competitions for individual players include the British Open Championships (1860), the British Amateur Championship (1885), and their American counterparts. Team competitions include the Canada Cup (teams of two professionals) and the Eisenhower Cup (1958; teams of four amateurs). Three competitions are played between the U.S.A. and Great Britain: the Walker Cup

(1922; amateurs), Ryder Cup (professionals) and Curtis Cup (women).

GOLGOTHA, see Calvary.

GOOD FRIDAY, the Friday immediately preceding Easter Sunday, sacred to Christians as commemorating the crucifixion of Jesus.

GORDON, Charles George (Chinese Gordon; 1833—85) British soldier and colonial official. He served in the Crimean War, participated in the capture of Peking in 1860, and suppressed the Taiping rebellion three years later. He became governor of the Equatorial Provinces of Egypt (1873) and governor-general of the Sudan (1877), displaying unusual abilities as an administrator. He was besieged at Khartoum during the Mahdi's revolt, and was killed two days before relief arrived.

GORKY, Maxim (1868—1936), Russian writer. Associated with revolutionary movements from the turn of the century, he wrote realistic works from a proletarian viewpoint. They include the tetralogy *Forty Years*, *Foma Gordeyev*, *The Mother* and the famous play, *The Lower Depths*. His best works were the semi-fictional autobiographies, *My Childhood*, *Out in the World* and *My Universities*. He sponsored the official Soviet policy of 'socialist realism' in literature.

GOSPEL, the 'good tidings' of salvation through Christ. The term subsequently came to denote the book in which the good tidings are contained; hence the first four books of the New Testament are commonly called the Gospels.

GÖTEBORG (Gothenburg), second largest city and chief seaport of Sweden Pop. (1960) 404,758. It is a commercial and industrial centre.

GOTHS, an East Germanic people from Gotland in south Sweden. By the 3rd century A.D. they were already living in the Ukraine. Early in the 4th century, they divided into the Visigoths or West Goths, who moved westwards in face of the advancing Huns, and the Ostrogoths or East Goths, who became their subjects. Under Alaric, the Visigoths. overran Greece and sacked Rome (410). In the 5th century, the Visigoths held all of Gaul and most of the Iberian Peninsula. Roderic, last of the Visigoths fell in battle against the Moors in Spain in 711. Forty years after the Ostrogoths freed themselves from the Huns in 453, their leader, Theodoric, became King of Italy. Their defeat by Justinian in the 6th century ended their existence as a separate people.

GOUACHE, a water-colour paint made opaque by mixing with white, which produces results similar to oil painting. It has the disadvantage of losing tone as it dries. It is the Continental equivalent of the English 'body colour'. See Water-Colour.

GOVERNMENT, the political organisation of a state. Through it, the state enforces its orders and administers its functions. It includes the executive, legislative, and judicial organs and the machinery of public administration, but in modern usage the term is used chiefly of the executive. Government may be based on the rule of a single person, a distinctive class, or derive its powers from the body of its subjects, as in a democracy.

GOYA, Francisco José de (1746—1828), Spanish painter. His outstanding work includes portraits, caricatures, paintings, drawings, and etchings of bull fights and street brawls. His *Family of Charles IV*, *Maja desnuda* (*The Naked*

Maja) and *The Disasters of War* are celebrated works.

GRACE, in Christian theology the unmerited gift of God's favour bestowed on sinful man.

GRAFTING, in horticulture, the union of parts of two plants so that they grow as one. The mature plant or root receiving the graft is called the stock. The part grafted on it (scion) may be a single bud or a twig bearing several buds. The scion and stock should belong to the same botanical family. The best time for grafting is in the winter or early spring when the scion is dormant and the stock just beginning to grow.

GRAMMAR, the science of the structure of a language and the rules which govern its use. It is concerned with word-formation, the parts of speech, the conjugation of verbs, the inflections of nouns to show case or number, and syntax or the construction of sentences. In a wider sense the term includes spelling, pronunciation, etymology and other subjects.

GRANADA, an ancient city in Spain, capital of the former province and Moorish kingdom of Granada. Pop. (1959) 145,169. Granada was the last Moorish kingdom of Spain, surrendered by Boabdil to Ferdinand and Isabella in 1492. The most famous of the Moorish buildings are the Alhambra (q.v.) and the summer palace (1319). The Royal Chapel (1506) contains the tombs of Ferdinand and Isabella; the cathedral dates from 1523.

GRAND ALLIANCE, War of the (War of the English Succession; 1688—97), a war between France and a coalition (the League of Augsburg) consisting of England, the Netherlands, Spain, Savoy, Sweden and the Holy Roman Empire. It was precipitated by Louis XIV's invasion and devastation of western Germany. James II of England had promised the French monarch support but his dethronement and the accession of William III (William of Orange) to the throne, completely altered the situation. Louis sent the deposed king to Ireland in 1689, where William defeated him at the Battle of the Boyne in July. An English naval victory at La Hogue decided that phase of the war, which ended in the exhaustion of both sides, the relinquishment by Louis of most of the territories he had won, and his recognition of William III as the rightful king of England.

GRAND BANK, an under-water plateau southeast of the coast of Newfoundland, east Canada. About 500,000 sq. miles in area, it is rich in codfish.

GRAND CANAL, a canal in China, at one time 1,300 miles long, running from near Peking to Hangchow. One section was built in 486 B.C., others in the 7th and 13th centuries A.D. Many parts of it are still in use, though much has silted up.

GRANT, Ulysses (1822—85), U.S. 18th President and commander-in-chief of the federal armies in the Civil War. After clearing the Mississippi River of Confederate troops and winning the Battle of Chattanooga, he was appointed supreme commander and subsequently engineered the final collapse of the Confederate armies. He did not distinguish himself as president (1869—77).

GRATTAN, Henry (1746—1820), Irish statesman and patriot. A member first of the Irish parliament and, later, of the British parliament, he fought untiringly for Irish independence and Catholic emancipation.

GRAVITATION, the force of mutual attraction between bodies in direct ratio to their mass and in inverse ratio to the square of the distance between them. In describing the force drawing other bodies towards the earth, the term gravity is commonly used. It is an important factor in space travel where its elimination brings about the state known as weightlessness.

GRAZ, a city in Styria, Austria, on the Mur River. Pop. (1959) 226,453. An ancient city in beautiful natural surroundings, it has interesting medieval buildings in the older part of the town and, with the help of hydro-electric power, has in modern times developed a wide range of industries.

GREAT BRITAIN, the main island of the British Isles, comprising England, Wales and Scotland (qq.v.) with adjacent small islands. Pop. (1961) 51,250,094; area 80,671 sq. miles. The name *Grande Bretagne* was given it by the French to distinguish it from Brittany *(Bretagne).* Together with Northern Ireland it forms the United Kingdom. Great Britain and the United Kingdom are frequently referred to abroad as 'England', but this is not acceptable to Scots, Welsh and Irish, still less is it acceptable to call them English; this creates difficulties as 'Briton' is usually reserved for the Ancient Briton. It is, however, permissible to speak of English literature and the English language. The following paragraphs deal with history from the time (1603) when James VI of Scotland became James I of Great Britain; earlier history will be found under England, Wales, Scotland and Ireland.

Elizabeth I was succeeded by James I (1603—25) who joined the crowns of England and Scotland. His son, Charles I, attempted to rule without parliament and impose the Anglican faith on the Scots, who were mainly Presbyterians. In 1642 civil war (q.v.) broke out between king and parliament, which ended in the execution of Charles in 1649 and the establishment of the Commonwealth. Led by Oliver Cromwell, England defeated the Netherlands and Spain, acquired new colonies and expanded the merchant fleet. Two years after Cromwell's death, Charles II was restored (1660) to the throne and pledged himself to preserve the rights of parliament. During his reign a dispute arose as to whether his Catholic brother, James, Duke of York, should be permitted to succeed to the throne; the Whigs opposed this, while the Tories favoured it, and succeeded in putting him on the throne as James II in 1685. His tolerance towards the Roman Catholics, however, made him very unpopular and, on the announcement of the birth to him of a son and heir who would exclude his Protestant daughter Mary from the succession, he was forced to flee. In the Glorious Revolution (q.v.; 1688) Prince William of Orange, who had married Mary, came to the throne; but the royal prerogative was circumscribed, the authority of parliament was broadened, and freedom of the individual was guaranteed. As an outcome of the Wars of the Spanish Succession (1701—13) against the Bourbons, Britain seized Gibraltar and a number of colonies in America and Africa. In 1714 George I of Hanover became king, and during his reign the system of cabinet government began to crystallise. In the Wars of the Austrian Succession (1740—48) and the Seven Years War (1756—63) Britain was able to expel the French from Canada and India and to establish its rule there. In the War of American Independence (1775—83), in which France and Spain joined, the American colonies were lost. The settlement of Australia began in 1788, and during the Napoleonic Wars French and Dutch colonies were conquered. At the Congress of Vienna (1815) Castlereagh agreed to the restoration of most of the French colonies and of Java, but retained Cape Colony, Malta, Ceylon and Trinidad.

With increasing wealth and possessions, and with an ever expanding overseas trade, Britain exploited its large resources in coal and iron to give the lead in laying the foundations of the Industrial Revolution. These developments led to the rise of a new middle class, growing rich from trade and industry but with no say in government. Parliament still consisted mainly of representatives of well-to-do landowners and of the 'rotten boroughs', constituencies which had been important in the Middle Ages but had dwindled into impoverished little hamlets. In 1832 a Reform Bill was at last enacted after much opposition, and was succeeded by others which greatly enlarged the franchise (q.v.). The next step was to improve the appalling conditions under which factory and mine workers, and especially children, were working. Progress in this sector was more the result of individual humanitarian effort than of legislative action. There was, however, a growing liberalisation of outlook, and revolution of the kind that broke out in Continental countries in 1848 was avoided.

The two great political parties who had dominated the 19th century, the Conservatives and the Liberals, were joined by a third, the Labour Party, first represented in parliament in 1899. Although it did not form a government until 1924, it had become the second major party before the Second World War and had caused the virtual extinction of the Liberals.

In the century preceding 1914 Great Britain did not interfere in the disputes of Continental countries, and emerged from its isolation only once, in the Crimean War (1853—55), in order to forestall Russian penetration in the Middle East. It did, however, fight a number of colonial wars. The last was in 1899—1902, when the Boers were defeated in the South African Wars and their territories annexed; these were granted autonomy in 1910 when the Union of South Africa came into being. Canada, Australia and New Zealand had already attained self-government. The rise of a unified Germany after 1870 confronted Britain with a serious rival for the rule of the seas, and forced it out of a policy of isolation into alliance with France and Russia. In the two World Wars that ensued Great Britain played a decisive role, but in the first suffered grievous losses in manpower and in the second had to sacrifice most of its overseas investments. The dependent countries of the British Commonwealth progressed rapidly towards the independence to which they had long been orientated, and first India and Pakistan (1947) and then Ceylon (1948) and numerous African colonies, commencing with Ghana (1957), attained full sovereignty within the Commonwealth, as did Cyprus and Malaysia; while Burma (1948), the Republic of Ireland (1949) and South Africa left the Commonwealth.

As part of a policy of integration with the West, Britain joined the North Atlantic Treaty Organisation in 1949. An application to join the European Common Market met with French opposition in 1962.

GREAT LAKES, a group of lakes in North America. Superior, Huron, Erie and Ontario lie between the U.S.A. and Canada, the international boundary passing through their centre; Michigan is entirely within the U.S.A. They are connected by rivers and Lake St Clair, and by the St Lawrence Seaway to the Atlantic. The lakes are rich in fish and, situated in the midst of a highly productive region containing abundant natural resources, carry a huge amount of ship-borne traffic. The total area is 96,000 sq. miles. See Lakes.

GREAT PLAINS, a vast lowland area running right through North America, from the Canadian prairies to the Gulf of Mexico, between the Rocky Mountains on the west and the Laurentian plateau and the Appalachian Mountains on the east. The Great Plains are virtually treeless, and it is thought that they may always have been grassland. The typical climate is one of cold winters and hot, dry summers.

GRECO, EL (Domenikos Theotocopoulos; 1541—1614), Spanish painter of Greek origin. Born in Crete (then Venetian), he was trained in the Byzantine art of icon painting and then became a pupil of Titian, settling in Toledo, Spain, before 1577. The elongated faces and limbs of his figures and the livid colouring heighten the emotional intensity of his ecstatic religious paintings, which were influenced by the spirit of the Jesuits and the Inquisition. His masterpiece is the *Burial of Count Orgaz* (Toledo); the *Agony in the Garden* is in the National Gallery, London.

GREECE, a European kingdom at the extremity of the Balkan Peninsula. Pop. (1961) 8,350,000; area 51,182 sq. miles. Except for the northeast, most of the country is mountainous, cut by deep valleys. The southern part consists of the Peloponnese Peninsula attached to the continental area by the Isthmus of Corinth, now traversed by a canal. Islands constitute a fourth part of Greek total territory. Agriculture is the main occupation although only 26% of the country is cultivable. Tobacco, olives, rice, currants, field crops and vegetables are grown. Mineral deposits include iron, copper, zinc, lead and silver. Coal and oil has to be imported. Industries include food processing, chemicals and textiles.

The recorded history of Greece goes back to the middle of the 8th century B.C. Early in its history, Greece consisted of small political units, usually in the form of city-states, which occasionally formed loose federations. By the end of the 6th century B.C., most of the city-states had achieved some form of democratic government. At the beginning of the 5th century the important Greek states were Sparta, Athens, and Thebes. In 480 B.C. Persian attempts to invade Greece were repulsed by the joint action of Athens and Sparta. As the power of Athens grew, a fruitless conflict with Sparta broke out at the same time as the rule of Pericles ushered in a period of wealth and unprecedented attainments in the arts and philosophy. In 405 B.C., Sparta put an end to Athenian supremacy, but was challenged in turn by a short period of Theban rule. Greece, exhausted by internal conflict, fell an easy prey in the middle of the 4th century to Philip of Macedon and his son, Alexander. Through conquests in North Africa and the Middle East, Alexander brought Greek culture to the Orient. At his death his empire fell to pieces and a final attempt by the Greeks of the Peloponnese to assert their independence in the Achaean League was only partially successful. In 146 B.C. Greece became a Roman colony, and later a part of the Byzantine Empire when the Roman world was divided. In 1453 it became part of the Ottoman Empire. An intellectual and political revival in the 18th century led

This beautiful 8th century Byzantine silk fabric is part of the shroud of St Siviard, now in Sens Cathedral, France. *Photo: Giraudon*

An 11th century Mohammedan fabric in Egyptian silk: part of the cope of St Mexme. Now in the Church of St Etienne, Chinon, France. *Photo: Giraudon*

Shown here is a scene illustrating the Battle of Hastings from the famous Bayeux Tapestry. The tapestry (q.v.), which is 231 ft long and 20 in wide, is embroidered in coloured wools on a coarse linen. It was made before the end of the 11th century, and no comparable work survives.
Photo: Giraudon

Dating from the 13th century is this exquisitely worked detail from an embroidered cope.

Photo: Victoria & Albert Museum

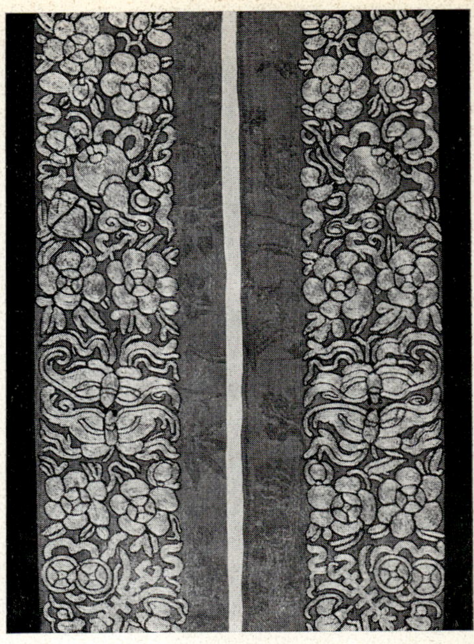

In China, embroidery developed along very distinctive lines: these decorations for the sleeves of a lady's robe are a typical example. 14th century. *Photo: Victoria & Albert Museum*

A detail from a very fine, large, 15th century French tapestry depicting a roe-deer hunt.

Photo: Victoria & Albert Museum. From the Chatsworth Collection. Crown copyright reserved

to the establishment of an independent Greek kingdom in 1829, aided by Britain, France and Russia. Although Greece gained territory in 1878 and in the Balkan Wars and the First World War, it lost certain areas in an unsuccessful attack on Turkey in 1922. From 1924—35 Greece was a republic. The country victoriously resisted an Italian invasion in 1940, but was soon devastated by the Germans. A revolutionary insurrection after the Second World War was suppressed. The capital is Athens (pop. 1961 565,084). Other important cities are Salonika (217,049) and Piraeus (186,014), the port of Athens.

GREEK CHURCH, see Orthodox Eastern Church.

GREENLAND, a Danish island between the Arctic Ocean and Baffin Bay. Pop. (1958) 28,000; area 839,782 sq. miles (over 80% glacier). It has a rugged, mountainous coast with deep fiords. The climate is arctic. Greenland has no large trees and produces vegetables in the south only. Fishing and hunting are important occupations. Greenland is the world's only source of natural cryolite; graphite is also mined. The capital is Godthaab.

GREENWICH, a metropolitan borough of London. Pop. (1961) 85,585. It was formerly the seat of the astronomical observatory, now in Sussex. Its meridian was adopted as the origin of the world's longitudes and zone time-system. Greenwich Hospital, in part designed by Wren, is now used as a naval college; the National Maritime Museum adjoins the Queen's House designed by Inigo Jones.

GREGORIAN CHANT, the official ritual music used in the liturgy of the Roman Catholic Church. It derives its name from Pope Gregory the Great, reputed to have made its final arrangement in the late 6th century.

GREGORY THE GREAT (*c.* 540—604), Pope from 590. A man of great learning, he was an efficient administrator, who strengthened the Church's temporal power as well as its spiritual content. He sent St Augustine to Britain.

GREGORY VII, St (Hildebrand *c.* 1020—85), Pope from 1073. In his efforts to make the papacy supreme within the church and to establish the church's supremacy over the state, he came into conflict with Henry IV of Germany. Although he forced Henry to seek absolution from him at Canossa, Henry eventually won and replaced him with Clement III.

GRENOBLE, a fortified city in south-eastern France. Pop. (1954) 116,400. Surrounded by mountains, it is near the junction of the Isère and Drac rivers. It has old churches and a famous university. The chief industry is kid gloves.

GREY, Charles, 2nd Earl (1764—1845), British statesman. One of the leaders in the impeachment of Warren Hastings, he also sought to impeach Pitt. In 1830 he became Whig prime minister. During his premiership the Reform Bill of 1832, the bill abolishing slavery throughout the Empire (1833), and the Poor Law Amendment Act (1834) were passed.

GREY, Lady Jane (1537—54), Queen of England for nine days. A great-granddaughter of Henry VII, she was proclaimed Queen on the death of Edward VI. On the arrival of Mary Tudor, she was deposed. Lady Jane and her husband were subsequently beheaded.

GREY OF FALLODON, Edward, 1st Viscount (1862—1933), British statesman.

He was under-secretary for Foreign Affairs (1892—95) and Foreign Secretary (1905—16). He strengthened Britain's alliance with France and opposed German expansion before the First World War. A mediator in the Balkan Wars, he tried to prevent war in 1914. From 1922 he was Liberal leader in the House of Lords.

GRIFFITH, Arthur (1872—1922), Irish political leader. He organised the Sinn Fein party in 1902. Arrested a number of times by the British, he was acting head of the Irish provisional Government in 1919. In 1921 he headed the delegation which signed the treaty with Britain recognising the dominion status of the Irish Free State.

GRIFFITH, David Wark (1880—1948), American pioneer film producer. He contributed much towards the progress of the early cinema, producing *Birth of a Nation*, *Intolerance*, *Broken Blossoms* and *Way Down East*.

GRIMM, Jakob (1785—1863) and Wilhelm (1786—1859), German philologists and folklorists. Jakob wrote important works on Germanic philology and folklore, formulating the law for sound changes in Indo-European languages. The brothers collaborated in publishing their famous collection of fairy tales.

GROMYKO, Andrei (1908—), Russian diplomat. He served as U.S.S.R. ambassador to Washington (1943—46), chief of the Soviet delegation to the U.N. in 1944, Soviet representative on the Security Council (1946—49), ambassador to Britain (1952—53), and U.S.S.R. Foreign Minister from 1957.

GROTIUS, Hugo (Huig van Groot; 1583—1645). Dutch jurist. An outstanding classical scholar and theologian, he became involved in theological controversy and political conflict, was condemned to death but escaped to Paris through the heroism of his wife, and there wrote *De jure belli et pacis*, a book which laid the foundations of international law.

GROZNY, a city in the R.S.F.S.R., in northern Caucasia, U.S.S.R. Pop. (1959) 240,000. It has important industries, manufacturing machinery and chemicals. Situated amid oilfields, it has refineries and pipelines to the Ukraine and the Black and Caspian seas.

GUADALAJARA, the second largest city in Mexico, capital of Jalisco state. Pop. (1960) 734,346. An educational and trading centre, it has important industries, producing textiles, foods, tinted brown glass, pottery, tooled leather, and gold and silver work. The city was founded in 1530.

GUADELOUPE, a French overseas *déparmentte* in the West Indies. Pop. (1959) 264,000; area 688 sq. miles. The colony consists of two main islands and five smaller dependencies. The chief products are bananas, sugar, rum, coffee and cocoa. The capital is Basse-Terre.

GUAM, the principal island of the Mariana Group in the North Pacific. Pop. (1960) 67,044; area 209 sq. miles. It is a self-governing U.S. possession of strategic importance, with a Polaris submarine base. A wide variety of tropical foods are grown. The capital is Agaña.

GUATEMALA, the northernmost Central American republic. Pop. (1960) 3,759,000; area 45,452 sq. miles. Mostly mountainous, Guatemala has dense forests along the coasts. The population is concentrated mainly along the Pacific slopes. Chiefly agricultural, it produces coffee, bananas, cotton, and chicle gum. There are rich reserves of dyewoods and cabinet woods. Conquered by Spain in 1524, Guatemala became independent in 1822. The capital is Guatemala City (pop. 1958 374,000).

GUAYAQUIL, port and largest city in Ecuador, on the Guaysa River. Pop. (1960) 295,791. It has diverse small industries and exports cocoa, coffee and Panama hats.

GUERNSEY, the second largest and westernmost of the British Channel Islands, in the English Channel. Pop. (1961) 45,126; area 24½ sq. miles. Famous for its distinctive breed of dairy cattle, it also exports tomatoes, grapes, early flowers, and stone.

GUIANA, see British Guiana; French Guiana; Surinam.

GUIDED MISSILE, a projectile the flight of which is radio- or radar-controlled partially or completely, either by its own internal mechanism or in response to signals from a distance. The homing, or target-seeking, missile reacts to stimuli from the target and adjusts its flight in order to hit it. Some guided missiles are powered by jet-propulsion engines; some are a combination of rocket and ramjet. They are classified as ground-to-ground, surface-to-air, air-to-surface, air-to-air and anti-submarine. Missiles can also be fired from submarines under water. The latest developments are missiles to destroy missiles.

GUILD, an association of artisans or merchants. In the Middle Ages guilds exercised complete control over the members of a trade, fostering and protecting their interests. No craftsman could work without becoming a member of his guild. From the 14th—16th centuries, guilds developed considerable power, political as well as economic. In England they lost their importance by the middle of the 17th century, becoming mere fraternal organisations

GUINEA, a republic of West Africa. Pop. (1961) 3,000,000; area 94,926 sq. miles. Mountainous in the interior, it consists of a humid plain in the south. The country has iron ore, diamonds and bauxite. Rice, oil palms, bananas, coffee and pineapples are grown. Formerly a French possession, it became independent in 1958. The capital is Conakry (75,000).

GUINEA, Portuguese, Portuguese colony in West Africa. Pop. (1960) 553,000; area 13,948 sq. miles. It consists of a low coastal region and numerous islands. Rice, palm-oil, groundnuts and hides are produced. The capital is Bissau.

GUINEA, Spanish, a Spanish colony in West Africa. Pop. (1960) 216,000; area 10,852 sq. miles. It consists of the islands of Fernando Po (q.v.) and Annobon, and the continental region of Rio Muni (capital Bata). Cocoa, coffee, fruit, vegetables and timber are produced.

GUINEVERE, the wife of King Arthur. A traditional feature of the legend about her is her infidelity with Lancelot.

GURKHAS, soldiers recruited in Nepal. They belong to various races, speaking Tibeto-Burmese and other languages and using an Indo-European *lingua franca*. Some of these races have a warrior tradition, of which the *kukri*, a curved knife, is a symbol, and have rendered notable service in the Gurkha Rifle Regiments, which took part in both

World Wars. The name Gurkha should properly be given only to the reigning house of Nepal.

GUSTAVUS II, Adolphus (1594—1632), King of Sweden. A highly cultured monarch, he was an able administrator and outstanding military leader. After emerging victorious from short wars with Denmark and Russia and a long struggle with Poland, he took an army to Germany in 1630 to help the Protestants against the Catholic League in the Thirty Years War. He fell in battle two years later, leaving Sweden a major power in Europe.

GUTENBERG, Johann (*c.* 1397—1468), German printer. He is credited with being the first European to have printed with movable type cast in moulds. His best-known work is a Bible which appeared *c.* 1456.

GWALIOR, a city in Madhya Pradesh, India. Pop. (1961) 300,513. The old city contains a huge fortress. There are textile industries; cereals and sugar-cane are grown in the district, which also has bauxite deposits.

GWYNNE, Nell (1650—87), English actress. She first achieved popularity in Dryden's *Secret Love, or the Maiden Queen.* Her lovers included Charles II, to whom she was faithful and bore two sons. She was buried at St-Martin-in the-Fields.

HAARLEM, a city in the Netherlands. Pop. (1960) 169,215. It is a world centre for flower bulbs and a market for dairy products. There are textile mills, breweries and printing establishments.

HABIT, a bodily or mental function which has become customary or automatic through frequent repetition. As familiarity increases, effort and intensity of feeling decrease. Habits are essential to the smooth and economical functioning of the organism. Bad habits indicate improper adaptation.

HADES, in Greek mythology, the lower world in which departed spirits dwelt. To enter Hades, the dead had to cross the river Styx on a ferryboat rowed by Charon, who collected a fee. Hades was originally the name of the ruler of this underworld; he was also called Pluto. His consort was Persephone, whom he had abducted from the upper world; she was the daughter of Demeter.

HADFIELD, Sir Robert Abbott (1859—1940), English metallurgist. He discovered manganese steel, silicon steel and other valuable steel alloys.

HADHRAMAUT, a region in East Aden Protectorate, South Arabia. Pop. 150,000; area 58,500 sq. miles. The area is mostly desert, with mountains along the coast. Wheat, tobacco, fruit and dates are grown in the valleys. It is under British supervision.

HADRIAN (76—138), Roman emperor from 117. He erected many fine buildings, but withdrew the borders of the empire in the East to the Euphrates. Travelling extensively, he visited Britain in 119 and had a wall built from Solway Firth to the mouth of the Tyne for protection against the Picts and Scots. He made important contributions to Roman law.

Hadrian's Wall (near Borcovicium)

HAGUE, THE ('s Gravenhage), governmental capital of the Netherlands. Pop. (1960) 606,110. The Palace of Peace houses the Court of International Justice. There are noteworthy historical buildings including the 17th-century Mauritshuis picture gallery. The city also has metallurgical industries. The suburb of Scheveningen is a seaside resort. The Hague Conferences of 1899 and 1907 laid down rules of warfare and set up the international court.

HAIFA, Israel's chief seaport, on the Mediterranean. Pop. (1961) 182,007. By Mt Carmel, it is an industrial centre with oil refineries, a car-assembly plant and steel and chemical factories.

HAILE SELASSIE I (1892—   ), Emperor of Ethiopia. The son of Ras Makonnen and a relation of the Emperor Menelik, as Ras Tafari he led the revolt fo the barons in 1916 which forced Menelik's successor to abdicate, becoming regent and in April 1930 emperor. From the first he sought to modernise and liberalise the country, though retaining the autocratic personal rule which circumstances dictated. The Italians invaded Abyssinia in 1935 and, after a fruitless appeal to the League of Nations, the emperor went into exile at Bath, England, for five years. When British forces retook Abyssinia, the emperor resumed his rule in 1941.

HAINAN, an island off southern China. Pop. (1953) 2,600,000; area 13,974 sq. miles. It has low coastland and densely forested mountains in the interior. Agriculture is the main occupation. The chief town is Kiungchow.

HAIPHONG, the chief seaport of North Viet-Nam. Pop. (1960) 367,000. An industrial and commercial centre, it produces tin, phosphates and machinery.

HAIR, filament-like modification of the epidermis or outer skin in mammals. In man very fine short hair is found in varying amounts over much of the body surface, but on the scalp it grows long (a length of 6 ft has been recorded). Individual hairs consist of a shaft and a root and grow in pits called follicles which lie in the true skin or dermis. There are three main types of human hair, woolly in Negroes, straight in Eastern races and waved in Europeans.

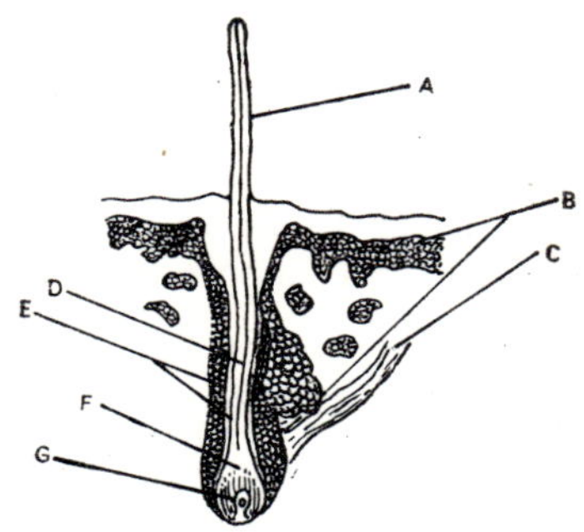

Human hair
A. Hair shaft B. Malpighian layer of epidermis C. Arrector pili D. Medulla E. Outer and inner root-sheath F. Root of hair-knob G. Papilla

Flaxen hair is found only among northern European races. Cases have been recorded of hair turning grey overnight under the stress of intense emotion; this is said to have happened to Marie Antoinette.

HAITI, a republic in the western third of the island of Hispaniola, West Indies. Pop. (1960) 3,505,000; area 10,204 sq. miles. Most of the country is mountainous. Coffee, sisal, bananas, cotton, tobacco and sugar are raised. There are some minor industries. Independent since 1804, it has experienced long periods of dictatorship. The population is almost entirely Negro, speaking a French dialect (Créole). The capital is Port-au-Prince (pop. 1957 200,000).

HALIFAX, Edward Wood, 1st Earl of (1881—1959), British politician. A Conservative member of parliament from 1910—25, he was subsequently (as Lord Irwin) Viceroy of India (1926—31), Foreign Secretary (1938—40) and Ambassador to the U.S. (1941—46).

HALLE, a city in East Germany, on the Saale River. Pop. (1960) 277,900. It has historical buildings, a university and medieval and Renaissance churches. Machinery, chemicals and foodstuffs are manufactured.

HALOGEN, a member of the family of active non-metals which includes fluorine, chlorine, bromine and iodine. They are never found uncombined in nature and form important salts and strong acids.

HAMADAN, a city in Iran. Pop. (1960) 122,000. An important trade and communications centre, it is famous for its rugs. It also has oil refineries. Known as Ecbatana in the 7th and 6th centuries B.C., it was the capital of the Medes.

HAMBURG, the chief seaport and second largest city in West Germany, on the Elbe River. Pop. (1960) 1,823,574. One of the oldest European ports, it has been the centre of German commerce since the founding of the Hanseatic League. It is also an industrial centre with shipyards and oil refineries and textile, metal and food factories. It has been completely rebuilt since 1945.

HAMILTON, a city in Ontario, Canada. Pop. (1961) 395,189. A hub of rail and highway communications and a port on Lake Ontario, it is the centre of Canada's steel industry. Textiles, machinery and metal goods are produced.

HAMILTON, Alexander (1757—1804), American statesman. An intimate of George Washington during the American Revolution, he later played a leading role in the formulation and adoption of the U.S. constitution in its present form. As Secretary of the Treasury in Washington's cabinet, he laid the foundation of American public finance. He was killed in a duel with the Vice-President, Aaron Burr.

HAMILTON, Emma, Lady (*c.* 1761—1815), mistress of Lord Nelson. She lived with Charles Greville and then married his uncle, Sir William Hamilton, who was posted as ambassador to Naples, where Nelson met her in 1798. She bore him a daughter in 1801. Lady Hamilton was the daughter of a blacksmith and became an actress; after the deaths of Hamilton and Nelson, she was arrested for debt, and she died in poverty.

HAMMARSKJÖLD, Dag (1905—61), Swedish statesman. He was Secretary-General of the U.N. from 1953 in succession to Trygve Lie. A skilful diplomatist, he was instrumental in forming the U.N. emergency forces in the Suez crisis of 1956 and the Congo in 1960. His conception of the U.N.'s independent role in such matters led to Soviet demands for his replacement by a 'troika' of three persons of different nationalities, but he continued to command a majority of the U.N. Assembly until his death in an air crash in Northern Rhodesia. He was posthumously awarded the Nobel Peace prize for 1961.

HAMMURABI, King of Babylonia of the 18th century B.C. He unified the Babylonian empire and did much to promote its development. He may have been responsible for the strict legal code which has survived on a large diorite block, now in the Louvre.

HAMPSHIRE, a maritime county in southern England; it includes the Isle of Wight. Pop. (1961) 1,336,084; area 1649 sq. miles. It is rolling country in which cereals, livestock and strawberries are produced. Industries include shipbuilding, aircraft, textiles, brewing and tanning. There are railway workshops at Eastleigh and an oil refinery at Fawley. The county town is Winchester, capital of Wessex and then of England until shortly after the Conquest. Southampton is a passenger and cargo port and Portsmouth is a naval base; Bournemouth is a seaside resort. The New Forest lies in Hampshire.

HAMSUN, Knut (1859—1952), Norwegian novelist. His most famous works were *Hunger* and *Growth of the Soil.* He received the Nobel Prize for literature in 1920. Pro-Nazi leanings during and after the Second World War damaged his prestige.

HANDEL, George Frederick (1685—1759), German composer, who after several visits to England finally settled there in 1716, becoming a naturalised English subject. He wrote an immense amount of music, including well over 40 operas and 32 oratorios. In Britain he is best known for the oratorio *The Messiah*, which has become a national institution; but several others, e.g. *Samson, Theodora* and *Jephtha*, are of almost equal merit. His operas are rarely heard, which is unfortunate as so much first-class music is buried in them, e.g. *The Faithful Shepherd. Music for the Royal Fireworks* and *Water Music* are among other compositions which, with the *concerti grossi*, have deservedly won fame. Beethoven and Mozart thought him the greatest composer the world had known, and the former particularly praised him for his genius in obtaining great effects with simple means.

HANGCHOW, a port and city in east central China, capital of Chekiang province, near the mouth of the Fuchun River. Pop. (1960) 700,000. It was the Kinsai described by Marco Polo as the finest city in the world, the Sung capital of the 12th and 13th centuries, and is still a beautiful city with island palaces and gardens. It is at the southern end of the Grand Canal (q.v.). The traditional industries of silk manufacture and tea processing flourish.

HANKOW, the largest inland port of central China, at the junction of the Han and Yangtze rivers, in Hupeh province. Pop. (1960) 809,000. Together with Hanyang and Wuchang, it constitutes the Wuhan conurbation, of which it is the largest unit. It manufactures machinery, textiles and chemicals.

HANOI, the capital of North Viet-Nam, on the Red River, Pop. (1960) 643,000. An ancient market town, with a modern town built in the French style, it has a large transit trade with Chinese Yunnan.

HANOVER, capital of Lower Saxony, West Germany, on the Leine River. Pop. (1960) 574,700. It was a member of the Hanseatic League, and a royal capital; it now has major industries, including vehicles, electrical equipment, chemicals, textiles and cigarette manufacture.

HANSEATIC LEAGUE, an association of North German towns which existed from the 13th to the middle of the 17th century for purposes of trade. With Lübeck as its centre, the League came to dominate foreign trade in the North and Baltic seas and as far as London and Novgorod. It possessed considerable political power at the peak of its development, but declined in the 15th century.

HAPSBURGS, the name of the dynasty that ruled large areas of Europe from 1273—1918. The family is first recorded in the 10th century as living at Castle Hapsburg, between Zurich and Basle. Rudolf I was elected King of the Romans in 1273, but abandoned Italy and added Austria to his German domains. The Hapsburgs ruled the Holy Roman Empire from 1438—1806, and took the title of Emperor of Austria from then until 1918. Charles V (1500—58) inherited Spain, the Spanish Netherlands, Naples, Sicily, Sardinia, the Spanish dominions in North Africa and America, and gained Bohemia and part of Hungary. The Spanish possessions were bequeathed to his brother Ferdinand, whose line died out in 1700, and the First World War ended the Austro-Hungarian Empire and Hapsburg rule.

HARBIN, the capital of Heilungkian province, in Chinese Manchuria. Pop. (1960) 1,200,000. On the Sungari River, it is a busy port. It is a railway junction on the Chinese Eastern Railway which links the Trans-Siberian Railway to Vladivostok. Locomotives, vehicles, foodstuffs and hides are produced.

HARDIE, Keir (1856—1915), British labour leader. A Scottish coal-miner, he became the first Socialist member of parliament. He founded the Independent Labour Party (1895), which he led in the House of Commons and which was one of the constituents of the Labour Party formed in 1900.

HARDY, Thomas (1840—1928), English novelist and poet. He is most widely known for his novels of 'character and environment' set in rural 'Wessex', then already in process of decay before the forces of industrialism. Of these *Under the Greenwood Tree*, *The Mayor of Casterbridge*, *Jude the Obscure* and *Tess of the D'Urbervilles* are perhaps the greatest. He wrote other more conventional novels, which are less successful. *The Dynasts* is a dramatic epic of the Napoleonic Wars. His lyric poetry shares the pessimistic outlook of the novels, stressing the absolute indifference of the gods who 'made sport with Tess'.

HARMONY, in music, the simultaneous combining of sounds of different pitch and the study of chords and their arrangement and relationship. Harmony seeks to create an overall sound structure in which each individual sound plays a distinctive role. The rapidity of the vibrations constituting a sound determines pitch. The difference in pitch between two tones constitutes an interval. A chord is a combination of two or more intervals.

HAROLD II (*c.* 1022—66), the last Saxon king of England. He ruthlessly suppressed Welsh rebellions when he ruled southern England as Earl of Wessex. In January 1066 he was elected king, and in September defeated an invading army of Norsemen under their king Harald Hardrada and Harold's brother, Tostig. Three days later William of Normandy began his conquest of England and Harold was killed in battle near Hastings.

HARRIMAN, Averell (1891—), American statesman. The son of a railway magnate, he served as Ambassador to Russia (1943—46) and Britain (1946), was adviser to President Truman on foreign policy, special representative in Europe (1948—50) under the Marshall Plan, Governor of New York (1955—58) and Ambassador-at-large under President Kennedy from 1961—63.

HARVARD University, the oldest American university, at Cambridge, Massachusetts. Founded in 1636, it was patterned upon English universities. In addition to the numerous faculties, the university has a number of libraries, research laboratories, museums, observatories and a university press.

HARVEY, William (1578—1657), English physician. He revolutionised medical science by his discovery of the continuous circulation of the blood in one direction, and of the pumping action of the heart.

HASTINGS, a seaside resort in Sussex, England. Pop. (1961) 66,346. It was one of the Cinque Ports and has some fine old buildings and the ruins of a Norman castle. Its name has been given to the battle, fought six miles away on Senlac Hill, Battle, in which William of Normandy defeated and killed Harold in 1066, becoming King of England.

HASTINGS, Warren (1732—1818), the first Governor-General of British India. He carried out a vigorous policy of consolidating British authority which gained him powerful enemies. On his return to England he was impeached but acquitted after a seven-year trial.

HATAY, see Antioch.

HAUPTMANN, Gerhart (1862—1946), German poet, dramatist and novelist. His works, which range from naturalism to poetic mysticism, include the play *The Weavers* and the novels *The Fool in Christ* and *The Heretic of Soana*. He was awarded the Nobel Prize for literature in 1912.

HAVANA, capital of Cuba. Pop. (1953) 785,485. Cuba's chief commercial centre and seaport, it exports mostly sugar. There are cigar and cigarette factories, textile mills, foundries and other industries. The city has notable public buildings.

HAVRE, LE, a seaport and commercial and industrial centre in northern France, at the mouth of the Seine. Pop. (1960) 139,800. Its industries include shipbuilding, machine shops, chemicals and sugar-refining.

HAWAII, a state (since 1959) of the U.S.A. in the North Pacific. Pop. (1960) 632,722; area 6423 sq. miles. Part of an archipelago 390 miles long, the state's main islands are Hawaii, Kahoolawe, Maui, Lanai, Molokai, Oahu, Kauai and Niihau. The island of Hawaii has an area of 4016 sq. miles and a population of 61,332. Tropical fruits (chiefly pineapples), vegetables and sugar-cane are grown. Mauna Loa (13,680 ft high) is the largest volcanic mountain in the world. The capital is Honolulu (pop. 294,179) on Oahu. The Hawaiian Islands were originally named the Sandwich Islands.

HAWTHORNE, Nathaniel (1804—64), American novelist. By portraying the atmosphere of Puritan New England, he achieved fame with *The Scarlet Letter*, *The House of the Seven Gables* and *The Blithedale Romance.*

HAYDN, Franz Joseph (1732—1809), Austrian composer. He displayed unusual musical ability at an early age. He composed oratorios (*The Creation* and *The Seasons*), operas, sonatas, masses and string quartets, and is considered the father of the symphony. In his symphonies, of which he composed 104, he made ingenious use of popular folk tunes. Mozart, who was 24 years younger yet died 19 years before him, greatly admired him, and each influenced the other's music.

HEAD, a distinct part in the bodies of higher animals housing the brain and principal sense organs of sight, hearing, smell and taste. It also contains the entrances to the alimentary and respiratory systems. In higher vertebrates, the shape of the head is determined by the skull which protects the brain. In man, it is an index to race.

HEATH, Edward Richard George (1916—), following junior offices in the Tory government, Heath became Government Chief Whip (1955–59), Minister of Labour (1959–60), and Lord Privy Seal (1960–63). He was elected leader of the Conservative Party in 1965.

HEAVY WATER, water in which each molecule contains an atom of hydrogen with double the atomic weight of ordinary hydrogen (see Deuterium). Known as deuterium oxide, it has properties differing from those of ordinary water. It serves as a moderator for slowing down high speed neutrons used in splitting atoms.

HEBRIDES (Western Isles), two island groups west of Scotland. Pop. (1960) 100,000; area 2850 sq. miles. The Outer and Inner Hebrides consist of more than 500 islands, most of them small and uninhabited. They are mostly rolling moorland used for pasturing livestock. Fishing, farming, the hand-weaving of tweeds, quarrying and distilling are the main pursuits. The largest islands of the Outer Hebrides are Lewis and Harris, forming one island, North and South Uist and Barra; in the Inner Hebrides are Skye, Rhum, Eigg, Mull, Iona, Jura and Islay. The chief town is Stornoway in Lewis.

HEDIN, Sven (1865—1952), Swedish explorer. Exploring uncharted areas of central Asia, he made valuable discoveries. He was strongly pro-German in both World Wars.

HEDONISM, a philosophic theory which holds that pleasure is the highest good. In its social aspects, it implies the greatest pleasure for the greatest number. In psychological theory, it postulates that an individual's behaviour is determined wholly by the desire for pleasure and the avoidance of pain.

HEGEL, Georg Wilhelm Friedrich (1770—1831), German philosopher. His system is known as Absolute or Objective Idealism, and is based on the logic of the dialectical method (see Dialectic) through which alone the Absolute can be understood. A statement about a thing taken in isolation can be only partly true, for that thing must be seen in its relationship to other things, and in that relationship lies its real nature. Thus a thing which is good in the circumstances of one culture or civilisation may be bad in another. Applying his triadic law of thesis, antithesis and higher synthesis to history (and in this influencing Marx), Hegel saw history as a succession of cultures of opposed nature merging into a higher culture knitting the ideals of both together, and so on to final perfection. In the same way family (thesis) and society (antithesis) merges into the State, which reconciles the warring needs of both. Hence Hegel, a strong Prussian nationalist, believed in a totalitarian state, a view which was manna from Heaven to the German nationalists of the 19th century, and to the Nazis.

HEIDELBERG, a city in Baden-Württemberg, West Germany, on the Neckar River. Pop. (1960) 127,444. It is famous for its old university and castle, and manufactures textiles, precision instruments, pianos and railway carriages.

HEILUNGKIANG, a province in Chinese Manchuria. Pop. (1959) 11,900,000; area 178,950 sq. miles. It is mountainous and has extensive forests. Coal is mined and electrical goods and generating plant manufactured. The capital is Harbin (pop. 1960 1,200,000).

HEINE, Heinrich (1797—1856), German poet of Jewish parentage. His *Buch der Lieder* and *Reisebilder* stamped him at once as a poet of considerable stature. An admirer of the French, he spent most of his life in Paris. His works include critical essays and satire.

HEJAZ, a region in northwest Saudi Arabia, on the Red Sea. Pop. (1960) 2,000,000; area 150,000 sq. miles. It consists of a narrow coastal region divided from plateaux by mountains. Dates, honey and hides are produced. Throwing off Turkish rule in 1916, it was independent until 1925. It contains the Moslem holy cities of Mecca (the capital) and Medina.

HELIGOLAND, an island in the North Sea off the mouth of the Elbe, West Germany. Area 130 acres. British from 1807—90, it was converted into a fortress by Germany. At the end of both the First and Second World Wars the fortifications were completely destroyed, after removal of the population.

HELMHOLTZ, Hermann von (1821—94), German physiologist and physicist, who became one of the founders of experimental psychology. He formulated a theory of the conservation of energy and invented the ophthalmoscope. He conducted important research into the problems of sensation, the focusing mechanism of the eye, the structure of the ear, the speed of transmission of impulses in nerve tissue and in electromagnetism.

HELSINKI (Helsingfors), capital of Finland. Pop. (1961) 457,121. A port on the Gulf of Finland, it is a commercial and industrial centre. Metal goods, textiles and saw-mill products are manufactured. It has a university.

HEMINGWAY, Ernest (1898—1961), American novelist and short-story writer. The exponent of a vigorous, active life, he developed a terse expressive style to capture it in his writing. His works include *A Farewell to Arms*, *For Whom the Bell Tolls* and *The Old Man and the Sea*. He received the Nobel Prize for literature in 1954.

HENDERSON, Arthur (1863—1935), British Labour leader and politician. Elected to parliament in 1903, he became chairman of the Labour Party five years later, serving in the Cabinet during the First World War. He was Home Secretary in 1924 and Foreign Secretary in 1929—31. Henderson was president of the World Disarmament Conference in 1932—33 and was awarded the Nobel Peace Prize in 1934.

HENRY I (1068—1135), King of England from 1100. A son of William the Conqueror, he made himself king while his elder brother Robert was away on the Crusades. He married an English princess, Matilda, and issued a charter promising to correct injustices. In 1106 he conquered Normandy, imprisoning Robert.

HENRY II (1133—1189), King of England from 1154. He was the first monarch of the House of Anjou or Plantagenet. Henry secured the return of several northern counties from Malcolm of Scotland and conquered Wales and southeast Ireland. A bitter controversy with Thomas à Becket ended in the latter's murder. He curbed the power of the barons which had waxed during his predecessor Stephen's reign.

HENRY III (1207—1272), King of England from 1216. His patronage of foreigners provoked a rebellion of barons. Failing to keep his agreement to institute reforms, he became involved in a war with the barons under Simon de Montfort which ended in his capture and subsequent release by his son Edward, after the Battle of Evesham.

HENRY IV (1367—1413), King of England from 1399. The son of John of Gaunt of the House of Lancaster. Banished from England by King Richard II, he later forced the latter to abdicate and was crowned king. He suppressed rebellions by the Percies and by Owen Glendower. He persecuted the Lollards and in his later years became increasingly tyrannical.

HENRY V (1387—1422), King of England from 1413. He commanded the army which invaded France and won the battle of Agincourt. His marriage to Catherine of Valois, daughter of Charles VI of France, made him French regent two years before his death.

HENRY VI (1421—71), King of England from 1422—61 and in 1470—71. Crowned King of France, he later lost all his French possessions except Calais. Economic unrest during his reign led to Jack Cade's rebellion. His struggle for power with the rival house of York in the Wars of the Roses ended in a Yorkist victory and his deposition and imprisonment (1465—70). He was restored briefly to the throne in 1470.

HENRY VII (1457—1509), King of England from 1485. The first Tudor monarch, he invaded England from his exile in Brittany and wrested the throne from Richard III. He instituted the Star Chamber, which he used to restrict the power of the nobles, and acquired great personal wealth. He defeated the pretenders Simnel and Warbeck.

HENRY VIII (1491—1547), King of England from 1509. Joining the Holy League against France in 1511, he led his troops to victory at the Battle of the Spurs. As arbiter, with Wolsey's help, between Francis I of France and Charles V of Spain, he met the former in person. His desire to divorce his wife, Catherine of Aragon, in order to marry Anne Boleyn involved him in a controversy with the Pope, which ended in a severance of all ties with the Church of Rome and the deposition of Cardinal Wolsey. Henry was declared supreme head of the Church of England and suppressed the monasteries, getting Thomas Cromwell to confiscate their properties. He remained, however, the Defender of the Faith, executing impartially both those Catholics who refused to recognise his new position, and Protestants. After having Anne beheaded, he married four more times, and was survived by his last wife, Catherine Parr. Anne was the mother of Elizabeth, Jane Seymour of Edward VI. Thomas Cromwell arranged his fourth marriage, with Anne of Cleves, but this was a complete disaster and Henry had Cromwell executed. He divorced Anne, but her successor, Catherine Howard, was also put to death. Henry completed the conquest of Ireland, but could not defeat the Scots and their French allies, and at last made peace with them.

HENRY IV of France (1553—1610), King of France and Navarre. The son of Antoine de Bourbon and the Queen of Navarre, he was the founder of the Bourbon dynasty. Brought up a Calvinist, he led the Huguenots against the Catholic League in the Wars of Religion as Henry of Navarre, but after the Massacre of St Bartholomew's Eve he became virtually a prisoner of the French court. On the death of Henry III in 1589 he became the nominal King of France, but it was not till he had renounced Protestantism in 1594 (saying 'Paris is worth a Mass'), that he reached the throne. In 1598 he issued the Edict of Nantes, which gave the Huguenots full freedom of worship and even made them eligible for public office. Under the guidance of his minister, Sully, Henry now restored order in France. He was assassinated by a Catholic fanatic.

HENRY the Navigator (1394—1460), Portuguese prince and grandson of John of Gaunt, renowned for his patronage of maritime expeditions and for his contributions to the science of navigation.

HENSCHEL, Sir George (1850—1934), German-born baritone, conductor and composer. He was the conductor of the Boston Symphony Orchestra (1881), but from 1884 settled in Britain.

HEPHAESTUS (Roman Vulcan), the lame Greek god of smiths and metalwork and of all those who use fire, important in a Bronze Age society. He was supposed to be the son of Hera and Zeus.

HEPPLEWHITE, George (d. 1786), English cabinet-maker of the 18th century. Lightness, delicacy and grace are the distinguishing characteristics of his work, which depended for its effect more upon inlay than carving. He popularised the winged easy-chair. Much prized among collectors are the smaller pieces, which include mahogany and satinwood knife-boxes, inlaid fire-screens, painted work tables and inlaid stands. His style owed its popularity to the conflicting tastes and changing ideals of the 18th century.

HERCULES (Greek: Heracles), in Greek and Roman mythology a demi-god, the personification of physical strength. He is the subject of many classical epic poems describing his adventures, particularly the 'twelve labours of Hercules'.

HEREDITY, the transmission of factors through reproduction which results in offspring resembling the parents. See Chromosome; Genetics.

HEREFORDSHIRE, an inland county in western England. Pop. (1961) 130,919; area 842 sq. miles. In the east are the Malvern Hills. The good grazing land accounts for the Hereford beef cattle and the Ryeland sheep. The county also produces fruit, grains and hops. There are quarries and factories producing farming-tools and paper. The county town is Hereford.

HERMES (Roman Mercury), the herald of Zeus and messenger of the gods. He wore the winged *petasus*, or travelling hat, and winged sandals, and carried the *caduceus*, a herald's staff entwined with serpents. He conducted the shades to the underworld, and was also the god of trade, cunning, theft, athletics and travel.

HERODOTUS (*c.* 485—425 B.C.), Greek historian and explorer, born in Halicarnassus. His title of Father of History is well earned by his nine-volume work, covering the history and geography of most of the known world, the fruits of his many travels, and an account of the Persian Wars.

HERSCHEL, Sir William (1738—1822), British Royal astronomer, of German birth. Trained as a musician, he turned his attention to astronomy and discovered the planet Uranus and two of its satellites, as well as two of Saturn's satellites. His studies covered many phases of astronomy from sun-spots to galaxies. He built his own telescopes, including a reflecting telescope with a focal length of 40 ft, for his observatory at Slough.

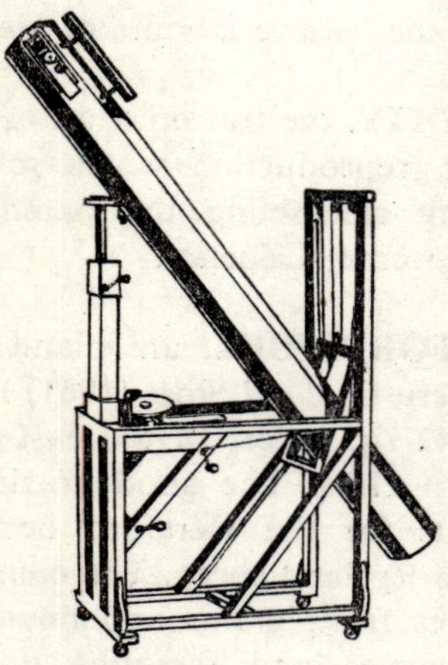
Herschel's reflecting telescope

HERTFORDSHIRE, an inland county north of London, England. Pop. (1951) 832,088; area 632 sq. miles. It is rolling country crossed by chalk ridges. An agricultural region, it produces mostly cereals and fruit. Livestock raising is important. There are iron foundries, breweries and tanneries. The county town is Hertford.

HIBERNATION, winter sleep among animals in a cold environment where there is food scarcity. Hibernating invertebrates and cold-blooded animals bury themselves throughout the winter with their body temperature almost the same as their surroundings. In some hibernating mammals (bat, dormouse, hedgehog), the temperature drops to a few degrees above that of the external environment, heart beat and respiration are down to a fraction of the normal and the body may lose as much as half its weight. This condition of full hibernation is called torpor. There are examples of partial hibernation; for example, the bear remains warm-blooded though respiration and circulation rates fall, and the polar bear produces young during hibernation. Squirrels and beavers emerge from hibernation when their stock of food runs out.

HIBERNIA, the ancient Roman name for Ireland (q.v.).

HIEROGLYPHICS, an ancient form of picture writing consisting of rough drawings which in an advanced form came to express ideas, both concrete and abstract, and, later, syllables and sounds. Hieroglyphics were first used by the ancient Egyptians and were also found among the Hittites, Minoans and Maya. Discovery of the Rosetta Stone in 1799 provided a key for deciphering Egyptian hieroglyphics. (Illus. facing.)

HIGHLANDS, Scottish, the mountainous region lying to the northwest of the geological fault running southwest from Stonehaven (Kincardine) to Helensburgh (Dumbarton) on the Clyde. To make way for sheep runs, the Highland landowners, in an operation known as 'The Clearances', from 1750 began expelling the crofters (small farmers), who migrated in large numbers to North America and elsewhere overseas. As 90% of the land was extremely poor grazing, it was turned into deer forest about 50 years later and most of it is fit for nothing else. The depopulation of the Highlands, for the geographical reason that most of the land is unsuitable for agriculture and is remote from the large markets, has continued ever since, though by developing hydro-electric power efforts are being made to attract industry. Afforestation is also being carried out and tourism has greatly developed.

The Gaelic speech has survived to a much greater degree than in Lowland Scotland, together with Highland dress, bagpipe music, and folk-dances and games.

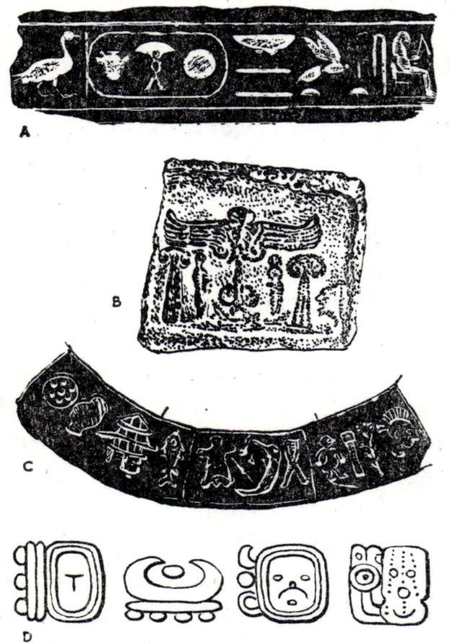

Hieroglyphic writing
A. Egyptian B. Hittite C. Minoan D. Mayan

HIMALAYA, a mountain chain extending for 1600 miles along the northern border of Pakistan and India, from the Indus to the Brahmaputra rivers. 150—200 miles wide, it forms a system of parallel and converging ranges generally running southeast from Kashmir and then east, and containing the highest peaks in the world. Vegetation varies from tropical jungle to snow-line plants. The region is particularly rich in birds. The highest peaks are Everest (29,028 ft), Godwin-Austen or K2 (29,250 ft) and Kanchenjunga (28,146 ft).

HINDEMITH, Paul (1895—1963), German composer. During the Nazi régime he went to live in the U.S.A., where he held a post at Yale University, returning to Germany after the war and later moving to Zurich. An accomplished player of string instruments, he was noted for his exceptional versatility, his works ranging from music for Disney cartoons to the opera *Mathis der Maler*, and for his explorations in the theory of music, on which he wrote many books.

HINDENBURG, Paul von (1847—1934), German general and statesman. He won his military laurels when he defeated the Russians at Tannenberg in the First World War. In 1916 he was appointed chief of the general staff. He was elected president of the Weimar Republic in 1925, in which capacity he dismissed the Chancellor Brüning and replaced him first with von Papen, and then (1933) Hitler. He was a leading exponent of the theory that the German army was stabbed in the back in the First World War by the pusillanimous civilians at home, thus keeping the German spirit of military aggressiveness alive for the Nazis to make use of later.

HINDU KUSH, a western extension of the Himalayan system along the Kashmir border into Afghanistan, southwest of the Pamir range. It is 350 miles long.

The highest point is Tirich Mir (25,263 ft), in Pakistan.

HINDUISM, the dominant religion of India and third largest of the world religions in numbers of adherents. It is as much a culture or way of life as a religion, for it knows neither a definite creed nor an historical founder. The main features are polytheism, behind which lies some kind of unity (Brahman, the Supreme Reality); a belief, shared with Buddhists, in reincarnation, the form (animal or human) of incarnation being determined by conduct in the previous life under the law of Karma, and with deliverance from the cycle of lives into Nirvana by attaining knowledge of the illusive nature of things (maya) by various paths of mysticism, often attended by rigid asceticism; a Brahman caste, who are custodians and interpreters of the sacred Sanskrit texts (Vedas; q.v.), but are not organised in any hierarchy; and the caste system. There have been several reform movements in the past century, the most notable being that led by Sri Aurobindo.

HIPPOCRATES (*c.* 460—377 B.C.), Greek physician to whom are attributed various writings on the art of healing known as the Hippocratic Collection, and who has therefore been called the 'Father of Medicine'. The Hippocratic Oath, still taken by physicians of several countries, laid down a code of ethics.

HIROSHIMA, a city on Honshu island, Japan. Pop. (1960) 285,712. It has textile industries. The first atomic bomb, dropped by the U.S. Air Force in August 1945, destroyed more than two-thirds of the city, killing 60,000 persons.

HISPANIOLA, an island in the West Indies. Area 29,536 sq. miles. The Dominican Republic occupies the eastern two-thirds; the rest belongs to Haiti. The name (*Espagnola*, 'Little Spain') was given to it by Columbus in 1492.

HISTOLOGY, the branch of biology which studies the types of cells present in the tissues of animals and plants, as opposed to cytology which studies the individual cell. Animal tissues include those of the nerves, muscles, blood vessels, bone, cartilage, skin and glands. Thin slices of material are examined by various methods of magnification, and in some cases changes can be watched on a television screen.

HISTORY, a systematic and impartial narrative of the story of man and of his political and social condition. History is not merely a collection of facts, for the facts must be evaluated and interpreted and the interpretations vary according to the historical school. The task of the historian is thus twofold: first, to gather the raw material; and secondly, to organise and interpret it.

HITLER, Adolf (1889—1945), Führer of the German Third Reich and leader of the National Socialist (Nazi) party. The son of an Austrian shoemaker, he lived in poverty in Vienna and Munich, turning his hand to many trades and trying unsuccessfully to train himself as an architect or artist. In this period he learnt to hate Jews, Slavs and Marxists. He won the iron cross as a lance corporal in the First World War. In Munich in 1920 he joined Röhm in a small party hostile to the Weimar Republic, the Versailles settlement and to Jews. Imprisoned after an unsuccessful attempt to overthrow the Bavarian government (1923), he wrote, with Hess, a two-volume work expressing his views *(Mein Kampf)*. During the economic crisis of the 1930s, the Nazi party rose to power and, after

Examples of 18th century French and 19th century English tapestries by the renowned artists François Boucher and Edward Burne-Jones respectively.

Photos: The Louvre and Victoria & Albert Museum

A 16th century embroidered head-dress.

Photo: Victoria & Albert Museum

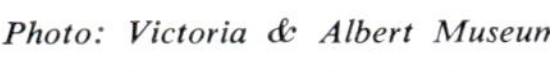

The largest tapestry ever made is Graham Sutherland's 'Christ in Glory'. Executed by weavers from the village of Aubusson in Central France for the new Coventry Cathedral in England, it measures 74′×40′.

Photo: P. W. & L. Thompson

Our planet is relatively small and insignificant yet the range of its natural geographical features is enormous. The vast snow and ice caps covering the North and South Poles present formidable conditions in which few creatures are able to live. *Photos: Brian Kemp*

The impenetrable tropical jungle forests of British Guiana. This mining settlement depends on aircraft to link it with the outside world. *Photo: Camera Press Ltd*

'Bush country', sparsely covered with stunted shrubs, is typical of vast areas of eastern and central Africa and Australia. This photograph was taken in Tanzania and shows the Pare Mountains in the background.

Photo: Central Office of Information.
Crown copyright reserved

his appointment as Chancellor, Hitler succeeded in outlawing all other parties and established a virtual dictatorship. In 1934 he had Röhm and many other rivals massacred. After swallowing up The Rhineland, Czechoslovakia and Austria, he led his country into the Second World War. By assuming complete control of the war, and by falling into insane rages when crossed, Hitler rendered conspicuous service to the Allies, e.g. by calling off the Battle of Britain, refusing to permit a withdrawal from Stalingrad, holding back the panzer reserves after D-day, the murder of Germany's ablest general, Rommel, and his choice for high office of such nonentities as Ribbentrop, Goering and Hess. Ensconced in a bunker in Berlin and surrounded by Russian troops, he ordered his armies to fight to the last man in the Bavarian Redoubt, and committed suicide with his mistress Eva Braun.

HITTITES, an ancient people of Asia Minor (Anatolia) who flourished from 2000—1200 B.C. During the height of their power (*c.* 1375) they ruled not only Asia Minor, but Syria and much of the Middle East and were threatening Egyptian territory there. Twentieth-century excavations have revealed a high standard of civilisation and art, and numerous cuneiform tablets have been deciphered which show that the Hittites spoke an Indo-European language.

HOBBES, Thomas (1588—1679), English philosopher. The founder of the empirical approach, he thought that the basic principle of all living things is self-preservation. To primitive man life was 'solitary, poor, nasty, brutish and short', and the only hope for him was to evolve a Social Contract by which he surrendered himself totally to an all-powerful ruler who would protect him. Such a ruler would retain power only so long as he was able, and revolt must not, therefore, be regarded as treason. Life is a condition of war of everyman against everyman, in which force and fraud are the two cardinal virtues. Egoism is the mainspring of man's conduct, and even unselfish actions are in reality disguised egoism. Hobbes was thus another father of totalitarianism. His pessimistic philosophy is contained in *Leviathan.*

HOCKEY, a British game, wholly amateur, in which teams of 11 try to get a small ball into the opponents' goal, using curved sticks with a striking surface on the left side only; the stick must not be lifted above the shoulders. An English Hockey Union was formed in 1875. Mixed teams of men and women also play. The game is particularly popular in India, Pakistan and the Netherlands.

HOGARTH, William (1697—1764), English engraver and painter. He was particularly known for his satirical engravings, and even his paintings such as *A Harlot's Progress* (1730—1) and *Marriage à la Mode* (1743—5) satirised contemporary society.

HOKKAIDO, the northernmost of the islands of Japan. Pop. (1958) 4,984,000; area 34,276 sq. miles. It is cold and mountainous, with dense forests. Coal, sulphur and iron are mined. Beans, potatoes and sugar-beet are grown. Fishing is very important. The chief city is Hakodate.

HOLBEIN, Hans (1497—1543), German painter and engraver, who settled in England in 1532 and became court painter to Henry VIII in 1536. Unfortunately all his major historical and religious paintings have been lost, and his chief surviving works are portraits. Many of these depict the sitter, at his request, in gorgeous costume, but Holbein's own taste was for the simplicity of such portraits as *Christina, Duchess of Milan* (National Gallery, London); many others are hung at Windsor Castle. He also painted excellent miniatures *(Mr Pemberton, Anne of Cleves)*, and a set of 51 plates of illustrations for the *Dance of Death* also survives. Another famous painting, *The Ambassadors*, is in the National Gallery, London.

HOLLAND, see Netherlands.

HOLLYWOOD, a suburb of Los Angeles, California, U.S.A. From 1910 it was the centre of the American film industry, but owing to technical developments it has lost its predominance.

HOLMES, Oliver Wendell (1809—94), American essayist and poet. From teaching and writing about medicine he turned to literature. He wrote poetry, novels and biographies but is best known for his light essays collected in *The Autocrat of the Breakfast Table* and similar works.

HOLY ALLIANCE, an agreement between the sovereigns of Austria, Russia and Prussia to conduct themselves in accordance with Christian principles. Signed in 1815 at the instigation of Czar Alexander I of Russia, it represented the solidarity of reactionary powers, and has little political importance.

HOLY COMMUNION, see Eucharist.

HOLY ROMAN EMPIRE (962—1806), the traditional name for the German empire. Although Charlemagne was the first crowned emperor (800) after the disintegration of the old Roman Empire, the official designation did not come into being until 926 when the German monarch Otto I was crowned emperor. In theory the empire was a single state with the emperor as ruler and the Pope as the religious head. However, from the outset several states (including France and England) refused to recognise any such authority, particularly as the emperors were invariably German (due to the fact that the electors were German). The last Holy Roman Emperor, Francis II of Austria, abdicated in 1806.

HOLY SPIRIT (Holy Ghost), in Christian theology, one of the three manifestations of the Godhead which is represented by the Trinity, the other two being God the Father, and the Son (Jesus Christ). The New Testament gives no precise definition of the term, and the doctrine of the Trinity was evolved in later centuries.

HOLYOAKE, Keith Jucka (1904—), New Zealand politician. He entered parliament in 1932, and became Minister of Agriculture in 1949. At the head of the National party, he became Prime Minister for a few months in 1957 and again from December 1960.

HOMER, the author, or the name traditionally given to the author, of the two great epics, the *Iliad* and the *Odyssey*. Nothing is certainly known about him; he is supposed to have been an Ionian Greek of Asia Minor, and Herodotus thought that he lived some 400 years before him, i.e. in the 9th century B.C. The first text of which there is any mention dated from the 6th century B.C. The *Iliad* relates the closing phases of the Trojan War (sometime before 1000 B.C.), caused by the Trojan Paris's abduction of the beautiful Helen, wife of Menelaus, King of Sparta. Under the leadership of Menelaus' brother, Agamemnon, the Greeks besieged Troy for 10 years. The poem opens with Achilles sulking in his tent after a quarrel with Agamemnon. After the Greeks have suffered initial reverses, Achilles is spurred to action by the death of his friend, Patroclus, and he slays Hector, son of Priam, King of Troy. Priam comes to beg for the body of his son. Odysseus introduces the Wooden Horse, full of men, into Troy, which falls. The *Odyssey* recounts the adventures of Odysseus on his way home to Ithaca. An ingenious yachtsman has recently charted this voyage, placing the Lotus Eaters on an island of Tunisia, Calypso on Malta, Nausicaa on Corfu and Scylla and Charybdis in the straits of Messina. Even in translation these tales have thrilled and charmed generations of readers throughout the world, whether following Odysseus across the wine-dark seas, or watching the gods and goddesses taking the most unsportsmanlike advantage of heroes locked in mortal combat. The Homeric Hymns are not by the author of these epics, they belong to a later age.

HONAN, a province in east central China. Pop. (1953) 44,214,594; area 64,545 sq. miles. Consisting of fertile plains intersected by mountains, it is traversed by the Hwang Ho (Yellow River). Grains, cotton, groundnuts and hemp are produced. Coal, iron, tin, lead and copper are mined. There are textile industries. The capital is Kaifeng.

HONDURAS, a republic in Central America. Pop. (1960) 1,950,000; area 43,277 sq. miles. Generally mountainous, it has fertile plateaux and river valleys. Bananas, coffee, timber, gold and silver are produced. Independent since 1838, it has had frequent revolutions. The capital is Tegucigalpa (pop. 1958 106,949).

HONG KONG, British colony and island off southeast China. Pop. (1961) 3,226,400; area 398 sq. miles. (including adjacent mainland and islands). An important commercial port, it has growing industries which include textiles, shipbuilding and iron and steel mills. The capital is Victoria. It serves as an entrepôt for China; there is acute overcrowding owing to the continued influx of refugees from China.

HONOLULU, capital of Hawaii. Pop. (1960) 294,194. On the island of Oahu, it has a good harbour and is an important focus of air and sea routes. The Japanese air attack on nearby Pearl Harbor brought America into the Second World War.

HONSHU, the largest and most important island of Japan. Pop. (1955) 67,000,000; area 88,919 sq. miles. It is mountainous (Fujiyama, 12,389 ft) and has valuable forests. Grains, tea, silk, cotton, fruit and vegetables are produced. Industries are diversified and include shipbuilding, metal equipment, chemicals and textiles. The largest cities are Tokyo, Osaka, Nagoya, Kyoto, Yokohama and Kobe, each of which has a population of over a million.

HOOD, Thomas (1799—1845), British poet and humorist. He had a gift for combining the humorous with the pathetic, and published some of his best poems in Punch; he excelled at punning. He edited several magazines.

HOPEI, a maritime province in east China. Pop. (1953) 35,984,644; area 54,154 sq. miles. Mountainous in the north and west, the rest of the province is a vast alluvial plain. The chief agricultural products are grains, fruit and livestock. It has coal and iron. Rugs, leather, textiles and jute are manufactured. The capital is Paoting. Other large cities are Peking and Tientsin.

HOPKINS, Sir Frederick Gowland (1861—1947), British biochemist. His most important work was concerned with proving that certain accessory factors are necessary to health. These later came to be known as vitamins. He shared the Nobel Prize for physiology and medicine with Christiaan Eijkman in 1929.

HOPKINS, Gerard Manley (1844—89), English poet whose innovations in metre and rhythm and sensitive use of language made a significant impact on the poets of the 1920s and '30s. In 1877 he was ordained priest and later became professor of Greek at University College, Dublin. He introduced sprung rhythm into his poetry, a method of manipulating syllables to achieve effects that had not been used since the time of the early Elizabethans.

HORACE (Quintus Horatius Flaccus; 65—8 B.C.), Roman poet. The *Odes*, in which he skilfully adapted to the coarser Latin tongue the lovely metres of Greek lyric poetry, provided the Latin 'tags' which were once freely bandied about the House of Commons *(Eheu fugaces, Postume, Postume, labuntur anni)*. Most of his other work was written in hexameters, and includes the *Satires*, which give an intimate and interesting picture of Roman life, and the more philosophical *Epistles*.

HORMONES, the chemical messengers secreted in vertebrates by the endocrine glands into the blood-stream; there are many kinds (see Endocrinology). For plant hormones see Auxins.

HORN, CAPE, the southernmost point of South America, in Chile. It was discovered by Lemaire and Schouten in 1616, and named after the latter's birthplace. It was dreaded by early navigators on account of the fierce storms that raged continually round it; the alternative was the Magellan Straits to the north, which were too narrow for easy navigation by sailing ships.

HORSE, a single-toed ungulate mammal with a long hairy tail, a mane, and callouses on the inner surfaces of the hind and fore legs. The modern horse is descended from the fox-size Eohippus of 45 million years ago, which had four toes on each front foot and three on each hind foot. Probably domesticated in Central Asia, horses were first used for hunting and war, and later as work animals. The use of horses in warfare gave a tremendous advantage to the armies with cavalry and charioteers. Various breeds now range in size from 200 to 2,220 lb. The average horse lives 18—20 years. Horses are now commonly used for riding, drawing loads and in such sports as racing and hunting.

HORSE RACING, in Britain, dates from at least the 12th century. The importation of stallions from Arabia and the East began in the 16th century, culminating in the importation of three horses from which all the world's bloodstock traces its ancestry. The Jockey Club was founded in 1752 and soon established itself as the controlling authority for racing on the flat. The first St Leger was run in 1778 and the first Derby in 1780. In flat-racing (from March to November) the main types of race are those for two-year-olds (only 5 furlongs at the beginning of the season), handicaps, weight-for-age and races subject to conditions (e.g. for fillies only, maidens at starting, apprentice races). Distances range from 5 furlongs to 2¾ miles. Horses are lined up by a starter before tapes which are raised when they are as nearly in line as possible, in contrast to the practice in the U.S.A. and other countries, where a starting gate is used.

Betting transactions are effected through bookmakers and the totalisator (on and off course) and betting shops.

The National Hunt Committee has, since 1866, controlled steeplechases over brush fences and water-jumps and hurdling over 3-ft hurdles. The season of racing 'over the sticks' fills the winter gap left by flat-racing. The Grand National (1839) at Aintree, Liverpool, is the principal race. The point-to-point meeting is run by a hunt and confined generally to horses that have been regularly hunted.

HOSPITAL, an institution for the diagnosis, treatment and care of persons suffering from illness or injury. Specialised hospitals provide services for childbirth, mental ailments and specific deformities and disorders. The first hospital in England was founded by the Archbishop of Canterbury in 900. The oldest existing hospital is the Hôtel de Dieu in Paris, founded in 660. In the ancient world, hospitals were connected with temples, and later, with monasteries. Many modern hospitals are now affiliated with medical schools and have facilities for research.

HOSPITALLERS, see Knights Hospitallers.

HOUPHOUËT-BOIGNY, Félix (1905—), President of the Ivory Coast. The son of a well-to-do planter and chief, he graduated from the Dakar Medical School and worked as a medical assistant on the Ivory Coast from 1925—40, when he began to take an interest in local politics. In 1946 he helped to form the Rassemblement Démocratique Africain (R.D.A.) of which he became President, and which was to come into power in seven African republics. From 1946—59 he represented his country in the French National Assembly, and was a member of the French Cabinet from 1956. He became Prime Minister in 1959 and President in 1960. He formed the Brazzaville group of French-speaking republics, which supports economic and political co-operation but not federation among African states.

HOUSE, a fixed, permanent structure for human habitation. Primitive man lived in trees and caves or built simple structures of saplings supporting roofs of leaves or branches. Huts of stone, clay bricks and timber were used to make homes in regions where these materials were available. Roman houses constructed around open courts had arrangements for heating the houses through hot air ducts. The Anglo-Saxons lived in structures built on wooden frames with turf for the roof, in which a hole was left for the smoke to escape. In the Middle Ages the big houses had a Great Hall, where the whole household lived, fed and slept. In Tudor times chimneys, glazed windows and plastered ceilings began to come into common use.

HOUSE OF COMMONS and House of Lords, see Parliament.

HOUSTON, a seaport in southeast Texas, U.S.A. Pop. (1960) 938,219. A leading cotton market and communications centre, it exports large quantities of petroleum. Its industries include oil refineries, shipbuilding, food processing, chemicals, textiles and lumber. It is the largest city in the southern states.

HOWRAH, a city in West Bengal, India, facing Calcutta across the Hooghli River. Pop. (1961) 514,090. A communications centre, it has jute, textile and shipbuilding industries.

HUDDERSFIELD, a city in the West Riding of Yorkshire, England. Pop.

(1961) 130,302. It has important woollen and other textile manufactures, and specialises in tweeds. There are chemical works, iron foundries and metallurgical industries.

HUDSON BAY, an inland sea in north-east Canada. Area 540,000 sq. miles. It is connected with the Atlantic and Arctic oceans. There is fishing and whaling. Navigation is possible only from June to October.

HUDSON, Henry (d. 1611), English navigator. After failing twice to find a North-East Passage across northern Europe to the East, Hudson turned westward, crossed the Atlantic and discovered the river, bay and strait which now bear his name. He died when a mutinous crew cast him adrift in a small boat.

HUGHES, Thomas (1822—96), English novelist. A social reformer, he published numerous works but is remembered mainly for his *Tom Brown's School Days*, a picture of life in an English Public School (Rugby).

HUGO, Victor (1802—85), French poet, novelist and dramatist, and a leader of the Romantic movement in France. Immensely prolific, his work plumbs the depths and reaches the heights; he excelled above all as a manipulator of words — the sense did not always reach the same standard. In lyric, epic and meditative poetry he was often supreme; his novels, such as *Les Misérables* and *Notre-Dame de Paris* inclined to melodrama and implausible characters; his plays were of no great value except for their occasional flashes of lyric poetry.

HUGUENOTS, the name given to the French Protestants in the 16th—18th centuries; the derivation of the word is uncertain. They were strong in southwest France, with leaders such as the Condés, Henry of Navarre and Coligny. The Massacre of St Bartholomew's Eve (1572) led to the Edict of Nantes (1598) which gave them full liberty of worship, but from 1624 Richelieu curbed their power and Louis XIV revoked the Edict (1685) and expelled the Huguenots, to the great loss of France and the gain of neighbouring countries, including England. Only after the Revolution were the Protestants of France allowed to live in peace.

HULL (Kingston-upon-Hull), a seaport in Yorkshire, England. Pop. (1961) 299,068. At the junction of the Hull and Humber rivers, it is an important fishing port as well as a commercial and industrial centre. There are several 14th-century buildings.

HUMANISM, a term the meaning of which evolved with the views it describes. It meant, successively, an education based on the Latin, and later the Greek, classics; the comparative study of classical, Christian and Hebrew thought; the whole movement of thought and the arts which led to the Renaissance and the Reformation; the reaction against Scholasticism; any system that was based on the belief that 'Man is the measure of all things', that undermined the absolute authority of the Church and of dogma, that liberated thought, and emphasised belief in human progress and the overriding importance of human welfare.

HUMBOLDT, Baron Alexander von (1769—1859), Prussian naturalist and explorer. He travelled extensively in South and Central America, and visited the Urals, studying the regions and their natural phenomena. His *Kosmos* covered the whole scientific knowledge of his time. The 30-volume *Voyage aux régions équinoxiales du nouveau continent*, which he wrote together with his fellow-scientist, Aimé Bonpland, is a complete record of their journeys.

HUME, David (1711—76), Scottish philosopher, economist and historian. He developed empiricism to its ultimate logical conclusion — scepticism. All knowledge consists of impressions and ideas, the latter being developed from the former. We must suspect any idea for which we cannot find an original sense-impression. On this basis he abandoned the ideas of self, of causality and the possibility of proof in ethics. He wrote sceptically also about religion (including miracles). He made valuable contributions to economics.

HUNAN, a province in south central China. Pop. (1953) 33,226,954; area 79,378 sq. miles. It is a hilly province which includes four large river basins. Growing rice and tea, it is also rich in minerals, producing coal, iron, tungsten and antimony. The capital is Changsha.

HUNDRED DAYS (March 20 to June 26, 1815), the period between Napoleon's entry into Paris after his escape from Elba, and his abdication after the Battle of Waterloo (June 18).

HUNDRED YEARS' WAR, the struggle between France and England between 1337 and 1453, with several intervals of peace. The first phase began when Edward III of England claimed the French throne and ended in 1360 in English victories at Crécy and Poitiers. Charles V of France renewed the fighting nine years later and regained much of the territory previously lost. Henry V defeated Charles VI at Agincourt and, having overrun Normandy in 1419, was recognised as heir to the throne of France. In the next 10 years England occupied most of France north of the Loire, only to have the tide turned by the victories of Joan of Arc and other successes. By 1453 only Calais remained in English hands. The war decimated France, destroying its feudal order and laying the groundwork for a new society, while it turned England's attention away from the Continent to the sea and colonial expansion.

HUNGARY, People's republic in central Europe. Pop. (1960) 9,977,870; area 35,919 sq. miles. Consisting mostly of large, treeless steppes, Hungary is bounded on the north by the foothills of the Carpathian Mountains. The Danube is navigable for its entire course through the country. About a tenth of Hungary is forested. Major crops are cereals, potatoes and sugar-beet. Fishing is important in the rivers and Lake Balaton. There are oil deposits. Coal, lignite, iron, bauxite and manganese are mined. Leading industrial products are cement, sugar, chemicals and textiles. Invaded by the Magyars in 896, Hungary became a powerful kingdom in 1342—82. Defeated by the Turks in 1526, Hungary accepted Hapsburg rule to escape Ottoman domination. Peace with the Ottoman Empire did not come until 1699. A revolt against the Hapsburgs in 1848 led by Louis Kossuth failed. In 1867 Hungary became part of the dual monarchy of Austria-Hungary. Following the collapse of the Austro-Hungarian Empire after the First World War, Hungary experienced brief republican and Communist régimes until the old kingdom was restored in 1920 without a king, under the regency of Admiral Horthy. First an ally of Germany in the Second World War, and later occupied by it, Hungary became an ally of the U.S.S.R. at the close of the conflict. The capital is Budapest (pop. 1960 1,807,299).

Other important cities are Miskolc (144,270), Debrecen (129,305) and Pécs (114,625).

HUNS, a people of Mongolian origin who terrorised Europe early in the 5th century A.D. Under Attila, they swept westward across the Rhine, ferociously sowing destruction wherever they went, until finally checked south of Châlons-sur-Marne in 451 by the Romans and Visigoths. The following year Attila was turned back from Italy after devastating many cities there. After Attila's death their empire collapsed, and by the end of the 8th century the Huns were no longer identifiable as a distinct nation.

HUNTING, fox-hunting with a pack of hounds as it is known today began in Britain in the 17th century. The first operation is to draw coverts; if the hounds, of which there may be from 20 to 80 couples, find a fox they drive him into the open, where the hunt followers join in, keeping well behind hounds. The fox may be caught and killed, or get to ground in an unstopped earth, or the hounds may lose the scent (check, be at fault). The hunting shires (Rutland, Leicestershire, Northamptonshire) are the homes of the most famous hunts, (Pytchley, Quorn, Belvoir and Cottesmore). Cub-hunting begins in August and fox-hunting in November.

Stag-hunting, once the sport of kings, and imported by the Normans, is now almost confined to three packs in Devon and Somerset. The season lasts for six weeks from August 12, and a similar period from the beginning of April. The quarry is the male of the red deer, which may be wild or carted (kept in a paddock, taken to the hunt in a cart, and brought back intact after the hunt). The deer-hound has been replaced by staghounds, which are specially trained foxhounds.

Beagling is the hunting of the wild hare, more elusive than the fox, on foot, with a pack of beagles or, in open country, mounted and with harriers, the latter being sometimes used to hunt the fox also. The season lasts from autumn until March.

Otter-hunting is also on foot, with otterhounds or foxhounds, from May to August.

HUNTINGDONSHIRE, an inland county in east central England. Pop. (1961) 79,879; area 366 sq. miles. Except for rolling hills in the south and west, it is mostly flat. A rich agricultural region, the county produces cereals, potatoes and sugar-beet. Livestock-raising and dairy farming are important. There are few industries except for the Fletton brickworks. The county town is Huntingdon.

HUPEI, a province in central China, in the Yangtze Valley. Pop. (1953) 27,789,693; area 71,955 sq. miles. Enclosed by mountains, it is intersected by important trade routes. Rice, wheat, cotton, tea, tobacco and silk are produced. There are iron and coal deposits, and metallurgical, textile, flour processing and cement industries. The capital is Wuchang.

HUSS, John (*c.* 1369—1415), Bohemian religious reformer and martyr. Arousing the animosity of the church by his defence of Wycliffe's doctrines and by his attacks on clerical abuses, he was excommunicated in 1410. Refusing to recant his convictions he was burnt at the stake.

HUXLEY, Aldous (1894—1963), English writer. The author of poetry, short stories and essays, he is famous for his brilliant novels of contemporary life. His works include *Crome Yellow*, *Antic Hay*, *Point Counter Point*, *Brave New World* and

Eyeless in Gaza. He spent his later years in California, where he produced works on the improvement of eyesight without glasses, oriental mysticism *(The Perennial Philosophy)* and the effects of taking the stimulant mescalin.

HUXLEY, Thomas Henry (1825—95), English biologist and palaeontologist. An early advocate of Darwin's theories, he published important studies on vertebrates and served on numerous royal commissions. He coined the term agnostic and applied it to himself.

HYDERABAD. (1) Capital of Andhra Pradesh state, India. Pop. (1961) 1,252,337 A walled city on the Musi River, it is a trade centre with textile manufactures. (2) City in West Pakistan. Pop. (1951) 241,801. Near the Indus River, it is a commercial and railway centre and manufactures silver and gold embroidery, textiles, silk, pottery and lacquered ware. It was the capital of the old Sind province.

HYDRAULICS, the science of applying the pressure of water or some other fluid, e.g. oil, to operate machines. Hydraulic machines are of two kinds: those transforming moving water into mechanical energy, such as water-wheels, turbines and motors, and those in which the liquid itself transmits power, as in presses, jacks and lifts.

HYDROCHLORIC ACID, a very active mineral acid produced by dissolving hydrogen chloride in water. It is important as a solvent for most metals and is the source of many valuable salts. It is present in the gastric juices.

HYDROGEN, see Elements.

HYDROGEN BOMB (thermonuclear or fusion bomb), entirely different from the atomic bomb, using nuclear fusion instead of nuclear fission. The explosion of an atomic bomb is, however, used in it to produce the very high initial temperature required to heat the explosive charge which, in the earlier hydrogen bombs, comprised two rare isotopes of hydrogen (deuterium and tritium). This heat causes atomic condensation of the kind that occurs in the sun when hydrogen is condensed into helium, releasing huge amounts of energy.

Hydrogen bombs with an explosive effect equivalent to ten million tons of TNT (i.e. 10 megatons) have been tested, compared with the 20,000 tons for the, first atomic bomb. In the cobalt bomb, which is believed to exist only in theory, a shell of cobalt round a hydrogen bomb would produce a form of cobalt which would remain intensely radioactive for several years, thus increasing and prolonging the danger from radioactive fall-out.

HYDROGEN PEROXIDE, a pure, colourless, oily liquid which decomposes easily into water and oxygen. A powerful oxidising agent, it is used as a bleach and disinfectant.

HYDROPONICS, the cultivation of plants in a water medium without soil. The water contains nutritive chemicals and means of support for the growing plant. Plants may also be rooted in sand and watered with chemical nutrients.

HYPNOTISM, a physiological state of increased suggestibility stemming from the operator's influence on the subject. Resembling sleep, it can be induced in trances of varying depth, depending on the subject. Individuals also vary as to their susceptibility. Hypnosis has a strong influence on many physiological and psychological functions, depending on the subject's degree of co-operation. In medicine, it is useful as an anaesthetic, as a diagnostic in uncovering suppressed memories, and for curing certain neurotic symptoms.

HYSTERIA, a neurotic disorder in which emotional conflicts are expressed in various physical symptoms. It can simulate any known physical disease. It may be so severe as to cause insanity.

IASI (Jassy), a city in Rumania. Pop. (1961) 124,715. A cultural and industrial centre, it produces textiles, chemicals, wines and tobacco. It was once the capital of Moldavia.

IBN SAUD, Abdul Aziz (1880—1953), founder of Saudi Arabia. Grandson of the Sultan of Turkish Nejd, his early life was spent in exile. He conquered Nejd in 1901 and became leader of the fanatic, reformist and nationalist Wahhabi movement. By 1914 he had conquered all Arabia except Hejaz, and during the First World War remained neutral in spite of Lawrence's support of his rival, the Hashimite King of Hejaz. By 1924 Ibn Saud had conquered Mecca and the Hejaz and in 1932 he was proclaimed king of a unified Saudi Arabia, a country which was transformed shortly afterwards by the discovery of vast oil resources. Ibn Saud joined the Allies in 1944 and a year later helped to found the Arab League, on which he was one of the more moderate influences.

IBSEN, Henrik (1828—1906), Norwegian dramatist and poet. He was appointed director of the Bergen National Theatre when he was only 23 years old, and in 1857 he became manager of a theatre in Christiania. He spent many years abroad in self-exile, following his government's refusal to grant him a pension. His bitterness is reflected in his first two great dramatic poems, *Brand* and *Peer Gynt*, together with his own inner uncertainties, which reappear in all his plays. He next turned to social problems in *Pillars of Society*, *A Doll's House*, *Ghosts*, *Hedda Gabler* and *The Master Builder*, moving from a simple realism towards a greater use of symbolism, and showing a growing pessimism about the fate of the idealist in the material-minded society of his day. He had great influence in Germany and, through Bernard Shaw's championship and William Archer's translations, an even greater influence in England, both on the content and the stagecraft of subsequent serious drama.

ICE AGE, a geological period, contemporary with the Pleistocene (see Geology) and beginning about a million years ago, during which ice-sheets and glaciers covered the continents as far south as Kiev, London and New York. The Ice Age was interspersed with warm periods, one of which may be our own. Neanderthal Man may have appeared in the last warm period, 10,000 to 25,000 years ago, and modern man after the last glacial period. Many very varied theories have been put forward to account for the Ice Age, but none is conclusive, and arguments continue.

ICELAND, an island republic in the North Atlantic. Pop. (1960) 178,000; area 39,709 sq. miles. It consists of highland plateau and volcanic mountains and most of the population lives in the coastal lowlands, which have temperatures in winter only a little below freezing point. Snowfields and glaciers cover more than 13% of the area. Hay, potatoes and turnips are raised, together with livestock. Fishing is the principal source of income. First settled in 874, it was an independent republic from 930—1262. After a period of Norwegian rule, it followed Norway into the union with Denmark, which ruled it until 1918, when it was granted home rule. In 1944 it achieved complete independence. The capital is Reykjavik (pop. 1961 73,388).

ICONOCLASTS, members of a movement in the Eastern Church during the 8th and 9th centuries, which attempted to prohibit the use and veneration of icons or pictures of Christ and of saints within the Church.

IDAHO, a northwestern state of the U.S.A. Pop. (1960) 622,856; area 83,557 sq. miles. Uneven and mountainous, with arid deserts, it has broad plateaux and deep canyons. A third of the state is forested. There is extensive irrigation. The principal crops are wheat, lucerne, sugar-beet and potatoes. Livestock raising is important. Mineral deposits include lead, zinc, silver and phosphates. Idaho became a state in 1890, 30 years after its first permanent settlements were founded. The capital is Boise (34,481).

IDOLATRY, the veneration or worship of images of created objects believed to have supernatural powers. Though it is usually associated with more primitive groups, vestiges of it can still be observed in many religious rites.

ILLINOIS, a northern state of the U.S.A. Pop. (1960) 10,081,158; area 56,400 sq. miles. Situated in the Mississippi valley and the basin of the Great Lakes, and fronting on Lake Michigan, it is generally level. The state is predominantly agricultural and produces maize, wheat, oats and other grains, potatoes and soya beans. Livestock raising is important. There are deposits of coal, lead and petroleum. The leading industries are meat packing, machinery and steel equipment. First settled by French explorers and missionaries in 1720, it came under English rule in 1763. In 1818 it became a state. Springfield (pop. 83,271) is the capital. Other cities of importance are Chicago (3,550,404), Rockford (126,606) and Peoria (103,162).

ILLUMINATED MANUSCRIPT, a manuscript with elaborate initial letters or

Opening of early English manuscript. The Winchester Bible

other ornamentation decorated with gold or silver leaf, or painted in colour, often with exquisite miniature paintings to illustrate the text. Arabian and Persian documents were similarly embellished. The art began to die out with the invention of printing.

ILLYRIA, an ancient mountainous region along the Adriatic coast as far inland as the Danube and Morava rivers. The Illyrians ruled Macedonia early in the 4th century B.C.

IMAGINATION, the faculty to see in the mind whatever is not perceived by the senses. It concerns not only past experiences but implies the creating of new events, persons, and scenes as the individual desires in order to give him certain satisfactions. It may be controlled or apparently spontaneous. Imaginative fancies are an indication either of avowed or unknown mental processes.

IMMACULATE CONCEPTION, a Roman Catholic dogma which asserts that the Virgin Mary was free of the taint of original sin from the moment of her conception. The doctrine was made official by the bull of Pius IX in 1854.

IMPERIALISM, the policy of extending national domination by acquisition of territories, colonies or protectorates through diplomatic, military or economical means. Motives may be strategic (protecting sea-routes, providing coaling stations, etc.), economic or missionary. Imperialist powers brought with them war, disease and the slave trade; they also brought eventual peace, the abolition of slavery, education, medical services, roads and railways, and a market which led to vastly improved standards in living conditions.

IMPRESSIONISM, an artistic concept which is based on seeking to capture immediate overall sensory impressions without going into details. Selecting subjects from their environment, the Impressionist painters mostly preferred working in the open air. The emphasis was on light and the use of colour, and their pictures rarely had any moral or sentimental implications. The founders of Impressionism, under the influence of Manet, were Monet and Pissarro working in the 1860s, joined by Renoir, Degas, Sisley and Cézanne.

INCAS, an Indian tribe of the Peruvian highlands. In the 12th century A.D. they began a series of conquests which reached their height in the early 16th century. At that time the Inca empire included what are now the countries of Peru, Argentina, Ecuador and Chile. The empire collapsed after the invasion of the Spaniards under Pizarro (1532). They attained a high standard of civilisation and political organisation, even though iron and the wheel were unknown to them.

Inca architecture. (Temple of Warriors, Chichén Itzá, Yucatan)

INDIA, the subcontinent that includes India, Pakistan, Ceylon, Bhutan and Nepal (qq.v.). Pop. 550,000,000; area 1,632,474 sq. miles. Enclosed by Himalayan and other mountain ranges to the north, it consists of alluvial plains in the northcentral area, the Deccan plateau further south, and the coastal lowlands, with the Eastern and Western Ghats behind them. The climate is monsoonal, and the rainy season lasts from June to October. The peninsula produces wheat in the north, rice in the south, and spices in Ceylon.

The Indus Valley civilisation, of unknown origin, reached from Sind to Gujarat during the period *c.* 2600—1500 B.C. It succumbed to Aryan invasions from 1600—1300 B.C. Buddhism originated in Nepal in the 6th century but gradually yielded to Hinduism except in Ceylon. In 327 B.C. Alexander the Great marched down the Indus to near Karachi, where he embarked, leaving behind numerous colonies (later absorbed) and an influence on Indian art. The period of Indian empires followed: the Mauryas from 322 B.C., based on Patna; the Guptas of eastern India (4th century A.D.), the Rajputs (9th century) and, in south central India, Vijayanagar (1336—1564). There were recurrent Moslem invasions from the 11th century, and in 1206 Delhi became the Mohammedan capital. In 1398 the Mongols under Timus overran India. The great Mogul Empire, which lasted, at least in name, until 1857, was established in 1526 by Babur, a descendant of Timur. Akbar the Great (1556—1605) became the ruler of a well-governed empire which extended over all of northern India. Mogul power reached its height and began to decline in the reign of Aurangzeb (1659—1707). For a century after the visit of Vasco da Gama in 1498, the Portuguese conducted nearly all the trade with India. At the beginning of the 17th century, the English and the Dutch supplanted the Portuguese traders, the Dutch later withdrawing to the East Indies. The first English trading-post was established at Surat, in 1612. The French had considerable influence in southern India during the 18th century. After taking Bombay from the Portuguese, the British made it their headquarters in 1687. From 1750 occurred constant clashes with Indian rulers. The French gradually yielded all India to the British and in 1858, one year after the suppression of a mutiny by Indian troops, the British Crown formally took over all possessions controlled by the British East India Company. The degree of self-rule varied in the native states and provinces, some being directly under the British Raj, and some governed by Indian princes. At the beginning of the 20th century aspirations for independence grew, and after the First World War, were given mass expression by Gandhi, who led the opposition to the British. His struggle culminated in the partition of India between Moslems and Hindus in 1947 and the establishment of the Indian Union and Pakistan as members of the British Commonwealth.

INDIA, Republic of, a republic in south Asia, member of the British Commonwealth. Pop. (1961) 436,424,429; area 1,174,000 sq. miles. The north country consists of a plain drained by the Ganges flowing south from the Himalayas. Assam, in the northeast, is drained by the Brahmaputra. A series of low-lying mountain ranges intersect the plateau of central India. The west coastal range in the south merges into plains (in the east) and steppes (in the west) as far as the sea. The Godavari and Kistna rivers flow eastward into the Bay of Bengal across the central plain. Agriculture is the main pursuit. Cereals, coffee, tea, cotton, sugar-cane, groundnuts and jute are the principal products. Livestock is raised, and wool produced for export. The leading industries are iron and steel, jute manufactures, rice milling, textiles, vegetable oil processing and engineering. There are deposits of coal, iron, manganese, copper, lead, mica, gold, silver and petroleum. The Union of India comprises 15 states and 6 Union Territories, replacing British India which had about 560 native states under its administration. The states constituting the Union are: Andhra Pradesh, Assam, Bihar, Gujarat, Jammu and Kashmir (about half of which is under Pakistani occupation), Kerala, Madhya Pradesh, Madras, Maharashtra, Mysore, Orissa, Punjab, Rajasthan, Uttar Pradesh and West Bengal. The French settlements of Chandernagore and Pondicherry were incorporated into India by agreement. The Portuguese areas of Goa, Damao and Diu were invaded and annexed in 1961. The capital is Delhi (pop. 1961 2,061,758). Other large cities are Bombay (Greater Bombay, 4,146,491), Calcutta (2,926,498), Madras (1,725,216) and Hyderabad (1,252,337).

INDIAN MUTINY (1857—59), a mutiny of the Bengal army, in which discipline had deteriorated. Complaints that grease on cartridges was made of animal fat, thus rendering them unclean to Hindu and Moslem alike, had been met, and the refusal of troops at Meerut to use cartridges which had been made in their own camp, to demonstrate that no animal fat was used, started the mutiny. British officers and their wives and children were massacred. The mutiny spread to Delhi, Lucknow and to Cawnpore, where, on the promise of safe-conduct, the British surrendered and were immediately massacred, as were those at Delhi. Indian troops rendered signal service in helping to quell the outbreak, which was in no sense a nationalist movement (although it has become convenient for nationalists to represent it as such); it was not backed by any popular uprising, except, for purely local reasons, in Oudh; Madras and Bombay were unaffected. The small forces available were able to end the main mutiny in 1858, but disorder continued for another year.

INDIAN OCEAN, a body of water extending from Africa east to Indonesia and Australia, and from Asia south to the Antarctic regions. Area 29,340,000 sq. miles. India divides it into the Arabian Sea and the Bay of Bengal. The greatest depth is 22,968 ft between Sumatra and Java.

INDIANA, a north central state of the U.S.A. Pop. (1960) 4,662,498; area 36,291 sq. miles. Situated in the Mississippi valley and Great Lakes basin, it is mostly rolling lowland. Its northwest corner fronts on Lake Michigan. Largely agricultural, it produces maize, cereals, soya beans, clover seed, apples, strawberries, tomatoes and water-melons. Indiana manufactures iron and steel equipment, and is a leading producer of coal and oil. First settled in 1732, it became a state in 1816. The capital is Indianapolis (pop. 476,258). Other large cities are Gary (178,320), Fort Wayne (161,776) and Evansville (141,543).

INDIANS, American, the aboriginal inhabitants of the Americas, mistakenly called 'Indians' by Columbus, who thought he had reached India. The theory generally accepted is that the Indians are of Mongoloid stock and migrated intermittently from Asia to

North American Indian

America by way of the Bering Strait as early as 20,000 years ago. A variety of languages and cultures exist among the Indians. Some, such as the Aztecs, Incas and Mayas, attained a high degree of civilisation. Contrary to popular belief, the Indian population of North America has in recent years increased rather than decreased, there now being over 556,000 in the U.S. and Canada; in Central and Southern America there are far more, but owing to the varying degrees of admixture with European and African races no estimate can be given.

INDIVIDUAL PSYCHOLOGY, a school of psychology based on the teachings of Alfred Adler (q.v.). It stresses the importance of social interdependence in the life of an integrated individual.

INDO-CHINA, a peninsula in southeast Asia, between India and China. It is occupied by the states which formerly constituted French Indo-China: North Viet-Nam, South Viet-Nam, Cambodia and Laos (qq.v.).

INDO-EUROPEAN (Aryan), the name of a family of languages which derived from a common language spoken before 2000 B.C., probably somewhere in eastern Europe or southern Russia. It includes some of the languages of northern India, Persian, Greek and Latin, Celtic (e.g. Welsh), Germanic (e.g. English, German), Romance (French, Italian, Spanish, etc.), Scandinavian, and Slavonic (e.g. Russian, Polish) languages. Among European languages which do not belong to this family are Etruscan, Basque, Magyar (Hungarian), Finnish and Turkish.

INDONESIA, Republic of, a state in southeast Asia consisting of the former Dutch possessions in the East Indies. Pop. (1960) 92,600,000; area 575,894 sq. miles. Indonesia comprises a chain of islands of which the principal ones are Sumatra, Java and Madura, Nusa Tenggara (Lesser Sundas), Maluku (Moluccas), Sulawesi (Celebes), and Kalimantan (Borneo), together with some 3000 smaller islands and islets. They mostly comprise mountains, swamps and thick jungles, with a hot humid climate. The islands produce rubber, sugar, rice, tea, coffee, palm oil, spices and copra. Cassava and sweet potatoes are staples. Fishing and the raising of livestock are important. There are deposits of tin, bauxite, coal, manganese and petroleum, and valuable timber is produced. Industries consist of textile plants, shipyards, chemical works and an automobile assembly factory. Most of the area was Moslem by the 15th century. The Dutch began trading with the islands in the 16th century and annexed them in 1602. Complete independence was achieved in 1949, and West Irian (West New Guinea) was added in 1963. The capital is Djakarta (pop. 1961 approx. 3,000,000). Other large cities are Surabaya (1,135,300), Bandung (951,900) and Semarang (444,800).

INDORE, a city in Madhya Pradesh, India. Pop. (1961) 395,035. A communications and trading centre, it has several textile factories.

INDUS, see River.

INDUSTRIAL REVOLUTION, the name given to the period which began in Britain in 1709 with improvements in the production of iron, and had far-reaching effects on industry, due to increased mechanisation made possible by new inventions. The development of the steam engine (1776), the invention of the spinning jenny (1764), and the power loom (1785), all helped to move industry out of homes and workshops into large factories. This had an enormous impact on the social scene and necessitated many readjustments.

INFERIORITY COMPLEX, a psychological term to describe a feeling of inadequacy felt by an individual which leads him to expect failure and to seek rational explanations for that failure. As an escape from reality it avoids, rather than copes with, real problems. A determined effort to compensate for such inferiority may often prove successful.

INFLATION, an increase in the amount of currency circulating in the country which brings about a rise in prices and a corresponding drop in the value of money. It takes more money to buy less commodities. Increased government borrowing, and the issue of currency coupled with a scarcity of goods, are the commonest causes of inflation. Although wages also rise, failure to keep pace with price increases deprives the rise of all benefit.

INGE, William Ralph (1860—1954), Anglican prelate and theologian. Dean of St Paul's Cathedral, he was called 'the gloomy dean' because of the pessimistic tone of his teaching and writing. He was a prolific author.

INNOCENT III (*c.* 1160—1216), Pope from 1198—1216. He was unceasing in his efforts to strengthen the temporal powers of the church and went so far as to depose Otto IV, emperor of the Holy Roman Empire. He promoted the Fourth Crusade, which was diverted to Constantinople.

INNS OF COURT, four law associations in London possessing an exclusive privilege of admitting persons to practice at the bar. The Inns, which are self-governing, can also disbar members. They are Inner Temple, Middle Temple, Lincoln's Inn and Gray's Inn.

INÖNÜ, Ismet (1884—), Turkish statesman. He joined Mustapha Kemal's movement and adopted his present name after defeating the Greeks at Inönü in 1921. He became the first Prime Minister of the Turkish Republic (1923—4, 1925—37), succeeding Kemal Atatürk as President in 1938 and winning the first open elections with ease in 1946. After defeat at the 1950 elections he led the opposition until the military *coup d'état* in 1960, and was elected Prime Minister again in 1961 at the head of a coalition government.

INORGANIC CHEMISTRY, the chemistry of substances of mineral origin. See Organic Compounds.

INQUISITION, an administrative tribunal of the Roman Catholic Church established in the 13th century to combat heresy. At first it was directed against the Cathari, Waldenses and Albigenses but in the 15th century it was particularly employed against the Moors and Jews of Spain. The Inquisition was a ready tool in the hands of temporal rulers, as it permitted torture, execution and confiscation of property. In the 15th century it had ceased to function, except in Spain, but the Pope re-established it in Rome in 1542.

INSECT, a branch of the animal kingdom consisting of invertebrates with segmented bodies and jointed legs. The body is divided into three distinct regions: head, thorax and abdomen. The legs (three pairs) and wings (one or two pairs or, in some cases, none) are attached to the thorax. Most insects reproduce by laying eggs, which undergo a series of changes after hatching. Before

Vast areas of the Andes Mountains in South America are still unexplored. As shown here, they frequently rise sharply out of the tropical jungles. *Photo: Katy Knopfler*

The Himalaya range of mountains, which separates Kashmir from the plains of Northern India, is not only the most massive in the world but includes the highest peaks. Although the lower slopes are clad with vegetation, snow permanently covers the heights. *Photo: India House*

The Sahara Desert (q.v.), which covers 3,500,000 sq. miles of North Africa, is virtually devoid of life and vegetation. *Photos: Michael Kettle and Radio Times Hulton Picture Library*

Japan also has many mountains, of which Mt Fuji, pictured here, is the most famous tourist attraction. *Photo: Japan National Tourist Association*

The course of the River Mississippi in America is constantly changing owing to the heavy silt deposits which build up on the bends and eventually form banks of new land. Attempts are being made to control this process, which can otherwise turn waterside cities into inland cities within a fairly short period of time. *Photo: United States Information Service*

The Victoria Falls, on the boundary between Zambia and Southern Rhodesia, are one of the world's most stupendous sights. Fed by the Zambesi River, they spread across 1860 yards and fall 355 ft at the centre. *Photo: Government of Zambia*

becoming a perfect adult, the insect is first a larva (a worm or caterpillar) and then a pupa (dormant, in a protective covering). Insects breathe air and live on vegetable matter, although some eat meat and others are parasitic. Insects are beneficial in pollination and soil formation and some, like the bee and the silkworm, are of economic importance; others are extremely harmful in spreading disease and destroying human food. The most numerous of living organisms, insects constitute three-quarters to five-sixths of all animal life.

INSTINCT, a psychological term often used to designate an innate disposition, or impulse to act, which does not have to be learned. What were formerly believed to be instincts in man are proved to have been learned at an early age.

INSULIN, a hormone, produced by a group of cells in the pancreas, which plays a major role in the metabolism of the body and its utilisation of sugars and fats. It is important in the treatment of diabetes, and is also used to increase the appetite.

INTELLIGENCE TEST, an objective test designed to measure innate ability or the capacity to adjust to new situations. It consists of a group of tests each of which measures some special ability. If a child of 8 answers all the questions which a child of 10 normally solves, its mental age is said to be 10 years old. The mental age divided by the physical, or chronological, age gives the Intelligence Quotient (I.Q.). An I.Q. of 90—110 is considered normal.

INTERNATIONAL LABOUR ORGANISATION (I.L.O.), established in 1919 under the League of Nations, is a body on which governments, employers and employees are directly represented. Its objects are to improve labour conditions and promote economic and social stability. In 1951 it published *The International Labour Code.*

INTERNATIONAL LAW, principles and rules which are binding in the relations between independent states. Such a code becomes binding when the great majority of states make it valid either by formal agreement or after extended application. The most recent development is for international bodies, such as the U.N., to enact international legislation. This is usually done by many nations signing treaties or conventions dealing with specific problems.

INVENTION, a device or method which did not exist previously or was unknown before, or its improvement. The exclusive right of an inventor to his product for a definite period of time is recognised by all nations in the form of a contract or patent. The most noteworthy inventions include the following:

Invention	*Inventor*	*Country*	*Year*
Adding machine	William S. Burroughs	U.S.A.	1888
Aeroplane	Wilbur and Orville Wright	U.S.A.	1903
Automobile	G. Daimler and others	Germany	1887
Bakelite	Leo H. Baekeland	Belgium, U.S.A.	1908
Barometer	Evangelista Torricelli	Italy	1643
Camera, Kodak	George Eastman	U.S.A.	1888
Carburettor, Spray	Charles E. Duryea	U.S.A.	1892
Cellophane	J. E. Brandenberger	France	1911

Invention	*Inventor*	*Country*	*Year*
Cotton Gin	Eli Whitney	U.S.A.	1793
Cyclotron	Ernest O. Lawrence	U.S.A.	1931
Daguerreotype	Louis Daguerre	France	1839
Diesel engine	Rudolf Diesel	Germany	1897
Dynamite	Alfred B. Nobel	Sweden	1862
Dynamo	Michael Faraday	Great Britain	1831
Electromagnet	William Sturgeon	Great Britain	1823
Engine, Internal Combustion	G. Daimler	Germany	1885
Filament, Tungsten	Irving Langmuir	U.S.A.	1915
Fountain Pen	Lewis E. Waterman	U.S.A.	1884
Guncotton	Christian Schönbein	Germany	1845
Gyroscope	Jean Léon Foucault	France	1852
Jet-propelled aircraft	Sir Frank Whittle	Great Britain	1930
Lamp, Incandescent	Thomas A. Edison	U.S.A.	1879
Linotype machine	Ottmar Mergenthaler	U.S.A.	1885
Lithography	Alois Senefelder	Bohemia	1796
Machine Gun	Richard J. Gatling	U.S.A.	1861
Mercury-vapour lamp	Peter C. Hewitt	U.S.A.	1912
Microscope, Compound	Zacharias Janssen	Netherlands	1590
Microscope, Electronic	Vladimir Zworykin and others	Germany	1939
Motion pictures	Thomas A. Edison	U.S.A.	1893
Motor, A. C.	Nikola Tesla	U.S.A.	1892
Ophthalmoscope	Hermann von Helmholtz	Germany	1851
Phonograph (Gramophone)	Thomas A. Edison	U.S.A.	1877
Photography, Colour	Gabriel Lippmann	France	1891
Power loom	Edmund Cartwright	Great Britain	1785
Printing, movable type	Johann Gutenberg	Germany	1440
Reaper	Cyrus McCormick	U.S.A.	1834
Revolver	Samuel Colt	U.S.A.	1835
Rubber, vulcanised	C. Goodyear	U.S.A.	1839
Steam engine	James Watt	Great Britain	1765
Tank, military	Sir Ernest Swinton	Great Britain	1914
Telegraph	Samuel F. B. Morse	U.S.A.	1837
Telephone	Alexander G. Bell	U.S.A.	1876
Television	J. L. Baird	Great Britain	1926
Transistor	J. Bardeen, W. Shockley, W. Brattain	U.S.A.	1948
Typewriter	Christopher Sholes, C. Glidden, S. Soule	U.S.A.	1867
Wireless, Telegraphy	Guglielmo Marconi	Italy	1895

INVERNESS, a maritime county in north central Scotland. Pop. (1961) 83,425; area 4351 sq. miles. Mountainous with numerous wooded areas, it is well drained. Grain, potatoes and turnips are raised. Textiles, chemicals, foodstuffs and sawmill products are the principal industries. The county town is Inverness.

INVERTEBRATES, an artificially constituted group consisting of all animals which have no backbone (see Vertebrates). It includes insects, spiders, crustaceans, shellfish, starfish and jellyfish, slugs, snails, oysters, the various worms, sponges and protozoa.

IODINE, see Elements.

ION, an electrically charged atom or group of atoms, formed when one or more electrons are detached by radiation or particle collision, leaving the atom electrically positive; the process is called ionisation and the result is a positive ion. A negative ion is formed when an atom accepts one or more extra electrons. Ions can be produced in gas by electric spark, X-rays, etc. The positive ion of hydrogen is the proton (q.v.). The ionisation that occurs through the absorption of radiation produces the photoelectric effect of the photo-cell.

IONESCO, Eugène (1912—), Rumanian-born playwright who came to Paris with his French mother at an early age. He writes plays the absurdities of which show up the absurdities of the *bourgeoisie*; he aimed to create a 'theatre of violence — violently comic, violently tragic'. A characteristic play was *Rhinoceros* (1958).

IONIA, the west coast of Asia Minor on the Aegean Sea, colonised chiefly by Achaeans from mainland Greece in the 11th and 10th centuries B.C. It was highly advanced and prosperous in the 8th—6th centuries B.C.

IONIAN ISLANDS, a chain of seven large islands in the Ionian Sea near the northwest coast of Greece. Pop. (1951) 228,119; area 752 sq. miles. They are generally mountainous with fertile plains in which tropical fruit, cotton and cereals are raised. Fishing is an important occupation. Manufactures include textiles, food and shipbuilding. Venetian from 1386—1797, they passed through the hands of the French, Russians and British, who returned them to Greece in 1864. The islands are: Corfu (Kerkyra, Corcyra), Paxos, Lefkas, Cephalonia (Kephallenia), Ithaca (Ithake), Zante (Zakynthos) and Kythera.

IOWA, a north central state of the U.S.A. Pop. (1960) 2,757,537; area 56,290 sq. miles. Consisting of rolling prairie, the state lies between the Mississippi and Missouri rivers. Iowa is a leading agricultural region producing maize, oats, wheat, barley, rye, soyabeans, potatoes, buckwheat and popcorn. It ranks first in livestock production in the country. There are coal deposits. First settled in 1788, it became a state in 1846. The capital is Des Moines (pop. 208,982). Other important cities are Cedar Rapids (92,035) and Sioux City (89,159).

IPSWICH, a town in Suffolk, England. Pop. (1961) 117,325. At the head of the Orwell estuary, it produces agricultural implements, electrical equipment and clothing, and has breweries, tanneries and engineering works. There are numerous buildings of historic interest.

IRAN (Persia), a kingdom in southwest Asia. Pop. (1960) 20,633,000; area 636,294 sq. miles. The country is a vast plateau enclosed by high mountains in the north and by lower ranges in the south. There are lowlands along the Caspian Sea and the Persian Gulf. A huge desert area crosses central Iran from northwest to southeast. Predominantly agricultural, it produces wheat, rice, barley, cotton, sugar-beet, tobacco, grapes, dates, oranges, olives and tea. In addition to petroleum Iran has other mineral deposits but they are little worked. Sturgeon, for caviare, are caught in the Caspian Sea. Livestock, especially sheep, are an important factor in its economy. Exports include cotton and carpets. The population is mostly Shi-ite Moslem. Until 1935 the country was called Persia. Ruled by the Assyrians, Medes, and Achaemenids, the Persians forged an empire from the Mediterranean and Aegean seas to the Indus River under Cyrus in the early part of the 6th century B.C. Later kings (Cambyses and Darius the Great) added Egypt, Macedonia, Thrace and the Punjab to the Persian domains. Persian attempts to conquer Greece in the first part of the 5th century B.C. were repulsed and they were forced to withdraw from Greece permanently. In 331—330 Persia fell to Alexander the Great. After his death most of the country came under the rule of the Seleucids, and later of the Parthians. In A.D. 226, a native dynasty, the Sassanids, achieved a degree of power, clashing frequently with the Byzantines. Islam overran Persia in the 7th century. Between the 11th and 16th centuries, the Seljuk Turks and Mongols gained power. An Anglo-Russian treaty in 1907 divided Persia into three spheres of influence — Russian, British and neutral. In 1921 General Riza Pahlavi seized control and was elected hereditary Shah in 1925. During the Second World War Anglo-Russian occupation was necessary in order to forestall German penetration. A Russian-inspired separatist movement in the northwest province of Azerbaijan after the war was frustrated by U.N. intervention. The capital is Tehran (pop. 1956 1,513,164). Other important cities are Tabriz (290,195), Isfahan (254,876), Meshed (242,165) and Abadan (226,103).

IRAQ, a republic in southeast Asia. Pop. (1960) 6,750,000; area 116,600 sq. miles. It consists of a broad central valley between the Tigris and Euphrates rivers, mountains in the northeast and desert in the west. Wheat, rice, dates, wool and cotton are the chief products. Iraq has rich petroleum deposits. Known from earliest times as Mesopotamia, it was the centre of the Sumerian, Assyrian and Babylonian empires. Cyrus of Persia conquered it in 538 B.C., and Alexander the Great in 331 B.C. Sassanid rule was overthrown by the Arabs in A.D. 637 and Iraq became the headquarters of the Abbasid caliphate. Mongols, Seljuks and Ottoman Turks ruled it (1534—1918) until it came under British mandate. In 1932 Iraq became an independent kingdom. A military junta seized power in 1958 and overthrew the monarchy. The capital is Baghdad (pop. 1962 552,047). Other important cities are Mosul (179,646) and Basra (164,623).

IRISH REPUBLIC, a republic comprising 26 counties of Ireland, in the British Isles. Pop. (1961) 2,814,703; area 26,600 sq. miles. Consisting of a central plain enclosed by mountains, it has numerous lakes and bogs. The principal crops are potatoes, turnips, mangolds, sugar-beet and cereals. Livestock-raising is important and fishing is an essential occupation. Industries are mostly food-processing, saw-mill products, tobacco, textiles and metals. Populated by the Celts, Ireland adopted Christianity in the 5th century at the persuasion of St Patrick. British domination began in the 12th century and was completed by 1603. The potato famine of 1846—48 undermined the country's straitened economy and led to large-scale emigration and more insistent demands for self-rule. Resentful at the delay in securing autonomy, the Irish rebelled in 1916. The Irish Free State was established in 1922 as a dominion, the six counties of Ulster in the northeast remaining a part of the U.K. In 1949 the Republic of Ireland was proclaimed and the last ties with the British Commonwealth severed. The capital is Dublin (Baile Atha Cliath) pop. (1961) 535,488. Other important cities are Cork (77,860) and Limerick (50,497).

IRKUTSK, a city in the R.S.F.S.R., in Eastern Siberia, on the Angara River near Lake Baikal, U.S.S.R. Pop. (1962) 385,000. It is an industrial city in the centre of the Lena gold fields. It manufactures mining machinery, machine tools, chemicals and plywood.

IRON AGE, the period following the Bronze Age when man began using iron for making weapons and implements. It began in the Aegean area *c.* 1000 B.C., but not until *c.* 700 B.C. north of the Alps, and 400 B.C. in Britain.

IRRAWADDY, see River.

IRVING, Sir Henry (John Henry Brodribb; 1838—1905), English actor. Closely associated with the Lyceum Theatre in London, he was noted for his part of Mathias in *The Bells* and in many Shakespearean roles.

IRVING, Washington (1783—1859), American writer and diplomat. Famous on both sides of the Atlantic, he wrote *History of New York by Diedrich Knickerbocker*, *The Sketch Book*, and several biographies and series of essays.

ISFAHAN (Aspadana), a city in Iran. Pop. (1956) 254,876. On the Zaindeh River, it is in the centre of a fertile oasis enclosed by mountains on three sides. Its commercial products include textiles and carpets. The city was Persia's capital in the Safavid period, and contains some magnificent buildings of the 17th century.

ISLAM, the religion founded by Mohammed, sometimes referred to as Mohammedanism. It is based on the tenet of monotheism, Allah being the one indivisible God, and Mahommed his prophet. The Jewish and Christian scriptures are recognised as sacred writings, but the ultimate revelation is contained in the Koran, a compilation of God's messages to Mohammed. A believing Moslem must pray five times a day, fast during the month of Ramadan, is required to give alms and, if possible, to make a pilgrimage to Mecca at least once in his lifetime. There are over 200,000,000 Moslems today.

ISMAILIA, a city in Lower Egypt on the Suez Canal, on Lake Timsah. Pop. (1960) 115,200. The city is mid-way along the canal, and is connected by rail to Suez, Port Said and Cairo.

ISOTOPES, chemically indistinguishable atoms with the same atomic number but whose nuclei differ slightly in atomic weight because they contain different numbers of neutrons. Nearly all elements found in nature are a mixture of isotopes; e.g. iron normally has 26 protons and 30 neutrons, but also occurs naturally with 28, 31 or 32 neutrons and can be artificially produced with 27, 29, or 33. In stable isotopes, of which the earth is largely composed, the neutrons and protons are so strongly held together by nuclear forces that they can only be changed artificially. In unstable isotopes there are too many protons and neutrons, or they are not present in the right proportion. There are about 50 of these occurring in nature (e.g. uranium, radium) and they are radioactive. Most stable isotopes can be rendered radioactive by altering the number of protons or neutrons (or both) through bombardment with protons from an accelerator (e.g. a cyclotron), neutrons from a nuclear reactor or alpha particles from another radioactive substance.

Radioactive isotopes have many uses; in tracer techniques to follow the course taken by an element in the human body or a plant; in medical diagnosis; in radiotherapy; in the detection of flaws in metal or leaks in pipes; in measuring the thickness of sheets of material, etc.

ISRAEL, a republic in southwest Asia, on the Mediterranean. Pop. (1961) 2,232,300; area 8050 sq. miles. Hilly in the north and central portions, it has a fertile coastal plain and a vast southern desert steppe. Cereals, citrus fruits, vegetables, potatoes, groundnuts, cotton and sugar-beet are grown. There are potash and bromine deposits in the Dead Sea. Industries include textiles, metal products, diamonds, plastics, chemicals, paper and electrical appliances. The state came into existence in 1948 in the Jewish areas of Palestine upon the termination of a British mandate. Immediately after its establishment it fought off invasions by six Arab states with whom armistice agreements were signed in 1949. The capital is the new city of Jerusalem (pop. 166,301). Other large cities are Tel-Aviv-Jaffa (386,612) and Haifa (182,007). See also Palestine.

ISTANBUL (Constantinople), a seaport and city of European Turkey, on the Bosphorus. Pop. (1960) 1,459,528. It was the capital of the Byzantine and Ottoman empires. There are some 800 mosques, of which the finest is St Sophia (built 532—8), originally a church, now a museum. The Suleiman Mosque, built by Suleiman the Magnificent, dates from the 16th century. The excellent harbour is known as the Golden Horn. Sublime Porte was the French translation of the Ottoman Turkish name for the centre of government.

ITALY, a republic in southern Europe. Pop. (1960) 50,700,000; area 116,235 sq. miles. Most of Italy consists of a peninsula 600 miles long extending into the Mediterranean. Mountainous, it has active volcanoes (Vesuvius, Etna, Stromboli). The Alps extend into the north of Italy and the Apennines form a range down the centre to the southern extremity, but the coastal areas are low-lying. Sicily, Sardinia, Elba and about 70 smaller islands are part of Italy. The principal crops are cereals, sugar-beet, potatoes, tomatoes, olives, citrus fruits, apples, pears, grapes and tobacco. Livestock raising is important. There are deposits of sulphur, mercury, iron and bauxite. The leading industries are textiles, chemicals and motor cars. From the 2nd century B.C., to A.D. 476, Italy's history is that of Rome. Ostrogoths, Byzantines, and Lombards invaded Italy in turn.

The northern cities united to form the powerful Lombard League (1154), and the south, at first occupied by the Saracens, came under the rule of the Normans who established the powerful kingdom of the Two Sicilies. By the 14th century the kingdom of Naples occupied southern Italy, the papal states extended diagonally across the peninsula, and city-states contended for control of the north. Such city-states as Genoa, Venice and Florence became the centres of the revival of arts and learning during the Renaissance. In the 15th and 16th centuries, France, Spain and Germany fought over various parts of Italy. In 1713 Austria, which had long sought to dominate various parts of the country, gained control of Milan, Naples and Sardinia. For a while, at the beginning of the 19th century, Napoleon ruled Italy, to be replaced by Austria after the Congress of Vienna. Repeated Italian uprisings against Austrian domination in the various duchies were vigorously suppressed. By the middle of the 19th century Sardinia emerged as the rallying point for Italian independence and unity. By 1860 Lombardy, Modena, Parma, Tuscany and Romagna had joined Sardinia which then proceeded to conquer Sicily and Naples. In 1861 Emmanuel II, King of Sardinia, was proclaimed king of a united Italy. Although allied with the Central Powers, Italy entered the First World War on the side of the Allies in 1915. In 1922 Mussolini imposed a totalitarian Fascist regime on Italy which later allied itself with Nazi Germany. Mussolini's dictatorship was overthrown in 1943 and a republic proclaimed in 1946. The capital is Rome (pop. 1961 2,160,773). Other important cities are Milan (1,447,006), Naples (1,139,411), Turin (926,629), Genoa (752,983) and Palermo (585,231).

ITO, Hirobumi, Prince (1841—1909), Japanese statesman. He is credited with transforming Japan into a modern world power. Four times prime minister, he introduced far-reaching political and social reforms.

IVAN IV (The Terrible; 1530—84), first Russian monarch to use the title of Tsar. He was notorious for his brutality towards nobles and lower classes alike. His army conquered Siberia but lost a war against Poland and Sweden.

IVORY COAST, a republic in West Africa. Pop. (1961) 3,300,000; area 124,503 sq. miles. Coastal lowlands give way to a forested zone and savannah in the interior. The principal products are coffee, cocoa, bananas and timber. There are diamonds and gold. Formerly part of French West Africa, it achieved independence in 1960. The capital is Abidjan (pop. 1960 177,500).

IZMIR (Smyrna), a city and port in Turkey, on the Mediterranean. Pop. (1960) 370,923. It is a railway and manufacturing centre, exporting sultanas and figs. Its history goes back to 1000 B.C.

JACKSONVILLE, a port and city in northeast Florida, U.S.A., on the St John's River. Pop. (1960) 201,030. A commercial and communications centre, it is the largest industrial city in the region. It has a naval air station and exports large quantities of timber and phosphates. Excellent beaches make it a popular winter resort.

JACOBINS, members of a political club which came to dominate the French Revolution at its height; the name comes from their hiring a building of the Jacobin (or Dominican) friars in Paris. Jacobin clubs were formed throughout the country and wielded great influence. Under the leadership of Robespierre the Jacobins became increasingly extremist, and were supported by the Paris mob and the Commune. They were responsible for the king's execution and the subsequent Reign of Terror; but eventually the National Convention turned on them, had Robespierre guillotined (1794) and disbanded the clubs. The Jacobins remained a force to be reckoned with until Napoleon came to power; and abroad the name Jacobin was for long a synonym for extremist.

JACOBITES, an English political faction which continued to support the claims of the House of Stuart even after its exile in 1688. Two major attempts were made to restore the Stuarts but both ended in failure. When the deposed James II died (1701), the Jacobites supported his son, the Old Pretender, but since he refused to turn Protestant his half-sister, Queen Anne, was succeeded by the Elector of Hanover, George I, in 1714. In 1715 the Old Pretender was crowned at Scone, but the revolt was suppressed. In 1745 Prince Charles Edward (Bonnie Prince Charlie, the Young Pretender) landed in the Western Highlands, defeated the Hanoverians at Prestonpans, and marched to Derby. Lacking support from the English, he had to retreat, and was defeated at Culloden Moor, near Inverness, by the Duke of Cumberland.

JAFFA, see Tel-Aviv-Jaffa.

JAIPUR, capital of Rajasthan state, north central India. Pop. (1961) 402,760. It is a communications and commercial centre with jewel-cutting, enamel and metal-work industries. The city is walled and surrounded by hills. It has an 18th-century observatory.

JAMAICA, an independent sovereign state of the West Indies, within the British Commonwealth. Pop. (1960) 1,613,148; area 4411 sq. miles. Mostly high plateau, it has mountain ridges running across it. The island has more than a hundred swift-flowing rivers. It produces sugar, bananas, rum, coffee, cocoa, pimento, fruit-juices and bauxite. The capital is Kingston (pop. 180,000). The Turks and Caicos Islands and the Cayman Islands are dependencies of Jamaica. From 1958—62 it was a member of the West Indies Federation.

JAMES, the son of Zebedee, brother of John the Evangelist and the first of the apostles to die a martyr's death. He was executed by Herod Agrippa (*Acts* XII. 1—2) about A.D. 44. He is said to have visited Spain.

JAMES I (1566—1625), King of England, Scotland and Ireland. The son of Mary, Queen of Scots, and Lord Darnley, and crowned James VI of Scotland, he succeeded Elizabeth to the English throne in 1603. Though a weak and incapable monarch, he asserted the divine right of kingship which brought him into conflict with parliament and sowed the seeds of the Civil War. He was thwarted in his desire to grant toleration to the Catholics by the disclosure of the Gunpowder Plot (1605). He authorised the English translation of the Bible (King James's Version) in 1611.

JAMES II (1633—1701), King of England, Scotland and Ireland. Fleeing from England before the execution (1649) of his father Charles I, James returned at the time of the Restoration (1660) and was made Lord High Admiral of England. In 1685 he succeeded his brother Charles II to the throne. After the birth of his son (1688), the Protestants — fearing the establishment of a Roman Catholic dynasty on the throne — sent a petition to William and Mary asking them to accept the crown (see Glorious Revolution). James escaped to France, where Louis XIV tried to help him back to the throne; he landed in Ireland but was defeated at the Battle of the Boyne; he returned to France, where he died.

JAMES, Henry (1843—1916), American-born novelist who was educated in Europe and naturalised as a British subject (1915). Many of his novels and short stories, such as *Daisy Miller* (1878) and *The Ambassadors* (1903), deal with Americans in Europe. He was a brother of William James.

JAMES, William (1842—1910), American philosopher and psychologist. His *Principles of Psychology* greatly stimulated interest in psychological problems. He developed the philosophy of pragmatism which aroused considerable discussion and controversy. His works include *The Will to Believe*, *Varieties of Religious Experience* and *The Meaning of Truth*.

JAMMU AND KASHMIR, State in northwest India. Pop. (1961) 3,583,585; area 92,780 sq. miles. It is traversed by the Himalayan ranges and has fertile valleys. Agriculture is the main occupation and silk is produced. There are textile industries. Although nominally a part of the Union of India, its status is disputed by Pakistan, which occupies the western and northern portion of the area (under the name of Azad Kashmir; capital, Muzaffarabad). About 85% of the population is Moslem but the rulers are Hindu. The capital is Srinagar; the winter capital, Jammu.

JAMSHEDPUR, a city in Bihar, India. Pop. (1961) 332,134. It is a centre of India's iron and steel industry, started there by the Tata family, and of engineering works.

JANISSARY, a member of an elite force of Ottoman Turkish soldiers organised in 1328. In time they became very powerful and influential. Sultan Mahmud II had them massacred in 1826, by which time they had become an undisciplined rabble.

JANSENISM, a movement which developed within the Roman Catholic Church during the late 17th century. It was based on the writings of a Dutch theologian, Cornelis Jansen (1585—1638), who emphasised the authority of the Bible and the early Church councils as against the present Church. Although anti-Protestant, Jansen took the Calvinist view that man is so degraded through Original Sin, and so corrupt, that free will (q.v.) is of no avail; only supernatural grace can bring salvation. This split the Church in France, and a furious controversy ensued between the Jesuits and the Jansenists, who were supported by Pascal and the theologians of the Port-Royal convent in Paris. Although declared heretical, Jansenism remained a powerful influence in France as late as the 19th century, and a Jansenist church still exists in Holland.

JAPAN, island kingdom in east Asia. Pop. (1960) 93,403,445; area 182,700 sq. miles. It consists of four main islands — Hokkaido, Honshu, Shikoku and Kyushu — and many small adjacent islands. They are all mountainous. The principal crops are rice, barley, wheat, soya-beans, tea, tobacco, flax and fruits. Much land is devoted to mulberry trees for silkworm farms. Fishing and livestock raising are important. Minerals include coal, copper, lead, iron, zinc, barite, bauxite, manganese, cadmium and petroleum. Industries include textiles, shipbuilding, iron and steel and engineering. The three main religions of Japan are Buddhism, Confucianism and Shintoism. The Ainu are the aboriginals and still survive. The Japanese probably arrived in the 1st century B.C. In the 5th century A.D., Japan was ruled by feudal lords nominally owing allegiance to the emperor. Buddhism, the Chinese script and other Chinese influences arrived in the 6—7th centuries. From the middle of the 8th century the country was ruled by military families or armed monastic communities with the emperor merely a figurehead. From 1190 to 1867 Japan maintained a dual government with emperor and shogun (military commander) ruling either jointly, or alone. The emperor could not remove the shogun, but the latter sometimes exiled the emperor. A Mongol fleet sent by Kublai Khan was defeated in the 13th century. The first Europeans to arrive in Japan were the Portuguese in 1542. Disputes over the practice of Christianity led to an edict in 1636 forbidding all contact with foreigners. In 1853 the American Commodore, Matthew Perry, re-opened Western relations with Japan. A civil war led to the restoration of real power to the emperor in 1867. In 1871 feudalism was abolished and the modernisation of Japan began. The country quickly became a modern power and defeated first China, and then Russia, in war, gaining territory from both. In 1931 Japan invaded Manchuria and later sought to engulf all China. In 1941 Japanese forces attacked American, British, Dutch and French possessions in the Far East and subsequently occupied a vast, rich area from the Philippines to India. By the end of 1942 the tide began to turn and the dropping of atomic bombs on Hiroshima and Nagasaki in August 1945 crushed Japan into surrender. Changes were introduced into the Japanese constitution depriving the emperor of his divine rights and democratising the political system. U.S. troops maintain bases in Japan. The capital is Tokyo (pop. 1962 10,003,055). Other important cities are Osaka (pop. 1960 3,011,553), Nagoya (1,336,780), Kyoto (1,204,084), Yokohama (1,143,687) and Kobe (979,305).

JAVA, the principal island of Indonesia. Pop. (1961, including Madura) 63,000,000; area 50,390 sq. miles. Consisting of plateaux, dominated by volcanic mountains, it is level in the north. The island produces rubber, petroleum, rice, cane-sugar, tea, coffee and quinine. The capital is Djakarta (pop. 1961 approx. 3,000,000). Hindu invaders settled in the 1st century B.C. The Dutch founded Batavia in 1619.

JAZZ, style of rhythmical syncopated music in which improvisation plays an important part. Growing in New Orleans in the 19th century out of American Negro folk-songs, it acquired distinctive rhythm and harmony.

JEANS, Sir James (1877—1946), English physicist and astronomer. A prolific writer, he published numerous works on applied mathematics, stellar dynamics, theoretical physics and cosmogony. In later years he wrote excellent popular works, such as *The Mysterious Universe*.

JEFFERSON, Thomas (1743—1826), American statesman, writer and third President of the United States. Elected as a member to the Continental Congress (1775), he made the first draft of the Declaration of Independence (1776). He was Vice-President from 1796—1800 and then served as President (1800—08).

JEHOL, a former province in northeast China. Pop. (1953) 5,160,822; area 72,008 sq. miles. In 1955 it was divided among Hopei and Liaoning provinces and the Inner Mongolian Region.

JELLICOE, John, 1st Earl (1859—1935), Commander of the Grand Fleet in 1914—16, he fought the German fleet at the Battle of Jutland. He was subsequently First Lord of the Admiralty for a year. He was made Admiral of the Fleet in 1920. From 1920—24 he was Governor-General of New Zealand.

JENNER, Edward (1749—1823), English physician and surgeon. He founded the science of preventive medicine with his discovery of a vaccine against smallpox. He also studied ornithology and geology, and was a fair musician and poet.

JEROME, St (Hieronymus; ***c.*** **340—420),** Christian Father, born in Dalmatia, and educated in Rome. In 386 he entered a monastery in Bethlehem and there translated the Old Testament from the original Hebrew into Latin. His translation of the Bible is the official version (Vulgate Bible) adopted by the Roman Catholic Church.

JERSEY, the largest of the Channel Islands, Great Britain. Pop. (1961) 63,345; area 45 sq. miles. The chief occupations are agriculture, fishing, granite quarrying, and the raising of the famous Jersey cattle. Tomatoes, potatoes, fruits and flower bulbs are exported. The capital is St Helier.

JERUSALEM, ancient holy city and capital of Palestine. Pop. (in Israel; 1961) 166,301. From the days of King David (1000 B.C.) it has been the spiritual and secular capital of Judaism. It is closely associated with the culminating activities of Jesus. According to Moslem theology, Mohammed visited heaven from Jerusalem. Destroyed by Babylonians and Romans, it was later the capital of a Crusader kingdom. It was under Turkish rule until 1917. The city was divided as a consequence of the Arab-Israel war of 1948, the new sections remaining in Israel and the old walled city becoming part of the Jordan kingdom (pop. 60,337).

JESUITS, members of the Society of Jesus, a Roman Catholic order founded in 1534 by St Ignatius Loyola. They are renowned for their studies in theology and their missionary and educational work; they were particularly active in the Counter-Reformation.

JESUS OF NAZARETH (*c.* 4 B.C.—A.D. 29). the founder of the Christian religion. Born in Bethlehem to the Galilean carpenter Joseph and his wife Mary, he was named Jeshua meaning 'God is salvation' (the name 'Jesus' being the Greek rendering of the Hebrew). Little is known of his life in Nazareth. At the age of 12 he accompanied his family on a Passover pilgrimage to Jerusalem. When he was about 30 years of age Jesus was baptised by his cousin, John the Baptist, and began his three-year ministry spent going from town to town in the Galilean area preaching and healing. He acquired a following among the common people, but does not seem to have set up a definite organisation, except for his 12 chosen disciples. At the end of the third year Jesus came to Jerusalem for the Passover, where he was welcomed by the masses as the Messiah but arrested by the Jewish Sanhedrin. The Romans, fearing a political uprising, crucified him, but his disciples reported having seen him on several occasions after his death.

B.C. denotes Before Christ; A.D. *(anno domini)* denotes 'in the year of Our Lord'. The year of Jesus' birth is generally given as 4 B.C. owing to inaccurate recording by historians, based on the Roman Calendar. The correction was not made until the 5th century.

JET PROPULSION, the application of Newton's third law of motion to the propulsion of vehicles by gas turbine with the use of an airscrew. The law states that to every action there is an equal and contrary reaction. Craft are propelled forward in this way by means of large quantities of expanding gases escaping to the rear through a nozzle. The gases are formed as the result of combustion in a chamber. Rockets are a form of jet engine. The turbo-jet is the standard type of jet aircraft, in which the combustion chamber is fed by an air compressor driven by the gas turbine. In the turbo-prop a gas turbine drives a propeller, but usually subsidiary power is provided by jet propulsion. In the ramjet, air is compressed solely by the forward speed of the aircraft, and there is no turbine; as it can operate only at high speed it must be launched from a parent aircraft or be fitted with an auxiliary engine for take-off.

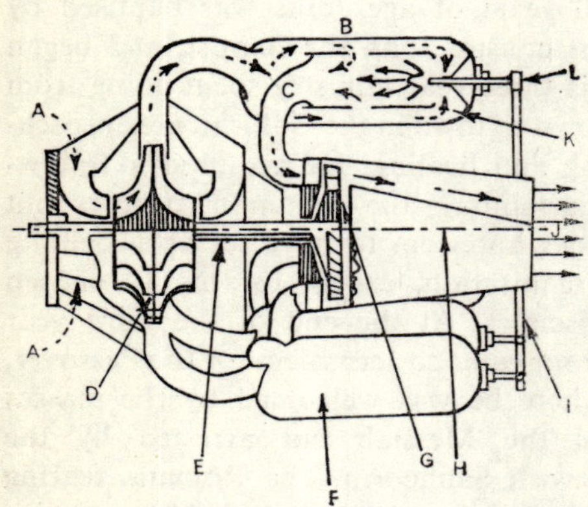

Whittle's jet engine
A. Air drawn in B. Compressed air flow C. Gases D. Air compressor driven by turbine E. Shaft F. Combustion cans G. Turbine H. Jet pipe and cone I. Fuel pipe from pump driven by turbine J. Jet K. Air mixes with fuel for burning L. Kerosene from fuel pump

JEWS, a people of mixed racial origin, predominantly Semitic, who were led by Abraham *c.* 2000 B.C. from east of the Euphrates to Canaan (Palestine), where they settled. After a period of famine they went to Egypt, where they stayed for 430 years, and were at first well treated. Later they were enslaved, and delivered by Moses (the Exodus) sometime between the 15th and 13th centuries; he brought them back to Palestine. The term Jew, strictly speaking, refers only to the tribe of Judah (6th century B.C.), but is commonly applied to all descendants of Abraham, also called Hebrews or Israelites. The Jews were held together by a religion, Judaism (q.v.), of which the main feature, unique at that time, was a belief in one God (monotheism).

In 586 Nebuchadnezzar captured Jerusalem and carried off the principal inhabitants to Babylon. The Babylonian Captivity lasted until they were freed by Cyrus in 538. Alexander the Great and his generals in the 4th century carried off many Jews to Alexandria, whence they spread over much of northeast Africa. In A.D. 70 Titus captured Jerusalem and hundreds of thousands of Jews scattered all over Europe (the Diaspora or Dispersion), and even to India and China. Their steadfast adherence to their ritual kept them apart from the Christian, Moslem and pagan communities among whom they lived, and this *apartheid* made them natural scapegoats in time of disaster. They had privileges but no rights, and were dependent on the favour of princes, who found them useful as moneylenders. Jews came to England as traders before the Norman Conquest. As a result of pogroms, Jews by the end of the Middle Ages had mostly moved into eastern Europe; Russian persecution moved them west again, and overseas to America.

The Jews were given full citizenship in France and America after the revolutions there, and in Britain in 1858. In the Second World War the Germans killed some six million Jews in concentration camps and gas chambers.

Despite persecutions, massacres and constant migrations, the Jews have managed to survive, with their faith, language and culture. Zionism has won its objective, and Jews are once more settled in their own state of Israel, though constantly menaced by the Arab world that surrounds their enclave. The total Jewish population of the world may be around 12 million (there are no reliable figures for Communist countries), of whom 2,000,000 are in Israel, 5,531,500 in the U.S.A., 450,000 in Great Britain and many others in Argentina and Morocco.

JINNAH, Mohammed Ali (1876—1948), Indian statesman. An active advocate of Indian independence, he headed the Moslem League for many years. In his later years he modified his views concerning Moslem-Hindu collaboration and pressed for a separate Moslem state. He was its first Governor-General when it came into existence under the name of Pakistan.

JOAN OF ARC, St (*c.* 1412—31), French heroine and martyr. Following instructions received from 'voices' she persuaded the dauphin of France to grant her a small army with which she proceeded to raise the siege of Orléans (1429), thus becoming the symbol of French resistance against the English. She was captured by the Burgundians who sold her to the English (1430); she was tried before a court of Inquisition presided over by a French bishop at Rouen, which sentenced her to death at the stake as a witch.

JOFFRE, Joseph Jacques (1852—1931), French military leader during the First World War. After a long career in the colonies, he was appointed Commander-in-Chief of the French Army in 1911. He held this post until the end of 1916, when he was dismissed by the politicians. They replaced him with Nivelle, who nearly lost the war. Joffre's greatest achievement was to save Paris at the Battle of the Marne in September 1914.

JOHANNESBURG, a city in Transvaal, Republic of South Africa. Pop. (1960) 1,110,905. In the midst of the Witwatersrand goldmining region, it is a financial, industrial and commercial centre and lies at an altitude of 5740 ft.

JOHN (1167—1216), King of England. The youngest son of Henry II, he attempted to usurp the throne during the absence of his brother (Richard the Lion-Heart) on the Crusades. John finally ascended the throne in 1199, but became involved in a conflict with the papacy. He was excommunicated (1212) but then recanted and accepted the Pope's nominee, Stephen Langton, for the archbishopric of Canterbury. Enraged, among other things, by John's repeated failures in France, the barons forced John to sign Magna Carta, which the Pope promptly declared null and void.

JOHN, Augustus (1878—1961), British painter. Born in Tenby, Wales, he studied at the Slade School, London. As an official artist in the First World War he made portraits of *T. E. Lawrence* and *Emir Faisal.* Other portraits include *Thomas Hardy*, *Lloyd George*, *Bernard Shaw* and *Dylan Thomas.* He was elected R.A. in 1928 but resigned, and was re-elected in 1946.

JOHN OF GAUNT, Duke of Lancaster (1340—99), son of Edward III and father of Henry IV, kings of England. From 1372—87, he assumed the title of King of Castile. One of England's most influential nobles, he defended the religious reformer John Wycliffe. Through Henry IV he was the founder of the Lancastrian dynasty; he was also an ancestor of Henry VII.

JOHN THE BAPTIST, St, a Jewish preacher, a cousin of the Virgin Mary, who made his appearance (*c.* A.D. 27) in the wilderness near the River Jordan and there exhorted the people to repent and prepare for the advent of the Kingdom of God. He baptised Jesus and is revered by Christians as the prophetic forerunner of the Messiah. John was beheaded by Herod Antipas whom he had denounced for marrying his brother's wife Herodias. In revenge, Herodias persuaded her daughter Salome to ask for John's head.

JOHN THE EVANGELIST, St, one of the 12 apostles, the son of Zebedee and the brother of James. A fisherman by trade, he became one of the apostles closest to Jesus. He is traditionally identified as the author of the Gospel of St John, the Epistle of St John and the Book of Revelation.

JOHNSON, LYNDON BAINES (1908—), U.S. President. Born in Stonewall, Texas, he entered Congress in 1937 as a New Deal Democrat, quickly showing his political ability. The day after Pearl Harbor he enlisted in the Navy, and was decorated for bravery. In 1948 he became a Senator and in 1953 the youngest man to lead his party in the Senate. Overwork led to a heart attack in 1955, but he made a complete recovery. After unsuccessfully contesting the 1960 presidential election he became Vice-President and, on the assassination of President Kennedy in 1963, 35th President. He was reelected in November, 1964.

JOHNSON, SAMUEL (1709—84), English lexicographer, essayist and critic. After a school which he had established failed, he determined to earn his living as a writer. He frequently contributed to periodicals, and in 1744 published the *Life of Savage*. From 1747—55 Johnson compiled the *Dictionary of the English Language*, which remained a standard work until the 19th century. His longest work is the ten-volume *Lives of the Poets* (1779—81). The *Journey to the Western Isles of Scotland* is a fascinating account of a trip he made with Boswell. He was, as presented by Boswell, a most extraordinary man: kind, learned, profoundly religious, a witty and brilliant conversationalist, he was also unkempt and very blunt; as an antidote for the melancholy to which he was a prey, he liked to have plenty of people around him in his house in Gough Square, whether they were such personalities as Burke, Sheridan, Reynolds and Goldsmith, his closest friends the Thrales, or people of no account whom he happened to have befriended.

JOHORE, a state in Malaya. Pop. (1961) 1,064,814; area 7330 sq. miles. It is at the southern extremity of the peninsula. Low-lying and thickly forested, it produces rubber, rice and copra. The capital is Johore Bharu, opposite Singapore.

JOLIOT-CURIE, Frédéric (1900—58) and Iréne (1897—1956), French scientists. Irène was the daughter of Pierre and Marie Curie. Husband and wife received the Nobel Prize for physics in 1935 for producing artificial radioactivity. The French government appointed Frédéric High Commissioner for Atomic Energy in 1946 but dismissed him in 1950 on account of his activities as President of the Communist-dominated World Peace Council.

JONES, Inigo (1573—1651), English architect who acquired such a reputation in Venice, where he was studying in 1604, that King Christian IV of Denmark invited him to design the two royal palaces of Rosenborg and Frederiksborg. In the following year he was appointed architect to the court of James I of England and in 1612 was engaged to prepare designs for a new palace at Whitehall. At this time he designed numerous stage sets for the theatre. Under Charles I he held the same office but after the Civil War was forced to pay considerable fines as a courtier. He died in poverty.

JONES, Paul (1747—92), American naval officer, born in Scotland. He did considerable damage to British shipping along the coasts of the British Isles during the American Revolution, even raiding Solway Firth. In command of a French squadron he captured two warships off the English coast in 1779. Later he fought for Russia against Turkey.

JONSON, Ben (1573—1637), English dramatist and poet. His famous works include *Every Man in His Humour*, *Volpone*, *The Silent Woman* and *The Alchemist*. His plays reflect the spirit of classical comedy.

JORDAN, see River.

JORDAN, a kingdom in southwest Asia. Pop. (1961) 1,752,095; area 34,750 sq. miles. Mostly desert in the east, it produces grain, fruit and grazing animals in the west. It is traversed by the River Jordan. Formerly (as Transjordan) a British mandate, it became independent in 1946. After invading Palestine in 1948, it annexed Arab areas there, comprising 2125 sq. miles (pop. 1953 745,786). The capital is Amman (pop. 1961 244,599).

JOSEPH, St, the husband of Mary, mother of Jesus. A carpenter by trade, he lived in the Galilean town of Nazareth. Very little is known of him, though it is generally assumed that he was considerably older than Mary and died before Jesus began his ministry.

JOSEPH OF ARIMATHAEA, a member of the Sanhedrin who, after the Crucifixion, requested and received permission to bury the body of Jesus in his own tomb. According to late medieval legend, he came to Glastonbury, in England, with the Holy Grail, in which was blood he had collected at the Cross; he was also said to have brought a thorn which he planted there, and which blossoms in mid-winter.

JOWETT, Benjamin (1817—93), English scholar and theologian. A famous master of Balliol College, Oxford, he wrote brilliant essays, one of which led to his being charged with heresy. He helped to popularise Greek literature by his translations of Plato, Thucydides and Aristotle.

JOYCE, James (1882—1941), Irish novelist. His early stories, *Dubliners* (1914), and the autobiographical novel *A Portrait of the Artist as a Young Man* (1916), established him as a considerable writer, but with the publication in Paris in 1922 of *Ulysses*, he emerged as probably the most original and influential novelist of the 20th century. In *Ulysses*, Joyce brought to perfection the technique of the internal monologue, or 'stream of consciousness', applying it to the re-creation of a single day in Edwardian Dublin, and to the analysis of the semi-autobiographical Stephen Dedalus, the Jewish salesman Leopold Bloom, his wife, and a brilliantly drawn host of minor characters. In *Ulysses*, as in the later and more abstruse *Finnegans Wake* (1939), Joyce enriched the language with portmanteau words, paradoxes, miraculous juxtapositions, puns, associations and parodies, and glosses on many cultural traditions. However, in *Ulysses*, though not, according to many critics, in *Finnegans Wake*, Joyce's grammatical innovations are never allowed to obscure the rich and complex beauty of his magnificent prose.

JUDAISM, the monotheistic religion of the Jews. Its foundations are the books of the Old Testament conceived as divinely inspired, and the subsequent teachings expressed in the codes and commentaries of the Talmud. Traditional Judaism is a way of life in which the details of living are carefully prescribed by the divine will. It has profoundly influenced Christianity and Islam, which borrowed freely from its ethical principles. Modern liberal movements have modified some of Judaism's traditional ceremonies.

JUDGE, the presiding official in a court of justice, whose duty it is to determine questions of law. In Great Britain and the U.S.A. judges are members of the legal profession. In England, judges of the High Court of Justice are appointed by royal patent while minor judicial officials, e.g. county court judges, are designated by the Lord Chancellor, who is himself selected by the Crown on the recommendation of the Government. In the U.S.A., Federal judges are appointed by the President, subject to the approval of the Senate. Other American judges are either appointed by the state governor or elected by the voters for a specific term of office.

JUDGMENT DAY, the theological name for the day on which all men — the living and the dead — will be judged according to their deeds before the throne of God. Predominant in Judaism, Christianity and Islam.

JULIAN (The Apostate; 331—63), Roman emperor. During a campaign in Gaul (357—60) his troops refused to obey an order from the Emperor Constantius to return, and proclaimed Julian emperor. He was marching on Constantinople when Constantius died, and thus his accession to the throne was accomplished without bloodshed. Julian had previously renounced Christianity and reverted to paganism. He was a great administrator and introduced many reforms. He believed in religious toleration, but the clamour of Christians for the persecution of heretics turned him against them, and he curbed their freedom. He was killed in battle in Persia.

JULIUS CAESAR, see Caesar, Gaius Julius.

JUNG, Carl (1875—1961), Swiss psychiatrist. At first an associate of Sigmund Freud, he later founded the school of Analytical Psychology which rejects the sexual origin of the neuroses and postulates the existence of a collective unconscious, which contains traces of ancient ways of thought inherited through the centuries. These he called archetypes; they express the needs and aspirations of humanity as contrasted with merely personal preoccupations, and include such concepts as death and resurrection, virgin mothers, etc. He classified the human personality on the basis of introversion and extroversion. He believed it was important for a man to develop that side of his nature which was less developed, e.g. the intellectual should give fuller rein to his emotions, the masculine man should develop the feminine side of his character, etc.

JUSTINIAN I (*c.* 483—565), Byzantine emperor from 527—565. Aided by his two brilliant generals Belisarius and Narses, he was able to restore and extend the boundaries of his empire. Justinian is best known as a legislator; he was responsible for the compilation of the Justinian Code.

JUTLAND (Jylland), Danish peninsula. Pop. 1,826,056; area 11,412 sq. miles. It is mostly lowland and rolling hills. Farming is the principal occupation. The chief town is Aarhus.

JUVENILE DELINQUENCY, the antisocial behaviour of children and adolescents. In many countries, it is handled by social agencies rather than courts. Broken homes, poor family adjustment or slum housing are often the cause. A life of crime frequently follows.

Another river, the Colorado in America, is responsible for another amazing phenomenon: the two-mile deep Grand Canyon has been formed by the action of the waters on the sandstone rock over a period of millions of years. *Photo: W. G. Carroll*

The boiling gases and molten rocks beneath the earth's surface burst through from time to time as volcanoes and hot water geysers. Japan and New Zealand are particular areas where these activities occur. The permanent hot water geysers illustrated are at Rotorua in New Zealand.

Photo: High Commissioner for New Zealand

The earth's atmosphere may become agitated by freak temperature and humidity conditions. Hurricanes and tornadoes result; this water spout is a form of tornado in which a huge column of swirling water is drawn up into the clouds above.

Photo: Radio Times Hulton Picture Library

Water vapour collects in the atmosphere in the form of clouds. Shown here is the cumulo-nimbus-capillatus variety from which showers fall. *Photo: Royal Meteorological Society*

A 4th century B.C. Persian silver plate showing a nobleman out hunting. He uses an elaborate stone-throwing bow. *Photo: Giraudon*

Greek foot soldiers, armed with spears, are protected with shields and headgear. *Photo: J. Powell*

The highly organised Roman armies spread the might of the Roman Empire across Europe, North Africa and the Near East. The Traiana Column in Rome. *Photo: Alinari*

In Europe, the Crusades (q.v.) of the 11th to 13th centuries saw the beginnings of the development of body armour. Even horses were provided with a fair amount of protective armour plating. *Photo: Wallace Collection*

KABUL, capital of Afghanistan. Pop. (1957) 310,000. Situated 7000 ft. above sea-level, it commands a number of strategic routes into India. In the centre of a rich fruit-growing district, it has light industries. Kabul was occupied by the British on several occasions during the Afghan Wars.

KAFKA, Franz (1883—1924), Austrian novelist born in Prague of Jewish parentage. Both his great novels, *The Castle* and *The Trial*, are unfinished; they both deal with the futility and confusion of modern man's life, their heroes wandering hopelessly about in a frightening dream world, never able to discover who is deciding their fate.

KAGOSHIMA, the chief port in southern Kyushu, Japan. Pop. (1960) 295,964. It manufactures pottery and glass and is a rice market.

KAIETEUR FALLS, a waterfall in British Guiana. The water falls 741 ft at a point where the Potaro River emerges from the Guiana highlands.

KAIFENG, capital of Honan province on the Hwango-Ho, central China. Pop. (1960) 450,000. A communications and trading centre, it occupies a strategic position. It is an ancient city enclosed by a wall.

KALAHARI DESERT, a large semi-arid desert in south central Africa, mostly in Bechuanaland. Area 200,000 sq. miles. The inhabitants, chiefly Hottentots and Griquas, graze sheep and cattle on its fringes. It lies at 3000—5000 ft above sea-level.

KALININGRAD (Königsberg), a port and fortress city in the R.S.F.S.R., U.S.S.R. Pop. (1962) 232,000. On the Pregel River, it is a fishing and commercial port. Manufactures include chemicals, metal products and textiles. Until 1945 it was the capital of East Prussia.

KAMCHATKA PENINSULA, a mountainous peninsula in eastern Siberia, between the Bering and Okhotsk seas. Pop. 6500; area 465,637 sq. miles. It has a cold damp climate. Rich in minerals, it has 13 active volcanoes. Fishing is the principal occupation.

KANAZAWA, a city in Honshu, Japan. Pop. (1960) 298,967. Manufacture of silk, porcelain, lacquerware and objects of inlaid bronze is responsible for its prosperity.

KANO, a town in Northern Nigeria. Pop. (1953) 130,000. The terminus of trans-Saharan camel routes, it has been an important commercial centre for many centuries. It is situated in a fertile agricultural region, and very large quantities of groundnuts, hides and skins are collected there for railing to the coast. The ancient mud walls, many yards thick and 13 miles in circumference, can still be seen.

KANSAS, a central state of the U.S.A. Pop. (1960) 2,178,611; area 82,276 sq. miles. Consisting almost entirely of an undulating plain, Kansas is predominantly agricultural. In addition to large quantities of wheat, it produces maize, grain sorghums, soya beans, oats, barley, rye, potatoes and flax. Livestock raising is important. There are deposits of coal, petroleum, lead and zinc. The principal industries are meat packing, transport equipment and oil refining. First settled in 1727, it became a state in 1861. The capital is Topeka (pop. 119,484). Other important cities are Wichita (254,698) and Kansas City (121,901).

KANSAS CITY, a city in Missouri, U.S.A., on the Missouri River. Pop. (1960) 475,539. A river port in the middle of an area rich in agricultural produce and mineral wealth, it is an important market for seed, hay and livestock. Its industries include flour mills, meat-packing plants and aircraft. It adjoins Kansas City, Kansas.

KANT, Immanuel (1724—1804), German philosopher. Kant studied at the University of Königsberg, receiving his degree in 1755. He was appointed lecturer, and in 1770 professor, at the same university. He is known as the founder of the school of critical philosophy. Kant's two most important works are *Critique of Pure Reason* (1781) and *Critique of Practical Reason* (1788). He distinguishes between the phenomenal world of things as they appear to us and the noumenal world of reality, or things-in-themselves, and holds that the nature of man's mind imposes its own pattern on the outside world and determines what we can know. In contrast to Hume, he claims that certain statements about the world are necessarily true. The will or reason is guided by the categorical imperative, the moral law or duty which is binding on all rational beings.

KAOHSIUNG, a seaport and city on the southwest coast of Formosa. Pop. (1962) 275,600. It is a commercial and industrial centre exporting rice and sugar. There are oil refineries.

KARACHI, Federal district and capital of Pakistan. Pop. (1961) 2,153,000. A seaport on the Indus delta, it exports wheat, cotton, wool and hides. There are important fisheries and industries. It has an international airport. Work began in 1961 on the building of a new capital, to be called Islamabad, near Rawalpindi.

KARAKORUM RANGE, a mountain chain in central Asia, west of the Tibetan plateau, in Kashmir. The highest peak is Godwin-Austen (K2), 28,250 ft.

KARELIAN AUTONOMOUS S.S.R., a republic of the R.S.F.S.R. between the White Sea and Gulf of Finland, U.S.S.R. Pop. (1959) 649,000; area 66,392 sq. miles. Lumbering and allied industries, fishing and shipbuilding are the main occupations. It is rich in minerals, especially mica. Part of the area was ceded by Finland after the 1940 Soviet-Finnish War. The capital is Petrozavodsk.

KARLSRUHE, a city in Baden-Württemberg, West Germany. Pop. (1960) 234,759. It is a centre of heavy industry and seat of the supreme court of the Federal Republic. It is an important focus of communications and is joined to the Rhine by a canal.

KARROO, Great and Little, transverse treeless plateau separated by mountain ranges and forming two successive terraces between the south coast and the high veld of the interior of Cape Province, Republic of South Africa. The Little Karroo, 30 miles long, is the southernmost and the Great Karroo lies at 2000—3000 ft above sea-level.

KASHMIR, see Jammu and Kashmir.

KASSEL, a city in Hesse, West Germany, on the Fulda River. Pop. (1960) 202,493. It manufactures optical instruments and railway equipment. Important museums and art galleries have survived much war damage to the old town.

KATANGA, a former province in the south of the Congo Federal Republic. Pop. 1,178,029; area 180,000 sq. miles. It is particularly rich in copper; other minerals include tin, cobalt, coal, iron, gold, platinum, diamonds, uranium and radium. The province attempted to secede from the republic when it achieved independence in 1960 but was restored to the federation with the help of U.N. forces and divided into three provinces. The capital was Elisabethville.

KATOWICE, a city in Poland. Pop. (1960) 269,000. A centre of metallurgical and chemical industries in former Upper Silesia, it is in the middle of a coal-mining region. It is an important railway junction. For a time it was known as Stalinograd.

KATTEGAT, an arm of the sea, between Denmark and Sweden. It links up with the Baltic through the Great and Little Belts and with the North Sea through the Skagerrak.

KAUNDA, Kenneth (1924—), Zambian politician. Born into a family of teachers, he was at first a schoolmaster and social welfare worker, becoming interested in politics in 1952. During a visit to India he was deeply impressed by Gandhi, whose doctrine of non-violence he adopted. He broke away from the African National Congress in 1958 and in 1960 was elected President of the United National Independence Party (U.N.I.P.). He became President of Zambia in 1964.

KAZAKHSTAN, a constituent republic of the U.S.S.R. Pop. (1959) 9,301,000; area 1,067,400 sq. miles. The second largest republic in the U.S.S.R., it is located in southwest Soviet Asia. Hilly in the centre, it is semi-desert with rolling steppes in the north and mountainous in the south and southeast. Its agricultural produce consists of grains, cotton, potatoes, vegetables and fruit. The area is famous for its livestock, especially sheep. It has rich deposits of coal, petroleum, tungsten, copper, lead, zinc, iron and other minerals. There are heavy engineering, chemical, textile, food and other industries. The capital is Alma-Ata (pop. 455,000). Other large cities are Karaganda (398,000) and Semipalatinsk (155,000).

KAZAN, capital of the Tatar Autonomous S.S.R. in the R.S.F.S.R. Pop. (1962) 711,000. On the Volga River, it is a major commercial and industrial centre producing chemicals, aircraft, heavy equipment, textiles, clothing and oil. It was founded in 1401 and became the Tatar capital of the Khanate conquered by Ivan the Terrible in 1552. Tolstoy and Lenin attended Kazan University.

KEATS, John (1795—1821), English poet. He started his career as an apothecary, but soon abandoned this for poetry. He published his first poems at the age of 22, and *Endymion* a year later. Other early but famous poems are *The Eve of St Agnes* and *La Belle Dame sans Merci*. In 1819 he became engaged to Fanny Brawne, and his passionate love for her found expression in the famous odes, *To a Nightingale*, *To a Grecian Urn* and *To Autumn*. Incurably ill with tuberculosis, Keats went to Italy in 1820, and his brief and crowded life ended there a few months later. Critics during his lifetime failed to recognise his genius but, from the time his *Letters* were published, he came to be accepted as one of the foremost English Romantic poets.

KEDAH, a state in Malaya, on the west side of the peninsula. Pop. (1961) 783,993; area 3660 sq. miles. Swampy and level, it produces rice, rubber, tin and tapioca. The capital is Alor Star.

KELANTAN, a state in Malaya on the west coast of the peninsula. Pop. (1961) 570,998; area 5750 sq. miles. Level in the north and hilly in the south, it produces iron, rubber, copra, cattle and areca nuts. The capital is Kota Bharu.

KELLY, William (1811—88), American inventor. Independently of Sir Henry Bessemer, he developed a process for converting pig-iron into steel in large quantities quickly and inexpensively.

KELVIN, William Thomson, 1st Baron (1824—1907), British physicist and mathematician. He made important investigations in the fields of thermodynamics and electricity. His inventions include major improvements in submarine telegraphy and navigation equipment. Kelvin's interests covered numerous branches of science. He was president of the Royal Society in 1890—95.

KENNEDY, Cape, a cape on the east coast of Florida, U.S.A. It is a base for testing and launching missiles and space satellites. It was previously known as Cape Canaveral, but was renamed in 1964 in honour of the assassinated president.

KENNEDY, John F. (1917—63), American statesman. Born into a Boston Irish family, he graduated from Harvard and in September 1941 enlisted in the Navy, serving with distinction and winning the Purple Heart for his conduct after a Japanese destroyer had rammed his motor torpedo-boat. After the war he entered politics as a Democrat, sitting in Congress as a Representative (1946—52) and as Senator for Massachusetts (1952—60). In 1960, in spite of being a Roman Catholic, he was elected President, the youngest in American history. From the start he showed courage and great energy in tackling the many crises that beset him, such as Negro unrest and the defiance of Southern governors on racial issues; during the Cuban crisis of 1962 he concluded an agreement with the U.S.S.R. removing international tension. He put forward a Grand Design for an Atlantic alliance of two equal partners (the U.S.A. and an enlarged European Community); he pressed on with a plan for an extension of tariff cuts (the Kennedy round); in July 1963 he signed the nuclear test ban agreement with the U.S.S.R. On November 22, President Kennedy was assassinated at Dallas, Texas, his putative assassin being himself assassinated two days later while still under interrogation by the police.

KENSINGTON, a residential suburb of West London. Pop. (1961) 170,891. It has numerous public buildings of interest including churches, educational institutions and Kensington Palace. The 275-acre Kensington Gardens adjoin Hyde Park.

KENT, a maritime county of southeast England. Pop. (1961) 1,701,083; area 1525 sq. miles. The central part is plateau and the North Downs cross the northern half of the county; there are forest ridges and Romney Marsh, reclaimed from the sea, in the south. It produces hops, fruit, field crops, vegetables and dairy products. Livestock raising is important. There are fisheries and diversified industries. The county covers approximately the same area as the Anglo-Saxon kingdom of that name, which existed from the 5th to the 9th century A.D. The county town is Maidstone which stands on the River Medway.

KENTUCKY, an east central state of the U.S.A. Pop. (1960) 3,038,156; area 40,395 sq. miles. Between the Ohio River on the north and the Mississippi on the west, it is generally plateau with mountains in the southeast. The chief crop is tobacco. Maize, wheat, hay, tobacco, soya beans and fruit are grown. Livestock is raised, especially horses. There are deposits of coal, petroleum and fluorspar. The leading industries are foods, tobacco, chemicals, machinery, transport equipment and metal goods. First settled in 1765, it became a state in 1792. The capital is Frankfort (pop. 18,226). The largest city is Louisville (390,639).

KENYA, a state of East Africa. Pop. (1961) 7,287,000; area 224,960 sq. miles. It is mountainous in the west and level in the coastal regions, with extremely varied climatic conditions. The main crops are coffee, cotton, maize, pyrethrum, sisal, tea and groundnuts. Livestock raising is important. Minerals include gold, sodium carbonate, copper, silver and salt. From 1952—56 African aspirations to independence assumed the form of violent outbreaks against the European settlers. The capital is Nairobi.

KENYATTA, Jomo (*c.* 1896—), Kenya statesman. He entered politics in 1922, joining the Kikuyu Association and its successors. After a visit to Moscow he settled in Sussex, England, until 1946, marrying an Englishwoman. During the Mau Mau campaign he was detained in 1952 and in 1954 sentenced to seven years' imprisonment. He was released in 1959 under restrictions as to place of residence which were lifted in August 1961. He became Prime Minister in May 1963.

KEPLER, Johannes (1571—1630), German astronomer. An assistant of Tycho Brahe in Prague, he founded the science of optics with his work *Dioptrics*. His most important works are *New Astronomy* and *The Harmonies of the World*. His three laws of planetary motion were the basis of Newton's discoveries concerning the solar system. They are: (1) the orbit of a planet is an ellipse with the sun as one of the foci; (2) the radius vector joining each planet to the sun sweeps over equal areas in equal times; (3) the square of the planetary period (the time for completing a circuit around the sun) is proportioned to the cube of the planet's distance from the sun.

KERENSKY, Alexander (1881—), Russian revolutionary. He was a member of the provisional government after the Czar was overthrown in 1917. He became premier of Russia, but could not hold the disgruntled Russian people together, and was ousted by the Bolshevik revolution.

KERRY, a maritime county in southwest Ireland, on the Atlantic Ocean. Pop. (1961) 116,405; area 1816 sq. miles. It is mountainous except for the north coast. The chief occupations are dairy farming, livestock raising, fishing and quarrying. There are textile manufactures. The county town is Tralee. The Killarney Lakes and 'Ring of Kerry' attract many tourists.

KEYES, Roger, 1st Baron (1872—1945), British naval officer. In the First World War he was Chief of Staff of the Eastern Mediterranean Squadron and later commanded operations against Zeebrugge and Ostend. He was Director of Combined Operations in 1940—41.

KEYNES, John Maynard, 1st Baron (1883—1946), British economist. He was chief representative of the Treasury at the Versailles Peace Conference but resigned because of disagreement with the prevailing views regarding reparations. He published his views in a famous work, *The Economic Consequences of the Peace* (1919), which immediately put him in the front rank of economists. A leading theoretician, he also exerted a profound influence on British fiscal policies. During the Second World War he was director of the Bank of England and chief negotiator for a loan from the U.S. He was a leading advocate of world-wide economic co-operation and one of the framers of the Bretton Woods agreement for the establishment of an international monetary fund and a bank for reconstruction and development.

In 1936 he published *The General Theory of Employment, Interest and Money*, in which he rejected the classical view that the economic system was self-regulating; he adovcated the control of recurrent crises, apparently endemic under capitalism, by credit and currency. It is a measure of his greatness that the ideas that then seemed revolutionary are now accepted as orthodoxy. In 1925 this many-faceted man married the Russian ballerina, Lydia Lopokova, and was guided by her in developing interest in ballet in Britain.

KHRUSHCHEV, Nikita (1894—), Russian statesman. Born near Kursk, the son of a Russian miner, he joined the Communist Party in 1918 and began his rise to power. In 1938 he was appointed first secretary of the Ukrainian Communist Party and became a full member of the Politburo in 1939. In 1953 he advanced to first secretary of the party and became Premier of the U.S.S.R. in 1958. He retired in the autumn of 1964.

KIANGSU, a maritime province in east China. Pop. (1953) 41,252,192; area 42,085 sq. miles. It is mostly level and well irrigated. It produces rice, cotton, tea and silk. Mineral deposits include coal, iron, marble, graphite and salt. There are diversified industries, chiefly textiles. The capital is Nanking. Other important cities are Shanghai, Soochow and Chinkiang.

KIDD, William (1645—1701), Scottish navigator and notorious pirate. Given a ship in New England for the purpose of hunting down French pirates in the Indian Ocean, he himself turned pirate. On returning to Boston to hand over some of his plunder to the authorities, he was arrested and subsequently tried and hanged in London.

KIEL, capital of Schleswig-Holstein, West Germany. Pop. (1960) 268,688. A port on the Baltic Sea and an industrial centre, it has shipyards and produces electrical equipment and textiles. Fishing is important.

KIEL CANAL, a canal in Schleswig-Holstein, West Germany, linking the North and Baltic seas. It is 45 ft deep and 61 miles long. It was opened in 1895.

KIERKEGAARD, Sören (1813—55), Danish philosopher and theologian who was bitterly opposed to the Lutheran Church in which he was brought up. He rejected the idea that religion consisted in assenting to a body of dogma; it is an approach to life to be worked out by each individual. He is one of the sources of inspiration of Existentialism.

KIEV, capital of the Ukrainian S.S.R., U.S.S.R. Pop. (1962) 1,208,000. On the Dnieper River, it is a cultural, commercial and industrial centre, with aircraft, automobile, machine-tool and other industries. In the 9th and 10th centuries it was the centre of a great empire; in the 11th, the capital of Russia.

KINDERGARTEN, an institution to further the development of children under school age. It is intended to introduce the children gradually to school life, arouse an interest in reading, develop manual skills and teach them how to get along with their fellows. Some kindergartens stress the need to become acquainted with the environment, and the development of self-expression. The trend is to integrate kindergartens with the curriculum of the early school grades.

KING, a male sovereign. In ancient times it was a title conferred on the most outstanding warrior. Kings formerly had absolute power over their subjects. Today the position is hereditary and its authority is generally limited.

KING, Mackenzie (1874—1950), Canadian statesman. He was born in Ontario and educated at Toronto, Chicago and Harvard. He entered parliament in 1908, was elected leader of the Liberal party in 1919, and was Prime Minister from 1921—30 and 1935—48. He took a leading part in many world conferences.

KINGSLEY, Charles (1819—75), English clergyman and novelist. In addition to advocating social and economic reforms, he wrote the historical novels *Hypatia* and *Westward Ho!* and the children's book *The Water Babies.*

KINGSTON, capital of Jamaica, West Indies. Pop. (1962) 180,000. It is a communications and commercial centre on the south side of the island, with an excellent harbour. It was rebuilt after an earthquake in 1907.

KIPLING, Rudyard (1865—1936), English poet and novelist. Born in Bombay, India, he was educated in England but returned to India in 1882, where he worked on the staff of a newspaper at Lahore. He was awarded the Nobel Prize for literature (1907). He portrayed the life of the British India of his day in *Plain Tales from the Hills* in prose, and in *Barrack Room Ballads* and *Departmental Ditties*, but his best account is the most famous — *Kim.* Other popular books are *Just So Stories* and the two *Jungle Books.*

KIRGHIZIA, a constituent republic of the U.S.S.R. in Central Asia. Pop. (1959) 2,063,000; area 76,460 sq. miles. Mountainous, with extensive plateaux, it has rich coal deposits. Mineral resources include oil, coal, uranium, sulphur, molybdenum, mercury, lead and tungsten. Livestock breeding is important. Agriculture is varied; much of the farmland is under irrigation. There are also diversified industries, including agricultural and mining machinery. The capital is Frunze (pop. 217,000).

KIRIN, a province in northeast China. Pop. (1953) 11,290,073; area 34,616 sq. miles. Mountainous, it has deposits of coal and iron. Grains and livestock are raised. The capital is Kirin. The most important town is Changchun, the rapidly growing railway junction through which much of Manchuria's trade passes.

KITCHEN, the part of the house where food is prepared. Cooking was formerly done over open fires in braziers or in hearths, and water was kept in containers filled outside the house. The introduction of water in the kitchen, first from a pump and later through plumbing, and the invention of cooking-stoves (using wood, coal, gas, oil or electricity as fuel) revolutionised the housewife's work. Whereas the kitchen still often serves also as an eating and living-room, the trend is to make it more compact and equipped with labour-saving devices.

KITCHENER OF KHARTOUM, Herbert, 1st Earl (1850—1916), British soldier and administrator. After a series of victories in Egypt and the Sudan where he inflicted several defeats on the Mahdi's forces culminating in the great victory at Omdurman, he succeeded Lord Roberts as supreme commander of the British forces in the Boer War. From 1902—09 he was Commander-in-Chief, India. In 1914 he became Secretary of State for War, in which capacity he raised three million volunteer soldiers. The Czar invited him to Russia for consultation; Kitchener sailed in H.M.S. *Hampshire*, which struck a mine off the Orkneys and sank with all on board.

KLEE, Paul (1879—1940), Swiss painter. Among the earliest artists to paint surrealistic fantasies, he later founded a German abstract school.

KLEPTOMANIA, compulsive stealing of an irrational nature. The stolen articles are neither wanted nor needed. The act of stealing is a substitute for expressing repressed wishes.

KNELLER, Sir Godfrey (1646—1723), German-born painter, who settled in London *c.* 1696. Outstanding as a portraitist, he was court painter to Charles II, William III and George I. He painted all these, and Queen Anne, Peter the Great, Louis XIV of France and numerous other celebrities of his time.

KNIGHTHOOD, a social and military institution made up of mounted warriors of noble birth. It was originally an integral part of the feudal social order, the knights being landowners. Knighthood reached its peak during and immediately after the Crusades, when it was governed by a series of codes and regulations; but it began to deteriorate by the beginning of the 15th century.

KNIGHTS HOSPITALLERS (Order of the Hospital of St John of Jerusalem), an order, originally of monks who had taken religious vows to protect pilgrims to Palestine and provide them with a hospice or rest-house in Jerusalem. It was founded *c.* 1087 and developed into a militant order which fought alongside the Crusaders. In 1291 it was driven from Jerusalem, and after a stay in Cyprus settled in Rhodes, where their impressive fortress can still be seen. The Pope transferred most of the property of the disbanded Templars to the Knights of Rhodes, as they were then called. The Turks expelled them from Rhodes in 1522 and they established themselves in Malta, which they administered until Napoleon drove them out in 1798. Rome is now the Order's headquarters.

The British Order dates from 1827; it relieves the sick in various ways, but its chief work is done through the St John Ambulance Association.

KNIGHTS OF THE ROUND TABLE, see Arthur.

KNIGHTS TEMPLARS (Knights of the Temple), a militant order of the Crusades which derived its name from the Temple at Jerusalem. Founded in 1118, it had by the 13th century developed into a fighting force of aristocrats, famous for their reckless courage. The Order acquired great wealth, which aroused the cupidity of Philip IV of France. They were accused of heresy, the Grand Master was burnt at the stake, and the Pope dissolved the Order (1307). In England Edward II confiscated their property.

KNOSSOS, an ancient Cretan city and the centre of Minoan civilisation. The great palace known as the Labyrinth was at the peak of its magnificence about 1450 B.C. It was destroyed twice, the second time in about 1400 B.C. See Aegean Civilisation.

Palace of Knossos

KNOX, John (*c.* 1515—72), leader of the Reformation in Scotland. He served as a chaplain to Edward VI, but left England (1553) when Mary Tudor came to power and went to Geneva where he met Calvin. In 1560 he was appointed minister of St Giles, Edinburgh, where he continued to preach until his death. He was chiefly responsible for the formation of the Presbyterian Church of Scotland.

KOBE, a seaport of southern Honshu, Japan. Pop. (1960) 1,113,901. An important shipbuilding port and commercial and communications centre, it has numerous diversified industries.

KOCH, Robert (1843—1910), German bacteriologist. He isolated the bacilli causing tuberculosis, anthrax, wound infections, cholera and other diseases. He made valuable contributions to the science of bacteriology, including improvements in culturing bacteria and staining techniques. In 1905 he was awarded the Nobel Prize for physiology and medicine for his development of the tuberculin test for tuberculosis.

KORAN, the sacred book of Islam. According to Moslem belief, it was divinely revealed to Mohammed by the Archangel Gabriel. Consisting of 114 suras, or chapters, written in classical Arabic, it proclaims the unity of God, denounces idolatry and lays down the basic tenets of Islam. It does not contain the utterances of Mohammed himself, some of which are interpretations of the Koran.

KOREA, a peninsula between the Sea of Japan and the Yellow Sea in the Far East, divided into two political units. It is mountainous in the east and consists of plains in the west. There are numerous rivers. The chief crops are rice, grains, beans, tobacco and cotton. There are deposits of coal and tungsten. In the north there is iron and petroleum. North Korea (pop. 10,600,000; area 46,814 sq. miles) is a People's Republic in the Soviet orbit; its capital is Pyongyang (pop. 700,000). South Korea (pop. 1960 24,994,117; area 38,452 sq. miles) is a republic allied to the West; its capital is Seoul (pop. 2,400,000). Under Japanese domination from 1907, it was divided into two states separated by the 38th parallel after Japan's defeat in the Second World War. North Korean forces invaded South Korea in 1950 but were repulsed, together with their Chinese allies, with the help of U.N. troops.

KOREAN WAR, on June 25, 1950, North Korean forces invaded South Korea, meeting with little opposition until the arrival of U.S. air forces two days later, when the U.N. Security Council voted military sanctions against the aggressor. A U.N. force, consisting chiefly of American, Australian and British troops under U.S. General Douglas MacArthur, carried out a successful counter-offensive in September which took them into North Korea. The entrance of superior numbers of Communist Chinese units into the war forced the U.N. forces to retreat and to continue limited offensives until two years of truce negotiations, were concluded in 1953. The truce line was approximately the 38th parallel dividing North and South Korea. The struggle in Korea was an important phase in the Cold War, with the U.S.S.R. supporting North Korea and Communist China against the Western democracies and the U.N.

KOSCIUSZKO, Tadeusz (1746—1817), Polish statesman and general. After serving under George Washington in the American War of Independence, he returned to his native Poland where he led a desperate defence against the invading Russians in 1792. Two years later, he led a short-lived insurrection against Russian rule. He attended the Congress of Vienna (1815) but could not obtain the liberation of his country.

KOSSUTH, Lajos (1802—94), Hungarian patriot and leader of the 1848—49 Hungarian revolution. He was proclaimed president of the short-lived Hungarian Republic in 1849, but was forced to flee in the same year and spent the remainder of his life in exile.

KRAKOW, a city and capital of medieval Poland on the Vistula River. Pop. (1961) 490,000. A commercial and cultural centre, it produces textiles, steel, machinery and chemicals. In the Second World War the city was almost completely destroyed, but it has been rebuilt with extensive industrial and residential suburbs.

KREFELD, a city in North Rhine-Westphalia near the Rhine, West Germany. Pop. (1960) 207,891. A communications and industrial centre, it produces textiles, machinery and chemicals.

KREISLER, Fritz (1875—1962), Austrian violinist. He composed a number of violin pieces, including *Caprice Viennois* and *Tambourin Chinois*, and an operetta, *Apple Blossoms*.

KREMLIN, a fortress in Moscow containing the offices of the central government of the U.S.S.R. Built in the 12th century, it consists of churches, palaces, museums, gardens and an arsenal, surrounded by walls. Outside is Red Square on one side and the River Moskva on another.

KRIVOI ROG, a city in the Ukrainian S.S.R., on the Ingulets River, U.S.S.R. Pop. (1962) 448,000. Surrounded by coal and iron mines, it is an important steel-producing city.

KRUGER, Paul (Oom Paul; 1825—1904), last President (1883—1900) of the Transvaal Republic. He was Vice-President of Transvaal when it was annexed by Britain in 1877, and played a leading role in seeking autonomy and keeping Uitlanders (non-Boers) out of the area.

KRUPP, Alfred (1812—87), German munitions manufacturer. A trained metallurgist, he was one of the first to utilise the steam-hammer and the Bessemer process for manufacturing steel to produce armaments. The Krupp family supplied Germany with armaments in both World Wars, manufacturing locomotives and heavy machinery in the interim. The Krupp empire was re-established in 1953.

KRYPTON, see Elements.

KUBLAI KHAN (1216—94), Mongol ruler of China. He completed the conquest of China begun by his grandfather, Genghis Khan. He established Buddhism as the state religion and fostered scholarship and the arts. He drove out the Sung, and established the Yüan, dynasty. Marco Polo visited his capital and served under him.

KUIBYSHEV, a city in the R.S.F.S.R., on the Volga River, U.S.S.R. Pop. (1962) 881,000. An important railway junction, it is a river port and a commercial and industrial centre. It also has oil refineries.

KU KLUX KLAN, an American secret terrorist organisation devoted to the idea of Protestant white supremacy. Anti-Catholic, anti-Jewish and anti-Negro, it flourished from 1866—69 and was revived in 1915; it is found in the south and in rural areas. Unwilling to leave its obscurantism in any doubt, it now also opposes foreign-born settlers, post-Darwinian thought, socialism and any form of Christianity more advanced than Fundamentalism.

KUMASI, a town in Ghana, West Africa. Pop. (1960) 220,922. Built on reclaimed swampland, it produces chiefly cocoa. It was the ancient capital of the Ashanti kingdom.

KUN, Bela (1886—*c.* 1936), revolutionary leader in Hungary in 1919. He began to transform the country into a Communist state, until he was defeated by a Rumanian army. He fled to the U.S.S.R. and was executed as a Trotskyist.

KUNMING, capital of Yunnan province, southern China. Pop. (1960) 500,000. A communications and commercial centre, it has important metallurgical industries producing articles of copper, tin and steel.

KUOMINTANG, the Chinese nationalist party founded in 1912 by Sun Yat-sen. By 1930 it controlled most of China, having broken with the Communists in 1927. Its power is now limited to Formosa.

KURIL ISLANDS, a chain of U.S.S.R. islands in the Far East, extending from Kamchatka to Hokkaido, Japan. Pop. 17,549; area 6000 sq. miles. They are mountainous and have dense forests, containing fur-bearing animals. There are sulphur deposits, and fishing is important. They were ceded by Japan to the U.S.S.R. following the Second World War.

KUWAIT, a shaikhdom on the northwest coast of the Persian Gulf. Pop. (1961) 321,000; area 6000 sq. miles. Mostly desert, it has since 1938 become the world's largest oil producer. It was formerly under British protection but achieved independence in 1961. British, and subsequently Arab League, troops were summoned to protect it against Iraqi designs of conquest.

KWANGSI-CHUANG, an autonomous region in southern China. Pop. (1953) 19,560,822; area 85,452 sq. miles. Consisting of transverse mountains cut by valleys, it has a subtropical climate. Rice, sugar, tobacco, indigo and silk are produced. The capital is Nanning.

KWANTUNG, a maritime province in southeast China. Pop. (1953) 34,770,059; area 85,447 sq. miles. Consisting of hills running parallel to the coast and valleys, it has a broad estuary on the China Sea. A leading silk producer, it also grows rice, tea and sugar. The capital is Canton.

KWEICHOW, a province in southwest China. Pop. (1953) 15,037,310; area 68,139 sq. miles. Much of it consists of densely forested mountains. Cereals, beans and tobacco are raised. Minerals include coal, copper, tin, lead, gold, mercury and iron. The forests include many tropical, rare, species of trees. The capital is Kweiyang.

KYOTO, a city in Honshu, Japan. Pop. (1960) 1,284,746. An industrial and cultural centre, it has numerous Buddhist temples, buildings of historical interest and a university. It was the imperial capital for over a thousand years, from its foundation in 793 until 1868.

KYUSHU, the southernmost of the main islands of Japan. Pop. (1955) 12,097,000; area 16,247 sq. miles. The island is mountainous; it produces cereals, sweet potatoes, fruits, hemp, and tea in the south. Minerals include coal, copper and antimony, and there are large metallurgical industries.The principal cities are Fukuoka, Kumamoto and Nagasaki.

LABOUR MOVEMENT, the organised activities of working-men to improve their conditions. It exists in a free society under capitalism where workers are aware of their distinct interests as opposed to those of other groups. Such movements generally engage in three kinds of activities: economic (trade unions), political (labour parties) and co-operative (non-profit organisations of workers).

LABOUR PARTY, the Independent Labour Party, formed in 1895, at first collaborated with the Liberals in politics. In 1906 it became part of the newly organised Labour Party, of which 29 members were elected to parliament. Up to the First World War it slowly gained in strength, supporting the efforts of Asquith and Lloyd George to secure the passage of social legislation. In 1924 the Labour Party formed a minority government under Ramsay MacDonald with the support of the Liberals. A second minority government was formed in 1929, but in 1931, in face of the growing financial and unemployment crisis, MacDonald formed a predominantly Conservative national government. This survived until 1935, but MacDonald lost the support of most of his party, which had gone into opposition. In Churchill's wartime administration of 1940—45 Attlee, Bevin, Morrison, Dalton and other leaders of the Labour Party served in high office. With the end of the war the party came into power with a large majority, and at once inaugurated a programme to nationalise basic industries and the Bank of England, and to provide comprehensive social services. With Clement Attlee as Prime Minister, it embarked on a policy of granting independence to India, Ceylon and Burma, and preparing the colonies for independence. Ernest Bevin made a great name for himself as Foreign Secretary, and was prominent in the counsels of the U.N. In 1951 the Labour Party lost its majority and again went into opposition during 13 years of Conservative rule. In a General Election in October 1964 the Labour Party was returned to power with a majority of four.

LABUAN, an island off the northwest coast of Borneo, administered as part of Sabah (North Borneo), Federation of Malaysia. Pop. 9000; area 35 sq. miles. It produces rice, rubber and coconuts. The capital is Victoria.

LACROSSE (French *la crosse*, 'the bishop's crozier'), originally an American Indian game, played by men and women, introduced into England from Canada (1867). A team (of 10 or 12) try to get a rubber ball through the opponents' goal, using a wooden 'crosse' which has a mesh pocket of hide and gut not more than 1 ft wide, with which the ball is caught, carried and thrown.

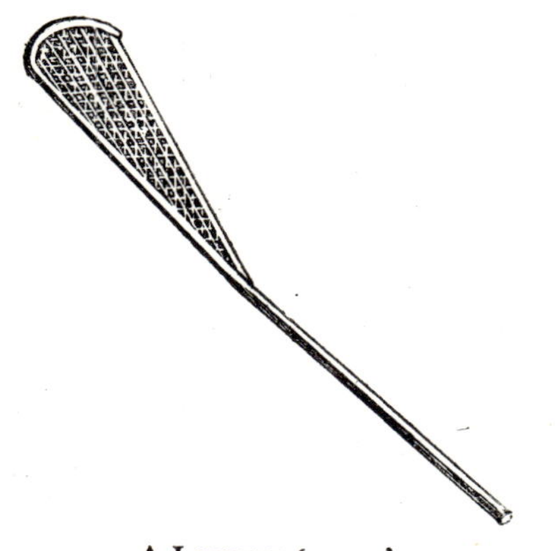

A Lacrosse 'crosse'

LAFAYETTE, Joseph Gilbert du Motier, Marquis de (1757—1834), French soldier and statesman. After serving in the American War of Independence, he commanded the National Guard in Paris during the early days of the French Revolution, opposing violence. He was a prisoner of the Austrians for five years until released by Napoleon. Between 1820 and 1830 he was a member of the Carbonari opposition to the restored Bourbons. Again commander of the National Guard in 1830, he helped put Louis Philippe on the throne.

LA FONTAINE, Jean de (1621—95), French poet and writer of fables. His chief work consists of his 12 volumes of *Fables*, in which he uses tales of animals, insects and plants, derived from Aesop, oriental tales and other sources, to portray the weaknesses of human nature. The fables are written with versatility and skill in free verse, and have charmed readers of all ages. The occasional lyrical passages show him to be a poet of the highest rank, and the later volumes, in particular, have great profundity of psychological insight

LAGERLÖF, Selma (1858—1940), Swedish novelist. She is famous for *The Story of Gösta Berling*, *Jerusalem* and *The Wonderful Adventure of Nils.* Awarded the Nobel Prize for literature in 1909, she was the first woman to be elected to the Swedish Academy.

LAGOS, capital of Nigeria. Pop. (1962) *c.* 450,000. It has an excellent harbour and is the terminus of the main railway from the north. Lagos is an important commercial centre, originally built on an island but now spreading widely over the adjacent mainland.

LAHORE, capital of West Pakistan, on the Ravi River. Pop. (1961) 1,297,000. A communications and industrial centre, it produces rugs, textiles, metal articles and foodstuffs. It is an ancient city and achieved great prominence in the empires of the Moguls and the Sikhs. It was the capital of the Punjab under British rule.

LAISSEZ FAIRE, an economic and political principle which holds that no state agency or government should interfere in the conduct of business, confining its activities to providing a judicial system with which to deal with contract breakers.

LAKE, a landlocked body of water in a depression. Water collects as the result of precipitation, springs, or the inflowing of rivers. The degree of salinity depends on the ratio between the rate of inflow and the rate of evaporation. The following are the world's principal lakes:

FRESHWATER LAKES

Name	*Location*	*Area sq. miles*	*Elevation above sea-level, ft*	*Maximum depth, ft*
Alberta	Central Africa	1,640	2,037	50
Amandjuak	Baffin Land	4,000	—	—
Athabasca	Alberta, Canada	3,058	699	Shallow
Baikal	E. Siberia, U.S.S.R.	12,150	1,515	5,413
Bangweulu	E. central Africa	1,900	3,700	15
Chad	Chad-Nigeria	8,000	850	20
Como	Italy	55.5	650	1,365
Constance	Switzerland, Germany, Austria	208	1,309	827
Dubawnt	Canada	1,600	—	—
Edward	Central Africa	1,500	3,000	—
Erie	U.S.A.—Canada	9,940	572	210
Geneva	France—Switzerland	225	1,230	1,095
Great Bear	Canada	12,000	391	270
Great Slave	Canada	11,170	495	650
Huron	U.S.A.—Canada	23,010	581	750
Koko Nor	Tibet	2,300	—	—
Ladoga	U.S.S.R.	7,100	55	730
Lake of the Woods	Ontario—Manitoba, Canada	1,485	1,058	—
Lucerne	Switzerland	49	1,435	700
Maggiore	Italy	82	636	1,220
Manitoba	Canada	1,817	813	12
Maracaibo	Venezuela	6,300	—	—
Michigan	U.S.A.	22,400	581	923
Mweru	Congo-Rhodesia	1,700	3,189	—
Neuchatel	Switzerland	90	1,420	472
Nicaragua	Nicaragua	3,100	—	—
Nipigon	Ontario, Canada	1,870	850	—
Nyasa	S. Africa	11,000	1,650	2,580
Onega	U.S.S.R. in Europe	3,764	125	408
Ontario	U.S.A.—Canada	7,540	—	—
Reindeer	S. central Canada	2,444	1,150	—
Superior	U.S.A.—Canada	31,820	622	1,302
Tanganyika	E. central Africa	12,700	2,534	4,708
Titicaca	Bolivia—Peru	3,200	12,507	892
Vänern	Sweden	2,149	144	292
Victoria Nyanza	E. central Africa	26,828	3,717	270
Winnipeg	Manitoba, Canada	9,398	712	70
Winnipegosis	Manitoba, Canada	2,086	831	38

SALT-WATER LAKES

Aral Sea	U.S.S.R.	24,635	155	222
Balkhash	U.S.S.R.	6,675	900	36
Caspian Sea	U.S.S.R.—Iran	169,300	−86	3,612

Name	Location	Area sq. miles	Elevation above sea-level, ft	Maximum depth, ft
Dead Sea	Israel—Jordan	340	−1,290	1,280
Eyre	S. Australia	3,700	−35	Shallow
Gavidnez	Australia	1,600	—	—
Great Salt Lake	Utah, U.S.A.	1,800	4,218	40
Issyk-Kul	U.S.S.R. in Asia	2,390	5,400	2,300
Koko-Nor	Central China	2,300	10,000	—
Rudolf	Kenya	3,500	1,230	—
Torrens	Australia	2,350	—	—
Urmia	Iran	1,795	4,184	50
Van	Turkey	1,453	5,643	—

LAKE DISTRICT, a region of beautiful lakes and mountain scenery in northwest England. It lies in Cumberland, Westmorland and northern Lancashire. Area 70 sq. miles. It includes the largest lake in England, Windermere (10 × 1 mile) and the highest mountain, Scafell Pike (3210 ft). The district is associated with the Lake Poets, Wordsworth, Coleridge and Southey; and De Quincey wrote the *Opium Eater* in Wordsworth's cottage at Grasmere.

LAMAISM, the modified form of Buddhism which developed in Tibet and Mongolia. Buddhism was introduced into Tibet in the 8th century A.D. where it evolved into a separate religion. The head of the sect and of the state was the Dalai Lama, believed to be an incarnation of Buddha. When a Dalai Lama died the country was searched for the new-born baby into whom his spirit had passed. The same procedure was used in choosing the second-in-command, called the Panchen or Tashi Lama. Up to a quarter of the male population were monks, whose task it was to collect taxes for their own maintenance. Formalised ritualism had proceeded to such a degree that it was thought efficacious to fly a flag, with a prayer inscribed on it, or to turn a prayer-wheel, similarly inscribed. The religion has been largely stamped out by the occupying Chinese forces.

LAMARCK, Jean Baptiste, Chevalier de (1744—1829), French naturalist. A precursor of Darwin, he held that characteristics acquired by an animal as part of its adjustment to its environment are transmitted to the offspring, a view not now generally accepted. His view was that a prolonged change in environment resulted in changed needs and new habits; e.g. some muscles might be used more than before and would become enlarged, while others might be used less and would eventually atrophy. He thought that the consequential changes in structure (in this case, of the muscles) could be passed on to subsequent generations as 'acquired characteristics'. He was influenced by Buffon and Erasmus Darwin, and in turn Charles Darwin acknowledged his debt to Lamarck.

LAMB, Charles (1775—1834), English essayist and critic. He wrote a number of critical works, but is best known for his essays published under the pen-name 'Elia': *Essays of Elia* (1823) and *Last Essays of Elia* (1833). He looked after his sister Mary after she had recovered from the insane fit in which she killed their mother, and together they compiled a book of précis for children of the plays of Shakespeare, *Tales from Shakespeare*. He was a life-long friend of Samuel Taylor Coleridge.

LAMBETH, a metropolitan borough of south London, England. Pop. (1961) 223,162. It contains the residence of the Archbishop of Canterbury, Lambeth Palace. Pottery and chemicals are manufactured. Four noted bridges cross the Thames into Lambeth.

LANARKSHIRE, an inland county in south central Scotland. Pop. (1961) 1,626,317; area 897 sq. miles. It consists of the Clyde Valley, moorlands in the east and west, and hills in the south. There are coal, iron, shale and fire-clay deposits in the north. Livestock, cereals and fruit are raised. Lanarkshire is an important manufacturing area for engineering, shipbuilding and textiles among other industries. The county town is Lanark. Glasgow, Motherwell, Airdrie, and Hamilton are in this county.

LANCASHIRE, a maritime county in northwest England, on the Irish Sea. Pop. (1961) 5,131,646; area 1875 sq. miles. It has a number of estuaries. Consisting of undulating terrain in the north and central part, it is hilly in the east. Cereals and livestock are raised. There are deposits of coal, iron, fire clay, copper and lead. Lancashire is traversed by a network of waterways. The county is mainly industrial, producing textiles, engineering products, chemicals and foodstuffs, etc. The county town is Lancaster. Liverpool and Manchester are its most important cities, with Bolton, Blackburn, Rochdale, Bury, Oldham, Accrington, Burnley and many other large industrial towns. The two chief seaside resorts are Blackpool and Southport.

LANCASTER, Duke of, see John of Gaunt.

LANCERS, mounted troops armed with light lances. Their modern use was introduced into European armies by Napoleon. British lancer regiments were in action during the Boer War and in the early stages of the First World War. Lance charges were employed primarily against infantry following an artillery bombardment.

LANCHOW, the capital of Kansu province, central China. Pop. (1960) 700,000. A commercial centre on the Hwang Ho (Yellow River), it is also an important railway junction. There are oil refineries.

LAND'S END, a cape in the extreme southwest of England, in Cornwall. Its granite cliffs facing the Atlantic Ocean are 60—100 ft high.

LANE, Edward William (1801—76), English Orientalist. A frequent visitor to Egypt, he is known for his *Arabic Lexicon* and his translation of *The Thousand and One (Arabian) Nights.*

LANG, Andrew (1844—1912), Scottish scholar and author. In addition to poetry, novels and fairy tales for children, he wrote prolifically on anthropology, history, folklore and literature.

LANGUAGE, like culture, is independent of race. One language may be spoken by a group of people who are racially distinct but find it convenient to adopt it, e.g. to extend trade; conquerors may impose their language on, or absorb a language from, the conquered; a language may absorb large vocabularies from several foreign languages and then, later, be purged of them, as happened with Turkish under Atatürk's reforms. A recent example of the genesis of a language is Bahasa Indonesia, a partly artificial modernisation of Malay with Dutch features, written in a Latin script, and already possessing

There exist early 14th century records of the discovery of gunpowder, which within the next one hundred years was being put to use in projecting stone cannon balls from primitive cannon. Shown here is a contemporary engraving of a later, Cromwellian, cannon.
Photo: Radio Times Hulton Picture Library

The navy developed short-range cannon for their fighting ships. This one dates from the late 18th century. *Photo: Ministry of Works. Crown copyright reserved*

By the time of the Crimean War (q.v.) cannon had become enormously powerful weaponry.
Photo: Imperial War Museum

As knowledge of mechanics and explosives increased, cannon became smaller, but more powerful and manoevrable. This cannon and its crew fought in the American Civil War. *Photo: U. S. Army photograph*

Based on French design, this 75 mm field gun was built in 1897. *U. S. Army photograph*

The First World War also saw the evolution of the tank, a heavily armoured small field gun able to manoevre at speed over difficult terrain. The very first models were actually armoured with old boiler plates.
Photo: Imperial War Museum

The First World War (q.v.) provided the stimulus for full-scale development of heavy field guns capable of firing 15″ explosive shells over long distances. *Imperial War Museum*

The ultimate development of the cannon is this rocket-propelled radio-controlled anti-tank shell.
Photo: Crown copyright reserved

a literature which is inspired by English and American literatures. It was rendered necessary by the welding into one political state of islands where some 250 distinct Indonesian languages were spoken. A foreign language may also be adapted by an aristocracy, e.g. French in Imperial Russia; and there are three kinds of Balinese, used according to the relative status of the person addressed. The fact that few people are going to give themselves the trouble of learning a difficult language spoken by a small group leads inevitably, as facilities for travel and communication improve, to the abandonment of minor languages and the growth of the *lingua franca*; it is for this reason that the artificial resuscitation of such languages (e.g. Irish) is foredoomed to failure.

Languages fall into three main classes: the inflectional, such as Latin and Greek (and Russian and Semitic languages), in which nouns have case endings and verbs have elaborate conjugations; the monosyllabic, such as Chinese, which are usually tonal; and the agglutinative, in which root words are modified by prefix and suffix (e.g. Japanese, Finnish).

The main families of languages (with typical examples) are:

Indo-European (the main languages of Europe, India, Persia and Russia).

Semitic-Hamitic (Hebrew, Arabic, Berber).

Ural-Altaic, which is subdivided into: Altaic (Turkish, Mongol); and Finno-Ugric (Finnish, Hungarian).

Sino-Tibetan (Chinese, Burmese, Siamese).

Malay-Polynesian (includes Melanesian and Micronesian).

Dravidian (the languages of southern India, e.g. Tamil).

Amerindian, a large subdivision ranging from Eskimo to Maya.

Negro, subdivided into: Bantu (Kikuyu, Swahili); and Sudanic (Yoruba).

In addition there are many languages which have so far defied classification, including Australian aboriginal languages, Basque, Ainu (Japanese aborigine); and ancient languages that have yet to be deciphered, e.g. Etruscan, early Cretan.

LANIER, Sidney (1842—81), American poet. In his *Science of English Verse* he put forward his theory that the techniques of music could be applied to poetry, and put them into practice with considerable success in his poems about his native state, Georgia.

LAOS, a kingdom in northwest Indo-China. Pop. (1962) 3,000,000; area 89,320 sq. miles. It consists of plateaux crossed by the Mekong River along which there are rice-producing alluvial plains. There are dense forests containing valuable timber. Tin is mined, but the country is economically underdeveloped. There are large Chinese and Vietnamese minorities. Since achieving its independence from French rule in 1949 Laos has been in the throes of a prolonged struggle for supremacy between Communist and anti-Communist factions. The capital is Vientiane.

LAO-TSE (b. *c.* 600 B.C.), Chinese philosopher. He appears to have formalised rather than founded the Chinese religious philosophy known as Taoism (q.v.) in a book later incorporated in the *Tao-Teh-King*. Nothing is certain about this legendary figure, who may have been a contemporary of Confucius.

LA PAZ, the seat of government of Bolivia. Pop. (1960) 347,394. It is 12,130 ft above sea-level and surrounded by mountains on three sides. La Paz is an important trading centre for agricultural and mining products. It has textile and clothing manufactures. It is the highest capital in the world and, since the proportion of oxygen in the atmosphere is so low, a fire brigade is not necessary. La Paz is connected by rail to the international port of Arica.

LAPLAND, an area in northern Europe extending across the Arctic regions of Norway, Sweden, Finland and the U.S.S.R. Pop. 100,000; area 130,000 sq. miles. Consisting mainly of mountains, forests, swamps and glacial lakes, it has many swift rivers valuable for hydro-electric power. The region is rich in fur-bearing animals. Reindeer are raised in the south. There are deposits of iron and copper. Lapps number about 30,000.

LA PLATA, a seaport and city of Argentina 35 miles south of Buenos Aires. Pop. (1958) 410,000. It is a beautifully laid-out cultural centre and a market for agricultural products. Cattle are exported and there is a meat-packing industry.

LA ROCHEFOUCAULD, François, Duc de (1613—80), French writer. His *Mémoires* possess considerable literary merit and historical value. He is chiefly famous for his *Maximes*, in which he developed his belief that all human virtues spring from self-interest, a situation which to him seemed natural. He was, however, depressed by man's intellectual and spiritual laziness. Samples may give the flavour of his maxims: 'We have all enough strength to bear the misfortunes of others', and 'It is good to prostrate oneself in the dust from time to time; it is not good to stay there'.

LASALLE, Ferdinand (1825—64), the founder of German Socialism. A nationalist, he believed that state action rather than revolution would improve the lot of the working classes, but in other respects was a Marxist. He was killed in a duel.

LAS PALMAS, the largest city of the Canary Islands. Pop. (1959) 177,746. On the north coast of Gran Canary, it is a commercial and tourist centre, exporting wine, fruit, vegetables, sugar and cochineal.

LAS VEGAS, a city in southeast Nevada, U.S.A. Pop. (1960) 64,405. It attracts tourists because of its gambling facilities; it is also a market for farm produce.

LAST SUPPER, the Passover meal celebrated by Jesus and his apostles on the eve of his Passion and Crucifixion, now observed as the sacrament of the Eucharist.

LATERAN COUNCILS, a series of five ecclesiastical councils held in the Lateran basilica in Rome (1123, 1139, 1179, 1215 and 1512—17). The third council declared that popes should be elected exclusively by the college of cardinals, and the fourth council preached the crusade against the Albigenses.

LATIMER, Hugh (1485—1555), English bishop and reformer. An ardent defender of the Reformation, he supported Henry VIII's divorce from Catherine of Aragon. After Mary came to the throne, he was burned at the stake as a heretic.

LATIN, an Indo-European language originally spoken in Rome and the district of Latium. In the first century B.C. it spread throughout the confines of the Roman Empire, later becoming the language of learning and of the Christian church in all except eastern Europe. Long after the various dialects spoken in all parts of Europe had developed into native vernaculars, it remained the language of scholarship and is still retained by the Roman Catholic Church in its rites and ceremonials. Vulgar Latin was spoken until about the 5th century A.D., and the next 500 years witnessed the evolution of French, Spanish, Italian and other Romance languages. Famous Latin writers of the classic period include Lucretius, Cicero, Virgil, Horace and Ovid.

LATTER DAY SAINTS, see Mormon.

LATVIA, a constituent Baltic republic of the U.S.S.R. Pop. (1962) 2,200,000; area 25,200 sq. miles. Consisting of rolling country with marshes and deep river valleys, it is predominantly agricultural. Cattle breeding and dairy farming are the chief pursuits. Cereals, flax and potatoes are raised. There are deposits of peat and gypsum. A quarter of the country is forested. Industries include metallurgy, cement, textiles and foodstuffs. Fishing is important. Independent from 1918—1939, prior to which period it was a part of Russia, it was annexed by the U.S.S.R. in 1940. The capital is Riga (pop. 620,000).

LAUD, William (1573—1645), Archbishop of Canterbury. An opponent of Puritanism, he unswervingly defended the authority of the Anglican church in England and Scotland, causing war with the Scots. He was found guilty of treason by the Long Parliament and beheaded.

LAUDER, Sir Harry (Harry MacLennan; 1870—1950), Scottish comedian. He was famous for his Scottish songs, such as *Roamin' in the Gloamin'* and *I Love a Lassie.*

LAUSANNE, a city in Switzerland, capital of Vaud canton. Pop. (1960) 123,300. On mountain slopes near Lake Geneva, it is bisected by the Flon River. It has historical buildings and is a commercial and industrial centre, producing precision instruments and foodstuffs. The Treaty of Lausanne (1923) made peace between the Allies and Turkey. The Lausanne Conference (1932) abolished German reparations.

LAVAL, Pierre (1883—1945), French politician. He served twice as Premier (1931, 1935), and three times as Foreign Minister (1931, 1934, 1935) of France. He became head of the Vichy government in 1942 and, thinking that there was no practicable alternative, embarked on a policy of half-hearted political collaboration with Nazi Germany. He was sentenced to death and executed in 1945.

LAVOISIER, Antoine Laurent (1743—94), French chemist. He discovered the properties of oxygen, explained the process of combustion and demolished the phlogiston theory. He formulated the law of the Conservation of Matter.

LAW, a body of rules for regulating human conduct which can be enforced by a politically organised society. In theocratic societies, the word of God as interpreted by the holy books was the only source of law. Generally, all existing laws developed from the customs of primitive peoples. The law of Continental Europe is based on Roman law which combines features of classical Roman law and Germanic law, while English Common Law (q.v.) is the basis of the law of most countries of the British Commonwealth and the U.S.A.

LAWN TENNIS, an outdoor game developed in 1874 from Real Tennis, played on a grass or hard court by two or four players with rackets tautly strung with gut. A hollow rubber ball is hit over a net not less than 3 ft high. Each rally is started by striking the ball diagonally into the opponent's service court. In a straight set, i.e. in which the opponent does not score, the scoring proceeds by the stages love-all, 15-love, 30-love, 40-love, game; at 40-all (40—40, called deuce) one side has to score two consecutive points to win, the first one resulting in the score (ad)vantage-server or vantage-striker. If each side scores a point after deuce, the score reverts to deuce. A set is won by the player who first wins six games, unless the score reaches 5-all, in which case the winner has to establish a lead of two games. A match is decided by the best of three sets (sometimes five for men). If the first service goes out or does not go over the net (a fault), the server may serve a second time; if it hits the net and falls into the correct court (a let), an extra service is allowed. The ball must be returned after one bounce, or volleyed before it has bounced. The doubles game is played on the full court but a singles game is restricted to a narrower area by the exclusion of the 'tram-lines' down each side.

The international tournaments are at Wimbledon (1877), Forest Hills (New York, 1924) and Paris (hard court). The international Davis Cup knock-out competition (1900) is open to teams of men from any country, but is usually won by the U.S.A. or Australia. Teams of women from the U.S.A. and Britain play for the Wightman Cup (1923). Early Wimbledon singles winners include Suzanne Lenglen (France; 1919—25), Bill Tilden (U.S.A.; 1920–21, 1930), Fred Perry (Britain; 1934–36), Helen Wills Moody (U.S.A.; 1927—29, 1932—33, 1935, 1938) The Frenchman Cochet and the Basques Borotra and Lacoste won all the men's singles between them from 1924—29. The Second World War deprived France and Britain of their high positions.

LAWRENCE, David Herbert (1885—1930), English novelist. Born in Nottinghamshire, the son of a coal-miner and a schoolmistress, Lawrence published his first novel at 26. *Sons and Lovers*, dealing with types of relationship between men and women — one of his obsessions — is largely autobiographical. After its publication he married Frieda, the former wife of a Nottingham professor, and wrote his masterpiece, *Women in Love*, exploring patterns of emotion in modern love. A visit to Australia resulted in *Kangaroo*, and a stay in New Mexico *Plumed Serpent*. His last major work was *Lady Chatterley's Lover*. He also wrote poems, and painted. Unable to shake off his Puritan industrial background, class-conscious and battling with tuberculosis, this irascible genius was a Puritan in outlook, and particularly in matters of sex; he thought that men should be guided by the instincts of the blood rather than by intellect, and yet feared that women in England and America were developing matriarchal tendencies which hampered the evolution of the male. While much of his thought degenerated in later years into an almost incomprehensible mysticism, he remained able to bring vividly to life any scene he described, including countries and communities, as Australia in *Kangaroo*.

LAWRENCE, Thomas Edward (1888—1935), British Orientalist and soldier. He organised Arab guerrilla sorties against the Turks during the First World War, describing his experiences in *Seven Pillars of Wisdom* and *The Revolt in the Desert*. In 1922 he joined the R.A.F. as 'J. H. Ross', then the Tank Corps as 'T. E. Shaw', from which he transferred to the R.A.F. again. He was killed in a motor-cycle accident. A mysterious, tortured soul, a man of action and also an archaeologist, translator of Homer and Fellow of All Souls, his motives have never been fathomed; he appeared both to court and to shun publicity, to be diffident and yet ambitious. Much has been written about him, but the picture does not grow clearer.

LEAD, see Elements.

LEAF, an organ of higher plants which manufactures food (sugars) from carbon dioxide and water through the action (photosynthesis) of sunlight and chlorophyll, which it possesses in large quantities. A common leaf consists of a stalk (petiole) from which emerges a flattened tip or blade, which is the food-making part. A system of veins branches out into the blade from the end of the petiole. These consist of xylem tissue, which bring water and minerals to the leaf cells, and phloem tissue which conduct manufactured foods out of the leaf and down into the stem. The forms and external structure of the leaves of different species of plants vary greatly; they may, for example, be modified into tendrils or spines. Leaves develop from buds on the stem.

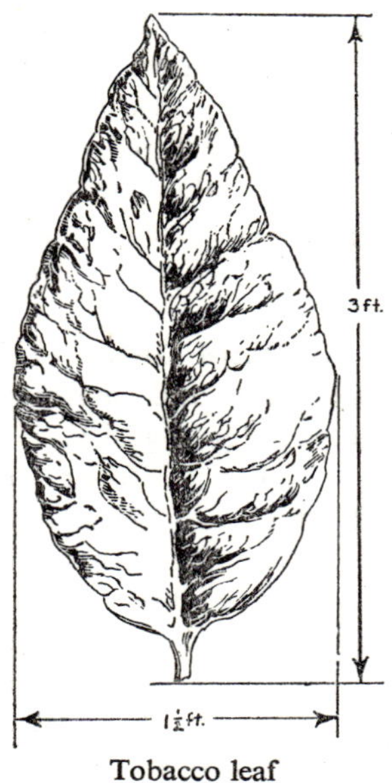

Tobacco leaf

LEAGUE OF NATIONS, an international organisation established by the Treaty of Versailles after the First World War. The main purpose of the League was to effect reconciliation in international disputes and thereby preserve peace. The League achieved considerable success in the social and economic spheres and intervened successfully in several conflicts between smaller nations, but it proved unable to settle disputes between the larger powers. Japan and Germany resigned in 1933 and the dying League was finally killed by Mussolini, who defied it over Abyssinia and withdrew Italy from membership in December 1937. The League was formally dissolved in 1946.

LEAP YEAR, a year containing an additional day (February 29). The extra day is added to compensate for the discrepancy between the solar year (365¼ days) and the calendar year (365 days). Years exactly divisible by 4 (or 400, in even-century years) are leap years.

LEASE-LEND, see Lend-Lease.

LEBANON, a republic in southwest Asia, on the Mediterranean. Pop. (1962) 1,626,000; area 3400 sq. miles. It is a mountainous country with the fertile Bekaa valley lying between two ranges. Lebanon is predominantly agricultural, producing cereals and fruit. There is iron ore, and textiles are manufactured. It became independent in 1941, after 20 years of a French mandatory régime. The population is half Christian and half Moslem. The capital is Beirut (pop. 500,000). Tripoli (100,000) is an oil pipeline terminus.

LECKY, William Edward Hartpole (1838—1903), Irish historian. He had a broad, liberal view of history. His leading works are *History of the Rise and influence of Rationalism in Europe, History of European Morals from Augustus to Charlemagne*, and his eight-volume *History of England in the Eighteenth Century*.

LE CORBUSIER (Charles-Édouard Jeanneret Gris (1887—1965), Swiss-born French architect. Advocating functional construction, he introduced revolutionary innovations into modern architecture and town planning. His famous works include *Towards a New Architecture* and *The City of Tomorrow*. He designed the immense block of flats near Marseilles known as *La Ville Radieuse*, helped to design the United Nations block in New York, and prepared the town plan of Chandigarh, the new capital of the Punjab, India.

LEE, Robert E. (1807—70), American general, leader of the Confederate armies in the American Civil War. Offered command of the Union Army, Lee preferred to remain loyal to his native state Virginia, although he opposed secession, and joined the Confederates. Although outnumbered and short of supplies, he managed to win several brilliant victories before he was forced to surrender to Grant at Appomattox Courthouse in April 1865. After the war Lee accepted the presidency of Washington (now Washington and Lee) College.

LEE, Sir Sidney (1859—1926), English literary critic. He edited the *Dictionary of National Biography* and the 20-volume *Cambridge Shakespeare*, and wrote several works on Shakespeare.

LEEDS, a city and county borough in the West Riding of Yorkshire, England. Pop. (1961) 510,597. On the Aire River, it is an important rail and water transport centre. Its manufactures include clothing, meat, leather, chemicals, glass, furniture, and heavy iron and steel equipment and machinery, including aircraft and locomotives. The city is near iron and coal deposits and an agricultural area.

LEEWARD ISLANDS, (1) a British crown colony in the West Indies consisting of the territories of Antigua, St Christopher-Nevis-Anguilla, Montserrat and the Virgin Islands. Pop. (1959) 137,421; area 423 sq. miles. The principal products are sugar, molasses, cotton, limes and fruit, vegetables, cotton seed, salt, charcoal, livestock, fish and vegetables; (2) a group of islands administered as part of the Netherlands Antilles consisting of St Maarten (shared with the French), St Eustatius and Saba. Pop. 3,742; area 74 sq. miles; (3) part of the Society Islands in French Polynesia, consisting of the islands of Huahiné, Raiatéa, Borabora, Tahaa and Maupiti. Pop. 19,400. Copra and fish are the principal products.

LEGHORN, see Livorno.

LEHÁR, Franz (1870—1948), Hungarian composer. He is known chiefly for his operetta *The Merry Widow*. *The Count of Luxembourg* and *Friederica* were less successful. His other works include sonatas, symphonic poems, marches and dances.

LEIBNIZ, Gottfried (1646—1716), German philosopher and mathematician. Mind and matter consist of wholly independent units of force (monads), no two of which are the same, though all act in conformity with a pre-established harmony. Leibniz classified the monads as unconscious (as in inanimate matter), conscious (as in animals) and self-conscious (as in man). He adopted the view, developed by a predecessor, that the relationship of mind and body can be compared to that of two synchronised clocks; if you see that every time the hand of one points to the hour the other strikes, you may think that one event causes the other. He also explored the nature of truth. His mathematical work was of the highest importance; he laid the basis for the theory of infinitesimal calculus. Leibniz made a fruitless attempt to reconcile the Roman Catholic and Protestant churches.

LEICESTER, Robert Dudley, Earl of (1532—88), English courtier and favourite of Queen Elizabeth. He was condemned to death for having supported the claims of Lady Jane Grey but was pardoned by Mary. In 1585—87 he commanded an unsuccessful expedition to the Netherlands and was captain of the English troops which had been put in readiness at Tilbury to resist the Spanish Armada (1588).

LEICESTER, a county town and borough of central England, on the Soar River. Pop. (1961) 273,298. It is the main centre of the hosiery trade, and also manufactures footwear, knitted goods, electrical goods and chemicals. The remains of a Roman town on the site have been excavated.

LEICESTERSHIRE, an inland county in central England. Pop. (1961) 682,196; area 832 sq. miles. It consists of valleys and plains alternating with low hills. Oats, wheat, turnips and dairy products are the chief crops. Livestock is raised. It is one of the hunting shires, with the Quorn, Pytchley, Belvoir and other famous packs. Coal, iron, slate and limestone are found. The county town is Leicester.

LEIDEN (Leyden), a city in west central Netherlands. Pop. (1960) 96,440. On the Old Rhine River, it is an old city with a famous university; in the 14th century it replaced Ypres as a weaving centre. Its botanical gardens are celebrated. Textiles are manufactured, and there are printing works.

LEIGHTON, Frederick, 1st Baron (1830—96), English painter and sculptor. His works dealt chiefly with subjects from antiquity. His best-known paintings include *Cimabue's Madonna Carried in Triumph through the Streets of Florence*, *Venus Disrobing*, *Hercules Wrestling with Death* and *Helen of Troy*. He also executed murals.

LEINSTER, the second largest province in the Irish Republic. Pop. (1961) 1,329,625; area 7,620 sq. miles. It is a maritime province on the Irish Sea in the east central part of the country. There are mountains and coalfields, but the province is predominantly agricultural, and livestock raising is important. There are numerous archaeological remains. Leinster comprises the counties of Carlow, Dublin, Kildare, Kilkenny, Leix (Laoighis), Longford, Louth, Meath, Offaly, Westmeath, Wexford and Wicklow.

LEIPZIG, a city of East Germany. Pop. (1960) 589,600. At the junction of the Elster and Pleisse rivers, it is a communications and industrial centre. It is famous for its book publishing, musical events and annual fairs. Textiles, machinery, precision instruments, paper, leather and foodstuffs are manufactured. It has an old university, and many interesting 15th- and 16th-century buildings escaped war damage.

LENA, see River.

LEND-LEASE, the name applied to an Act of the U.S. Congress (1941) which authorised the president to send material aid to other Allied nations in the Second World War. The value of the aid given is estimated at £12,000 million.

LENIN, Nikolai (Vladimir Ilyich Ulyanov; 1870—1924), Russian statesman and leader of the Revolution. Born into a cultured middle-class family, Lenin began to study Marxism when a law student; his brother was executed for plotting to kill the Czar. Lenin was exiled to Siberia (1897—1900), where he married and wrote a book. From the time of his release until 1917 he lived in various European countries, except for a return in disguise for the abortive 1905 Revolution. He broke with the majority of his friends in the Russian Social Democrat Party in 1903 and led the Bolshevik (majority) party from that time, expelling the Menshevik opposition from the party in 1912. In 1917 the Germans, wishing to weaken Russia, allowed Lenin and his colleagues to return to Russia from Switzerland through Germany in a sealed train. Lenin went into hiding at first but soon overthrew the Kerensky Government, ruling Russia until his death. During those years he made peace with Germany (Treaty of Brest-Litovsk), defeated the White Russian counter-revolution, founded the Third International, partitioned the estates among the peasants and introduced the New Economic Policy. He worked at fever pitch, and this, combined with the effects of a wound from a would-be assassin in 1918, resulted in paralysis and a premature death. His embalmed body lies in the mausoleum in Red Square, Moscow. He wrote numerous books, marked by his practical and undogmatic approach to current problems.

LENINGRAD (St Petersburg 1703—1914; Petrograd 1914—24), a seaport and city in the R.S.F.S.R., at the mouth of the Neva River, U.S.S.R. Pop. (1959), 2,888,000; with suburbs, 3,300,000. Built on numerous islands, it is an important cultural and industrial centre. It produces synthetic rubber, chemicals, ships, steel, metal goods, paper, machinery and textiles. It has a university, theatres, art galleries, libraries, museums and other cultural institutions. Founded by Peter the Great as his capital, it had become a leading economic centre by the 19th century. It was the scene of revolutionary activity in the Czarist period.

LENT, the period of 40 days which ends on Easter Sunday. Lent is a time of penitence and is marked by abstention and by fasting.

LEO X (1475—1521), Pope from 1513—21. A son of Lorenzo de Medici (The Magnificent), he was made a cardinal at the age of 13. Though he was a great patron of the arts (Raphael painted his portrait), he failed to recognise the need for reform and considered it sufficient to excommunicate Luther.

LEO XIII (1810—1903), Pope from 1878—1903. A capable and energetic leader, he championed the working class and acted as a mediator in the political life of many countries. He did much to prepare the Roman Catholic Church for the 20th century.

LEÓN, a province in northwest Spain, an independent kingdom until 1230. Pop. (1960) 584,594; area 5,937 sq. miles. There is an arid central plain, with mountains to the north, northwest and south. Cereals are grown and much of the land is occupied by cattle ranges. There are coal and iron mines: in Roman times the hills were worked for gold. The capital is León.

LEONARDO DA VINCI (1452—1519), Italian painter, sculptor, scientist, engineer, architect and musician. The most versatile genius of all time, Leonardo delved into all aspects of modern science, conscientiously recording (in his 'mirror' writing) and illustrating all his observations in notebooks. More than 7000 pages from these notebooks are still extant. His most famous paintings are the *Last Supper* (1495—97), *Mona Lisa* (1504) and the *Virgin of the Rocks* (versions in the National Gallery, London and the Louvre). There are, however, only some 16 paintings which can be attributed to him with certainty, and no sculpture. Above political loyalty, he worked for Lorenzo the Magnificent at Florence, for Cesare Borgia as a military engineer, for Ludovico Sforza at Milan, and died in a château near Amboise, France, provided for him by Francis I.

LÉOPOLDVILLE, capital of the Federal Republic of the Congo, above the rapids on the Congo. Pop. (1958) 389,547. It is a commercial and industrial centre producing textiles and metal goods.

LEPIDUS, Marcus Aemilius (d. 13 B.C.), Roman politician and member of the second triumvirate (43) with Augustus and Mark Antony. He was deposed in 36, after having tried to annex Sicily.

LEPROSY, a chronic contagious disease caused by a micro-organism resembling that of tuberculosis, which enters the body through a mucous membrane or the skin and may affect the skin, the nerves, or both. Not all forms are contagious and it is not transmitted by those who have had it. In ancient times it was often confused with other diseases. The disease can usually be cured if it is taken early enough, but left to run its course it usually results in progressive disfigurement to the face and loss of the extremities, though it may die out of its own accord after many years. It is now chiefly found in Africa, India and China, and also in Iceland, but was once common in Europe.

LESSEPS, Ferdinand, Vicomte de (1805—94), French diplomat and engineer. He was the leading spirit in organising a company to construct the Suez canal and personally supervised the work. He later headed a company to build a canal across the isthmus of Panama, but failed and was convicted of misappropriating funds.

LESSING, Gotthold (1729—81), German dramatist and critic, author of the comedy *Minna von Barnhelm* (1767) and champion of religious tolerance, as in his major work *Nathan der Weise* (1779). His *Laokoon* deals with the philosophy of aesthetics.

LEVERHULME OF THE WESTERN ISLES, William Hesketh Lever, 1st Viscount (1851—1925), English soap manufacturer and philanthropist. The founder and chairman of Lever Brothers, which later became Unilever Ltd, he established the model industrial town of Port Sunlight. He also introduced a profit-sharing plan for his employees and presented Lancaster House to the British people to house the London Museum. He spent much time and money on trying to raise the standard of living in the island of Lewis with Harris, in the Hebrides, but met with a poor response from the local inhabitants.

LEWIS, Sinclair (1885—1951), American novelist. Satirising the small-town middle class of the Middle West where he was born, he was the first American to receive the Nobel Prize for literature (1930). He refused the Pulitzer prize in 1926. His works include *Main Street*, *Babbitt*,

Arrowsmith, *Elmer Gantry*, *Dodsworth* and *Kingsblood Royal*.

LHASA, capital of Tibet, China. Pop. 30,000. It was a Buddhist centre with numerous lamaseries, shrines and temples. The palace (Potala) of the Dalai Lama was built on the side of a cliff. Europeans were for a long time rarely able to enter the city.

LIAONING, a maritime province in Chinese Manchuria. Pop. (1953) 18,545,147; area 26,372 sq. miles. Mountainous in the centre, it has rich iron and coal deposits. Liaoning, developed in turn by the Japanese and the Russians, is the main centre of China's rapidly expanding heavy industry, the main industrial towns being Shenyang (formerly Mukden, now the capital of the province), Anshan, Fushun, Penki and Dairen. Dairen is also one of China's chief ports, and nearby Port Arthur is a naval base.

LIBEL, the publication in writing or some other permanent form (e.g. film, record) of a defamatory statement about another. Defamation in a spoken or non-permanent form is called slander. In cases of libel, the person whose reputation has been attacked may sue for damages without being required to prove that he has suffered actual harm from the libellous statement. Criminal libel is a libel that might cause a breach of the peace. In civil libel it is a defence to prove that the statement was true, but not in criminal libel, unless its publication can be shown to have been in the public interest.

LIBERAL PARTY, a British political party which grew out of the old Whig party in the 1830s. It advocates moderate reform, supporting social legislation as well as private enterprise. Until 1885 it was the dominant party in parliament; in the 1906 elections the party won its last great victory at the polls. Until the First World War it was the leading rival of the Conservative Party. In the 1964 general election, only nine liberal members were elected to parliament.

Gladstone advocated Irish Home Rule; Joseph Chamberlain split the party by opposing it, though he split the Tory party with his proposals for tariff reform. Asquith and Lloyd George introduced unemployment insurance and old age pensions, but fell out during the First World War, and the party slowly disintegrated, partly because their main aims had already been achieved.

LIBERALISM, a political philosophy which stands for the freedom of the individual, free enterprise, free trade and the fullest development of democratic institutions. Where in former times it opposed government intervention, it now advocates state measures to improve the lot of the population.

LIBERIA, a republic in West Africa. Pop. (1961) 1,250,000; area 43,000 sq. miles. Mostly covered by dense forests, it has extensive swamps along the coast. The principal crops are rice, cassava, coffee and sugar-cane. The Firestone Plantation Company operates large rubber plantations. Important minerals are diamonds, gold and iron. The capital is Monrovia (pop. 80,000). Liberia was founded for freed American slaves in 1847 and has enjoyed U.S. patronage ever since. Government is mostly in the hands of the 15,000 descendants of the original settlers from the U.S.A.

LIBRARY, a collection of books and the building which houses them. The establishment of libraries was given a tremendous impetus by the invention of printing. Modern libraries now include special services for students, including microfilm and gramophone records. The British Museum was founded in 1753, the Cambridge University Library in 1444 and the Bodleian Library at Oxford in 1602. The Science Library and the Patent Office Library, both in London, contain large collections of scientific works. The Library of the Victoria and Albert Museum is the British national art library. England's first public library was established in 1601. Since 1850, public libraries have been opened in all the large centres of the U.K., helped by the munificence of Andrew Carnegie. The finest library in Europe is the Bibliothèque Nationale in Paris. There are huge libraries in Moscow and Leningrad; the leading American library is the Library of Congress, Washington.

LIBYA, a Moslem kingdom in North Africa comprising Tripolitania, Cyrenaica and Fezzan. Pop. (1961) 1,195,000; area 679,360 sq. miles. It consists of a coastal zone along the Mediterranean suitable for agriculture, a mountainous area, and deserts in the south, in which there are scattered oases. Dates, olives, oranges, cereals and grapes are grown. Occupied by Italy in 1921, Libya became independent in 1951. The joint capitals are Tripoli (pop. 1962 184,000) and Benghazi (70,533). Libya is without minerals or industry, and is therefore dependent on foreign financial and technical aid.

LIDDEL HART, Basil Henry (1895—), British author and military historian. After serving in the army during and after the First World War, he wrote on military topics for the press. Some of his suggestions for infantry training and organisational reforms for the armed forces were adopted. He has written works on military subjects, including biographies of outstanding soldiers.

LIDICE, a mining village in Czechoslovakia, west of Prague. In 1942 the Germans completely destroyed it in retaliation for the killing of the German occupation governor, Reinhard Heydrich. All 187 male inhabitants were executed and many of the women and children were killed elsewhere.

LIE DETECTOR, an instrument for recording graphically changes in blood pressure, pulse rate, respiration, muscular pressure and contraction, and electrodermal response (a change of electrical potential on the skin) which are likely to result from feelings of guilt.

LIECHTENSTEIN, an Independent principality in central Europe. Pop. (1960) 16,495; area 62 sq. miles. Mostly mountainous, it produces wheat, wine, fruits and livestock in the valleys. The capital is Vaduz (pop. 3500). Switzerland administers some of the services and there is a local legislature. Much of the revenue is derived from the sale of stamps, issued in small numbers to ensure scarcity value, and the registration of companies wishing to evade the company legislation of their homelands.

LIÈGE (Luik), a Belgian city at the junction of the Meuse and Ourthe rivers. Pop. (1961) 153,978. It has many bridges, historical buildings, a cathedral and a university. In the centre of a coal-mining region, it is an important manufacturing town, producing arms, machinery, metal goods, chemicals, glass and textiles.

LIGHT, an electromagnetic wave travelling through space which stimulates the eye to cause vision. Light travels at a speed of 186,000 miles per second (in a vacuum, more slowly through a medium). Light rays show the direction in which light is moving. When travelling in a uniform medium, they move in straight lines. They are capable of reflection from a surface and can be refracted or bent when they cross a boundary between two different media. White light sent through a prism is dispersed into colours of varying wavelengths, from the shortest, violet, to the longest, red. The sources of light are chemical heat, induced heat, fluorescence, phosphorescence, nuclear reactions and biochemical reactions.

LIGHTHOUSE, a building erected on a prominent part of a coast equipped with a powerful light to warn and guide mariners at night. Lights may be fixed, revolve slowly, or flash on and off at regular or irregular intervals, of varying combinations either singly or in groups. There are also lighthouses using coloured lights. Modern lighthouses now have radio beacons by which ships equipped with a radio compass may determine their bearings.

LIGHTNING, an electrical discharge in the atmosphere appearing as a bright flash either between two clouds, between different parts of the same cloud, or between a cloud and the earth in either direction. Rapid motion of the air and fast-condensing water vapour produce electricity in the atmosphere. When excessive electric potential is built up, a spark leaps between two poles with opposite charges (see Electricity). This lightning flash is followed by thunder which is caused by the violent expansion of the air and its compression around the path taken by the flash.

LILLE, a city in northeast France, on the Deule River. Pop. (1962) 199,033. An industrial and commercial centre, it has famous textile factories. Iron, sugar and chemicals are also produced. It was occupied for four years by the Germans in both World Wars. It is an educational centre with a university and other specialist schools.

LIMA, capital of Peru, at the foot of the Andes on the Rimac River. Pop. (1961) 1,700,000. A cultural and commercial centre, it has an old university and ancient palaces and churches. It manufactures iron and copper products, textiles, pottery, dyestuffs and furniture. Founded in 1535 by Pizarro, it was for a long time the centre of Spanish rule in South America. The port is Callao, seven miles away.

LIMERICK, an inland county of Munster province, Irish Republic. Pop. (1961) 133,025; area 1064 sq. miles. It is generally level, but hilly in the northeast, southeast and southwest, the east forming part of the fertile Golden Vale of Ireland. Oats and potatoes are the principal crops; livestock raising and dairy farming are important. There are considerable salmon fisheries. The country has limestone and lead. The county town is Limerick.

LINCOLN, Abraham (1809—65), American statesman and 16th President. Born and reared in the wilderness of the state legislature of Illinois from 1834—1840 and studied law at the same time. In 1858 he opposed Stephen Douglas for the Senate, and though he lost the election, he gained great popularity. In 1860 Lincoln was elected President, and the Southern States seceded from the Union, plunging the country into a Civil War. Lincoln guided the Union, with a sure hand, but was assassinated in a Washington theatre shortly after the victory of the North. His powers of oratory may be gauged from his Gettysburg address, which included the famous words: 'We highly resolve that these dead shall not have died in vain;

that this nation, under God, shall have a new birth of freedom; and that government of the people, by the people, for the people, shall not perish from the earth'.

LINCOLNSHIRE, a maritime county of east central England, on the North Sea. It consists of three administrative divisions: in the southeast, Holland (pop. 1961 103,388); in the west, Kesteven (135,317); and in the north, Lindsey (504,678). Total area 2,665 sq. miles. It is hilly, except for Holland, which grows large quantities of tulips. Cereals are grown. Livestock raising is important. There is some fishing, and agricultural machinery and leather goods are manufactured in Lindsey. The county town is Lincoln.

LINDBERGH, Charles Augustus (1902—), American aviator. He was the first man to make a solo flight across the Atlantic. In May 1927 he flew from New York to Paris in a monoplane, *The Spirit of St Louis.*

LINNAEUS, Carolus (Karl von Linné; 1707—78), Swedish botanist and naturalist. He laid the foundation for the modern system of biological nomenclature, establishing principles for classifying plants and animals according to species and genera. His most famous work is *Systema Naturae.*

LINOTYPE, a machine for setting type moulds and arranging them in lines of the proper length for printing. It is operated by a keyboard similar to that of a typewriter. Molten metal is forced into a slot containing brass matrices which have been released into place by pressure on the appropriate keys. The metal is cooled rapidly, leaving a slug which is trimmed to exact size and placed with others to form a column of type. Film-setting is fast replacing Linotype.

LIP READING, a method to enable persons with hearing disorders to understand words spoken by others from the movements of the lips and the mouth.

LIPPI, Fra Filippo (*c.* 1403—69), Florentine painter who particularly excelled in frescoes. One of the best examples of his work is to be found in the Prato Cathedral, near Florence. His heavenly figures are delightfully human, and he had a great feeling for flowers. His natural son, Filippino Lippi (1457—1504) was almost as famous as his father, but his paintings varied greatly in merit.

LIPPMANN, Gabriel (1845—1921), French physicist. He devised a technique for photographing in colour for which he was awarded the Nobel Prize for physics in 1908.

LIQUEUR, an alcoholic drink made from a grain spirit or brandy flavoured by fruits or plants with sugar added. Fruit liqueurs are made from cherries, apricots, peaches, blackberries and other fruit. The plant liqueurs include absinthe, anisette, crème de menthe and kümmel. Liqueurs are usually served at the end of a dinner.

LIQUID, a state of matter having volume but no shape, which conforms to that of the container. The other two states of matter are solid and gaseous. Liquids do not expand like gases and they cannot be compressed into a space smaller than their normal volume. A liquid changes to a solid when cooled to its freezing point and becomes a gas when heated to its boiling point. Water, for example, freezes at 0°C (32°F) and boils at 100°C (212°F).

LIQUORS, Alcoholic, these include fermented and distilled drinks. Fermented drinks are made from grapes or other fruit. The term is applied to wines and beers. Distilled drinks are made by distilling the essence of a liquid containing alcohol. Whisky is made from fermented grain mash, brandy from wine or fermented fruit mash, rum from molasses or fermented sugar-cane juice, and vodka from fermented wheat mash.

LISBON, capital of Portugal on the Tagus River. Pop. (1960) 802,230. It has a large port and is an industrial centre. It has a varied overseas trade. Its industries include sugar refineries, textiles, chemicals, paper, tobacco and iron goods. Romans, Huns, Visigoths and Moors ruled the city in turn, the Moors being expelled in 1147. From 1580—1640 it was under Spanish domination. Lisbon was virtually destroyed in the earthquake of 1775, and thus has no ancient buildings of note.

LISTER, Joseph, 1st Baron (1827—1912), English surgeon. He introduced the use of antiseptics in surgical operations. Lister was president of the British Association for the Advancement of Science and of the Royal Society.

LISZT, Franz (1811—86), Hungarian pianist and composer. He studied first in Vienna (1821) and then in Paris (1823) where he met Chopin, Berlioz and Paganini. Liszt was the leading piano virtuoso of his day, and wrote over a thousand compositions including the *Hungarian Rhapsodies* and the *Liebesträume*.

LITHIUM, see Elements.

LITHOGRAPHY, a printing process making use of stone (or zinc or aluminium plates) for reproducing the subject. The subject is drawn or imprinted directly on the stone — usually limestone — with a greasy crayon which will accept ink but reject water. The drawing is transferred from the inked parts to a dampened sheet of paper by pressure.

LITHUANIA, a constituent Baltic republic of the U.S.S.R. Pop. (1962) 2,800,000; area 31,600 sq. miles. Much of the country is undulating plain, with many bogs and marshes, and considerable forest. Grains, potatoes and vegetables are the principal crops. Livestock is raised and timber is an important product. Cement, textiles, sugar and shoes are manufactured. The capital is Vilnius (pop. 235,000). Kaunas is another large city (214,000). It was part of Poland from 1385 to 1795, then Russian and from 1918 to 1940 independent; it was then incorporated in the U.S.S.R.

LITTLE ENTENTE, a political and economic alliance formed by Czechoslovakia, Rumania and Yugoslavia after the First World War, chiefly for the preservation of their territorial integrity. It had close ties with France. Nazi Germany put an end to its existence.

LITURGY, derived from the Greek *leitourgia* meaning 'public service', it has subsequently come to denote an established form of public worship or ritual.

LITVINOV, Maxim (1876—1952), Soviet diplomat. After the abortive attempt to overthrow the Russian government in 1905, he escaped to England. Under the Bolshevik régime he was appointed envoy to Great Britain, and became foreign minister in 1930, but was removed from office in 1939. From 1941—43 he was ambassador to the U.S., but fell into disfavour in 1946 and disappeared from the political scene.

LIVER, the largest gland of the body, weighs about 3 lb. and lies below the right lower ribs. It is supplied by the blood with digested foodstuffs from the intestines and makes them suitable by metabolism (q.v.) for absorption by the cells; these products are passed back into the blood-stream, any excess being stored in the liver, which also stores an emergency supply of blood. It secretes bile into the intestines to aid in the digestion of fats, and manufactures a substance which aids blood-clotting.

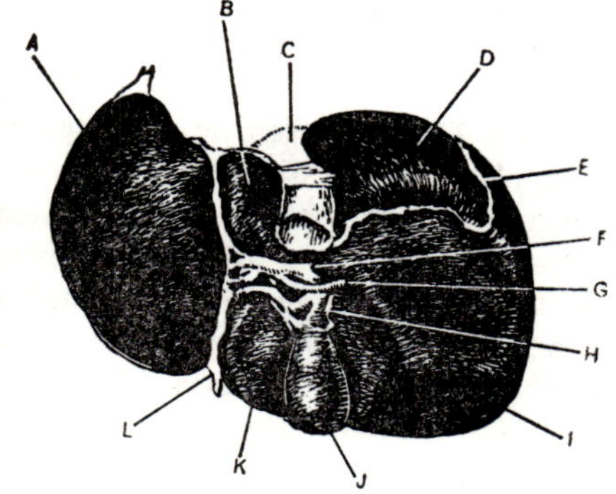

Human liver (viewed from below and behind) A. Left lobe B. Caudate lobe C. Inferior vena cava D. Bare area E. Coronary ligament F. Portal vein G. Common bile duct H. Cystic duct I. Right lobe J. Gall bladder K. Quadrate lobe L. Umbilical fissure

LIVERPOOL, a city and county borough in Lancashire, England, on the estuary of the Mersey. Pop. (1961) 747,490. England's second largest port, it is linked to Manchester and the east coast by canals. Liverpool is a communications and industrial centre. There are iron and steel mills, tobacco factories, sugar refineries and diversified light industries. It is a large milling centre and oil-seeds are processed. Liverpool has two large new cathedrals, an Anglican, designed by Sir Giles Scott, and a Roman Catholic, designed by Lutyens.

LIVINGSTONE, David (1813—73), Scottish missionary and African explorer. On three trips into the heart of Africa, he discovered Lakes Ngami, Nyasa, Shirwa, Bangweulu and Mweru, the upper course of the Congo, the Victoria Falls and the Luluaba River. He vigorously fought slavery. H. M. Stanley joined him for six months in an exploration of northern Tanganyika. Livingstone died in Northern Rhodesia.

LIVORNO (Leghorn), an Italian port and city in the Mediterranean. Pop. (1961) 159,973. The third largest port in the country, it has shipbuilding, oil refining and metal-work industries.

LLOYD GEORGE, David, 1st Earl (1863—1945), British liberal statesman. The son of a Welsh schoolmaster, he became a solicitor and then entered parliament in 1890, retaining his seat for 54 years. In 1908 he became Chancellor of the Exchequer; the rejection of his 'people's budget' by the House of Lords resulted in the abolition of the veto power of that house. In this budget he introduced old age pensions, and in 1911 he was responsible for the foundation of the Welfare State by introducing health and unemployment insurance. As Minister of Munitions in 1915 he energetically remedied the scandalous shortage of arms and ammunition which had hampered the British Expeditionary Force in France. By 1916 he had decided that the war could not be won under Asquith and, in a series of manoeuvres which are still the subject of speculation and controversy, replaced him as the head of a coalition government. His able and tireless leadership was a major factor in winning the war. As one of the Big Three at Versailles he played a leading part in framing the Peace Treaties. These were later to come in for much criticism, as was his pro-Greek policy, but to reconcile the conflicting and voluble claims of half a hundred national and racial groups was a task which could not be achieved to the satisfaction of all, or even of the majority. Lloyd George was dogged by other crises, such as the unexpected post-war slump, the ill-advised intervention in the Russian Revolution, and troubles in Ireland. Any premier was bound to fall in such circumstances, and in 1922 he fell. The Conservatives withdrew from the coalition, and even the reuniting of Asquith's and Lloyd George's followers could not bring the Liberal Party back to life and power. The 'Welsh Wizard', whose emotional oratory and personal fascination had held the country in their spell, gradually faded from the political picture, and his most important re-appearance was to help unseat Neville Chamberlain in 1940. He wrote his *War Memoirs* and other books.

LLOYDS, a London association of marine underwriters, which issues all kinds of insurance except life. It publishes a daily list of world-wide shipping reports and its annual Shipping Register contains information on the port facilities and ships of all nations. The name derives from its origin at Lloyd's Coffee-house in 1689. The expression 'A.1 at Lloyd's' comes from the system of classifying ships, A.1 being the highest class of wooden ship in the early days. The Lutine bell is rung for an important announcement, such as the sinking of a ship; the bell was salvaged from the frigate *Lutine* which sank in 1799.

LOCARNO PACT, an agreement signed by Great Britain, France, Germany, Belgium and Italy in 1925 guaranteeing the German-French and German-Belgian frontiers and pledging the solution of disputes by peaceful means. Germany was then admitted into the League of Nations and the French agreed to demilitarise the Rhineland. In 1936 Hitler broke the pact by marching into the Rhineland.

LOCKE, John (1632—1704), English philosopher. Locke was an early proponent of the empirical method of reasoning, his major work being *Essay Concerning the Human Understanding* (1690) His ideas exercised great influence on subsequent philosophical and political thought. He was a champion of religious toleration and the natural rights of man to life, liberty and property; he held that sovereignty depends on the will of the governed, a view which helped to justify the Revolution of 1688.

LOCOMOTIVE, a vehicle operated by steam, electricity or diesel oil for hauling rolling stock along a railway track. Steam-powered locomotives are run on coal, the reciprocating motion of pistons moved by expanding steam being converted into rotary motion. The first steam locomotive was built by the English inventor Richard Trevithick in 1803. George Stephenson built the *Rocket* in 1829 and the *Planet* in 1831. The disadvantages of the steam engine are that it takes so long to get up steam, and has to be taken out of service for cleaning at frequent intervals. The electric locomotive has replaced it in countries where hydro-electric power is plentiful, and the diesel-electric locomotive is replacing it elsewhere.

LOCUST, a destructive migratory grasshopper. Locusts fly in huge swarms which darken the sky, and devour anything green on which they alight. They can lay waste extensive areas, leaving them completely devoid of vegetation. The wingless young (hoppers) are just as

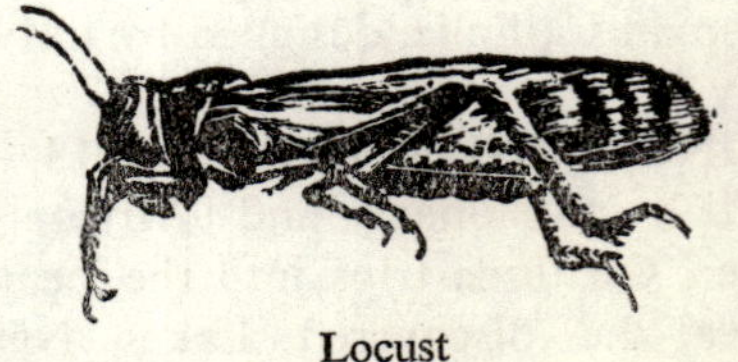
Locust

In the 16th century the usefulness of a portable 'hand cannon' was realised, but first examples were cumbersome, inefficient and liable to explode. *Photo: Ministry of Works. Crown copyright reserved*

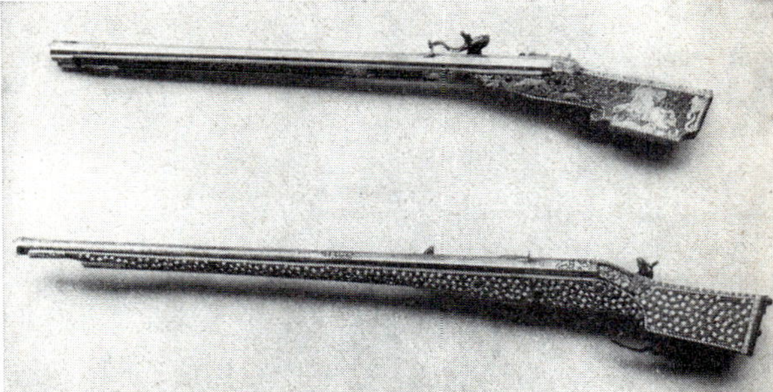

The arquebus was a refinement of the hand cannon which was fired from a rest. It led eventually to the development of the rifle. The photographs show early 16th, late 16th and early 17th century examples. *Photos: Victoria & Albert Museum*

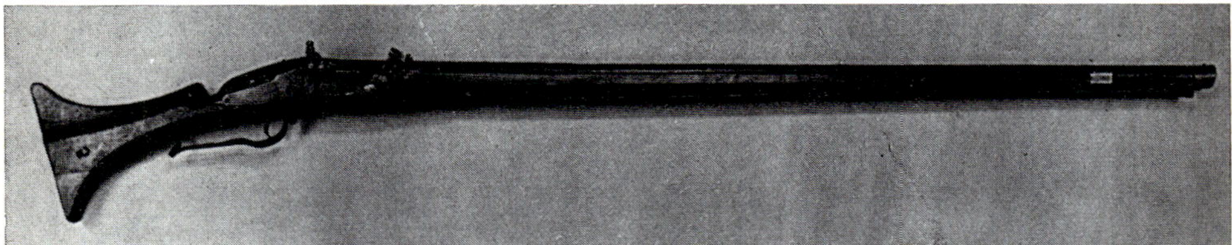

In the 17th century muskets were produced. They were hand guns designed for use by infantry soldiers. Mounted soldiers of the same period carried the shorter-barrelled carbines, shown in the lower photograph. *Photos: Ministry of Works. Crown copyright reserved*

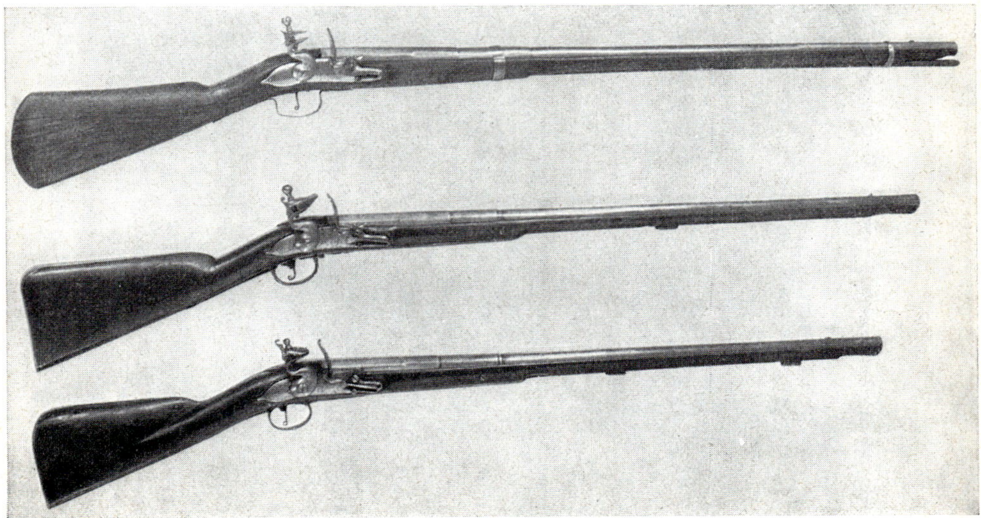

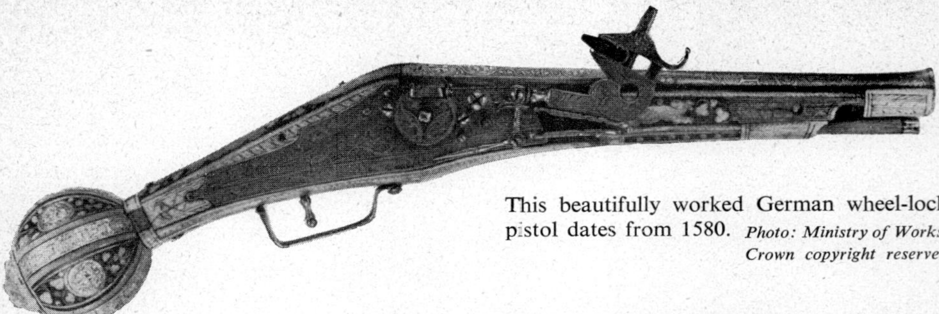

This beautifully worked German wheel-lock pistol dates from 1580. *Photo: Ministry of Works. Crown copyright reserved*

A pair of flint-lock duelling pistols of the 18th century. *Photo: Ministry of Works. Crown copyright reserved*

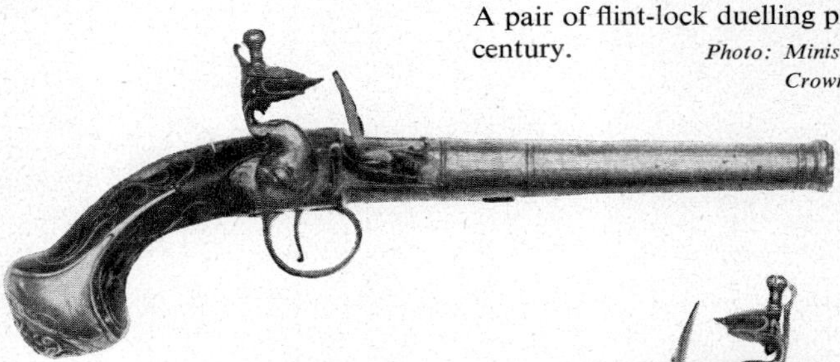

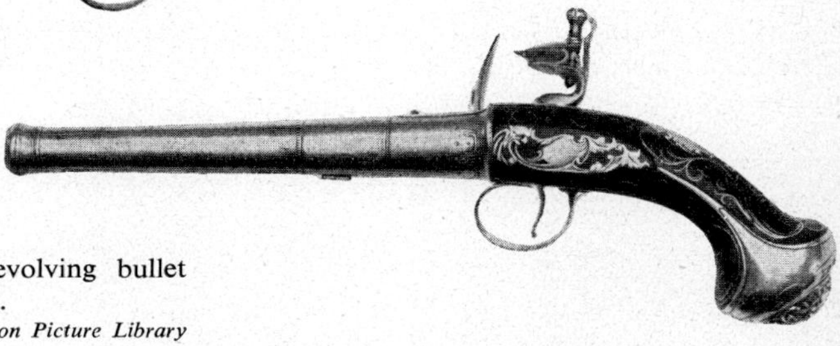

The earliest revolver with revolving bullet chamber was patented in 1835.
Photo: Radio Times Hulton Picture Library

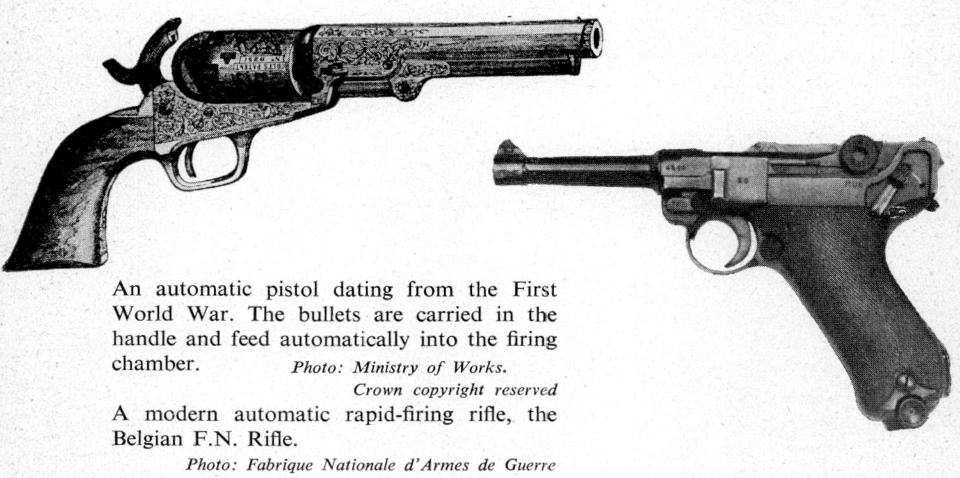

An automatic pistol dating from the First World War. The bullets are carried in the handle and feed automatically into the firing chamber. *Photo: Ministry of Works. Crown copyright reserved*

A modern automatic rapid-firing rifle, the Belgian F.N. Rifle.
Photo: Fabrique Nationale d'Armes de Guerre

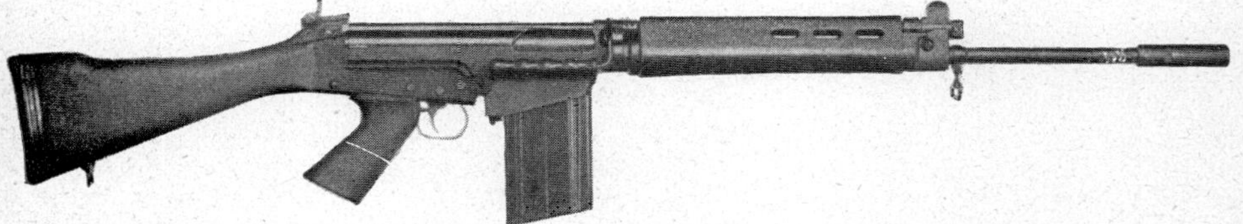

destructive, marching in hordes and devouring as they advance. The menace of locust-caused famine has been diminished by the scientific study of their habits; they migrate only in years when favourable conditions have led to overpopulation, and they can be destroyed by prompt action before they leave their breeding-grounds.

LODZ, a city in central Poland. Pop. (1961) 723,000. It is a leading cotton textile centre and also manufactures paper, chemicals, leather and metal goods.

LOFOTEN ISLANDS, a group of mountainous islands off the northwest coast of Norway. Pop. 30,000. Inside the Arctic Circle, the group consists of five large islands and several smaller ones. Cod, herring and lobster fishing is the principal occupation.

LOGIC, the science of reasoning which attempts to ascertain the principles on which valid reasoning is dependent. The founder of this study was Aristotle, who developed the syllogistic form of reasoning. Applying a general principle to a particular instance is called deductive or *a priori* reasoning; the process, fundamental in scientific research, of formulating a principle or law from the element or elements common to a mass of data, is called inductive or *a posteriori* reasoning.

LOGISTICS, the branch of military science concerned with providing the means for conducting warfare. It means manufacturing and supplying the proper equipment to the men who need it when and where they require it.

LOLLARDS, the name (possibly meaning 'mutterers') given to the followers of John Wycliffe (q.v.), after whose death in 1384 they were persecuted as heretics by Henry IV. Lollardy helped to prepare the way for the Reformation, remaining strong in London and East Anglia.

LOMBARD STREET, a short street in the city of London occupied by financial establishments and banks. It takes its name from the Italian merchants and moneylenders who settled there in the 13th century.

LOMBARDY, a region in northern Italy. Pop. (1961) 7,390,492; area 9190 sq. miles. In the middle of the depression between the Alps and the Apennines, it is well irrigated and fertile. Grains, flax, mulberry trees and grapes are grown. There are deposits of copper, zinc and iron. Alabaster, marble and granite are quarried. Rich in hydro-electric power, it is a leading industrial centre producing foodstuffs (especially cheese), silks, rayon, engineering equipment, motor cars and wines. Lombardy contains or adjoins all the Italian Lakes, and is drained by the Po. The main industrial towns are Milan, Pavia and Novara. It has been a centre of Italian political, commercial and cultural life since the late Middle Ages. The Germanic Lombards occupied northern and central Italy in 568. Charlemagne conquered them in 773 and became King of the Lombards. They were converted to Christianity and absorbed into the Italian population, their language dying out by the 9th century.

LOMOND, LOCH, largest and most beautiful of the Scottish lakes. Area 28 sq. miles. It lies 20 miles north of Glasgow and drains into the Clyde at the southern end. It contains about 30 wooded islands. Ben Lomond (3192 ft) dominates it to the northeast. The lake abounds with game fish.

LONDON, capital of the United Kingdom and the British Commonwealth of Nations, on the Thames. Pop. (1961) 8,171,902 (Greater London). A new Greater London Council comprises 33 boroughs, including the City of London, covering an area of 700 sq. miles. It is a major intellectual, cultural, financial, commercial and industrial centre. The City of London extending over an area of 675 acres with a population of 4771 is the business and commercial centre. Among the more famous buildings are Wren's St Paul's Cathedral, Westminster Abbey, the Houses of Parliament (rebuilt in the 19th century), the Tower of London (built by William the Conqueror), the Guildhall in the City (rebuilt after destruction in an air raid), St James's Palace, Buckingham Palace, Lambeth Palace (seat of the Archbishop of Canterbury), famous hospitals such as St Bartholomew's, St Thomas's and Guy's, and the government offices in Whitehall. Cultural institutions include the British Museum and Library, the nearby London University, the Natural History Museum, the Victoria and Albert Museum, the Festival Hall (containing two concert halls), the National and National Portrait Galleries in Trafalgar Square, the Tate Gallery and the Wallace Collection. London is particularly well provided with open spaces: Richmond Park, Regent's Park containing the Zoo, Kew Botanical Gardens and, nearer the centre, Hyde Park and Kensington Gardens.

In its extensive docks, stretching downstream from London Bridge to Gravesend, the Port of London, the greatest port in the world, handles much of the country's trade in sugar, tea, rubber, timber, etc. Industry is extremely diversified and the city is the largest market in England.

London was of no significance during the Roman period, except as a ford. Early in the 7th century it was under the East Saxons. Devastated by the Danes, it did not become an important town until the reign of Alfred towards the end of the 9th century. William the Conqueror granted a charter to London, making it subject only to the king. In the 12th century the Hanseatic merchants established their headquarters in the city and two centuries later it had become the leading commercial centre in England. The city continued to expand in all directions in the subsequent centuries. In 1665 the plague took a toll of 10,000 victims, and a year later more than 13,000 houses were destroyed in the Great Fire. By the 20th century London had become the undisputed centre of world commerce and had spread out into great suburban districts. During the First World War it was bombed several times by German aircraft with little effect, during the Second World War it was the principal target of German air attacks against England. By July 1941 over a million houses had been damaged and 375,000 people were registered as homeless. Devastation returned in 1944 and 1945 when the city was subjected to severe attacks by flying bombs and rockets. Reconstruction began immediately following the cessation of hostilities.

LONDON, a city in south Ontario, Canada, in the county of Middlesex and on the Thames River. Pop. (1961) 181,283. It is a railway junction and the financial, distributing and industrial centre of a rich agricultural region. It has a university and other institutions of higher education, and St Paul's Cathedral. Textiles, foodstuffs, metal equipment, electrical goods and shoes are manufactured.

LONDON, UNIVERSITY OF, established in 1836, is composed of 37 more or less independent colleges scattered throughout London, with the main building in Bloomsbury. It has eight faculties and an internal enrolment of over 20,000 students.

LONG BEACH, a city in southwest California, U.S.A. Pop. (1960) 344,168. It has a good harbour and an eight-mile promenade and bathing beach. A naval base, it has the world's largest dry dock. There are oil wells near by and it has oil refineries, fish-canning factories, and automobile and aircraft plants.

LONGFELLOW, Henry Wadsworth (1807—82), American poet. Famous for his long poems, *Evangeline*, *The Song of Hiawatha* and *The Courtship of Miles Standish*, he won more critical praise for his short, simple lyrics. A teacher of European languages, he introduced Americans to European literature and legends.

LONG ISLAND, an island along the coast of the states of New York and Connecticut, U.S.A. Pop. (1960) 6,358,328; area 1680 sq. miles. It is part of New York state. The western third, containing the thickly inhabited boroughs of Brooklyn and Queens, belongs to New York City. The other two-thirds are rural, with seaside resorts. There are some beautiful estates. The eastern part grows potatoes and cauliflower and is famous for its poultry, especially ducks, and for oysters.

LONG PARLIAMENT, the parliament convened by Charles I in 1640 and which continued in being during the Civil War. In 1642 the Royalists withdrew from it and in 1648 the Parliament was purged of Presbyterians by the army (Pride's Purge); the 50 remaining members (known as the 'Rump parliament') condemned Charles to death (1649). The Long Parliament was dismissed by Cromwell in 1653 but reassembled in 1659 to begin the negotiations which led to the Restoration, dissolving itself in 1660.

LOPE DE VEGA, see Vega, Lope de.

LORD, in Britain an honorary title, used as a less formal substitute for the full title of marquesses, earls, viscounts and barons (e.g. the Marquess of Londonderry may be referred to as Lord Londonderry); and for the courtesy titles (their fathers' second title) of the eldest sons of dukes, marquesses and earls (e.g. the eldest son of the Duke of Bedford is the Marquess of Tavistock, referred to informally as Lord Tavistock) — the younger sons of dukes and marquesses (but not earls) being referred to by Christian and surname (e.g. Lord John Russell, a younger son of a Duke of Bedford). The title is given to bishops (Lord Bishop of Liverpool), and to Judges of the High Court. There are various special uses, e.g. Lord Chancellor, Lord Chamberlain, Lords of the Treasury, Lords of the Admiralty, Lord Mayor, Lord Provost, etc. See also Parliament.

LORD'S SUPPER, see Last Supper.

LORRAINE, a region in eastern France, an ancient kingdom, a duchy of the Holy Roman Empire, and a former French province. It became part of Charlemagne's empire, and was then included in Upper Lotharingia. By the 14th century it was regarded as French and in 1766 it became formally part of France. In 1870, after the Franco-Prussian War, Lorraine was, with Alsace, lost to Germany and restored in 1918. It now consists of the *départements* of Meuse, Moselle, Meurthe-et-Moselle and Vosges. The chief towns are Nancy, Metz, Verdun and Épinal.

LOS ALAMOS, a town in New Mexico, U.S.A. Pop. (1960) 12,993. Because of its isolated position, it is the headquarters of American atomic energy research, chiefly in its military application.

LOS ANGELES, a city in southwest California, U.S.A., on the Pacific Ocean. Pop. (1960) 2,479,015. The third largest city in the U.S.A. and the largest west of Chicago, it has the largest area of any municipality in the country (455 sq. miles). It is an important port and industrial and commercial centre. The city's industries include aircraft, automobile assembly plants, food processing, oil-well equipment, tyres, furniture, fish canning and textiles. The suburb of Hollywood is the centre of the American motion-picture industry. Los Angeles has many museums and institutions of higher learning, and numerous large parks. Settled by Spaniards in 1781, it became a permanent part of the U.S.A. in 1847.

LOUIS IX (St Louis; 1214—70), King of France from 1226—70. He was a just and wise ruler and frequently served as mediator in conflicts between various rulers, including Henry III of England. He fought bravely in the Fifth Crusade in Egypt, but spent four years in Saracen hands; on the Sixth Crusade he died in Tunis.

LOUIS XIV (Le Roi Soleil; 1638—1715), King of France. The son of Louis XIII, he ascended the throne at the age of five, and the country was ruled till his death in 1661 by the avaricious Mazarin. In 1660 Louis married the Infanta Maria Theresa of Spain, who died in 1683. Mazarin was not replaced, and Louis took affairs into his own hands *(L'état c'est moi)*, exacting subservience from the aristocracy, whose revolts (the Frondes) he quelled, and appointing his ministers from the *bourgeoisie.* He had the services of Colbert until his death in 1683; this able minister reorganised the army and navy of which Louis was to make much use, developed Canada and founded Louisiana. He also reformed taxation, improved agriculture and introduced state-owned industry. In 1672 France invaded the Republic of Holland, and in spite of strong opposition, led by William of Orange, secured some gains. Louis revoked the Edict of Nantes in 1685, which drove many Huguenots to England and other Protestant countries. William of Orange formed the League of Augsburg, or Grand Alliance, of England, Holland and Sweden, and another war ensued in which the French were victorious on land but defeated at sea. In 1700 Louis accepted the Spanish throne on behalf of his grandson Philip (v); this, combined with his support for the Old Pretender, his attempt to exclude the British from the Spanish Indies, and a further attack on the Dutch, led to the War of the Spanish Succession (1701—13), which after Marlborough's victories at Blenheim, Ramillies and Malplaquet, ended French dominance of Europe. In the Peace-treaty of Utrecht Louis had to recognise the Protestant succession in England and abandon the claim of Philip V of Spain to the French throne. The continual wars all but ruined French finance and trade.

During Louis' reign the arts and sciences were patronised, the palace of Versailles was built, and French literature was enriched by Molière, Racine, La Fontaine and many others. Louis was much influenced by a succession of mistresses, including Louise de la Vallière, who retired to a convent, Mme de Montespan, and Mme de Maintenon, whom he eventually married in 1683, and who brought a more religious outlook to his old age.

LOUIS XV (1710—74), King of France. The great-grandson of Louis XIV, he succeeded to the throne at the age of five, the Duke of Orleans acting as regent until 1723. Idle, frivolous and extravagant, Louis left affairs to Cardinal Fleury (d. 1743) and then to his various mistresses, especially Mmes de Pompadour and du Barry. France lost Canada and India and reached the verge of bankruptcy under an exceptionally corrupt régime. Louis did his best to precipitate the 'deluge' which he correctly prophesied would follow his reign.

LOUIS XVI (1754—93), King of France from 1774—92. He ascended the throne at a critical period. Turgot and Necker tried to restore the country's finances but were foiled by the refusal of the aristocracy to submit to the very slight amount of taxation which would have saved France from bankruptcy. Louis was forced to summon the States-General, and from that time he was unable to stem the tide of events that swept on to the Revolution (see French Revolution). In 1791 he attempted to flee, but was apprehended. The monarchy was abolished in 1792 and the next year Louis was sentenced to death at the guillotine, together with Marie Antoinette.

LOUIS NAPOLEON, see Napoleon III.

LOUIS PHILIPPE (1773—1850), King of the French. He fought on the side of the French Revolution, adopting, with his father the Duke of Orleans, the surname Égalité. Later he came under suspicion and fled into exile. After the Bourbons had been driven out he was elected king in 1830. His régime was corrupt, reactionary and, in foreign affairs, timid and in 1848 Louis was deposed and the Second Republic formed.

LOUISIANA, a south central state on the Gulf of Mexico, U.S.A. Pop. (1960) 3,257,022; area 48,523 sq. miles. Generally flat, it is crossed by the Mississippi River from north to south. Frequent flooding has necessitated the construction of extensive river works. One-third of the total area is delta. The principal crops are sugar-cane, maize, sweet potatoes, soya-beans, pecans, cotton and strawberries. There are sulphur and petroleum deposits. Industries include oil refining, chemicals, lumber, food and paper. First settled by French settlers in 1699, it bears the name originally applied to a vast region which extended as far as the Canadian border, and was purchased from France in 1803. Louisiana became a state in 1812. The capital is Baton Rouge (pop. 152,419). Other important cities are New Orleans (627,525) and Shreveport (164,372).

LOUISVILLE, a city and port in Kentucky, U.S.A., on the Ohio River. Pop. (1960) 390,639. Louisville is chiefly important for its trade in tobacco and whisky. There are also oil refineries, chemical and synthetic rubber plants and other industries. Louisville's situation at the junction of several major railways has promoted an extensive distributive trade in livestock and other products. There is an old-established university.

LOURDES, a town in southwest France. Pop. (1954) 15,829. At the foot of the Pyrenees, it has become a notable place of pilgrimage for Roman Catholics since the Virgin Mary appeared to a peasant girl, aged 14, in a cave above the town in 1858; since then other apparitions have been reported, and a spring discovered which has miraculous powers. Lourdes is visited in some years by over a million people. Slate and marble are quarried.

LOURENÇO MARQUES, capital of Mozambique (Portuguese East Africa). Pop. (1962) 48,000. It is a principal port for all southeast Africa. The city is an important railway terminus of lines from the Transvaal and Rhodesia, and a coaling station.

LOUVRE, the chief museum of art antiquities in Paris. The site has a long history: a fortress was built there in 1200, and a palace in the 16th century, added to by Catherine de' Medici, and Louis XII and XIV: this became derelict in the 18th century and was occupied by squatters, removed by Napoleon, who began the work of restoration. Napoleon III continued the interrupted work, but much damage was done in the 1871 riots. The building now houses Greek, Roman, Egyptian and Oriental antiquities, and has a fine sculpture department; it is however chiefly famous for its magnificent collection of paintings, of which the best known is the *Mona Lisa*. The collection of sculpture includes the *Venus de Milo* and the *Winged Victory of Samothrace.*

LOW, Sir David (1891—1963), British caricaturist. Born in New Zealand, he achieved an international reputation in London with his satirical and editorial cartoons. He was the creator of Colonel Blimp whose sayings, delivered in the nude from a Turkish bath, went round the world: 'There's only one way to stop these bullying aggressors — find out what they want us to do, and then do it'; 'Hitler only needs arms so that he can declare peace on the rest of the world,' etc.

LOYOLA, ST IGNATIUS OF (*c.* 1491—1556), Spanish priest and the founder of the Society of Jesus (Jesuits). While recovering from a wound which he received as a soldier, he read the lives of the saints, and then dedicated his life to Christian service. He founded the Society of Jesus in 1534, and Pope Paul III gave it official status in 1540. Ignatius wrote the book *Spiritual Exercises.*

LÜBECK, a port and city in Schleswig—Holstein, West Germany, at the junction of the Wakenitz and Trave rivers. Pop. (1960) 231,495. An industrial city producing ships, machinery and chemicals, it was the leader of the Hanseatic League. Many of its fine buildings, dating back to the 12th century, were destroyed or very badly damaged during the Second World War.

LUBLIN, a city in Poland. Pop. (1960) 181,000. A centre of the grain and cattle trade, it has a large textile industry. Soap, flour, tobacco and leather are also produced. It was already in existence in the 10th century. During both World Wars it was occupied by the Germans. Lublin was the capital of the Polish provisional government from July 1944—June 1945.

LUCERNE, a city in Switzerland, on the banks of the Reuss River as it flows out of Lake Lucerne. Pop. (1961) 70,600. Commanding a view of snow-covered mountain peaks, it is a favourite tourist centre. The town has medieval towers, walls, and an old bridge with a wooden roof. The Cathedral (rebuilt 1633) was part of a Benedictine monastery around which the town grew.

LUCKNOW, the capital of Uttar Pradesh, India, on the Gumti River. Pop. (1961) 662,196. A communications centre, it has a large university. Manufactures consist of copper ware, chemicals, textiles, pottery, clay moulding and silver ornaments. The city was the site of a heroic defence by Sir Henry Lawrence in the 1857 mutiny.

LUCRETIUS (*c.* **99—55 B.C.**), Roman philosophical poet famed for his masterpiece *De Rerum Natura* (On the Nature of Things), the first great hexameter poem in Latin, in which he expounds the Epicurean philosophy, based on the theory that the universe is the result of a combination of atoms, an idea derived from Leucippus through Democritus.

LUDDITES, the name applied to industrial rioters in England in 1811—12, who demolished new textile machinery. The name is derived from Ned Ludd, an imbecile, who destroyed several stockingframes. Twelve Luddites were executed.

LUDENDORFF, Erich von (1865—1937), German general. After brilliant achievements on the Eastern Front during the First World War, he was transferred to the Western Front where he made a desperate attempt to win the war before the American troops arrived. Failing to do so, he advocated surrender and was removed from command.

LUDWIG, Emil (1881—1948), German biographer. He wrote popular biographies of Napoleon, Goethe, Jesus, Lincoln, Franklin Roosevelt, Beethoven, Freud, Hitler and others.

LUDWIGSHAFEN, a city in Rhineland-Palatinate, West Germany, on the Rhine. Pop. (1960) 159,732. An industrial centre and river port, it produces chemicals, heavy metal equipment, diesel engines and glass.

LUNG, one of a pair of respiratory organs in the chest cavity of man and the higher animals. The left lung has two lobes, and the right one, three. The lobes are subdivided internally into lobules consisting of tiny air-sacs (alveoli), blood vessels, nerves and lymphatic tissues. In the alveoli, which contain blood vessels connected to arteries and veins, oxygen breathed in through the nose or mouth replaces carbon dioxide eliminated as waste by the body.

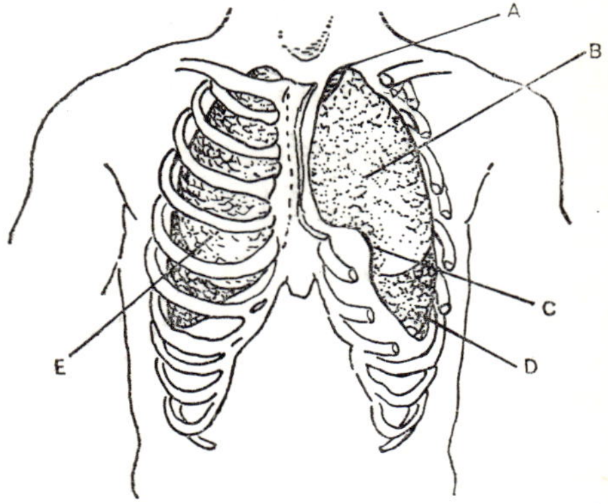

Human lung
A. Apex of left lung B. Upper lobe C. Cardiac notch D. Lower lobe E. Right lung

LUNIK, one of three moon rockets launched in 1959 by the U.S.S.R. I (January) entered a solar orbit between Earth and Mars and was the first rocket to escape Earth's gravity. II (September) landed on the moon 35 hours after take-off. III (October) circumnavigated the moon, photographed the hidden side, and returned to orbit the Earth. In April 1963 Lunik IV missed the moon by 5,300 miles and went into orbit round the Sun (see illustration overleaf).

LUTHER, Martin (1483—1546), German leader of the Reformation. Luther spent three years in an Augustinian monastery. He believed in justification by faith, i.e. that God's forgiveness is won through faith and not through good works, and still less through buying a written statement of pardon for sin (indulgence). As a professor of philosophy at the University of Wittenberg he nailed to the university church door 95 theses against the selling of indulgences by the church,

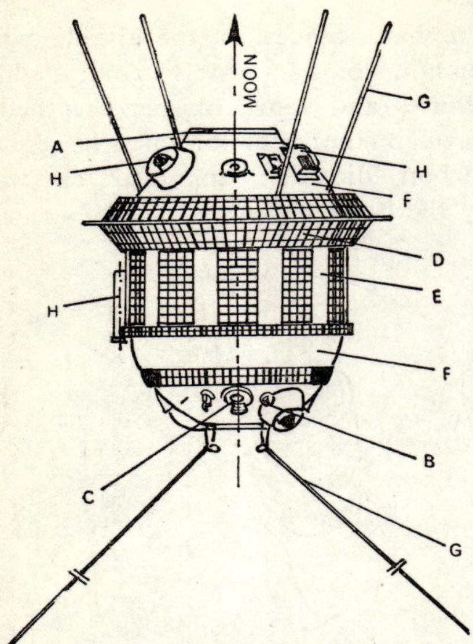

Russian Moonshot Satellite
A. 'Porthole' for camera lenses B. Gyro C. Solar transducer (transformer of sun power) D. Sections of solar battery E. Gratings of heat-regulating system F. Thermal screens G. Aerials H. Research instruments

and was excommunicated in 1520. He publicly burned his bull of excommunication and defended his views before the Diet of Worms (1521). Luther then began preaching and organising the reform movement. He made a translation of the Bible which played a large role in shaping the modern German language.

LUTHERANISM, the theological system based on the teachings of Luther. The beliefs of the Lutherans are based on the Augsburg Confession (1530) drafted by Melanchthon, and Luther's *Shorter Catechism*. They differ from those of the Calvinists, especially on Consubstantiation (see Eucharist). The Lutherans are strongest in Germany and Scandinavia, and emigrants from those countries have formed a strong community in the Middle West of the U.S.A.

LUTHULI, Albert (1899—), Zulu chief and politician. President of the African National Congress until it was banned in 1960, he has consistently fought *apartheid* in South Africa. He was awarded the Nobel Peace prize in 1960, and elected Rector of Glasgow University in 1962. He has published an autobiography, *Let My People Go*.

LUXEMBOURG, a grand duchy in Western Europe. Pop. (1961) 319,526; area 999 sq. miles. For the most part hilly, it has fertile soil in the south. The principal crops are oats, wheat and potatoes. Cattle are reared for dairy produce. Luxembourg has deposits of iron, and metallurgical and agricultural industries. Luxembourg (pop. 1961 71,667) is the capital, and the headquarters of the European Coal and Steel Community.

Luxembourg became a duchy in 1354, was placed under the Duke of Burgundy in 1443, incorporated in the Austrian Netherlands in 1713, annexed by France in 1794, linked with the Netherlands crown in 1815, and became independent in 1890.

LUXOR, a village in Upper Egypt on the Nile. Pop. 5,000. It is a tourist centre from which the antiquities of Thebes (q.v.) can be visited. These are at Luxor itself, at Karnak and on the other side of the Nile.

LUZON, the largest island in the Philippines. Pop. 4,000,000; area 40,420 sq. miles. The island is mountainous and has luxuriant tropical vegetation. Rice, sugar cane, tobacco, Manila hemp and coconuts are important crops. Copper and gold are mined. There is a textile industry. The two largest cities of the Philippine republic, Manila and Quezon City, are in Luzon.

LVOV, a city in the Ukrainian S.S.R., on the Peltev River, U.S.S.R. Pop.

(1962) 447,000. A cultural, communications and industrial centre, it has Catholic and Greek Orthodox cathedrals. It manufactures textiles, foodstuffs, chemicals, metal equipment and sawmill products and has oil refineries. The city was Polish until 1772 and again from 1920—39.

LYDIA, an ancient country in the west of Asia Minor. It flourished under Croesus (q.v.) and then passed through the hands of a succession of rulers, finally becoming a Roman province. The capital was Sardis.

LYMPHATIC SYSTEM, an arrangement of ducts, glands and vessels, parallel and co-extensive with the blood circulatory system, for distributing the lymph which bathes and nourishes the tissues. Lymph nodes throughout the system filter out bacteria. Lymph is colourless or yellowish and is derived from blood plasma; it oozes through the walls of the capillary vessels of the blood system, is collected by the lymphatic system, and returned to the blood.

LYNCHING, punitive execution carried out by mob violence accompanied by varying degrees of brutality, usually with the tacit approval, if not direct participation, of local officials. Originally a method of administering justice in the sparsely settled territories of the old American West, it became a form of terror employed by certain sections of the white community in the South against Negroes, often for some petty offence, or no offence at all. The identity of the Lynch who gave his name to the practice is unknown, the gap being filled by various conflicting speculations.

LYONS, a city in central France, at the junction of the Saône and Rhône rivers Pop. (1962) 535,784. A communications and commercial centre, it is an important river port. There is a Roman arena, several medieval churches and a university founded in 1808. Chiefly a silk manufacturing city, it now also produces clothing, chemicals, textiles, automobiles, electrical appliances and metal goods. Founded in 40 B.C., it was the capital of Celtic Gaul, and later of Burgundy.

MACAO, a Portuguese colony on the south China coast, at the mouth of the Canton River. Pop. (1962) 188,000; area 5 sq. miles. An important harbour, it is a leading distribution centre for fish and opium. It is 40 miles west of Hong Kong.

MACARTHUR, Douglas (1880—1964), American soldier. As commander of the U.S. forces in the Philippines, he gallantly defended the islands against the Japanese in 1940—41. In 1942 he was appointed supreme commander of the Allied forces in the southwest Pacific, and in 1945 received the surrender of the Japanese and was in supreme command of Japan until 1951. Commissioned to lead the U.N. troops in Korea (1950), MacArthur was removed from his command by President Truman in 1951 for his outspoken criticism of the administration's policy, particularly of the prohibition of air attack on enemy lines of communication in China.

MACARTHUR, John (1767—1834), pioneer of the wool industry in Australia. Born in Plymouth, he went to Sydney in 1790 and joined the New South Wales Corps of police. After hearing his fervent advocacy of the prospects of wool production in Australia, Lord Campden, Secretary of State, gave him some merinos from the royal flocks and made a grant to him of 5000 acres of land. With these sheep he founded Australia's main source of wealth; in 1817 he also planted the first vineyard, thus starting Australia's wine trade. A fiery character, he was in continual trouble, over a duel with a senior officer, a clash with a Governor over a rum-manufacturing monopoly and so on. Finally he was arrested by Governor Bligh (of the *Bounty*), released by his Corps, and himself arrested Bligh, keeping him in prison for two years. Later he became sufficiently domesticated to sit in the colony's Legislative Council (1825—32), but he died insane.

MACAULAY, Thomas Babington, 1st Baron (1800—59), English historian, politician, poet and essayist. He was a Whig member of parliament and served as Legal Adviser to the Supreme Council in India. While there, he wrote his famous minute on Indian education (1835) which resulted in English becoming the only medium for higher education. On his return in 1839 he was made Secretary of State for War. He published *Lays of Ancient Rome* in 1842, when he was already at work on his *History of England*, the last volume of which came out in 1855. Possessed of a phenomenal memory which enabled him to quote verbatim whole paragraphs that he had read only once, he took great pains in assembling his material and wove it into a most readable history; he could not, however, conceal his Whig bias, nor had he imaginative insight into the springs of human action in times other than his own.

MACDONALD, James Ramsay (1866—1937), British labour leader. One of the founders of the Labour Party, he became its first Prime Minister in 1924. His government fell the same year when he lost Liberal support by trying to establish closer relations with the U.S.S.R. He formed the second Labour government in 1929, but in 1931, in face of the financial crisis, he formed a coalition government dominated by the Conservatives, with himself as Prime Minister and Snowden as Chancellor of the Exchequer; this was regarded by most of the Labour Party as 'the great betrayal' and from that time MacDonald was viewed with distrust, and eventually ostracised, by his former colleagues. In 1935 he yielded place to the Conservative, Baldwin.

MACDONALD, Sir John Alexander (1815—91), Canadian Conservative statesman. Born in Glasgow and brought to Ontario as a child, he qualified as a lawyer and in 1844 became a member of the Canadian House of Assembly. He entered the Cabinet in 1847 and became Prime Minister (1857—58), showing vigour and imagination, and leading the movement for federation. As Attorney-General he secured the passage of the North America Act (1864) which established the Dominion of Canada, of which he became the first Prime Minister (1868—73 and 1878—91).

MACEDONIA, an ancient country north of Greece. Under Philip II and Alexander the Great it became a world power. In A.D. 146 it was reduced to a Roman province. It is now divided among three Balkan countries: (1) Yugoslav Macedonia is a constituent republic of the federation, pop. (1960) 1,387,000; area 10,598 sq. miles. Mostly mountainous, it produces cereals, tobacco and cotton. The capital is Skopje. (2) The prefecture of Macedonia in northeast Greece is mountainous in the west and flat in the east. Pop. (1951) 1,690,455; area 10,219 sq. miles. Cereals, tobacco, fruit and opium are grown, and fishing is important. The principal city is Salonika. (3) Bulgarian Macedonia is a small mountainous district in the extreme southwest of the country. Pop. (1946) 252,258.

MACHIAVELLI, Niccolò (1469—1527), Italian diplomat and author, famed for his analysis and description of the art of ruling set forth in his best-known book, *The Prince*. His ideal of a ruler was an autocrat, unrestrained by religious or moral scruples, whose acts would be dictated by expediency.

MACKENZIE, see River.

MACKENZIE, William Lyon (1795—1861), Canadian journalist and politician. Born near Dundee, he came to Canada in 1820 and entered the Assembly of Upper Canada in 1827. After the failure of a rising of radicals led by him in 1837 at Toronto, he fled to the U.S.A. returning later to become a member of parliament (1851—58). He was the grandfather of Mackenzie King (q.v.).

MACMILLAN, Harold (1894—), British statesman. Educated at Oxford, he served in the First World War and entered parliament in 1924. He negotiated the peace between the Greek government and the rebels in 1945. From 1955—57 he was Chancellor of the Exchequer and became Prime Minister in 1957. He resigned from the premiership in 1963 because of ill-health.

MADAGASCAR, see Malagasy Republic.

MADEIRA, the largest of a group of Portuguese islands in the Atlantic Ocean, about 390 miles west of Morocco. Pop. (1962) 269,769; area 315 sq. miles. Constituting the Portuguese district of Funchal, the archipelago is mountainous. Tropical fruit, wine, sugar-cane and bananas are produced on the terraced slopes and in the lowlands. The capital is Funchal, a popular winter resort.

MADHYA PRADESH, a state in central India. Pop. (1961) 32,394,375; area 171,201 sq. miles. Mountainous in the north, it is flat in the south. There are dense forests. Main agricultural crops include rice, cotton, jute, oil-seeds and pulses. There are deposits of manganese, coal, marble and limestone. Textiles are manufactured. The capital is Bhopal.

MADRAS, a state in southern India, on the Bay of Bengal. Pop. (1961) 33,650,917; area 50,110 sq. miles. A plateau enclosed by mountains on three sides, it is the hottest part of India. Cereals, tobacco, cotton and groundnuts are grown. Timber, iron, gold and silver are produced. There are textile industries. The capital is Madras (pop. 1,725,216), a commercial centre and seaport on the coast. Other towns of importance are Madurai, Trichinopoly and the second port, Cochin.

MADRID, the capital of Spain, on the Manzanares River. Pop. (1960) 1,966,070. Situated on a high plateau in the middle of the country, Madrid is the cultural, communications and financial centre of Spain. It has famous museums, art galleries and a university. Foodstuffs, engineering products, porcelain and chemicals are manufactured. Captured from the Moors by Alphonso VI in 1083, it became the capital of Spain in 1561.

MADURA, an Indonesian island north of Java, from which it is administered. Pop. 1,962,500; area 1770 sq. miles. The island is hilly, with many arid areas and agriculture is not important. Cattle are bred for the paddy-fields of Java. The only other sources of income of any importance are fishing, salt mines and teak forests. The inhabitants are Moslem. The capital is Pamekasan.

MAETERLINCK, Maurice (1862—1949), Belgian dramatist, poet and essayist, recipient of the Nobel Prize for literature (1911). He was the author of the plays *Pelléas et Mélisande* and *L'Oiseau bleu*. He also wrote a series of imaginative works on natural history, of which *The Life of the Bee* is best known.

MAFEKING, a town in Cape Province, Republic of South Africa (pop. 5813), where 700 British defenders successfully held off a Boer siege from October 12, 1899 until they were relieved on May 17, 1900. The lifting of the siege gave rise to boisterous celebrations in London, from which derives the word *mafficking*.

MAFIA, a secret society in Sicily which wields great power through the extortion of protection money, ransom and blackmail. Originally *mafia* meant the hostility to the law traditional to Sicilians. The Mafia in the 15th century consisted of various unorganised bands, each operating in its own territory. This form of gangsterism was revived in 1860, suppressed under the Fascist régime and has since been revived again. By opposition to all measures of social or material reform that might improve the conditions of the ignorant peasantry on whom they batten, and by such devices as threatening to cut off water supplies in an arid country, the Mafia do immense harm. Danilo Dolci (b. 1925), an Italian architect, has been trying since 1952 to end their power, with the minimum of help from the government.

MAGDEBURG, a city in East Germany, on the Elbe. Pop. (1960) 260,618. Magdeburg is a river port, with good rail communications. In the middle of a large sugar-beet area, it has developed sugar refining; it also has an important zinc refinery, iron and steel plants, and manufactures a wide range of precision instruments, electrical machinery and chemicals. An influential member of the Hanseatic League, it was sacked and the inhabitants massacred in the Thirty Years War; in 1680 it became Prussian.

MAGELLAN, Ferdinand (*c.* 1480—1521), Portuguese navigator. In the service of Charles V of Spain, he sailed westward in 1519 to seek the Spice Islands. He was killed in the Philippines, which he reached by sailing through the Magellan Straits of South America. The voyage across the Pacific took 98 days, during which no land was sighted except for two barren islands; supplies ran out and scurvy claimed many of the crews. One ship discovered Borneo; another, under del Cano, was the only ship to round the Cape of Good Hope and return to Spain (1522), thus completing the first circumnavigation of the globe.

MAGI, the Greek form of the ancient Accadian title given to their high priests, and adopted in Babylonia and

Assyria. In later times they degenerated into itinerant magicians, but the name seems to have been used also for astrologers generally. The three kings, or wise men, who were guided by a star to come to Bethlehem from the East (Matt. ii. 1—12) and offer their presents of gold, frankincense and myrrh at the Nativity, had become known by the Middle Ages by the names Melchior, Kaspar and Balthasar (Daniel), the youngest of them usually represented in paintings as a black man.

MAGIC, the art of influencing natural phenomena by supernatural means. Spirits, religious rites and forces in nature have been used to perform magic. Incantations and amulets are part of the magical instruments surviving in many religions. Magic has been classified as productive (e.g. of rain), protective (e.g. against sickness) and destructive (black magic).

MAGNA CARTA, the charter reluctantly signed by King John (1215) in deference to his barons. Immediately after signature he persuaded the Pope to declare it null and void. The Magna Carta has been widely misunderstood. In the main it restored rights to the barons, not to the people generally; even the famous clause regarding unlawful arrest is specifically limited to freemen — it did not apply to the villeins. The charter did, however, restore certain rights to merchants, the Church and some towns, and sought to regulate weights and measures.

MAGNESIUM, see Elements.

MAGNETISM, the property of attracting iron possessed by certain substances. Such substances include nickel, cobalt and various iron alloys. Magnetism can be produced in iron or steel by rubbing it with a magnet; by placing it alongside a magnet; or by inserting a bar of (soft) iron inside a coil of insulated wire through which an electric current is run. Lodestone is a natural magnet. When suspended freely, a magnetic needle turns in a north-south direction corresponding to the earth's magnetic lines of force. Magnets have poles of high magnetic intensity. Opposite poles attract each other; like poles repel. Magnetism is believed to be due to the arrangement of the molecules of a substance, or to the movement of the electrons.

MAGNITOGORSK, a city in the R.S.F.S.R., on the Ural River, at the foot of the Ural Mountains, U.S.S.R. Pop. (1962) 333,000. The site of magnetic iron ore mines and of great iron and steel works, it is one of the most important industrial towns in the Soviet Union. Other industries include chemicals, building materials and foodstuffs.

MAHARASHTRA, a state in India, on the Arabian Sea. Pop. (1961) 39,504,294; area 118,903 sq. miles. Formed in 1960 from the former Bombay state, it produces cotton, rice and groundnuts. It has also textile, chemical, engineering and foodstuffs manufactures. The capital is Bombay (q.v.). Poona and Sholapur are important towns.

MAHLER, Gustav (1860—1911), Austrian (Bohemian) composer. Although he conducted most of his life, he was basically a composer. The themes of his ten symphonies, the last of which was unfinished, are nature, man's search for spiritual regeneration, and reconciliation with life as we find it.

MAINE, a state of New England, U.S.A. Pop. (1960) 969,265; area 33,215 sq. miles. Generally hilly, the state has hundreds of lakes and large forests; the latter support paper and sawmill industries. Principal crops are potatoes, blueberries, maize, peas, beans, oats, hay and apples. Poultry-raising is important. Minerals include mica and feldspar. The state has many holiday resorts, catering especially for hunters. First settled in 1623, it was a part of Massachusetts until 1820, when it was admitted to the Union. The capital is Augusta (pop. 21,619). The largest cities are Portland (72,566) and Lewiston (40,804).

MAINZ, the capital of Rhineland-Palatinate, West Germany, at the junction of the Rhine and Main rivers. Pop. (1960) 129,627. A commercial and industrial centre, it produces foodstuffs, cement, machinery and optical glass. It has an ancient cathedral, several 14th- and 15th-century buildings and Roman remains. Founded in 13 B.C., it was a big town as early as the 10th century A.D.

MAJORCA, the largest of the Balearic Isles. Pop. (1960) 270,000; area 1405 sq. miles. Mountainous in the north and west, it is in general very fertile. Grain and tropical fruit are grown. Brandy, wines, oil, fruit and textiles are exported, but the island depends mainly on the tourist industry.

MALABAR, the west coast of India from Goa to Cape Comorin. Rice, coconuts, rubber and spices are grown in the area, which has numerous sand-dunes and lagoons. Coimbatore and Trivandrum are the largest cities, and the chief port is Cochin.

MALACCA, a state in Malaya, on the west coast of the peninsula. Pop. (1961) 335,127; area 640 sq. miles. Consisting of hills, valleys and jungles, it has swampy coastal regions and a hot, humid climate. Rubber, tapioca and rice are grown. Fishing is important. The capital is Malacca.

MALAGA, a city in southern Spain. Pop. (1961) 301,048. Almost enclosed by mountains, it is a Mediterranean port exporting citrus, tropical fruit, grapes and wine. Chemicals and textiles are manufactured. Of Phoenician origin, it was for centuries a Moorish town, and a principal port of the kingdom of Granada.

MALAGASY REPUBLIC (Madagascar), an island republic in the Indian Ocean, off the southeast coast of Africa. Pop. (1961) 5,487,000; area 227,800 sq. miles. Mountainous and traversed by valleys, the island has a tropical climate. The chief agricultural products are manioc, rice, maize, sweet potatoes, vanilla, coffee and groundnuts. The breeding of cattle and other livestock is important. There are valuable woods in the forests; graphite, mica, quartz and beryl are mined. There are textile and food industries. Under varying degrees of French control since 1883, it became independent in 1960. The capital is Tananarive (pop. 1960 247,917). Other important towns are Majunga (34,119) and Tamatave (39,627).

MALAWI, formerly Nyasaland, a British protectorate in southeast Africa, west of Lake Nyasa, is now a self-governing state within the Commonwealth, having achieved independence in 1964. Pop. (1963) 2,921,100; area 49,177 sq. miles. It consists of a series of plateaux separated by lowlands. The main occupation is agriculture. Tobacco, tea, cotton and livestock are the principal products. There are no minerals which could be exploited economically, and no industry. The area was known as British Central Africa from 1893—1907. The capital is Zomba. Nyasaland had to be subsidised from the revenue of the Federation of Rhodesia and Nyasaland which it left in 1962, and its economic future as an isolated state must be a matter for anxiety.

MALAYA, States of, a federated unit of the Federation of Malaysia, under an elected Paramount Ruler, Yang di-Pertuan Agong. Pop. (1963) 6,900,000; area 50,700 sq. miles. The federation consists of the states of Johore, Kedah, Kelantan, Negri Sembilan, Pahang, Perak, Perlis, Selangor and Trengganu, together with the former British Straits Settlements of Malacca and Penang. It is mountainous, covered with dense forests, and swampy in the west. The population is concentrated on the west and east coastal plains. Rice, rubber, palms and tea are grown. Livestock breeding and fishing are important occupations. Tin, iron, coal, bauxite, tungsten, ilmenite and gold, are all found. The Federation achieved independence in 1957 after years of varying degrees of British control. The capital is Kuala Lumpur (pop. 1962 316,230). Other large cities are George Town (234,903) and Ipoh (125,770). Nearly 40% of the inhabitants are Chinese.

MALAY ARCHIPELAGO, a group of tropical islands extending 4,800 miles from the Bay of Bengal to the Solomon Islands in the Pacific Ocean. It includes Indonesia, the Philippines, New Guinea and the Bismarck Archipelago.

MALAY PENINSULA, a peninsula in southeast Asia, 700 miles long and 200 miles at its widest point. It extends from the Isthmus of Kra to Singapore Strait and consists of the southern portion of Thailand, the States of Malaya, and Singapore.

MALAYSIA, an independent federation in southeast Asia, and a member of the British Commonwealth. Pop. (1962) 9,748,812; area 127,449 sq. miles. It was formed in September 1963 from the States of Malaya (the nine Malay states and the Straits Settlements of Penang and Malacca), Sabah (formerly North Borneo) and Sarawak. There is an elected paramount ruler, the Yang di-Pertuan Agong. The federal capital is Kuala Lumpur. For further details see under the constituent states.

MALDIVE ISLANDS, a group of 13 coral atolls and 300 uninhabited small islands in the Indian Ocean, southwest of Ceylon. Pop. (1961) 90,000; area 115 sq. miles. Fishing and commerce are the principal occupations. Coconuts, copra, millet and fruit are exported. The people are Moslems. The islands are self-governing but under British protection. The capital is Male.

MALENKOV, Georgi Maximilianovich (1902—   ), the Russian Communist leader who succeeded Stalin as Prime Minister of the Soviet Union in 1953 but resigned in 1955 after assuming responsibility for the failure of the agriculture programme.

MALI, a republic in West Africa. Pop. (1961) 4,100,000; area 460,200 sq. miles. Consisting of a part of the Sahara in the north, it lies in the Senegal and Niger valleys in the south. Millet, rice, sorghum, maize, groundnuts and cotton are grown. Livestock breeding is important. There are a number of irrigational projects. The capital is Bamako (pop. 1961 120,000). Formerly French Sudan, it became independent in 1960 and was, for a year, federated with Senegal. Mali was the name of an empire, with its capital near Bamako, which flourished from the 13th to the 17th centuries.

MALMÉDY, a town in Belgium. Pop. 6200. It is the chief town of a district which was part of Prussia from 1815—

1919. After the First World War it was restored to Belgium, together with the town of Eupen.

MALMÖ, a port and city in southern Sweden. Pop. (1961) 229,388. Opposite Copenhagen, on the Sound, it was a Hanseatic port in the Middle Ages. It exports agricultural and dairy products, chemicals and timber. Its industries include shipbuilding, machinery, foodstuffs, textiles, rubber goods and tobacco. There are several medieval buildings.

MALORY, Sir Thomas (d. *c.* 1471), English writer. He wrote the prose epic *Morte d'Arthur* which contains the famous tales of the King Arthur legend. It consists of eight separate romances, being shortened versions, very freely adapted in the later romances, of the 13th-century French legends. Malory has not been identified with any certainty; he appears to have written some of the work in prison, and it is thought that he may have been a Warwickshire knight of that name who was sentenced to imprisonment on various serious charges, and escaped from prison more than once.

MALRAUX, André (1895—), French novelist. He worked in the propaganda department of the Third International and then under the Kuomintang, depicting the life of Chinese revolutionaries in *Les Conquérants* and *La Condition humaine.* He travelled in Indo-China, Persia and Afghanistan, and then organised an air corps for the Spanish government, serving as a pilot in the Civil War *(L'Espoir).* He served in a French Tank Corps in 1939, was taken prisoner and escaped to unoccupied France, where he led a brigade of the Free French Forces *(Le Temps du mépris).* He then abandoned communism and became Minister of Information under de Gaulle (1944—46). Since then he has written a three-volume work on the plastic arts, *Psychology of Arts.* Since 1960 he has been Minister of State for Cultural Affairs under the Fifth Republic.

MALTA G.C., a self-governing British colony and chief island in the Maltese archipelago, in the Mediterranean. The inhabited islands are Malta, Goza and Comino: Pop. (1961) 328,854; area 122 sq. miles. It was an important British naval base. The islands produce cereals, fruits, potatoes and onions. Textiles, clothing and foodstuffs are the main industries. Fishing is important. Conquered by the Arabs in 870, the islands belonged to Sicily from 1090—1530, when they became the property of the Knights of St John, who ruled them until 1798. Brief Napoleonic domination was followed by annexation to Britain in 1814. The capital is Valletta. Malta suffered severely during the Second World War, being under constant air attack and with difficulty kept supplied with food by convoys that had to run the gauntlet of the Mediterranean. For their bravery in these circumstances, the community was given the exceptional award of the George Cross. Political quarrels have marked the post-war period.

MALTA, Knights of, see Knights Hospitallers.

MALTHUS, Thomas Robert (1766—1834), English clergyman and political economist. In his studies of population, he reached the conclusion that population increases out of all proportion to the increase in means of subsistence. He recognised the existence of natural checks on population growth and advocated voluntary birth control. He also published many important papers on political economics.

An aerial view of Calder Hall, the first nuclear power station in the world to produce electricity on a full commercial scale (see Nuclear Reactor). *Photo: United Kingdom Atomic Energy Authority*

Drawing of the prefabricated nuclear power plant at Sundance, Wyoming. Constructed in sixteen sections, the plant is capable of producing 1000 kilowatts of electrical energy for a period of two years without refuelling. *Photo: United States Information Service*

A heavy moveable lead container used for transporting highly radioactive material within an atomic research station. *Photo: United Kingdom Atomic Energy Authority*

Close-up of a heavy lead container used for carrying low power radioactive materials.
Photo: United Kingdom Atomic Energy Authority

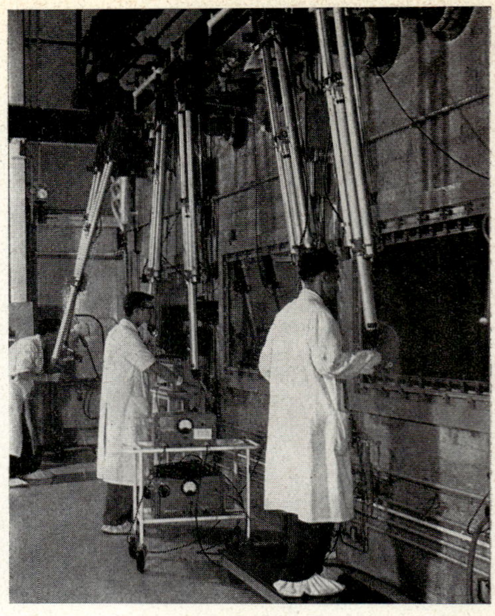

Three 'hot caves' used for isolating fission product isotopes (q.v.) for industrial radiography and medical therapy units. Each cave consists of a large steel drybox surrounded by 3ft thick concrete walls. Viewing is through a 3ft thick zinc bromide window.
Photo: United Kingdom Atomic Energy Authority

Photograph taken from the interior of a 'hot cave' showing radioactive materials being automatically manipulated from outside the 3ft thick zinc bromide window.
Photo: United Kingdom Atomic Energy Authority

MAMELUKES, Turkish, Mongol and Caucasian slaves in Egypt who overthrew the sultanate (1250) and established their own rule in both Egypt and Syria. The Mameluke reign lasted until 1517, and though marked by political intrigue, brought many cultural benefits to its subjects. They survived as part of the Turkish army to fight in Egypt against Napoleon.

MAMMAL, a branch of the animal kingdom consisting of warmblooded vertebrates whose females have mammary glands for nourishing the young. Mammals have a heart with four chambers and breathe through lungs. Most of them have coverings of hair and bear living young, except for the duck-billed platypus and spiny anteater. The most important Orders, with examples, are: Marsupials (kangaroo); Insectivores (shrews, hedgehogs); Chiroptera (bats); Primates (man, monkeys, lemurs); Edentates (armadillos); Lagomorphs (rabbits); Rodents (rats, squirrels); Cetaceans (whales, porpoises); Carnivores (dogs, cats, bears); Proboscidea (elephants); Perissodactyls (hoofed; horse, rhinoceros); Artiodactyls (cloven-hoofed mammals); non-ruminants (camel, hippopotamus), and ruminants (cattle, deer).

MAN, Isle of, British island in the Irish Sea. Pop. (1961) 48,151; area 227 sq. miles. Hilly, with wooded valleys, the island has a mild climate. Chiefly agricultural, it produces cereals, turnips and potatoes. Tourism, fishing and livestock breeding are important occupations. The chief town is Douglas.

The Isle of Man and some Scottish islands were nominally under Norway, until the last King of Man and the Isles died in 1266. Thereafter Man was in turn under Scotland, England, the Earls of Derby and the Dukes of Atholl. In 1866 it was given home rule under a Lieutenant-Governor appointed by the Crown, with a Legislative Council and a House of Keys (one of the world's oldest legislative assemblies), which together form the Tynwald Court. This passes laws subject to Royal assent.

MANAGUA, the capital of Nicaragua. Pop. (1962) 236,000. On the shore of Lake Managua, it is a communications and commercial centre. The city was seriously damaged by earthquakes in 1931 and 1936.

MANCHESTER, a city and county borough in Lancashire, England, on the River Irwell. Pop. (1961) 661,041. A seaport with extensive facilities and the terminus of the Manchester Ship Canal, it is a communications, commercial and industrial centre in a coal-mining region with ample hydro-electric power. Its cultural institutions include a university, libraries, art galleries and the Hallé Orchestra. Chiefly a cotton trade and textile centre, it also produces engineering goods, heavy machinery and transport equipment, chemicals, rubber goods, paper products and foodstuffs.

MANCHESTER SHIP CANAL, a waterway in northwest England linking Manchester with the Irish Sea. It was opened to traffic in 1894. Starting in the Mersey estuary at Eastham, it is 35½ miles long with a minimum depth of 28 ft and a width of 172 ft at the surface. There are several series of locks.

MANCHURIA, a former territory in northeast China, now divided into nine provinces: Antung, Liaopei, Sunekiang, Hokiang, Nunkiang, Hsingan, Heilungkiang, Kirin and Liaoning. Pop. (1947) 35,161,181; area 464,567 sq. miles. Mountainous in the east and northwest, it has a vast alluvial plain in tne southwest.

Its principal products are soya beans, cereals, coal, iron, gold, silver, zinc, copper, lead and tungsten. Livestock raising and fishing are important. There are valuable forests. It is the most highly industrial region of China, producing two-thirds of the country's iron and steel, and much of its heavy machinery. Occupied by the Japanese in 1931, it was a puppet state, known as Manchukuo, until taken by Soviet troops in 1945 and restored to China. The capital was Changchun (after Mukden), now called Shenyang.

MANDALAY, a city in Upper Burma, on the Irrawaddy River. Pop. (1960) 203,000. It is a river port and commercial centre. There are numerous pagodas and Buddhist monasteries, which are visited by many pilgrims. Silk and gold-ware are produced. The city was the capital of Upper Burma in the mid-19th century. It was severely damaged during the Second World War.

MANET, Édouard (1832—83), French painter. He exhibited with Monet, Pissarro and Whistler in 1863, but, although he was friendly with them and with Renoir and Sisley, he was not a member of the Impressionist group. He travelled extensively, and many of his pictures were of Spanish scenes. He made much use of black to heighten the contrast between light (the principal person in a picture) and shadow. Among his famous pictures are *Déjeuner sur l'herbe*, *Olympia* and *The Fife-player*. After the Franco-Prussian War, in which he served as an officer in the National Guard, he began to paint in the open air and in his later work adopted Impressionist techniques. *A Bar at the Folies-Bergère* was painted in 1882. He also executed pastels and engravings.

MANGANESE, see Elements.

MANHATTAN, an island off the east coast of New York state, U.S.A., at the mouth of the Hudson and East rivers. Pop. (1960) 1,698,281. Manhattan is the core of New York, containing Broadway, Wall Street, Fifth Avenue, Central Park, Times Square, the Metropolitan Opera House, the United Nations building and the characteristic skyscrapers of 'downtown' New York. A Dutch fort was built at the southern end of the island in 1614, on a site said to have been bought from the Indians for $24.

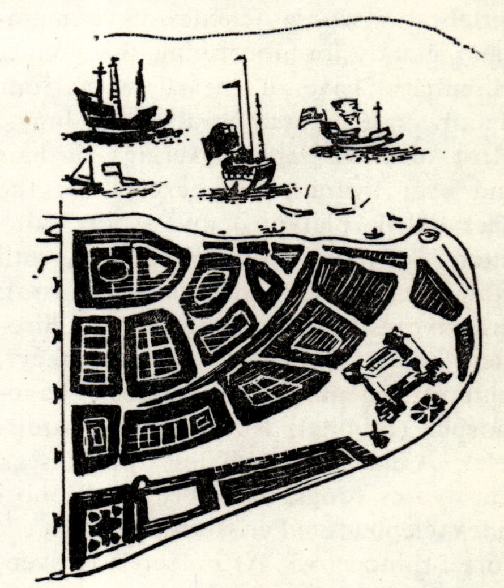

Plan of 17th-century Dutch fort built on southern end of Manhattan Island

MANICHAEANS, the followers of Mani, a Persian, who founded (3rd century A.D.) a religion strongly influenced by Gnosticism and based on the teachings of Buddha, Jesus and Zoroaster. It spread to India and China, the Middle East, North Africa and southern Europe. After almost dying out, Manichaeism was revived and influenced the Bogomils and Cathari (see Albigenses). The main tenet was that the material world is an invasion of the world of light by the powers of darkness. The believer was enjoined to practise a rigorous asceticism to assist in the battle of light against darkness.

MANILA, the largest city and capital of the Philippines, in the island of Luzon. Pop. (1960) 3,006,627, including Quezon City and Pasay City. The main business area is on the north side of the River Pasig; the old town on the south bank was completely destroyed during the Second World War, and new administrative buildings have been erected there. The new capital-designate, however, is to be Quezon City, which adjoins Manila to the northeast, and where the university is sited. Manila has one of the largest land-locked harbours in the world. The first settlement was made by Spaniards from Mexico in 1571.

MANITOBA, a province in central Canada, with the Hudson Bay to the northeast. Pop. (1961) 921,686; area 246,512 sq. miles. The whole province is studded with lakes, the largest of which, Winnipeg, Winnipegosis and Manitoba, are in the south, which consists of rolling prairies; in the north there are some low mountain ranges and around Flin Flon on the western border are rich mineral deposits. Wheat and other cereals are the principal crops. Livestock raising and fishing are important, and furs and forest products a valuable source of income. There are deposits of copper, gold, zinc, silver, nickel, uranium and petroleum. The main industries are meat packing, iron and steel, petroleum products, transport equipment and clothing. The first permanent settlement in the region was in 1812. Before it became part of the Dominion of Canada in 1870, the area was known as the Red River Settlement. The capital and only large city is Winnipeg (pop. 475,989).

MANN, Thomas (1875—1955), German novelist. A Nobel Prize winner in 1929, he emigrated from Nazi Germany to the U.S.A. in 1933, returning in 1952. His major works are *Buddenbrooks* (1901), *The Magic Mountain* (1927), the tetralogy, *Joseph and his Brethren*, *Dr Faustus* and *Felix Krull* (1954). He also wrote many short stories. Mann is probably the most outstanding novelist that Germany has produced.

MANNHEIM, a city in Baden-Württemberg, West Germany, at the junction of the Rhine and Neckar rivers. Pop. (1960) 305,544. An important river port, it is a leading industrial city. Its manufactures include chemicals, textiles, flour metallurgical products and tobacco.

MANSFIELD, Katharine (1888—1923), New Zealand author. *Bliss*, *The Garden Party* and the *Dove's Nest* are her chief collections of short stories. She was educated, and spent many years, in London, where she married Middleton Murry; she died in France of tuberculosis. Her main work consists of her vivid short stories, of consummate craftsmanship; her *Journal* and *Letters* are equally vital.

MANSLAUGHTER, the killing of another person by unlawful means but without malice aforethought. It can either be voluntary, as in a quarrel, or involuntary, e.g. through negligent driving. In Britain and the U.S.A. manslaughter is a felony with a maximum penalty of life imprisonment.

MANSON, Sir Patrick (1844—1922), British physician and parasitologist. After engaging in medical practice in Hong Kong, he helped to found the London School of Tropical Medicine. He was the first to discover how mosquitoes spread malaria.

MANZONI, Alessandro (1785—1873), Italian novelist. A leading figure in the Italian Romantic movement, he became famous with his *I Promessi Sposi* (The

Betrothed), set in 17th-century Lombardy under Spanish rule, and containing a memorable picture of Milan stricken by plague.

MAO TSE-TUNG (1893—), Chinese Communist statesman. The son of a peasant family, he became the acknowledged leader of China's Communist party in 1931. After the victory of the Communist army in 1948—49, he became Chairman of the People's Republic of China in 1950, a post he held until his resignation in 1958. He has been the Chairman of the Central Committee of the party since 1936. He has written several books, including *The New Democracy*.

MAORI, a Polynesian word meaning 'native of the soil'. It is applied to the inhabitants of New Zealand found there by the early Dutch explorers. They appear to represent an invasion of the 14th century by Polynesians who settled and perhaps intermarried with earlier

Maori canoe

inhabitants. They are a remarkable race who have moved in a short time from a Stone Age culture to full integration into the New Zealand community, of which their natural dignity has made them respected members; there is no racial barrier or colour-consciousness, and intermarriage with European settlers has been common. There are now about 150,000 Maoris, about the same number as, according to tradition, the original invaders. Nearly all live in North Island, with some 5,000 in South Island.

MARACAIBO, a city and port in northwest Venezuela, at the mouth of the large freshwater Lake Maracaibo. Pop. (1961) 421,166. The centre of the country's oil production, it also exports sugar, cacao and hides. It was founded in 1571 and was for many years an important cultural centre of South America.

MARALINGA, a desert region in the west central portion of South Australia. It is the testing ground for British and Australian atomic weapons.

MARAT, Jean-Paul (1743—93), French revolutionary, doctor and scientist. He was a leading opponent of the Girondists, and was assassinated by a Girondist adherent, Charlotte Corday.

MARCONI, Guglielmo (1874—1937), Italian physicist and engineer. The first to make use of electromagnetic waves for wireless telegraphy, he sent signals between Penarth and Weston-super-Mare in Great Britain, in 1896, a distance of 9 miles. In 1901 he received the signal 'S' in Newfoundland sent by an assistant in Cornwall, a distance of 2100 miles. In 1909 he shared the Nobel Prize for physics with Karl Braun.

MARCUS AURELIUS (121—180), Roman emperor from 161—180. He was a humanitarian who made sweeping reforms for improved social conditions. His persecution of Christians was to him the just punishment for subversive heretics. He expounded the Stoic philosophy in his *Meditations*.

MARGARET OF ANJOU (1430—82), Queen consort of Henry VI of England.

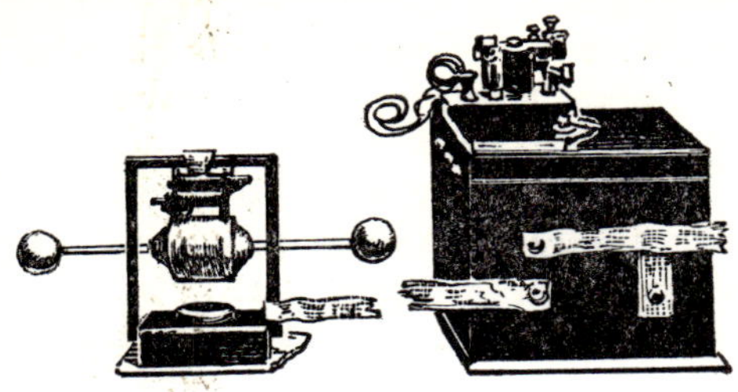

Marconi's first wireless transmitter (1895)

During Henry's period of insanity (1453—55) she was the virtual ruler of England. She led the Lancastrians in the Wars of the Roses but was eventually captured at Tewkesbury and imprisoned. In 1476 she was allowed to return to France, where she died in poverty.

MARIA THERESA (1717—80), Empress of Austria and Queen of Hungary and Bohemia. The daughter of Emperor Charles VI, she inherited on his death in 1740, by virtue of the Pragmatic Sanction (q.v.), the Hapsburg dominions of Austria, Hungary and Bohemia, and in 1745 became co-regent of the Holy Roman Empire with her husband, Francis I, who died in 1765. Her succession as a young and inexperienced female seemed a good opportunity to her neighbours, and, breaking their promises, Bavaria, Prussia, Naples, France and Spain disputed it. Charles of Bavaria invaded Austria and Bohemia, and was elected Emperor as Charles VII; Frederick of Prussia annexed Silesia, the most valuable of the Hapsburg territories. In the War of the Austrian Succession (1740—48) which followed, Britain and Holland helped Maria Theresa against Prussia and France. By the Treaty of Aix-la-Chapelle Maria retained all her possessions except Silesia and parts of Italy. In the Seven Years War (1756—63) she failed to regain Silesia. In 1772 she tried to prevent, and then joined in, the first Partition of Poland, gaining Galicia. She devoted her last 17 years to internal reform. A benevolent despot, she improved education, codified the laws, abolished torture and preached religious toleration, except for the Jesuits. She had 16 children, one of whom was Marie Antoinette; her eldest son succeeded his father as Emperor and his mother as Hapsburg ruler. Beautiful, pious, unforgiving and an efficient administrator, she was the first to unify the Hapsburg rule.

MARIANA ISLANDS, an archipelago in the Western Pacific. Pop. 44,000; area 450 sq. miles. Consisting of about 15 islands, both volcanic and coral atolls, the group produces sugar, copra and phosphates. Fishing is important. The chief islands are Guam, Saipan, Tinian and Rota. Discovered by Magellan in 1521 and called by him the Ladrones Islands, they were a Spanish possession until 1899. The U.S.A. then took Guam and Germany purchased the remaining islands, which after the First World War became mandated to Japan. In 1947 the U.S.A. was given a U.N. trusteeship over the Japanese islands. The capital is Saipan.

MARIE ANTOINETTE (1755—93), Queen of France. The daughter of Maria Theresa, she married (1770) the Dauphin of France (later Louis XVI) and entered into the dissolute life of his pleasure-seeking court. The unpopularity she incurred by the mere fact of being Austrian was deepened by her frivolity, extravagance and flouting of French etiquette. She was easily suspected of encouraging her vacillating husband to refuse concessions, of being responsible for the abortive flight to Varennes (see French Revolution), of plotting foreign intervention and betraying French plans to the enemy. When arrested with the king, she faced her accusers and went to the guillotine commanding the admiration even of her enemies.

MARIINSK CANAL, a waterway system in the R.S.F.S.R., U.S.S.R., 350 miles long. It connects the Volga with Lake Onega and, linking up with other waterways, provides inland water transport between Moscow and Leningrad.

MARK, St, John Mark, the companion of St Paul on the latter's first missionary journey (Acts xii. v. 25) and, according to tradition, the author of the Gospel of St Mark which was dictated by St Peter.

MARK ANTONY, see Antony, Mark.

MARLBOROUGH, John Churchill, 1st Duke of (1650—1722), English general and statesman. Son of Sir Winston Churchill, he married in 1677 Sarah Jennings (1660—1744), a friend of Princess Anne. He was made a baron by James, Duke of York, and defeated Monmouth at Sedgemoor (1685). In 1688 he deserted the Royalists for William of Orange, excusing himself on the ground, which was true, that he was after all a Protestant. William rewarded him with an earldom. By 1691 he was insuring himself against a Stuart restoration by intriguing with the Jacobites, and the following year he was put in the Tower on evidence subsequently proved to have been forged. In 1698 he was restored to favour and, on Anne's accession in 1702, made a duke. Marlborough commanded the English and Dutch forces in the War of the Spanish Succession, winning famous victories at Blenheim, Ramillies, Oudenarde and Malplaquet (1709). The Tories ousted the Whigs in 1710, Anne and Sarah quarrelled, Mrs Masham, a tool of Harley, replaced Sarah, and Harley replaced the Duke, who was found guilty by parliament of embezzlement and forced to flee to Holland. He returned in 1714, welcomed by George I who restored all his honours, but he was already a sick man and with his wife retired to Blenheim Palace, given him by Queen Anne.

Marlborough never lost a battle, and showed a remarkable grasp not only of tactics but of the grand strategy of land and sea forces. In money matters he was certainly mean, but it is difficult to assess the truth of the many attacks on his probity in view of the disreputable character of his enemies and the bias of Whig historians.

MARLOWE, Christopher (1564—93), English dramatist. Chiefly concerned with the conflict between reason and faith, he exerted considerable influence on Shakespeare. His outstanding works include *Tamberlaine*, *Doctor Faustus*, *The Jew of Malta* and *Edward* II, which first revealed the potentialities of English blank verse on the stage. A member of a group of free thinkers, he became involved in London's underworld, and perhaps acted as a government spy. A warrant was issued for his arrest as an atheist, but before it could be executed he was killed in a 'drunken tavern brawl', which may, however, have been stage-managed.

MARMORA (Marmara), the sea separating Asia Minor from European Turkey. It has an area of 4500 sq. miles, a length of 175 miles and a maximum depth of 4250 ft. The Bosporus links it to the Black Sea, and the Dardanelles to the Aegean. It is the ancient Propontis.

MARQUESAS, an island group in French Polynesia. Pop. 4170; area 480 sq. miles. The largest islands are Nuka-Hiva and Hiva-Oa. Sugar-cane, bananas and copra are produced. The chief town is Atuoua, the burial place of Paul Gauguin, the French artist. When discovered in 1595, the islands had a population of 100,000. Disease brought by Europeans destroyed them almost entirely.

MARRAKESH, a city in Morocco, at the foot of the Great Atlas Mountains. Pop. (1960) 243,134. A trading centre, it produces textiles and foodstuffs. Marrakesh is the southern capital of Morocco; it is said to have had a population of 700,000 in the 13th century. The old town is very dilapidated, but its geographical position gives it great potentialities for future development.

MARRIAGE, social recognition of the union of a man and woman as husband and wife. Legally, it is a contract involving certain responsibilities. The forms of marriage include monogamy, polygamy, polyandry and group marriage. In endogamous marriage one may marry only within one's group, while exogamy forbids marriage inside the group. In a morganatic marriage the inferior partner and the children may not inherit the spouse's titles or estate. In Christian societies the Church has always regulated matrimonial relations and discouraged civil ceremonies, which are binding in most countries. A Common Law marriage is one in which the couple can prove that they have been living together for a definite period. Generally, the law forbids marriages between persons within specified degrees of kinship. In 1935, English law granted women equal rights in the marriage relationship in regard to ownership of property and certain other matters.

MARS, the fourth planet from the sun in our solar system. It is about 141,700,000 miles from the sun and the shortest distance between it and the earth is 34½ million miles. Moving at an average speed of 15 miles per second, it takes 687 days to complete a revolution around the sun. Its diameter is 4215 miles and it has two small satellites. Mars has a thin atmosphere and polar caps which vary in size with the seasons. Most of its surface has a reddish or orange colour, representing desert areas, but there are greenish patches which change in area and colour, and may be due to some primitive form of vegetation. The existence of fine straight lines (canals) has not been conclusively demonstrated. Any life on Mars would be very primitive; though the temperature may reach 50° F. at noon, night temperatures are very low, and there appears to be no oxygen present.

MARSEILLES, a French city and port on the Mediterranean. Pop. (1962) 783,738. A commercial and industrial centre, it manufactures ships, aircraft, glass, chemicals and wines, and has oil refineries. It is the country's principal port. Among the interesting buildings is the *Ville Radieuse* of Le Corbusier (q.v.). One of the oldest cities in Europe, it was colonised by the Greeks in the 7th century B.C. Julius Caesar captured it in 49 B.C. After the decline of the Roman Empire, it was ravaged by Goths, Burgundians, Franks and Saracens. It became part of France in 1481.

MARSHALL ISLANDS, an archipelago in the North Pacific Ocean. Pop. (1961) 15,399; area 150 sq. miles. The chief crop is coconuts. Ruled by Germany until the First World War, the islands were a Japanese mandate until the end of the Second World War when they became an American trusteeship. The islands of Bikini and Eniwetok are testing sites for U.S. atomic bombs.

MARTEL, Charles, see Charles Martel.

MARTINIQUE, an island in the French West Indies. Pop. (1960) 274,000; area 420 sq. miles. Mountainous and dominated by the volcanic Mt Pelée, which destroyed the old capital of St Pierre in 1902, the island produces sugar-cane, rum, bananas and pineapples, and rum is exported. The population is mostly Negro and mulatto. It has been French since 1635. The new capital is Fort-de-France (60,648).

MARX, Karl (1818—83), German Socialist philosopher. Educated at the University of Jena, he became the editor (1842) of the *Rheinische Zeitung* of Cologne, which was suppressed because of its liberalism. Marx went to Paris, where he met Friedrich Engels and became a convert to Socialism. Together they wrote *The Communist Manifesto* (1848) for the League of Communists. In 1848 he emigrated to England where he spent the rest of his life. In 1864 he was instrumental in founding, and largely directed the policy of, the International Working-men's Association, which later became known as the First International. The first volume of his book *Das Kapital* was published in 1867. The other two volumes were written by Engels from Marx's notes and published posthumously. See Communism.

MARY (Blessed Virgin Mary), the mother of Jesus. Betrothed but not yet married to the Galilean carpenter Joseph, Mary was visited (according to Luke, but not Matthew) by the angel Gabriel and informed that she would conceive and bear 'the Son of the Highest'. Mary appears from time to time in the New Testament narratives of Jesus' ministry. She has been especially venerated by the Roman Catholic and Orthodox Eastern churches as having intercessory powers for sinners. See Immaculate Conception.

MARY QUEEN OF SCOTS (1542—87), Queen and last Catholic ruler of Scotland. The daughter of James V of Scotland, she inherited the throne when she was six days old. At the age of 16 she married the 14-year-old dauphin who became Francis II of France. He died two years later and Mary returned to Protestant Scotland, where she was crowned. In 1565 she married Darnley (q.v.) and after his assassination she married Bothwell (q.v.) who, although formally acquitted of the murder, was everywhere regarded as guilty. The Scottish barons rose and forced her to abdicate. She was held prisoner, but in 1568 escaped and fled, against advice, to Elizabeth for protection. Elizabeth kept her in custody for the rest of her life. She was constantly accused of plotting against the Queen and finally found guilty. She was executed at Fotheringay Castle.

MARY (1867—1953), Queen consort of George V of England. Daughter of the Duke and Duchess of Teck, she married in 1893. She became especially popular during the First World War for her services on behalf of wounded soldiers.

MARY I (1516—58), Queen of England from 1553—58. After her father, Henry VIII, divorced her mother, Catherine of Aragon, Mary was declared illegitimate. On the death of Edward VI (1553) she succeeded to the throne, although Lady Jane Grey, whom Edward VI had been persuaded to nominate as his successor, had been proclaimed a few weeks earlier. She had Lady Jane executed, together with her husband and father. An ardent Catholic, she married Philip II of Spain, who left her after a year. The extent of her responsibility for the persecutions of Protestants which gave her the name 'Bloody Mary' is not clear. Cranmer, Latimer and Ridley were among those who went to the stake. Her last three years were spent in illness and misery. At Philip's persuasion she entered into a war with France which lost her Calais and probably hastened her end.

MARY II (1662—94), Queen of England, Scotland and Ireland (1689—94). The elder daughter of James II and the consort of William III, she was appointed joint sovereign with her husband after her father had been deposed.

MARY MAGDALENE, a woman of Magdala possessed of demons who was healed by Jesus. She was present at the Crucifixion and was among the group of women who found the sepulchre empty on the first Easter Sunday. It was to her that the risen Christ first appeared.

MARYLAND, South Atlantic state, U.S.A. Pop. (1960) 3,038,156; area 10,577 sq. miles. It has a coastal plain merging with a central hilly region which becomes mountainous in the west. Tomatoes, cereals, hay, potatoes and tobacco are the principal agricultural products. Poultry and other livestock are important sources of income. Chesapeake Bay, which almost bisects the state, produces large quantities of sea-food. Coal, sand and gravel are the chief mineral products. The principal industries are steel manufacturing and copper smelting. First settled in 1634, Maryland was one of the original 13 states. The capital is Annapolis (pop. 23,385). Baltimore is the largest city (929,024).

MASARYK, Jan (1886—1948), Czech statesman and son of T. Masaryk (q.v.), he was connected with the embassies in Washington and London before becoming, in 1940, Foreign Minister to the Czech government that was provisionally reconstituted in London that year. His broadcasts to occupied Czechoslovakia during the war brought him popularity and he was invited to continue as Foreign Minister after the revolutionary events of February 1948. He held the office until his death one month later, when he threw himself from his office window.

MASARYK, Thomas (1850—1937), Czechoslovak patriot and statesman. In Paris during the First World War, he organised the movement for Czech independence. He was elected president of the Czechoslovak Republic in 1918 and served in this capacity till 1935. He had in earlier life made his name as a sociologist and philosopher.

MASCAGNI, Pietro (1863—1945), Italian operatic composer. Famous as a conductor, he is best known for his opera *Cavalleria Rusticana.*

MASEFIELD, John (1878—), English poet laureate, dramatist and novelist. He was appointed poet laureate in 1930. His outstanding poetic works include *Salt Water Ballads* and *On the Hill* and the long poems *The Everlasting Mercy, The Widow in the Bye Street* and *The Dauber.*

MASERS (Lasers), a discovery of the 1950s with vast potentialities. The original maser (microwave amplification by stimulated emission of radiation) was employed to amplify very high-frequency signals without the generation of background noise. It was found that the same principles could be applied to the propagation of light. Ordinary light beams are neither continuous nor well focused (they are 'incoherent'), and thus range and sharpness are limited; they also lose intensity by passing through a medium. In the optical maser (sometimes called laser: *l* for light, the term microwave no longer being appropriate) a device was made to propagate coherent light, highly focused over a long range, which absorbs energy from an intervening medium to emerge brighter than before. This can be beamed vast distances through a telescope, and in one experiment illumined an area of the moon no more than three miles across. It can also be focused to a needle of intense light which has vaporised an industrial diamond.

The potentialities of lasers are still being explored. Among them are: use in a radar warning system of far greater range and accuracy than orthodox radar, or to measure interplanetary distances to within an inch.

MASS, the English term for the Latin *Missa* which is used chiefly by the Roman Catholic Church to denote the service of the Eucharist (q.v.). There are four distinct types: the Pontifical, High, Sung and Low Mass.

MASSACHUSETTS, a northeastern state, on the Atlantic Ocean, U.S.A. Pop. (1960) 5,148,578; area 8257 sq. miles. Hilly and generally low in the east, it consists of a plateau merging into mountains in the west. In the southeast is the low and occasionally marshy peninsula of Cape Cod. Ample hydroelectric power and transport facilities have made the state predominantly industrial. Its principal manufactures include textiles, footwear, foundry and machine shop products, chemicals, foods, building materials, rubber goods, sawmill products and shipbuilding. The cod fisheries are of great importance. Dairy products, poultry, fruit and vegetables are produced. There are 40 colleges and universities in the state. First settled in 1620 by the Pilgrim Fathers, at Plymouth, the state played a leading part in the struggle to secede from the mother country. The capital is Boston (pop. 697,197). Other important cities are Worcester (186,587), Springfield (174,463) and Cambridge (107,716).

MASSENET, Jules Émile Frédéric (1842—1912), French composer. He was professor of composition at the Paris Conservatory. In addition to cantatas, overtures, orchestral suites, and an oratorio, he wrote the operas *Le Cid*, *Thais* and *Hérodiade (Salome)*, and his masterpiece *Manon* (1884).

MASSEY, Vincent (1887—), Canadian Liberal statesman. Born at Toronto, and educated at Toronto and Oxford universities, he served as Minister to the U.S.A. (1926—30), High Commissioner in the U.K. (1935—46) and delegate to the League of Nations Assembly from 1936. He became the first Canadian-born Governor-General in 1952. His brother is the actor, Raymond Massey.

MASSEY, William Ferguson (1856—1925), New Zealand Conservative statesman. Born in Northern Ireland, he went to New Zealand when young, where he was a member of parliament from 1894 till his death. He was Prime Minister (1912—22) and a member of the Imperial War Cabinet (1917—18).

MASTERS, Edgar Lee (1869—1950), American poet, author of the *Spoon River Anthology* (1915), written in free verse and contrasting the real characters of various Middle Western worthies with the eulogies that appeared on their tombstones.

MATERIALISM, a school of philosophy which holds that only matter is actually existent and that therefore the soul of man is not supernatural, but simply the effect of the physical organisation of the body. Democritus in ancient times, and Hobbes in more modern times, were leading exponents of this view.

MATHEMATICS, the science of quantities and magnitudes and their interrelationships organised in a logical pattern. Pure mathematics, which deals with logical variables, includes arithmetic, algebra, and the study of infinity and the infinitesimal. The mathematical aspects of mechanics, physics, geodesy and geophysics, and astronomy are included in the realm of applied mathematics. Widely applicable in numerous fields, mathematics is considered the principal source of rational science.

MATISSE, Henri (1869—1954), French artist. A master of line and colour, he was a leader of the Fauves (q.v.). A lithographer and sculptor as well, his famous works include the interior designs in the chapel of St Marie du Rosaire, near Nice.

MATO GROSSO, a state in southwest Brazil. Pop. (1960) 910,262; area 487,482 sq. miles. The largest state in the country, it consists of a vast plateau bearing the same name which divides the Amazon and Paraguay river systems. Cattle-ranching is the chief occupation. It has large undeveloped deposits of gold, silver, lead, manganese, platinum and diamonds. The capital is Cuiabá.

MATTHEW, St, one of the apostles of Jesus (probably identical with the Levi of Mark and Luke). A tax collector (publican) by profession, he is traditionally regarded as the author or editor of the Gospel of St Matthew.

MAUGHAM, William Somerset (1874—1965), English author and dramatist. His novels include *Of Human Bondage*, *The Moon and Sixpence* and *Cakes and Ale*. His best work is contained in his short stories, mostly acid in tone, written in a taut economical style which has won him many admirers; four of the best were filmed as *Quartet*. He had the unendearing practice of including in his work vitriolic and recognisable portraits of his not always voluntary hosts during his travels in the east. His plays include *Our Betters*; he also wrote essays.

MAU-MAU, a terrorist underground movement of the Kikuyu tribes in Kenya which waged ruthless warfare against Europeans in the colony from 1952—57; the core of the movement were probably nationalists fighting for independence, but they were joined by large numbers of thugs whose atrocities it will take a long time to forget. The revolting oaths which members were made to take may have been confined to the thug element, or the account of them may have been exaggerated during the extreme tension of that time, when European settlers, especially those living on isolated farms, carried on with great bravery though in constant danger.

MAUPASSANT, Guy de (1850—93), French novelist and short-story writer. Influenced by Flaubert, he wrote stories in a strongly realistic vein and established his reputation with the masterly short story *Boule de Suif* (1880). His better-known works include *Bel Ami* (1885) and *A Woman's Life* (1883). Maupassant attempted suicide in 1891 and was committed to an asylum where he remained till his death.

MAURIAC, François (1885—), French novelist and dramatist. Probing deeply into the conflicts besetting the Roman Catholic, he wrote *The Kiss to the Leper*, *Génitrix*, *The Desert of Love*, *Thérèse Desqueyroux* and *Viper's Tangle*. He also wrote poetry, biographies and essays. In 1952 he was awarded the Nobel Prize for literature.

MAURITANIA, Islamic Republic of, a republic in northwest Africa, on the Atlantic Ocean. Pop. (1961) 727,000; area 419,230 sq. miles. Part of the western

Sahara, it consists of a sandy plain with scattered hills. The chief products are cattle, gum, salt, beans and dried fish. There are considerable deposits of iron and copper. A French possession from the end of the 19th century, it became independent in 1960. Its territory is claimed by Morocco. The capital is Nouakchott.

MAURITIUS, a British island colony in the Indian Ocean, 500 miles east of Malagasy. Pop. (1961) 687,450; area 805 sq. miles. Mostly flat, it is mountainous in the south. Its chief crop is sugar. Tea, tobacco and timber are important products. Abandoned by the Dutch, who first settled it in 1598, the island became French in 1710, and was occupied by the British in 1810. The capital is Port Louis (pop. 104,016).

MAUROIS, André (Émile Herzog; 1885—), French biographer, novelist and essayist. His works include biographies of Shelley, Byron and Disraeli. A shrewd but kindly critic of the British, his experiences as an interpreter in the British Army in the First World War produced *Les Silences du Colonel Bramble.*

MAYA, an American Indian people who inhabited the region southeast of Mexico. The Old Empire began in A.D. 317, reached its peak in the 8th century and ended 200 years later. It was succeeded in the 10th—11th centuries by the New Empire in the northern part of Maya territory, in Yucatan. It was marked by the infiltration of the Toltecs who introduced a Mexican culture (the Plumed Serpent — Quetzalcoatl — and human sacrifice). This empire prospered for 200 years; there was civil war in 1194 and it came to a virtual end in 1441. When the Spaniards arrived in 1527 they found it in an advanced state of disintegration. The basis of both empires was the shifting cultivation of rich soil in freshly cleared forest. The Maya had no metal, a fact which makes their achievements in farming and building the more remarkable. Crops were divided one-third each to nobles, priests and farmers. There are still some two million Maya-speaking people, on the whole little changed except outwardly. There are very numerous remains of their astonishing buildings, huge temples, truncated pyramids, and even some impressive mural paintings. The Maya invented an extremely accurate calendar system and a type of hieroglyphic script.

Mayan pyramid

MAYFLOWER, a three-masted, double-decked English merchant ship of about 180 tons which brought the Pilgrim Fathers from England to Plymouth (New England) after a three months' voyage in 1620. There were 102 passengers on board.

MAZARIN, Jules (1602—61), an Italian by birth, took French nationality in 1639 and was nominated by Richelieu as his successor. He prosecuted the Thirty Years War with vigour and, during Louis XIV's minority, consolidated the power of the monarchy after defeating a revolt by the nobles (the Fronde). He amassed an enormous fortune, some of which he used to patronise the arts.

Mayflower

MECCA, the most important holy city of the Moslem world, and the capital of Hejaz, in Saudi Arabia. Pop. (1962) *c.* 150,000. It lies east of its Red Sea port of Jidda, in a narrow valley surrounded by rocky hills. The birthplace of Mohammed, it is a centre of pilgrimage visited annually by more than 125,000 Moslems. The most important rite of the pilgrims is to walk seven times around the Ka'aba, a massive, cube-like structure whose construction is attributed to Abraham. Non-Moslems are not permitted inside the city. A contract was placed in 1963 for the rebuilding of the railway to Maan (and Damascus), disused since it was severed in the First World War by troops under Lawrence of Arabia.

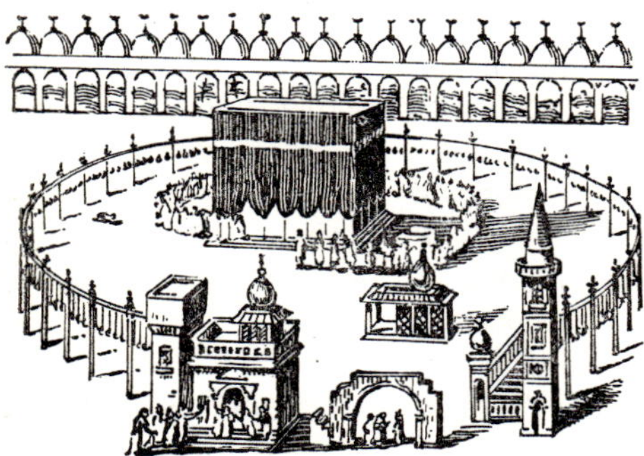

Ka'aba at Mecca

MEDELLIN, a city in Colombia, South America. Pop. (1962) 690,710. A communications and commercial centre, it is an important industrial city. It manufactures textiles, metal goods, leather, foodstuffs and tobacco products. There is a university, and many interesting buildings survive from the colonial period.

MEDICI, one of the leading families in Italy during the 14th—16th centuries. They rose to power under Giovanni (1360—1429), a Florentine banker who amassed a huge fortune. Among the more prominent members of the family were: Cosimo de Medici (1389—1464), Lorenzo the Magnificent (*c.* 1449—92), the popes Leo X, Leo XI and Clement VII, and Catherine de Medici of France. The Medici line came to an end in 1737.

MEDICINE, the science concerned with the restoration and preservation of health. The careful observations of Hippocrates and his rejection of prevalent views regarding the supernatural origins of disease marked a turning point in the medicine of the ancients. The work of Claude Bernard, William Harvey, Louis Pasteur, Joseph Lister, Robert Koch and many other research scientists of the 19th century laid the foundation of modern medicine. The invention of sensitive machines and instruments, the discovery of new drugs such as insulin and antibiotic substances, new techniques for diagnosing ailments, increasing specialisation, and rigorous requirements for persons studying medicine, have made it possible to cure diseases which in past years exacted a heavy toll of human life and suffering. Experimentation and the utilisation of other branches of science are a distinguishing feature of modern medicine.

The introduction of health programmes under government direction in many countries, e.g. the National Health Service in Great Britain, has made medical services available to people who might otherwise be deprived of such benefits for lack of financial means.

MEDINA, a Moslem holy city in the Hejaz, Saudi Arabia, about 200 miles north of Mecca. Pop. 50,000. The second-holiest city in Islam, it was the scene of Mohammed's activity after his flight from Mecca. He is traditionally said to be buried under the El Haram mosque. Non-Moslems may not enter the city.

MEDITERRANEAN, the largest enclosed sea in the world, on the shores of Europe, Africa and Asia. About 2300 miles long, its width varies from 1200 to 100 miles, its total area being about 1,000,000 sq. miles; it is almost tideless. The maximum depth is 15,564 ft. It communicates with the Atlantic Ocean by the Strait of Gibraltar; with the Black Sea, through the Dardanelles, Sea of Marmora and the Bosporus; and with the Indian Ocean, by the Suez Canal and Red Sea. The principal rivers draining into it are the Rhône, Po, Ebro and Nile. Its chief islands are the Balearic Islands, Sardinia, Corsica, Sicily, Malta, Crete, Cyprus, and the Ionian and Greek archipelagos. The Mediterranean has been a centre of civilisation, a highway of commerce, and a focus of power politics since the dawn of history.

MEERUT, a city in Uttar Pradesh, India. Pop. (1961) 283,878. An important rail junction, it has factories for processing cotton and manufacturing chemicals, flour and soap. Dating back to 250 B.C., the city was taken by Moslem invaders in 1191. The first outbreaks of the Indian Mutiny (1857) took place in Meerut.

MEKNÈS, a city in Morocco. Pop. (1960) 177,100. One of the capitals of the country, it is a commercial and industrial centre. Leather and earthenware are manufactured.

MEKONG, see River.

MELANCHTHON (1497—1560), the adopted name of a German theologian and close friend of Martin Luther. He was largely responsible for the formulation of the Augsburg Confession (1530). See Lutheranism.

MELANESIA, Western Pacific islands comprising the Bismarck Archipelago, Solomon Islands, New Hebrides, and the Louisiade, Santa Cruz and Loyalty islands as far as, and including, New Caledonia and the Fiji Islands. The inhabitants are short, dark, with frizzy black hair and negroid features; they are akin to the Papuans of New Guinea, with some Polynesian blood.

MELBOURNE, a city in Australia, capital of Victoria, at the mouth of the Yarra River. Pop. (1961) 1,907,366. A seaport with many beautiful suburbs, it is a cultural and commercial centre. It has large livestock markets.

MEMORY, the mental retention and reproduction of events previously experienced. The intensity of a memory depends on when it was retained and under what emotional circumstances, the frequency of its repetition, the degree of interference by other memories, the motivation for its recall, and the age and ability of the individual. Unconscious memories also exert a decisive influence on the personality.

MEMPHIS, a city and port in Tennessee, U.S.A. Pop. (1960) 497,524. On the Mississippi River, it is an important commercial and distributing centre. It is a road and rail junction with a large cotton market. Memphis is a leading producer of cotton-seed products and is a distributing point for hardwood timber, steel products, drugs and chemicals. The city has many institutions of higher learning.

MENDEL, Gregor Johann (1822—84), Austrian botanist and abbot. He established the fact that heredity is governed by certain mathematical laws. Mendel demonstrated that hybrids resulting from the crossing of two species exhibit the dominant traits of one parent but their offspring display those of both grandparents, in the proportion 3 : 1. His work, unnoticed during his lifetime, was rediscovered in 1900.

MENDELÉEV, Dmitri Ivanovich (1834—1907), Russian chemist. He compiled the Periodic Table of elements, classifying them according to atomic weight. He found that certain groups of elements in this table had similar properties, and was able to predict the existence and properties of elements unknown at the time, three of which were discovered before he died.

MENDELSSOHN-BARTHOLDY, Felix (1809—47), German musician and composer, grandson of the philosopher Moses Mendelssohn. He began composing when only 12 years of age. In 1835 he was appointed director of the Gewandhaus concerts in Leipzig, and in 1841 became the King of Prussia's Kapellmeister. Among his more famous works are: *Songs without Words* (1833), *Midsummer Night's Dream* (1843), the oratorio, *Elijah* (1846), the Violin Concerto and the Fourth (Italian) Symphony.

MENDOZA, a city in Argentina. Pop. (1954) 115,161. At the foot of the Andes, in a wine-producing district, it lies on two rivers and is connected to Valparaiso by a railway over the Andes. The principal occupations are wine-making and fruit-drying. It also has cement plants and oil refineries. Founded in 1562, it belonged to Chile until 1776.

MENSTRUATION, the periodic discharge of bloody fluid from the uterus. In women, it begins at puberty between the ages of 11 and 16 and continues normally until middle age. Occurring once in every 28—30 days, it takes place about 14 days after ovulation and lasts for 3—6 days. It is caused by the elimination of the lining of the uterus (endometrium) when no fertilised egg is attached to it. Pregnancy suspends menstruation.

MENTAL DEFICIENCY (called in U.S.A. Feeblemindedness), the possession of a sub-normal intellect, is defined in British law as arrested or incomplete mental development existing before the age of 18. In law the mentally defective are classified as follows (the percentage of normal intelligence being shown in brackets): idiots (0—20%), those unable to guard themselves against common physical dangers; imbeciles (20—50 %), unable to manage their own affairs, and cannot be taught to do so; feeble-minded, formerly called simpletons, and in U.S.A. morons (70 %), requiring protection, both for their own sakes and for others', and having the mental age of 10; morally defective, any of the above classes, with added vicious or criminal tendencies. Cretins are in a class apart, since the cause is physical (thyroid deficiency) and the condition is accompanied by marked physical symptoms.

MENTAL HYGIENE, the application of psychology and psychiatry to the prevention of mental disorders and the furthering of mental health. It strives to teach the individual how to avoid conflicts and achieve personal happiness and social usefulness, and is also concerned with treating instability and faulty adjustment.

MENZIES, Sir Robert Gordon (1894—), Australian lawyer and statesman. He was first elected to the Federal House of Representatives in 1934, serving as Attorney-General from 1934—39, and as Prime Minister from 1939—41, when he was defeated by the Labour party. He formed a new Liberal party in 1943, and was again Prime Minister from 1949. When re-elected in 1963, at the head of a Liberal-Country party coalition, he had almost doubled the record for length of tenure of the Australian premiership.

MERCATOR, Gerardus (Gerhard Kremer; 1512—94), Flemish geographer, mathematician and cartographer. He developed the science of map projection for many different kinds of map. His principal work was his *Atlas*, a word he introduced. Mercator's projection is a method of map projection still used on nautical charts, as it enables all compass bearings to be shown as straight lines.

MERCIA, an ancient Anglo-Saxon kingdom in central England. Founded about 582, it was independent until about 827, when it merged with the kingdom of Wessex. Tamworth was the royal, and Lichfield the ecclesiastical capital.

MERCURY, see Elements.

MEREDITH, George (1828—1909), British novelist and poet. The keynote of his work is a horror of the commonplace; his characters move in an intellectual, aristocratic world where a careless phrase or gesture may spell doom. His best novels are *The Ordeal of Richard Feverel*, *Beauchamp's Career*, *The Egoist* and *Diana of the Crossways*. His best verse is in *Modern Love*.

MESHED, a city in northeast Iran. Pop. (1956) 242,165. Situated 3197 ft above sea-level, on the Kashaf River, it is a communications and trading centre for the entire region and the centre of pilgrimage for Shi'ite Moslems. Manufactures include silks, carpets and cotton goods.

MESOPOTAMIA, the region in southwest Asia between the Tigris and Euphrates rivers. Its southern and more important portion lies in the modern state of Iraq; here were located the ancient countries of Sumer, Akkad and Babylonia. Assyria was located in the North.

MESSIAH, a Hebrew word meaning 'anointed', which in the Old Testament was applied to any King of Israel. Later it came to mean to the Jews the ruler who would one day establish the Kingdom of God on earth; to the Christians this was Christ, the Greek word for Messiah (see Christ).

MESSINA, a city in Sicily. Pop. (1961) 251,423. An important port in the centre of a rich fruit-growing region, it has fruit-extract industries and silk manufactures. Fishing is a leading occupation. An ancient city, it suffered severe earthquakes in 1783 and 1908. It is on the Strait of Messina, a 19-mile-long body of water separating Italy from Sicily.

MEŠTROVIĆ, Ivan (1883—1962), Yugoslav sculptor. He executed subjects from Slavonic folklore, mythology and religion, and designed numerous war memorials. His bust of *Masaryk* is in the Tate Gallery, London. He lived in

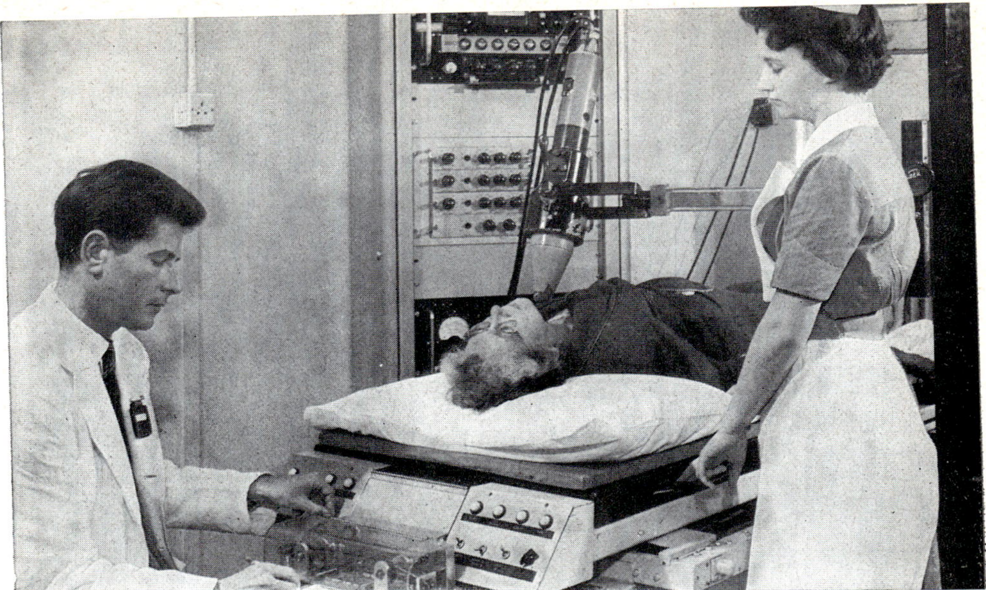

In order to trace the size and shape of this patient's thyroid gland a minute tracer dose of radioactive iodine, which concentrates in the gland, has been administered. By means of the scintillation counter held over the neck a colour picture of the gland is printed at the operator's end of the couch.

Photo: United Kingdom Atomic Energy Authority

Scintillation counters are also used in the detection of brain tumours. Here the patient is given an intravenous injection of a radioactive isotope which is taken up more by the tumour than by the normal brain.

Photo: United Kingdom Atomic Energy Authority

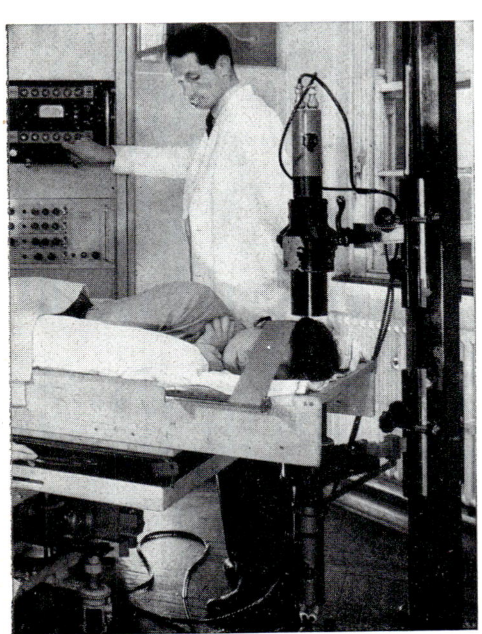

Two pairs of scintillation counters are used here for the study of heart and lung function. In this case air containing minute quantities of radioactive oxygen is administered to the patient.

Photo: United Kingdom Atomic Energy Authority

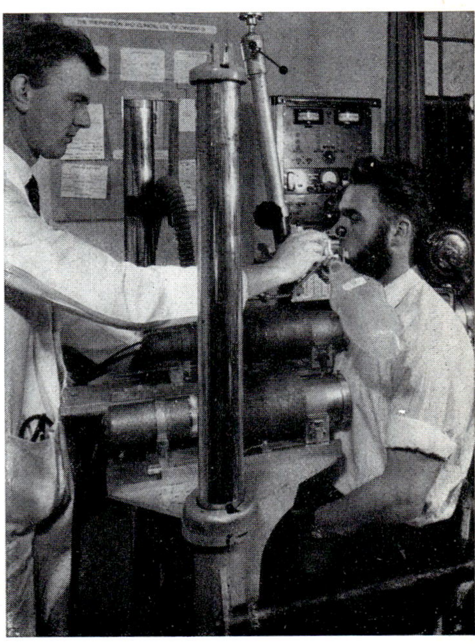

A steam generating heavy water reactor under construction. Essentially an experimental machine for study of the system, this reactor will produce 300,000 kilowatts of heat and will supply 100,000 kilowatts of electrical energy.

Photo: United Kingdom Atomic Energy Authority

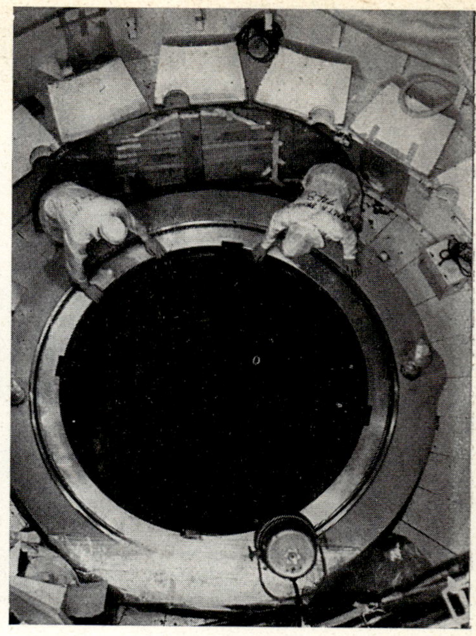

Looking down into the core of the nuclear reactor aboard the N.S. *Savannah*, the first atomic powered merchant vessel built.

Photo: United States Information Service

The N.S. *Savannah* passing down river at Camden, New Jersey, for its first sea trials.

Photo: United States Information Service

France and England during the First World War, and later went to live in the U.S.A.

METABOLISM, the chemical processes necessary for the survival of the living organism. It includes the breaking down of substances into simpler forms, breathing, digestion, the repair and growth of cells, photosynthesis (q.v.) and reproductive functions.

METAL, a chemical element whose distinctive characteristics are a bright lustre, hardness, opaqueness, ductility, malleability, conductivity of heat and electricity, fusibility and high specific gravity. These characteristics vary considerably in different metals. The atoms of metallic elements have one, two or three electrons in their outer shell which they give up during chemical actions, producing positive ions. Copper is the oldest known metal, and iron the most important (see Elements).

METAPHYSICS, the branch of philosophical thought which investigates the nature and essence of the basic concepts (first or primary principles) such as matter, time and space, and the purpose of creation or 'the meaning of life'. The name is derived from the title of Aristotle's book on the subject, *meta ta phusika*. The subject has two main divisions: Ontology, the study of Being, of what really exists and whether it is material, mental, ideal or spiritual; and Epistemology, the study of how anything can be known.

METCHNIKOV, Ilya (1845—1916), Russian biologist. He discovered the process of immunity against diseases. His *Immunity in Infectious Diseases* was published in 1901. In 1908 he shared the Nobel Prize for Physiology and Medicine with the bacteriologist Paul Ehrlich.

METEOROLOGY, properly the study of the physics of the atmosphere, but popularly used as the equivalent of weather forecasting. The study of the weather involves observations of atmospheric pressure, temperature, visibility, wind strength, humidity, precipitation (rain, snow, hail), cloud and sunshine. Lines are drawn on meteorological maps linking places with equal atmospheric pressure (isobars), temperature (isotherms), rainfall (isohyets), etc. A front is the boundary at the earth's surface between two air masses of different temperature, and it brings changes in the weather. In a cold front a cold mass of air is driven towards a mass of warm air, which rises sharply above it. Atmospheric pressure rises, temperature falls, and there may be heavy showers. The surface of a warm front is driven up over the cold air mass at a less steep angle, leading to considerable rainfall at first; then the wind changes, temperature rises and rainfall diminishes. Warm fronts are common in high latitudes during the winter. A depression is a region of low pressure, up to 2000 miles across and moving at any speed from very slowly to 700 miles a day; strong winds blow round it, anti-clockwise in the north, clockwise in the south. They bring much cloud, rain and unsettled weather generally. An anticyclone is a high-pressure region with lighter winds blowing in the reverse direction to those of the depression. They bring fine weather in the summer, but fog in the winter.

METEORS, small particles which enter the earth's atmosphere and are heated to incandescence before being totally consumed (shooting stars). What falls to earth is called a meteorite. Meteors and meteorites are stony or metal fragments, mostly iron. They are generally believed to be remnants of shattered planets. Some meteors move in swarms round the sun; the earth passes through some of these each year, e.g. the Geminids in December, the Perseids in August and the Leonids about November 14.

METHODISM, the name given to the various churches and organisations which trace their origin to the Holy Club, founded at Oxford in 1729 by Charles Wesley, which was in derision called 'methodist' by fellow students. The spiritual birth of Methodism may be said to be the religious experience undergone by John Wesley in 1738. These two elements — the 'method' and organisation of the Holy Club and the evangelistic fervour of a personal religious experience — combined to make up the spiritual genius of Methodism. Today there are some 750,000 Methodists in Britain, where the organisation is presbyterian, and over ten million in the U.S.A., where it is episcopal. In 1932 the principal British sects, Wesleyan, Primitive and United Methodists, became one Church.

METRIC SYSTEM, a system of weights and linear, surface, and solid measurements based on decimal units. The following are the English equivalents of metric denominations:

1 centimetre $= \frac{1}{100}$ of a metre
= 0.3937 in.
1 metre = 3.28 ft.
1 litre = 1.76 pint.
1 sq. metre = 10.7639 sq. ft.
1 hectare = 2.471 acres.
1 gram = 0.353 oz. avdp.
1 kilogram = 1,000 grams
= 2.2046 lb.
1 metric ton = 1,000 kilograms
= 1.1023 short tons.

METTERNICH-WINNEBURG, Prince von (1773—1859), Austrian statesman. Ambassador to the court of Napoleon in 1806, he became the Chancellor and Minister of Foreign Affairs from 1809 until 1848 when he was forced by the revolution to flee to England. He presided over the Congress of Vienna (1814—15) and, in his later life, became the leading force for Conservatism in Europe, ruthlessly repressing any signs of liberalism or national independence.

MEXICAN WAR (1846—48), the conflict between the United States and Mexico which arose from the former's annexation of Texas (1845). The Americans conducted the war on two fronts; the northern under General Zachary Taylor, and the southern under General Winfield Scott. In both theatres the Americans were victorious and Mexico was forced to cede California, Nevada, Utah and parts of Arizona, Colorado, New Mexico and Wyoming to the U.S. for a compensation of $15 million.

MEXICO, a federal republic in Central America. Pop. (1960) 34,625,903; area 763,944 sq. miles. Situated between the Gulf of Mexico and the Pacific Ocean, Mexico consists of a series of plateaux enclosed on each side by mountain ranges nearly parallel to the coasts. The Yucatan peninsula in the southeast is low-lying and covered with dense jungle. Enjoying a wide variety of climatic conditions, Mexico grows grains, cotton, sugar, bananas, winter vegetables, tobacco, sisal and coffee. Livestock breeding and timber reserves are important. There are considerable deposits of petroleum, silver, lead, gold, coal, iron, zinc, graphite, manganese, sulphur, barytes, cement and other minerals. Although mining is the principal industry, more than 95% of the mining properties are foreign-owned. Before the arrival of the Aztecs, whose empire was conquered by Spain in 1519—21, the Mayas and Toltecs ruled the area. A war lasting from 1810—21 secured Mexican independence. From then until 1877, there were two emperors and a large number of dictators and presidents. Mexico lost large areas north of the Rio Grande to the U.S.A. After the lengthy dictatorship of Porfirio Diaz which ended in 1911, Mexico embarked on a period of far-reaching reforms. The capital is Mexico City (pop. 1960 3,223,606). Other leading cities are Guadalajara (734,346), Monterrey (596,993) and Puebla (287,952).

MEXICO CITY, the capital of Mexico. Pop. (1960) 3,223,606. Situated 7460 ft above sea-level, it is an important communications and distributing centre. Lack of cheap power has hampered its industrial development. Manufactures include tobacco, leather goods, soap, textiles, and work in gold and silver. Mexico City is the cultural centre of the nation and has several institutions of higher learning. Under the Aztec name of Tenochtitlan, it had a notable history before the Spaniards conquered and nearly destroyed it in 1521.

MEYERBEER, Giacomo (Jakob Liebmann Beer; 1791—1864), German operatic composer. A child prodigy, he composed church and incidental music, cantatas, an overture, an oratorio, and notable French and Italian operas, including *Robert le diable*, *Les Huguenots* and *L'Africaine.*

MIAMI, a city in southeast Florida, U.S.A. Pop. (1960) 291,688. A communications centre and seaport, it is adjacent to the celebrated winter resort of Miami Beach, which is an independent city (pop. 61,740). Its manufactures include metallurgical products, foodstuffs, furniture, chemicals and building materials. It has Agricultural and Mechanical colleges.

MICHELANGELO (Michelagniolo Buonarroti; 1475—1564), Italian sculptor, architect, painter and poet. An artist of wonderful range and power and one of the leading personalities of the Italian Renaissance, he composed sonnets, designed the dome of St Peter's in Rome, executed unsurpassed sculptures, notably *David*, and painted the story of the *Creation* on the ceiling, and the *Last Judgment* on the altar wall, of the Sistine Chapel in Rome.

MICHELSON, Albert Abraham (1852—1931), American physicist. He determined the velocity of light, using an interferometer he had invented. His demonstration that there were no relative movements between the earth and the ether paved the way for Einstein's theory of relativity. He was the first American to be awarded the Nobel Prize for physics (1907).

MICHIGAN, a north central state, U.S.A. Pop. (1960) 7,823,194; area 58,216 sq. miles. The state is divided by Lakes Michigan and Huron into Upper Peninsula, having a rough hilly surface, and Lower Peninsula, a low, gently rolling terrain. Mining and lumbering are the main occupations in the Upper Peninsula; agriculture and manufacturing in the Lower. The state has over 11,000 lakes. The principal crops are hay, cereals, sugar-beet, potatoes, soya beans and fruit. Livestock breeding is important. Michigan is predominantly industrial, primarily producing automobiles but also aircraft parts, engines, boilers and refrigerators. There are valuable fisheries. Iron, copper, cement, salt, gypsum and petroleum are found. First settled in 1668, it became a state in 1837. The capital is Lansing (pop. 1960 107,807). Other leading cities are Detroit (1,670,144), Flint (196,940) and Grand Rapids (177,313).

MICRONESIA, western Pacific islands, comprising the Mariana, Palau, Caroline, Marshall and Gilbert groups. The inhabitants are not racially distinct, but a mixture of Polynesian, Melanesian, Indonesian and Malayan races.

MIDDLESBROUGH, a municipal and county borough, North Riding of Yorkshire, England, on the Tees estuary. Pop. (1961) 157,308. In the midst of a large coal, iron and limestone region, it is an important port. The principal industries are iron and steel manufactures, shipbuilding and chemicals. The city experienced considerable growth in the last century because of improved transport facilities and the construction of blast furnaces.

MIDDLESEX, a county in southeast England, most of it part of metropolitan London. Pop. (1961) 2,230,093; area 232 sq. miles. It is mostly built up but there is some market gardening. Manufacturing includes metal works, breweries and chemicals. The county town is Brentford, but it is administered from the Guildhall, Westminster.

MIDLOTHIAN, a county in east central Scotland, on the Firth of Forth. Pop. (1961) 580,332. Mostly hilly, it produces grains, turnips and potatoes. Coal, limestone, fireclay and oil shales are found. Dairy farming and fishing are important. There are paper mills. The county town is Edinburgh.

MILAN, a city in Lombardy, North Italy, on the Olona River. Pop. (1961) 1,580,978. In the middle of a fertile plain, it is Italy's principal financial and industrial city and a commercial and communications centre. Its varied manufactures include heavy metallurgical equipment, automobiles, electrical appliances, chemicals, textiles, porcelain, musical and surgical instruments, and furniture. Milan is a publishing and music centre. There are a number of historic buildings, many severely damaged in the Second World War, and a university. In A.D. 303 Milan became the capital of North Italy. It was ravaged by Attila in 452 and by the Goths in 639. In 1395 it became a duchy, and was under Austrian rule from 1714 to 1796. Napoleon made it the capital of the kingdom of Italy in 1805, until it was restored to Austria in 1815. United with Sardinia in 1859, it became incorporated into Italy in 1861.

MILK, a secretion from the breasts or udders of mammals containing most substances essential to proper nutrition. In western cultures, man generally uses cow's milk as a beverage. Rich in vitamins (especially A and B-complex), it also contains fat, carbohydrates, proteins and important minerals, making it the most complete food.

MILL, John Stuart (1806—73), English philosopher and economist. Subjected to a severe and rigorous educational training, he followed in the footsteps of his father James Mill as a Utilitarian philosopher. His best-known works are: *Principles of Political Economy* (1848) *System of Logic* (1843) and the *Essay on Liberty*.

MILLAIS, Sir John Everett (1829—96), English painter. Chiefly known as a portraitist, he won fame with his paintings of historical subjects and landscapes. He was a founder of the Pre-Raphaelite movement in England. His work exhibits painstaking effort and a sense of the dramatic.

MILLET, Jean François (1814—75), French painter. His early life on a farm at Barbizon is reflected in most of his work. His outstanding paintings include *The Winnower*, *The Gleaners* and *The Angelus*.

MILLIKAN, Robert Andrews (1868—1953), American physicist. He carried out important experiments on the electrical nature of the electron, measuring its charge. His studies of cosmic rays earned him international recognition. He was awarded the Nobel Prize for physics in 1923.

MILNER, Alfred, 1st Viscount (1854—1925), German-born English statesman. From 1897—1905 he was High Commissioner for South Africa. Failing to reach an agreement with the Boer States, he advocated war. He served as Secretary for War in 1918, securing the appointment of Foch as supreme commander. He recommended the grant of independence to Egypt.

MILTON, John (1608—74), English poet. He studied for the ministry at Christ's College, Cambridge, but decided to devote himself to poetry and spent six years (1632—38) developing his intellectual powers. During the Civil War he allied himself completely with the Independents and wrote a number of prose tracts in their defence. By 1652 Milton was completely blind and had to dictate his works. Though he wrote against the Restoration, he escaped punishment at the hands of Charles II. His great masterpiece, *Paradise Lost*, was begun about 1658, completed in 1665 and published in 1667. It is a blank verse epic written in a latinised style, dealing with the revolt of the angels and the fall of man; it is dominated by Satan, the embodiment of the sin of pride. Milton received £5 for this poem. In 1671 he published a lesser work, *Paradise Regained*, on the subject of the temptation of Christ. One of the greatest of Milton's other poems is *Samson Agonistes*, on the death of Samson. Others to achieve particular fame were *L'Allegro*, *Il Penseroso* and *Lycidas*.

MINAS GERAIS, an inland state in southeast Brazil. Pop. (1960) 9,798,880; area 224,701 sq. miles. On Brazil's great central plateau, it is crossed by numerous mountain ranges. Its principal crops are coffee, sugar, maize, tobacco, cotton, rice and manioc. Cattle breeding is important. Rich in mineral resources, it produces gold, iron, copper, zinc, manganese, platinum and diamonds. There are metallurgical, textile and food manufactures. The capital is Belo Horizonte (pop. 1960 693,328).

MINDANAO, the second largest of the Philippine islands. Pop. 3,500,000; area 36,537 sq. miles. Mountainous, with numerous lakes, it has dense forests in the interior providing valuable timber. There are rich deposits of copper and gold. Hemp, rice, coffee, sugar-cane and coconuts are grown. Livestock is raised. Zamboanga and Davao are the principal cities.

MINDORO, an island in the Philippines. Pop. 172,000; area 3759 sq. miles. It has a damp hot climate favouring the dense growth of a large variety of tropical woods. Hemp, cotton, sugar-cane, tobacco and rice are grown. There are copper, gold, sulphur and coal deposits. The capital is Calapan.

MINERALOGY, the science dealing with the occurrence, characteristics, chemical composition, classification and uses of minerals. It is a branch of geology. Minerals may be defined as natural, inorganic substances of homogeneous chemical composition which are generally, with the important exception of mineral oils, solid and of a crystalline structure. They are most easily identified by their degree of hardness, pattern of cleavage along definite planes, form of breaking off, streaking, lustre, colour, specific gravity and transparency. Most rocks are not minerals but mixtures of different varieties. A few are elements but most of them are chemical compounds. Minerals possess great economic importance as ores, fuels, building materials, abrasives, chemicals, and precious and semi-precious stones.

MINNEAPOLIS, a city in southeast Minnesota, U.S.A., on the Mississippi River. Pop. (1960) 482,827. It is an important flour-milling city and the financial, commercial, industrial and distributing centre of the northwestern states. Its industries include linseed products, artificial limbs, jewellery, textiles, foodstuffs and metal goods. It is a large butter marketing centre and a railway junction.

MINNESOTA, a north central state on Lake Superior, U.S.A. Pop. (1960) 3,413,864; area 84,068 sq. miles. Mostly mountainous, the state is a rich source of iron. The Mississippi rises in the northern portion and forms its southeastern border. There are more than 10,000 lakes in Minnesota. A leading livestock producer, the state ranks first in the U.S. in the production of butter and maize. It has valuable forests. Settled in the first quarter of the 19th century, it became a state in 1858. The capital is St Paul (pop. 313,411). Other leading cities are Minneapolis (482,827) and Duluth (106,884).

MINORCA, one of the Spanish Balearic Islands in the Mediterranean. Pop. 60,000; area 283 sq. miles. Fruits, olives and cereals are grown. Livestock breeding is important. The capital is Mahón.

MINSK, capital of Byelorussia, U.S.S.R., on the Little Svislocha River. Pop. (1962) 599,000. An industrial centre, it manufactures automobiles, engineering products and textiles. It has a number of historic buildings and important educational and scientific institutions. It was founded in 1066.

MISSILE, Guided, see Guided Missile.

MISSISSIPPI, south central state, on the Gulf of Mexico, U.S.A. Pop. (1960) 2,178,141; area 47,716 sq. miles. Its west boundary is the Mississippi River, and the state is generally hilly, with a humid sub-tropical climate. The chief product is cotton. Tung nuts, pecans, sweet potatoes, cereals and sugar-cane are raised. Livestock breeding and timber are important sources of income. There are petroleum deposits. Mississippi has the third largest Negro population in the U.S.A. The capital is Jackson (pop. 144,422).

MISSOURI, a north central state, U.S.A. Pop. (1960) 4,319,813; area 69,674 sq. miles. Mountainous in the central portion, it consists mostly of prairies and plateaux, except for the southeastern lowlands. The Mississippi is the state's eastern boundary, and the Missouri traverses it from west to east, after forming the northern half of its western border. Missouri has a humid sub-tropical climate and produces maize, soya beans, wheat, oats and cotton. It is a leading livestock producer. Minerals include coal, lead, lime, barytes, iron and copper. In lead production Missouri ranks first among the states of America. The state's largest industries are food processing and the manufacture of transport equipment. The capital is Jefferson City (pop. 28,064). The largest cities are St Louis (750,026) and Kansas City (475,539).

MITTELLAND CANAL, an inland system of canals and rivers across North Germany linking the Dortmund-Ems Canal in the northwest of West Germany with the Elbe at Magdeburg in East Germany, and from there, via Berlin, with the Oder at Frankfort on the Polish border.

MOBILE, a seaport and city in Alabama, U.S.A., on the Gulf of Mexico. Pop. (1960) 202,779. A leading communications centre and cotton market, Mobile has important industries, producing sawmill and petroleum products, and building materials.

MODENA, a city in North Italy. Pop. (1961) 139,496. There are numerous palaces, churches, museums, and an old university. Modena is a communications centre with a trade in farm products. Textiles and leather goods are manufactured.

MODIGLIANI, Amedeo (1884—1920), Italian painter. His work is distinguished by emphasis on line and distortion for greater effect. He produced sculpture exhibiting African and Cubist influences.

MOGULS (Persian and Arabic form of 'Mongol'), a Mohammedan dynasty of India founded in 1524—26 by Babur, a descendant of Genghis Khan and Tamerlane. Babur conquered most of northern India and established his capital at Delhi. The greatest of the Mogul emperors were Akbar (1542—1605), Shah Jahan, who completed the Taj Mahal in 1647, and Aurangzeb (1618—1707), after whose death the Mogul Empire began to decay. The last of the line was imprisoned by the British in the Indian Mutiny (1857).

MOHAMMED (*c.* 570—632), the founder of the Islam religion, born at Mecca and, in the eyes of his followers, the last and greatest of God's prophets to mankind. He became manager to a rich widow, Khadija, 15 years his senior. In 595 he married her; their only surviving child was Fatima, from whom sprang the successors of the Prophet acknowledged by the Shi'ite sect. In 610 he received his first revelation from the angel Gabriel, and *c.* 616 proclaimed himself Prophet and, while in trance, dictated the Koran to secretaries. He had few followers in Mecca and in the face of derision and persecution he fled to Medina ('the Flight', Hegira, properly Hijra) in 622, regarded ever since as the first year of the Mohammedan era. By war and diplomacy his following increased, and he finally conquered Mecca in 630, setting up a Mohammedan state there. Within a century of his death Islam spread from India and China to Spain, one of the most astonishing achievements in history. See Islam.

MOLDAVIA, a constituent republic of the U.S.S.R. in southeast Europe. Pop. (1962) 3,100,000; area 13,200 sq. miles. Hilly, with dense forests in the north thinning out in the central portion, it consists of steppes in the south. Wheat, maize, sunflowers, grapes, sugar-beet, potatoes and vegetables are grown. Fishing is important. The principal industrial products are wine, tobacco and foods. The capital is Kishinev (pop. 214,000). The country consists mostly of the former Rumanian province of Bessarabia, annexed by the U.S.S.R. in 1940. The name Moldavia formerly applied to a principality which combined with Wallachia to form the kingdom of Rumania.

MOLECULE, the smallest quantity of a substance possessing its characteristics. It usually consists of two or more atoms of the same (e.g. hydrogen, oxygen) or different elements (e.g. carbon dioxide). The molecules of inert gases (e.g. argon) or mercury vapour are identical with their atoms.

MOLIÈRE (Jean Baptiste Poquelin; 1622—73), French dramatist. His most distinguished works are satirical comedies of manners, and many of his characters have become immortal as types. His famous plays include *School for Husbands*, *School for Wives*, *The Miser*, *Tartuffe*, *Don Juan* and *The Misanthrope*.

MOLOTOV, Vyacheslav Mikhailovich (1890—), Soviet statesman. He served as Premier of the Soviet government from 1930 to 1941, and as Minister of Foreign Affairs from 1939 to 1949 and again from 1953 to 1956. He was removed from office and expelled from the Politburo for leading an 'anti-party' group (1957). Though he was appointed Russian delegate to the International Atomic Energy Agency in 1960, he had to go back to Moscow to defend himself against various charges in 1961, and did not return to his post.

MOMBASA, a town of Kenya, East Africa. Pop. 102,000. It is built partly on the south offshore island of Mombasa and partly on the mainland. The landlocked harbour of Kilindini is the best in East Africa and exports rubber, ivory and hides. Mombasa is the terminus of the Kenya-Uganda Railway.

MONACO, an independent principality on the Mediterranean, enclosed by France, under whose protection it is. Pop. (1956) 20,422; area 8 sq. miles. It is divided into three parts: Monaco-Ville, La Condamine, and Monte Carlo. Most of the principality's income is derived from the tourist trade and the gambling concessions at Monte Carlo. Olive oil, perfumes, liqueurs and oranges are produced.

MONASTERY, a community bound by religious vows and living apart from the world, devoting their time to meditation and prayer; also the buildings in which they live. The habit of life grew from that of the solitary hermit; monasteries are pre-Christian in origin and are found under other religions, e.g. Buddhism; huge monasteries existed under the régime of Lamaism in Tibet. The Christian monastery consisted of a church, cloister, chapter-house, dayroom, dormitory, refectory and cellar. The workshops, infirmary and abbot's or prior's house were in separate buildings. A fine example of a monastery, though in ruins, is Fountains Abbey in Yorkshire. An abbey is a large monastery in the charge of an abbot or abbess; a priory is a smaller monastery under a prior or prioress.

Monte Cassino

Christian monasteries were founded in Egypt and the Eastern Empire in the 4th century; Iona was founded by St Columba in the 6th century. The first of the great European monastic orders was the Benedictine; St Benedict built Monte Cassino in Italy *c.* 520, and introduced a monastic Rule which was adopted by later orders. The

Cluniac order (910) was a reformed Benedictine order in which all monasteries were subject to the authority of a mother institution. The other great orders were the Cistercians (1098), the Augustinian Canons (11th century) and the Carthusians (1084). The four great mendicant orders — Franciscans, Dominicans, Carmelites and Augustinians — had no monasteries but worked 'in the world'.

At the dissolution of the monasteries in England (1536—39), monasteries were turned into churches or cathedrals, sold or given to individuals or demolished.

MONET, Claude (1840—1926), French Impressionist painter. His landscapes are remarkable for their representation of the interplay of light. His finest paintings include *The Cathedral at Rouen* and *London: the Parliament*. The term Impressionism (q.v.) is derived from his painting *Impression: soleil levant.*

MONEY, an object which serves as a medium of exchange or a means of making payment, a unit of account or measure of value, and a convenient way for storing wealth. Although cowrie shells, amber, and elephant tail bristles serve these purposes among primitive peoples, metals, especially gold and silver, have come to be widely used as money because of their beauty or durability. All the various kinds of money used in one country are issued in fractions or multiples of a standard unit (e.g. pound sterling, dollar, franc) defined in terms of a specific quantity of a certain metal, usually gold.

MONGOLIA, the name given to the traditional home of the Mongols in central Asia. It contains the Gobi Desert in the central portion and is enclosed by huge mountain ranges. Politically the region is divided between the Chinese autonomous region of Inner Mongolia (pop. 1953 6,100,104; area 347,000 sq. miles; the capital is Huhehot), and Outer Mongolia, now the Mongolian People's Republic (pop. 1963 1,018,000; area 591,121 sq. miles). The latter subsists mostly on stock breeding, the total cultivated area being only about 300 sq. miles. Mineral deposits consist chiefly of coal and petroleum. The capital is Ulan Bator (pop. 1963 218,000). A Chinese province until 1911, Outer Mongolia declared its independence in 1921, and immediately established friendly relations with the U.S.S.R.

MONK, George, 1st Duke of Albemarle (1608—70), English general and admiral. Captured (1644) by the Parliamentarians while fighting for Charles I, he promptly joined forces with Cromwell (1647—60). In 1660 he worked to bring about the Restoration and was rewarded by being commissioned as an admiral.

MONMOUTHSHIRE, a county in southeast Wales, north of the Severn. Pop. (1961) 443,689; area 546 sq. miles. Mountainous in the north, it is flat in the south. Livestock breeding is important. Fruit and grains are grown. There are many coal mines in the western portion. Iron, limestone, sandstone and fire-clay are also found. Industries are mostly metallurgical. There are numerous ancient relics. The county town is Newport.

MONOCOTYLEDONS, the smaller sub-group of angiosperms consisting of plants which are usually herbaceous and often have bulbs, corms, tubers or rhizomes. The leaves have parallel veins and the roots are unbranched; the parts of the flowers are in threes or multiples of three, and there is only one seed-leaf. The stem is usually straight, green and non-woody.

MONRAVIA GROUP, a group of 20 newly independent African states not in the Casablanca group (q.v.), formed in 1961. They represent a more moderate trend in African political opinion.

MONROE, James (1758—1831), American statesman and fifth President of the United States. He served as Senator (1790—94), minister to France (1794—96), Secretary of State (1811—16), and was elected President in 1816. He formulated the Monroe Doctrine in a message to Congress (1823) in which he opposed any further attempts at the colonisation of the Americas by the European powers.

MONTAIGNE, Michel Eyquem de (1533—92), French essayist. His essays dealt with every aspect of man's existence and pleaded for tolerance, moderation and reason. The English translation of his *Essays* by John Florio (in 1603) exerted a profound influence on English writers, including Shakespeare.

MONTANA, a northwestern state of U.S.A. Pop. (1960) 674,767; area 147,138 sq. miles. The eastern two-thirds of the state consist of plains and the rest is in the Rocky Mountains. The principal crops are wheat and barley. Livestock raising and timber are important. Minerals include gold, silver, copper, lead, zinc, chromite, coal, phosphate rock, manganese and petroleum. First settled in 1809, it became a state in 1889. The capital is Helena (pop. 20,227). The largest city is Great Falls (55,357).

MONTE CARLO, a town in Monaco. Pop. 11,000. Overlooking the Mediterranean, it is famous primarily for its gambling casino, which supplies most of the principality's revenue. There is a cathedral, a medieval Genoese and Renaissance palace and an oceanographic museum built in 1910 by Prince Albert.

MONTENEGRO, a federated republic of Yugoslavia, on the Adriatic Sea. Pop. (1961) 489,000; area 5331 sq. miles. Mountainous, it is mostly devoted to livestock breeding. Cereals, potatoes, tobacco, grapes, olives and figs are grown. An independent principality and later kingdom, Montenegro fought many wars against the Turks who sought to subjugate it. In 1919 it became part of Yugoslavia. The capital is Titograd (pop. 22,000).

MONTERREY, a city in Mexico, capital of Nuevo Léon. Pop. (1960) 596,993. A railway and commercial centre, it has smelters cement works, foodstuffs factories and cotton mills. There are institutions of higher learning.

MONTESQUIEU, Baron de la Brède et de (1689—1755), French writer and political theorist. He is particularly known for his *Lettres persanes* (1721), a criticism of French life, and *L'Esprit des Lois* (1748), a monumental work of 31 volumes, in which he developed the view that constitutional liberty is based on the separation of legislative, judicial and executive powers.

MONTEVIDEO, capital of Uruguay, on the Río de la Plata estuary. Pop. (1959) 900,000. A communications centre and seaport, it has numerous meat-processing industries. There is also a petroleum refinery, and cement, textiles, shoes, paper and glassware are manufactured. The city is noted for its large number of parks, especially an unusually large rose garden. Montevideo was settled in 1726.

MONTFORT, Simon de, Earl of Leicester (*c.* 1208—65), French-born English general and statesman. Originally an adviser to Henry III, whose sister he married, he fell out with the king and became leader of the popular party. In the ensuing revolt he enjoyed initial success, but was defeated and killed by Prince Edward at the battle of Evesham.

MONTGOMERY, Bernard, 1st Viscount (1887—), British soldier. From 1939—40 he commanded the 3rd division in France, and in 1942 he led the British Eighth Army in Egypt in its offensive against Rommel which began with the attack at El Alamein, and ended with the surrender of the German forces in Africa. Montgomery led the Eighth Army in the invasions of Sicily and Italy (1943), and was appointed (1943) commander of the British forces in the Normandy invasion. From 1945—46 he served as commander-in-chief of the British occupation forces in Germany.

MONTREAL, a city in Quebec, Canada, at the junction of the St Lawrence and Ottawa rivers. Pop. (1961) 2,109,509. A leading communications, commercial and industrial centre, it is the nearest North American port to Europe. Some 65% of the population is French-speaking. The principal industries are chemicals and the smelting of non-ferrous metals. Other leading products are iron and steel manufactures, pulp and paper, textiles, ships, aircraft, electrical apparatus, foodstuffs, tobacco, paints and rubber goods. The harbour has vast facilities for exporting grain. Montreal has a large fur market. There are many old buildings and churches; McGill University was founded in 1821. Founded by a Frenchman in 1642, it was occupied by the British in 1760. The city was for a period the capital.

MOON, the satellite of a planet, commonly applied to the Earth's only natural satellite. The Earth's moon is about 238,857 miles away from it, completing its elliptical orbit around it in 29½ days. It shines by reflected sunlight and only one side is visible from the earth. The moon's diameter is 2160 miles. Since it has no atmosphere, it is subject to extremes in temperature. The surface is covered with tens of thousands of craters of various sizes. The portion of the moon visible from the earth changes as its angle with the sun varies. In 1959 the U.S.S.R. launched an 860-lb. rocket which landed on the moon 35 hours after take-off. Since then, both the U.S.S.R. and U.S.A. have sent a number of instrument-bearing rockets to the moon. See Lunik.

MOORE, George (1852—1933), Irish novelist. His work includes the novels *Confessions of a Young Man*, *Esther Waters*, *Sister Teresa*, *The Brook Kerith*, and a number of plays.

MOORE, Henry (1898—), English sculptor, born in Yorkshire. His massive, simple works of abstract sculpture include a *Madonna* at St Matthew's, Northampton, a memorial to the Airborne Forces, at Arnhem, and a figure for the Unesco headquarters building in Paris. The Tate Gallery and the Victoria and Albert Museum have examples of his work. As official war artist he also made drawings of scenes in air-raid shelters (1940—42).

MOORE, Thomas (1779—1852), Irish poet. His best-known works are the songs in his *Irish Melodies. Lalla Rookh*, *Loves of the Angels* and the prose romance, *The Epicurean*, also met with much success. He wrote a life of Byron, whom he knew well.

MOORS, the name given to the Mohammedans of northwest Africa who invaded

Spain in 711, and by 718 had almost completed its conquest. They were finally expelled from Spain in 1492 with the fall of Granada. They were not a homogeneous race, but a mixture of Berbers, Arabs and Syrians, with the Berbers predominating.

MORAVIA, a region in central Czechoslovakia. Pop. 3,135,180; area 10,351 sq. miles. Mountainous, it is crossed by the Morava River. Chiefly agricultural, it produces cereals, flax, sugar-beet and hay. Stock-raising and dairying are important. There are coal and iron mines and diversified industries. The largest city is Brno.

MORAY FIRTH, an arm of the North Sea on the northeast coast of Scotland. It is 16 miles wide at its entrance and is nearly 40 miles long.

MORE, Sir Thomas (1478—1535), English author and statesman. After several years of living an ascetic life, he became a member of parliament. He held a number of positions and succeeded Wolsey as Lord Chancellor. For refusing to recognise Henry VIII as head of the English Church, he was beheaded. An outstanding humanist, he is famous for his *Utopia*, describing an ideal state. The Roman Catholic Church canonised him in 1935. His day is July 9.

MORMONS (or The Church of Jesus Christ of Latter-Day Saints), a religious group founded in New York state by Joseph Smith (1805—44) who was given an ancient record by an angel which he subsequently translated into English *(Book of Mormon)*, and which is accepted by Mormons as having equal spiritual authority with the Old and New Testaments. The original, written in 'reformed Egyptian', was handed back to the angel. Smith was murdered, and was succeeded by Brigham Young, who led the trek to Salt Lake, then not part of the U.S.A. A feature of the early days of the movement was polygamy; this was abolished in 1890.

MOROCCO, a kingdom in northwest Africa, on the Atlantic Ocean and the Mediterranean Sea. Pop. (1961) 11,626,000; area 171,305 sq. miles. Mountainous in the north, it consists of a plain along the Atlantic coast. It is predominantly agricultural, producing cereals, citrus fruit, olives and vegetables. Livestock breeding is important. There are deposits of phosphates, coal, iron, lead, antimony and manganese, Fishing is a leading source of income. From 1912—1956 it was mostly French, with a small portion belonging to Spain. In 1956 it became independent, incorporating also the former international zone of Tangier. The population consists of Berbers and Arabs. The king resides at Rabat (pop. 224,901), but Fez (215,812), Marrakesh (241,900) and Meknès (177,100) are also considered capitals. The largest town is Casablanca.

MORRISON, Herbert, Baron (1888—1965), British politician and Labour leader. A member of parliament from 1923, he was chairman (1928—29) of the National Labour Party, Leader of the House of Commons (1945—51) and Foreign Secretary for a short period in 1951. He was also Leader of the London County Council (1933—40). He was made a life peer in 1959.

MORSE, Samuel (1791—1872), American artist and inventor of the telegraph. A portrait painter and president of the National Academy of Design, of which he was a founder member. He invented the electromagnetic recording telegraph and developed a system of signals for sending and receiving messages.

MOSCOW, the capital and largest city of the U.S.S.R. and the R.S.F.S.R., on the Moskva River. Pop. (1962) 6,296,000. It is a communications, commercial and industrial centre. Moscow has educational and scientific institutions and is a drama and music centre. The Kremlin citadel is the political nerve centre of the U.S.S.R. and of world Communism. There are heavy industries manufacturing transport equipment, engines, automobiles and aircraft. Precision tools, textiles, chemicals and foodstuffs are some of the principal products. Moscow was the old capital of Russia until the 18th century. It has numerous historic buildings and monuments. In 1812 the Russians burned the city in order to deprive Napoleon of a base. Moscow again became the capital in 1918.

MOSES, Hebrew leader, prophet and lawgiver. Born to a Hebrew woman but raised at the Egyptian court, Moses rejoined his people when he killed an Egyptian who was maltreating a Hebrew slave. He fled to Midian, but returned to Egypt at God's command to lead the children of Israel out of their bondage and into the Promised Land. Moses was the leader of his people during their 40 years' sojourn in the Wilderness and it was through him that God gave the Ten Commandments to the children of Israel.

MOSLEM, see Islam.

MOSUL, a city in northern Iraq, on the Tigris. Pop. (1962) 340,541. It lies in the middle of rich oilfields and in a grain-growing region. A railway and trade centre, it is the starting-point of an oil pipeline to Tripoli, Lebanon.

MOTOR CAR, see Automobile.

MOUNTAIN, a mass of earth or rock towering above the surrounding land. Groups of mountains are called ranges, systems, chains or cordilleras. Mountains are classified as folded, faulted, volcanic, or residual. Mountains strongly affect the climate of neighbouring regions. They also have strategic, social and economic importance. Usually unfit for cultivation, they may contain minerals and be covered with valuable forests as far as the timber-line. The world's highest peaks are Everest, Godwin-Austen, and Kanchenjunga. The following are the world's principal mountains (an asterisk denotes an active volcano):

Name	*Range*	*Location*	*Height in ft*
Anconcagua	Andes	Argentina-Chile	22,835
Ararat	—	Turkey	17,212
Cayambe	Andes	Ecuador	19,170
Chimborazo	Andes	Ecuador	20,557
Citlaltepetl	—	Mexico	18,700
Cook	Southern Alps	South Island, N. Z.	12,349
Cotopaxi*	Andes	Ecuador	19,344
Demavend	—	Iran	18,500
Dhaulagiri	Himalaya	Nepal	26,795
Elbruz	Caucasus	U.S.S.R.	18,468
Erebus*	—	Antarctica	13,202
Etna*	—	Sicily	10,758
Everest	Himalaya	Nepal	29,028
Fairweather	St Elias	Canada	15,287
Fujiyama	—	Japan	12,385
Gannet Peak	Rockies	Wyoming, U.S.A.	13,785

Name	Range	Location	Height in ft
Godwin-Austen (K2)	Karakoram	India	28,250
Huascaran	Andes	Peru	22,205
Jungfrau	Bernese Alps	Switzerland	13,667
Kanchenjunga	Himalaya	Nepal	28,146
Kenya	—	Kenya	17,040
Kilimanjaro	—	Tanganyika	19,565
Llullaillaco	Andes	Argentine-Chile	22,148
Logan	St Elias	Yukon, Canada	19,850
McKinley	Alaska	Alaska	20,320
Matterhorn	Alps	Switzerland-Italy	14,780
Mauna Kea	—	Hawaii	13,796
Mauna Loa*	—	Hawaii	13,680
Mercedairo	Andes	Argentina	21,883
Minya Konka	—	Szechuan, China	24,900
Mont Blanc	Alps	France	15,781
Monte Rosa	Pennine Alps	Italy-Switzerland	15,217
Muztagh	Kunlun	Sinkiang, China	23,890
Muztagh Ata (K5)	Pamirs	Sinkiang, China	24,388
Ojos Del Salado	Andes	Chile	23,293
Pike's Peak	Rockies	Colorado, U.S.A.	14,110
Popocatepetl	—	Mexico	17,887
Rainier	Cascades	Washington, U.S.A.	14,410
Ruwenzori	Ruwenzori	Congo-Uganda	16,795
St Elias	St Elias	Alaska-Canada	18,008
St Gotthard	Alps	Switzerland	10,490
Sanford	Rockies	Alaska-Canada	16,208
Simplon	Alps	Switzerland	11,117
Stalin Peak	Pamirs	Tadzhikistan, U.S.S.R.	24,590
Stromboli*	—	Lipari Islands, Italy	3,040
Tocorpuri	Andes	Bolivia	22,182
Tolima	Andes	Colombia	17,109
Tupungato	Andes	Argentina-Chile	21,489
Vesuvius*	—	Italy	4,260
Whitney	Sierra Nevada	California	14,495

MOUNTBATTEN of Burma, Louis, 1st Earl (1900—), British sailor. He entered the navy in 1913 and was a captain by 1937. Appointed Chief of Combined Operations in 1942, he trained the Commandos. From 1943—46 he served as Supreme Allied Commander in southeast Asia. He was the last British viceroy of India (1947), was advanced to First Sea Lord in 1955, and in 1959 became Chief of the Defence Staff. See Battenberg.

MOUTH, in man, the opening through which food is taken into the body and from which speech issues. The mouth cavity, extending from the lips to the throat, contains the tongue, gums, teeth and salivary glands. Its roof consists of the hard and soft palates and it is bounded below by muscles and soft tissue under the tongue.

MOZAMBIQUE, Portuguese colony on the southeast coast of Africa. Pop. (1960) 6,230,000; area 298,000 sq. miles. Its principal products are sugar, cotton, copra, sisal and cashew nuts. Gold, coal, graphite and mica are mined. There are rich forests. It was discovered by Vasco da Gama in 1498 and first colonised in 1505. The capital is Lourenco Marques.

MOZART, Wolfgang Amadeus (1756—91), Austrian composer. His musical, genius became apparent when he was still a small child. He was 15 when his opera *Mitridate* was successfully produced in Milan. While he was concert master and organist at Salzburg, he composed the highly original serious opera *Idomeneo*. His greatest comic operas are the *Marriage of Figaro*, *Don Giovanni* and *The Magic Flute*. From his vast output it is possible to single out only a few works: the *Haffner*, *Prague* and *Jupiter* symphonies, the piano concertos, the Clarinet Concerto, the last three horn concertos, the Clarinet Quintet, the Mass in C minor and the Requiem. He was pre-eminent in every form of music, and as pianist, organist, violinist and conductor. He used up all his powers on music and was unable to manage his own life. One of the two greatest composers the world has known, he died young and in poverty.

MUKDEN, see Shenyang.

MÜLHEIM, a city and port in North Rhine-Westphalia, West Germany, in the Ruhr. Pop. (1960) 181,288. It is an important communications, coal and iron centre. It has large metallurgical industries in addition to manufacturing textiles, foodstuffs and building materials.

MUNICH (München), capital of Bavaria, West Germany. Pop. (1960) 1,101,400. The third largest city in Germany, and important for its industries, it is chiefly famous for its museums and buildings, many of them very badly damaged in the Second World War. The magnificent collections of Old Masters in the Old and New Pinakotheks, both completely destroyed, were transferred to the Haus der Kunst; the Deutsches Museum houses a great scientific collection; classical antiquities are in the Glyptothek, and there is a Bavarian National Museum. The finest churches are the Cathedral (Frauenkirche) and the Asamkirche. The Zoo is famous, and there is a huge English Garden. There is also an ancient university and the rococo castle of Nymphenburg. Munich is well known for its lager beer, and other major activities include printing and publishing, the making of optical and other precision instruments, electrical engineering, locomotives and vehicles. Munich is a Catholic town, with a history going back to at least the 12th century. It was the birthplace of the Nazi Party and later became the capital of the movement. In September 1938 the Munich Pact was signed here.

MUNSTER, largest province in the Irish Republic, on the Atlantic Ocean and St George's Channel. Pop. (1961) 848,368; area 9475 sq. miles. Predominantly mountainous, it is divided into the six counties of Waterford, Clare, Cork, Kerry, Limerick and Tipperary. Barley, corn and potatoes are grown. Dairy farming is important. Coal is mined. There were two kingdoms here before the English conquest. The most important towns are Limerick, Waterford, Cork, the capital, and Cobh, its port.

MÜNSTER, a city in North Rhine-Westphalia, West Germany, on the Dortmund-Ems Canal. Pop. (1960) 175,406. A commercial, communications and industrial centre, it manufactures machinery, leather goods and copper products. It has a university.

MURCIA, a city in southern Spain, on the Segura River. Pop. (1961) 249,738. The market centre of a rich fruit-growing region, it manufactures textiles, foodstuffs and silk. It is the capital of the province of Murcia which was part of an ancient kingdom of the same name. The city has relics of the Moorish period.

MURMANSK, a city in the R.S.F.S.R., on the Barents Sea, U.S.S.R. Pop. (1962) 245,000. The largest city inside the Arctic Circle, it is an ice-free port, the centre of a large fishing fleet, and a naval base. It is the seat of Soviet polar research. There are shipyards and factories for fish processing.

MURRAY, see River.

MUSCAT AND OMAN, a sultanate in the southeast corner of Arabia. Pop. (1957) 550,000; area 82,000 sq. miles. It consists of a coastal plain, mountains and a plateau. Dates are exported and camels bred. There are pearl fisheries.

MUSIC, a combination of rhythmic sounds pleasing to the ear. Musical tones are produced by similar vibrations following one another at regular intervals. The three characteristics of a musical tone are pitch (either high or low, depending on the frequency of vibration), intensity or loudness (depending on the distance through which the vibrating body — string, air column, metal or stretched skin — swings), and timbre or the quality peculiar to individual instruments. Rhythm, melody (a succession of single tones of varying pitch), harmony and tone quality are the basic elements of music. Primitive man devised three groups of musical instruments: wind, percussion and string. The leading musical forms are cantata, chamber music, concerto, mass, oratorio, overture, passion, rondo, sonata, song and symphony.

MUSSOLINI, Benito (1883—1945), Italian dictator (called *Il Duce*) and leader of the Fascist party in Italy. He entered politics as a Socialist and founded (1914) the daily *Il Popolo d'Italia*, which later became his official mouthpiece. He organised the Fascist party in 1921 and engineered its 'March on Rome' (1922) which resulted in a *coup d'état* that placed him in complete control of the government. In 1940 he entered the Second World War on the side of Nazi Germany. Mussolini was deposed by his own countrymen (1943) and executed by partisans.

MUSSORGSKY, Modest Petrovich (1839—81), Russian composer. He is noted particularly for the opera *Boris Godunov*. His other well-known works include *Pictures from an Exhibition* and *A Night on the Bare Mountain*.

MYSTICISM, a term for the religious practices (and their results) which aim at a spiritual union with God bringing insight into the mysteries of the universe and the sources of wisdom. Mystics are found in all religions, but especially among Christians, Mohammedan Sufis, Buddhists and Hindu *yogi*, and there is a remarkable uniformity in their accounts of such experiences. These include a preliminary period of the darkest despair, followed by a sudden illumination, in which distinctions between past and present, good and evil, subject and object, and all opposites disappear in a higher synthesis. The techniques also show basic similarities — long preparation, meditation, prayer and asceticism. Among the most famous mystics are Jakob Boehme, Meister Eckhart, St John of the Cross, St Theresa and the author of *The Cloud of Unknowing*.

MYTHOLOGY, the study of myths; also a collective term denoting a body of myths and usually applied to the myths of a national, ethnical or religious group.

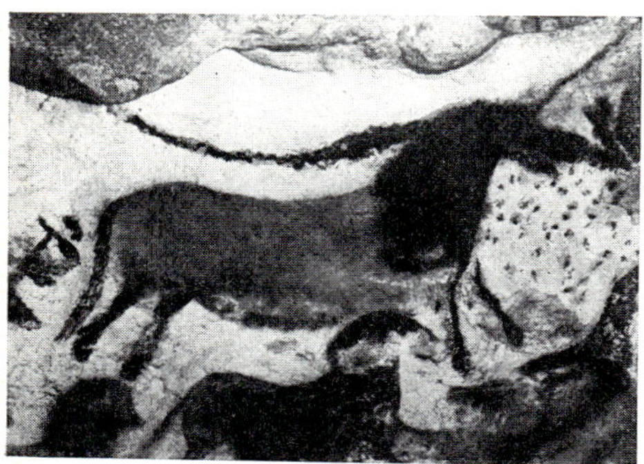

Among the earliest existing records of man's attempts at illustrating events from his life are these hunting scenes drawn *c.* 12,000 B.C. in caves at Lascaux, France.

Photo: Photographic Archives, Paris

For centuries society in Europe has centred on the Christian Church. So too, for centuries, have European artists portrayed their impressions of biblical scenes. Illustrated here is a Head of the Archangel, a Russian icon dating from the 12th century. *Photo: Larousse*

A detail showing the angels playing music, from the altar-piece painted by the Van Eyck (q.v.) brothers in 1432. *Photo: A. C. L.*

The powerful imagery of Gothic symbols is illustrated in this crucifixion painting by Matthias Grünewald (*c.* 1460-1528).

Photo: Paul Hamlyn Library

One of the most famous paintings by Leonardo da Vinci (q.v.), his *Madonna of the Rocks*.
Photo: Trustees of the National Gallery

The Florentine mannerist painter Agnolo Bronzino (1503-72) was one of the most significant portrait painters of his period. Illustrated is his *Eleonora di Toledo*.
Photo: The Wallace Collection. Crown copyright reserved

The Flemish painter Pieter Brueghel the Elder (q.v.) completed his *Adoration of the Kings* in 1563. *Photo: Trustees of the National Gallery*

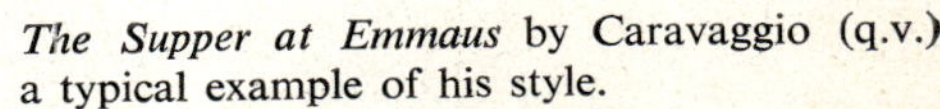

The Supper at Emmaus by Caravaggio (q.v.) a typical example of his style.
Photo: Trustees of the National Gallery

NAGASAKI, a seaport in Kyushu, Japan. Pop. (1960) 344,079. Enclosed on three sides by hills, it is an important shipbuilding centre. The manufacture of enamel and lacquer ware is a leading pursuit. About 40% of the city was destroyed by the second atomic bomb explosion in the Second World War.

NAGOYA, a seaport in Honshu, Japan. Pop. (1960) 1,591,914. It is a railway, financial and commercial centre, and is the seat of the Atsuta shrine, the second most sacred holy place in Japan. The city has numerous educational institutions. Important industries include ceramics, clocks and watches, woollen goods, textiles, machinery, lacquer ware, glass and cement.

NAGPUR, a city in Maharashtra, India. Pop. (1961) 643,186. Famous for its Hindu temples, it is a railway and commercial centre. Its manufactures include textiles and metallurgy.

NAIROBI, capital of Kenya. Pop. (1961) 297,000. It lies at the southeast corner of the Kenya highlands, 330 miles by rail from the port of Mombasa. The Nairobi National Park, a game reserve, is in the vicinity.

NANCHANG, capital of Kiangsi province, China, on the Kan-Kiang. Pop. 480,000. It is a market for tea, rice and cotton and the centre of commerce for the province. There are a number of institutions of higher learning.

NANCY, a city in northeastern France, on the Meurthe River. Pop. (1962) 133,532. An administrative, commercial and industrial centre, it manufactures machinery, textiles and foodstuffs. The former capital of the duchy of Lorraine, it was embellished by the Polish father-in-law of Louis XV, Stanislas Leczinsky. The old ducal palace has been much restored and now houses a fine museum. Points of interest are the Place Stanislas, the zoo and rose garden of Pépinière, and the Place de la Carrière.

NANKING, capital of Kiangsu province, China, on the Yangtze River. Pop. (1957) 1,419,000. A river port and communications centre, it produces fine porcelain, silk, damask and tapestries. The suburb of Siakwan is the business area. The walled city was founded by the Ming dynasty in the 13th century, and was their capital until 1421. The Taiping rebels destroyed many of the old buildings in 1864. Chiang Kai-shek made it his capital from 1928 to 1937, when it was looted by the Japanese and the inhabitants massacred. Chiang returned briefly from 1946 to 1949. Near the city are the Ming tombs (rifled) and the mausoleum of Sun Yat-sen.

NANSEN, Fridtjof (1861—1930), Norwegian statesman and arctic explorer. In 1888 he crossed the icefields of Greenland on foot, and in 1893—96 led an expedition into the northern Arctic. Nansen was active in the peaceful movement for Norwegian independence from Sweden, and received the Nobel Peace Prize in 1922 for his work in repatriating war prisoners.

NANTES, a city in northwestern France on the River Loire. Pop. (1962) 246,227. An important port since the 16th century, it is a commercial and industrial centre. Shipbuilding, metallurgy, chemicals, stained glass and foodstuffs are the chief industries. The cathedral dates from 1434 and the castle was founded in 938. Here, in 1598, Henry IV issued an edict granting Protestants religious freedom and civil rights. This Edict of Nantes was revoked by Louis XIV in 1685.

NAPLES, a city in southern Italy, on the Tyrrhenian Sea. Pop. (1961) 1,179,608 An important port and commercial centre, it has shipyards, oil refineries, and metallurgical, chemical and food industries. It is at the foot of Mt Vesuvius. There are many ancient buildings, and churches, and the National Museum of antiquities from Pompeii and Herculaneum nearby. The island of Capri lies across the bay. Under Roman rule it was a centre of learning and a summer resort. In 1282 it became the capital of the Kingdom of Naples, and in 1799 of the Napoleonic Parthenopean Republic.

NAPOLEON I (Bonaparte; 1769—1821), Emperor of the French, 1804—14. He was born at Ajaccio, the son of a Corsican lawyer, and became an artillery officer. During the Revolution he was a moderate Jacobin and a friend of Robespierre. In 1793 he distinguished himself in the siege of Toulon, and quelled a Royalist rising in Paris in 1795. In the same year he displayed his generalship by defeating the Austrians in three battles in Italy, where he formed the Cisalpine Republic. The Directory (see French Revolution) were by this time growing apprehensive of his increasing influence in Paris, and were glad to send him to Egypt and Syria; his dreams of conquering India were ended by Nelson's success at the Battle of the Nile. In 1799 Napoleon returned to Paris, overthrew the Directory and became First Consul, and later Consul for life. He returned to Italy to defeat the Austrians at Marengo, making peace with them in 1891 and with Britain in 1802.

He was now free to attend to home affairs. He conciliated the Church by a Concordat with the Pope; reorganised education with a system of *lycées* and a national university; built a series of military roads; fostered trade and industry; founded a national bank; and codified the law. After the discovery of a plot against him, a national plebiscite was held and he became Emperor; titles and honours were restored and the Legion of Honour established. Of his brothers, Louis, the father of Napoleon III, was made King of Holland in 1806; Joseph became King of Naples (1806) and of Spain (1808); Jerome was made King of Westphalia (1807). He had married Joséphine in 1796 but, as she produced no heir, divorced her and married the daughter of the Emperor of Austria, Marie Louise, in 1810, by whom he had one son, the King of Rome (Napoleon II).

The Napoleonic Wars (q.v.) ended in Napoleon's abdication and exile to Elba. He escaped for the brief Hundred Days (q.v.) and was then exiled to St Helena, where he died.

It is ironic that the valuable and permanent legacy of this great general lay in his domestic reforms; his masterly victories in the field were later seen to have achieved nothing except the death of perhaps a million people.

NAPOLEON III (1808—73), Emperor of the French from 1852—70. The nephew of Napoleon I and the son of Hortense de Beauharnais his life was one long disastrous attempt to restore the glories of the Napoleonic era, though he had none of Napoleon's abilities. He was in prison from 1840—46 for conspiring against Louis Philippe, but escaped to London. He seized his chance with the revolution of 1848 and was elected President of the Second Republic. After a *coup-d'état* in December 1851 a plebiscite was held and he became emperor. The following year he married Eugénie, who presided over the glories of the court of the Second Empire. Napoleon III's rule was autocratic; police, spies, censorship and corruption were its main features. In 1849, in pursuit of glory abroad, he defended the Pope against the republicans. He joined in the Crimean War, helped to found the new Kingdom of Italy, and tried to establish a satellite empire in Mexico. He managed to alienate Italy and Austria, and was outmanoeuvred by Bismarck into precipitating the disastrous Franco-Prussian War, in which he was captured at Sedan (1870). Napoleon and Eugénie spent the rest of their lives in exile at Chislehurst, England.

NAPOLEONIC WARS (1803—15), which followed the French Revolutionary Wars, began after Napoleon became emperor. Pitt formed a coalition with Russia, Austria and Sweden in response to Napoleon's threat to invade England — a threat removed by Nelson's victory at Trafalgar (October 1805). On land Napoleon defeated the Austrians and Russians at Austerlitz (December 1805). Prussia then joined the war and, after its defeat at Jena (1806), the French occupied Berlin, making peace with Russia at Tilsit in 1807. Napoleon tried to blockade Britain into surrender by instituting the Continental System, whereby European countries were forbidden to trade with it; and to enforce the blockade he occupied Portugal and put his brother Joseph on the Spanish throne. The Spaniards revolted (see Peninsular War), and when Alexander failed to observe the ban on British trade Napoleon invaded Russia with the Grand Army of 360,000 men (1812), defeated the Russians at Borodino and entered Moscow. But Moscow was set on fire and the Russian winter closed in. In its retreat from Moscow the Grand Army was badly mauled at Beresina. Prussia and Austria were encouraged to attack the weakened French and, in the War of Liberation, defeated them at Leipzig (1813) and drove them out of Germany. Napoleon abdicated (April 1814) but escaped from Elba (March 1815) and in the Hundred Days (q.v.) was again defeated at Waterloo.

NASSER, Gamal Abdul (1918—), Egyptian statesman. He fought in the Second World War, and in Palestine against the Israelis (1948—49). In 1952 he led the Free Officers' revolt which deposed King Farouk, becoming Deputy Premier in 1953 and Prime Minister from 1954—56. As President in 1956 he nationalised the Suez Canal and pressed on with land reform and the financing of the High Dam at Aswan. Nasser formed the United Arab Republic with Syria in 1958, and has taken a leading part in Pan-African affairs.

NATAL, a province in the Republic of South Africa, on the Indian Ocean. Pop. (1960) 2,979,920; area 33,578 sq. miles (including Zululand). Consisting of a series of mountain ranges decreasing in height towards the coast, Natal is not very fertile. Sugar-cane is the chief crop. Cereals, fruit and vegetables are grown. Fishing is important. There are rich coal reserves. Most of the 340,235 (1960) Europeans are descendants of original

British settlers. The capital is Pietermaritzburg.

NATIONALITY, in Britain the Nationality Act of 1948 governs the grant of British citizenship, which carries with it the right to vote and to enter certain professions (e.g. the law) closed to aliens. Anyone born in the United Kingdom or a British colony is a British citizen. Those born in the Commonwealth are now called 'Commonwealth citizens', and can become British citizens by registration, as can citizens of the Republic of Ireland. Aliens can obtain citizenship by naturalisation without losing the citizenship of their home country. Women no longer acquire British citizenship automatically by marriage to a British citizen.

NATURAL SELECTION, see Darwin; Evolution.

NAVARRE, a province and former kingdom of northern Spain. Pop. (1960) 402,042; area 4055 sq. miles. In the north it is mountainous; along the Ebro valley grain and apples are grown and livestock reared. The kingdom was founded in the 9th century, and incorporated into Spain in 1833. The capital is Pamplona.

NAVIGATION, the art of directing a vessel on its course. In ancient times it was done by the guidance of heavenly bodies, conspicuous landmarks along coasts, and the release of land birds. The re-discovery of the compass in the 12th century, and of the cross-staff and astrolabe in the 15th, were major steps in the development of navigational aids, further greatly improved by the invention of the marine sextant and chronometer in the 18th. Radio and radar devices now supplement astronomical methods.

NAVY, the ships of a nation built and maintained specially for purposes of war and national defence. In the 9th century Alfred the Great formed a navy for protection against Viking raids and for offensive attacks against their harbours. The English Navy became a powerful force in the reign of Elizabeth I, crushing the Spanish armada in 1588. Although occasionally challenged by Dutch or French fleets, the British Navy was mistress of the seas until after the First World War, when the U.S.A. equalled its power. The U.S. Navy emerged as the world's greatest seapower after the Second World War. The chief classes of modern naval vessels are the destroyer, the submarine, the cruiser and the aircraft carrier. Aircaft carriers and submarines play a leading role in the naval establishment of world powers.

NAZARETH, a town in northern Israel. Pop. (1961) 25,066. It was the home of the family of Jesus and is associated with his early life.

NAZISM, a political movement propagated by the so-called National Socialist German Workers' Party which dominated Germany from 1933—45. The Nazi Party was founded in Bavaria shortly after the 1918 revolution. Its goals were the unification of all German-speaking peoples, the extermination of the Jews, and the conquest of *Lebensraum* for the German people. Among its early leaders were Hitler, Hess and Rosenberg. An abortive attempt to overthrow the Bavarian government in 1923 led to the dispersion of the party, but from 1924—30 Hitler reorganised it and it rapidly gained in strength. In 1933 Hitler was appointed chancellor and the Nazis set about systematically suppressing all other parties. The Nazi Party ruled Germany throughout the Second World War but was dissolved by the Allies in 1945.

NEANDERTHAL MAN, a race of man which occupied parts of Europe, West and Central Asia and North Africa about 10,000—25,000 years ago. It was distinguished by the heavy brow-ridge, sloping forehead, short, thick neck, and receding chin. This type of primitive man lived in caves, possessed fire and stone tools, and depended chiefly on game for food. Neanderthal man probably appeared in the last warm period of the Ice Age and modern man *(Homo sapiens)* after the last glacial period; they may be divergent forms with a common ancestor.

Neanderthal man

NEBRASKA, a north central state of U.S.A. Pop. (1960) 1,411,330; area 77,227 sq. miles. Most of the state is rolling prairie, with the Bad Lands to the north and west. Important for its agricultural products, it grows maize, wheat, oats, barley, rye and potatoes, and breeds livestock. Petroleum, natural gas and cement are produced. Meat-packing is the principal industry. Railway rolling stock, farm machinery, precision instruments and flour are manufactured. The first Europeans were Spaniards who reached the region in 1541. It was part of the Louisiana Purchase and in 1867 became a state, 20 years after it was first settled. The capital is Lincoln (pop. 1960 128,521). The largest city is Omaha (301,598).

NEGRO, a member of a race of mankind distinguished by dark skin colour, crinkly or woolly hair, broad nose, and pronounced jaw and lips. Adaptation to tropical and sub-tropical climatic conditions accounts for the emergence of this type. The term is applied specifically to dark-skinned peoples of Africa south of the Sahara, and to their descendants elsewhere, e.g. in the U.S.A. and West Indies.

NEHRU, Jawaharlal (1889—1964), Indian nationalist leader and statesman. Educated in England, he returned to India to practise law. He joined the Indian National Congress and became a follower of Mahatma Gandhi. In 1947 Nehru became Prime Minister of India, an office he held until his death in 1964.

NEJD, the central region of Saudi Arabia. Pop. 4,000,000; area 424,600 sq. miles. Mostly a desert plateau, it produces dates, cereals, coffee, pearls, hides, wool and petroleum. Livestock raising is important. The largest city is Riyadh (pop. 150,000), the capital of Saudi Arabia. Nejd is the home of the Wahhabis, who under Ibn Saud imposed their domination over most of Arabia.

NELSON, Horatio, 1st Viscount (1758—1805), English admiral. He lost his right eye in 1794 and his right arm in 1797. After receiving promotion for gallantry in the Battle of Cape St Vincent (1797) against the combined French and Spanish fleets, he won an overwhelming victory against Napoleon's fleet in the Battle of the Nile (1798) and destroyed the Danish fleet at Copenhagen in 1801. In 1805 he engaged the French fleet under Villeneuve at Trafalgar and, though mortally wounded, lived to learn of the English victory. See also Hamilton, Lady.

NEOPLATONISM, the name given to a philosophical school of thought based on Plato, Aristotle, Pythagoras and other sources, which flourished particularly in Alexandria and Athens from the 2nd to the 6th centuries. It was an attempt by Graeco-Roman philosophers, led by Plotinus, to combat Christianity.

NEPAL, a kingdom in the Himalayas. Pop. (1961) 9,407,127; area 54,362 sq. miles. The northern portion contains the world's highest mountain peaks — Everest, Kanchenjunga and Dhaulagiri. In the southern lowlands rice, wheat, maize and millet are grown. Jute, timber, medicinal herbs and oilseeds are important products. Livestock breeding is widespread. There are jute and sugar mills and match, glass and ceramics factories. The capital is Katmandu (pop. 195,260). The Gurkhas moved eastwards into Nepal in the 18th century.

NERO (37—68), Emperor of Rome. The adopted son of Claudius, he became emperor in 54. During his last 13 years he was responsible for the murder of, among very many others, his mother, Claudius' son Britannicus, his two wives, and Seneca and Lucan. His main interests were in athletics and the arts. He ran, acted, sang and erected magnificent buildings for himself. He is thought to have set fire to Rome and then, to divert suspicion, to have blamed the Christians, whom he burnt or threw to the lions in the public 'games'. Revolts eventually got under way, in England, Judaea, Gaul, Spain and Africa, and the army mutinied. Condemned to death by the Senate, he shrank from suicide and ordered a servant to kill him, saying, with apparent sincerity: 'Ah! What an artist perishes with me'.

NERVOUS SYSTEM, the communications system of the body which transmits impulses and co-ordinates and integrates its activities and functions. It has two main divisions. The central nervous (or cerebrospinal) system, consisting of brain, cerebellum and spinal cord, is equivalent to the conscious mind; it commands the muscles directly via the motor nerves, or indirectly through the autonomous nervous system. The latter, corresponding to the unconscious mind, controls the organs, e.g. the heart, the intestinal muscles, and regulates the body temperature, digestion, etc. It is divided into antagonistic systems, the sympathetic, which, for example, accelerates the heart, constricts the arteries (producing pallor), contracts the pupils and, in general prepares the body for fight or flight; and the parasympathetic, which slows the heart, etc., and in general produces relaxation. Thus emotional states influence bodily actions, a view which is the basis of the psychosomatic approach to medicine. The nerves, long fibres made up of nerve cells smaller than a pin-head, are all duplicated: afferent nerves which bring in messages from eyes, ears, skin, etc., and efferent nerves which carry commands to muscles. In reflex actions there is a sort of short-circuit between incoming message and outgoing command.

NESS, LOCH, a lake in Inverness, in the Highlands of Scotland. Enclosed by high hills, it is a link in the Caledonian Canal connecting the east and west coasts of Scotland. It is 22½ miles long and very deep, and has for long been associated with the legend of an aquatic prehistoric monster.

NESTORIANISM, the doctrine of the Syrian Patriarch of Constantinople, Nestorius (d. *c.* 451), that Christ had a twofold personality, and that Mary was not the Mother of God, but of a man who became Christ. Cyril, the Patriarch of Alexandria, was his fanatical opponent, and won the day at the Council of Ephesus (431). Nestorius was excommunicated for heresy, but a large group of his followers remained true to him. A Nestorian Church still survives today in Iraq, Syria and Persia.

NETHERLANDS, a kingdom in Western Europe, on the North Sea. Pop. (1960) 11,480,000; area 13,025 sq. miles. Flat, except for hills in the southeast, it requires dykes to keep the water out of that half of the country which is below sea-level. The principal crops are cereals, peas, flax, potatoes and sugar-beet. Livestock raising, dairy farming, market gardening, flower and bulb cultivation, and fishing are important. There are deposits of coal and petroleum. Highly industrialised, the Netherlands produces textiles, clothing, chemicals, foodstuffs, building materials and ships. The region was once part of Charlemagne's empire and was later dominated by Burgundy and by the Austrian Hapsburgs. In the 16th century it came under Spanish rule. The suppression of political freedom and of the Protestant movement by Philip II of Spain led to a revolt in 1568. In 1579 the seven northern provinces (the United Provinces) federated to form the Union of Utrecht, the beginning of the modern state of the Netherlands. By mid-17th century the country's independence was completely established and the Dutch began to achieve prominence as a great sea and colonial power. In the following century, however, their power declined. From 1795, the region was ruled by France, first as the Batavian Republic and later as a kingdom, part of the Napoleonic Empire. In 1814 all the provinces of the Netherlands and Belgium were merged into one kingdom; but in 1830 Belgium withdrew. Neutral in both World Wars, the country was invaded and ravaged by the Germans in 1940. The Netherlands East Indies threw off Dutch rule after the Second World War and formed the Republic of Indonesia. The capital is Amsterdam (pop. 1960 869,602). The seat of government is The Hague (606,110). Other large cities are the port of Rotterdam (729,852) and Utrecht (254,186).

NETHERLANDS ANTILLES, two groups of islands in the Caribbean Sea. Pop. (1960—61) 188,914; area 403 sq. miles. The largest is the Leeward group, the smaller the Windward Islands. Oil refining is the principal occupation. The capital is Willemstad on Curaçao.

NEUROSES, a vague term for mental disorders not so severe as psychoses, e.g. hysteria, obsessions, phobias and morbid anxiety. They are due to a failure to face life and a desire to find excuses for evading its obligations and unpleasantnesses. In hysteria the excuses may take the form of deafness, inability to read or paralysis, the characteristic feature being that the patient is far less worried about his disability than would be expected (*la belle indifférence*).

The phobias are numerous, such as a morbid dislike of some animal, the fear of being shut in (claustrophobia) or of crowds (agoraphobia). Neurasthenia is a favourite complaint of neurotics: it does not exist, nor has the state of nerves anything to do with any neurosis, and it follows that 'nerve tonics' do no good.

NEUTRALITY, in international law, the legal status of a state which remains at peace in time of war between other states. A neutral state must maintain complete impartiality towards all belligerents. The warring nations are obliged on their part to respect neutral territory, territorial waters, air-space and nationals.

NEUTRON, an atomic particle which has no charge but is some 1840 times as heavy as an electron. Neutrons are found in the nuclei of all atoms except hydrogen. See Isotope; Proton.

NEVADA, a western state of the U.S.A. Pop. (1960) 285,278; area 110,540 sq. miles. The state consists almost entirely of a vast plateau. Livestock raising, the farming of hay, wheat, barley, maize and potatoes, and mining and lumbering, are the principal occupations. Nevada is a leading producer of gold, silver, copper and manganese. First settled in 1851, it became a state in 1864. The capital is Carson City (pop. 5163). The largest cities are Las Vegas (64,405) and Reno (51,470).

NEW BRITAIN, the largest island in the Bismarck Archipelago, southwestern Pacific Ocean. Pop. (1961) 109,961; area (with adjacent small islands) 14,600 sq. miles. It is mountainous and has a number of active volcanoes. Copra and cocoa are exported.

NEW BRUNSWICK, a province of the Dominion of Canada, on the Atlantic Ocean. Pop. (1961) 597,936; area 27,985 sq. miles. Consisting of rolling terrain with a plateau in the northwest and hills in the southeast, it has many lakes. The chief agricultural products are cereals, potatoes, hay and roots. Blueberries, strawberries and other fruit are raised. Livestock breeding is important. Forest products and fisheries provide a substantial source of income. There are various minerals, including iron, copper, lead, zinc, manganese and petroleum. Fish, dairy and other foods are produced. There is a pulp and paper industry. The population is predominantly of British origin. First explored in 1604, it was under French rule until 1713. New Brunswick was separated from Nova Scotia and became a province in 1784. The capital is Fredericton (pop. 1961 19,683); the largest city is St John (95,563).

NEW CALEDONIA, a French island in the southwestern Pacific Ocean. Pop. (1958) 72,478; area 8,548 sq. miles. The island is mountainous and produces timber, coffee, copra, maize, fruit and vegetables. Livestock is raised. There are large deposits of nickel, chrome and iron. Half the population is Melanesian. The capital is Nouméa.

NEW DELHI, see Delhi.

NEW ENGLAND, the six northeastern states of the U.S.A.: Maine, Vermont, New Hampshire, Massachusetts, Connecticut and Rhode Island. Founded on a tradition of English Puritanism, they represented the leading intellectual force in the U.S. until well into the 19th century.

NEW GUINEA, an island in the southwestern Pacific Ocean, divided between Australia (the eastern portion) and Indonesia (West Irian, q.v.). Area 312,329 sq. miles. Mainly mountainous, it has jungle-covered swamps in the south. There are numerous rivers. The Australian portion consists of the U.N. trust territories of New Guinea (pop. 1958 1,341,268; area 93,000 sq. miles) in the northeast; and Papua (pop. 1958 487,150; area 90,600 sq. miles) in the southeast. Both parts have adjacent islands, the trust territory including the Bismarck Archipelago and the Solomon Islands. Papua produces rubber and coconuts; New Guinea has gold and timber. Cocoa, coffee, rice and groundnuts grow. The capital is Port Moresby.

NEW HAMPSHIRE, a northeastern state of U.S.A. Pop. (1960) 606,921; area

9304 sq. miles. The state consists of forest-covered mountains, long valleys and numerous lakes. The principal crops are hay, potatoes, vegetables and apples. Livestock is raised. Manufactures consist of textiles, leather goods, paper and sawmill products. It is a popular holiday centre. First settled in 1623, it was one of the original 13 states. The capital is Concord (pop. 28,991).

NEW HAVEN, a city and port in Connecticut, U.S.A. Pop. (1960) 152,048. A communications and commercial centre, it manufactures firearms, tools, watches and textiles. It is the seat of Yale University.

NEW HEBRIDES, an island group in the southwestern Pacific Ocean, jointly administered under an Anglo-French condominium. Pop. (1960) 60,374; area 5,700 sq. miles. Valuable timber, sugarcane, copra, cocoa, coffee and frozen fish are produced.

NEW JERSEY, a middle Atlantic state of the U.S.A. Pop. (1960) 6,066,782; area 7836 sq. miles. Hilly in the north, it consists of a plain sloping towards the sea in the south. The principal occupations are livestock breeding, market-gardening, fruit growing, forestry, and flower cultivation. The leading crops are maize, wheat, potatoes, peaches, blueberries, cranberries and apples. There are deposits of zinc, iron and various sands. The chief industries are chemicals, petroleum refining, nonferrous metals, automobiles, meat packing and shipbuilding. First settled in 1638, it was one of the original 13 states. The capital is Trenton (pop. 114,167). The largest cities are Newark (405,220), Jersey City (276,101), and Paterson (143,663).

NEW MEXICO, a southwestern state of the U.S.A. Pop. (1960) 951,023; area 121,666 sq. miles. Traversed by the Rocky Mountains from north to south, the state consists of plains in the eastern portion. It has a semi-arid climate, making irrigation necessary. The principal crops are hay, maize, grain, sorghums and cotton. Livestock breeding is important. There are large deposits of uranium, potash, pumice and perlite. Other leading deposits are petroleum, natural gas, copper, zinc, lead, beryllium, gold, silver and manganese. Food manufacturing, sawmill products, printing, and transport equipment are the principal industries. There are large American Indian reservations. The state is used for atomic energy tests. First settled in 1598, it belonged to Spain until 1821, and then to Mexico. It became U.S. territory in 1848 after the Mexican War, and entered the Union in 1912. The capital is Santa Fé (pop. 34,676). The largest city is Albuquerque (201,189).

NEW ORLEANS, a city in southeast Louisiana, U.S.A., on the Mississippi delta. Pop. (1960) 627,525. A large seaport, it is a communications, financial and shipping centre. Cotton, rice, sugar, grain and lumber are the principal exports. Industries consist of petroleum refining, shipbuilding, food packing and processing, textiles and furniture. Founded by the French in 1718, it also experienced a brief period of Spanish rule. French influence has left its stamp on the old quarters of the city as well as on the population. There are 18th-century buildings, art galleries, and two universities.

NEW SOUTH WALES, a state in southeastern Australia. Pop. (1961) 3,916,907; area 309,433 sq. miles. Traversed by the Great Dividing Range from north to south, it consists of sloping plateaux in the west. The principal crops are grains, potatoes, hay, tobacco, rice, sugar-cane, tropical fruit and grapes. Livestock, especially sheep breeding and dairy farming are important. There are large forest tracts, coal deposits, silver, lead, zinc, sulphur, titanium and other minerals. There are also iron and steel industries, textile plants, and factories for manufacturing clothing, footwear, foodstuffs, sawmill products and paper. The first settlement was at Port Jackson in 1788. The capital is Sydney (pop. 1961 2,181,211), the largest city in Australia. Other leading cities are Newcastle (208,905) and Greater Wollongong (131,758).

NEW TESTAMENT, the collection of 27 books which make up the distinctively Christian part of the Bible. It consists of the four Gospels, one book of Early Church history (Acts), a number of epistles, and the apocalyptic Revelation. See Bible.

NEW YORK CITY, a city and seaport in New York state, on the Atlantic Ocean, U.S.A. Pop. (1960) 7,781,984. The largest city in the U.S.A. and the largest in the world under a single municipality, it is a leading financial, commercial and communications centre. It consists of the boroughs of Manhattan, Bronx, Brooklyn, Queens and Richmond. The focal point is Manhattan, the island on which the original town was founded as New Amsterdam in 1624. The world's tallest buildings and Wall Street, the country's financial centre, are situated in Manhattan. The city has numerous parks, libraries and museums. There are many churches of all denominations. New York City has a number of universities and is also a centre for music and the theatre. Its leading industries include furs, clothing, foodstuffs, metal and machine-shop products, cosmetics, machinery, footwear, and chemicals, but there is a large variety of other industries. New York City leads the U.S.A. in publishing. Much of American wholesale and retail business is carried on in the city. Some of the largest bridges in the world link Manhattan to its environs. Dutch until 1664, the city was the capital of the U.S.A. from 1785–90 and the capital of New York state until 1797.

NEW YORK STATE, a middle Atlantic state of the U.S.A. Pop. (1960) 16,782,304; area 49,576 sq. miles. Mountainous in the northeast and southeast, it consists of a plateau with alternating ridges and valleys. There are many rivers and lakes. Dairy farming, livestock raising, the cultivation of field crops, apples and other fruit, cabbages, onions and potatoes are the leading agricultural pursuits. Maple-sugar is a major product. Minerals consist of iron, cement, petroleum, gypsum, titanium, talc, abrasive garnet, wollastonite, emery and building stone. The chief industries are clothing, printing and publishing, foodstuffs, iron and steel equipment, aircraft, locomotives, typewriters, electrical appliances, photographic and optical goods, and wines. From 1609—64 the region was under the rule of the Dutch, who ceded it to the English. It was one of the 13 original states. The capital is Albany (pop. 129,726). The largest cities are New York (7,781,984), Buffalo (532,759), Rochester (318,611) and Syracuse (216,038).

NEW ZEALAND, a member of the British Commonwealth of Nations in the South Pacific Ocean. Pop. (1961) 2,414,064; area 103,736 sq. miles. It consists of North Island (area 44,281 sq. miles) and South Island (58,093 sq. miles), the two principal islands, Stewart Island (670 sq. miles), the Chatham Islands (372 sq. miles) and minor islands (320 sq. miles). North and South Islands are mountainous, with active volcanoes and numerous lakes. The principal crops are wheat, oats and barley. Livestock breeding and dairy farming are important occupations. The leading industries are foodstuffs, wool, sawmill, products, chemicals, sheet metal, clothing, machinery, automobile assembly, and printing and publishing. There are deposits of gold, silver, tungsten, coal, petroleum, and building sand and stone. The principal exports are dairy products, meats and wool. In the 12th and 13th centuries the Maoris, a Polynesian people, settled the islands. European settlement began in the early years of the 19th century. There were frequent wars with the Maoris who finally yielded in 1871. New Zealand has advanced social legislation. The capital is Wellington (pop. 150,537). Other leading cities are Auckland (448,218), Christchurch (220,322) and Dunedin (105,053).

NEWARK, a city and port in New Jersey, U.S.A., on Passaic River and Newark Bay. Pop. (1960) 405,220. A communications, financial, industrial and commercial centre, it is the seat of numerous insurance companies. A wide diversity of articles are manufactured, ranging from aircraft to cosmetics. The city has many parks and numerous educational institutions. It was settled in 1666. Its proximity to New York City accounts for some of its intensive business activity in the distributing and retail fields.

NEWCASTLE, a city and port in New South Wales, Australia, at the mouth of the Hunter River. Pop. (1961) 208,905. On the outskirts of a large coal-mining region, the city has extensive metallurgical industries. There are shipyards and engineering works.

NEWCASTLE-UPON-TYNE, a county borough and port in northeast England, on the River Tyne. Pop. (1961) 269,389. A leading centre for exporting coal, it also has shipyards and heavy industries. Locomotives, turbines, chemicals, lead, glass and copper wares are manufactured. Five bridges link the city to Gateshead across the river. There is a 12th-century castle keep, and the 13th-century Black Gate is a museum.

NEWFOUNDLAND, a province of the Dominion of Canada. Pop. (1961) 457,853; area 156,185 sq. miles. It consists of the island of Newfoundland (area 42,734 sq. miles) in the Atlantic Ocean and the eastern portion of the Labrador peninsula. The island is a rugged plateau with numerous lakes and rivers. Fishing is the chief occupation. Sealing and lumbering are important. There are large deposits of iron, and lead, zinc and copper are mined. Newsprint and pulp manufacture are the leading industries. Discovered by John Cabot in 1497, Newfoundland island became a Crown Colony in 1583, a dominion from 1917, and Canada's tenth province in 1949. The capital is St John's (pop. 1961 90,838). See Labrador.

NEWMAN, John Henry (1801—90), English Cardinal. Vicar (1828) at St Mary's, Oxford, and a leader of the Oxford Movement, he joined the Roman Catholic Church in 1845, and was appointed Cardinal in 1879. He is the author of the hymn *Lead, Kindly Light*, and of the spiritual autobiography *Apologia pro Vita Sua* (1864).

NEWPORT, a city and county borough in Monmouthshire, Wales, on the Usk River. Pop. (1961) 108,107. A port for exporting coal and steel, it manufactures steam engines, machinery, chemicals, plastics and aluminium goods. There are shipyards capable of building the largest type of tanker.

NEWSPAPERS, daily, evening or weekly, derived from hand-printed newsletters published in England in the 16th century. There were English weekly newspapers in the 17th century, although no domestic news could be printed until 1641 because of the Star Chamber's censorship. The oldest newspaper still in existence is the *London Gazette* (1665). The first daily was the *Daily Courant* (1702). Although heavily taxed from 1712 till the mid-19th century, English papers grew in numbers and circulation. *The Times* began appearing, as the *London Universal Register*, in 1785, and the *Observer* in 1791. Popular journalism, started by the *Daily Telegraph* in 1855, was brought to the masses by the *Star* (1855) and Harmsworth's *Daily Mail* (1896), which passed the million circulation mark during the Boer War. Then followed the great days of the Press Lords (Northcliffe, Rothermere, Beaverbrook and Kemsley), in whose footsteps Roy Thomson now follows. Rising costs have led to ever increasing dependence on advertising, amalgamations, financial mergers, and the virtual impossibility of starting a new paper with any hope of success.

NEWTON, Sir Isaac (1642—1727), English philosopher, mathematician and physicist. His formulation of the laws of gravitation and of motion won him special distinction. He discovered the binomial theorem while still a student, and then shared with Leibniz the distinction of discovering the calculus. He invented the reflecting telescope and made important discoveries in optics; his theory of the nature of light, however, misled many generations of physicists. His influence on philosophic thought was revolutionary. He wrote *Philosophiae Naturalis Principia Mathematica* and *Opticks*. He became President of the Royal Society in 1703.

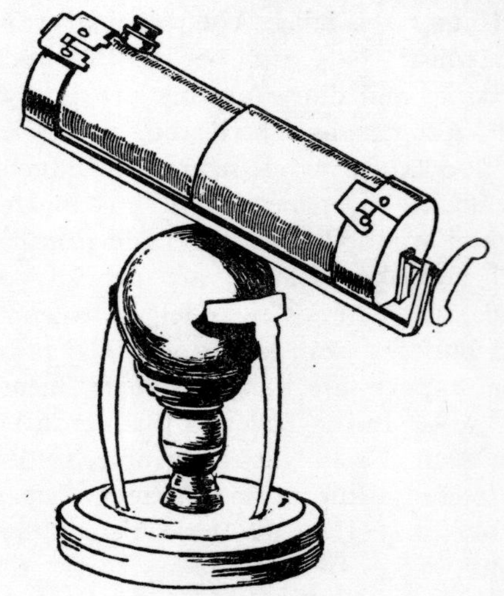

Newton's telescope

NIAGARA FALLS, a waterfall 168 ft high on the Niagara River, which forms part of the Canadian-U.S.A. boundary. Hydro-electric power has been developed from it.

NICAEAN COUNCILS, two ecclesiastical councils held at Nicaea. The first, convened by Constantine (325) to combat Arianism, adopted the Nicene Creed and the second (787), under the Empress Irene, condemned the iconoclasts.

NICARAGUA, the largest Central American republic, between the Caribbean Sea and the Pacific Ocean. Pop. (1960) 1,501,538; area 57,145 sq. miles. It is mountainous in the west, with fertile valleys; the east coast is swampy and more than half the country is jungle. Coffee, cotton, sugar-cane, cocoa, maize, beans and tropical fruit are grown. Livestock breeding is important. Gold, silver, copper and precious stones are found. There are local industries, including matches, cigarettes, textiles and dairy products. Independent since 1838, Nicaragua has had a number of unstable governments. U.S. troops were stationed there from 1912—25 and at intervals until 1933. The capital is Managua (pop. 198,939).

NICE, a French city on the Mediterranean. Pop. (1962) 294,976. A popular winter resort, it has a port. There are metallurgical, textile, and food industries. It became French in 1860.

NICHOLAS, St (d. *c.* 352), a bishop in Asia Minor about whom very little is known. His day (December 6) was observed by Dutch Protestants, who called him Sint Klaas; they took the custom with them when they emigrated to America, where the name became corrupted to Santa Claus and coupled with Christmas celebrations.

NICHOLAS II (1868—1918), the last Czar of Russia. He came to the throne in 1894. During his reign Russia was humiliatingly defeated by Japan, the 1905 Revolution was ruthlessly put down, and the management of the Russian armies, especially of the medical services and supply generally, in the First World War was hopelessly inefficient. In addition, his wife was under the influence of the rascally monk Rasputin. Forced to abdicate in 1917, the Czar, together with his family, was executed the following year by the Bolsheviks.

NICKEL, see Elements.

NIETZSCHE, Friedrich (1844—1900), German philosopher, author of *Thus Spake Zarathustra* (1883—85), *Beyond Good and Evil* (1886), and *The Will to Power*, published posthumously. An unlikely follower of the mild Darwin, Nietzsche took his conception of the survival of the fittest and developed his own theory of the ideal Superman, beyond good and evil, conscious of his noble, heroic mission to drag the rest of the world, willy-nilly, along the path he mapped out for it. He never ceased to inveigh against the slave morality taught by Christianity; compassion and self-sacrifice are the virtues of the servile, the weaklings, who may be disregarded. Nietzsche died insane.

NIGER, see River.

NIGER, a republic in West Africa. Pop. (1961) 2,870,000; area 458,995 sq. miles. The north is part of the Sahara. There is sufficient water only in the thickly forested southwest, through which the River Niger flows. Millet, groundnuts (which form 90% of exports), beans, manioc, cotton and rice are cultivated. There is considerable livestock. Salt, natron, tin and gum arabic are produced. Formerly a French territory, it became independent in 1960. The capital is Niamey (pop. 30,030).

INGERIA, Republic of, a republic and member of the British Commonwealth in West Africa, on the Atlantic Ocean. Pop. (1961) 35,752,000 (figure subject to revision); area 356,669 sq. miles. Consisting of dry savannah in the north, it is mostly plateau in the interior with lagoons and tropical forests in the coastal region. Groundnuts, cotton, hides and skins, tin and columbite are produced in the north; palm products, cocoa, timber and rubber in the south. Coal, gold, petroleum and tantalite are also found. Industries consist of textiles, foodstuffs, plywood and ceramic products. Under British administration since the last quarter of the 19th century, it became independent in 1960. The territorial divisions are Northern, Eastern, and Western Nigeria, with a Mid-West state formed from two western provinces in 1963. The federal capital is Lagos (pop. 1962 450,000). Other large cities are Ibadan (600,000), Ogbomosho (139,535) and Kano (130,173).

NIGHTINGALE, Florence (1820—1910), English nurse and founder of modern nursing. A volunteer nurse in the appalling conditions of the Crimean War, her efforts were so successful that the death rate among the sick and wounded fell from almost 50% to around 2%. She devoted the rest of her life to reforming, and raising the status, of the nursing service. In 1907 she was awarded the Order of Merit, the first woman to be so distinguished.

NILE, see River.

NITROGEN, see Elements.

NKOMO, Joshua (*c.* 1916—), Rhodesian politician. Born in Matabeleland, he became an auctioneer and estate agent in Bulawayo. After becoming President of the African National Congress he lived in London in exile, returning in 1960 as President of the National Democratic Party (N.D.P.).

NKRUMAH, Kwame (1909—), Ghanaian statesman. Educated at Achimota College and Lincoln College, Pennsylvania, he was a schoolmaster from 1931—34. He went to London in 1945, where he met George Padmore and started his political career, becoming general secretary of the United Gold Coast Convention Party in 1947 and founding the Convention People's Party in 1949. After a civil disobedience campaign in 1950 he was sent to prison, where he still was when elected to the Gold Coast Legislative Council in 1961. Released by the Governor, Sir Charles Arden-Clarke, with whom he was on good terms, he became Prime Minister of the Gold Coast in 1952 and of independent Ghana in 1957. In 1960 he became President, with the title Osagyefo (Victorious Leader). He considers that, in its present stage of development, Socialism is best suited to his country, and has fought hard, against considerable opposition, for a United States of Africa. His books include *I Speak of Freedom* and *Africa Must Unite* (1963).

NOBEL, Alfred Bernhard (1833—96), Swedish chemist and inventor. He patented more than a hundred inventions, the chief among them being dynamite, blasting gelatine and a smokeless gunpowder. On his death he left a fund of nearly £2,000,000 for awarding five annual prizes to persons making outstanding contributions in chemistry, physics, physiology or medicine, literature and the cause of world peace.

NORFOLK, a maritime county in eastern England, on the North Sea. Pop. (1961) 561,980; area 2,055 sq. miles. Consisting of a rolling plain, it has numerous shallow lakes in the east known as the Broads. The principal crops are wheat and other grains, potatoes, clover and hay. Sugar beet, vegetables and fruit are also cultivated. Dairy farming and fishing are important. The leading industries are fish-canning, textiles, footwear, agricultural implements and flour. The county town is Norwich.

NORFOLK, a port and the largest city in Virginia, U.S.A. Pop. (1960) 305,872. A communications and industrial centre, it is a large naval base. Nearby beaches make it a favourite resort. Norfolk's industries include shipbuilding, automobile assembly, aircraft parts, tools, metal products, chemicals and foodstuffs.

NORMAN CONQUEST (1066—71), the conquest of England by William the Conqueror (Duke of Normandy), which led to the downfall of the old Anglo-Saxon dynasty and which, by virtue of bringing England into closer relationship with the Continent, ushered in a period of social and cultural enlightenment for the English.

NORMANDY, a former French province on the English Channel. It consists of chalky plains in the north, the Seine valley, and the fertile cornlands of the south. There are deposits of iron ore; wool and cotton weaving are important pursuits. The Normans or Northmen conquered the region in the 10th century A.D. In 1066 Duke William II suppressed rebellious elements and then invaded England. From 1417—50 Normandy belonged to England and then reverted to France. The Allies' first invasions of German-occupied France were carried out in Normandy in 1944.

NORTH AMERICA, the continent in the northern half of the western hemisphere. Pop. (1959; including Central America) 261,000,000; area 9,355,000 sq. miles. From north to south the continent consists of the gently-rolling Laurentian Upland, the Hudson Bay Lowland, the Atlantic and Gulf of Mexico Coastal Plain, the northeast-southwest Appalachian Highlands, the Central Lowland, and the Great Plains as far as the Rocky Mountains. Beyond the Rocky Mountains are the Cordilleran Plateaux and the Pacific Coast Range. The climate varies from arctic to tropical in Central America, and the vegetation varies accordingly. Most of the rivers drain into the Atlantic Ocean. The continental divide runs along the Rocky Mountains. Possessed of great forest and mineral wealth, it drew many European settlers after its discovery by Columbus in 1492. The earliest inhabitants were American Indians and, in the far north, Eskimos. Most of the native cultures were annihilated with the coming of Europeans. The earliest settlers were Spaniards in the south; French in the St Lawrence and lower Mississippi valleys; and English on the east coast. Large numbers of African slaves were imported during the 17th—19th centuries. Politically North America is divided between Canada, the U.S.A., Mexico, and the countries of Central America. The island of Greenland belongs to Denmark and those of St Pierre and Miquelon to France.

NORTH ATLANTIC TREATY ORGANISATION (N.A.T.O.), a military alliance for mutual security. Formed in 1949, it consists of Belgium, Canada, Denmark, France, the German Federal Republic, Great Britain, Greece, Iceland, Italy, Luxemburg, Netherlands, Norway, Portugal, Turkey and the U.S.A.

NORTH BORNEO, see Sabah.

NORTH CAROLINA, an Atlantic state of the U.S.A. Pop. (1960) 4,556,155; area 52,712 sq. miles. The state consists of a coastal plain, the Piedmont Plateau in the central portion, and the Appalachian Highlands in the west. It has a humid subtropical climate. The principal products are tobacco, maize, poultry, pigs, cotton and groundnuts. There is a large variety of minerals, chiefly mica, feldspar, silica, millstones, kaolin clay and pyrophyllite. Lumbering is important. The leading industries are textiles, cigarettes, electrical machinery and furniture. The first English colony in America was established on Roanoke Island in 1585. One of the 13 original states, it was a member of the Confederacy during the Civil War. It is the most advanced Southern state. The capital is Raleigh (pop. 93,931). Other leading cities are Charlotte (201,564), Greensboro (119,574) and Sinston-Salem (111,135).

NORTH DAKOTA, a north central state of the U.S.A., on the Canadian border. Pop. (1960) 632,446; area 70,665 sq. miles. Part of the Great Plains, it rises gradually towards the west. The principal crops are barley, rye and wheat. Flax seed, potatoes, hay, oats and maize are also cultivated extensively. Livestock raising is important. There are coal and petroleum deposits. The main manufactures are dairy products. First settled in the 1760s, it became a state in 1889. The capital is Bismarck (pop. 27,670). The largest city is Fargo (46,662).

NORTH POLE, the northern axis of the earth and the centre point of the Arctic Circle. It consists of ice above water two miles deep. It was first reached by Rear-Admiral Robert Peary of the U.S. Navy in 1909.

NORTHAMPTON, a city and county borough, Northamptonshire, England, on the Nene River. Pop. (1961) 105,361. It is a footwear manufacturing centre. There are also iron foundries and breweries. It has some old churches. Several parliaments met here during the 12th—14th centuries.

NORTHAMPTONSHIRE, a Midland county, England. Pop. (1961) 398,132; area 998 sq. miles. The Soke of Peterborough (pop. 74,442; area 84 sq. miles) in the northeast is an administrative county consisting of reclaimed fenland. The county is hilly in the west and southwest, where the rivers have their sources. Livestock breeding and dairy farming are important. Wheat and other grains, potatoes, turnips and sugar-beet are the principal crops. Shoes, iron products, silks, paper and flour are manufactured. There is some timber and building stone. In ancient times the county was part of Mercia. Northampton is the county town.

NORTHCLIFFE, Alfred Harmsworth, 1st Viscount (1865—1922), British newspaper proprietor. In 1888, six years after founding the weekly, *Answers*, he bought the *Evening News*. He founded the *Daily Mail* in 1896 and the *Daily Mirror* in 1903. Northcliffe became principal owner of the *Times* in 1908, managing it until his death, when it was sold. The *Daily Mail*, which at one time sold at a halfpenny, was the first paper to exceed two million in circulation. In it were to be found the germs of most of the features of the modern newspaper.

NORTHERN IRELAND, a self-governing constituent of the United Kingdom. Pop. (1961) 1,425,462; area 5,238 sq. miles. It consists of the six counties of Antrim, Armagh, Down, Fermanagh, Londonderry and Tyrone. These, with the counties of Cavan, Donegal and Monaghan (in the Irish Republic), formed the old province of Ulster, a chief centre of English, and later Scottish, settlement. Northern Ireland came into existence with the Treaty of 1921 which established the Irish Free State. It has its own parliament (House of Commons and Senate) at Stormont, near Belfast, and a Governor appointed by the Crown; it also returns 12 members to the House of Commons in London. A quarter of the land is mountain or bog. The chief crops are oats, potatoes, fruit (in Armagh) and flax. Industry is mainly located at Belfast, the capital, where there is shipbuilding and the manufacture of aircraft and linen. Roman Catholics form the largest single religious group, but are outnumbered by the Protestants, who are divided into various denominations, of which the Presbyterian is the largest.

NORTHERN TERRITORY, the north central division of Australia. Pop. (1961) 43,304 (including 16,165 aborigines); area 523,620 sq. miles. Consisting of a gently-rising surface from the coast, it is mostly desert in the south. Beef-cattle

El Greco's (q.v.) highly emotional *Cleansing of the Temple.*

Photo: Trustees of the National Gallery

The remarkable portrait by Velasquez (q.v.) of Pope Innocent x, which astounded the art world.

Photo: Anderson-Giraudon

Rembrandt's (q.v.) wonderful ability to portray old age is illustrated in his magnificent *Abraham Dismissing Hagar and Ishmael.*

Photo: Victoria & Albert Museum

The 17th century Dutch painter Jan van Huysum specialised in minutely detailed and elaborately composed flower studies. *Flowers in a Vase.*

Photo: The Wallace Collection. Crown copyright reserved

Mr & Mrs Andrews is a typical example of the work of Thomas Gainsborough (q.v.), the English portrait and landscape painter.

Photo: Trustees of the National Gallery

J. M. W. Turner's (q.v.) *Snowstorm at Sea* illustrates one aspect of this remarkable painter's diversified range of subjects.

Photo: Trustees of the National Gallery

Ingres (1780-1867) was the leader of the neo-Classical school and in opposition to Delacroix and the Romantic school. His most successful works were portraits; newly discovered photography greatly influenced him. A detail from his painting *Madame Moitessier*.

Photo: Trustees of the National Gallery

Eugène Delacroix (1798-1863) was the leader of the Romantic school in France. His large canvases were painted in a broad free manner, full of brilliant colour and violent movement. *The Good Samaritan.*

Photo: Victoria & Albert Museum

The French Impressionist Camille Pissarro (1830-1903) was the most unwavering of the Impressionist group. He was strongly influenced by Corot (q.v.). *Jardin des Tuileries, Matin, Printemps.*

Photo: Marlborough Fine Art Ltd

raising is the leading occupation, and there is a pearl-fishing industry. There are mineral resources including gold, copper, tungsten, uranium, mica and manganese. First a part of New South Wales and later South Australia, it was placed under Commonwealth administration in 1911. The capital is Darwin (12,480). Alice Springs (3000) is in the heart of the area.

NORTHUMBERLAND, a county in northeast England, on the Scottish border and the North Sea. Pop. (1961) 818,988; area 2019 sq. miles. It consists of high moors in the central portion, with the Cheviot Hills on the border. The principal rivers are the Tweed and the Tyne. Oats, barley, potatoes, and sheep are raised. There are large coal deposits in the south. Lead, zinc, building stone and fireclay are found. The leading industries are shipbuilding, chemicals, engineering and glass. There is a Roman wall. Newcastle-upon-Tyne (pop. 1961 269,389) is the county town.

NORTHUMBRIA, one of the seven Anglo-Saxon kingdoms of England, extending along the east coast from Yorkshire to Berwick. It was formed by Æthelfrith (reigned 593—617) through the union of the kingdoms of Bernicia and Deira. The kingdom was the leading power in England until 685. In 920 it acknowledged the supremacy of Wessex. Northumbria was finally absorbed into England towards the end of the 11th century.

NORTHWEST TERRITORIES, a region of northern Canada between Yukon Territory and Hudson Bay. Pop. (1961) 22,998; area 1,304,903 sq. miles. Mining, fishing and trapping are the chief occupations. There are deposits of gold, silver, pitchblende and petroleum. Fishing is important. The population consists of Europeans, American Indians and Eskimos. The region is divided into the districts of Keewatin, Mackenzie and Franklin, the latter in the Arctic Archipelago.

NORWAY, a kingdom in northwest Europe, in Scandinavia. Pop. (1960) 3,583,000; area 124,556 sq. miles. Consisting of a central plateau with forested mountains, it is cut by deep fiords on the west coast. There are numerous lakes, rivers and glaciers. The northern portion is within the Arctic Circle. There is arable land in the southeast on which hay, potatoes and cereals are grown. Stock raising and trapping fur-bearing animals are important. The forests are a leading source of income. Fishing and the production of whale oil are important occupations. There are deposits of iron, aluminium, nickel, copper, zinc and other minerals. The most important industries are pulp and paper, canning, and electro-chemical and electro-metallurgical manufactures. The history of Norway diverges from that of the rest of Scandinavia with the period of the Vikings in the 9th—11th centuries. After a brief period of Swedish domination, Norway was a Danish province for nearly 600 years, down to 1814, when another union with Sweden was effected. In 1905 Norway became independent. Neutral during the First World War, Norway was under German occupation from 1940—45. In the post-war period Norway became a member of the North Atlantic Treaty Organisation. The capital is Oslo (pop. 1961 477,121). The next largest city is Bergen (115,914).

NORWICH, a city and county borough, Norfolk, England, on the Wensum River. Pop. (1961) 119,904. It has an important livestock market. Footwear and clothing are the leading manufactures. There are iron foundries and chemical, engineering and foodstuffs factories. There is a fine Norman Cathedral (1096), and many 16th-century houses.

NOSE, a bony compartment serving to warm, moisten and filter air breathed into the respiratory system, and as the organ of the sense of smell. The external part consists of bone and cartilage with openings for the nostrils. The interior above the roof of the mouth is divided into two parts by the nasal septum and opens into the throat. Its mucous membrane contains the receptors for the sense of smell. In human beings the nose is relatively inefficient as an organ of smell, having little discrimination.

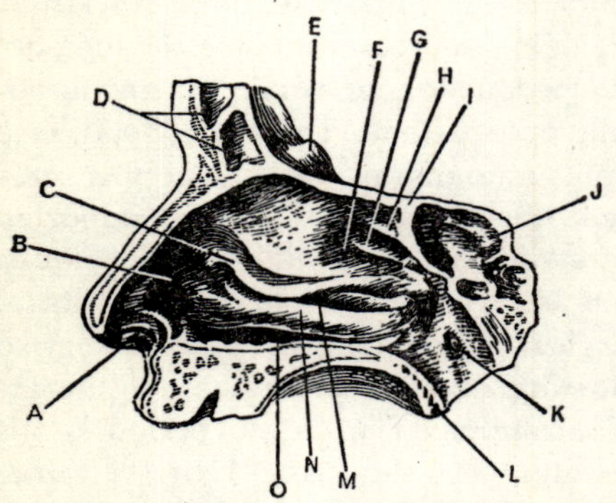

Human nose (lateral wall of right nasal cavity) A. Vestibule B. Nasal cavity C. Middle nasal concha D. Frontal sinus E. Crista galli F. Superior meatus G. Superior concha H. Supreme concha I. Opening of sphenoidal air cells J. Sphenoidal air cells K. Auditory tube L. Soft palate M. Middle meatus N. Inferior nasal concha O. Inferior meatus

NOTTINGHAM, a city and county borough, Nottinghamshire, England, on the Trent River. Pop. (1961) 311,645. A communications centre, it manufactures lace, hosiery, silks, metal and leather goods, bicycles and tobacco. An important Danish borough in the 9th century, it has a number of old buildings; the Castle is a museum and art gallery; the Elizabethan Wollaton Hall houses a natural history museum, and Newstead Abbey, Byron's home, is nine miles to the north. There is a 19th-century Roman Catholic cathedral, and a university.

NOTTINGHAMSHIRE, a Midland county in England. Pop. (1961) 902,966; area 844 sq. miles. Generally flat, it is drained chiefly by the Trent River. On its fertile soil wheat, oats, barley, root-crops and grasses are grown. Cattle raising and dairy farming are leading occupations. There are deposits of coal and building stone. The principal manufactures are textiles, lace, iron and steel, machinery, bicycles and motors. The county town is Nottingham.

NOVA SCOTIA, a maritime province in southeastern Canada. Pop. (1961) 737,007; area 21,068 sq. miles. It consists of a peninsula and Cape Breton Island connected by a causeway. The main peninsula is hilly and cut by transverse valleys. There are many small rivers. Dairy farming, poultry raising and fruit growing are the main pursuits. Forestry and fishing are important sources of income. The principal minerals are coal, gypsum and barytes. Settled by the French early in the 17th century, it was called Acadia. In 1713 it became a British possession, and in 1867 one of the four original provinces of the Dominion. The capital and largest city is Halifax (pop. 1961 183,946).

NOVAYA ZEMLYA, a group of Russian islands in the Arctic Ocean. Area 35,000 sq. miles. There is much wild life on the two main islands. Lead, copper and zinc are found. Fur trapping, whaling, sealing and fishing are principal occupations. It is a site for atomic tests. Except for a few coastal settlements, the islands are uninhabited.

NOVOSIBIRSK, a city in the R.S.F.S.R., on the Ob River, U.S.S.R. Pop. (1962)

985,000. The largest and most important industrial and communications centre in western Siberia, with a large hydroelectric station, it has numerous educational and cultural facilities. Manufactures include meat packing and processing, textiles, sawmill products, metallurgical works, machinery and chemicals.

NUBIA, a region in northeast Africa, between the Libyan desert and the Red Sea, corresponding to northern Sudan. It was part of ancient Ethiopia. The Nubian desert, extending from the Nile River to the Red Sea, covers an area of 90,000 sq. miles.

NUCLEAR FISSION, the breaking up of the nucleus of a heavy atom into two or more unstable nuclei of approximately equal mass. This produces an enormous release of energy, unchecked in the atomic bomb, but kept under control in the nuclear reactor (q.v.). If, for example, the unstable natural isotope of uranium known as U235 (having 143 neutrons and 92 protons) is bombarded with neutrons, some nuclei temporarily gain an extra neutron, rendering them even less stable. These nuclei split into two or more fission fragments plus two or three neutrons; the extra neutrons promote disintegration in other nuclei, in a chain reaction. The total mass of fission products is less than that of the original nucleus; the missing mass has turned into atomic energy, in accordance with Einstein's formula $E = mc^2$ (see Relativity). Nuclear fission was discovered in 1939.

NUCLEAR FUSION, see Hydrogen Bomb.

NUCLEAR PARTICLES, fundamental particles such as the neutron, proton, electron (qq.v.), of which there are believed to be nearly a hundred. Each kind has its anti-particle (see Positron). Mesons of different kinds, negative and positive, are found in cosmic rays. Neutrons are emitted together with beta particles; they have no charge and no mass, and are highly penetrative.

NUCLEAR PHYSICS, the study of the nucleus of atoms and its radiations (the study of its surrounding electrons is the subject of atomic physics). It has led to the development of nuclear power and the atomic bomb. Experiments centre round the bombardment of nuclei with artificially accelerated particles. One of the main problems is to elucidate the nature (still unknown) of the strong forces which hold together the protons and neutrons of a nucleus; they do not resemble the electrical attraction found between electrons and nucleus.

NUCLEAR REACTOR (atomic pile), a device to control the energy released in nuclear fission (q.v.) by the use of moderators (e.g. graphite, heavy water) which slow down the neutrons; excess neutrons are absorbed at a controllable rate, and thus the chain reaction is kept at the constant level required. The nuclear reactor is used to produce heat to generate steam for turbines at electric power stations, to provide power for ships or aircraft, and to produce a plutonium isotope used in the atomic bomb. Materials irradiated in a reactor acquire new properties. In Britain the Atomic Energy Authority's plant at Calder Hall, mainly engaged in making plutonium, began also to feed electricity into the National Grid in 1956. The first of several civil nuclear power stations to do this was that at Berkeley, Gloucestershire, in 1962.

NUCLEAR WEAPONS (see Atomic Bomb; Hydrogen Bomb) produce blast, heat-flash, gamma-ray flash and radioactive fall-out. Nuclear warheads either atomic or thermonuclear, can be fitted to intercontinental ballistic missiles. Nuclear artillery (tactical nuclears) consists of rockets and artillery which propel nuclear weapons over a comparatively short range, and is employed on or near the battlefield in support of ground forces. The largest nuclear weapons are classified in megatons; a megaton is the explosive force equivalent to a million tons of TNT.

NUCLEIC ACIDS, complex organic compounds containing nitrogen, with huge molecules. There are two types: DNA (deoxyribonucleic acid) found in all cell nuclei, and RNA (ribonucleic acid) in cytoplasm, the living substance that surrounds the nucleus. They occur as nucleoproteins, i.e. combined with proteins. Chromosomes are coiled DNA molecules, which vary with the species and carry the genes; they act as transmitters of hereditary qualities from generation to generation by means of a code of 'instructions' or 'specifications', which can be arranged in an infinity of permutations and combinations; these are passed on by DNA to RNA.

NUCLEUS, the central core of an atom, where most of its mass is concentrated, around which the electrons revolve. The whole atom has 10,000 times the diameter of its nucleus. It consists of two types of fundamental particle, the positive proton and the neutral neutron, bound together by strong nuclear forces, and thus has a positive charge. The atomic weight of an atom depends on the mass number, i.e. the total number of protons and neutrons. Isotopes (q.v.) are atoms of the same element having different numbers of neutrons.

NUMIDIA, an ancient country in North Africa, between Carthage and Mauretania. It corresponds to Algeria.

NUREMBERG (Nürnberg), a city in Bavaria, West Germany, on the Pegnitz. Pop. (1960) 448,900. A commercial and industrial centre, it is in the midst of a rich agricultural region. Its manufactures include metal and electrical equipment, chemicals, automobiles, toys and sawmill products. It was a favourite venue for monster Nazi rallies, and after the Second World War, in which the many magnificent medieval buildings were destroyed or badly damaged, it was the scene of the trials of war criminals.

NYERERE, Julius (1922—), Tanganyikan statesman. Educated at Makerere College and Edinburgh University, he taught in Roman Catholic schools and then founded the Tanganyika African National Union in 1954. He led the elected members in the Legislative Council, becoming Chief Minister in 1960 and then Premier. In January 1962 he resigned office, and became the first President of the new republic in December of that year. He stands for moderation, racial harmony and an East African federation.

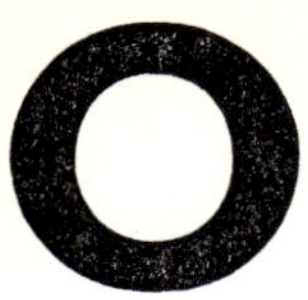

OAHU, the most important island in Hawaii. Pop. (1960) 500,409; area 604 sq. miles. It is a popular tourist centre and grows sugar and pineapples. The largest city is Honolulu (294,179).

OAK RIDGE, a town in Tennessee, U.S.A. Pop. (1960) 27,009. A centre for all phases of atomic energy research, it was here that the first atomic bombs were produced.

OAKLAND, a city and port in California, U.S.A., on San Francisco Bay. Pop. (1960) 367,548. A communications, commercial and industrial centre, it exports fresh and canned fruit. There are shipyards, oil refineries and sawmills. Manufactures include foodstuffs, automobiles, chemicals and electrical equipment. There are many educational and cultural institutions. Oakland is connected to San Francisco by the remarkable Transbay Bridge.

OB, see River.

OBERAMMERGAU, a town in Bavaria, West Germany. Pop. (1960) 4655. It is famous for its presentation of the Passion Play every 10 years, in which local inhabitants play most parts. Finely carved wooden and ivory objects are made.

OBERHAUSEN, a city in North Rhine-Westphalia, West Germany. Pop. (1960) 256,495. An important iron and steel centre in the Ruhr, it produces chemicals, furniture and glass.

OBSERVATORY, Astronomical, an institution, or building, for studying the heavenly bodies. It is usually equipped with permanently mounted telescopes and other instruments for conducting observations and research and for recording results. A library and photographic laboratory provide services essential to modern observatories. The Royal Observatory at Greenwich was completed in 1675. The largest telescope in the world is a 200-in. reflector at the Mt Palomar Observatory in California, U.S.A. Other famous observatories are Mt Wilson (California), Yerkes (Wisconsin) and Manchester University's experimental station at Jodrell Bank, which uses a radio telescope, and is the largest of its type in the world, able to trace solar systems millions of light years away.

OCEANIA, a region comprising all the island groups of the Pacific. It includes Micronesia, Melanesia, Polynesia and Australasia. Pop. 14,800,000; area 3,201,000 sq. miles.

OCEANOGRAPHY, the science of the oceans, it deals with the vast body of knowledge as applied specifically to seas, including chemistry, physics, biology, geography and geology. Its province embraces the study of ocean currents; the composition, temperature and density of sea-water; the depth of the ocean floor, the nature of the sediment found there, and all kinds of marine life. Bathyspheres, depth-sounding apparatus and sea-floor samplers are employed.

ODENSE, a city in Denmark, capital of the island of Fyn. Pop. (1960) 111,145. An industrial port, it is one of Denmark's oldest cities. Manufactures include foodstuffs, textiles and machinery.

ODER (Odra), see River.

ODESSA, a city and port in the Ukrainian S.S.R., on the Black Sea, U.S.S.R. Pop. (1962) 704,000. An educational and cultural centre, it is also a holiday resort. It produces ships, aircraft, munitions, chemicals, foodstuffs, clothing and machinery. Broad stone stairways lead up from the sea.

ODYSSEUS (Ulysses), one of the legendary heroes of the Trojan War who is especially known for his 10 year period of wandering described in Homer's epic poem, the *Odyssey*.

OFFA (d. A.D. 796), King of Mercia. During his long reign he regained control of Kent, Wessex, East Anglia, Powys in Wales and a region south of the Humber; by his daughter's marriage he allied himself with Northumbria. A code of law known to Alfred the Great was compiled by him. He signed a commercial treaty with Charlemagne. The remains can still be seen of Offa's Dyke, which ran from the mouth of the Dee to that of the Wye, and was built of stone and earth to keep out Welsh marauders.

OFFENBACH, Jacques (1819—80), German-born French composer of operettas. In addition to the famous *Tales of Hoffmann*, he wrote *Orpheus in the Underworld*, *La Belle Hélène*, *La Vie Parisienne* and many other operettas.

OHIO, see River.

OHIO, a north central state, on Lake Erie, U.S.A. Pop. (1960) 9,706,397; area 41,122 sq. miles. Generally flat, it has a low-lying northeast-southwest ridge. The principal crops are maize, oats, wheat, soya beans, potatoes, tobacco, apples and grapes. Livestock raising is important. There are extensive deposits of coal, petroleum, natural gas, lime, sand and gravel. It is a leading industrial state producing pig-iron, steel, tyres, paper, motors and metal products. The capital is Columbus (pop. 471,316). Other large cities are Cleveland (876,050), Cincinnati (502,550), Toledo (318,003) and Akron (290,351).

OIL WELL. Following seismic soundings of the sub-strata, a tapering hole is drilled in sections and strengthened with steel linings from a derrick erected overhead. When the oil is eventually reached, the derrick and drilling rig are replaced by a pump which draws the crude oil to the surface. It is subsequently refined and stored in tanks.

OKLAHOMA, a south central state of the U.S.A. Pop. (1960) 2,328,284; area 69,919 sq. miles. Mostly level plain, it has wooded mountains in the east. Predominantly agricultural, it produces maize, wheat, grain, sorghums and cotton. Livestock raising is important. There are extensive deposits of petroleum, natural gas and gypsum. The leading industry is petroleum refining. Zinc smelting, meat packing and flour milling are also important. Set aside as Indian Territory in 1834, Oklahoma was thrown open to settlers in 1889. It became a state in 1907. The capital is Oklahoma City. The other large city is Tulsa (261,685).

OKLAHOMA CITY, the capital and largest city of Oklahoma, U.S.A., on the North Canadian River. Pop. (1960) 324,253. It is a centre for communications, finance, commerce, shipping and wholesale trade. In a rich oil-producing area, it has livestock and cotton markets, and extensive stockyards. Its chief industry is oil refining and processing. Other industries include aircraft, steel, oil-field supplies and meat packing. The city was settled in a single day in 1889, when 10,000 persons claimed sites in the area on the throwing open of the Indian Territory to white settlement.

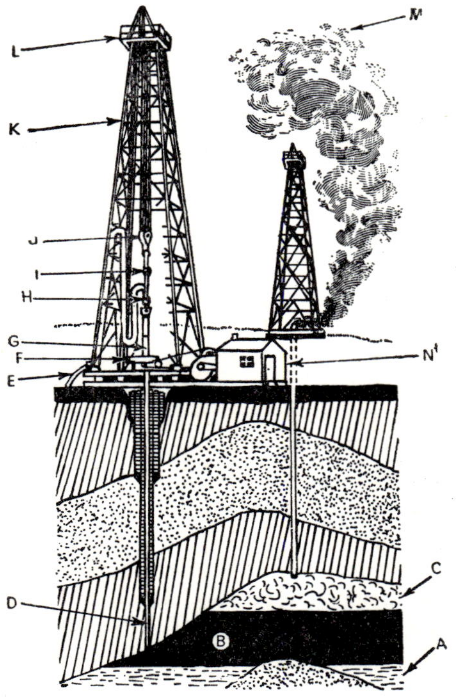

Oil well
A. Water B. Oil in porous rock C. Gas collects here D. Drill pipe boring down E. Flexible mud hose F. Rotary table G. Kelly H. Swivel I. Hook J. Travelling block K. Derrick L. Safety platform M. Gas burning N. Engine house

OLD PRETENDER (1688—1766), or James Edward Francis Stuart, the son of James II and half-brother of Queen Anne, landed in Scotland six weeks after the outbreak of the first Jacobite rebellion in 1715. After the defeat of the Jacobites (q.v.) he returned to France and then lived in Rome on a pension from the Pope. His son was the Young Pretender (q.v.).

OLD TESTAMENT, a collection of 39 books sacred to Jews and Christians alike, which contains Jewish law, history, prophecy, poetry and narratives from the pre-Christian era. It is written largely in Hebrew (with a few chapters in Aramaic) and took — in contrast to the New Testament — several centuries to evolve. See Bible.

OLDENBURG, a city in Lower Saxony, West Germany. Pop. (1960) 121,618. It is a railway junction and manufacturing centre with food processing and light industries. There are timber, grain and livestock markets. Buildings of interest include a Gothic church and a ducal palace.

OLDHAM, a city and county borough, Lancashire, England, on the River Medlock. Pop. (1961) 115,426. A cotton textile centre, it also has foundries and engineering works.

OLIVIER, Sir Laurence (1907—), British actor and producer. His first stage appearance was as Katherine in *The Taming of the Shrew* at Stratford in 1922. In 1951 he appeared with Vivien Leigh (from whom he was divorced in 1961) in the leading roles of *Antony and Cleopatra* and Shaw's *Caesar and Cleopatra*, played for a season on alternate nights. His Macbeth at the Stratford Memorial Theatre in 1955 put him in the first rank of actors. Other notable parts include Archie Rice in John Osborne's *The Entertainer* (1957). He produced and played in three very successful Shakespearean films, *Henry V*, *Richard III* and *Hamlet*. In 1962 he was appointed the first artistic director of the British National Theatre.

OLYMPIC GAMES, international amateur athletic contests held every four years, reviving a custom observed in Olympia, ancient Greece, from 776 B.C. to A.D. 394. The first modern games were held in Athens in 1896. Subsequent meetings took place in Paris (1900), St Louis, U.S.A. (1904), London (1908), Stockholm (1912), Antwerp (1920), Paris (1924), Amsterdam (1928), Los Angeles (1932), Berlin (1936), London (1948), Helsinki (1952), Melbourne (1956), Rome (1960) and Tokyo (1964). The 1964 games covered more than 50 different events. The 1968 Olympics are scheduled to be held in Mexico City.

OLYMPUS (Olimbos), a mountain in Thessaly, Greece, 9730 ft high. The ancient Greeks regarded it as the dwelling place of the gods.

OMAHA, the largest city in Nebraska, U.S.A., on the Missouri River. Pop. (1960) 301,598. A port and railway junction, it is also a large meat-packing and livestock centre. There are many insurance companies. Omaha has oil refineries and flour and cereal mills, and manufactures farm machinery, paints and ball-bearings, as well as smelting and refining silver and gold. It has several institutions of higher learning.

OMAR KHAYYAM (d. *c.* 1123), Persian poet, astronomer and mathematician. He is famous in Europe chiefly for his epigrammatic quatrains known as the *Rubáiyát*.

OMDURMAN, a town in the Sudan. Pop. (1956) 130,000. A commercial centre, on the Nile, it is a market for ivory, gum arabic, cattle and camels. General Kitchener decisively defeated the Khalifa here in 1898, in a battle in which Winston Churchill charged with the 21st Lancers.

OMSK, a city in the R.S.F.S.R., U.S.S.R. Pop. (1962) 650,000. In western Siberia, on the Irtysh and Om rivers and the Trans-Siberian railway, it is a commercial and industrial centre. Industries include automobile assembly, farm implements, silk mills and chemicals.

O'NEILL, Eugene (1888—1953), American dramatist. His preoccupation with psychological conflicts and his deep insight and theatrical skill made him outstanding among American playwrights. His works include *Beyond the Horizon*, *Anna Christie*, *Strange Interlude*, *Mourning Becomes Electra*, *Emperor Jones*, and *The Iceman Cometh*. He was awarded the Nobel Prize for literature.

ONTARIO, an east central Canadian province, bordering on the Great Lakes and Hudson Bay. Pop. (1961) 6,236,092; area 412,582 sq. miles. It consists of a flat peninsula in the southeast, and a forested region with numerous lakes and rivers in most other areas. The principal crops are grain, soya beans, hay and fruit. Livestock breeding and dairy farming are important. Forest products and fisheries are a leading source of income. There are deposits of gold, nickel, copper and uranium. The rivers provide considerable hydro-electric power. Manufactures include iron products, non-ferrous metals, foodstuffs, chemicals, textiles, leather and rubber goods, electrical apparatus, machinery, newsprint and wood pulp. The first permanent settlement was in 1673 at what is now Kingston. From 1791—1867 it was called Upper Canada. The capital is Toronto (pop. 1,824,481). Other important cities are Hamilton (395,189), Ottawa, the federal capital (429,750), Windsor (193,365) and London (181,283).

OPERA, a play set to music. It may include arias, duets, trios, quartets, choruses and recitatives with orchestral accompaniment. Scenery, costumes, and often dancing and spectacular scenes, are distinctive features. Grand opera is opera, usually tragic, in which there is no spoken dialogue. In the French *opéra comique* the dialogue is spoken; the adjective has lost all significance. Light opera is intended chiefly for entertainment. *Opéra bouffe* is farcical opera; *opera buffa*, classical Italian comic opera.

OPERETTA, a short opera, generally in a light vein. Devised by Jacques Offenbach, it is intended primarily to amuse. The story is usually sentimental and frivolous. Much spoken dialogue is employed and the music is light and attractive. W. S. Gilbert and Sir Arthur Sullivan wrote outstanding operettas.

OPIUM, the dried juice extracted from the unripe capsules of the opium poppy. It is chewed or smoked, mainly in the east, in order to produce a state of elation followed by dreamy sleep. Addiction leads to mental and physical deterioration. It is used in medicine as a sedative and analgesic, especially in the form of its alkaloid derivatives, morphine and codeine.

OPIUM WAR (1840—42), the armed conflict between China and Great Britain over the former's refusal to permit the import of opium. Britain received indemnities, including Hong Kong.

OPORTO, a city and port in Portugal, on the Douro River. Pop. (1960) 303,424. It is a commercial and industrial centre with an Atlantic port at nearby Leixoes. Its principal export is port wine. Manufactures include textiles, wines, jewellery, tobacco and leather goods.

ORAN, a city and port in Algeria, on the Mediterranean Sea. Pop. (1960) 300,000. A commercial, communications and industrial centre, it has a large harbour. There are markets for cereals, livestock, wool, hides and wines. At the end of the 15th century it was a leading Mediterranean commercial centre but shortly afterwards became a pirate stronghold. The French occupied Oran in 1831.

ORANGE FREE STATE, an inland province of the Republic of South Africa. Pop. (1960) 1,386,547; area 49,647 sq. miles. It consists of rolling plains devoted to stock raising, grains, fruit and tobacco. It is one of the world's leading producers of gold; there are also deposits of diamonds and coal. First settled in 1810, it became an independent Boer republic in 1854. It played an important part in the South African War and was annexed to the Crown as the Orange River Colony in 1900. In 1910 it was merged in the Union of South Africa. The capital is Bloemfontein (pop. 1960 140,924, including 61,213 Whites).

ORATORIO, a drama with biblical text set to music for solo voices, chorus and orchestra, on a larger scale than a cantata. It makes no use of scenery, costumes or action. Among the most famous oratorios are Handel's *Messiah*, Mendelssohn's *Elijah* and Dvořák's *Stabat Mater*. English oratorios have been written by Alexander Mackenzie *(Rose of Sharon)*, Hubert Parry *(Judith, Job)*, C. V. Stanford *(Eden)*, Elgar (*The Apostles* and *Dream of Gerontius*) and Stainer *(The Crucifixion)*.

ORCHESTRA, a group of musicians playing various types of instruments under the direction of a conductor. A modern symphony orchestra may have as many as a hundred players. The principal sections of an orchestra are strings, woodwind instruments, brass and percussion instruments. The strings are divided into first and second violins, violas, cellos and double basses. Woodwind includes flutes, oboes, clarinets and bassoons, usually in pairs. Trumpets, horns and trombones form the basis of the brass section, and kettledrums of the percussion, augmented in later years by bass and side-drums, triangle and cymbals. Saxophones, brass and percussion instruments dominate a jazz orchestra.

OREGON, a northwestern state of the U.S.A., on the Pacific Ocean. Pop. (1960) 1,768,687; area 96,891 sq. miles. Rolling plateau in the eastern areas, it consists of two parallel north-south mountain ranges in the west; the southeast and south centre is arid. Grains, fruit, vegetables, livestock and dairy foods are the principal agricultural products. Oregon has important fisheries, especially salmon. There are small deposits of nickel, gold, silver, copper, lead, mercury, building stone and uranium. Hydro-electric power makes considerable industry possible, chiefly timber products, machinery, metalwork, chemicals, paper and food processing. First settled in 1830, it became a state in 1859. The capital is Salem (pop. 49,142). The largest city is Portland (372,676).

ORGANIC COMPOUNDS, chemical compounds containing carbon, combined with hydrogen (hydrocarbons) and often also with oxygen, nitrogen and other elements. Groups containing carbon, oxygen and hydrogen are carbohydrates (q.v.), alcohols, aldehydes, ketones, ethers and esters. Groups containing nitrogen include amines, amides, nitro-compounds, amino-acids, proteins (q.v.), purines and alkaloids. The molecules of organic compounds are often very complex and contain a large number of atoms arranged either in an open chain (aliphatics) with or without branches, or in a ring (cyclic compounds). Substances with the same molecular formula but different molecular arrangements are called isomers. Organic chemistry is the chemistry of organic compounds (originally of substances produced by living organisms). See Inorganic Chemistry.

ORGANISATION FOR ECONOMIC CO-OPERATION AND DEVELOPMENT (O.E.C.D.), formed in 1961 by the members of the O.E.E.C. (q.v.) with the U.S.A. and Canada as additional members, to achieve economic improvements in Europe and an expansion of world trade. Paris is the headquarters.

ORGANISATION FOR EUROPEAN ECONOMIC CO-OPERATION (O.E.E.C.), an organisation formed originally in 1948 by 16 European countries to administer Marshall Aid after the Second World War. In 1961 it was replaced by the Organisation for Economic Co-operation and Development (q.v.).

ORGANISATION OF AMERICAN STATES (O.A.S.), formed in 1948 by the republics of the American continent for the pacific settlement of disputes in the Western Hemisphere and the promotion of inter-American understanding.

ORIGEN (*c.* 185—254), one of the early Church Fathers. Born and educated at Alexandria, he became the head of a school in Caesarea where he taught for 20 years. He wrote a great number of theological works, including a commentary on the Old Testament.

ORINOCO, see River.

ORKNEY ISLANDS, an island group in the North Sea forming a Scottish county north of Scotland. Pop. (1961) 18,743; area 360 sq. miles. Consisting of 29 inhabited islands, the group produces grain, turnips, potatoes and livestock. Fishing is important. There are numerous archaeological remains. The capital is Kirkwall.

ORTHODOX EASTERN CHURCH (Greek Church), the Church of the Eastern Roman Empire after Constantinople was made the capital was at first part of the Catholic Church under the Papacy, and became known as the Greek Orthodox or Byzantine Church. Rivalry and dissension grew between the Patriarch at Constantinople and the Pope at Rome and, as the Papacy grew weaker, the Eastern Church became more insistent on its rights and stubborn over its doctrine; in particular Constantinople rejected the doctrine of clerical celibacy and objected to the wording of the Nicene Creed. The result was the Great Schism of 1054; Leo IX excommunicated the whole Church, which then established itself independently under the name Holy Orthodox Catholic Apostolic Eastern Church, implying by this title that it was the only true Church. Under Ottoman rule the patriarch was allowed to supervise all the Greeks in the Turkish Empire; the patriarchate also absorbed other Christian communities, including those in the Balkans, Alexandria and Russia. Russia broke away in 1448 and, since the Czar claimed to be heir to the Byzantine emperors, Russia claimed, and still claims, to be head of the Orthodox Church. After the Turkish Revolution Atatürk allowed the Patriarch of Istanbul to remain the nominal head of the Church, which has communities in the Balkans, the Near East, Russia, Japan and elsewhere. Church services are held in Old Greek or Church Slavonic; icons are used; the saints and the Virgin are revered but not worshipped; there is singing, but no instrumental music. Monasteries are numerous, the most famous being Mount Athos. There are over five million adherents in the New World alone, and no reliable estimate can be made of the much greater number in the Old.

OSAKA, a city and seaport in Honshu, Japan. Pop. (1960) 3,011,553. A leading commercial and industrial centre, it produces textiles, foodstuffs, ceramics, chemicals, paper and metallurgical products. There is a large shipbuilding industry.

OSLO, capital of Norway. Pop. (1960) 465,000. A commercial, communications and industrial centre, it has an important port on the Skagerrak. Famous for its scenic beauty, it is the leading cultural and financial centre in Norway. Manufactures include foodstuffs, textiles, sawmill products, chemicals and machinery.

OSMIUM, see Elements.

OSMOSIS, the process of the diffusion of liquids or substances in solution through animal or plant membranes. In this way the hairs of plant roots absorb

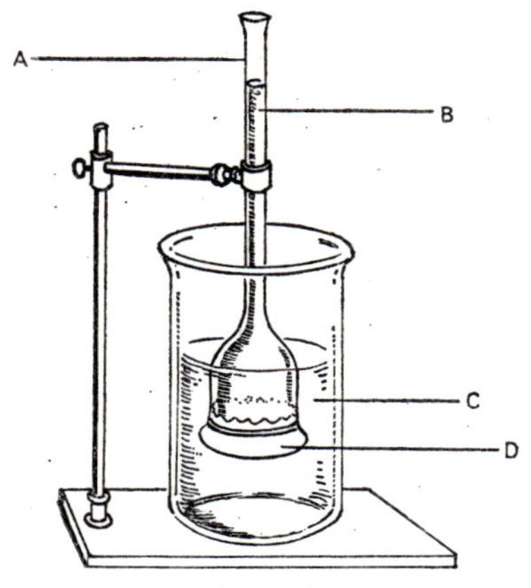

Osmosis
A. Thistle funnel B. Salt solution C. Water
D. Parchment paper or fish bladder

soil water and liquids reach the leaves of plants.

OSNABRÜCK, a city in North Rhine-Westphalia, West Germany, on the Hase River. Pop. (1960) 134,636. It is an industrial centre manufacturing machinery, iron and steel products, chemicals, textiles and musical instruments.

OSTRAVA, a city in Moravia, Czechoslovakia. Pop. (1959) 231,698. In a large coal-mining district, it is a highly industrialised centre producing iron and steel, machinery, chemicals and petroleum products.

OTTAWA, capital of Canada and of the Ontario province, on the junction of Ottawa and Rideau rivers. Pop. (1961) 429,750. In the centre of abundant hydro-electric developments, it manufactures varied sawmill products, metal goods, furniture, clothing and dairy foods.

OTTOMAN EMPIRE, see Turkey.

OVID (Publius Ovidius Naso; 43 B.C. — A.D. 17), Roman poet. Distinguished for his elegiac verse, he wrote *Ars Amatoria* on the art of love, in which he recounts, with no great reverence, stories from Greek and Roman mythology, and the *Heroides,* fictitious love-letters from legendary heroines. He spent his last nine years in exile, probably because Augustus found him too frivolous, and there wrote the *Tristia* and *Letters from Pontus.*

OXFORD, city, municipal and county borough in England at the junction of the Thames (Isis) and Cherwell rivers. Pop. (1961) 106,124. A religious, educational and trading centre, it has also become a manufacturing city. There are iron and steel works, an automobile factory, printing and publishing. Oxford is famous for its university, of which the oldest foundations are University College (1249) and Balliol (1262). There are four women's colleges, the Bodleian Library (1597), the Old Ashmolean Museum, the Sheldonian Theatre, Christ Church cathedral and many churches.

OXFORDSHIRE, a south midland county, England. Pop. (1961) 309,458; area 749 sq. miles. Lying between the Cotswolds and the Chilterns, the county consists of rolling uplands with peaceful villages in the valleys, and considerable areas of woodland. Predominantly agricultural, it produces cereals, pasture crops and sugar-beet. Livestock breeding and dairy farming are important. Blankets, automobiles, gloves, paper and agricultural tools are manufactured. The county town is Oxford, earlier called Oxenford. Chipping Norton is a particularly attractive town, and Blenheim Palace, where Winston Churchill was born, lies to the north of Oxford.

OXYGEN, see Elements.

P

PACIFIC OCEAN, the largest mass of water in the world, bounded by the Americas, Asia and Australia. Its maximum length from north to south is 8300 miles and its greatest width 11,000 miles, with an overall area of 63,801,700 sq. miles. The deepest ocean, the average depth is nearly 3 miles, and the maximum 37,800 ft, in the Marianas Trench. It has underwater mountains reaching a height of 11,500 ft in the Bering Sea. There are countless islands, mostly in the southwest.

PADEREWSKI, Ignace Jan (1860—1941), Polish composer, pianist and statesman. He wrote two operas, a symphony, a concerto and various piano pieces, but achieved greater fame as a concert pianist. He worked hard for the freedom of his country during the First World War, and after it ended was Premier until December 1919. He then returned to music, living abroad; but in 1939 he resumed political activity, becoming chairman of the Polish National Council in Paris.

PADUA, a city in northern Italy, on the Bacchiglione River. Pop. (1961) 198,403. A communications centre and agricultural market, it produces chemicals, automobiles, foodstuffs, agricultural machinery and beer. The city has numerous bridges, arcaded streets and open squares. The 13th-century Basilica of S. Antonio is one of the finest Italian churches; other churches have frescoes by Giotto and Mantegna.

PAGANINI, Niccolò (1782—1840), Italian violinist and composer. A child prodigy, he showed such remarkable skill as a violin virtuoso that he was popularly supposed to have sold his soul to the Devil.

PAHANG, a state of Malaya. Pop. (1961) 354,316; area 13,280 sq. miles. On the east coast of the Malay peninsula, it is mostly mountainous. The chief products are rubber, rice and coconuts. There are deposits of tin and gold. British influence began in 1887. The capital is Kuala Lipis.

PAINE, Thomas (1737—1809), English-born revolutionary, agitator and writer. His two pamphlets *Common Sense* and *Crisis* (1776) exerted influence on the revolutionary movement in America. After the conclusion of the War of Independence, he wrote *The Rights of Man,* for which he was condemned in England on a charge of treason. He then fled to France where he worked on behalf of the French revolutionaries, but became a victim of intrigue during the Reign of Terror and narrowly escaped the guillotine; he was put in prison, where he wrote the anti-clerical and deist *The Age of Reason,* which was not well received. He returned to America an embittered man, and died in poverty.

PAINTING, the application of a coloured powder mixed with an adhesive to a flat surface in order to depict objects, persons, scenes or mental states. Its purpose is most often to impart a truth, evoke pleasure, portray life as it is or express some aspect of the painter's personality. The type of adhesive — the yolk of an egg, linseed oil, a glue, or some combination of these — determines the kind of painting, e.g. oil, fresco, gouache, tempera or water-colour. The basic elements of painting are drawing, composition, the interaction of light and shade (chiaroscuro), and colour. The availability of certain materials, the cultural climate of the time, and the effect desired by the artist give rise to specific schools of painting. Each painter develops his own style which reflects his individuality. Modernist art spurns mechanical representation, and strives to convey the spirit or essence of a subject.

PAKISTAN, a Moslem republic in the Indian sub-continent, consisting of two provinces separated by a thousand miles of Indian territory. Pakistan is a member of the British Commonwealth. Pop. (1961) 93,812,000; area 360,780 sq. miles.

West Pakistan (pop. 40,815,000; area 300,839 sq. miles) is a plain with mountains in the west and north. The Indus river flows down into the Arabian Sea. Predominantly agricultural (through irrigation), it produces wheat, cotton, barley, sugar-cane, millet, rice, maize, fodder crops, fruit and dates. Livestock breeding and forestry are important occupations. There are deposits of coal, limestone, gypsum, natural gas and iron. Cotton weaving is an important manufacture. The capital is Lahore (pop. 1,297,000).

East Pakistan (pop. 50,844,000; area 54,501 sq. miles) is low-lying fertile country. Mostly agricultural, it produces rice, pulses, wheat, barley, tea, tobacco, sugar-cane and jute. Fishing and forestry are important. Textiles, sugar, matches, aluminium, glass, jute and hosiery are the leading industries. The capital is Dacca (pop. 1958 600,000).

Pakistan became a dominion in 1947, after the partition of India. The capital is Karachi (pop. 2,153,000). Other important cities are Chittagong (294,000) and Hyderabad (241,801).

The possession of Kashmir (with Jammu) is in dispute between India and Pakistan; rather less than half the territory is occupied by Pakistan. A new capital of Pakistan is being built at Islamabad, near Rawalpindi (237,219), where the President and the Ministries have temporary headquarters.

PALESTINE, an ancient country in southwest Asia, bordering on the Mediterranean. Pop. (1948) 1,739,624; area 10,429 sq. miles. Now divided between Israel, Jordan and Egypt. Part of southern Palestine was settled by the Israelites (see Jews) under Abraham *c.* 2000 B.C. and again, after the return from Egypt, under Moses between the 15th and 13th centuries. In *c.* 1000 B.C. King David made Jerusalem his capital and ruled all Palestine except the coastal strip held by the Philistines. After King Solomon's death, this kingdom split into two: Judah (with Jerusalem as capital) and Israel (Samaria), the latter being conquered by the Assyrians in 721. The country passed successively under the rule of Babylon (586—538), Persia, Alexander (333), Rome (66 B.C.; Titus destroyed Jerusalem in A.D. 70 and renamed Judaea [Judah] Palestina), Persia (614—629), Byzantines, Islam (640), the Crusaders (11th century), Egypt (1187—1517), Ottoman Turks, and finally Great Britain, which administered it, from 1922 as a mandated territory under the League of Nations, from 1917 to 1948. Then, on the recommendation of the U.N., it was partitioned between Israel and Jordan (qq.v.).

PALESTRINA, Giovanni Pierluigi da (*c.* 1524—94), Italian composer. He composed numerous masses, motets, hymns, magnificats, litanies and madrigals, and was appointed singer in the papal choir by Pope Julius III. His works include the *Stabat Mater* for eight voices, and the *Missa Papae Marcelli.*

PALGRAVE, Sir Francis (1788—1861), English historian, author of *Rise and Progress of the English Commonwealth* (1832) and *History of Normandy and England* (4 volumes, 1851—1864).

PALM SUNDAY, the Sunday immediately preceding Easter commemorating Christ's triumphal entry into Jerusalem. It marks the beginning of Holy Week.

PALMERSTON, Henry, 3rd Viscount (1784—1865), English statesman. Secretary of War from 1809 to 1828, he then served as Foreign Secretary (1830—41, 1846—51) but was dismissed for his open approval of Napoleon III's *coup d'état.* Palmerston became Prime Minister (1855—58, 1859—65) and it was under his leadership that the Crimean War and the Indian Mutiny were ended. In his foreign policy he tried to curb France and Russia, against whom he defended the interests of Belgium and Turkey. This made him unpopular with Queen Victoria.

PALMYRA (Tadmor), an ancient city in an oasis of the Syrian desert 150 miles northeast of Damascus. Founded by Solomon on an important trade route between the Mediterranean and Mesopotamia, it prospered under Roman rule in the 2nd century A.D., after the fall of Petra, and under Queen Zenobia it was the capital of an empire which included Egypt, Asia Minor and Syria. Palmyra passed out of history with its destruction by the Romans in A.D. 273. The ruins of a temple and a colonnaded street can still be seen.

PAMIRS, a high mountain plateau in Central Asia, in the Tadzhik S.S.R. known as the 'Roof of the World'. Covering an area of 150 miles square, it has an average elevation of 12,000 ft. Stalin Peak is 24,590 ft high; it was climbed in 1962 by an Anglo-Russian expedition, and has recently been renamed Mt Communism. The Pamirs are at the focal point of several major ranges; the Himalaya, Hindu Kush, Kunlun, Karakorum and Tien Shan.

Ruins at Palmyra, Syria (Triumphal Arch)

PAMPAS, a region of grassy plains in Argentina extending from the Rio Negro in the south to the Gran Chaco in the north and from the Andes to the Atlantic. Beef cattle and sheep are raised in vast numbers and cereals, lucerne and flax grown. In the eastern half the characteristic tall coarse pampas grass is found.

PANAMA, a republic in Central America. Pop. (1960) 1,053,000; area 28,575 sq. miles (excluding the Canal Zone). The narrow strip of the Canal Zone, under U.S. administration, divides the country into two, and is a gap in the mountain range which traverses the whole of Panama. The westward slopes are only sparsely inhabited; the eastern have dense rain forest, in the clearings of which bananas, rice, cocoa, coffee and coconuts are grown. Livestock raising is important Formerly a part of Colombia, Panama became independent in 1903. The capital is Panama City. Panama has, nominally, a huge merchant fleet, consisting of ships of all nations whose owners seek to avoid the stricter regulations of their own countries.

PANAMA CANAL, a waterway connecting the Atlantic and Pacific oceans across the isthmus of Panama. Under construction from 1907—14, it is situated in the Canal Zone (area 648 sq. miles) leased to the U.S.A. The canal is 50 miles long, ranges in bottom width from 300—1,000 ft and has a minimum depth of 41 ft. It has 12 pairs of locks in each direction. The average time to traverse it is 7—8 hours.

Plan of Panama Canal

PANAMA CITY, capital of Panama, at the Pacific extremity of the Panama Canal. Pop. (1960) 238,980. A commercial centre, it is one of the oldest towns in the Americas.

PANKHURST, Emmeline (1858—1928) a militant English suffragette. In 1903 she founded the Women's Social and Political Union, which did not hesitate to resort to window-breaking, arson and bombing in order to achieve its goal, which was attained in 1918 when women received the right to vote. She was assisted by her daughters, Dame Christabel and Sylvia; the latter subsequently worked for Abyssinian independence.

PAPACY, the office of the Bishop of Rome (the Pope), who is supreme head of the Roman Catholic Church. According to Church tradition, St Peter was the first Bishop of Rome and the Popes are his successors.

PAPER, a material made from cellulose fibres of vegetable origin, which is matted or felted into thin sheets. Most paper is made from wood pulp. Other raw materials include rags, old papers, cotton linters, esparto grass, jute, straw and hemp. The first English paper-mill was built about 1490, but paper was made in China as early as the first century A.D.

PAPIER MÂCHÉ, a term covering varied forms of utilising paper pulp, glue and paste which are pressed, moulded and dried into the desired shape. Masks, dolls' heads, mirror and picture frames are some of the smaller products which can be created from this process, although it was used in the 18th century as a substitute for plaster in internal architectural decorations.

PAPUA, see New Guinea.

PARACELSUS, Philippus Aureolus (1493—1541), Swiss physician, mystic

Faa Iheihe, painted by the French post-Impressionist Paul Gaugin (q.v.) in the South Sea Islands, where he spent much of his life.

Photo: Director of the Tate Gallery

A detail from Georges Braque's (q.v.) *La Calanque*, painted in 1907 during his experiments with Cubism.

Photo: Marlborough Fine Art Ltd

A typical example of Grant Wood's (q.v.) 'American Gothic' style of painting.

Photo: The Art Institute of Chicago. Friends of America Art Collection

Metamorphosis of Narcissus by the Spanish Surrealist painter Salvador Dali (q.v.).

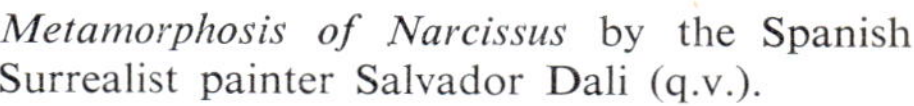

Photo: Director of the Tate Gallery

Jackson Pollock's (q.v.) *Stenographic Figure*, painted in 1942 and one of the earliest in his very characteristic abstract style.

Photo: Marlborough Fine Art Ltd

Georges Mathieu's (*b.* 1921) *Everard des Barres entre à Clairvaux* is an example of his abstract work. Closely associated with the American neo-expressionist painters, he is opposed to abstract formalism.

Photo: Marlborough Fine Art Ltd

Robert Rauschenberg (*b.* 1925), one of the leaders of contemporary Pop-art, yet of a pronouncedly individual style. Illustrated here is his *Tracer*, painted in 1964.

Photo: Pierre Golendorf

and alchemist, *né* von Hohenheim. The first to suggest that chemistry is important in the study of disease, he introduced numerous chemical remedies, including laudanum.

PARAGUAY, an inland republic of South America. Pop. (1960) 1,760,000; area 157,006 sq. miles. It consists of vast tropical forests in the east and grassy plains in the west. The principal crops are maize, manioc, cotton, sugar-cane and groundnuts. Livestock breeding is important. The forests yield timber, yerba maté (Paraguay tea) and tannin. Iron, copper and manganese are mined on a small scale. After achieving independence from Spain in 1814, Paraguay was ruled by a succession of dictators. From 1865—70 Paraguay fought a war against Argentina, Brazil and Uruguay which cost it half a million men. A war with Bolivia in 1932—35 resulted in the acquisition of four-fifths of the Gran Chaco district in the north. The capital is Asunción (pop. 201,340).

PARAMARIBO, capital of Surinam, on the Surinam River. Pop. (1962) 118,000. A port on the Atlantic Ocean, it exports balata gum, sugar, cocoa, bauxite, timber and rubber. It became an English settlement in 1640 and alternated between English and Dutch ownership until 1815, when it was finally awarded to the Netherlands.

PARANÁ, capital of Entre Rios province, Argentina. Pop. (1956) 183,897. A port on the Paraná River, it is a commercial centre of growing importance. It was founded by colonists from Santa Fé in 1730. From 1853—1862 it was the capital of Argentina.

PARIS, capital and largest city of France, on the Seine. Pop. (1962) 2,811,171. It is the French cultural, financial, communications, commercial and industrial centre. The Right Bank, in the main, is a noisy city, the Left Bank preserves more of the dignity and calm to be expected of the cultural capital of Europe, best seen, however, in the two islands in the Seine, the Ile de la Cité (with the 12th-century Notre Dame and a rewarding flower market) and the Ile St Louis. On the Left Bank are the Latin Quarter (with the Sorbonne University, founded 1253) and Montparnasse, both of which have yielded place as the centre of artistic life to Montmartre, crowned by the Sacré Coeur, a delightful quarter ruined by heavy traffic and extortionate prices. The Louvre (q.v.) takes pride of place among the museums and art galleries, but there is a wonderful collection of Impressionist and other modern painting in the Jeu de Paume in the Tuileries Gardens. The Opéra, Opéra-Comique and the Comédie Française (two theatres) are the main homes of opera and drama. The luxury shops are in the area round the Place Vendôme, and the Arc de Triomphe commemorates Napoleon at the commencement of the once fashionable Champs Elysées. Among the many parks are the Jardin du Luxembourg, Bois de Boulogne, Jardin des Plantes and Parc Monceau. The remains of many famous people lie in the Père-Lachaise cemetery. The Eiffel Tower (984 ft) is a useful viewpoint and landmark.

Industries include automobiles, luxury and fashion goods, perfumes, book publishing, chemicals, machinery, Sèvres porcelain, tobacco, textiles and foodstuffs. Clovis, King of the Franks, made Paris his capital at the beginning of the 6th century. In 987 Hugh Capet made the city the capital of France. From 1420—1436 Paris was under English rule. Under Louis XIV Paris became the literary centre of Europe. In 1814 and

1815 the city was occupied by the Allies. The Prussians besieged it in 1870—71. It was twice in danger of German conquest during the First World War and was frequently bombarded. During the Second World War it was declared an open city and was occupied by the Germans from 1940—44. In 1951 Paris celebrated the 2000th anniversary of its foundation.

PARLIAMENT, the legislature of the United Kingdom of Great Britain and Northern Ireland, is composed of the sovereign, the House of Lords (lords spiritual and temporal) and the House of Commons. Its origins are complex and its development into a legislative body was the result of a long process of evolution. The parliament convened by Simon de Montfort in 1265 marked the first occasion that knights and burgesses were represented. In the early years the powers of parliament grew by a process of bargaining, as the kings who needed financial support for their undertakings were forced to accede to some of its demands. The beginnings of the modern parliament may be placed during the reign of Edward III (1327—77) when two distinct bodies (later to become the House of Lords and the House of Commons) were created. By 1399 parliament had sufficient power to depose the king. Charles I was executed and James II deposed by Act of Parliament. The House of Commons began its rise to prominence in 1832 and, by 1911, the House of Lords had lost even its powers of veto. The British House of Commons has become the model for a great number of parliamentary governments overseas.

PARMA, a city in northern Italy, on the Parma River. Pop. (1961) 140,844. A trading centre for livestock, grain and dairy produce, it manufactures textiles, glass, metal goods and tobacco products. There is an 11th-century cathedral and other historical buildings Founded by the Etruscans, it later became a Roman colony. In 1545 it became the capital of the Duchy of Parma.

PARNELL, Charles (1846—91), Irish political leader. In 1878 he organised the Land League, and he became president of the Home Rule Confederation (1880). He lost his position as the majority leader of his party when he was named co-respondent in a divorce suit (1890).

PASCAL, Blaise (1623—62), French mathematician and religious writer, one of the outstanding minds of the 17th century. In 1654 he became a monk at Port Royal. He defended Jansenism (q.v.) in his *Provincial Letters* (1656—57). His *Pensées* are a series of brief 'thoughts' scribbled on odd scraps of paper and published, in considerable disorder, after his death; from them it is possible to piece together his philosophy. He was obsessed by the puniness of man, 'the weakest thing in nature' under the 'eternal silence' of the stars, at the mercy of fortuitous circumstances (If Cleopatra's nose had been shorter, the whole face of the world would have been different); man's only hope was to turn to God. He tried to move the worldly by a direct appeal to the heart, 'which has reasons better than those of Reason', e.g. by his proposition that either there is a life after death or there is not, and thus it is but simple prudence to conduct oneself on the supposition that there is.

PASSION PLAY, a dramatic presentation of the Passion of Jesus Christ. They were common in the Middle Ages and several, the most publicised of which is that at Oberammergau, are still staged.

PASSOVER, the Jewish festival which

lasts for nine days at the full moon nearest to the spring equinox. Traditionally it commemorates the passing over of the Israelites at the slaying of the firstborn in Egypt (Exodus xii), but it is probably a combination of earlier festivals. The essential feature was the sacrifice and eating of a lamb. The first day is now celebrated with a family feast.

PASTEUR, Louis (1822—95), French scientist, and founder of bacteriology and microbiology. His investigations into the process of fermentation led to major discoveries in bacteriology and the development of pasteurisation (the use of heat to kill micro-organisms in food, particularly milk). He saved the French silkworm industry by discovering a method of controlling silkworm disease, and developed vaccines for chicken cholera, anthrax and hydrophobia.

PATAGONIA, the southernmost region in Argentina, east of the Andes. Consisting of an arid plateau, it serves mostly for grazing sheep. There are no metallic ores, but petroleum is found in two places in sufficient quantities to supply Argentina's needs; there is one small coalfield. The Tierra del Fuego region is shared with Chile.

PATENT, the exclusive right granted by a government to an inventor to manufacture, use and sell his invention for 16 years. Patents are granted by the Patents Office if they are satisfied that the idea is new, that the applicant is 'the true and first' inventor, or importer, and if, after publication of the application, no objection has been raised.

PATHOLOGY, the study of the causes and nature of disease, and of the bodily changes produced by it, primarily through the microscopic examination of diseased tissue. It includes the study of inflammation, wounds, tumours, the part played by the endocrine glands, and post-mortem work.

PATRICK, St (*c.* 389—461), a missionary to Ireland and its patron saint, probably born in Wales. Captured and enslaved by Irish pirates, he managed to escape to Scotland. He returned to Ireland, however, as a missionary and by the time he died had spread Christianity throughout all Ireland, and set up missions to convert the peoples of the continent of Europe to Christianity. Although his own accounts have survived, the details of his career are in the highest degree obscure, and much legend naturally grew around him, such as his ridding Ireland of snakes.

PAUL, St (*c.* A.D. 3—67), Christian apostle and missionary to the Gentiles. Paul (Hebrew name, Saul) was a Roman citizen and Pharisee born of Jewish parents in Tarsus. At first a persecutor of the Christians, he was converted to Christianity on the road to Damascus, when he heard a voice saying: 'Saul, Saul, why persecutest thou me?' He made three missionary journeys (recounted in the Acts of the Apostles) through Asia Minor and Greece, preaching both to Jews and Gentiles. It was Paul who made of Christianity a unique, independent religion instead of a Jewish sect, for he insisted that Gentile converts had no need of first becoming Jews through circumcision. It was, however, Paul who developed the doctrine of Atonement which has been a stumbling-block to so many. According to one tradition, he died a martyr's death at Rome in the Neronian persecution.

PAUL VI (né Giovanni Montini; 1897—), elected Pope in 1963. Born near Brescia, took orders in 1920; joined Vatican Secretariat, becoming one of the two

Pro-Secretaries (1952). He became Archbishop of Milan in 1955.

PAVLOV, Ivan (1849—1936), Russian physiologist. His work on the physiology of digestion won him the Nobel Prize in 1904, but he is best known for his theory of the conditioned reflex (q.v.).

PEARL HARBOR, a city and port in Oahu island, near Honolulu, Hawaii. Eighteen U.S. naval vessels were struck by bombs in a surprise attack by Japanese airplanes on December 7, 1941, on the naval base and military installations. This attack, made without declaration of war, brought the U.S. into the Second World War.

PEARSON, Lester Bowles (1897—), Canadian Liberal statesman. After education at Oxford University as a Rhodes scholar, he became a professor of history. He was the Canadian Minister for External Affairs (1948—57), playing a prominent part in the founding of N.A.T.O. and being primarily responsible for the sending of the U.N. emergency force to Egypt during the Suez crisis, for which he was awarded the Nobel Peace prize in 1957. He became Prime Minister in 1963.

PEARY, Robert (1856—1920), U.S. Arctic explorer. After discovering that Greenland was an island and investigating the culture of its Eskimos, he was first to reach the North Pole, in 1909.

PEEL, Sir Robert (1788—1850), English statesman. He entered the House of Commons in 1809 as a Tory, served as Home Secretary (1822—30) and finally as Prime Minister (1834—35, 1841—46). He opposed the Reform Bill of 1832. He was the originator of the London Constabulary (Peelers) and revived Pitt's income tax in 1842 to bring order to the country's finances. In the face of the Irish potato famine he repealed the Corn Laws (q.v.) in 1846, thereby dividing his party, and he supported Free Trade. Disraeli described Peel as the greatest member of parliament that ever lived.

Peeler

PEKING, capital of China. Pop. (1958) 5,420,000. The older part of Peking consists of two walled cities. The Manchu Inner City is surrounded by 14½ miles of wall, 50 ft high and 40 ft wide at the top. It contains the Imperial City, also walled, six miles in circumference, and within this again is the Forbidden City, containing the 15th-century Imperial Palace. Within the Imperial City also lie lakes and gardens, and the Kublai Khan Palace. The Hall of Classics, the Temple of Confucius and a large Buddhist lamasery are in the outer part of the Inner City, where also, after the Taiping Rebellion, the Dowager Empress gave permission for the foreign legation quarter to be built. Adjoining the Inner City to the south is the other main part of old Peking — the 'Chinese' or Outer City, which has within its walls the Temple and Altar of Heaven. The business quarter is also here. Outside the old cities (which cover a total area of 25½ sq. miles) are residential suburbs to the west, and the industrial quarter to the east. Peking is the focus of railway lines from all parts of China, and from Russia, and is at the terminus of the Grand Canal. There are several universities.

Towns have existed on the site since the 12th century B.C., and Peking, under various names, has been a capital of some part of China, with few breaks, from the 10th century A.D. Genghis Khan captured it in 1215 and Kublai Khan made it the Mongol capital in 1267 — this was the city praised by Marco Polo. Peking, as it now is, was designed by a Ming Emperor in 1421. It was the Manchu capital from 1644—1911 and thereafter of the republic until 1928. The Communists restored it to its former status in 1949.

PELOPONNESOS, the mountainous peninsula which forms southern Greece. Pop. (1961) 1,090,822; area 8,356 sq. miles. It is attached to the mainland by the Isthmus of Corinth through which a canal has been cut. In ancient times the peninsula was dominated by Mycenae, and then by Sparta.

PELOPONNESIAN WAR (431—404 B.C.), the war between the Peloponnesian confederacy led by Sparta and a maritime league of city-states under Athens. The war resulted from growing friction and jealousy between Athens and Sparta. Athens was finally defeated by Lysander at Aegospotami, and lost once and for all her position of political leadership in Greece.

PENANCE, in the Roman Catholic Church, is a sacrament, consisting of the confession of sin, the grant of absolution by a priest, if he is satisfied that the penitent is duly contrite, and the imposition of a task or punishment in atonement.

PENANG, a state of Malaya. Pop. (1960) 633,127; area 400 sq. miles. It consists of the island of Penang (formerly Prince of Wales Island) and the adjacent area on the west coast of the Malay peninsula. The principal products are coconuts, spices, tin and rubber. The capital is Penang (Georgetown), a port which handles traffic railed from Burma and Thailand, in addition to the tin and rubber of Malaya.

PENICILLIN, a antibiotic drug extracted from a soil mould, which can destroy germs. It is effective against blood poisoning, syphilis, pneumonia and other diseases. Sir Alexander Fleming discovered it in 1928. It has several disadvantages: it can produce strains of bacteria which are immune to its effects; it can produce allergy; it is subject to the law of diminishing returns; and its indiscriminate use is highly undesirable. For example, in a case of fever, penicillin might be prescribed: if the fever is due to viral pneumonia the penicillin will not cure the disease, but it will mask its symptoms and seriously delay proper treatment.

PENINSULAR WAR (1808—14), one of the major campaigns in the Napoleonic Wars (q.v.), in which the combined British, Portuguese and Spanish forces under the leadership of the future Duke of Wellington drove the French out of the Spanish-Portuguese peninsula. It followed a Spanish revolt against the rule of Joseph Bonaparte, whom Napoleon had made King of Spain. Sir

Arthur Wellesley (later Viscount, and then Duke of Wellington) drove Junot out of Portugal and then left the command to Sir John Moore, whose invasion of Spain failed. Moore retreated to Corunna, where he was killed and the British troops evacuated (1809). Wellington returned, again cleared Portugal, and invaded Spain; but this invasion also was a failure. In 1813 Wellington defeated Joseph at Vittoria and followed the French into France, defeating Soult at Toulouse a week after Napoleon's abdication.

PENN William (1644—1718), English Quaker and founder of the American colony of Pennsylvania. The son of Admiral Sir William Penn, he became a Quaker preacher. Happy to rid England of Quakers, Charles II made him a grant of land in North America. Penn founded Philadelphia, made protective treaties with the Indians and welcomed all immigrants fleeing from oppression, whatever their persuasion. He died in England.

PENNINE CHAIN, a range of hills in northern England running north-south from the Cheviots to northeast Derbyshire, where it forms the Peak District. It is higher in the north (Cross Fell 2930 ft) than in the south (Kinderscout 2080 ft).

PENNSYLVANIA, a north Atlantic state of the U.S.A. Pop. (1960) 11,319,366; area 45,333 sq. miles. The Allegheny Mountains run diagonally across the state from the northeast. Buckwheat, cereals, potatoes, tobacco, mushrooms, vegetables, fruits and flowers are cultivated. Stock raising is important. Minerals include large deposits of coal; there is also petroleum and natural gas. The state is a leading producer of iron and steel, and manufactures include locomotives, engines, boilers, motor vehicles, blast furnaces and textiles. First settled in 1682 by William Penn (q.v.), it was one of the original 13 states. The capital is Harrisburg (pop. 79,697). The largest cities are Philadelphia (2,002,512) and Pittsburgh (604,332).

PEPYS, Samuel (1633—1703), English diarist. He began his *Diary* in 1660 and kept it, in shorthand, until his sight began to give him trouble in 1669. This period covers the Restoration, the Plague, the Fire of London and the Dutch War, and Pepys, who as a high and very efficient official of the Navy Board knew everyone, is a unique source of sidelights on these great events. His financial dealings, his philanderings, his quarrels with his wife and his oft-repeated vows (as often broken) are all recorded with disarming frankness. The manuscripts passed into the hands of Magdalene College, Cambridge, and remained unknown and undeciphered until 1819; parts were published in 1825.

PERAK, a state of Malaya, on the west coast of the Malay peninsula. Pop. (1960) 1,362,983; area 8030 sq. miles. Consisting mostly of forested mountains, it has rich tin deposits. Other minerals include tungsten, gold, silver, lead, iron, copper, zinc, arsenic and titanium. There are extensive rubber plantations, and sugar, tobacco, rice, tea, coffee and vanilla are grown. The first English settlement was made in 1795. The capital is Ipoh.

PERICLES (*c.* 490—429 B.C.), Athenian statesman. Although a member of the Athenian aristocracy, he became the leader of the democratic party and — after 444 — the most influential minister in Athens. He used the funds of the Delian League to repair the ravages wrought by the Persians in Athens, building the Parthenon and the Propylaea, and commissioning the gold and ivory statue of Athene by Phidias. He also led the Athenian forces in the early stages of the Peloponnesian War (431—29).

PERSIA, see Iran.

PERSPECTIVE, the method employed in drawing to make an object on a flat surface appear three-dimensional as seen from any fixed point. The basic principle is that, although parallel lines do not meet, they appear to do so, at a vanishing point or points on the horizon. Brunelleschi, Uccello and Piero della Francesca laid the foundations of this study in the 15th century.

PERTH, a burgh in Perthshire, Scotland, on the Tay River. Pop. (1961) 41,199. A rail centre, it has a dyeing industry and manufactures linen, carpets, glass and ink. Formerly called St Johnstoun, it was the capital of Scotland until 1437. Scone Palace is near by. There is a 13th-century church.

PERTH, capital of Western Australia. Pop. (1961) 419,755. A financial and commercial centre, it produces foodstuffs and engineering products. The city has Anglican and Catholic cathedrals. Its port is Fremantle, 12 miles away.

PERU, a republic on the northwest coast of South America. Pop. (1961) 10,016,232; area 482,258 sq. miles. It comprises from west to east, a coastal desert; a central region of high Andean peaks interspersed with plateaux and with forested eastern slopes; and the Amazonian plains. The principal agricultural products are cotton, sugar, wool, hides, skins, coffee and rice. There is considerable livestock. Wild rubber is gathered, and fisheries are important. Peru has extensive mineral deposits including petroleum, silver, lead, copper, gold, vanadium, iron, zinc and coal. The leading industries are textiles, footwear, cement, rubber products, chemicals, plastics, steel and glass. The centre of the Inca empire, it was conquered by the Spaniards in 1531—33, and became the most important Spanish viceroyalty in South America, gaining independence in 1824. The capital is Lima (pop. 1,700,000). Other important cities are Callao (135,244), Arequipa (392,352) and the ancient Inca capital of Cuzco (68,483).

PERUGINO (Pietro Vannucci: ***c.*** **1446—1523),** Italian painter. A leading Umbrian artist of the early Renaissance, he painted numerous religious subjects and frescoes, including *Christ Giving the Keys to St Peter* in the Sistine Chapel, Rome, and *Crucifixion with Saints* (Florence) Raphael was his pupil.

PESHAWAR, a city in West Pakistan, on the Bara River. Pop. (1951) 151,776. It is an important trading centre near the Khyber pass, commanding the main route between Afghanistan and India.

PESTALOZZI, Johann Heinrich (1746—1827), Swiss educational reformer. Concerned with the moral and religious training of peasant children, he advocated developing the personality from within, making use of concrete objects for instruction, and proceeding from the known to the unknown. He was unfortunate and not very practical, and had to contend with much jealous or bigoted opposition. However, the ideas set out in his books lived on to be incorporated in the primary education systems of many countries.

PÉTAIN, Henri Philippe (1856—1951), French soldier and politician. Promoted to Commander-in-Chief of the French

Army after his successful defence of Verdun in the First World War, he became Premier (1940) and remained as the aged and muddled head of the Vichy government throughout the Second World War. In 1945 he was convicted of treason for his co-operation with the Germans and condemned to death, but the sentence was subsequently commuted by General de Gaulle to life imprisonment.

PETER, St, one of the 12 chosen apostles of Jesus. A fisherman by trade, he left his work to follow Jesus and became one of the most favoured disciples. Peter was not only the spokesman of the early Church but, according to Roman Catholic tradition, was also the first bishop of Rome, where he died a martyr's death in Nero's reign.

PETER THE GREAT (1672—1725), Czar of Russia. He devoted his energies to the westernisation of Russia and largely succeeded in bringing his hitherto backward country into a position of leadership among the nations of Europe. After working incognito in the dockyards of Western Europe, he came home to reorganise the fleet, the army, education, the alphabet, the calendar and the law; he shaved off the beards of his *boyars* and placed the Church under his control. He sent the regent, his half-sister, to a convent, locked up his first wife, murdered his son, and raised his low-born ex-mistress to the throne, to succeed him as Catherine I. To acquire ice-free ports he fought Sweden to gain the Baltic region where he built his new capital, St Petersburg (later Leningrad), conquered Azov from Turkey and Baku from Persia.

PETER THE HERMIT (*c.* 1050—1115), French monk and hermit whose zealous preaching helped arouse enthusiasm for the First Crusade. He himself led an unruly mob of peasants across Europe in 1096, of whom many died on the way and the rest were slaughtered by the Turks. Peter, disgusted with their lack of discipline, had abandoned them before this disaster, and returned to found a monastery in the Low Countries.

PETRARCH, Francesco (1304—74), Italian poet. Known today chiefly for his *Rime*, love lyrics inspired by his adoration, from a distance, of a married woman called Laura. Their style was imitated by many generations of Italian poets. Most of his works, and his letters, were written in Latin and dealt with graver subjects, as in his *Secretum*, a dialogue between Petrarch and St Augustine.

PETROL (U.S. 'gasolene'), a colourless, highly volatile liquid with a characteristic odour obtained by the fractional distillation of petroleum. When mixed with air in a carburettor and compressed by a piston it forms the explosive mixture which, ignited by electric spark, provides the motive power in an internal-combustion engine. The petrol used for this purpose is usually a mixture of natural and cracked gasoline. The latter is produced by catalytic cracking, which breaks down complex hydrocarbons into simpler compounds in the presence of a catalyst. With the introduction of higher-compression engines, the antiknock value of the fuel used became increasingly important. The cracked gasoline improves this, as do other additives such as tetra-ethyl lead. The value is indicated by the octane rating, e.g. 90-octane petrol contains 90% knock-free fuel. The higher the octane rating the greater the wastage of petroleum, and hence the higher the cost.

PETROLEUM, an oily, inflammable liquid mixture consisting of hundreds of hydrocarbons, occurring underground in sedimentary rocks. It is usually discovered by drilling up to 2½ miles or more, and it is brought to the surface either by gas pressure or pumps. The components have different boiling-points, and, the various categories (or fractions) are extracted by fractional distillation in an oil refinery, which yields in descending order of refinement: petrol, paraffin (kerosene), diesel oil, paraffin wax, and heavy residues such as viscous lubricating oils and bitumen. Other products include benzine, glycerine, p.v.c. for plastics, acetone for synthetic fibres, petroleum jelly (petrolatum), cosmetics, fertilisers, insecticides and weed-killers. Natural gas may be found in association with liquid petroleum (as casinghead gas) or alone; from it are obtained natural gasoline, ethylene (for alcohols, ethers, polyethylene plastic) and many other organic compounds used in drugs, chemicals, plastics and synthetic rubber.

Col. Drake drilled the first oil well at Titusville, Pennsylvania, in 1859. The major producers today are countries round the Gulf of Mexico (U.S.A., Venezuela), round the Persian Gulf (Kuwait, Saudi Arabia), and U.S.S.R.

PHILADELPHIA, the largest city in Pennsylvania, U.S.A., at the confluence of the Delaware and Schuylkill rivers. Pop. (1960) 2,002,512. Centrally situated on the Atlantic coast, it is a financial, communications, commercial and industrial centre in the vicinity of iron and coal deposits. A major port, it manufactures textiles and textile machinery, steel products, transport equipment, radios, electrical appliances, automobile parts, locks, bearings, foodstuffs and petroleum products, as well as a large variety of other goods, such as paper and books. There are extensive shipyards. It has museums and institutions of higher learning. Having played a leading role in the American War of Independence, it has numerous historical landmarks. The first settlers, in 1638, were Swedes and Finns. In 1681 William Penn founded the city and gave it its name. From 1790—1800 it was the capital of the U.S.A.

PHILATELY, see Stamp Collecting.

PHILIP II (1165—1223), King of France from 1180—1223. In a series of wars with England, he conquered nearly all the English possessions in France, and made France a major political power in Europe.

PHILIP II (382—336 B.C.), King of Macedon. Seizing the throne in 359 he organised a powerful and efficient army and after the battle of Chaeronea (338) had all Greece under his control. He was assassinated as he was preparing to invade Persia. His conquests paved the way for his son, Alexander the Great.

PHILIP II (1527—1598), King of Spain, Portugal, Naples and Sicily. His second marriage was to Mary I of England. He was responsible for the building of the Spanish Armada, whose defeat (1588) left England in control of the seas.

PHILIP V (1683—1746), King of Spain from 1700—1746 and founder of the Spanish Bourbon dynasty. He was the grandson of Louis XIV and his succession to the Spanish throne was one of the causes of the War of the Spanish Succession. Philip was an extremely weak ruler who was completely under the influence of his second wife, Elizabeth Farnese.

PHILIPPINES, The, a republic in the western Pacific, consisting of over 7,000 islands and islets. Pop. (1960) 27,473,000; area 115,707 sq. miles. Only 462 islands have an area exceeding 1 sq. mile. Volcanic and mountainous, the largest are

Luzon (40,420 sq. miles) and Mindanao (36,537 sq. miles). Nine others vary in area from about 1000—5000 sq. miles. Principal crops are rice, Manila hemp, copra, sugar-cane, maize and tobacco. Lumbering and fishing are important. The leading minerals are copper, gold, silver, lead, zinc, chromite, iron, manganese, quicksilver, coal and building stone. A Spanish possession from 1565, the islands were ceded to the U.S. in 1898, two years after the outbreak of a revolt against Spain. From 1942—44 they were occupied by the Japanese. In 1946 the Philippines became independent. The capital is Manila (pop. 3,006,627 including Quezon City where a new capital is being built). Other important towns are Cebu (209,000) and Bacolod (126,200).

PHILOSOPHY, a word of Greek origin which means literally 'the love of wisdom'. Philosophy is the universal science which is concerned with the explanation of general phenomena by seeking to comprehend their basic causative principles, i.e. the ultimate reality, and with considering how, if at all, such knowledge can be attained. Philosophy can also be regarded as the bringing of a critical, open mind to the examination of any aspect of life — e.g. morality, politics, religion, aesthetics— in order to probe into its significance and its relation to life in general.

Early Greek philosophers speculated on the nature of the material universe, and some of them developed a remarkable atomic theory (Leucippus and Democritus in the 5th century B.C. whose theories were put into verse by Lucretius). Others concentrated on ethics, and from them the Romans adopted two contrasting schools of thought—the Epicureans who thought that the aim of life was the pursuit of happiness, and the Stoics, who faced life with fortitude and tried to live in conformity with reason. The two main streams of philosophy derive from Plato, who postulated a world of abstract ideas of which we see only the shadows, and from Aristotle, the logician, analyser and classifier. In the history of the Christian Church the views of Aristotle, through the advocacy of Thomas Aquinas, soon displaced those of Plato, and were accepted as orthodox by the Roman Catholic Church.

With the Renaissance European philosophy divided into Rationalism which rejected revelation and intuition as sources of knowledge, but held that some knowledge rests on self-evident truths or innate ideas, and constructed various ideal worlds on this basis; and the Empiricism of the English philosophers Locke, Berkeley and Hume, who thought that knowledge was based only on what is perceived by the senses, or experience. In the Rationalist stream were Descartes—who taught that there were two independent worlds of mind and body—Spinoza and Leibniz. The contrast between the changing world of appearance and the ideal world of reality was stressed by Kant and Hegel, the Idealists; and a more mystical element was introduced by Kierkegaard. Even more practical than the Empiricists were the Pragmatists, led by William James, while Wittgenstein and the Logical Positivists demolished most preceding theories by denouncing as futile all attempts to explain the universe, since the only statements we can usefully make are those verifiable by experience.

PHNÔM-PENH, capital of Cambodia, on the Mekong River. Pop. (1962) 403,000. A communications and commercial centre, it trades in agricultural products, rubber and skins. It is connected by rail to Bangkok.

PHOBIA, an irrational obsessive fear. It can be attached to any kind of object or situation and stems from an unconscious conflict involving an early fear-producing experience. Recall of the original repressed situation, and the re-evaluation of it, usually causes the phobia to disappear.

PHOENICIA, an ancient maritime country on that part of the Syrian coast which extended from the Orontes River in the north to the city of Akko (modern Acre) in the south. Phoenicia was not a united kingdom but rather a number of independent city-states forming a loose confederacy which relied primarily on trade and commerce. The Phoenicians founded colonies in various parts of the Mediterranean region and at Cadiz. The chief towns were Tyre and Sidon. Phoenicia declined with the growth of the Greek empire.

PHONETICS, the study of the speech sounds of a language or dialect, or of language in general. Sounds are either consonants produced by a speech organ obstructing the escape of air from the lungs, or vowels, exhalations modified in the oral cavity. Voiced consonants are pronounced by vibrating the vocal cords (e.g. *b*); whereas unvoiced, or voiceless, consonants are produced without this vibration (e.g. *p*). Consonants are classified according to the organs which produce them.

PHOSPHATES, the salts of phosphoric acid. They are vital to the life and growth of plants and animals. The term generally refers to phosphate fertiliser or calcium phosphate, the main constituent of animal bones.

PHOSPHORUS, see Elements.

PHOTOGRAPHY, the fixing of the image of an object on a sensitised surface by the effects of light. The image is focused on sensitive film inside a light-tight compartment by means of a lens. Immersion of the film in an alkaline solution produces a negative in which the bright parts of the original object appear light and the light areas dark. Any number of positive prints may be made from the negative by exposure to light which restores the light values of the original object. Orthochromatic monochrome film is sensitive to blue, violet and green, and panchromatic to all colours including red. Colour films are used to produce either a positive print in colour or a transparency for display in a projector. The applications of photography are numerous: astronomy; air photography (in reconnaissance, mapping, forestry work, archaeology); spectography; infra-red, ultra-violet and X-ray photography in medicine and industry; tracking nuclear particles; and slow-motion and time-elapse cinematography (in the latter exposures are made at long intervals but projected at normal speed, giving a speeded-up picture of e.g. plant growth).

PHOTOSYNTHESIS, the formation of carbohydrates (q.v.) from carbon dioxide and water, using energy absorbed from sunlight by the green pigment, chlorophyll, found in almost all plants except fungi. It is probable that fats and proteins are also indirectly the products of photosynthesis.

PHYSICS, is traditionally defined as the study of the properties of matter and energy, but the definition has become blurred by modern developments, e.g. biophysics links biology and physics, while nuclear physics studies the atomic nuclei and their radiations, but molecules may be the subject of chemistry. Physics has expanded to include not only the classic heat, light and sound, electricity and magnetism, and thermodynamics, but also low-temperature physics, crystal physics, cosmic rays, the quantum theory, wave mechanics and many other fields.

PHYSIOLOGY, the study of all the life processes of plants and animals and of the functions of their various organs and tissues. Physiology overlaps sister sciences, but the main divisions of study include the muscular, circulatory, respiratory, reproductive, excretory and nervous systems, embryology and endocrinology (in part), metabolism, nutrition, growth, photosynthesis, vision, hearing, taste, smell and touch.

PICARDY, an ancient province of northern France, between Artois and Normandy, represented today by the Somme *département* and neighbouring regions, especially of Aisne and Oise. It is a country of orchards, sugar-beet, dairy farming and veal production, with textiles as the chief manufacture. The capital was Amiens; other towns are Beauvais, Cambrai and St Quentin. The battles of Agincourt and Crécy, and in 1916 the Battle of the Somme, were fought here.

PICASSO, Pablo (1881—   ), Spanish painter, born in Malaga, studied art in Barcelona and matured in Paris. He passed under many influences and through many styles. His 'blue' period (1900—04) was characterised by pictures in which blues and blacks predominate. In his next stage he turned to painting actors and harlequins in pinks and fawns. In his *Demoiselles d'Avignon* (1907) he began semi-abstract painting in which nudes are broken up into planes, sometimes with several aspects of the same subject presented simultaneously. This led up to Cubism, which he developed with Braque, painting 'not what you see but what you know is there'. It was at this stage that Negro influences began to appear. After experiments with collage and Surrealism Picasso began to paint monumental nudes with increasing distortion *(The Three Dancers)* and in *Guernica* (1936), inspired by the Spanish Civil War, expressed his horror of war. Among his many other activities, Picasso has painted scenery for Diaghilev and designed ceramics.

PILATE, Pontius, Roman procurator of Judaea and Samaria (26—36), who presided at the trial of Jesus. According to the Gospels he was very reluctant to authorise the crucifixion, saying 'I find in him no fault at all' and 'I am innocent of the blood of this just person', and he 'washed his hands before the multitude', but yielded to the clamour of the Jews. As there was so much unrest in his province, he was later recalled to Rome, but nothing is certainly known of his later history.

PILGRIM FATHERS, English separatists from the Church of England and others who accompanied them to America in 1620. They first went to the Netherlands in 1608 and later migrated to North America in the *Mayflower* and founded Plymouth colony, in Massachusetts.

PILSUDSKI, Józef (1867—1935), Polish statesman. Active in the movement for Polish independence, he was dictator of Poland from 1919—22 and from 1926 to his death.

PINERO, Sir Arthur Wing (1855—1934), British playwright. He wrote popular plays, of which *The Second Mrs Tanqueray* (1893) was made particularly famous by the acting of Mrs Patrick Campbell.

PIRACY, armed robbery committed against a vessel on the high seas. Any nation seizing the offenders may try and punish them. Piracy has a long history, but the most famous pirates were those who, often with the encouragement of their governments, preyed on Spanish shipping in the Caribbean during the 17th and 18th centuries, and were variously called buccaneers, freebooters or filibusters. Among them were Sir Henry Morgan and Capt. Kidd. The Corsairs, or Barbary pirates, were a highly organised band made up of many nationalities who operated from North Africa from the 16th century up to 1830.

PIRAEUS, Greek port and city on the Mediterranean. Pop. (1951) 186,014. The port of Athens since ancient times from the 6th century B.C., it was destroyed in 86 B.C. and virtually ceased to exist until its revival in 1830. It is a commercial and industrial centre producing textiles, machinery and tobacco products.

PIRANDELLO, Luigi (1867—1936), Italian dramatist and novelist. Interested in unique problems of the individual, he wrote *Six Characters in Search of an Author*, *As You Desire Me*, and other plays. He also wrote a large number of short stories.

PISA, a city in northern Italy, near the Tyrrhenian Sea. Pop. (1959) 86,974. It has beautiful Renaissance buildings including the famous Leaning Tower of the cathedral, which took 200 years to complete, a university and a museum.

PITCHBLENDE, a mineral of major importance, the principal source of uranium and radium. There are important deposits in the Congo region of central Africa, northwest Canada and Czechoslovakia.

PITT, William (The Elder), see Chatham, Earl of.

PITT, William (The Younger; 1759—1806), English statesman. Second son of the Earl of Chatham, he entered parliament in 1781. In 1783, when only 24 years of age, he was appointed Prime Minister. He served in this capacity until 1801, one of the longest tenures of this ministry in British history. Pitt's greatest achievements were his economic reforms, but most of his energies were necessarily directed towards the war against the French. It was he who set up the great European coalitions against Napoleon which, though he did not live to see their ultimate success, brought about the downfall of Napoleonic France. His cautious measures of reform ensured that there would be no parallel in Britain to the French Revolution. He resigned in 1801 on George III's refusal to approve any degree of Catholic Emancipation, but after Addington's failure he was recalled as Prime Minister in 1804, and lived to hear of the victory at Trafalgar. He never married.

PITTSBURGH, a city in southwest Pennsylvania, U.S.A. Pop. (1960) 604,332. A port on the Ohio River, it is a major industrial and communications centre in the midst of a region rich in coal, petroleum and natural gas. In addition to extensive steel mills, it has railway shops, shipyards, oil refineries, coke plants and limestone quarries. Manufactures include electrical equipment, ceramic ware, aluminium, chemicals, and iron and steel products.

PIUS XI (né Achille Ratti; 1857—1939), Pope from 1922—39. Renowned as a theologian, he reorganised the Vatican library and encouraged the pursuit of ecclesiastical studies. In 1929 he effected the Lateran Treaty with Mussolini by which the independence of the Vatican State was ensured, but he openly denounced totalitarianism.

PIUS XII (né Eugenio Pacelli; 1876—1958), Pope from 1939—58. He proclaimed the dogma of the Assumption of Mary (1950) and reformed the Holy Week ritual (1956). He was an outspoken critic of totalitarianism.

PIZARRO, Francisco (1470—1541), Spanish conqueror of Peru. He made himself master of the last Inca kingdom with great brutality and treachery, plundering the country of vast wealth. He was murdered by supporters of a former partner of his, Diego de Almagro, whom he had executed.

PLANET, one of the nine heavenly bodies revolving in elliptical orbits round the sun. Planets are huge globes visible because of reflected sunlight, and are identifiable by their steady light in contrast to the twinkling of stars. In order of distance from the sun, they are as follows:

Name	*Mean distance from sun (miles)*	*Mean orbital velocity (min./sec.)*	*Mean diameter (miles)*
Mercury	36,000,000	29.8	3,100
Venus	67,280,000	21.8	7,700
Earth	93,000,000	18.5	7,918
Mars	141,710,000	15.0	4,213
Jupiter	483,900,000	8.12	86,840
Saturn	887,100,000	6.00	71,520
Uranus	1,785,000,000	4.23	31,690
Neptune	2,797,000,000	3.37	31,000
Pluto	3,675,000,000	2.95	3,600

PLANT, a living organism of the vegetable kingdom. Plants are divided into the following major groups (phyla): Thallophytes, simple plants reproducing by spores and division, and having no stem, leaf or root (algae, fungi); Bryophytes, moss-like plants (liverworts, mosses); Pteridophytes, plants with vascular tissue and true roots (ferns, clubmosses, horsetails); and Spermatophytes, the seed-bearing plants, subdivided into Gymnosperms (e.g. conifers) and Angiosperms, the flowering plants. Angiosperms are again subdivided into monocotyledons (grasses, lilies, orchids) and dicotyledons (all other flowering plants).

PLANTAGENETS, a name which is used to denote the dynasty (also referred to as Angevin) which ruled England from 1154—1485. It derives from the *planta genista* (broom), a sprig of which was the badge of Geoffrey of Anjou who, by his marriage in 1129 to Maud (or Matilda), daughter of Henry I, became the father of the first of the Plantagenet Kings of England, Henry II. The dynasty includes the houses of Lancaster and York. The last king was Richard III.

PLASTICS, a group of materials, derived from natural and synthetic organic substances, which during the process of manufacture become a soft, dough-like mass which can be shaped into a permanent form by heat and pressure. They consist of derivatives of chemicals, cellulose, coal, petroleum and proteins which can be moulded, cast, extruded, laminated, blown or formed into shape. They are tough, durable, water- and heat-resistant. Those produced by polymerisation fall into two groups: thermoplastic, which soften on heating and harden on cooling, and are usually soluble in organic solvents; and thermosetting which, once formed, do not soften on re-heating. Plastics have an immense number of industrial applications, including electrical insulation, paints, adhesives, artificial textile fibres, mouldings, buttons, synthetic rubber and safety glass.

PLATINUM, see Elements.

PLATO (*c.* 427—347 B.C.), Greek philosopher, the pupil of Socrates and the teacher of Aristotle. After the death of Socrates (399) Plato travelled to Egypt, Italy and elsewhere, but returned (*c.* 386) and founded the Academy, where he taught for the next 40 years. Plato's philosophy is expounded in a series of dialogues between Socrates and his pupils, and it is not always easy to decide which views were derived from Socrates and which were Plato's own. The *Apology*, *Crito* and *Phaedo* describe the trial and death of Socrates, the last dealing with the immortality of the soul. The *Symposium* examines the nature of Love. In the *Republic* and *Laws* Plato describes the ideal state, ruled by philosopher-kings (who are not allowed to own any property of their own), assisted by auxiliaries (or executives); the rest of the state consists of the producers. If Plato had lived today he would have likened our state to that of a cinema audience, who can see all things depicted on a screen, but these are but shadows of the real objects, which we never see. They are the Ideas or Forms, eternal, unchanging, knowledge of which can only be obtained through reason, not through the senses or by scientific experiment. Man's mind consists of three elements, Desire, Emotion and Reason, and the good life consists in freeing ourselves from the dominance of Desire and developing Reason.

Plato's dialogues are works of art which would be read as literature even if the ideas they contain were not of such absorbing interest. His influence on all philosophy was immense, as also on early Christianity until the influence of Thomas Aquinas brought Aristotle to the fore. His Academy continued in being until A.D. 529.

PLOVDIV, a city in Bulgaria, on the Maritsa River. Pop. (1959) 171,391. A trading centre for the surrounding agricultural region, it manufactures leather, foodstuffs, textiles, attar of roses and wood products. It was called Philippopolis by Philip of Macedon and was the capital of Thrace in Roman times.

PLUTARCH (A.D. 46—120), Greek author and biographer, best known for his *Parallel Lives*, the biographies of 46 famous Greek and Roman statesmen, arranged in pairs for purposes of comparison.

PLUTONIUM, see Elements.

PLYMOUTH, a seaport, city and county borough in South Devon, England, on Plymouth Sound. Pop. (1961) 204,279. It is a naval base, second in size only to Portsmouth, and port-of-call for ocean liners. There are extensive fisheries, some industry and considerable export-import trade. Plymouth became a leading port during the reign of Elizabeth I. There are shipyards, and fish canning is a leading industry. The centre of the town was completely destroyed during the Second World War, and has been rebuilt with an imaginatively designed shopping area and civic centre.

POE, Edgar Allan (1809—49), American poet, critic and short-story writer. The melodiousness and haunting rhythm of his poems made him famous. They include *The Raven*, *Annabel Lee*, *The Bells* and *Ulalume*. His stories are permeated by a sense of the macabre. In *The Murders in the Rue Morgue* Poe produced the first modern detective story.

POET LAUREATE, an honorary appointment conferred by the British sovereign on a poet attached to the court. He is expected to write poems on important national events and personalities. Since John Dryden, the following have been awarded the title: Thomas Shadwell, Nahum Tate, Nicholas Rowe, Lawrence Eusden, Colley Cibber, William Whitehead, Thomas Wharton, Henry James

Pye, Robert Southey, Wordsworth, Tennyson, Alfred Austin, Robert Bridges and John Masefield (from 1930).

POETRY, a formalised expression of thought or emotion making use of such devices as rhyme, rhythm, metre and figures of speech. It uses emotive words rich in associations, in a compact shorthand style which sometimes conveys several layers of meaning. It employs imaginative insight to lend significance to human experience and speaks to the heart with an intensity heightened by indirection and innuendo. There are many forms of poetry: the long epic of heroic deeds; the shorter ballad telling a traditional tale and, like the epic, originally passed on by word of mouth; the lyric, in origin a short accompanied song expressing the poet's feelings; the ode, a lyric in the form of an address to a person or thing (e.g. to Autumn); the elegy, a lyric of lament; the sonnet, a fourteen-line poem conforming to a strict rhyme pattern; the pastoral, an idealised picture of shepherd or rustic life, used as a vehicle for a more profound theme; and satire, in which the attack is sharpened by being confined to a rigid metrical pattern, as in the heroic couplet.

POISON, a substance causing a harmful or deadly effect on a living organism. Chemically, it may be an acid, alkali, gas, metal or glucoside. Poisons affect the body either by causing inflammation or corrosion or by acting on the neuromuscular system or the blood. The effects vary under certain conditions. There are antidotes for counteracting some of them. Toxin is poison set up in the body by bacteria.

POLAND, a people's republic in eastern Europe, on the Baltic Sea. Pop. (1962) 30,323,900; area 121,131 sq. miles. Most of the country is lowland, with the Carpathian Mountains in the south. The principal crops are cereals, potatoes, sugar-beet, tobacco and hops. Livestock raising and fishing are important. Poland produces coal, coke, iron, steel, cement, chemicals and fertilisers, aluminium, copper, lead, zinc, petroleum and natural gas. Textiles, footwear and soap are important manufactures.

Boleslas I extended the borders of his father's domain to include Bohemia, Moravia and Saxony and took the title of king in 1024. This empire soon broke up into a number of small duchies. In 1410 Ladislas broke the power of the Teutonic Knights and reached the Baltic. Although a great power until the 17th century, Poland was racked by internal discord which led to three partitions of the country (1772, 1793 and 1795) among Austria, Russia and Prussia. After the First World War, Poland regained its independence to become embroiled immediately in a war with Russia which enabled it to extend its borders. In 1939 Poland was invaded by Germany. The country was subsequently devastated by the German armies attacking the Soviet Union. After the Second World War, Poland entered the Soviet orbit, ceding territory in the east to the U.S.S.R. and gaining former German areas in the west, including Silesia with its large coal deposits. The capital is Warsaw (pop. 1,171,000). Other important cities are Lódz (723,000), Wroclaw (Breslau, 443,000), Krakow (490,000) and Poznan (418,000).

POLICE, a body of officers for the maintenance of law and order and the prevention and detection of crime. The present system in England was introduced by Sir Robert Peel in 1829, and has four chief divisions: county, borough, city of London, metropolitan police of Greater London. In totalitarian states,

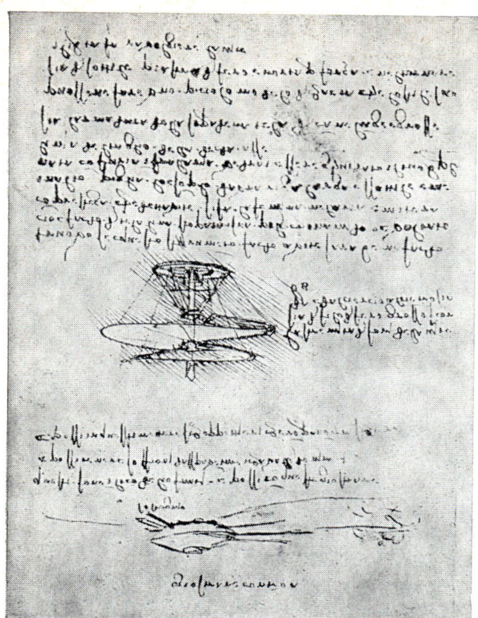

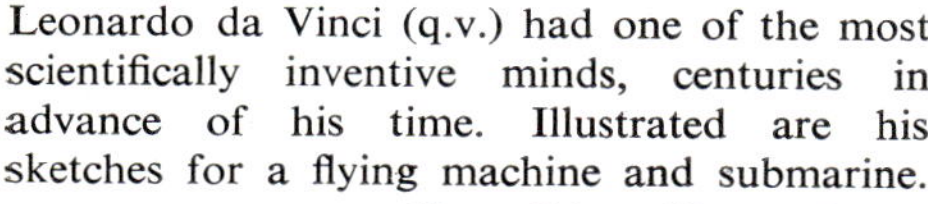

Leonardo da Vinci (q.v.) had one of the most scientifically inventive minds, centuries in advance of his time. Illustrated are his sketches for a flying machine and submarine.

Photo: Science Museum, London

Napoleon I devised plans in 1803 for invading Britain by balloons (q.v.) capable of carrying '3000 men and some horses'.

Photo: British Council

The first dirigible balloon, driven by propeller, was constructed and flown by Frenchman M. Henry Giffard in 1852.

Photo: Science Museum, London

Airships are still in use today, mainly for scientific investigation of meteorological data. Illustrated is the U.S.S. *Akron*, in flight over New York City. *Official U. S. Navy Photograph*

The original motor-driven heavier-than-air machine built by the American Wright brothers (q.v.) and first flown in December 1903. *Photo: Crown copyright. Science Museum, London*

the police act as an arm of repression and terror.

POLIOMYELITIS (Infantile Paralysis), a notifiable virus infection of the nerves of movement, usually affecting a limb. Commonest among children, and occurring in minor epidemics after a spell of hot weather, it can be carried by persons who have had a very mild attack without knowing it. Preventive inoculation has made great progress in recent years.

POLITICAL SCIENCE, the study of the nature, functioning, and structure of government. Its province includes the form of government; the making and administration of laws; the political system; social and economic phenomena; international relations; and the purposes of the state.

POLLINATION, the method by which flowering plants transfer the grains containing the male element (pollen) from the stamen (see Flower) to the pistil of the same or another flower. The pollen grains adhere to the sticky surface of the stigma and germinate to form a new plant. They may be carried by the wind, insects, birds, or snails, etc.; or they may simply fall to the ground. Cross-pollination is the transfer of the pollen to the stamen of the flower of another plant of the same species, the resulting offspring usually being more vigorous than in self-pollination.

POLLOCK, Jackson (1912—56), an American painter and leader of the Abstract-Expressionist movement. He painted in a vigorous style with twisting, labyrinthian lines characterising his work.

POLO, a Persian game on horseback, played also in India, China and Japan, and introduced to England by Indian Army officers in 1869. It is also found in the U.S.A. and Argentina. It is played by teams of four on a ground of about 300 × 160 yds, with polo sticks (long canes with wooden striking heads, resembling a croquet mallet in shape), which are used to send the 5 oz. ball through a goal 8 yds wide. The game lasts an hour, broken up into short periods called chukkas. Since riding schools in Britain have started hiring out trained polo ponies and providing facilities for learning the game, the number of players has greatly increased.

POLO, Marco (*c.* 1254—1323), Venetian traveller. Together with his father and uncle, he went via Persia and the Gobi desert to China, where he was employed in the service of Kublai Khan, the Tartar Emperor. Later, captured in a war with Genoa, he dictated the story of his adventures to another captive.

POLONIUM, see Elements.

POLYNESIA, a division of the Pacific islands between and including Hawaii, Easter Island and New Zealand. They are roughly distributed in two parallel east-west chains, of either volcanic or coral origin. The climate is tropical and there is abundant seasonal rainfall. The inhabitants are light brown and tall and have wavy black hair. Their population has declined by about 90% since the 18th century.

POMERANIA, a region in Poland and East Germany, on the Baltic Sea. It was formerly a Prussian province subsisting chiefly on agriculture, fisheries and shipbuilding. The chief town was Stettin.

POMPEII, an ancient Italian city near Mt Vesuvius and Naples. It was destroyed by a volcanic eruption in A.D. 79 and buried under layers of lava and ashes. Rediscovered in 1748, it has yielded

Pompeiian street, as uncovered from lava

invaluable information about life in ancient Rome.

POMPEY THE GREAT (Gnaeus Pompeius; 106—48 B.C.), Roman general. He won fame by clearing the Mediterranean of pirates, defeating Mithridates of Pontus and annexing Syria and Palestine. Faced by the hostility of the Senate on his return to Rome, he joined Caesar and Crassus in forming the First Triumvirate (60) and married Caesar's daughter Julia. After Julia's death (54) rivalry developed between Pompey, heading the conservative senatorial party, and Caesar. Civil war broke out, and at the Battle of Pharsalus (48) Pompey was decisively defeated by Caesar's forces. He fled to Egypt, where he was assassinated.

POONA, a city in Maharashtra, India, at the confluence of the Mutha and Mula rivers. Pop. (1961) 721,134. A commercial centre, it manufactures cotton, paper, rice, sugar and iron goods. There are many educational institutions. The city contains temples and palaces dating from the 16th—19th centuries, when it was a Mahratta capital. Lying at 1800 ft, it is the hill station for Bombay and was an important military station under the British *raj*.

POPE, Alexander (1688—1744), English poet. The principles guiding his poetry are set forth in his poem *Essay on Criticism*. His translation of Homer brought him much wealth. Most of his work is satire, nearly all of it written in the heroic couplets which he developed to perfection. His *Essay on Man* is a philosophical poem, *the Rape of the Lock* is a mock-heroic tale of contemporary life, the *Dunciad*, as so many of his poems, an attack on his rivals. Made oversensitive by his hunch back, he quarrelled with many of his friends, and his reputation suffered from the attacks of the Romantic poets, who did not approve of him or his poetry. He is now established among the great Augustan poets.

PORT ARTHUR (Liu-Shun), a port and city in south Laioning, northeast China. Pop. 137,100. Leased to Russia in 1897, it was occupied by Japan in 1905. The U.S.S.R. occupied it in 1945 and restored it to China in 1954. It is linked to the adjacent city of Dairen (q.v.), to form Lüta. It was for a time a joint Russo-Chinese naval base.

PORT ELIZABETH, a port and city in Cape province, Republic of South Africa, on Algoa Bay. Pop. (1960) 270,815. A rail, industrial and commercial centre, it exports wool, mohair, skins and fruit. Industries include sawmill products, chemicals and food processing.

PORTO ALEGRE, a seaport in southeastern Brazil, capital of Rio Grande do Sul province. Pop. (1960) 641,173. At the mouths of five rivers, it is a major communications, commercial and industrial centre with shipyards and factories producing textiles, iron products, footwear, chemicals, foodstuffs, paper and furniture. One of the most up-to-date cities in Brazil, it has a large German-speaking element.

PORT OF SPAIN, capital of Trinidad. Pop. (1960) 121,150. A port of call for numerous ships, it exports agricultural products and asphalt.

PORTLAND, the largest city in Oregon, U.S.A., on the Willamette River. Pop. (1960) 372,676. Commanding a view of snow-covered mountain peaks, it is a communications, industrial, financial and commercial centre. Its port serves the entire Columbia River basin. Portland leads in the processing of lumber. Other products are aluminium, textiles, machinery and lumbering equipment. There are a number of institutions of higher learning.

PORTSMOUTH, a city and county borough, Hampshire, England, on Portsea Island. Pop. (1961) 215,198. A major naval base and arsenal, it manufactures light engineering products and aircraft. Portsmouth itself is a naval garrison town, the dockyards are at Portsea, while Landport and Cosham are residential areas, Southsea is a seaside resort and Spithead is the anchorage. All these are in the borough; across the harbour is Gosport.

PORTUGAL, a country on the west side of the Iberian peninsula, Europe. Pop. (1960) 9,124,000; area 35,490 sq. miles (including Madeira and the Azores). It has highlands in the northeast which slope down to the sea, and coastal plains and river valleys opening on to the Atlantic Ocean. The principal crops are grains and potatoes. Portugal is a leading wine producer and source of cork. Fishing and livestock raising are important. There are deposits of coal, cement, copper, kaolin, iron ores and manganese.

Portugal was part of Spain until the middle of the 12th century. Portuguese expansion began with Alfonso III (1248—79) who gave the country most of its present boundaries. By the middle of the 16th century, Portuguese navigators had given their country a vast empire in South America, Africa, Indo-China and Malaya. After 60 years of Spanish occupation (1581—1641), Portugal began to decline as an imperial power. Civil strife during the 19th century ended in the expulsion of the king in 1910 and the establishment of a republic. Since 1932 Antonio Salazar has been dictator. The capital is Lisbon (pop. 790,434). Other important cities are Oporto (284,842), Setubal (44,235) and Coimbra (42,640). See also Angola; Guinea, Portuguese; Mozambique.

POSEIDON (Roman Neptune), the Greek god of the sea, who joined his brothers Zeus and Hades in the overthrow of Kronos. The trident, perhaps originally a thunderbolt, was his chief symbol, together with the dolphin and the horse. Triton was his son.

POSITRON, the positively charged counterpart of the electron (an anti-electron). When these two types of particle collide they are usually annihilated and produce gamma rays; in the reverse direction, pairs of electrons and positrons can be produced by gamma rays. When a proton changes into a neutron a positron is formed and beta radiation results.

POSTAL SERVICES, a service for the dispatch of letters to and from England was inaugurated during the reign of Elizabeth I. In 1840 Sir Rowland Hill introduced the penny postage stamp, the first in the world. Pillar boxes appeared in London in 1857. Subsequent expansion of the services include postal and money orders, savings banks, telegraph and telephone communications, insurance stamps and payment of pensions. The Universal Postal Union, with its main office in Berne, regulates the international distribution of mail.

POST-IMPRESSIONISM, a name, introduced in 1910, for the artistic reaction away from the naturalism of the Impressionists towards a new stress on the importance of the subject, colour, form and solidity. The leaders of the movement were Cézanne, Van Gogh and Gauguin.

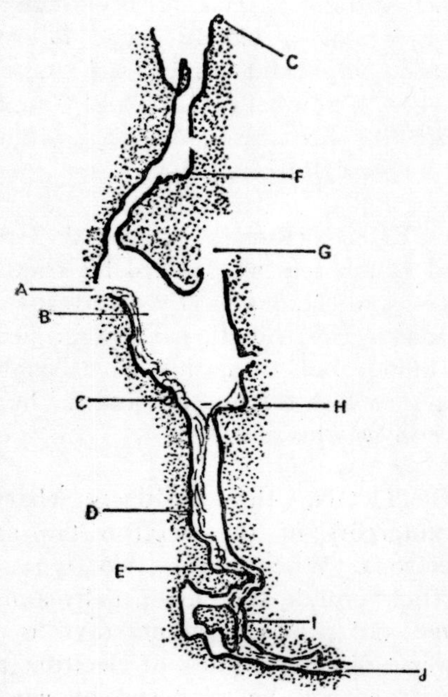

Pot-holer's underground shafts and caverns (cross-section of La Henne Morte)
A. Stream B. 590 ft C. Winch D. 328 ft pitch and waterfall E. Lake at 1246 ft F. 290 ft G. Unexplored H. Underground camp chamber I. 130 ft waterfall J. Sump 1460 ft

POT-HOLING, the exploration of underground shafts and caverns worn by water in chalk or limestone country. In Britain, Derbyshire and Yorkshire are rich in suitable sites, and new underground rivers and caves are still being found there, often bizarre, and even beautiful, with their stalagmites and stalactites. In September 1962 a French geologist spent over two months down a 400-ft pot-hole in the Alps, studying the effects of prolonged exposure.

POTSDAM, a city in East Germany, 18 miles southwest of Berlin, on an island in the Havel River. Pop. (1960) 115,163. From the time of Frederick the Great it was the capital of Brandenburg and the site of Hohenzollern glory; the Sans Souci Palace survived the Second World War. Churchill, Truman, and Stalin met here in 1945 to discuss problems arising out of the defeat of Nazi Germany.

POTTERY, objects made from clay, sand, chalk, calcified bones, ground flints, etc., and hardened by fire. Pottery making is one of the oldest arts. Before the invention of the potter's wheel, earthenware vessels were made either by scooping out the centre of a ball of clay or by placing coils of clay one above the other. Earthenware is opaque and porous and may be glazed or unglazed. China is translucent and in its best forms made of china clay. Pottery includes tiles, bricks, drainpipes, porcelain insulators, etc. Ceramics is the name given to artistic pottery.

POUND, Ezra (1885—), American poet and critic. He spent many years in Europe and founded the Imagist school of poetry in England. The bulk of his later work is included in his *Cantos*. For broadcasting for Mussolini from Italy during the Second World War, he was arrested and committed to a mental hospital from 1945—58.

PRAGMATIC SANCTION, an imperial or royal edict concerning Church or State, especially that by which the Emperor Charles VI, having no male heir, proclaimed Maria Theresa his successor and emphasised the indivisibility of his dominions (1713). Although they had previously promised to respect it, several European powers, led by Frederick the Great, disputed it as soon as the emperor died; this led to the War of the Austrian Succession (q.v.).

PRAGUE (Praha), capital of Czechoslovakia, on the Vltava River. Pop. (1961) 1,003,000. It is a communications, educational, cultural, commercial and industrial centre. Its industries include machinery, leather, chemicals, glass, footwear and foodstuffs. Prague was the capital of Bohemia; the old town, on the left bank, contains the 16th-century royal palace, Hradčany, 240 ft above the river, and the cathedral of St Vitus. The university was founded in 1348.

PRAYER, addressed to God or, in the Roman Catholic Church, to the Virgin Mary, saints or angels, as intercessors, may be spoken or thought, communal or solitary, and its content may be adoration, thanksgiving, confession or petition. Prayers for the dead are permissible for those who believe in Purgatory. The implications of a belief in the efficacy of a petition, even a disinterested petition on behalf of another, are difficult to fit into a theological system.

PRAYER BOOK, The Book of Common Prayer, an English translation and simplified adaptation (*c.* 1549) of medieval Catholic liturgical books. It is now, although in revised form, the service book of the Anglican Church. A revised prayer book failed to obtain parliamentary approval in 1928.

PREDESTINATION, the view that man is predestined by God to salvation or damnation. It was preached by St Augustine in its most extreme form and was adopted by Calvin and Luther. St Thomas Aquinas took a middle course, holding that although man was born to original sin he can be saved by divine grace provided he co-operates; he is free to choose to do so, but God foresees that some will not so choose, and predestines them to damnation. See Determinism.

PREGNANCY, the period between the fertilisation of the ovum in the female mammal (conception) and the separation of the fully developed being from the body of the mother. In humans, it lasts for 280 days or nine calendar months. Initial symptoms are the cessation of menstruation, enlargement and sensitivity of the breasts, fatigue and sometimes nausea. In about the fourth month the abdomen begins to increase in size.

PRE-RAPHAELITE BROTHERHOOD, originally a nickname for a group of English painters (Holman Hunt, Millais, Rossetti and Burne-Jones) founded in 1848. The movement was based more on disapproval of Raphael than on their proclaimed admiration for the Italian primitives who preceded Raphael (about whom they knew little). They at first tried to recapture the high seriousness and the meticulous fidelity to Nature that they attributed to the primitives, and used bright colours and the outdoor study of background detail. Later, except for Hunt, they turned to a romantic medievalism which had little connection with their original aims, but they kept the name Pre-Raphaelite even after it had ceased to have any meaning. After a few years the group broke up.

PRESBYTERIANISM, a system of ecclesiastical government by elected presbyters (elders) who are subdivided into two groups, the ministers and the lay-elders. Though Calvin is generally recognised as the father of modern Presbyterianism, its adherents regard it as being the form of church government practised by the early Church. Today the Presbyterian Church numbers over

40 million members throughout the world. The established church in Scotland is Presbyterian, and it was mainly from Scotland that the movement spread overseas to the U.S. and the Dominions. Welsh Presbyterianism, however, had a separate origin.

PRESIDENT, the head of a republic. There are two main types. In the French type, widely imitated on the Continent, the President was, until President de Gaulle became President of the Fifth Republic, mainly a figure-head. The other main type is the American, a form imitated in South America and elsewhere. The American President is formally elected in the January following each leap-year by electors from every state in the Union. On taking office he becomes the country's chief executive and the commander-in-chief of all the armed forces. As members of the House of Representatives are elected for two-year terms and Senators for six, the President cannot rely on support from Congress during his four-year term, and his plans may be frustrated. In 1951 it was enacted that a President may not serve more than two terms of office.

PRETORIA, administrative capital of the Republic of South Africa and capital of Transvaal province. Pop. (1960) 422,590. A communications, commercial and industrial centre, it produces metallurgical articles. It has a university. The government buildings were designed by Sir Herbert Baker (1910—13); the Voortrekker Monument is another prominent landmark. The streets and parks have numerous jacaranda trees, and the time of their flowering is celebrated by a festival week.

PRETORIUS, Martinius Wessels (1818——1901), South African Boer statesman. President of both the South African (Transvaal) and Orange Free State republics, he served, together with Paul Kruger and Petrus Joubert, as administrator of the Transvaal after its annexation by Britain in 1877.

PRIEST, one who has the authority to perform the rites and rituals of a given religion. In the Christian Church a priest occupies a position above that of deacon but below that of bishop. The priest has the right to administer the sacraments and to pronounce absolution.

PRIESTLEY, John Boynton (1894—), British novelist, dramatist and essayist. His novels *The Good Companions* and *Angel Pavement*, and the play *Dangerous Corner*, are among his best-known works.

PRIESTLEY, Joseph (1733—1804), English clergyman and scientist. He discovered oxygen and carbon monoxide and invented carbonated drinks. His work in gases led him to discover methods for producing ammonia, nitrous oxide, sulphur dioxide and hydrogen sulphide. A Liberal, he emigrated to the U.S.A. to escape the public hostility he aroused by his sympathy with the French Revolution.

PRINCE EDWARD ISLAND, a Canadian island province in the Gulf of St Lawrence. Pop. (1961) 104,629; area 2184 sq. miles. Generally flat with hills in the centre, it is mostly agricultural. The chief crops are hay and clover, grains, seed potatoes, fruit and turnips. Livestock breeding, dairy farming and oyster fishing are important. Industries include canning, sawmill products, food processing and fox raising. The capital is Charlottetown (pop. 18,318).

PRINTING, the production of an impression by the transfer of ink. There are three main types of process for accomplishing this: letterpress or typographic printing, in which the ink is transferred from a raised image; intaglio or gravure printing which makes use of a plate in which recesses have been incised for filling with ink; lithography, in which the image is made in greasy ink on a flat absorbent stone. Collotype is used in reproducing work of the finest detail, and silk screen is a method using stencils on silk, wire gauze, etc. Typesetting can be by Linotype, which casts whole lines (slugs), used in newspapers and books; Monotype, which casts single letters, used in tabular and other complicated work; or a newer method, photo-typesetting which makes use of photographic film. Printing was known to the Chinese before the 10th century A.D. There is some controversy as to who first invented printing in Europe in the 15th century but the credit is usually given to Johann Gutenberg.

PRISON, a place where persons are confined against their will for violations of the law. The modern aim is not detention merely for the purposes of punishment and isolation but also in order to rehabilitate the offender and prepare him to assume a useful position in society. To avoid mixing young offenders with older criminals, the imprisonment of persons under 21 is discouraged; the aim is wherever possible to substitute, particularly for short prison sentences, committal to Borstal schools, where trade and industrial training is given to those aged 15—20, or to detention centres and remand homes (age 14—20), or attendance for not more than three hours a day at attendance centres (age 12—20). For habitual offenders sentences of corrective training or preventive detention can be imposed. The distinction between simple imprisonment, penal servitude and imprisonment with hard labour was abolished in 1948.

PRIVY COUNCIL, in Britain, a body of advisers to the Crown. In earlier days the Privy Council exercised great power but it now has mainly a formal function. The Judicial Committee of the Privy Council is the final court of appeal from colonial courts. When the sovereign signs an Order-in-Council, three members of the Privy Council must be present. Members of the Cabinet must be Privy Councillors. The Lord President of the Council is always a prominent member of the Cabinet. Privy Councillors are styled 'The Right Honourable' and have the letters P.C. after their names.

PROKOFIEV, Sergei (1891—1953), Russian composer. A skilled conductor and outstanding pianist, he wrote operas *(The Love of Three Oranges)*, ballets *(Romeo and Juliet)*, symphonies *('Classical' Symphony)*, chamber music and the musical tale *Peter and the Wolf.*

PROPAGANDA, the attempt to mould the opinions of people for the purpose of influencing their behaviour. The organs used to make propaganda techniques effective include the press, radio, television, motion pictures and posters. The techniques are based on the psychological manipulation of human nature to induce people unconsciously to change their attitudes. Advertising is today the commonest form of a technique which derives its name from a Papal Committee set up in 1622 and called the College for the Propagation (Latin *propaganda*) of the Faith.

PROPHET, one through whom the God makes known his revelations. In the Judaeo-Christian tradition the Old Testament prophets played a major role in the spiritual development of the religion. The major prophets were Isaiah, Jeremiah, Ezekiel and Daniel.

PROTEINS, complex organic compounds composed of carbon, hydrogen, oxygen and nitrogen, each molecule containing hundreds or thousands of the molecules of 20 different amino-acids. Every species of living thing has kinds of protein peculiar to itself. In the nitrogen food cycle, proteins are synthesised from carbon dioxide, water, soil nitrates, ammonium salts, etc., and eventually break down into these components again. They are found in some viruses, muscle, haemoglobin (in blood), and as hormones (insulin) or as enzymes (pepsin). Fibrous proteins are structural materials in skin, hair, wool, etc. Common proteins are egg albumen and casein in milk.

PROTESTANTISM, a name applied originally only to the followers of Martin Luther who 'protested' (in the Late Latin sense of 'bear public witness') against the decree of the Catholic states passed at the second Diet of Speyer in 1529 to ban Luther's teachings, but subsequently used to denote all the churches which broke off relations with Rome at the time of the Reformation. The two main divisions are Lutheran and Calvinist (or Reformed; q.v.). At first the tendency was to subdivide into more and more sects but when it was realised that harm resulted from this, especially in the mission field, there was a reaction towards amalgamation, which still proceeds.

PROTON, one of the two main types of nuclear particles (q.v.), having a positive electrical charge equal to the negative charge of an electron, and 1840 times its mass. The atomic number of an element is the number of protons in its atomic nucleus (which, since an atom as a whole is neutral, is the same as the number of electrons). The alpha particle and the nucleus of helium both comprise two protons and two neutrons bound together. The proton is the nucleus of the ordinary hydrogen atom (which alone has no neutron).

PROUST, Marcel (1871—1922), French novelist. His one work is his 15-volume novel *Remembrance of Things Past.* Confined to his room by asthma, Proust devoted his last 10 years to the reconstruction, in infinite detail, of his life from childhood to the years when he was frequenting the artistocratic *salons* of Paris. In simple language, but in gently meandering sentences of sometimes immense length, he explores the subtleties of thought and emotion in a world where time does not exist, for he held, with Bergson, that the past continues to exist, and that events do not happen to us but we come to pre-existing events. Proust's influence, small during his lifetime, has since become very great.

PROVIDENCE, capital of Rhode Island, U.S.A., at the mouth of the Providence River. Pop. (1960) 207,498. It is a seaport and a communications, commercial, industrial and cultural centre. Industries include machine tools, textiles, textile machinery, rubber goods, jewellery and silverware. It is the seat of Brown University and of the first Baptist meeting-house.

PRUSSIA, a former kingdom and German state. Pop. (1938) 41,762,040; area 113,545 sq. miles. On the Baltic and North seas, it comprised nearly two-thirds of pre-war Germany. Its history is closely associated with that of the mark of Brandenburg and the house of Hohenzollern. It came into existence through the union of the territories of the Teutonic Knights and the Elector of Brandenburg in 1618. Frederick William (1640—88) strengthened the independence of his realm and laid the foundation of Prussia's greatness. During the reign of Frederick the Great (1740—86), Prussia's rivalry with Austria resulted in her acquisition of Silesia, and her emergence as a military power after being victorious in the Seven Years War (1756—63). Prussia then began to assume leadership in German affairs. Overrun by Napoleon, the kingdom regained most of its territories after 1815. The first step towards German unity was taken when Prussia united all Germany in a customs union (Zollverein) in 1834. Prussian victories over Austria (1866) and France (1870) paved the way for the union of all Germany under William I in 1871, with Bismarck as Chancellor. Prussia took the lead in German expansion in the period up to the First World War; but afterwards it became a state with dwindling influence in German affairs, and much of East Prussia was ceded to Poland. With the end of the Second World War Prussia ceased to exist and the area was divided between East and West Germany. The principal cities included Berlin, Cologne, Essen, Frankfurt-on-Main and Düsseldorf.

PSALMS, the collection of 150 hymns and psalms incorporated in the Book of Psalms, one of the books of the Old Testament. They are traditionally ascribed to King David, but while some were written before the Exile, others were composed as late as the 2nd century B.C. It is unlikely that any of them were written by David.

PSYCHOANALYSIS, a term applied to a method of diagnosis and treatment of psychological disorders, and also to the theory on which it is based. The three leading theorists are Freud, Adler and Jung (qq.v.), who respectively stressed the role of 'sex', aggression and the collective unconscious in the early development of personality.

The mind is regarded as having three parts: the id (Latin, 'it'), the seat of the unconscious primitive drives of 'sex' and aggression; the ego, the conscious mind which seeks to adjust the id to the hard facts of reality; and the super-ego, the censor which has unconsciously absorbed the ethical standards imparted by the parents through praise, blame and example. The super-ego tries to discourage thoughts and behaviour that will not win social approval, and if it is disregarded a feeling of guilt or ostracism results. Unless a proper balance is struck between these three parts, neurotic behaviour (see Neurosis) will be the outcome.

The term 'sex' (or libido) is used in psychoanalysis in a very wide sense to include wants, appetites and positive feelings, in contrast to 'aggression', the negative desire to destroy, hurt, etc. The id may express itself covertly in many ways, e.g. exhibitionism, sadism, masochism; or be sublimated (i.e. diverted) into socially useful and approved ways (e.g. the potential sadist may become a boxer or a surgeon); or disguise itself as its opposite (as in the case of the extreme puritan, who is shrinking in horror from his own sexuality). The ego uses many tricks to effect its adjustments, e.g. compensation to cover a feeling of inferiority (see Adler); projection (accusing others of our own faults, which in extreme cases may lead to persecution mania); rationalisation (manufacturing apparently reasonable excuses for unreasonable conduct). Psychosomatic medicine (q.v.) has thrown much light on the processes by which a person who has emotional reasons for not wanting to hear becomes deaf, or who, under the strain of prolonged frustration, may develop various diseases and disabilities.

The basic method of psychoanalytic

treatment is to discover the patient's early emotional history, by getting him to talk uninhibitedly about his past, saying anything that comes into his head; by the analysis of his dreams; and by building up a picture by deductions from his free association of ideas, lapses of memory, slips of the tongue, etc. The psychiatrist then tries to teach the patient how to resolve past (usually childhood) conflicts in the light of present mature experience.

Although individual theorists may seem to carry some ideas to extremes, and although psychoanalytic treatment of an individual may be prolonged, expensive and in the long term ineffective, it is incontestable that psychoanalysis as a whole has permanently transformed psychology, medicine and social attitudes, and greatly enriched our lives.

PSYCHOLOGY, the science of the individual and his adjustment to his environment. An outgrowth of philosophy and physiology, it was at first equated with a study of the mind. Later schools denied the possibility of being able to measure the mind objectively through the introspective investigation of individual faculties and pointed out that only a person's behaviour could be studied scientifically (see Behaviourism). Gestalt psychology (q.v.) teaches that there is a natural tendency to find significant patterns among sensations and an ability to learn by insight. In the course of time, basic principles were laid down to explain various types of human behaviour and were applied to such fields as education, vocational guidance, personnel selection, mental health and social movements. Particular fields of study include the assessment of intelligence, the classification of personality types and their relation to physique, the processes of learning, memory, the conditioned reflex (q.v.), and perception.

PSYCHOSIS, a severe disease, especially a derangement of the mental processes, amounting to insanity. There are two chief types. In schizophrenia the victim lives in a world increasingly divorced from reality, with progressive disorder of feeling, thought and action. He suffers from delusions and hallucinations, hearing voices which give him instructions he must obey. This used to be called dementia praecox, as it was first observed in young adults. The condition responds to treatment with insulin and tranquillisers. In popular usage the term schizophrenia is applied to split personality, an extremely rare condition in which a person's mental life is divided between two sub-personalities, the actions of one being to some extent unknown to the other, as in the case of R. L. Stevenson's Dr Jekyll and Mr Hyde. The other chief type is manic depression, in which the patient alternates between wild elation and melancholia, both without cause. In paranoia there are no hallucinations but a deeply ingrained persecution complex; the sufferer is able to produce the most plausible and detailed evidence to back up his assertion that he is the victim of persecution.

PSYCHOSOMATIC MEDICINE, the branch of medicine that studies the effect of emotional factors (especially worry) on bodily conditions, as in gastric ulcer. high blood-pressure, some skin diseases, exophthalmic goitre (see Endocrinology). Physicians have been converted in increasing numbers to the view that both physical and mental factors are present in many, if not all, diseases, and that therefore the search for and removal of the emotional cause is of the first importance. Intensive study is now being devoted to this subject.

PTOLEMY (Claudius Ptolemaeus; *c.* A.D. 100—170), Greek astronomer, mathematician and geographer. His theory (described in his *Almagest*) that the earth is the centre of the universe influenced astronomical thought down to the 16th century.

PUBLIC OPINION, the dominant attitude on some current event or issue. The intensity of the attitude held is an important factor in determining the extent to which the opinions really reflect public feelings. In democracies, public opinion moulds the government; the reverse is true in a totalitarian state. An individual's attitude towards a problem or occurrence is determined by such factors as education, environment, age, sex, religion, national and racial forebears, economic status and occupation. Various kinds of pressure groups are always attempting to influence public opinion.

PUCCINI, Giacomo (1858—1924), Italian operatic composer. He achieved widespread fame with his operas *Manon Lescaut*, *La Bohème*, *Tosca* and *Madam Butterfly*, and the unfinished *Turandot*.

PUEBLA, a city in southern Mexico on the Atoyac River. Pop. (1960) 287,952. A communications, commercial and industrial centre, it commands a view of four snow-covered mountains, including Popocatepetl (17,887 ft). It is in the midst of an agricultural and mining region. Textiles, footwear, glass and cigarettes are manufactured and there are distinctive local handicrafts. The town was founded in 1531 and has many fine colonial buildings, including the oldest theatre in the Americas. An Aztec pyramid is near by.

PUERTO RICO, a U.S. self-governing island commonwealth in the West Indies. Pop. (1960) 2,349,544; area 3423 sq. miles. Most of the island is mountainous. There are large sugar-cane plantations, and pineapples, tobacco, cotton and coconuts are also grown. Iron ore is the only important mineral. The principal industries are concerned with processing agricultural products. Discovered by Columbus in 1493, Puerto Rico was a Spanish possession until 1898, when it became U.S. territory. It became self-governing in 1952. Spanish is the mother tongue of most of the population, which is about 25% Negro. The capital is San Juan (pop. 432,377). The other large city is Ponce (114,286).

PUGWASH MOVEMENT, started by Bertrand Russell and others, and inspired by Einstein, this movement, which was named after the Canadian town where the first conference was held, brings together scientists of many nations to confer periodically as individuals on the means of diverting science from destructive to constructive purposes, and on international co-operation between scientists. In 1958 it issued the 'Vienna declaration' on the dangers of nuclear bombs, whether clean or dirty, and of radiocative fall-out.

PUNIC WARS (264—146 B.C.), a series of three separate wars waged between Rome and Carthage. They were a result of increased commercial competition between the two leading powers of the Mediterranean. In spite of the brilliant leadership of the Carthaginian general, Hannibal, Carthage was defeated and completely destroyed, leaving Rome unchallenged in its power.

PUNJAB, a region in the northwest of the Indian sub-continent. In the Indus plain, it is watered by five rivers which combine to form the Indus. Cereals, cotton and sugar are the principal crops.

It was divided in 1947 between India and Pakistan. East Punjab is a state in the Indian Union with a population which is two-thirds Hindu; pop. (1961) 20,298,151; area 47,084 sq. miles; the capital is Chandigarh. West Punjab has been incorporated into West Pakistan; the leading city is Lahore.

PURITANISM, a term applied in the 16th and 17th centuries to numerous dissenting groups holding very varied opinions on religious reform. They may be divided into two main bodies: those who wished to eliminate the last traces of Romanism from the Anglican Church, but who regarded themselves as Anglicans; and those who wished to substitute government by elders (i.e. Presbyterianism) for government by bishops. By the 17th century, Baptists, Unitarians, Quakers and many others were all called Puritans, a name which was eventually replaced by those of Dissenter or Nonconformist. In general it can be said that Puritans stood for austerity (strict observance of the Sabbath, no church music, no incense); some were not merely against bishops but anticlerical. After the Restoration they asked for religious toleration, but themselves showed little tolerance, e.g. in America.

PUSAN (Fusan), a city and port in southeastern Korea. Pop. (1960) 1,162,614. A commercial centre, it trades in silks, hides, beans, rice and dried fish. It was a major base of operations for U.N. forces in the Korean War.

PUSHKIN, Aleksandr (1799—1837), Russian poet and novelist. He wrote lyric poetry, long narrative poems, short stories and a novel, *The Captain's Daughter*, but his greatest works are the romance *Eugene Onegin* and the drama *Boris Godunov*, both in verse. Pushkin was the first to develop a distinctively Russian poetic style; his poetry is characterised by a simplicity which conceals supreme artistry.

PYONGYANG, capital of North Korea, on Taedong River. Pop. (1962) 940,000. In the midst of a coal and iron mining region, it is an industrial and commercial centre.

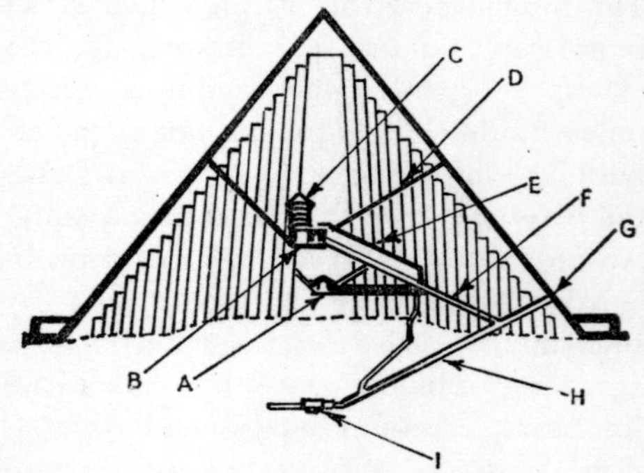

Egyptian pyramid of Cheops at Giza
A. Queen's Chamber B. King's Chamber C. Five chambers over King's Chamber D. Air channel E. Grand gallery F. Ascending corridor E. Entrance H. Descending corridor I. Chamber in rock foundation

PYRAMIDS, the Egyptian pyramids are huge stone or brick structures containing passages and rooms, erected by the Pharaohs as royal tombs. The most important are at Giza and Saqqara on the west bank of the Nile. The largest, built by Khufu (Cheops) about 2900 B.C., is 481 ft high and covers 13 acres. The other two large pyramids in the same area, built by Khafra (Chephren) and Men-kau-Ra (Mycerinus), are smaller. There are altogether 70 pyramids in Egypt.

PYRENEES, a mountain range in southwest Europe forming the boundary between France and Spain. It extends for 270 miles from the Bay of Biscay to the Gulf of Lyons. The highest point is Pic d'Anéto (11,174 ft).

PYTHAGORAS (*c.* 570—500 B.C.), Greek philosopher and mathematician. Born in Samos, he emigrated *c.* 530 to Croton in southern Italy, where he founded a religious community which wielded political power. Their doctrine was taken from the Orphic Mysteries, and the school, which existed until *c.* 300 B.C., influenced Socrates and Plato. Pythagoras believed in reincarnation, and thought that the soul was purified by study and ascetic living, including a vegetarian diet. The main studies were in mathematics, the mathematics of music (e.g. the relation of the intervals) and medicine. The attribution of the famous Euclidean theorem to Pythagoras may perhaps be well grounded. Much legend grew up about the Pythagoreans, whose aims were of a religious rather than political order.

QATAR, an independent shaikhdom on the Persian Gulf. Pop. (1962) 40,000; area 4,000 sq. miles (approximate figures). Some three-quarters of the population live in the capital city of Doha; conditions elsewhere, in the arid desert land, being very primitive. Qatar is one of the richest oil-producing areas of the Middle East, and in recent years development of facilities for this industry has been rapid. A modern port has been constructed at Umm Said on the east coast.

QUAKERS, see Friends, Society of.

QUANTUM THEORY, a fundamental theory of matter and motion which arose from the discovery that nuclear particles (q.v.) behave both as electromagnetic waves and as particles (see Electromagnetic Waves). According to the Uncertainty (or Indeterminacy) Principle, the more precisely the position of a particle is measured the less precisely can its momentum be measured, and vice versa. A set of mathematical rules was worked out for calculating the behaviour of fundamental particles in accordance with this principle. They form the Quantum Theory, which has led to very great advances in knowledge of physical phenomena. This theory, in turn, was further developed in the theory of wave mechanics.

QUARTER DAYS, four days on which rents and other quarterly payments fall due and tenancies end. In Britain (except Scotland) they are March 25 (Lady Day), June 24 (Midsummer), September 29 (Michaelmas) and December 25. The corresponding days in Scotland, called Term Days, are February 2, May 15, August 1, November 11.

QUEBEC, capital of Quebec Province, and the oldest town in Canada. Pop. (1961) 357,568. Situated at the first narrows on the St Lawrence River, which are spanned by a bridge, it has excellent docks handling grain and timber. There is considerable industry, including iron foundries and pulp and paper mills. The old town is by the river; the upper town, on a bluff overlooking the river, has the Parliament Buildings and the Laval University with its museum and library. Founded by the French in 1608, the town's population is still mainly French-Canadian. Quebec was taken by Wolfe in the Battle of the Heights of Abraham (1759), in which both Wolfe and the French general, Montcalm, were killed.

QUEENSLAND, a state of northeastern Australia. Pop. (1961) 1,518,859; area 670,500 sq. miles. The state includes the Torres Strait Islands, with a population of Melanesians, and extends to within 10° of the equator. The central grassy plains are separated from a narrow coastal strip by the forested Great Dividing Range; the Great Barrier Reef, the largest coral reef in the world, runs parallel with the coast. The leading crop is sugar-cane, grown in the coastal strip with labour mainly of Italian descent. Wheat, fodder crops, bananas and pineapples are the other main crops. There are huge cattle ranches, dependent on artesian wells, in the north; sheep are reared for wool in the south. Uranium, lead, zinc, and silver are mined near Mt Isa, copper at Mt Morgan, and bauxite, coal, tungsten and gold elsewhere. A convict settlement was established at Brisbane in 1824, joined by free settlers from 1842. Brisbane is the capital.

QUEMOY, a Nationalist-held island off the Chinese mainland. Pop. (1962) 90,000, of whom some 40,000 are troops stationed there for the defence of Formosa.

QUEZON CITY, the designated capital of the Philippines, still under construction. See Manila.

QUITO, capital of the Republic of Ecuador. Pop. (1962) 267,798. The town, built mainly in a picturesque, colonial style, is situated in a valley on the central plateau of Ecuador, some 9000 ft above sea-level. Products include hides, timber, religious pictures and carving and other products of folk arts and crafts. There are several large monastic institutions and a university. It has suffered repeatedly from earthquakes.

RABAT, the administrative centre of Morocco, on the Atlantic Ocean, at the mouth, of the Bu-Regreg River. Pop. (1960) 224,901. It produces textiles and leather goods. The King of Morocco normally resides here.

RABELAIS, François (*c.* 1494—1553), French satirical writer and physician. His early years were spent as a monk and his last as the curate of Meudon, near Paris; nevertheless, the chief target of his satire is the Church. In his uproariously comic *Gargantua and Pantagruel* he lays about him in the interests of humanism, especially on the subject of education and monastic training. Like James Joyce, he found the existing language inadequate and coined a marvellous treasury of ludicrous words; the coarseness of some passages was but in keeping with the spirit of his times.

RACHMANINOV, Sergei (1873—1943), Russian composer, pianist and conductor. He left Russia in 1917 to live in Switzerland and the U.S.A., and his nostalgia for the country house life of Russia is the source of much of the melancholy in his music. A lesser Tchaikovsky, he wrote music of great beauty but lacking profundity. His greatest, but lesser known, works are the Third Symphony, the *Études-Tableaux* and the Vesper Mass. More popular are the Second and Third Piano Concertos and the Rhapsody on a Theme by Paganini.

RACINE, Jean (1639—99), French dramatist. Corneille wrote of heroic clashes between love and duty, in which duty triumphs; less sublime, Racine shows us heroes destroyed by love, moving stoically to disaster which they know they cannot avert. His simple, exquisite, sometimes incantatory lines show a more delicate sensitivity than Corneille's, and a more profound insight into the psychology of his more human and more universal characters. Among his most characteristic plays are *Andromaque, Phèdre, Britannicus* and the later religious play, *Athalie.*

RADAR, a radio device for detecting and determining the position of aircraft, vessels and other objects. It utilises radio waves for the detection of reflecting surfaces. The waves sent out from the transmitter are reflected from the object and return to the receiver which is able to follow its movements. The name, derived from Radio Detection And Ranging, indicates both its original military objectives and its difference from the earlier radio direction finding,

Principle of radar

which depended on co-operation from the object detected. The theory of radar had been known for many years, but it was Robert Watson-Watt's proposals in 1935 which led to its being applied in time to provide Britain with early warning of German air attacks.

RADIATION, the emission of energy in the form of a beam of rays, particles or waves. The term is applied to sound, and to the emission of alpha and beta particles and neutrons, but more usually refers to electromagnetic waves (q.v.) such as light, gamma rays, radio, X-rays, radiant heat, etc.

RADIO, an abbreviation for radio telegraphy, formerly called wireless telegraphy. The term is applied to the various methods of communication by radio waves, which are electromagnetic waves with a wavelength between 18 miles and a small fraction of an inch. In common usage this wide range is divided into long, medium and short wavebands and V.H.F. (very high frequency, i.e. very short wave). The longer the wave the greater the range; the shorter the wave the greater the freedom from atmospherics. The waves are reflected, with greater or lesser efficiency, by various layers of the ionosphere; the Telstar artificial communications satellite is used to reflect microwaves so that they can be used in long-range communication. Radio waves are normally radiated in all directions, but they can be focused in a particular direction by radio beam. The term radio may mean broadcasting, radio telegraphy, radio telephony, the transmitting set, the receiving set or the message sent.

The radio transmitter emits a continuous carrier wave of a definite frequency, to which the receiving set must be tuned. The sound is converted by the microphone into electrical impulses which are superimposed on the carrier wave (modulation); the receiving set amplifies these signals and converts them back into sound through a loudspeaker (or telephone receiver).

RADIOACTIVITY, the emission of certain forms of radiation during the disintegration (decay) of the unstable atomic nuclei of certain elements. The radiation may consist of positively charged alpha particles (consisting of two protons and two neutrons), negative beta particles (which are electrons forced out when a neutron is converted into a proton), positrons (produced when a proton is converted into a neutron), or gamma rays (the result of excitation during the process of achieving stability). All elements in the periodic table above bismuth (atomic number 83) are radioactive. Other elements may be rendered radioactive artificially by bombardment with beams of nuclear particles, especially neutrons, but also alpha particles, protons and gamma rays. Considerable amounts of energy are given off in the process and the atoms change to atoms of a different element (see Alchemy). The radiations penetrate substances opaque to light, darken a photographic film, ionise gases, etc. The rate of decay is measured in terms of the half-life, i.e. the time required for the number of radioactive atoms to drop to half the number originally present. Becquerel discovered beta-particle radioactivity in uranium in 1895; the following year Pierre and Marie Curie discovered the intensely radioactive element radium. The artificial production of radioactivity was achieved by the Joliot-Curies in 1934.

RADIUM, see Elements.

RAEBURN, Sir Henry (1756—1823), Scottish portrait painter. He was appointed by George IV as His Majesty's Limner in Scotland, where he painted many portraits of distinguished men and women.

RAILWAY. Before the first steam locomotives came into operation on colliery lines, animals were used to pull wagons loaded with minerals on wooden rails. In 1825 the Stockton and Darlington Railway inaugurated the railway era by providing the first public service for passengers and freight. In the 1830s steam trains began service in France, U.S.A., Belgium, Germany and Russia. In a short time railways emerged as the most efficient means of moving large numbers of people and goods over considerable distances, and by 1874 the British railway system was virtually complete. In 1948 it was nationalised. The first underground railway (London) was built in 1863 and the first electric train (Brighton line) ran in 1883. Hydroelectric power was used in Northern Ireland in the 1880s and became the chief source in Alpine regions and Sweden. In the U.S.A., where oil was

A model of George Stephenson's (q.v.) 'Rocket' steam locomotive which first ran in 1829.

Photo: Crown copyright. Science Museum, London

The Daimler Motor Co., founded at Kannstatt, Germany, in 1890, was one of the first companies to build successful high-speed internal-combustion engines. This model was built by them in 1895 (see Automobile).

Photo: Science Museum, London

One of the earliest typewriters (q.v.) was this model built in 1875 by the American Remington company.

Photo: Crown copyright. Science Museum, London

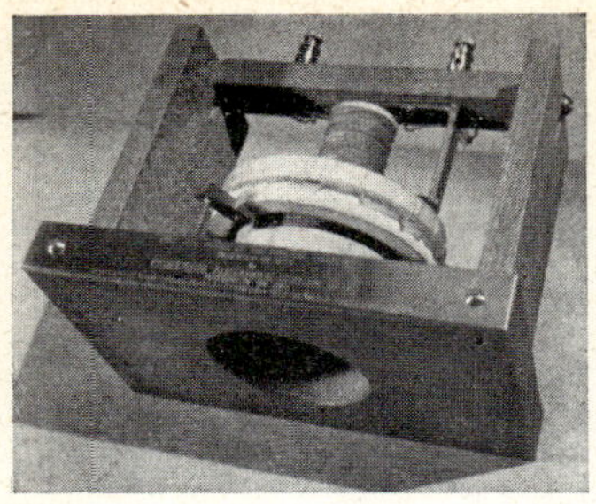

A model of the original telephone (q.v.) invented in 1875 by Alexander Graham Bell (q.v.).

Photo: By courtesy of H. M. Postmaster-General

Among the important inventions of the American, Thomas Edison (q.v.), was the phonograph; his original equipment is illustrated here.

Photo: Crown copyright. Science Museum, London

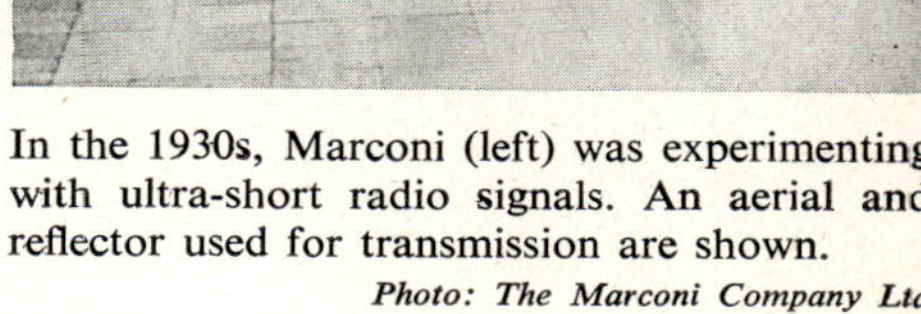

In the 1930s, Marconi (left) was experimenting with ultra-short radio signals. An aerial and reflector used for transmission are shown.

Photo: The Marconi Company Ltd

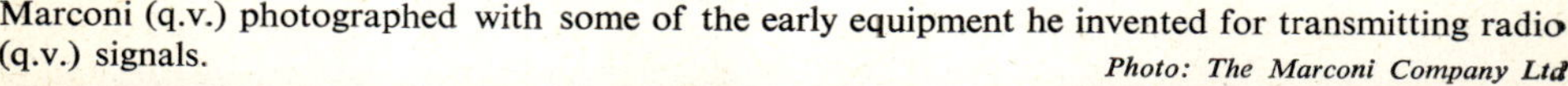

Marconi (q.v.) photographed with some of the early equipment he invented for transmitting radio (q.v.) signals.

Photo: The Marconi Company Ltd

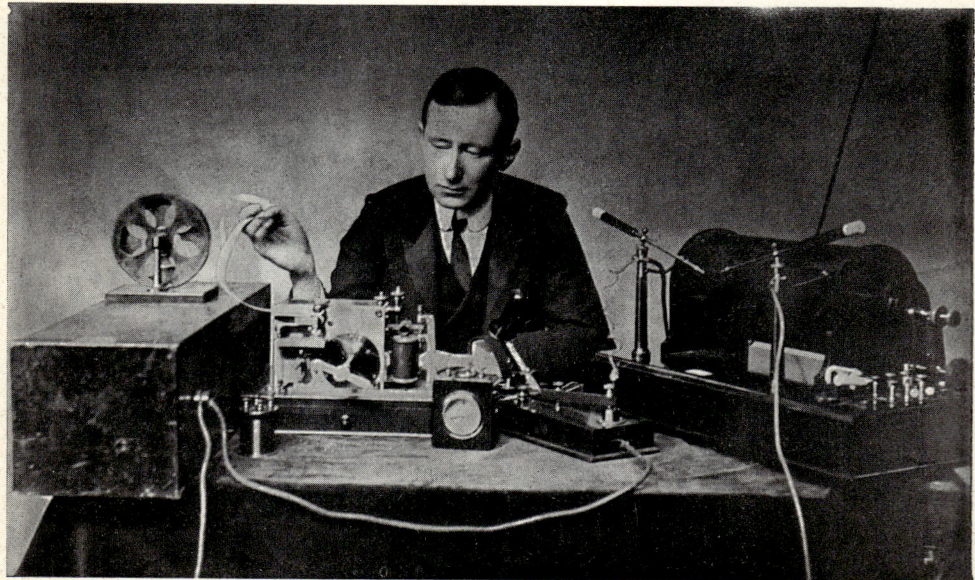

The crude equipment of John Baird's (q.v.) television system, first demonstrated in 1926.

Photo: Crown copyright. Science Museum, London

Huge radio telescopes have been used during recent years for making more accurate astronomical measurements than previously were possible. They are also used to track satellites and rockets. *Photo: Aerofilms, Ltd*

An American astronomy satellite, used for detecting and measuring cosmic gamma radiation in space.

Photo: United States Information Service

The late 18th and early 19th century explorers in Australia found the aborigines using boats constructed of timbers lashed together that had changed little since prehistoric times.

Photo: Radio Times Hulton Picture Library

The Phoenicians (q.v.) were one of the earliest civilisations to develop the wood-built sailing ship. These models were reconstructed from wall paintings in Thebes and show small and large, long-range, merchant ships. *c.* 14th century B.C.

Photos: Haifa Maritime Museum

In Roman times their ships (q.v.) ranged throughout the Mediterranean and North Atlantic. Illustrated is a merchant ship, with more sophisticated sails than the Phoenicians used.

Photo: Crown copyright. Science Museum, London

ROMAN MERCHANT SHIP
SECOND CENTURY A.D.

After the 16th century the power and wealth of European countries depended largely on their supremacy at sea. Shown are Spanish galleons (fighting ships armed with cannon) of 1561.

Photo: Science Museum, London

plentiful, the diesel engine was early introduced. Railways, with their heavy capital and maintenance charges, were badly hit by the growth of road transport for heavy goods, and in the 1950s began to hit back with differential freight rates and the rail-van system, giving door-to-door service.

RALEIGH, Sir Walter (*c.* 1552—1618), English courtier and adventurer. Leicester introduced him to court, and he soon became a favourite of Elizabeth, who sent him on the first colonising expedition ever sent out from England. This was to Virginia; it was not a success, as Raleigh had no administrative abilities, but he won immortality by bringing back tobacco and potatoes. His arrogance and Leicester's jealousy began to lose him Elizabeth's favour, and soon after James I came to the throne he was put in the Tower on a trumped-up charge of treason. On paying a bribe of £1500 he was released after 12 years and sent on a gold-hunt to Guiana; he returned old, sick and empty-handed and James had him executed. Raleigh wrote the entrancing *History of the World* (while in prison), and the *Discoverie of Guinea*, in which he described the inhabitants of the non-existent El Dorado (who had, he said, no heads). He also wrote some good poems.

RAMAN, Sir Chandrasekhara Venkata (1888—), Indian physicist. Experimenting with monochromatic light passing through a transparent substance, he discovered that some of the light diffused from the original path exhibited frequencies either higher or lower than the primary beam, due to the light gaining energy from, or losing it to, a vibrating molecule (Raman effect). He was awarded the Nobel Prize for physics in 1930.

RAMESES II, Egyptian Pharaoh from *c.* 1292—1225 B.C. Son of Seti I, he seized the throne from his elder brother. After a famous but indecisive battle at Kadesh (1290) fought to regain Asia Minor from the Hittites, he signed a treaty with them against the Assyrians. He nearly ruined Egypt by his huge building programme, which included the Abu Simbel temples, the great hall at Karnak, and the Rameseum, where the broken remains of his colossal statue, inscribed 'My name is Ozymandias, King of Kings', moved Shelley to write a famous Ichabodean poem. Apart from his name of Ozymandias, he was the Sesostris of Greek writers, perhaps the Rhampsinitos of Herodotus, and has even been identified with the Pharaoh of the Exodus.

RAMSAY, Sir William (1852—1916), British chemist. He discovered the inert gases argon, helium, krypton, neon and xenon. In 1904 he received the Nobel Prize for chemistry.

RANGOON, capital of Burma, near the mouth of the Irrawaddy River. Pop. (1960) 723,000. It is Burma's chief port, exporting mainly rice. A centre of Burmese religious life, it contains the gold-covered Shwe Dagon pagoda, in addition to Hindu temples and Moslem mosques. There are textile industries, and handicrafts include ivory and wood carving.

RAPHAEL (Raffaello Sanzio; 1483—1520), Italian painter. Leonardo, Michelangelo and Raphael were the three masters of the High Renaissance (1500—27), when Italian painting reached its perfection of grace and simplicity. His main work was the frescoes for the Stanze, a series of small rooms in the Vatican, of which the finest are *The School of Athens* and *The Disputation*;

his most famous work is the *Sistine Madonna* (Dresden). He designed tapestries which still hang in the Vatican, and the cartoons for them are in the Victoria and Albert Museum. Also in London, in the National Gallery, are the *Knight's Dream* and *St Catherine.*

RARE EARTHS, a group of 15 metal elements bearing a close resemblance to one another and, in many properties, to aluminium. They are of comparatively rare occurrence and very difficult to separate and extract. Some of them are used in ceramics, lighter flints, coloured glass and arc-light carbons.

RASPUTIN, Gregor (*c.* 1873—1916), an illiterate Russian monk who became the leading influence at the court of Nicholas II. By appearing to heal the haemophilia of the Crown Prince Alexis, Rasputin attained a dictatorial hold over the royal family, who willingly followed his every command. Rasputin (debauchee) was the name given to him because of his doctrine 'Sin that ye may be forgiven', which led to Roman orgies in the palace and to his assassination by a group of Russian nobles.

RAT, a common rodent. The largest of the species, the Brown, Hanover or Norwegian rat, is believed to have come originally from western China, and has almost displaced the Black rat in Europe. Rats eat almost anything and are now found everywhere. They cause considerable damage to crops and property, and greatly influenced history as the carriers of disease.

RATIONALISATION, the attempt to make what one says and does appear rational. Distinct from reasoning, it starts with a wished-for conclusion and supplies excuses to justify it. It may be entirely unconscious.

RATIONALISM, in philosophy, the view that truth can be attained by reason alone, without recourse to experiment and observation, on the one hand, or to intuition and revelation on the other; it represents the views of the Continental philosophers, Descartes, Spinoza and Leibniz, in contrast to the English Empiricists.

In theology Rationalism is the view that reason is the ultimate authority, not faith.

In the 19th-century the name Rationalist was given to agnostics and freethinkers.

RAVEL, Maurice (1875—1937), French composer. A leader of the Impressionist movement, he wrote chamber music, piano pieces, ballet music *(Daphnis et Chloë)*, the popular *Boléro* and a one-act comedy *L'Heure espagnole.*

RAWALPINDI, a town in West Pakistan, on the Leh River. Pop. (1961) 340,175. Of strategic importance, it is a communications, commercial and industrial centre. Its industries include locomotive works, an oil refinery and an iron foundry. It is the temporary seat of government pending the completion of the new capital of Pakistan at Islamabad near by.

RAWLINSON, Sir Henry Creswicke (1810—95), British diplomat and archaeologist. While serving as a diplomat in the Middle East, he copied and interpreted the trilingual inscription of Darius I at Behistun, which facilitated the decipherment of cuneiform inscriptions.

RAYLEIGH, John William Strutt, 3rd Baron (1842—1919), British physicist. He determined the densities of the gases in the atmosphere and did important research in acoustical vibrations, optics, capillarity and electromagnetism

Together with Sir William Ramsay he discovered argon. He received the Nobel Prize for physics in 1904.

READE, Charles (1814—84), British novelist and dramatist. His most famous work is *The Cloister and the Hearth*, an historical novel about the parents of Erasmus. He was also the author of *It is Never Too Late to Mend* and *Hard Cash.*

READING, a city and county borough, Berkshire, England, at the confluence of the Thames and Kennet rivers. Pop. (1961) 119,870. It is a railway centre and market for agricultural produce. The chief manufacture is biscuits. Market gardening and seed production are important. The modern university is famous for its faculty of agriculture.

REALISM, in literature and the arts, is a reaction against both Classicism and Romanticism; at first taking the form of the faithful rendering of contemporary life, it soon came to mean, as with Zola, the dwelling on squalor and the seamy side of life in an endeavour to shake the complacency prevalent in the middle and upper classes in the late 19th century.

In philosophy Realism has two opposite meanings: the everyday view that what we see is real; and a philosophy which holds that what we see is illusory and that Ideas (see Plato) are the only true realities.

RED CROSS, an international organisation set up originally to relieve suffering in war. The movement was started by Henri Dunant, a Swiss, in 1864, and it took as its symbol a red cross on a white ground, the reverse of the Swiss national flag. In war Red Cross staff are treated by civilised belligerents as neutral, and buildings or vehicles marked with the Red Cross are immune from attack. The organisation tends the wounded and tries to help prisoners of war. The activities of the Red Cross have spread to peacetime, e.g. in dealing with refugees, sudden disasters (e.g. an earthquake), epidemics, famine, etc., and in training people in First Aid.

REFLECTION AND REFRACTION. When some form of radiation (e.g. light) strikes a surface and is turned back to the original medium, reflection takes place. Refraction is the bending of a form of radiation from its original direction when it passes from one medium to another (e.g. from air into glass or water).

REFLEX, an involuntary muscular or glandular action resulting from the stimulation of a sensory nerve. A conditioned reflex is one that has been acquired through associating a specific stimulus with a certain result.

REFORMATION, the religious revolution of the 16th century which established Protestantism. In the 14th and 15th centuries the Church had vigorously suppressed all attempts at reform (see Huss; Wycliffe) and so, in the 16th century, the reform movement assumed the proportions of an open revolt. It was both a revivalist movement aiming at a return to the teachings of the early Church, and a revolt by the people of northern Europe against the privileges and pretensions of a priesthood dominated by the Latin races of the south. Among the many streams of discontent that converged to produce Luther, Zwingli and Calvin (qq.v.) were disgust at the immorality of the priests; resentment, deepened by the growth of nationalism, against papal authority, especially in political matters; envy of the great wealth of the Church, which aroused the cupidity of hard-pressed monarchs; and opposition to Church doctrines and practices born of new thinking in a humanistic and sceptical age. Among those points that came under attack were the celibacy of the clergy, monasticism, transubstantiation (see Eucharist), the adoration of the Virgin Mary and the saints, and the Church's teachings on the major issues of free will and predestination, and justification by works and faith. The reformers wanted the Bible and services in the vernacular instead of in Latin which the majority could not understand; and they wanted to join in congregational singing.

The occasion of Luther's protest in 1519 was the mass campaign to collect money for the rebuilding of St Peter's, Rome, by the sale of indulgences for the remittance of sins; a more enlightened age was revolted by the idea that one could buy one's way into Heaven. The Emperor Charles v found that feelings were too strong for conciliation, and the Pope had lost the power to repress the movement. At the Peace of Augsburg (1555), by which time both Luther and Zwingli were dead, Germany was divided according to the persuasion of the ruling princes, into a Protestant north and west and a Catholic south and east. Lutheranism had already been established in Scandinavia, and in Britain Henry VIII's personal quarrel with the Pope had come to a head in the Act of Supremacy in 1534, followed by the dissolution and looting of the monasteries. The Anglican Church, however, was completely opposed to Lutheranism, though it was adopted in Scotland through the advocacy of John Knox. Holland was inspired to wage a war of independence, and the Huguenot minority in France won a measure of freedom by the Edict of Nantes (1598). In Bohemia, Poland and Hungary Lutheranism was crushed in the 17th century. Rome tried to stem the tide of Protestantism by the Counter-Reformation (q.v.), without much success.

REFORMED CHURCHES, the name given to those churches of the Reformation which followed the theological teachings of Calvin rather than those of Luther. Generally speaking they have a presbyterian form of ecclesiastical government and reject the more elaborate ritual of the Lutheran churches The Reformed Churches are strongest in the Netherlands, Scotland, France, Poland, Switzerland and the U.S.A. They reject consubstantiation (see Eucharist) and regard the Lord's Supper as a commemorative meal only.

REIGN OF TERROR (1793—94), the name given to that period of the French Revolution (q.v.) when the radical Jacobins controlled the government and summarily guillotined those opposing them. It came to an end with the overthrow and execution of Robespierre.

REINCARNATION (Transmigration of Souls, Metempsychosis), the belief that after death the soul will be reborn in another human being or animal. The status in the next life is determined by conduct in this life. The belief is found in Pythagoras, Plato, Buddhism, Hinduism and Plotinus.

RELATIVITY, the basic principle of theories formulated by Einstein after the discovery by Michelson and Morly of inconsistencies when the laws of classical physics are applied to bodies moving at velocities near that of light. It was found that the relative speed of light is unaffected by the motion of its observer. Einstein decided that time and space are not absolute but relative to the observer, and that it is impossible to determine absolute motion. He predicted that light rays passing near the sun would be deflected as if by gravitation, and this has since been conclusively demonstrated.

Einstein's special theory is based on events as they appear to observers in a state of uniform motion relative to one another. It dealt with the physics of particles moving near the velocity of light. He found mass and energy interchangeable in certain conditions according to the formula $E = mc^2$, where E is energy, m is mass and c the velocity of light in centimetres per second. This formula shows that a small mass gives great energy, as in the energy of the sun's rays, the atomic bomb and the nuclear power station. Mass is a function of its velocity, i.e. increases with speed. It is thought that some particles (the photon and neutrino) may have no mass when at rest and derive their mass solely from their energy. It was also found that a body moving with very high velocity experiences a contraction in length in the direction of motion.

Einstein's later general theory, based on events as they appear to observers not in relative uniform motion, provided a four-dimensional geometry of space-time which gave a new conception of, among other things, the theory of gravitation.

RELIGION, a term which refers to man's belief in and reverence for a Divine Being. It is a phenomenon common to all cultures and societies and a great number of systems have developed which give expression to man's religious feelings. In the more primitive cultures it is sometimes difficult to differentiate between religion and magic, the two elements being often intermingled. The major religions of the world today are Christianity, Islam, Buddhism, Hinduism, Brahmanism, Judaism and Zoroastrianism. Taoism is less a religion than a religious philosophy, and Confucianism is a code of behaviour.

REMBRANDT, Harmensz van Rijn (1606—69), Dutch painter and etcher. Prodigious in output, he covered a wide range of subjects in his portraits, drawings, etchings and prints, ranging from genre pictures, groups, portraits, still-lifes, to landscapes and representations from the Bible and mythology. He was a master of light and shade, and he excelled in the portrayal of old age. There is a long series of self-portraits made throughout his career, showing him in opulence, poverty and sad old age. One of his best known pictures was *The Night Watch*, made for a company of defence volunteers, and he painted many such groups, e.g. the *Staal Meesters* for the Guild of Drapers. Among his many notable etchings are *Three Trees* and *Christ Healing*. He broke new ground with such still-lifes as *The Slaughtered Ox* and *Studies of a Sirloin of Beef*.

RENAISSANCE (rebirth), the emergence of Western Europe from the Middle Ages in the 15th—16th centuries under the inspiration of the rediscovery of Latin and Greek art, literature, science and thought. It was assisted by the growth of a wealthy middle class which could replace the Church as the patron of arts and letters, and which was imbued with a spirit of humanism and scepticism. The sack of Constantinople (1453) brought a flood of Byzantine scholars and Greek manuscripts to the West after Arabic scholars had already handed on the traditions of Greek science and thought. The discovery of America deepened the inquisitive urge to find out everything that could be known which was the hall-mark of the Renaissance, and the invent on of printing accelerated the spread of the new outlook.

In art the Renaissance started in

Florence, but its spirit moved on to produce religious revolution in Germany (see Reformation) and the outburst of poetry in Elizabethan England. The Florentine Giotto (1266—1337) began the artistic rebirth which ended with the death of Titian (1576), but it is usual to restrict the term Renaissance to a narrower period: the Early Renaissance, *c.* 1420—1500, in which the chief figures were Piero della Francesca, Uccello, Pollaiuolo and Botticelli; and the High Renaissance, *c.* 1500—27 (the date of the Sack of Rome), when Michelangelo, Leonardo, Raphael and Titian attained the balanced serenity and harmony which was the culmination of Renaissance art.

In architecture there was a revulsion from the Gothic, which was regarded as barbarous (hence the disparaging name). Brunelleschi and Palladio were the first to study the buildings of ancient Rome, and the result was the introduction of the rounded arch and the classical orders of architecture. This change reached most countries in the 16th century. In England, Elizabethan and Jacobean architecture was less influenced, although the pointed Gothic arch disappeared, and it was left to Inigo Jones, the Adam brothers and Christopher Wren to eliminate Gothic influences until the Gothic Revival of *c.* 1830.

In literature the characteristics of the new age were a heightened appreciation of style, and a substitution of individualistic self-expression for the ideals and abstractions of the Middle Ages. In Italy the emphasis was on aesthetic appreciation and the art of living, in northern Europe on learning for its own sake and the humanist approach to theology (as in Erasmus). Progress in philosophy and science was to come later when the new learning had been further digested.

RENAN, Ernest (1823—92), French philosopher, historian and philologist. He is particularly known for his work on the historical life of Jesus (*La Vie de Jésus*, 1863).

RENI, Guido (1575—1642), Italian painter. A master of the Eclectic school, he painted *Aurora*, *The Crucifixion of St Peter*, *Ecce Homo*, and *The Rape of Helen*.

RENO, a city in Nevada, U.S.A. Pop. (1960) 51,470. It is famous for its simplified divorce procedures, gambling resorts and skiing.

RENOIR, Pierre Auguste (1841—1919), French painter. Influenced at first by the Impressionists, he later developed a style of his own. He painted figures, portraits, still-lifes and landscapes. His favourite subject in later life was the female nude figure.

REPRODUCTION, the production of a new individual member of a species by an organism or organisms of the same species. Asexual or vegetative reproduction, the splitting of an animal into two parts of equal size, each of which can become an adult, is common among one-celled organisms. Bisexual reproduction in its higher forms involves the fusion of a non-motile egg cell by a motile sperm cell. The egg (ovum) is produced by the female and the sperm by the male. Some animals, e.g. snails and worms, can produce sperms and eggs simultaneously; others are male at one stage of life and female at another. In parthenogenesis (virgin birth) no sperm is needed; male bees are thus produced from unfertilised eggs, though female bees are formed in the normal way. Most animals, unlike man, can reproduce only at certain seasons of the year.

REPTILES, a class of cold-blooded vertebrate animals breathing air. Reptiles first appeared on the earth about 220,000,000 years ago and were the dominant form of life in the Mesozoic era (the Age of Reptiles) (see Geology). The class includes alligators, crocodiles, turtles, lizards, and snakes. Their bodies have scales or horny plates. The young are hatched from eggs. Most are carnivorous. Reptiles are the link between the amphibians on the one hand and birds and mammals on the other.

REPUBLIC, a form of state in which elected representatives of the people exercise sovereignty for a fixed period. Some modern dictatorships also call themselves republics. England was a republic from 1649—60 under the Commonwealth.

REPUBLICAN PARTY, one of the two major political parties in the United States. It was founded in 1854 to oppose the extension of slavery into the territories. First Republican president was Abraham Lincoln, who was succeeded consecutively by five others. The most recent Republican president was Eisenhower (1953—61), elected after 20 years of Democratic rule.

At first a progressive party, it became more and more conservative, and after the First World War isolationist. It is supported by business interests, and is strongest in the northeast and midwest.

RESINS, amorphous solids exuded from plants. A compound of carbon, hydrogen, and oxygen, they soften on heating and are soluble in alcohol, ether and certain oils. Synthetic resins are plastics. Hard resins include mastic and copal; soft resins, camphor, turpentine (from which rosin is obtained) and frankincense. Some resins are found in fossil form, e.g. amber.

RESTORATION, in English history, the restoration of the monarchy under Charles II (1660). Many Royalists were disappointed to find that it was by no means a return to the days of Charles I. The chief feature was that parliamentary government was restored, and a beginning of the party system was seen. There was a natural reaction against the austerity and simplicity of life under the Commonwealth, carried to extremes in the Restoration plays of Wycherley, Congreve and Dryden.

RESURRECTION, a rising or reawakening from the dead. The term refers to the bodily resurrection of Jesus from the dead, which is one of the basic tenets of the Christian Church, and also to the general resurrection of the dead at the Day of Judgment, an event clearly foretold by Christ, but left by him as a mystery which we cannot, and perhaps are not meant to, comprehend.

RÉUNION, a French island in the Indian Ocean between Malagasy and Mauritius. Pop. (1960) 330,000; area 970 sq. miles. The island is divided by a chain of mountains and a plateau. The principal crop is sugar-cane. The French occupied it in 1638 and remain the dominant part of the population. The capital is St Denis.

REUTER, Paul Julius, Baron von (1816—99), German-born British journalist. He founded a news agency in London in 1851 which immediately began to utilise newly developed telegraphic facilities. It is now a world-wide service.

REVIVAL, Religious, an upsurge of religious fervour and activity in a particular area which spreads rapidly, arouses feelings of contrition in the indifferent and restores them to divine grace.

REYNOLDS, Sir Joshua (1723—92), English portrait painter. He painted, with the help of many assistants, more than 2000 portraits and historical paintings, much of his best work being in the National Gallery, London. He was the first president of the Royal Academy, and did more than anyone to raise the status of the painter in England. During the earlier part of his career he painted in the classical style under the influence of his close study of the Italian masters; but in 1781 he visited the Low Countries and, influenced in particular by Rubens, he used a warmer style. Due to his experiments with paints and varnish many of his portraits have deteriorated. He painted almost everyone of note and was at his best with men and children.

RHEIMS, a city in northeast France, on the Vesle River. Pop. (1962) 138,576. The champagne centre of the world, it also has dye works, breweries, distilleries and textile factories producing celebrated woollen goods. In the cathedral, under construction from 1211—1430, 36 French kings were crowned; it has been restored after the very heavy damage suffered in the First World War. The Germans surrendered all their forces here to the Allies in May 1945.

RHINE, see River.

RHODE ISLAND, a state of New England, U.S.A. Pop. (1960) 859,488; area 1214 sq. miles. The state consists of a plateau sloping down towards the sea. The principal agricultural pursuits are dairy and poultry farming and market gardening. Rhode Island is predominantly industrial, producing textiles, machinery, metal goods and jewellery. Fishing is important. First settled in 1636, it was one of the 13 original states. The capital is Providence (pop. 207,498).

RHODES, Cecil John (1853—1902), British businessman and colonial statesman. He became Prime Minister of the Cape in 1890, and his ambition was to form a South African federation and to see a Cape to Cairo railway running through all-British territory. He was instrumental in occupying Basutoland and went on to annex Matabeleland and Mashonaland, thus founding the Rhodesias. His complicity in the Jameson Raid led to his resignation from the premiership in 1896. As head of the Kimberley diamond firm of De Beers and of Goldfields of South Africa he made a huge fortune, most of which he left to found the Rhodes scholarships to Oxford University. Groote Schuur, his home, was bequeathed as a residence for South African premiers.

RHODESIA AND NYASALAND, Federation of, a political association in central Africa which consisted of Southern Rhodesia, Northern Rhodesia (now Zambia) and Nyasaland (now Malawi), formed in 1953 and brokenup in 1962. Pop. (1960) 8,220,000; area 487,630 sq. miles. Northern Rhodesia wa dependent on copper, Southern Rhodesiashad a more balanced economy, and Nya saland had to be subsidised by the rest of the federation. Inter-unit communications were not good, and the whole area was dependent for export trade on ports all of which are over a thousand miles from the Copperbelt, in Portuguese Angola and Mozambique, and in South Africa. The Kariba dam on the border provided the Rhodesias with hydro-electric power, and the Wankie collieries supplied coal for the railways; otherwise the economies were not complementary. The main purpose of the federation was to provide a unit large and stable enough to attract investment. Founded initially for economic reasons, it was disrupted by political considerations.

RHODESIA, SOUTHERN, British self-governing colony in central Africa. Pop. (1963) 4,070,500, including 221,000 Europeans and 19,500 Asians and Coloureds; area 150,333 sq. miles. The main crops are tobacco, sugar, maize and tea; ranching and dairying are extensive. Minerals include asbestos, gold, chrome ore, coal (at Wankie) and some copper. Industry is expanding and already includes electrical equipment, radios, fertilisers, cement and textiles; but the most important sector processes local products — ferro-chrome, iron and steel, paper, pulp, dyestuffs, sugar, etc. Half the country is set aside as native reserves. Tourists visit the Zimbabwe ruins, the game reserves and the eastern highlands. The capital is Salisbury, and Bulawayo is an important centre.

RHODIUM, see Elements.

RHONDDA, a town in Glamorganshire, Wales. Pop. (1961) 100,314. It is the centre of a coal-mining district in a narrow valley.

RICHARD I (Coeur-de-Lion; 1157—99), King of England from 1189—99. While returning from the Third Crusade he was taken captive (1192) by Leopold I of Austria, and released only after being heavily ransomed (1194). Richard spent only a few months of his reign in England, which was ruled by Hubert Walter, Archbishop of Canterbury. Richard's brother John created much disorder, and the king himself drained his country of wealth in his efforts to hold his Angevin inheritance. He was killed in an obscure squabble with a vassal in France.

RICHARD II (1367—1400), King of England from 1377—99. Son of Edward the Black Prince, he took over as a minor a country which was in disarray after the Black Death and he had to quell the Peasants' Revolt of 1381. He proved himself an unstable and tyrannous ruler and, although he regained control for some years after quelling a rising of the barons, he was finally forced to abdicate by his cousin the Duke of Hereford (later Henry IV), and in 1400 was probably murdered.

RICHARD III (1452—85), King of England from 1483—85. As Duke of York he distinguished himself in the Wars of the Roses. When his brother Edward IV died he became Protector to his nephew, Edward V. On the pretext that Edward IV's sons were illegitimate he secured the crown for himself; it then transpired that both Edward V and his brother (the Princes in the Tower) were dead, and their murder has been traditionally attributed to Richard. The records of his reign are, however, confused and contradictory, and he seems to have been a brave man and an efficient king. In 1485 Henry Tudor, Earl of Richmond, led a rebellion in which Richard was defeated and slain at Bosworth, the earl being crowned Henry VII on the battlefield.

RICHARDSON, Sir Owen Willans (1879—1959), British physicist. He was the founder of the science of thermionics and also performed important work in spectroscopy, radiology and photo-electric emission. In 1928 he was awarded the Nobel Prize for physics.

RICHARDSON, Samuel (1689—1761), English novelist. He developed his stories by the use of letters to reveal character and unfold the plot. His best work is the immensely prolix and somewhat sentimental *Clarissa*. Fielding, of whom he was jealous, detected the prurience that lay beneath his sanctimonious tales of seduction and attacked him in parodies, but Richardson has his established place as a psychological novelist.

RICHELIEU, Cardinal (1585—1642), French statesman. He reconciled Marie de' Medici and her son, Louis XIII, after the latter had put to death the favourites she had installed in power during her regency, and it was to her that Richelieu owed his rapid advancement to Cardinal. When he became Chief Minister, however, he pushed her into the background and virtually ruled France until his death. In order to achieve his objective of establishing an absolute monarchy, he crushed both the nobles and the Huguenots, though he granted the latter toleration and civic rights. He reorganised the civil service, army and navy and then turned his attention to reducing the menace of the Hapsburgs. He subsidised Sweden and the Protestant princes of Germany against Austria, and brought France into the Thirty Years War. By the time he died France was strong and the monarchy secure. Richelieu founded the French Academy and rebuilt the Sorbonne. Cold-blooded intrigue and an efficient spy system kept this permanent invalid in power.

RICHMOND, capital of Virginia, U.S.A., on the James River. Pop. (1960) 219,958. It is a communications, educational, financial and commercial centre. A seaport and tobacco market, it manufactures flour, iron goods, tobacco products, foodstuffs, chemicals and machinery. From 1861—65 it was the capital of the Confederate States of America.

RIDING, a pastime of which the popularity in Britain since the war has immensely increased, especially among the young, leading to the establishment of riding schools all over the country, and of organised pony-trekking holidays, with rough hacking through moorland scenery in Scotland and elsewhere. Gymkhanas also attract increasing numbers of competitors for the mounted competitions. See Show Jumping.

RIDLEY, Nicholas (*c.* 1500—55), English reformer. He was appointed Bishop of London, where he founded three hospitals. A leader in the Reformation, he helped to compile the English Prayer Book. Ridley supported Lady Jane Grey, and was subsequently burnt at the stake at the orders of Mary.

RIGA, capital of the Latvian S.S.R., on the Baltic Sea, U.S.S.R. Pop. (1962) 620,000. It is a commercial, communications and industrial centre with diverse manufactures, shipyards and a port.

RIGHTS OF MAN, Declaration of the, a fundamental document adopted by the French National Assembly in 1789, which enumerated the inalienable liberties of the individual, guaranteeing the rights to freedom, property, security and resistance to oppression, and the freedom of speech, the press and worship. The will of the people was established as the ultimate source of government.

RILKE, Rainer Maria (1875—1926), Austrian poet. Born in Prague and educated at Berlin and Munich universities, he travelled extensively in Europe. After a mystical experience in Russia and a period as secretary to Rodin, he settled in Switzerland, where he wrote his finest poetry, *Sonnets to Orpheus* and the *Duino Elegies*. One of the great modern poets, he tried to communicate as much as was possible of a mystic's view of God and the universe.

RIMBAUD, Arthur (1854—91), French poet. All his poems were written between the ages of 16 and 19. Through the poem *Le Bateau ivre* he won the friendship of Verlaine, who later published his poems under the title *Les Illuminations*, thinking he was dead. Rimbaud at 19 abandoned literature, travelled in many lands, took a commercial post in Aden and then became a trader in Abyssinia. He died in a Marseilles hospital after a leg amputation.

RIMSKI-KORSAKOV, Nikolai (1844—1908), Russian composer. He left the Navy in 1873 to accept a teaching post, managing, as he confessed, by sheer hard work to keep just ahead of his pupils (although he had already written a great opera *Sadko*, which contains the haunting 'Chanson Hindou'). Much of his work is based on Russian history and legend. Among his works are the popular *Capriccio espagnol*, the operas *The Snow Maiden* and *Le Coq d'Or*, the symphonic suite *Scheherazade*, choral works, songs and piano pieces.

Ring (Etruscan)

RING, a circular band of metal worn on the finger as an ornament, talisman or pledge of faith. It is held to symbolise eternity and is endowed with supernatural powers in the folklore of many peoples. In ancient Rome the ring was a symbol of rank. Betrothal rings date back to ancient Egypt and were adopted by Christians in the 2nd century, later being used as wedding rings.

RIO DE JANEIRO, former capital of Brazil, on the Atlantic Ocean. Pop. (1960) 3,307,163. It has a magnificent natural harbour, dominated by two peaks, the Sugar Loaf (1230 ft.) and Corcovado. Manufactures include textiles, chemicals, foodstuffs and tobacco products.

RIO GRANDE, see River.

RIVER, a stream of running fresh water resulting from springs, rain or melting snow or glaciers in a catchment area and flowing from a higher elevation to a lower one. Cataracts or rapids are formed where the bed is uneven. When it reaches its base level, a river no longer deepens its channel but widens it. The speed of flow diminishes at the mouth and may form alluvial deltas. The total area drained by a river and its tributaries is called a river basin. The boundary between head streams flowing into different river beds is the watershed or divide. A continental divide is the boundary between river systems flowing towards opposite sides of a continent. The importance of rivers lies in their being sources of water and hydro-electric power, arteries of navigation, and the centre of fertile valleys. The following is a list of the world's principal rivers:

Name	*Location*	*Source*	*Outlet*	*Length* (miles)
Amazon	S. America	Glacier-fed lakes, Peru	Atlantic	3,900
Amu Darya (Oxus)	Central Asia, U.S.S.R.	Pamir Mts., U.S.S.R.	Aral Sea	1,500

Name	Location	Source	Outlet	Length (miles)
Amur	N.E. Asia	Confluence of Shilka and Argon rivers	Sakhalin Gulf	2,900
Arkansas	U.S.A.	Central Colorado	Mississippi	1,450
Athabaska	Alberta, Canada	Canadian Rockies	Lake Athabaska	765
Brahmaputra	India–Pakistan	Himalaya	Bay of Bengal	1,680
Clyde	Scotland	S. Lanark	Irish Sea	100
Colorado	U.S.A.–Mexico	Colorado, U.S.A.	Gulf of California	1,450
Columbia	Canada–U.S.A.	Columbia Lake, British Columbia	Pacific	1,241
Congo	W. Equatorial Africa	Between Lakes Nyasa and Tanganyika	Atlantic	2,900
Danube	S.E. Europe	Black Forest, W. Germany	Black Sea	1,725
Darling	Australia	Eastern Highlands	Murray River	1,160
Dnieper	S. European R.S.F.S.R.	Valdai Hills, U.S.S.R.	Black Sea	1,400
Don	S.E. European R.S.F.S.R.	Lake Ivan, U.S.S.R.	Sea of Azov	1,100
Dvina	Latvia–R.S.F.S.R.	Vologda Region, U.S.S.R.	White Sea	1,000
Euphrates	S.W. Asia, Iraq	Dumlu Dagh, Turkey	Persian Gulf	1,700
Fraser	British Columbia, Canada	Canadian Rockies	Georgia Strait	750
Ganges	India	Himalaya	Bay of Bengal	1,540
Hwang Ho (Yellow)	China	E. Kunlun Mts, W. China	Gulf of Chihli	2,700
Indus	Pakistan	Himalaya	Arabian Sea	1,700
Irrawaddy	Burma	N'mai and Mali rivers, N.E. Burma	Bay of Bengal	1,250
Jordan	Israel–Jordan Syria	Mt Hermon, Syria	Dead Sea	200
Lena	Siberia	Baikal Mts, U.S.S.R.	Arctic Ocean	2,800
Mackenzie	N.W. Territories Canada	Finlay River, British Columbia	Beaufort Sea (Arctic Ocean)	2,514
Mekong	Indo-China	Tibetan Highlands	S. China Sea	2,500
Mississippi	U.S.A.	Lake Itasca, Minnesota	Gulf of Mexico	2,348
Missouri	U.S.A.	Jefferson and Madison rivers, Montana	Mississippi	2,466
Murray	Australia	Australian Alps, New South Wales	S. Indian Ocean	2,310
Niger	W. Africa	Sierra Leone border	Gulf of Guinea	2,600
Nile	Central and N.E. Africa	Lake Victoria, E. Africa	Mediterranean	4,160
Ob	N.W. Siberia	Altai Mts, U.S.S.R.	Gulf of Ob	3,200
Oder	E. Germany–Poland	Carpathian Mts, N. Czechoslovakia	Baltic Sea	550
Ohio	E. U.S.A.	W. Pennsylvania	Mississippi	981
Orange	S.W. Africa	Basutoland	Atlantic	1,300
Orinoco	S. America	Sierra Parima, Venezuela–Brazil border	Atlantic	1,700
Ottawa	Ontario–Quebec, S.E. Canada	Laurentian Divide	St Lawrence	696
Peace	British Columbia, Alberta, W. Canada	British Columbia	Slave River	1,065

Name	*Location*	*Source*	*Outlet*	*Length* (miles)
Paraguay	S.E. S. America	Mato Grosso, Brazil	Paraná River	1,500
Paraná	E. S. America	Paranaiba and Grande rivers, S.E. Brazil	Rio de la Plata, Atlantic	2,450
Rhine	N.W. Europe	S. Switzerland	North Sea	800
Rio Grande	S.W. U.S.A.	San Juan Mts, Colorado	Gulf of Mexico	1,800
St Lawrence	U.S.A.–Canada	Great Lakes	Atlantic	750
São Francisco	E. Brazil	S.W. Minas Geraes, Brazil	Atlantic	1,800
Seine	France	Plateau de Langres, E. central France	English Channel	480
Shannon	Ireland	Cuileagh Mts, N. central Irish Republic	Atlantic	250
Syr Darya	Central Asia, U.S.S.R.	Tien Shan Mts	Aral Sea	1,200
Tagus	Portugal-Spain	E. central Spain	Atlantic	565
Tay	Scotland	Ben Lui, the border of Perthshire and Argyllshire	North Sea	118
Thames	England	Cotswold Hills, Gloucestershire	North Sea	215
Tiber	Italy	Tuscan Apennines	Mediterranean	240
Tigris	S.W. Asia	Taurus Mts	Euphrates	1,150
Ural	R.S.F.S.R.	S. Ural Mts, U.S.S.R.	Caspian	1,400
Vistula	Poland	Carpathian Mts	Baltic Sea	630
Volga	R.S.F.S.R.	Valdai plateau, U.S.S.R.	Caspian	2,300
Yangtze	China	Tibetan plateau	China Sea	3,100
Yenisei	Mongolia–Siberia	Tannu Ola Mts, W. Mongolia	Arctic Ocean	2,800
Yukon	Alaska–Canada	Lewes and Polly rivers, N.W. Canada	Bering Sea	1,800
Zambezi	S. Africa	Zambia	Indian Ocean	1,600

RIVIERA, a narrow strip of coast in southern France and northwest Italy, at the north end of the Ligurian arm of the Mediterranean. It is noted for its resorts.

ROBERTS, Frederick Sleigh, 1st Earl (1832—1914), British soldier. Educated at Sandhurst, he began his military career in 1851. He served in India where he won the V.C., took part in the Afghan War (1878—79), was promoted Field-Marshal (1895), commanded the army against the Boers (1899—1900) and became (1900) commander-in-chief of the British Army.

ROBESPIERRE, Maxmilien (1758—94), French revolutionary. Elected to the Third Estate (1789), he became a leader of the Jacobin Club. In 1793 he was elected to the Committee of Public Safety, but his brutal and dictatorial measures aroused the wrath of the opposition and he was guillotined. See French Revolution.

ROBIN HOOD, a figure in English folklore and literature who was supposed to have existed in the 14th century, or somewhat earlier. Living in Sherwood Forest with his band of outlaws, he robbed the rich to help the poor.

ROBOT, a machine designed to perform the work of a man. In Karel Čapek's drama *R.U.R.* (1920), where the term was first used, Robots are artificially made men. The term is sometimes applied to automatic devices.

ROCHDALE, a town and county borough in Lancashire, England, on the Roch River. Pop, (1961) 85,785. A manufacturing centre, it produces textiles and engineering goods. The first cooperative society was established here in 1844.

ROCHESTER, a city in New York, U.S.A., on Lake Ontario. Pop. (1960) 318,611. A port and communications centre, it produces cameras, precision instruments and various kinds of specialised equipment.

ROCK, see Geology.

ROCKEFELLER, John Davison (1839—1937), American industrialist. He founded the Standard Oil Company, which gained control of most of the American petroleum industry. One of the world's richest men, he contributed more than $500,000,000 to philanthropic enterprises.

ROCKETS, self-propelled air projectiles carrying their own fuel, are used as weapons of war, for upper atmosphere research and as space probes. The propellant may be solid, as in bazookas and rocket-assisted take-off, or liquid, usually liquid oxygen and another liquid (alcohol, nitric acid, etc.) stored separately. The rocket is propelled forward by the ejection of gases from burning fuel through a nozzle at the rear (see Jet Propulsion), and it was the discovery that the resultant thrust was effective even in a vacuum that led to the development of space rockets.

The first liquid-fuel rocket was fired in Massachusetts in 1826. The first long-range rocket weapon was the German V2

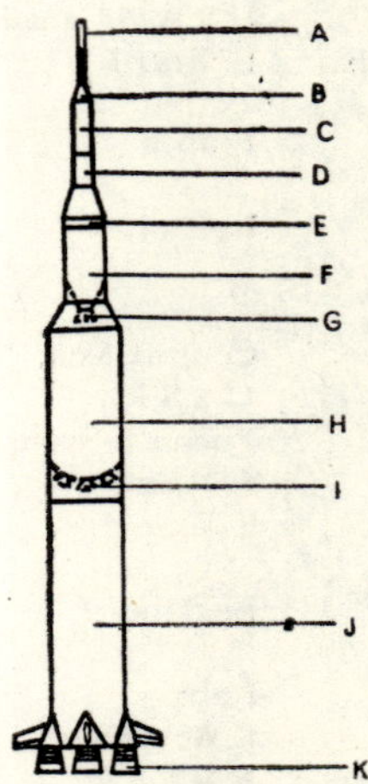

Space rocket (Saturn V)
A. Escape shaft B. Command module C. Service module D. Lunar Excursion module E. Instrument unit F. S.IV B. stage G. S.II engine H. S.II stage I. S.II engine J. S.K. stage K. F.I. engine

designed by Wernher von Braun and used with devastating effect against London towards the end of the Second World War. The fuel was alcohol and liquid oxygen; developing 600,000 h.p., it carried a ton of explosive 200 miles at a peak speed of 3500 m.p.h. The German team responsible for it continued their work after the war in Russia and the U.S.A. It was von Braun who developed the American *Jupiter.*

For very long range rockets two or more stages are used, which fall away when their fuel is exhausted. The I.R.B.M. (Intermediate Range Ballistic Missile) *Jupiter C* was used to launch the first American satellite; it weighed 18 tons and had a range of 3300 miles. Rockets with a range of over 6,000 miles are called Inter-continental Ballistic Missiles (I.C.B.M.). The first, *Atlas*, put into production in 1959, was powered by a cluster of rockets and used to launch satellites. The *Polaris*, produced in 1961, can be launched from land or submarine. In 1962 the U.S. *Nike-Zeus* anti-missile missile hit a target believed to be travelling at 16,000 m.p.h. at a height of 600 miles. British rockets have included *Black Knight*, *Skylark*, *Blue Streak* and *Blue Steel*.

When rockets are used in research, data may be tape-recorded or photographed or, in space research, radioed back to earth. A Soviet rocket hit the moon in 1959. The U.S. *Mariner* II operated by radio control was launched in 1962; it passed within 21,000 miles of Venus and radioed back data from a distance of 36 million miles. In the same year a Soviet rocket was launched towards Mars. Retro-rockets (subsidiary rockets firing backwards or at an angle) are used to slow down a rocket and manoeuvre it into orbit round a planet. A launching velocity of 18,000 m.p.h. is needed to escape the atmosphere, of 25,000 m.p.h. to escape gravity, and of 100,000 m.p.h. to escape the solar system. See also Guided Missile.

ROCKY MOUNTAINS, a mountain system extending along the western region of North America for 4000 miles from Alaska to New Mexico. The maximum width is about 300 miles. The highest peaks are Mt Logan (19,850 ft) in Alaska and Mt Elbert (14,431 ft) in Colorado.

ROCOCO, basically a style of gay, fanciful and exuberant interior decoration developed from the Baroque in the early 18th century in the Catholic countries of southern Europe where Baroque had prevailed. Its characteristic is a profusion of curvilinear decoration, overwhelming but charming. In architecture, examples are to be found in many Bavarian churches, the Frauenkirche at Dresden and the San Souci

Rococo (detail). Hôtel de Soubise, Paris

Palace at Potsdam. Watteau, Fragonard and Boucher represent the style in painting. Louis XV furniture, porcelain, gold and silver ware and sculpture also showed its influence.

RODIN, Auguste (1840—1917), French sculptor. His exquisite modelling of the human figure reveals a deep sense of beauty. His most famous works are *The Kiss*, *The Thinker* and *The Burghers of Calais*.

ROLLAND, Romain (1866—1944), French writer. He wrote plays, lives of Beethoven, Handel, Gandhi and others, and novels, of which the most famous is the 10 volume *Jean-Christophe*. He received the Nobel Prize for literature in 1915. He was a pacifist in the First World War and later became a Communist.

ROMAN CATHOLIC CHURCH, the Protestant name for the Catholic Church which acknowledges the supreme authority of the Bishop of Rome (the Pope). According to Roman Catholic belief, Jesus himself established the church with Peter as its head, and the Pope is the spiritual successor of Peter (see Apostolic Succession). The Roman Catholic Church is the largest single Christian Church in existence today.

The chief differences between the Roman Catholic and other Christian Churches are: the use of Latin and the Latin Vulgate in the services; the absence of congregational singing; the emphasis on the Mass (see Eucharist); the belief that faith without deeds is, in the words of the Council of Trent, 'dead and unprofitable'; confession to a priest; the canonisation of saints; prayers to the Blessed Virgin Mary and the saints; readiness to believe in contemporary miracles, e.g. the efficacy of a pilgrimage to Lourdes; teachings on Purgatory; monasticism; and the administration of extreme unction to the dying. The Church is authoritarian and insists on strict discipline. The traditional teachings of the Apostles may be interpreted by the Pope, as in the pronouncements on the Immaculate Conception (1854), the Infallibility of the Pope (1854) and the Assumption of the Blessed Virgin (1950). The Catholics are strongest in southern Europe, and are strongly anti-Communist. Divorce and birth control are not approved.

ROMAN EMPIRE, which was founded *c.* 29 B.C. by Augustus and lasted until A.D. 476, reached its widest extent under Trajan (d. 117), when it comprised not only the Mediterranean region but Gaul, Britain, Germany as far as the Danube, the Balkans, Asia Minor, Armenia and Mesopotamia. No significant additions were made after this date, and Mesopotamia was lost by Trajan's successor. The golden age of the empire also dates from Trajan's time, and lasted until the death of Marcus Aurelius in 180, from which year Gibbon dates the beginning of the decline of Rome. Franks, Goths (who killed the Emperor Decius in 251) and Parthians contributed to a century of war and disorder, deepened by the economic crisis caused by Rome's inability to find money or men to guard its extensive frontiers. Diocletian (284—305) reorganised the empire as a centralised bureaucracy; he also persecuted the Christians. Constantine the Great (ruled 306—337) preferred to make allies of the Christians and underwent conversion. He moved his capital to Byzantium, renamed Constantinople, thus facilitating the split of the over-large empire into two (Eastern and Western) soon after his death (see Byzantine Empire). Within a brief period of 45 years Rome was sacked by the Visigoths under Alaric (410) and the Vandals (455) and threatened by Attila and the Huns. Romulus Augustulus was deposed in 476 and the Western Empire ceased to exist.

ROMANTICISM, an artistic and literary movement which arose in 18th-century Europe in reaction against the prevailing classical standards. It regarded the expression of the artist's feelings as being of more importance than form or traditional rules of aesthetics. It grew out of a deepening knowledge of history and the world, a recognition of the changes being brought about by the Industrial Revolution, and an assimilation of the lessons of the French Revolution, Rousseau was its philosopher, and a liberal outlook, together with a new interest in, and sympathy for, the common people was a main feature. In literature the great figures were Goethe, Schiller, Heine, Wordsworth, Shelley, Keats, Byron, Hugo, Lamartine, Manzoni; in music Weber, Schumann, Wagner, Brahms; in art Delacroix and Géricault.

ROME, capital of Italy, on the River Tiber. Pop. (1961) 2,160,773. The Vatican (q.v.) lies on the west bank and the modern city, with the remains of Ancient Rome, is mainly on the east bank. The

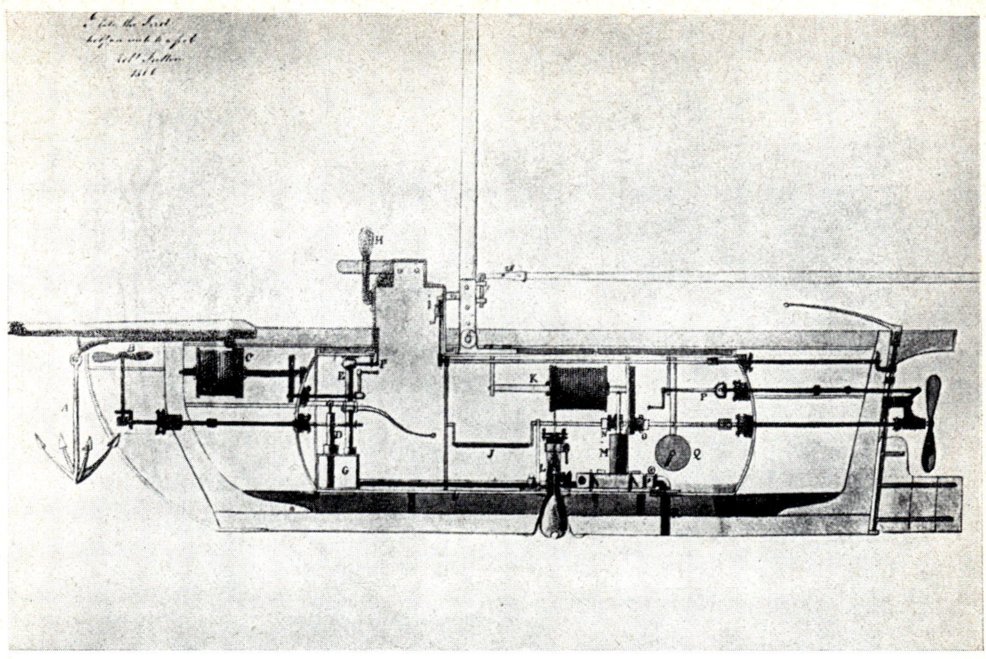

Following the plans outlined by Leonardo da Vinci, the American inventor Robert Fulton (q.v.) published this design for a submarine in 1804. *Official U. S. Navy photograph*

A model of the sailing ship H.M.S. *Victory*, the flagship from which Horatio Nelson (q.v.) directed the Battle of Trafalgar in 1805. *Photo: Crown copyright. Science Museum, London*

By 1840 ships relied for propulsion not only on their sails but on the auxiliary power of steam driven paddles. This model is of the P.S. *Britannia*. *Photo: Lent to the Science Museum, London, by The Cunard Steam Ship Company*

Sails gone, these elegant American paddleboats plied the Mississippi river in the 1850s. *Photo: Science Museum, London*

antiquities include the Colosseum (A.D. 80), the Roman Forum, with the Arch of Titus, and four other forums, the well-preserved Pantheon (27 B.C.), Castel Sant' Angelo (A.D. 136), built as a mausoleum by Hadrian, and the remains of the Temple of Castor and Pollux. Apart from St Peter's and St John Lateran (which is older), there are a great many beautiful churches and palaces, many built or rebuilt in the 17th and 18th centuries. The great squares and their Renaissance and Baroque fountains are a characteristic feature. The Villa Borghese has a fine collection of 16th-17th century paintings, and the Vatican museum is one of several. The equestrian statue of Marcus Aurelius is another landmark. Rome was traditionally founded in 753 B.C. It came under papal rule in the 8th century. Rome became the capital of United Italy in 1870. Industries include engineering, textiles and printing.

ROMMEL, Erwin von (1891—1944), German soldier. He was a brave and respected general, though not a military genius. He commanded the Afrika Corps in North Africa and then served in France until he was wounded. Hitler accused him of plotting against him and forced him to commit suicide.

ROMNEY, George (1734—1802), English painter. He painted portraits and historical subjects. He painted many pictures of Lady Hamilton in classical poses. His work is considered inferior to that of his contemporaries, Gainsborough and Reynolds.

RÖNTGEN, Wilhelm Konrad von (1845—1923), German physicist. His most important contribution to science was his discovery of X-rays, which led to the foundation of radiology and modern electronics. He was awarded the Nobel Prize for physics in 1901.

ROOSEVELT, Franklin Delano (1882—1945), American Democratic statesman and 32nd President of the United States. He entered politics in 1910 and was struck down by poliomyelitis in 1921; he made a brave recovery to become Governor of New York in 1928. Elected (1932) to the Presidency in the midst of an economic depression, he instigated a vigorous programme (the New Deal) to put the American economy back on its feet, meeting with considerable opposition, especially from the Supreme Court, even to such enlightened measures as the establishment of the Tennessee Valley Authority. He was, however, re-elected in 1936, and when war broke out, he allowed Britain to buy arms on a 'cash and carry' basis, although America was neutral. In 1940 he broke all precedents by being elected for a third term, and began preparing the reluctant nation for the inevitable war, introducing Lease-Lend to aid the Allies. He was elected for a fourth term in 1944, but died suddenly of a stroke, just before the end of the war.

ROOSEVELT, Theodore (1858—1919), American Republican statesman, soldier and 26th President of the United States. He was elected (1900) as Vice-President, becoming President when McKinley was assassinated in 1901, and was re-elected for a second term. He fought unceasingly against the big monopolies, secured the Panama Canal Zone for the U.S., and strictly enforced the Monroe Doctrine. After his retirement he took to big game hunting. He wrote several books.

ROSES, Wars of the (1455—85), a series of wars between the ruling house of Lancaster (descendants of John of Gaunt) and the Yorkist descendants of Edward II, named from the emblems worn (red rose for Lancaster, white for York).

After several defeats, the Yorkists won, and Edward IV gained the throne in 1461 with the help of Warwick 'the King-maker', who later turned against him and was killed at the Battle of Barnet (1471). Richard III seized the throne in 1483, but the Lancastrians, under Henry Tudor, rose against him and defeated him at Bosworth Field (1485). Henry became King Henry VII and united the two families by marrying Elizabeth of York, but Yorkist rebellions continued until 1497.

ROSETTA STONE, a slab of basalt found in 1799 in the Nile Delta by one

Rosetta Stone

of Napoleon's officers, and now in the British Museum; it provided the first key to the interpretation of Egyptian hieroglyphs. Dating from 196 B.C., it is written in hieroglyphs, demotic Egyptian and Greek.

ROSS, Sir James Clark (1800—62), Scottish polar explorer. He located the North magnetic pole, and in the course of an expedition in Antarctic waters discovered Victoria Land and the sea and island named after him.

ROSS, Sir Ronald (1857—1932), British bacteriologist. A surgeon in the Indian Medical Service, he discovered that female *Anopheles* mosquitoes are the carriers of the malaria parasite. He was awarded the Nobel Prize for physiology and medicine in 1902.

ROSSETTI, Christina Georgina (1830—94), English poet, the sister of Dante Gabriel Rossetti and the youngest of Gabriele Rossetti's four children. Her better-known works include *Goblin Market, The Prince's Progress* and *New Poems.*

ROSSETTI, Dante Gabriel (1828—82), English painter and poet. One of the founders of the Pre-Raphaelite Brotherhood, he painted *Mona Vanna*, *Girlhood of Mary Virgin* and *Beata Beatrix.* His poetical works include *The Blessed Damozel* and a volume of poems published in 1870 from manuscripts which he had buried in his wife's grave. In both poems and paintings he was inspired by Dante and medieval themes.

ROSSINI, Gioacchino (1792—1868), Italian operatic composer. He composed over 20 operas, his most famous being *The Barber of Seville* and *William Tell.* For the last 40 years of his life he wrote no more opera, but in his final years he composed pieces which were used by Respighi in the ballet *La Boutique Fantasque.*

ROSTAND, Edmond (1868—1918), French poet and dramatist. His greatest work is the romantic drama in verse *Cyrano de Bergerac.*

ROSTOV, a city and port in the R.S.F.S.R., on the Don delta, U.S.S.R. Pop. (1962) 661,000. It is a communications, commercial and industrial centre manufacturing agricultural machinery, metal products and vehicles. There are oil refineries and a grain market.

ROTTERDAM, a seaport in the Netherlands, at the junction of the Maas and Rotte rivers. Pop. (1960) 729,852. The largest port in Europe, linked with the North Sea at the Hook of Holland by a ship canal, and served by numerous inland waterways, it handles much of the trade of West Germany and Belgium. Its many industries include shipbuilding, chemicals, oil and sugar refining, margarine and clocks. Rotterdam was very heavily damaged during the Second World War, among the fine buildings destroyed being the 15th-century church, the Groote Kerk.

ROUEN, a city and port in France, on the River Seine. Pop. (1962) 123,474. Situated 78 miles from the mouth of the Seine, at the head of its tidal section and at the lowest bridgeable point, Rouen is one of the largest ports in France, handling wine, grain, etc. It is an important textile town, with other industries such as chemicals, engineering and oil refining. Rouen was the capital of Normandy; William the Conqueror died, and Joan of Arc was burned, there. The old buildings were badly damaged in the Second World War, but an exceptionally skilful restoration of the 13th-century cathedral, one of the finest in France, was completed in 1956.

ROUNDHEADS, a term of contempt applied in the time of Charles I to the London mob, who wore their hair short, in contrast to the luxuriant growth affected by the gentry. The term came to be applied, without literal justification, to all supporters of parliament against the Royalist Cavaliers in the Civil War. In so far as it implied that the two sides belonged to different classes it was completely misleading.

ROUSSEAU, Jean Jacques (1712—78), French writer and philosopher. He was dependent on a series of patrons, the first of whom, Mme de Warens, became his mistress. He left her in 1740 and had five children by a servant girl, all put in a foundling home. When his books put him in danger of arrest, he fled to Berne and then to England, where he was taken up by Hume, with whom he quarrelled (as with most people). He returned to France and in 1778 moved to the château of the Marquis de Girardin, where he died of a stroke and in a state of mental instability.

Rousseau was perverse, inconsistent and sentimental, and his whole personal life was a miserable failure; yet he was the inspiration of the Romantic movement, started the literature of introspection and psychological analysis, introduced the idea of the Noble Savage, unspoilt by civilisation (and even based a theory of education on it in his novel, *Émile*), and converted the French, and others, to a love of the beauties of Nature *(La Nouvelle Héloïse)*. Among his other seminal ideas were: society must be regenerated by the abolition of inequality; government is by consent *(The Social Contract*, the contradictions in which have inspired both the French Revolution and dictators); man is fundamentally good and must turn to God, but not through a church shrouded in the trappings of theology. His posthumous *Confessions* leave the reader pondering on the disparity between the man and his ideas.

RUANDA-URUNDI, formerly a U.N. trust territory under Belgian administration in central Africa. See Burundi; Rwanda.

RUBBER, an elastic solid obtained from the inner bark of several tropical and semi-tropical trees. In its natural form it is a milky fluid known as latex which becomes resistant to water when it coagulates. Pure rubber consists mostly of the hydrocarbon caoutchouc with small quantities of resin and protein. By treating it with sulphur and heating (vulcanisation) rubber acquires great strength, and resistance to solvents and extremes of heat and cold. Synthetic rubbers are produced from petroleum, alcohol, salt, natural gas and other substances. Originally collected from wild trees in Brazil and Bolivia, it is now produced in plantations in Malaysia, Indonesia, Ceylon, West Africa and elsewhere. Gutta-percha and balata are similar substances, and crepe rubber is raw, unvulcanised sheet rubber.

RUBENS, Peter Paul (1577—1640), Flemish painter. The greatest Baroque artist of northern Europe, he was prolific (using many assistants) and versatile. His works include the Medici cycle of decorations for the Luxembourg Palace, Paris, *Descent from the Cross* (in Antwerp Cathedral), genre pictures *(The Kermesse)*, landscapes, classical themes *(Judgment of Paris)* and portraits of his two wives, Isabella Brandt and Hélène Fourment *(Chapeau de Paille)*.

RUBIDIUM, see Elements.

RUBINSTEIN, Anton (1829—94), Russian pianist and composer. He possessed unusual piano-playing technique. His works include operas, oratorios, symphonies, piano pieces, songs and chamber music.

RUHR, the chief industrial district of West Germany, in the Ruhr valley. Situated in a rich coalfield area, it uses iron ore from Spain, Luxembourg and Sweden for its vast steel works, which include Krupps. The major towns are Bochum, Duisburg, Essen, Dortmund and Düsseldorf. The area was occupied in the 1920s by French troops.

RUMANIA, a people's republic in southeast Europe, on the Black Sea. Pop. (1960) 18,360,000; area 91,671 sq. miles. It has mountains in the north and central region, flanked by plains. The principal crops are maize, wheat and sugar-beet. There are deposits of petroleum, salt, coal, natural gas, lignite, iron and copper. The principal industrial products are chemicals, foodstuffs and textiles. Long an outpost of the Roman Empire, known as Dacia, it suffered from numerous invasions for a thousand years. In the 14th century the principalities of Wallachia and Moldavia were founded. From the 16th century to 1821 they were governed by Turkey. In 1859 both principalities were united under Alexander Cusa to form modern Rumania. After the First World War Rumania gained Transylvania, Bukovina and Bessarabia. The capital is Bucharest (pop. 1960 1,291,251).

RUPERT, Prince (1619—82), Royalist general and admiral. The son of the Elector Palatine of Bohemia and Elizabeth, daughter of James I, he came to England to serve under his uncle, Charles I, in the Civil War. He was a brilliant but erratic commander of cavalry, and won many battles. From 1648—53 he commanded a Royalist fleet of privateers. After the Restoration he served with distinction as an admiral in the Dutch Wars.

RUSKIN, John (1819—1900), British author and art critic. His works include *Modern Painters*, *The Seven Lamps of Architecture*, *The Stones of Venice*, and *Unto This Last*. He was an active supporter of social reform, and deplored the effects of industrialisation on society.

RUSSELL, Bertrand, 3rd Earl (1872—), English philosopher and mathematician. Educated at Cambridge, he was imprisoned during the First World War for his pacifist activities. He was awarded the Nobel Prize for literature in 1950. He has written on mathematical logic, philosophy, social problems (e.g. marriage) and, in the spirit of Mill and Bentham, on politics. He is a leader of the Campaign for Nuclear Disarmament. Among his better known works are *A History of Western Philosophy* (1945) and *Freedom and Organization* 1814—1914 (1934).

RUSSIA, see U.S.S.R.

RUSSIAN HISTORY. A Norseman, Rurik, founded the first dynasty in Novgorod, in 862. Vladimir the Great, who adopted Christianity, made Kiev the political centre of a large area. Overrunning Russia in the 13th century, Mongols ruled the country for 200 years and left a permanent mark on it. The rising into pre-eminence of the Muscovite principality culminated in the emergence of Ivan the Great, who threw off the Mongol yoke and took the title of Czar. The 16th century, one of territorial expansion for Russia, was marked by the cruelties of Ivan the Terrible. The westernisation of the country began with Peter the Great (1682—1725) and was continued by Catherine II (1762—96). Russia continued to expand, constantly acquiring additional territory on her borders. Napoleon's attempt to conquer Russia in 1812—13 failed. Alexander II extended Russia's empire to the Pacific Ocean and central Asia. Repressive policies at home, paralleled by expansionist foreign policies, led to increasing popular resentment throughout the 19th century. Russia's defeat by Japan in 1905 resulted in violent unrest and forced Nicholas II to agree to a representative assembly, from which, however, all liberal elements were excluded. Corruption, misery and suffering increased during the First World War and sparked off a revolution early in 1917 (see Russian Revolution).

RUSSIAN REVOLUTION (1917—20), the conflict which brought about the overthrow of the Czar and resulted in the establishment of the Bolshevik Government in Russia. The first stage began in 1917 with a workers' riot in Petrograd (Leningrad) and mutiny by troops in that city. The Duma (parliament) then resisted the Czar's orders to dissolve itself. On March 15, Nicholas II abdicated, the provisional government under the leadership of Prince Lvov and Kerensky assumed control, promised the Russian people freedom and eventual peace, and attempted to continue an unpopular war. When the Russian troops faced defeat, the Bolsheviks — led by Lenin and Trotsky — organised the October Revolution and gained complete control. See U.S.S.R.

RUSSIAN SOVIET FEDERAL SOCIALIST REPUBLIC (R.S.F.S.R.), far the largest of the constituent republics of the U.S.S.R. Pop. (1962) 122,100,000; area 6,310,594 sq. miles. Extending from Europe through Siberia to the Far East, it occupies three-quarters of the Union (most of it in Asia), and has over half its population. Most of it consists of a vast plain, with a highland plateau east of the Yenisei. The capital is Moscow.

The northwest (chief cities: Leningrad, Kaliningrad, formerly Königsberg) contains one-tenth of Soviet industry, of which the chief features are steel, armaments, heavy electrical equipment, machine tools, automobiles, textiles and shipbuilding. Agriculturally, it is a dairy farming area; there are few minerals.

The west (chief cities: Kalinin, Smolensk) is important for timber, and has textile and machinery industries. Agriculture includes dairying and the growing of potatoes and flax.

The Moscow Region (Moscow, Yaroslavl) has a third of the Union's industry (half of it around Moscow), including machine tools, ball-bearings, steel, aircraft, vehicles, textiles and chemicals.

The north (Archangel, Murmansk) stretches beyond the Arctic Circle and includes the Karelo-Finnish area. It is rich in timber and iron and has a variety of non-ferrous metals. Shipbuilding and iron and steel industries predominate.

The Black Earth Region (Voronezh — Kursk) produces a surplus of agricultural products, including potatoes, sugar-beet, flax, sunflowers and tobacco. Industry is of relatively minor importance, but there are aircraft and synthetic rubber works.

The Don and North Caucasus Region (Rostov, Krasnodar) is important for livestock and arable farming. It shares the Donbas coalfield and industrial area with the Ukraine to the west. There is petroleum and natural gas, and manufactures include agricultural machinery, textiles and shipbuilding. The Black Sea coast is famous for holiday resorts.

The Volga Valley (Gorky, Kuybyshev, Kazan, Volgograd (formerly Stalingrad) and Saratov) includes part of the Ural industrial area. Timber is plentiful, and sunflowers, sugar-beet, vines and tobacco are grown. There are oilfields, with natural gas, and manufactures of steel, tractors, aircraft, vehicles and ships.

The Ural Region (Sverdlovsk, Chelyabinsk, Perm, Magnitogorsk) lies astride the traditional boundary between Europe and Asia. There is much iron ore; non-ferrous metals, oil, asbestos and diamonds are also mined.

One of the major industrial areas, it uses coal from the Kuzbas, second in importance only to the Donbas, and uses iron from the Ural region. Metal refineries and chemicals are among the industrial activities, lead and zinc are mined, and grain and livestock raised.

East Siberia (Krasnoyarsk, Irkutsk) comprises one-third of the area of the U.S.S.R. but contains only 3% of the population. It has enormous reserves of coal, and is the chief source of coal, diamonds and gold. It also produces iron ore, platinum, furs and softwoods. There is an important industrial area north-west of Irkutsk, producing iron and steel, aircraft, armaments, locomotives and rolling stock.

The far east (Vladivostok, Khabarovsk), the coastal area stretching from China to the Bering Strait, comprises one-eighth of the Union but is sparsely inhabited. Oil is obtained from the Russian part of the island of Sakhalin Other products are hard- and soft-woods, furs, coal, iron, gold and tin. There is a growing industrial area at Komsomolsk on the Amur, producing iron and steel, with oil refineries and shipbuilding elsewhere.

RUTHERFORD, Ernest, 1st Baron (1871—1937), New-Zealand-born British physicist. He conducted important investigations in radioactivity and the structure of the atom and was the first to transmute an element, producing hydrogen from nitrogen. He made the Cavendish Laboratory, Cambridge, the world centre of research in nuclear physics. He received the Nobel Prize for chemistry in 1908.

RUTLANDSHIRE, a Midland county, the smallest in England. Pop. (1961) 23,956; area 152 sq. miles. Livestock, dairy products and cereals are grown. The county town is Oakham.

RWANDA, an independent republic in central Africa. Pop. (1962) 2,634,000; area 10,169 sq. miles. It is a mountainous, predominantly agricultural and cattle-breeding country. Until 1962 it was part of the U.N. Trust Territory of

Ruanda-Urundi, under Belgian administration since 1919, and previously German. The capital is Kigali. The majority of the people are of Bantu stock, and the wealth of the country lies in its flocks and herds.

RYUKU ARCHIPELAGO, an island group between Japan and Formosa. Pop. (1960) 882,000; area 921 sq. miles. Formerly Japanese, they are under U.S. control. The capital is Naha, on Okinawa, the largest island.

S

SAAR, a territory of West Germany. Pop. (1961) 1,072,000; area 991 sq. miles. It is important for its coal mines and iron and steel production. It was under League of Nations administration from 1919—35, but was then restored to Germany after a plebiscite. Occupied by France after the Second World War, it was reunited to Germany in 1957. The capital is Saarbrücken (pop. 111,600).

SABAH, a unit of the federation of Malaysia. Pop. (1960) 454,421; area 29,387 sq. miles. The country is very mountainous and well forested. Rice, hemp and tobacco are grown; exports include rubber, copra and hardwoods. The capital is Jesselton, which has a good harbour, as have Labuan and Sandakan. Until 1963 Sabah was the British colony of North Borneo.

SACRAMENT, in Christian theology a religious ceremony regarded as the outward and visible sign of an inward and spiritual grace. The Roman Catholic and Eastern Churches recognise seven: baptism, the Eucharist, matrimony, confirmation, penance (confession and absolution), extreme unction and Holy Orders. The Anglican Church recognises the first two without specifically rejecting, as some other Protestant churches reject, the other five.

SACRIFICE, the religious act of consecrating and presenting an offering to a deity. In Christian theology the death of Jesus is regarded as the final and ultimate sacrifice.

SAHARA, the desert region of North Africa. Pop. 2,500,000; area 3,500,000 sq. miles. Geographically, the Sahara is regarded as including not only the Libyan (Western) Desert, but also the two deserts, Arabian and Nubian, east of the Nile, the total area comprising a quarter of the continent. In common usage the term is restricted to the area west of the Nile. Fringed by the Saharan Atlas range on the north, it also contains the Ahaggar (10,000 ft) and Tibesti (11,000 ft) ranges in the interior. The surface varies from sand dunes to the more extensive rocky wastes, with scattered oases where dates are grown. In modern times vast resources of oil and natural gas have been found in the Algeria-Tunis zone, and large deposits of iron ore further west. The great potentialities of the area, combined with the lack of traditional boundaries in an area which until recently was almost exclusively French, have led to strained relations between Tunisia, Algeria, Morocco and Mauritania.

SAIGON, capital of South Viet-Nam, on the Saigon River. Pop. (1958) 1,799,175 (with Cholon). It is a seaport, and a commercial and industrial centre producing textiles and foodstuffs.

SAINTE-BEUVE, Charles Augustin (1804—69), French critic and poet. He analysed Jansenism in his *History of Port-Royal*. A vast number of acute and intelligent essays contributed to periodicals were collected and published under such titles as *Causeries du Lundi*; they deal with writers, historical characters and politicians of many countries.

ST ÉTIENNE, capital of Loire, France, on the Furens River. Pop. (1962) 203,633. In a coal-mining region, it has metallurgical, rifle, motor-cycle, textile and glass industries.

ST HELENA, British volcanic island in the South Atlantic. Pop. (1961) 4648; area 47 sq. miles. Flax is a leading product. Napoleon died in exile in St Helena in 1821 and Boer leaders were imprisoned here in 1900. The capital is Jamestown.

ST HELENS, a city and county borough in Lancashire, England. Pop. (1961) 108,348. Linked to the Mersey by a canal, it is a glass-manufacturing centre with foundries, chemical works and copper-smelting plants.

ST LAWRENCE SEAWAY, an enlarged waterway linking the Great Lakes and the Gulf of St Lawrence in the Atlantic, opened in 1959. The existing waterway was improved by widening the canals, building new locks, raising bridge levels and the creaton of an artificial lake, thus

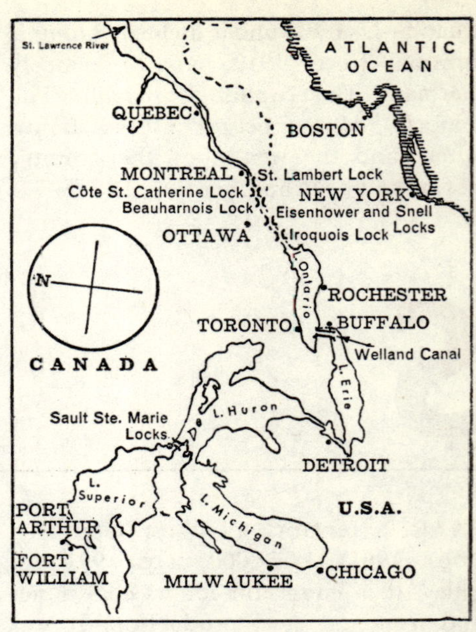

St Lawrence Seaway development

providing a seaway with a minimum depth of 27 ft. Whereas previously ocean-going ships had to load and unload their cargoes at Montreal, which was served by smaller Lake vessels from the west, it is now possible for ocean vessels of up to 9000 tons to proceed straight through the Seaway as far as Duluth, at the western end of Lake Superior, and for Lake vessels of 25,000 tons to come down as far as Montreal. Provision was also made for new major sources of hydro-electric power.

ST LOUIS, a city in Missouri, U.S.A., on the Mississippi just below its confluence with the Missouri. Pop. (1960) 750,026. Originally a fur-trading post, and now served by 25 railways, it is a market and distributing centre for grain and livestock. Its leading industries include brewing, steel, oil refining, footwear, meat-packing and the processing of alumina.

ST PAUL, capital of Minnesota, U.S.A.,

on the Mississippi, facing Minneapolis. Pop. (1960) 313,411. A communications centre in a rich agricultural region, it is a wholesale and retail distributing point for the American northwest. There are diversified industries, including meat-packing, metal products, publishing, furs and sawmilling.

SAINT-SAËNS, Charles Camille (1835—1921), French composer. A child prodigy, he produced music as a tree produces apples, to use his own phrase. Of his vast output, little has any profundity but some works have survived because of their pleasing melodies, e.g. *Le Rouet d'Omphale*, *Le Carnaval des animaux*, the opera *Samson and Delilah*, the symphonic poem *Danse macabre*, the Third Symphony and the Piano Concertos.

SAKHALIN, a mountainous island of the U.S.S.R., in the Pacific off the Siberian coast and north of Japan. Pop. (1959) 649,000; area 29,630 sq. miles (with adjacent islands). Its principal products are oil, coal, fish and timber. The southern half was ceded to Russia by Japan in 1875, recovered by Japan following the Russo-Japanese War of 1904—5, and restored to the U.S.S.R. in 1945.

SALADIN (1137—93), Sultan of Egypt as Salah ad-Din, succeeding the last Fatimid Caliph. He defeated the Second Crusade in the Battle of Hattin (1187), leaving only Tyre and Antioch in Christian hands. He united Palestine, Syria and Mesopotamia under Egypt. In the Third Crusade Richard I defeated Saladin and in the subsequent peace regained some of the territory lost, and also the right of pilgrims to free access to Jerusalem.

SALAMIS, an island near the Piraeus, Greece. In 480 B.C. Themistocles defeated the Persian fleet in the narrow waters between the island and the mainland; this battle, with the land battle of Plataea (479), ended Xerxes' invasion of Greece.

SALISBURY, capital of Rhodesia. Pop. (1962) 277,000. It is the centre of a gold-mining and tobacco-growing area. There are rail-links to South Africa and Beira (Mozambique), and an international airport.

SALISBURY, Robert Arthur Talbot Gascoyne-Cecil, 3rd Marquess of (1830—1903), British statesman. He was Foreign Secretary from 1878—80, and later served as Prime Minister (1885—86, 1886—92, 1895—1902), but resigned at the conclusion of the Boer War. He succeeded Disraeli as Leader of the Conservative Party in 1881. In foreign affairs his policy was based on the avoidance of entangling alliances.

SALONIKA, see Thessaloniki

SALT LAKE CITY, capital of Utah, U.S.A., on the Jordan River. Pop. (1960) 189,454. On a mountain slope not far from Great Salt Lake, it is the headquarters of the Mormon religion. It is a commercial, financial and industrial city producing nonferrous metals, petroleum products and canned meat.

SALZBURG, a town in Austria on the Salzach River. Pop. (1961) 108,114. A bishopric since A.D. 700, dominated by an ancient citadel, the fine old town has a 17th-century cathedral, the Franciscan Church, and a unique shopping centre of narrow medieval streets. As Mozart's birthplace, with an annual international music festival, and as a gateway both to Tyrol and to the lakes of Salzkammergut, it is much frequented by tourists.

SALVADOR, EL, see El Salvador

SALVATION ARMY, an international evangelical organisation which grew from a mission founded in the 1860s by William Booth in the East End of London, its present semi-military name and organisation dating from 1878. With the aid of military bands, street-corner services and the periodical *War Cry*, its uniformed men and women officers have brought Christianity to slum-dwellers in many countries, and with great courage have carried out valuable rehabilitation and charitable work, undeterred by the most forbidding urban areas.

SAMARIA, a region of ancient Palestine, now in Jordan, between Galilee and Judaea. The town of Samaria was from the 10th to 8th centuries B.C. capital of the Kingdom of Israel.

SAMARKAND, a city in the Uzbek S.S.R., U.S.S.R., in Central Asia. Pop. (1962) 215,000. A walled oasis town, it became capital of Tamerlane's empire in 1370, when it was known as the Golden City. The ruins of his mausoleum and summer palace still remain. It was an early Mohammedan centre, and has many mosques and minarets. After the Mongols, Samarkand was ruled by the Chinese and then by Bokhara, coming under Russian administration from 1868. There are textile and engineering works.

SAMOA, an island group in the south central Pacific comprising the Republic of Western Samoa and American Samoa. They are essentially rugged mountain tops covered with thick vegetation and under heavy rainfall. Copra, cocoa, yams, oranges, pawpaws and bananas are the principal products. Western Samoa (pop. 1961 113,567; area: 1130 sq. miles) consists chiefly of the large islands of Savai'i (700 sq. miles) and Upolu (430 sq. miles). German until their occupation by New Zealand forces in 1914, they became independent in 1961; the capital is Apia. American Samoa comprises the islands of Tutuila and the Manua group (pop. 1960 20,051; area 76 sq. miles). The Treaty of Berlin of 1899 gave the U.S.A. rights over the islands. The capital is Pago Pago.

SAN ANTONIO, a city in south central Texas, U.S.A., on the San Antonio and San Pedro rivers. Pop. (1960) 587,718. In a cattle-raising and oil-producing region, it is an industrial and communications centre. San Antonio is a winter resort and a major air base (including Randolph Field). The city has stockyards, oil refineries and food processing plants.

SAND, George (Lucile Aurore Dupin; 1804—76), French Romantic novelist. Her numerous works include *Indiana*, *Lélia* and a long autobiography. She was an intimate of Alfred de Musset, Chopin, Sainte-Beuve, Balzac, the elder Dumas, Flaubert and Liszt.

SAN DIEGO, a city in California, U.S.A., on the Pacific Ocean. Pop. (1960) 573,224. It has a fine harbour and is an important naval and fishing base. Industries include tuna-packing, food processing and aircraft.

SAN FRANCISCO, a city and port in California, U.S.A., on the Pacific. Pop. (1960) 742,855. It is a commercial, financial and industrial centre and has an important agricultural market, with oil refineries and industries producing metallurgical articles, chemicals and foodstuffs. It has numerous parks, museums and churches. Founded by Franciscan friars in 1776, it began to develop rapidly after the discovery of gold in California in 1848, the year when it passed from Mexico to the U.S.A. The city has a large Chinese quarter. The largest single-span bridge in the world was constructed (1937) across the Golden Gate, the entrance to San Francisco Bay; and another famous bridge, the Transbay, links the city to Oakland. The city suffered heavy damage in two fires in the 1850s and in the earthquake of 1905. In 1945 an international conference here drew up the United Nations Charter.

SAN JOSE, a city in California, U.S.A. Pop. (1960) 204,196. A rapidly growing communications and industrial centre, it is in the midst of a rich fruit-growing region. Food processing, chemicals, steel and mercury works form its main industries. Lick Observatory is near by.

SAN JUAN, capital of Puerto Rico, on the Atlantic. Pop. (1960) 431,705. A commercial city, it has a busy port and food-processing industries. It was founded in 1510 and remains of the original fortifications survive, with many 16th-century buildings.

SAN MARINO, a republic in central Italy on the Adriatic. Pop. (1962) 17,000; area 38 sq. miles. It claims to be the oldest and smallest republic in the world and is under Italian protection. It produces barley, wine, cattle and building stone. The capital is San Marino, on a mountain 2500 ft high. San Marino declared itself neutral in the Second World War, but was occupied by the Germans.

SAN SALVADOR, capital of El Salvador, on the Asalquate River. Pop. (1960) 252,591. It manufactures textiles, foodstuffs and cigars. The city has suffered from frequent earthquakes. It was founded in 1525.

SANTA CLAUS, see Nicholas, St

SANTA FÉ, a city in central Argentina, on the Paraná. Pop. (1954) 219,620. A major port, it is also a commercial centre. Founded in 1573, it has many ancient churches. Argentina's constitution was adopted here in 1853.

SANTAYANA, George (1863—1952), American poet, philosopher and educationalist. He gave up (1912) his position as professor of philosophy at Harvard University, and during the Second World War he settled in a monastery in Italy, where he died.

SANTIAGO, capital of Chile. Pop. (1960) 1,169,481. A modern skyscraper city, beautifully situated on a plain at the foot of the Andes, it is a financial, commercial and cultural centre. Its manufactures, which include textiles, machinery, chemicals, clothing and foodstuffs, account for half the industrial production of Chile. The town was founded in 1541.

SANTIAGO DE CUBA, a city and port in Cuba. Pop. (1960) 166,384. An industrial and commercial centre, it was the capital of Cuba from 1523—56. Industries include iron foundries, tanneries, sawmills and rum distilleries. There is an important university.

SANTOS, a city and port in Brazil. Pop. (1960) 265,753. It is the world's largest coffee port and also exports rice, sugar, rum, hides and manufactured goods. Paraguay has been granted a free-port zone here.

SÃO FRANCISCO, see River.

SÃO PAULO, capital of São Paulo state, Brazil, on the Rio Tieté. Pop. (1960) 3,776,581. The second largest city in South America and a major communications, commercial and industrial centre, it has large cotton and coffee exchanges. The principal manufactures, based on local hydro-electric power, are textiles, rubber, chemicals, automobiles, metal and electrical goods and foodstuffs. The city has the largest cathedral (1954) in South America, accommodating a congregation of 8000.

SARAJEVO, capital of Bosnia and Herzegovina, Yugoslavia. Pop. (1961) 143,117. The assassination here of Archduke Francis Ferdinand in June 1914 was the immediate cause of the First World War. A gruesome museum by the site of the crime commemorates the young assassin.

SARAWAK, a unit of the Malaysian Federation on the island of Borneo. Pop. (1961) 769,034; area 47,071 sq. miles. The principal products are rubber, timber, sago, oil, rice, pepper, gold and bauxite. The capital is Kuching. Sir James Brooke, formerly of the Indian Army and the East India Company, visited Sarawak in 1840 and helped to quell an insurrection against the Sultan of Brunei, who thereupon made Brooke Rajah of Sarawak. The title became hereditary in the Brooke family until 1946, when Sarawak was made a British colony.

SARDINIA, Italian island and autonomous region south of Corsica. Pop. (1961) 1,413,289; area 9302 sq. miles. Mountainous, it is mostly devoted to grazing. Agricultural products consist of wines, olive oil, cereals, tobacco and citrus fruit. Fishing and dairy farming are important. The south has deposits of lead, zinc, lignite, tin and iron. From 1720 until it united with Italy in 1861, it was ruled by the house of Savoy. The capital is Cagliari.

SARGENT, John Singer (1856—1925), American painter. Born in Florence, educated in Paris and, from 1884, resident in London, he painted some murals (e.g. for the Boston Public Library), but is best known for his portraits, which included Theodore Roosevelt, Joseph Chamberlain, Ellen Terry, the Wertheimer family and a full-length portrait of Lord Ribblesdale.

SARTRE, Jean Paul (1905—), French philosopher, novelist and dramatist. An atheist, a Communist and one of the leaders of post-war Existentialism (q.v.), he has a horror of the irrationality of man, of which he sees evidence all around him, and pours scorn on bourgeois morality. In the struggle for freedom, violence is inevitable. These are obtrusively the themes of his plays, such as *The Flies*, *Crime passionel* and *In Camera* (in which the three characters discover that 'Hell is other people'). His philosophical works are *Being and Non-Being* and *Existentialism*; his basic tenet is that man must work out his own system of ethics and must have the courage to choose freely for himself how he will behave.

SASKATCHEWAN, a west central province of Canada. Pop. (1961) 925,181; area 251,700 miles. From north to south it consists of a rocky forested region with numerous lakes, a belt of forests, and vast prairies devoted chiefly to wheat. Fur trapping, lumbering and fishing are important. There are deposits of copper, gold, cadmium, silver, zinc, selenium, petroleum, coal and uranium. Most of the industries process the food resources of the province. There are tanneries, oil refineries and railway shops. Sawmill products, metal goods, electrical equipment, automobiles, chemicals and textiles are manufactured. The capital is Regina (pop. 112,141).

SATANISM, a cult which venerated Satan. It flourished especially in Germany and Austria during the Middle Ages and its members were believed to practise sorcery and witchcraft.

SATELLITE, a small planet revolving around a larger one. The earth has one, Mars two, Neptune two, Uranus five, Saturn nine, and Jupiter twelve.

SATIRE, an attack on the morals and manners of contemporary society, usually aiming at correction. Ridicule by exaggerated caricature and a barely concealed snarl are perhaps the distinctive ingredients. Among the great satirists were Juvenal, Molière, Swift *(Gulliver's Travels)*, Voltaire *(Candide)* and Dryden. In more recent times George Orwell's *Animal Farm* and Aldous Huxley's *Brave New World* deserve mention.

SAUDI ARABIA, a kingdom comprising most of the Arabian peninsula. Pop. *c.* 6,000,000; area *c.* 600,000 sq. miles (the boundaries are not defined). Mostly desert, it produces dates, cereals, pearls, hides and livestock. Almost the only source of income is petroleum. Saudi Arabia comprises the states of Hejaz, Nejd and Asir, united into one kingdom by Abdul Aziz Ibn Saud after a series of conquests from 1919—27. It contains the most sacred shrines in Islam at Mecca and Medina. The duality of the state is recognised in the fact that there are still two capitals, Riyadh (Nejd) and Mecca (Hejaz). The importation of slaves is regulated.

SAVAGE, Michael Joseph (1872—1940), New Zealand statesman. Born in Australia, he went to New Zealand in 1907 as a miner and was active in trade union affairs. He entered the New Zealand parliament in 1919, became leader of the Labour party in 1933, and the first Dominions Labour Prime Minister (1935—40), in which capacity he introduced social security measures.

SAVONAROLA, Girolamo (1452—98). A Florentine religious reformer and Dominican friar. He fearlessly denounced corruption and vice and was largely responsible for causing the overthrow of the Medici in Florence (1494) and the setting up of a short-lived republic. In 1497 he was excommunicated by Pope Alexander VI, whom he had criticised. The Florentines grew tired of him, and he was arrested, tortured, hanged and burnt.

SAVOY, House of, the ruling dynasty of the kingdom of Italy from 1861 till 1946. The house goes back to the 11th century. Amadeus was created Duke of Savoy in 1416, and under his rule the duchy reached its greatest extent. A successor, Victor Amadeus II, became King of Sardinia in 1720; and in 1861 Victor Emmanuel II became the first king of a united Italy.

SAXONS, a Teutonic people who lived in north central Germany in the 2nd century A.D. They came into conflict with neighbouring tribes, and in the 5th and 6th centuries some of them settled in the south of England (see Anglo-Saxons). Those who remained in Germany (the Old Saxons) extended their domain southward, encompassing the territory later included in the kingdom of Saxony; they were finally conquered by Charlemagne.

SAXONY, a region in East Germany, a former kingdom and state. At one time the region extended to the borders of Poland in the north. Later the name applied only to the electorate and subsequent kingdom of Saxony, which was a portion of the original area. Dresden was the capital of the kingdom, of which Frederick Augustus I became king in 1806. As a consequence of supporting Napoleon, the king lost more than half his domain, which became the Prussian province of Saxony. The kingdom of Saxony sided with defeated Austria in the Seven Weeks War of 1866 and was compelled to join the North German Federation. A part of the German empire in 1871, it became a state in the republic established after the First World War. After the Second World War, Saxony became a part of the German Democratic Republic. Lower Saxony (pop. 1961 6,641,000; area 18,226 sq. miles) is a state in West Germany; the capital is Hanover.

SCANDINAVIA, a region in northwest Europe comprising Norway, Sweden, Denmark and Iceland, whose peoples share a common racial origin.

SCAPA FLOW, a strait in northern Scotland enclosed by the Orkney Islands, with an anchorage of about 60 sq. miles. The German naval vessels interned here after the First World War were scuttled by their crews in 1919.

SCEPTICISM, a philosophical school of thought which holds that the ultimate truth is unattainable by man. The earliest exponent of Scepticism was Pyrrho of Elis (3rd century B.C.).

SCHILLER, Johann Friedrich von (1759—1805), German dramatist and poet. Educated at the Military Academy at Stuttgart, he gave up all thought of a career as an army surgeon and devoted himself to literature. After writing some plays he turned to the study of history and of Kant's philosophy and published a history of the Thirty Years War. In 1794 Goethe invited him to Weimar and persuaded him to take up poetry again. In the last six years of his life he produced his greatest dramas, *Wallenstein*, *Mary Stuart*, *The Maid of Orleans* and *William Tell.* It was also at Weimar that he wrote his famous ballads. One of Schiller's odes was adopted by Beethoven for the choral finale to his Ninth Symphony.

SCHLEGEL, August Wilhelm von (1767—1845), German poet and literary critic. He established the reputation of Shakespeare in Germany by his excellent translations of 17 of his plays.

SCHLESWIG-HOLSTEIN, state and former Prussian province in the northern portion of the German Federal Republic, on the North and Baltic seas. Pop. (1960) 1,289,984; area 6047 sq. miles. Cereals, potatoes, cattle, fish, textiles and iron and steel are the principal products. For long an area of contention between Denmark and Germany, the region was awarded to Germany by a plebiscite in 1920. The capital is Kiel. North Schleswig (Slesvig) elected to become Danish.

SCHOLASTICISM, the term used to describe the Christian theology and philosophy of the *doctores scholastici* (doctors of leisure) of the Middle Ages from the 9th—15th centuries. It was primarily concerned with the reconciliation of logic and human reason with the teachings and traditions of the Church. Anselm, Abélard, St Thomas Aquinas and Duns Scotus were among the most influential Schoolmen.

SCHOPENHAUER, Arthur (1788—1860), German philosopher. His philosophy is deeply tinged with pessimism and he himself was drawn towards the mystic teachings of Buddhism. There is no meaning in life and no escape from sorrow and pain, except in the contemplation of beauty and the annihilation of desire. His major works are *The World as Will and Idea* (1819) and *The Two Fundamental Problems of Ethics* (1841).

SCHUBERT, Franz (1797—1828), Austrian composer. He was a child prodigy, and had composed the *Erlking* by the age of 18. An outstanding master of melody he wrote about 600 songs; *Die Schöne Müllerin* and *Die Winterreise* contain some of the finest. Although the songs are his most characteristic contribution, Schubert found time in his brief life to show his mastery in other forms, e.g. the Eighth (Unfinished) and Ninth symphonies, the Octet, the two quintets, the quartets, piano sonatas and the incidental music for *Rosamunde*.

SCHUMANN, Robert (1810—56), German composer. Inspired by Romantic poetry, he composed most of his best music before he was 33. He excelled in the song (especially the *Dichterliebe* cycle to Heine's poems) and the shorter piano pieces, but in the more substantial forms (symphony, cantata, opera) he was much less successful, except in the famous Piano Concerto in A minor. From 1843 his mental health deteriorated, and in 1854 he attempted suicide.

SCHWEITZER, Albert (1875—1965), French musician and physician, born in Alsace. Educated at the universities of Strasburg, Paris and Berlin, where he took doctorates in philosophy, theology, music and medicine, at the age of 35 he abandoned the brilliant prospects that lay before him in Europe to found a hospital in Lambaréné, Gabon, then in French Equatorial Africa, returning to Europe for brief visits only, during which he would demonstrate that he was one of the best interpreters of J. S. Bach, a fine organist, and, incidentally, a skilled repairer of the organ. He wrote numerous works on theology, especially on the Kingdom of God; on philosophy, in which he expounded his theory of Reverence for Life; and on his life and work at Lambaréné. He was awarded the Nobel Peace Prize in 1952 and an honorary O.M.

SCOTLAND, the northern part of the island of Great Britain. Pop. (1961) 5,178,490; area 29,796 sq. miles. From north to south it consists of the Highlands (Ben Nevis, 4406 ft, the highest peak in Great Britain); the fertile Central Lowlands, supporting most of the population; and the Southern Uplands merging into the Cheviot Hills (q.v.). The principal crops are oats and barley, potatoes, root crops and fruit. Livestock raising and fishing are important. There are deposits of coal and shale oil. Main industries are textiles, iron and steel production, transport equipment, machinery, shipbuilding, engineering, distilling, brewing, sugar refining, dyeing and tobacco products.

Scotland's original inhabitants were the Picts. Known in ancient times as Caledonia, after the departure of the Romans in the 5th century it was occupied in the west by Scots originating in Ireland, in the southwest by Britons and in the southeast by the Angles. Union of the Picts and Scots under Kenneth MacAlpin in 844 gave birth to the kingdom of Scotland. After the Norman conquest of England in 1066 and the marriage of Malcom III to a Saxon princess, the English language and Norman-English institutions began to gain a foothold in the country. During the intermittent periods of English rule attempts to achieve independence were frequently made. Wallace, at first successful (1297), was subsequently defeated at Falkirk. In 1314 Robert

Bruce at Bannockburn freed Scotland from English rule. James I, who became king in 1406, was a capable sovereign but was held prisoner in England for 18 years. James IV was defeated and killed by the English at Flodden Field in 1513. His granddaughter, Mary Queen of Scots, ascended the throne after the defeat of her father by the English at Solway Moss in 1542. Forced to abdicate by a rebellion, she fled to England where she was held prisoner by Queen Elizabeth I and subsequently beheaded. James VI of Scotland, Mary's son, and closest kin to Elizabeth, succeeded her in 1603 as James I of Great Britain, France and Ireland. Charles II was invited by the Scots to become their king after the execution of his father in 1649, but his armies were defeated by Cromwell's soldiers. In 1660, he was restored to the throne of England and Scotland. At his death in 1685, he was succeeded by his brother James VII of Scotland and II of England, who was deprived of his throne by the Revolution of 1688. Commercial jealousy between England and Scotland made it necessary to unite the parliaments of both countries in 1707, thus reconciling the two peoples. The capital is Edinburgh (pop. 1961 468,378). The leading commercial and industrial city is Glasgow (1,054,913).

SCOTT, Robert Falcon (1868—1912), English Antarctic explorer. He made several surveys of Antarctica, discovering King Edward VII Land and sounding the Ross Sea. In 1912 he reached the South Pole by sledge shortly after Amundsen. He died on the return journey, with his four companions.

SCOTT, Sir Walter (1771—1832), British Romantic novelist and poet. A prolific writer, he achieved popularity in a short time with his poems and historical novels. The former include *Minstrelsy of the Scottish Border*, *The Lay of the Last Minstrel*, *Marmion*, and *The Lady of the Lake*. The latter comprised the *Waverley* series (*Rob Roy*, *Ivanhoe*, etc.).

SCULPTURE, artistic expression in three dimensions. It includes carving in stone, ivory, wood and bone; modelling in wax, clay or other soft substances; casting in bronze; shaping in metals and other materials, and construction. The two basic techniques consist of subtraction — cutting away parts of the material in order to impart to the remainder the form which the artist's imagination wishes to bestow upon it, and addition — creating a form by modelling a soft substance and building it up to the desired appearance. The sculptor must never lose sight of the possibilities and limitations of his material if he wishes to bring to life the idea to which he is striving to give a visible, tangible form. Sculptured forms range from images in the round to incisions and low relief.

SEA, a large area of ocean enclosed by well-defined land boundaries or a large salt lake (see Lake). The following are the principal ocean seas:

Name	*Location*	*Area (sq. miles)*	*Greatest depth (ft)*
Adriatic	S. Europe	60,000	—
Andaman	S.E. Asia	308,000	12,392
Baltic	N.W. Europe	163,000	1,380
Bering	Alaska—Siberia	875,800	13,422
Black	S.E. Europe	165,000	—

Name	*Location*	*Area (sq. miles)*	*Greatest depth (ft)*
Caribbean	Central and S. America	1,049,500	22,788
E. China	China—Ryuku	482,300	9,126
Hudson Bay	N.E. Canada	475,800	600
Irish	Ireland—Great Britain	75,000	850
Japan	Japan—Korea	389,100	12,276
Mediterranean	Europe—Asia—Africa	1,000,000	13,564
Mexico, Gulf of	U.S.A.—Mexico	618,200	12,744
North	Great Britain—Europe	222,100	2,165
Okhotsk	E. Siberia	589,800	11,400
Persian Gulf	Iran—Arabia	89,000	—
Red	S.E. Asia—N.E. Africa	169,100	7,254
St George's Channel	Ireland—Wales	8,000	—
South China	E. Indian Archipelago	895,400	18,090
White	N.E. R.S.F.S.R., U.S.S.R.	45,000	—
Yellow	China—Korea—S. Japan	240,000	300

SEATTLE, port and largest city in Washington, U.S.A. Pop. (1960) 557,087. A communications, commercial and industrial centre, it is a major gateway to the Pacific, Canada and Alaska. Lumbering, fishing and the manufacture of aircraft, iron and steel, light metals, foodstuffs and textiles are its main pursuits. It is also an educational centre.

SECURITY COUNCIL OF THE U.N. has five permanent members (France, U.S.S.R., U.K., U.S.A. and Formosa) and six others who are elected for two-year periods by the General Assembly. It sits continuously and has two main responsibilities, to promote the peaceful settlement of disputes and to stop aggression. Action must be approved by seven members, including all five permanent members, who thus have a power of veto.

SEINE, see River.

SEMANTICS, the scientific study of meaning. It seeks to discover the true meaning behind words and the way in which they are used.

SENECA, Lucius Annaeus (The Younger; *c.* 4 B.C.—A.D. 65), Roman stoic philosopher. He was Nero's tutor and, for a time, one of his most influential advisers. Charged with conspiracy, Seneca, at the express wish of Nero, committed suicide.

SENEGAL, a republic in West Africa, south of the Senegal River. Pop. (1961) 2,973,000; area 80,695 sq. miles. Mostly sandy plain, it produces millet, rice, groundnuts (which account for 90% of exports), oil-cake, phosphates, cement and titanium. Formerly a French territory, it became independent in 1960 and was later a member of the short-lived Federation of Mali. The capital is Dakar (pop. 300,000).

SEOUL, capital of South Korea, on the Han River. Pop. (1960) 2,400,000. A religious and cultural centre, it manufactures metallurgical products and textiles.

SERBIA, a federated republic of Yugoslavia and former kingdom in southeast Europe. Pop. (1960) 7,593,000; area 33,930 sq. miles. It consists of plains in the north and rugged mountains in the rest of the country. The principal crops are grain, sugar-beet, grapes, tobacco and rice. Livestock raising is important in the highlands. Natural resources consist of timber, coal, lead, zinc, silver, lignite and copper. Under Stephen Dusen, Serbia ruled most of the Balkans. After the Battle of Kossovo (1389) it came under Turkish domination and was constantly in revolt. After an uprising in 1804—16 led by Karageorge and Obrenovich, Serbia became an autonomous principality and was thereafter torn by dynastic rivalries between the members of these two families, exacerbated by Russian and Austrian interference. In 1882 it became an independent kingdom. In the Balkan Wars (1912—13) Serbia doubled its territory. Serbia's refusal to accept Austria's outrageous demands following the assassination of Archduke Francis Ferdinand at Sarajevo in 1914 was the pretext for the Austro—German alliance, starting the First World War, in which it was overrun by Austrian and Bulgarian troops. After the war it became the nucleus of the Serb-Croat-Slovene kingdom (1918). The capital is Belgrade (pop. 542,000). See Yugoslavia.

SERVOMECHANISM, a device by which a low power input is highly amplified (often hydraulically) to a predetermined quantity of output, any error being corrected by feedback (q.v.); in control engineering (see Automation) the principle is applied to the control of the positioning of a work-piece, or the velocity of a machine, etc.

SEVASTOPOL, a port and city of the Ukrainian S.S.R., on the Black Sea, U.S.S.R. Pop. (1962) 169,000. It is an industrial centre with shipyards and a naval base. It fell to British, French and Turkish troops after a 349-day siege in 1855. In 1941—42 it held out for 250 days against German attacks.

SEVEN WONDERS OF THE WORLD, in the ancient world, were traditionally the Pyramids of Egypt, the Hanging Gardens of Babylon, the Temple of Diana at Ephesus, Phidias' statue of Zeus at Olympia, the Mausoleum at Halicarnassus in Asia Minor, the Colossus of Rhodes and the Pharos lighthouse at Alexandria.

SEVEN YEARS WAR (1756—63), the war waged by Frederick the Great of Prussia and Britain against Austria, France and Spain. The struggle resulted in the recapture of Silesia from Prussia and in the triumphal emergence of Britain as a colonial power in Canada and India, after Wolfe's capture of Quebec and Clive's victory at Plassey.

SEVILLE, a city in Spain, on the Guadalquivir River. Pop. (1960) 450,213. A communications and industrial centre, it is a major river port. There are many remains of the Moorish occupation and it is noted for its magnificent cathedral (1402). It manufactures textiles and chemicals. Capital of the Vandal empire, it became a flourishing centre in the subsequent Moorish period.

SEYCHELLES, a British colony in the Indian Ocean consisting of 92 islands and islets. Pop. (1960) 41,425; area 156 sq. miles. The principal products are copra, guano and spices. Fishing is important. The capital is Victoria on the main island of Mahé.

SHACKLETON, Sir Ernest (1874—1922), British Antarctic explorer. In 1909 he came within 111 miles of the South pole, the nearest until then, and discovered the location of the South magnetic pole.

SHAKESPEARE, William (1564—1616), English poet and dramatist. Born in Stratford-on-Avon into a family of prosperous tradesmen and farmers, he was probably educated at Stratford Grammar School. Little is known of his early life. In 1582 he married Anne Hathaway, eight years his senior. A few years later he was working in a London theatre, and must soon have begun adding to and altering plays, as in 1592 he was already being attacked as a jack-of-all-trades by a rival playwright. About this time he came under the patronage of the young Earl of Southampton, to whom he dedicated his early poems *Venus and Adonis* and *The Rape of Lucrece*. By 1594 he was a member of London's leading company of actors, the Lord Chamberlain's (later the King's) men, for whom he wrote his plays. By 1597 he was prosperous, able to buy a good house in Stratford, the owner of the Globe and the part-owner of the Blackfriars Theatre. Between 1610 and 1612 he seems to have retired to Stratford, where he died. His contemporaries describe him as a gentle and convivial soul who frequented the Mermaid Tavern with Ben Jonson and others.

The chronology of the plays is much disputed, but the greatest probably fall into the following periods: 1594—95, *Romeo and Juliet*, *Midsummer Night's Dream*, *Merchant of Venice*, *Richard* II, *Henry* IV, *Henry* V; 1599—1604, *Julius Caesar*, *Hamlet*, *Othello*, *As You Like It*, *Twelfth Night*; 1605—08, *Lear*, *Macbeth*, *Antony and Cleopatra*; the *Sonnets* were published, in mysterious circumstances, in 1609, and *The Tempest* in 1611.

The qualities of England's greatest poet that have excited the greatest admiration are the richness of his Elizabethan vocabulary, with its wealth of imagery and metaphor, his lyric poetry, his creation of so wide a range of immortal characters depicted with such subtlety and insight, and his illumination of the major themes which preoccupy thinking man — the problem of good and evil (e.g. in *Julius Caesar* and *Macbeth*), the fall from greatness to disaster (e.g. *Othello* and, supremely, in *Lear*) or the nature of kingship (in *Henry* IV and *Henry* V). The place of Shakespeare in literature was defined by Matthew Arnold: 'Others abide our question. Thou art free.'

SHANGHAI, a port and city in Kiangsu, eastern China, near the estuary of the Yangtze River. Pop. (1958) 7,100,000. The largest city in China, it is a financial, commercial and industrial centre. Its manufactures include metallurgical products, chemicals, textiles, foodstuffs and paper. Capture of the city by Chinese Communists in 1949 eliminated all foreign interests.

SHANNON, see River.

SHANTUNG, a province in eastern China, on the Yellow Sea. Pop. (1957) 54,030,000; area 56,447 sq. miles. Except for mountains in the central peninsula, it is mostly fertile plain. Grain, silk, fruit, livestock, coal, copper, iron and lead are its principal products. The province played a significant role in Chinese history, and before the First World War was leased in part to Germany. The capital is Tsinan.

SHASTRI, Lal Bahadur (1904—), Indian politician. During a lifetime's active political career, he held a wide variety of ministerial offices between 1948—64. He was elected Indian Prime Minister in 1964, following the death of Nehru (q.v.).

SHAW, George Bernard (1856—1950), Irish dramatist and critic. He wrote intellectual comedies and philosophical plays with a moral. His works include *Candida*, *Mrs Warren's Profession*, *Man and Superman*, *Pygmalion*, *Heartbreak House*, *Major Barbara*, *St Joan*, and

John Bull's Other Island. He received the Nobel Prize for literature in 1925. The witty prefaces to his plays are as important as the plays themselves. His early musical criticism had great merit, and it was he who popularised Ibsen in England. His interests were very varied including Lamarckism, vivisection, vaccination, vegetarianism, spelling reform, Shakespearean criticism, and so forth.

SHEFFIELD, a city and county borough, West Riding, Yorkshire, England, at the junction of the Sheaf and Don rivers. Pop. (1961) 493,954. The principal English cutlery centre since the 14th century, it is also a major steel manufacturing city. Industries include naval equipment, hydraulic presses, rails, axles, instruments, firearms, leather, paper and chemicals. Silver-plating, electro-plating and type-founding are important.

SHELLEY, Percy Bysshe (1792—1822), English poet. A radical thinker, and ardent supporter of political freedom and social justice, he was in constant difficulties with authority. The last four years of his life were spent in Italy, where he wrote his famous philosophical poems *Prometheus Unbound* and *The Cenci.* Other important works are *Alastor*, *The Revolt of Islam*, the elegy *Adonais* on the death of Keats and the lyric drama *Hellas*, but he is most widely known for his odes, such as those to Autumn, the West Wind and a Skylark.

SHENYANG (Mukden), a city in Liaoning, northeast China. Pop. (1956) 2,290,000. It is connected by rail to Port Arthur, the Trans-Siberian Railway, Peking and Korea. One of China's principal engineering centres, it manufactures heavy machinery, cables and electrical equipment, besides having a wide range of lesser industries. It was the Manchu capital until they invaded China in the 17th century.

SHERATON, Thomas (*c.* 1751—1806), next to Chippendale the most famous English furniture designer and cabinet-maker. His slender forms and sweeping curves were characteristic, and his extensive use of satinwood differentiated his furniture from most of that which had preceded it. He designed many beautiful sideboards and bookcases, and the variety of the backs and legs of his chairs produce an impression of lightness and grace that has never been surpassed. The remarkable series of volumes of designs for furniture which he published during the last sixteen years of his life were not a commercial success and he lived in extreme poverty.

SHERIDAN, Richard Brinsley (1751—1816), Irish dramatist and politician. His most famous comedies are *The Rivals*, *The School for Scandal* and *The Critic.* He became a member of parliament in 1780 as an ardent Whig of no great ability, and held minor offices from time to time.

SHETLAND ISLANDS, an island group northeast of the Orkneys, forming a separate county of Scotland. Pop. (1961) 17,809; area 551 sq. miles. Of the 100 islands, 27 are inhabited, the largest being Mainland. Fishing and the raising of livestock, including the Shetland pony, are important. Fine knitted goods are manufactured. Oats, barley, potatoes and turnips are grown. The chief town is Lerwick.

SHINTOISM, the Chinese name, meaning 'the way of the gods', given by Chinese Buddhist missionaries to the primitive religious beliefs they found in Japan in the 6th century. Later the name was applied to the combination of

Buddhism, emperor worship, ancestor and nature worship which became the Japanese state religion until 1945.

SHIP CANALS, The most important ship canals are the Suez Canal (1869) 101 miles long and 197 ft wide, and the Panama Canal (1914), 50 miles long and 300 ft wide, both of which have shortened sea routes by immense distances. Improvements to the St Lawrence Seaway (q.v.), completed in 1958, enable ocean-going vessels of up to 9000 tons to reach Duluth, Minnesota. Other ship canals include the Kiel (1895; 150 ft wide), Manchester (1894; 120 ft) and Corinth (1893; 72 ft).

SHIPS, the first of which we have any knowledge was a Minoan ship of the 3rd millennium B.C. A model sailing ship was found in Tutankhamen's tomb (1300 B.C.). The Viking long-ship, with one square sail, high bow and stern and very little freeboard, was used on voyages to Iceland and America. The first decked ship was Henry VII's *Great Harry*, square rigged, with a high poop and a displacement of 1500 tons. Steam propulsion was introduced at the beginning of the 19th century, at first auxiliary to sail, with paddle-wheel propulsion. A paddle-wheeled ship crossed the Atlantic in 1838. Various types of screw propulsion were tried from 1836. By 1840 iron had replaced wood, and the first steel hull was built in 1858. The *Great Eastern* (1859), designed by Brunel, was nearly 700 ft long, with a displacement of 18,900 tons. Parsons's steam turbine appeared in 1897, followed by ships fired by oil instead of coal, the German diesel ships of the 1920s, and the gas turbine in 1956. The first nuclear-powered merchant ship, the U.S.S. *Savannah*, made her maiden voyage in August 1962. After the Second World War the most important class of ship became the oil-tanker; the Japanese built one which, with a displacement of 69,000 tons, could carry over 100,000 tons of oil.

SHIRAZ, a city in southern Iran. Pop. (1956) 169,088. A trade centre in a region producing grapes, cereals and sugar-beet, it is known for its wine, carpets and brocades. It is beautifully situated on a plain 5000 ft above sea-level, surrounded by mountains.

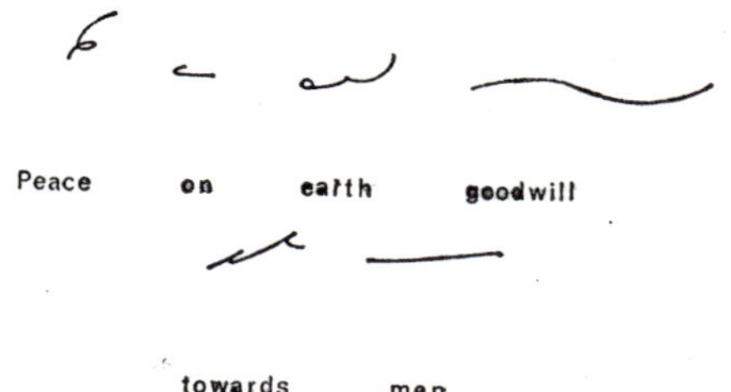

Shorthand-writing (Gregg) with 'translation'

SHORTHAND, a system of rapid writing using symbols for the purpose of recording speech. The two most popular systems are Pitman and Gregg, the first using shading to differentiate between characters. In 1912 an Irish stenographer, Ward Stone, invented the stenotype machine for recording dictation accurately according to a phonetic system of spelling.

SHOSTAKOVICH, Dmitri (1906—) Russian composer. His works include symphonies (especially fine are the Fifth, Seventh, and Tenth), operas, ballets, piano pieces, and music for motion pictures.

SHOW JUMPING, like riding, has enjoyed an immense increase in popularity in recent years, no doubt aided by television programmes. Entrants individually complete a circuit of varied jumps, including water-jumps, walls, double fences, etc. Faults are awarded for falls, touching or displacing obstacles and refusing, and there is often a time limit, with bonus points for speed. At some shows there is a competition in dressage, i.e. horsemanship, or the art of training a horse in obedience, balance, etc., a development from the *haute école* or highly schooled training for which the Spanish Riding School in Vienna is famous. Displays of show jumping are given at the International Horse Show, Dublin, the International Horse Show and the Horse of the Year Show, both at the White City, London, the Royal Richmond Horse Show and the Royal Windsor Show.

SHROPSHIRE (Salop), a county in western England. Pop. (1961) 297,313; area 1347 sq. miles. Hilly in the south and west, it has coalfields on the eastern border; cattle and sheep are raised and crops include cereals and sugar-beet. There are numerous Roman remains. The county town is Shrewsbury.

SIAM, see Thailand

SIBELIUS, Jean (1865—1957), Finnish composer. His work includes seven symphonies, a violin concerto, choral works, tone poems *(Finlandia)*, songs, and violin and piano compositions. The main theme of his more important works was the hostile forces of Nature; he was not very interested in human beings. Mystery surrounds Sibelius, for he composed much that was trivial, a little that was great, and almost nothing after 1925 that he did not burn.

SIBERIA, a region of the U.S.S.R. consisting of the Asian portion of the R.S.F.S.R. and the northern area of Kazakhstan republic (q.v.). It stretches from the Urals to the Pacific. Area 5,200,000 sq. miles. The chief rivers are the Ob, Yenisei and Lena flowing into the Arctic, and the Amur flowing into the Pacific. In the south it is crossed by the Trans-Siberian railway (1903), which runs from Chelyabinsk through Omsk, Novosibirsk and Irkutsk to Vladivostok. The climate varies from extreme cold (as low as −94 °F). in the northern tundras to burning heat in the arid steppes of the south. Gold is mined in quantity in the Lena valley and by Lake Baikal, and the diamond mines of Yakut are said to be as rich as those in South Africa. For industrial development see R.S.F.S.R. The area was originally inhabited by ancestors of the American Indian races who migrated across the Bering Strait, and then by Mongoloid peoples, Tungus, Yakuts, Samoyeds and others, who still form an element in the population, which has been increasingly Russianised since the first colonisation of the 18th century.

SICILY, an Italian island in the Mediterranean separated from the mainland by the Straits of Messina. Pop. (1961) 4,711,783; area 9926 sq. miles. It is mountainous in the north with plains and hills in the central portion; the volcanic Mt Etna is in the northeast. It produces wines, oranges, almonds, olives and corn. Fishing is important. There are deposits of building stone, salt, sulphur, borax, mercury and petroleum. Important since Greek and Carthaginian times, it became a Norman kingdom in the 11th century. Later, it passed to the German emperors and the house of Anjou. Intermittently, Sicily, together with Naples, was part of the Kingdom of the Two Sicilies and was usually under Spanish rule, except for a period under Napoleon. In 1861 Sicily was united with the Kingdom of Italy. The capital is Palermo (pop. 587,063).

SIDNEY, Sir Philip (1554—86), English soldier and poet. A favourite at the court of Elizabeth I, he wrote *Arcadia*, *Apologie for Poetrie*, *Defence of Poesie*, and the sonnet sequences *Astrophel and Stella*. He was governor of Flushing and was fatally wounded fighting the Spaniards at Zutphen.

SIERRA LEONE, an independent state in West Africa, and a member of the British Commonwealth. Pop. (1961) 2,400,000; area 27,925 sq. miles. Generally hilly, it produces palm products, rice, coffee, cocoa, groundnuts, ginger, kola nuts and cassava. There is fishing and livestock breeding. Iron, diamonds and chrome are mined. The country has palm-oil and rice mills. A British possession from 1787, it first served as a settlement for freed slaves. In 1961 it became independent. The capital is Freetown.

SIKHS, a religious sect founded in 1499 by Nanak in the Punjab, which for five hundred years had suffered from being on the invasion route of Moslem conquerors, who had already converted half the Hindu population to their religion. Himself under the influence of Mohammedan Sufi mysticism, Nanak preached that all the people of the Punjab were one, neither Hindu nor Moslem. The Sikhs were forced by persecution into becoming a highly militant community who harried not only the Mogul authorities, but Persian and Afghan invaders and the Marathas. They had a temple at Amritsar, a bible (the *Granth Sahib*), and were distinguished by their long hair and ritual articles of dress. The Sikhs were brave warriors, who fought two wars with the British in the 1840s and thereafter served with distinction in the Indian Army. At the Partition they were again involved in fighting with the Moslems, and many migrated to India from West Punjab when it came under Pakistani rule.

SIKKIM, a state under a Maharajah protected by India, in the eastern Himalayan foothills. Pop. (1961) 161,080; area 2745 sq. miles. Rice, maize, millet, apples and oranges are the principal crops. There are dense tropical forests. Sikkim lies on the main trade routes between India and Tibet; the people are mainly Nepalese and of the Buddhist religion. The capital is Gangtok.

SILESIA (Polish Śląsk; Czech Slezsko), a region in east central Europe on either side of the Oder River, mostly in southwest Poland, with a portion in north central Czechoslovakia. Cereals, fruit and sugar-beet are raised. There are rich deposits of coal, zinc, lead, arsenic and iron. Industries include metals, chemicals, armaments, textiles, cement, glass and ceramic ware. Part of Prussia from 1740 until the First World War, it was divided among Germany, Poland and Czechoslovakia in 1919. After the Second World War the former German portion was awarded to Poland. The leading Polish cities are Katowice and Wroclaw (Breslau).

SILICON, see Elements.

SILK, a strong fibre produced by silkworms in the process of providing themselves with a protective covering, or cocoon. The larva of the silk moth which feeds on mulberry leaves produces most commercial silk. According to the Chinese, the industry was founded there in 2600 B.C. Silkworm eggs were smuggled out of China and brought to Europe in A.D. 550.

SILO, an airtight building or tower in which compacted green crops (grass, lucerne, sugar-beet tops, pea-haulm, etc.) are stored for the winter feeding of livestock. Controlled fermentation takes place and the temperature has to be kept near an optimum level for good results. (Illustrated overleaf.)

SINGAPORE, independent state and member of the British Commonwealth, at the southern tip of the Malay peninsula. Pop. (1960) 1,652,000 (mainly Chinese); area 291 sq. miles. It is a naval, military and air base, and a major commercial centre. The principal exports are rubber, tin and coffee. Occupied by the British since 1819, it achieved independence in 1959. The capital is Singapore (pop. 953,000), which is the trade and commercial centre for Malaya and Indonesia, and manufactures rubber products, footwear and furniture.

SINKIANG-UIGHUR, an autonomous region in western China. Pop. (1957) 5,640,000; area 705,962 sq. miles. It is mountainous, with vast deserts, and produces cotton, cereals, wool and silk. There are petroleum deposits and other untapped mineral resources. The capital is Urumchi (Tihwa).

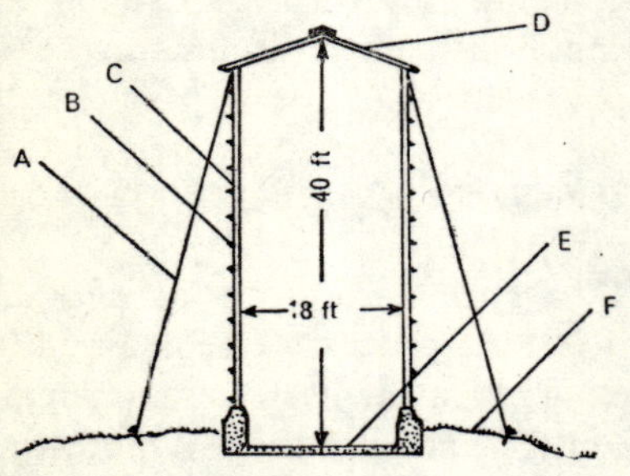

Silo (section). The type used for corn ensilage
A. Anchor B. Iron bands C. Creosoted staves D. Roof E. Concrete base F. Ground level

SINN FEIN, an Irish nationalist party (the name meaning 'ourselves alone') which was founded by Arthur Griffith in 1905, and played a major role in the establishment of the Irish Free State (1921).

SITWELL, Edith (1887—1964), English poet and critic. Her work, which is generally rhetorical, includes *The Mother and Other Poems*, *Gold Coast Customs*, *Green Song*, *The Song of the Cold*, and *The Canticle of the Rose*. Her brother Osbert (1892—) wrote an autobiography in five volumes, satirical poetry and novels; and her brother Sacheverell (1897—), art criticism and travel books.

SKIN, a protective covering of the body which serves as an organ of sensation, breathing and regulation of body temperature; it also absorbs and secretes. The skin consists of two basic layers, the dermis or true skin and the overlying epidermis. The dermis is attached to underlying areas by the subcutaneous tissue. Nails, feathers, hair, hoofs, beaks and horns are modifications of skin.

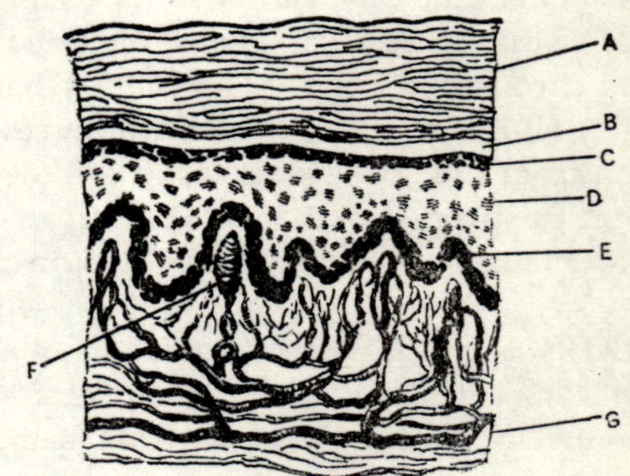

Human skin tissue
A. Corneal layer B. Stratum lucidum C. Stratum granulosum D. Stratum mucosum E. Stratum germinativum F. Nervous papilla of corium G. Blood vessels and nerves

SKYSCRAPER, an unusually tall building constructed on a steel frame. Congestion, lack of space in cities, and the invention of the lift hastened its development. The Empire State Building in New York is 1472 ft in height.

SLAVERY, an institution found in many early societies, originally supplied by prisoners of war; ancient Greece and Rome were dependent on it. A modified form of slavery was feudal serfdom, under which a serf was not free to leave his master, although he could not be sold and his master was obliged to provide him with land and a livelihood. Serfdom died out in England in the 13th century, in France with the Revolution and in Russia not until 1861.

Arabs were the leading slave traders, carrying them from East Africa to the Middle East and India; slavery was a recognised Mohammedan institution and indigenous in Africa, where wars were often merely slave-raids. The Spanish and Portuguese were the first Europeans to join in, exporting slaves from West Africa in the 15th century, first to their own countries and then to the West Indies and America. The English entered the trade in 1562 (Hawkins), and were followed by France, Sweden and Denmark, all with governmental support. By the 18th century the number of slaves who survived the Atlantic passage reached 100,000 a year.

To the Quakers belongs the honour of at last arousing the public conscience in England. Wilberforce, Clarkson, Zacchary Macaulay and others persuaded parliament to accept gradual abolition of the trade in 1792, and the abolitionists were supported by Pitt, Burke and Fox; in 1811 slave trading became a felony. Other countries followed suit and after the American Civil War Lincoln declared slavery illegal in 1865. It now survives only in Saudi Arabia.

SLAVS, a very large ethnic group speaking closely related Indo-European languages, usually classified as East Slavs (Russians, Ukrainians), South Slavs (Bulgars, Serbs, Croats, Slovenes) and West Slavs (Wends, Czechs, Slovaks, Moravians, Poles, Silesians and Pomeranians). For hundreds, and perhaps thousands, of years they kept out of harm's way, being a peaceable people, in inaccessible places such as the Pripet marshes and the Carpathians, but in about the 5th century they were forced to start on their widely dispersed migrations to the regions they now occupy. They are remarkable for their strong sense of nationhood, which has caused them to be a permanent nuisance to all their would-be rulers.

SLEEP, a state in which the organism withdraws from normal phenomena in its environment. Sensitivity, metabolic rate, pulse beat, respiration, blood pressure and muscular tension are diminished. Sleep enables the body to rebuild its stores of energy and replace worn-out cells and is induced by relaxation and fatigue. Recent researches indicate that dreams are an essential accompaniment, that if a person is prevented from dreaming his health suffers. On the other hand long hours of deep sleep are not essential, and much of the malaise that accompanies insomnia is due either to unnecessary worry about the imagined effects of loss of sleep or to the worry which led to it. An Italian, Dr Pavoni, is said not to have slept for 60 years, and used to specialise in taking night calls.

SLOANE, Sir Hans (1660—1753), British physician and naturalist. As physician to the Governor of Jamaica, he collected 800 new species of plants. His library of 50,000 volumes, several thousand manuscripts, coins, pictures and curios formed a beginning of the British Museum.

SLOVAKIA, a part of Czechoslovakia. Pop. (1949) 3,816,037; area 18,902 sq. miles. Consisting mostly of the Tatra group of Carpathian Mountains, it is largely agricultural, producing wheat, maize and grapes. Stock breeding is important. Industries include oil refining, textiles, metallurgy and chemicals. It was a German-sponsored 'independent' state from 1939—45. Bratislava (Pressburg) was the capital, and, under the name Pozsony, was capital of Hungary from 1541—1784.

SLOVENIA, a federated republic of Yugoslavia. Pop. (1960) 1,598,000; area 6266 sq. miles. Mostly mountainous, it has valuable forests. Livestock raising and dairy farming are important. Grain and fruit are cultivated. There are deposits of iron, coal, mercury, lead, zinc and alumina. Industries include metal smelting, especially of iron and steel. Textiles, glass, cement and foodstuffs are manufactured. The capital is Ljubljana (pop. 155,000).

SMETANA, Bedrich (1824—84), Czech composer, pianist and conductor. He composed operas *(The Bartered Bride)*, chamber music, a series of symphonic poems *(My Country)*, and piano pieces.

SMITH, Adam (1723—90), Scottish political economist. He is remembered chiefly for his *Wealth of Nations*, a work on economic theory based on developments before the Industrial Revolution and the emergence of large-scale business enterprises. It laid the basis of economics as a social science.

SMOKING, the use of tobacco for smoking originated among the aborigines of the western hemisphere and was introduced into England in the 1560s, spreading rapidly. Pipes and cigars were the first forms of smoking. Smoking is habit-forming and recent world-wide experiments have proved that it is a major factor in the development of lung cancer and other malignant diseases.

SMOLLETT, Tobias (1721—71), Scottish picaresque novelist. His best work is *Humphrey Clinker*. He also wrote several novels of adventure at sea, including *Roderick Random* and *Peregrine Pickle. Travels to France and Italy* gives a wonderful picture of the insular Smollett abroad — and hating it.

SMUTS, Jan Christiaan (1870—1950), South African statesman, philosopher and soldier. He was an outstanding Boer Commando leader in the South African War. An advocate of Anglo-Boer co-operation, he later headed various ministries in the Union of South Africa, commanded forces against German South West Africa during the First World War, and was a member of the Imperial War Cabinet. He was premier from 1919—24 and from 1939—48. In 1941 he was created field-marshal. Smuts was an active supporter of the League of Nations and of the United Nations. In philosophy he believed in creative evolution, expounded in *Holism and Evolution* (1926).

SMYRNA, see Izmir.

SNOW, Sir Charles, Baron (1905—), English novelist and scientist, appointed Parliamentary Secretary to the Ministry of Technology in 1964. Author of the *Strangers and Brothers* novel sequence, he also wrote *The Two Cultures* (1962) in which he put forward the view that Western society is increasingly divided into two camps, the scientists and the literary intellectuals, who do not understand each other's outlook.

SOAP, a cleansing substance made from a caustic alkali (potash or soda) and acids present in animal or vegetable fats. Soap removes dirt by causing the oils in the greasy particles to separate into tiny globules which are carried off by water, by lowering the surface tension of water, and by sucking the soiling matter off in foam. Soap is known to have been used in Ancient Greece.

SOCIALISM, a term covering widely divergent political and economic theories all of which have in common opposition to capitalism, the removal of social and economic inequalities, the taking over by the state of at least some basic industries and services (the traditional phrase is 'the means of production, distribution and exchange'), a planned economy (as opposed to *laissez-faire*), the abolition of colonialism, and in general the subordination of individual to community interests. To a Communist, Socialism is a clearly defined transitional stage on the way to true Communism (q.v.) and the Socialism of Western Europe is unworthy of the name.

The term was first used of Robert Owen's experimental 'village of co-operation' at New Lanark in 1834, dismissed by Marx as Utopianism; the idea goes back many centuries and was developed by French thinkers before the Revolution; the organisation was mainly the work of German Socialists in the 19th century. The British Fabian movement adopted an even more cautious approach through the political education of intelligent public opinion. British Socialism, based on trade union support, proceeds by a limited programme of nationalisation and the provision of social securities and wider educational opportunities.

SOCIOLOGY, the study of the origin, development and nature of human societies and institutions. It is concerned with all the general group activities of man and all phenomena which make man a social being. The great problem of this young science has been to discipline itself to restrict its operations to the scientific, objective study of facts, eschewing all temptations to indulge in ideological speculation.

SOCRATES (469—399 B.C.), Greek philosopher. Though he himself left no written works, his life and teachings are fully recorded by his pupil, Plato. Socrates was made (406) one of the Senate of Five Hundred in Athens, but was subsequently sentenced to death on a charge of impiety and corrupting the young. His method was to get to the root of a matter by question and answer (dialectic), gradually eliminating the inconsistencies and irrationalities in his hearers' views and assumptions, and assisting them to arrive at the truth — acting, as he said, as a midwife at the birth of true ideas.

SODIUM, see Elements

SOFIA, capital of Bulgaria. Pop. (1959) 671,192. On an upland plain, it is a railway and industrial centre, producing foodstuffs, leather, silk, textiles, tobacco, chemicals and engineering products. An old city, it was under Turkish domination from 1382 till 1878. The Church of St Sophia dates from the 6th century.

SOIL EROSION, the removal of the top layer of fertile soil by the action of wind and rain, aggravated by drought, when the wind blows away the powdery soil, and over-cultivation, especially on unterraced sloping ground. Soil erosion caused immense damage in the prairie states of the U.S. in the 1930s, forming 'dust bowls'; common in Asia and Africa.

SOLAR SYSTEM, the sun and all the heavenly bodies that move round it in nearly circular orbits, and in nearly one plane. These bodies are the nine planets and their satellites, the asteroids (most of which lie between the orbits of Mars and Jupiter), comets, meteors and particles of matter.

SOLINGEN, a city in North Rhine-Westphalia, West Germany, on the

Wupper River. Pop. (1960) 168,455. It is a manufacturing centre famed for its iron and steel industry and its cutlery.

SOLOMON, King of Israel from *c.* 973—*c.* 933 B.C. The son of David and Bathsheba, he extended the borders of Israel. He burdened his country with harsh taxation to pay for the extravagances of his semi-Oriental court and for grandiose buildings, such as the Temple. He married a daughter of the Pharaoh of Egypt, and was said to have been the father of Menelek, King of Abyssinia, by the Queen of Sheba. Heathen practices were introduced by his foreign wives. At his death, and as a direct result of his misrule, civil war broke out which ended in the permanent partition of Israel into the Kingdom of Judah in the south and the kingdom which retained the name of Israel in the north.

SOLOMON ISLANDS, an island group in the South Pacific. The northern islands are an Australian trusteeship territory; the largest island is Bougainville (pop. 1961 56,330; area 4100 sq. miles). The southeastern islands are a British protectorate (pop. 114,350; area 11,500 sq. miles); the largest island is Guadalcanal (area 2500 sq. miles) and the most populous is Malaita (pop. 46,000). The islands are all mountainous and produce bananas, pineapples, sweet potatoes, cocoa, copra, timber, trochus shell and kauri gum. They were the scene of heavy fighting against the Japanese, who occupied them in the Second World War.

SOMALIA, a republic in East Africa, on the Indian Ocean. Pop. (1961) 1,990,000; area 246,200 sq. miles. It consists mainly of an elevated plateau sloping down towards the coast and is mostly stony, dry land. Devoted primarily to stock raising, it produces bananas and cotton. It was formed in 1960 by the merger of the British protectorate of Somaliland and the Italian colony of Somalia. It is predominantly Moslem. The capital is Mogadishu.

SOMALILAND, FRENCH, a colony on the Gulf of Aden, East Africa. Pop. (1961) 81,000; area 8900 sq. miles. The principal occupation in this desert region is stock raising. Coffee, hides and salt are produced. The capital, Djibouti, is a leading port for the interior.

SOMERSET, a county in southwest England, on the Bristol Channel. Pop. (1961) 598,556; area 1620 sq. miles. It is ringed with hills (Exmoor, Quantocks, Mendips and Blackdown), the central plain being devoted mainly to sheep and cattle farming. Fruit growing and fishing are important. There are deposits of building stone, slate and clay. Industries are few, and include textiles, copper and iron products, bricks, cider and paper. There are numerous Roman remains. The county town is Taunton.

SOOCHOW (Wuhsien), an ancient city and port in Kiangsu, eastern China. Pop. (1960) 474,000. A communications centre on the Grand Canal, it is traversed by canals running through the city. Trade and the manufacture of engineering products and textiles are leading pursuits. It was formerly a treaty port.

SOPHOCLES (*c.* 495—406 B.C.), Athenian dramatist. He wrote over a hundred plays, of which only seven survive; these include *Ajax*, *Antigone*, *Oedipus Rex*, *Electra*, *Philoctetes* and *Oedipus Coloneus*. He took over Greek drama from Aeschylus, whom he defeated in the dramatic contest in 468, and developed it with assurance and skill, having none of the doubts about the role of the gods in human destinies that were felt by his successor, Euripides, who defeated Sophocles in 441. His characters face a choice between duty to the state and duty to the gods, and only in *Philoctetes* is there an element of psychological conflict in the mind of the hero. In 440 Sophocles served as a general under Pericles in the Samian War.

SOUL, the human spirit in man, reflected in his intelligence, will and personality, as opposed to the material body. By some Christian writers the immaterial side of man is divided into two parts, the spirit and the (lower) soul, the seat of intelligence or mind.

SOUND, waves of vibratory motion through a medium, e.g. air. All sound waves travel at a speed of 1130 ft per second at 68°F., slowing down at lower temperatures and increasing in speed as the temperature rises. Sound waves can be reflected, refracted or diffracted. The human ear can perceive sound-waves vibrating between 20 and 20,000 times a second, the equivalent of 10 octaves; a child can probably hear up to 40,000, but this figure is reduced steadily throughout life; in his forties a man of average hearing has the upper limit reduced by about 160 a year, which reduces the appreciation of music and leads to difficulties in distinguishing sounds, particularly the initial consonants of unfamiliar words and names. A mouse squeaks at about 100,000 c.p.s (cycles per second — vibrations per second); a bat at up to 150,000 c.p.s. Sound is measured in decibels (intensity) or phons (loudness). Water is a good conductor of sound; an explosion off western Australia was picked up by a hydrophone in Bermuda 223 minutes after it occurred.

SOUTH AFRICA, Republic of, an independent state. Pop. (1960) 15,982,664, including 3,067,000 Whites; area 472,685 sq. miles. Mostly plateau, except for a narrow coastal area in the south-eastern portion, it is traversed by two east-west mountain ranges separated by depressions. The principal crops are wheat, barley, oats, mealies (maize), potatoes and Kaffir corn. Tobacco, sugar-cane, fruit and vegetables are also cultivated. Livestock breeding, whaling, fishing and viticulture are important pursuits. There are rich deposits of gold, diamonds, coal, copper, tin, asbestos, manganese, platinum and chrome. The leading industries are foodstuffs, metals, clothing, chemicals, machinery, textiles and electrical appliances. What was until 1961 the Union of South Africa was formed in 1910 by the union of the provinces of the Cape of Good Hope, Natal, the Transvaal and the Orange Free State. A little over half the white population are of Dutch descent (Boers) and live mostly in the interior and in the north. Dutch settlers first came to South Africa in 1652. British settlers arrived in the first quarter of the 19th century. The chief bone of contention between the British and the Boers was the question of slavery, abolished by Britain in 1833. Between 1835—37, about 10,000 Boers *(Voortrekkers)* struck out for the north and established a number of independent republics. Friction between Boers and British mounted and, after a series of incidents, the Boers declared war in 1899. Their defeat marked the annexation of all their territories by Britain in 1902. South Africa became a republic and withdrew from the British Commonwealth in 1961. The country's principal problems are the continued friction between the two elements of the white population, and the Boer-dominated government's policy of *apartheid.* The administrative capital is Pretoria (pop. 422,590) and the legislative capital Cape Town (745,942). Other leading cities are Johannesburg (1,110,905), Durban (655,370), Port Elizabeth (270,815).

SOUTH AMERICA, the continent in the southern portion of the Western Hemisphere, between the Atlantic and the Pacific. Pop. (1959) 137,000,000; area 6,889,000 sq. miles. About 3200 miles wide and 4600 miles from north to south, it consists of the Andes Mountains along the entire west coast, the Guiana highlands in the northeast, Brazilian highlands in the east and the Patagonian highlands in the south, all being interspersed with plateaux. There are lowlands along the coasts and flanking the three great rivers, the Amazon, Orinoco and Paraná. The climate is essentially warm but varies with the altitude and proximity to the equator. Vegetation is dense and varied. There are numerous deposits of gold and silver, nitrates, manganese, tin, copper, coal, iron and petroleum. The original inhabitants ranged from the highly civilised Incas to tribes in various stages of primitive culture. European settlers were mostly Portuguese in the east and Spaniards elsewhere. Negro slaves from Africa added still another racial element. Politically South America consists of Argentina, Bolivia, Brazil, British Guiana, Chile, Colombia, Ecuador, French Guiana, Paraguay, Peru, Surinam, Uruguay and Venezuela.

SOUTHAMPTON, a seaport and county borough, Hampshire, England, on a peninsula between the Itchen and Test rivers and the English Channel. Pop. (1961) 204,707. One of the best natural harbours in Great Britain, it is a port of call for the largest passenger ships. The leading industries are shipbuilding and engineering.

SOUTH AUSTRALIA, a state of the Australian Commonwealth, in the south central portion. Pop. (1961) 969,258; area 380,070 sq. miles. Consisting of two north-south mountain ranges in the southeast, it is a vast plain in the northwest with extensive barren areas. The principal crops are cereals, hay, vines and fruit. Livestock, mainly sheep, is an important item. The leading minerals are iron, uranium, pyrite, gypsum, salt, building stone and coal. The chief manufactures are machinery, metals, foodstuffs, sawmill products, clothing, paper, textiles and chemicals. The capital is Adelaide (pop. 587,656 with suburbs).

SOUTH CAROLINA, a south Atlantic state of U.S.A. Pop. (1960) 2,382,594; area 31,055 sq. miles. Low-lying in the east, it forms part of the Piedmont Plateau in the western half and is mountainous in the northwest. The chief crops are maize, oats, wheat, peaches, cotton, groundnuts and tobacco. Livestock is raised. There are deposits of kaolin, cement, clay and other non-metallic minerals. The state is becoming increasingly industrialised and produces textiles, asbestos, and sawmill and steel products. First settled in 1670, South Carolina was one of the original 13 states. It seceded from the Union in 1860 and precipitated the Civil War by an attack on Federal troops in Fort Sumter in April 1861. The capital is Columbia (pop. 97,433).

SOUTH DAKOTA, a north central state of U.S.A. Pop. (1960) 680,514; area 77,047 sq. miles. Divided by the Missouri River, it is an undulating plain in the east and barren rough plateau in the west. Predominantly agricultural, South Dakota produces cereals, flax seed and potatoes. Livestock raising and dairy farming are important. Rich in gold, it has deposits of silver, gypsum, beryl, iron uranium and feldspar. The leading industries are meat packing and butter. Settled in the mid-19th century, it became a state in 1889. The capital is Pierre (pop. 10,108). The largest city is Sioux Falls (65,024).

SOUTH-EAST ASIA TREATY ORGANISATION (S.E.A.T.O.), a collective-security organisation formed in 1954 by an alliance between Australia, New Zealand, Pakistan, the Philippines, Thailand, France, Britain and the U.S.A., later joined by Cambodia, Laos and Vietnam. Bangkok is the headquarters of the organisation.

SOUTH WEST AFRICA, nominally, mandated territory administered by the Republic of South Africa, on the Atlantic. Pop. (1961) 525,064; area 318,261 sq. miles. Consisting of a desert coastal strip and barren areas in the east, it is mostly arid plateau, good only for livestock grazing. Karakul sheep are an important source of income. Cheese and butter are exported. There are deposits of diamonds, copper, tin, vanadium concentrates, lead, tungsten, iron, manganese, salt and lithium. Annexed by Germany in 1888, it was occupied by troops of the Union of South Africa in 1915. The capital is Windhoek (pop. 1960 36,049).

SOVIET UNION, see Union of Soviet Socialist Republics.

SPACE FLIGHT. Man's first venture into space was made when a member of the U.S.S.R. air force, Major Yuri Gagarin, travelled in orbit round the earth on April 12, 1961. In a capsule weighing 4¾ tons he completed the orbit in 89 minutes, travelling at heights between 109 and 187 miles. The first American to emulate this feat was Col. Glenn in February 1962; and the first woman was a Russian, Valentina Tereshkova, in June 1963. The difficulties that had to be overcome were the launching by multi-stage rocket (see Rockets), the problems of travelling in a condition of weightlessness, and the accuracy which had to be achieved in order to bring the space craft down in a predetermined area so that its occupant could be rescued in time. All these have been satisfactorily solved. The next step is the construction of a launching platform in orbit round the earth, from which space ships can be launched on more distant journeys. While it has been found that the danger from meteorites had been exaggerated, the danger of exposing man for prolonged periods to cosmic radiation, and still more to solar radiation, has yet to be assessed. Experiments have been carried out in the U.S.A. and the U.S.S.R. in preparation for projects to put a man on the moon, but expenditure is immense, and scientific value debatable.

SPAIN, a state in southwest Europe, in the Iberian peninsula. Pop. (1960) 30,128,000; area 189,855 sq. miles. Mostly plateau, it is crossed by mountain ranges and river valleys. It is predominantly agricultural, producing grain, olives, potatoes, vegetables, sugar-cane, sugar-beet, tobacco, grapes, citrus and other fruit. Livestock, lumbering and fishing are important. Silk, honey, wine and turpentine are produced. Rich in minerals, Spain has deposits of coal, lignite, iron, copper, potash, lead, manganese, sulphur, zinc, mercury and ilmenite. The chief manufactures are textiles, metallurgical products, chemicals, paper, cork, cement, pig-iron and steel. From 201 B.C. Spain was part of the Roman Empire and grew prosperous until overrun by barbarians early in the 5th century A.D. In 711—14 the Moors swept away the weak Visigoth kingdom and occupied almost the entire country. Under them, Spanish civilisation outstripped that of most of Europe. The

Moors, however, divided into several small states in 1031, were finally driven out in 1492 by the Christian kingdoms of Aragon, Castile and Navarre. Aragon and Castile were united by the marriage of Ferdinand of Aragon and Isabella of Castile in 1469, and their conquest of Granada and Navarre brought all Spain under their rule in 1512. This was a period of exploration and the acquisition of great wealth abroad and oppression at home. Ferdinand's grandson, the Hapsburg Charles v of the Holy Roman Empire, made Spain a powerful absolutist state. The decline of Spain as a world power began with the defeat of the Spanish Armada sent by his son, Philip II, to destroy England. Disastrous wars with the British and French in the early part of the 19th century further impoverished the country and made it eager for liberal reforms. In 1820 Spain lost her American colonies, and in a war with the U.S.A. in 1898 she lost Cuba and the Philippines. The last king of Spain was Alfonso XIII, who reigned from 1902 until his deposition in 1931. From 1923—30 General Primo de Rivera made himself dictator with the king's sanction. The republican régime established in 1931 was again victorious at the 1936 elections, and introduced reforms. It was opposed by the Church, the army and land-owning groups, who supported a rebellion by Gen. Franco. After a civil war of great ferocity (July 1936—March 1939) in which Franco had Nazi and Fascist support, he established a corporate state. Neutral in the Second World War, Spain favoured, but did not assist, the Axis. The capital is Madrid (pop. 1,975,666). Other large cities are Barcelona (1,503,312), Valencia (543,736) and Seville (424,757).

SPANISH SUCCESSION, War of the (1701—14), a war precipated by Louis XIV's acceptance of the Spanish throne on behalf of his grandson, Philip of Anjou (Philip v). Spain ruled the Spanish Netherlands (Belgium), the Balearic Islands, Milan, Naples and Sicily, and the prospect of the French controlling the western seaboard of Europe and the trade route through the Mediterranean alarmed the British and Dutch; while the Austrians, who in previous negotiations had been promised a share of the Spanish dominions, were equally upset. Imprudently, Louis by his first acts exacerbated the situation, and even recognised the Old Pretender as James III of England, and so war broke out. In campaigns in the Spanish Netherlands, Marlborough won four great victories, Blenheim (1704), Ramillies, Oudenarde and Malplaquet (1709); an Allied invasion of Spain was unsuccessful, although Madrid was twice occupied. At sea Gibraltar and Port Mahon (Minorca) were taken. The Treaty of Utrecht (1713) ended French supremacy in Europe. While Philip v retained the Spanish throne, Austria was given the Spanish Netherlands, Milan, Naples and Sicily; Louis abandoned his championship of the Stuarts and recognised the Protestant succession in England; England kept Gibraltar and Minorca, and won Nova Scotia and Newfoundland.

SPECTRUM. The visible spectrum is the band of colour produced by bending a beam of white light through a prism. The colours range from red, with the longest wavelength, to violet, with the shortest, in the sequence of a rainbow. The invisible or electromagnetic spectrum consists of infra-red, heat, and radio waves beyond the red; and of ultra-violet, X-rays, gamma rays and cosmic rays beyond the violet.

SPEECH. Speech sounds are formed by a breath of air causing the vocal cords in the throat to set up vibrations

A photograph of the S.S. *Great Eastern* (1858), one of the most controversial ships ever built and a commercial failure. She had not only sails and paddles, but a four-bladed propeller in addition.

Photo: Science Museum, London

By the mid 19th century iron started to be used in ship construction. This Portuguese iron-clad, the *Vasco da Gama* (1867), was a fighting ship propelled by sails and twin screws (propellers).

Photo: Crown copyright. Science Museum, London

The S.S. *Cutty Sark* (1869) was the last Clipper ship. Clippers were sleek, very fast grain transporters that relied solely on vast sail area for propulsion. *Photo: Crown copyright. Science Museum, London*

The First World War saw the virtual end of sailing ships and introduction of all-metal, heavily armed and powerful fighting ships. Illustrated is an early battleship, the U.S.S. *Indiana*.

Official U. S. Navy Photograph

A model of the British First World War battleship, H.M.S. *Barham*, 1914.

Photo: Lent to the Science Museum, London, by John Brown Co. Ltd

which produce resonance in the mouth. See Language, Phonetics.

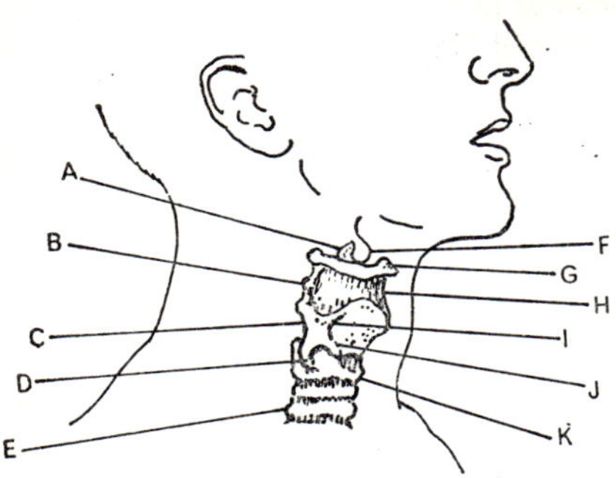

Human vocal system (Larynx)
A. Epiglottis B. Cartilage triticea C. Superior cornu of thyroid cartilage D. Inferior cornu of thyroid cartilage E. Trachea F. Back of tongue G. Hyoid bone H. Thyro-hyoid membrane I. Superior tubercle J. Oblique line K. Cricoid cartilage

SPENCER, Herbert (1820—1903), English philosopher. Though trained to be a civil engineer, he left this profession in 1845 to devote himself to writing. An agnostic, and having no appreciation of the arts or literature, he tried to fit sociology, ethics and psychology into a rather mechanical evolutionary framework; he believed that human progress was inevitable, and therefore opposed all governmental interference.

SPENSER, Edmund (*c.* 1552—99), English poet. His greatest work is the *Faerie Queene*. He first attracted attention with *The Shepheardes Calendar*. His other works include *Astrophel, Amoretti* and *Epithalamion*.

SPEZIA, LA, a city in northern Italy, on the Ligurian Sea. Pop. (1961) 121,191. It is a commercial port and naval base with shipyards, oil refineries, an arsenal and maritime industries.

SPINOZA, Benedict (1632—77), Dutch philosopher. The son of a Portuguese Jew, he incurred the suspicion of the Jewish community in Amsterdam and was excommunicated (1656), but he continued his philosophical studies and supported himself by grinding lenses. His greatest work (published posthumously) is the *Ethics*, in which he set out a series of axioms (in what Hume described as a gloomy region of hideous hypotheses) from which he deduced a tidy, serene, pantheistic philosophy based on the acceptance of Necessity.

SPIRITUALISM, a cult which holds that it is possible to communicate with disembodied spirits, a belief which has existed from ancient times. The earth is surrounded by a series of concentric spheres of increasing purity, through which the spirits of the dead progress until they are finally absorbed in God. It is during its stay in the lowest sphere that the spirit can be contacted through a medium at a séance.

SPITSBERGEN (Svalbard), a group of islands belonging to Norway in the Arctic Circle. Pop. (1956) 4276; area 24,294 sq. miles. There are deposits of coal, iron, zinc, phosphates, copper and asbestos. The islands are used as a sealing and whaling station. The Russian population outnumbers the Norwegian.

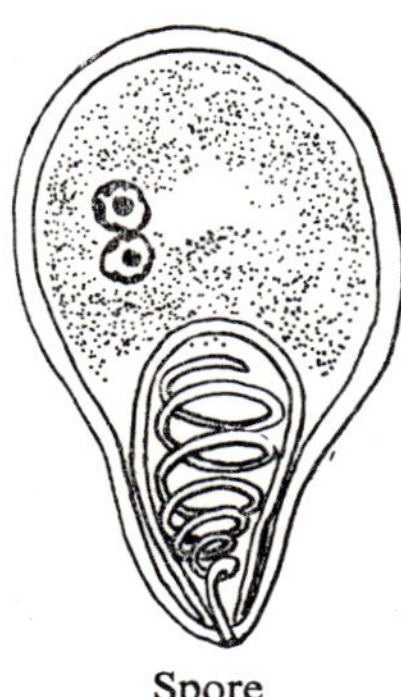

Spore

SPORE, a simple, asexual, usually one-, but sometimes multi-celled reproductive body, generally of microscopic size, which becomes detached from the parent and is carried in huge numbers by wind, water, etc., to a new site to give rise to a new individual, directly or indirectly. This form of reproduction is found in protozoa, bacteria and among plants, particularly ferns, fungi and algae.

SQUASH RACKETS, a game developed at Harrow in the 1850s from Rackets, a similar game played in a larger court. It is a fast racket-and-ball game played in a closed court. Only the server scores, but the service changes after a winning shot by the receiver. The ball is taken on the volley or after one bounce. If a player impedes an opponent there is a let.

STAËL, Madame Germaine de (1776—1817), French novelist and critic. Exiled by Napoleon, she returned to France in 1815. Her works include the novels *Delphine* and *Corinne*; and in *De l'Allemagne* she introduced the French to German literature.

STAFFORDSHIRE, a Midland county of England. Pop. (1961) 1,733,887; area 1153 sq. miles. Hilly in the north, it is rich in coal deposits throughout, with iron in the south. Cattle raising and dairy farming are important. Predominantly industrial, it brews beer and manufactures iron and steel products, chemicals, footwear and textiles. The Black Country towns of Wednesbury, Willenhall, Wolverhampton, West Bromwich and Walsall are in the south. In the north is the famous Potteries district around Stoke-on-Trent, and Izaak Walton's Dovedale forms the northeast boundary with Derbyshire. The county town is Stafford.

STAMP COLLECTING, about 20 years after the issue of the first postage stamp in England (1840), stamp collecting was well on its way to becoming an international hobby. Collectors are especially interested in rare issues, errors, and stamps with unusual circumstances surrounding their appearance. Stamps are distinguished from each other by difference in design, colour, means of separation from one another, printing methods, types of paper, types of gum and variations in cancellation if the stamp has been used. King George V was a great philatelist, and the collection now owned by Queen Elizabeth II is probably the most valuable in the world.

STANLEY, Sir Henry Morton (1841—1904), British African explorer. He wrote several books about his journeys during which he found David Livingstone, whom he joined in exploring Lake Tanganyika. He made extensive trips in Central and East Africa and discovered the Ruwenzori Mountains and Lake Albert Edward.

STAR, a heavenly body giving off its own light, such as the Sun. The naked eye can see about 5000 stars in the entire sky. Most stars are single but about 20% of those observable are double stars revolving around a common centre of gravity. There are also large clusters moving together through space. Stellar energy is believed to arise from a chain of nuclear explosions, by which it is estimated that the Sun, for example, may lose four million tons a second. A nova is a star that flares up, its brightness increasing up to a millionfold in a matter of days, and then fades; in supernovae the brightness may increase one thousand millionfold. Stars do not vary very greatly in mass, but the range of density is enormous and some giant stars are several hundred times the size of the Sun. Temperatures at the surface range from 1200°C. in red stars to 100,000°C. in the bluest.

STAR CHAMBER, an English tribunal which from 1487 had special powers to try offences against the Crown. It became a powerful weapon in the hands of unscrupulous monarchs (e.g. Charles I) and was abolished in 1640.

STARCH, a white granular substance found in all green plants, chiefly in cereals, peas and potatoes. Insoluble in water, it is the plant's reserve food supply. Most commercial starch is produced either from potatoes, rice, maize or corn. It is used chiefly for food, laundry stiffening, the preparation of glucose and dextrin, and in printing and finishing various cloths. Starch is a carbohydrate.

STATE DEPARTMENT, the executive department of the U.S. government in charge of foreign relations. It was established in 1789 and has the Secretary of State at its head.

STATISTICS, quantitative data arranged in a form suitable for analysis. The facts or information are expressed in numbers which represent certain tendencies and relationships. Statistics make it possible to form judgments based on summaries of large bodies of facts.

STEAM-ENGINE, a machine for utilising the expanding power of steam in order to convert it into mechanical energy capable of doing work. In the most common type, steam applies pressure alternately to either side of a piston which is forced back and forth inside a hollow cylinder. The piston is connected to a revolving flywheel. In a steam turbine, which provides greater power, steam under pressure causes a rotor to revolve. James Watt was a leading inventor of the steam-engine.

STEEL, a compound of iron and carbon which is stronger, finer, harder, smoother and more elastic than iron. It rusts less easily and takes a higher polish. Steel is often combined with other metals to form alloys adapted to various special purposes. While high-carbon steel is harder, low-carbon steel is the more widely used. The Bessemer process makes it possible to produce large quantities of steel quickly from cast iron.

STEELE, Sir Richard (1672—1729), English essayist and politician. He was the founder of *The Tatler* (1709—11) and *The Guardian* (1713), and with Addison was one of the leading contributors to *The Spectator* (1711—12).

STENDHAL (Henri Beyle; 1783—1842), French novelist. A worshipper of great men of action, he served in the retreat from Moscow, and his disappointment in hopes of high office under Napoleon was but the first of the many frustrations of his career. Writing in a plain and precise style, he focused his talent on human character and the analysis of motive, in novels with plots verging on the absurd, such as *Le Rouge et le noir* and *La Chartreuse de Parme.*

STEPHEN (*c.* 1094—1154), King of England. A grandson of William I, he usurped the throne on the death in 1135 of Henry I, the prior claims of whose daughter, Matilda, he had previously acknowledged. Matilda landed in England in 1139, and the subsequent intermittent civil war ended in the Treaty of Wallingford (1153) by which, under pressure of the Church, he yielded place to Henry II, son of Matilda.

STEPHENSON, George (1781—1848), English engineer. Long years of experiment led to his construction in 1825 of a steam locomotive capable of hauling 38 carriages of passengers and freight at a speed of 12 miles per hour. The

Rocket followed in 1829. His name is associated with the founding of England's railway system.

STERNE, Laurence (1713—68), English novelist. He took holy orders and became a prebendary of York in 1738. He wrote humorous, cynical but rather brutal novels, such as the rambling *Tristram Shandy*, in which the famous Uncle Toby refights his Flanders campaigns and tries to evade Widow Wadman, and *A Sentimental Journey*, based on his travels in France.

STETTIN, see Szczecin.

STEVENSON, Robert Louis (1850—94), Scottish writer. In 1888 he settled in Samoa, where he died. He wrote verse, books of travel *(Travels with a Donkey in the Cevennes)*, essays *(Virginibus Puerisque)*, short stories *(New Arabian Nights)*, the children's favourite pirate book, *Treasure Island*, and many novels — *The Strange Case of Dr Jekyll and Mr Hyde*, *Kidnapped*, *The Black Arrow*, *The Master of Ballantrae* and, his best though unfinished, *Weir of Hermiston*. He also collaborated with his stepson in *The Wrong Box*.

STOCK EXCHANGE, a market for dealing in stocks and shares, which are held or obtained by the jobbers. Brokers are the middlemen, remunerated by brokerage (commission), between the public and the brokers. The chief buyers tend to be institutions such as insurance companies and pension funds. Dealings are in government securities; debenture and preference stock, which are fixed-interest loans, the latter with the right to pass the dividend if the company fails to earn an adequate profit; and Ordinary shares, the holders of which are theoretically the owners of the company, with rights to a share in the profits, if there are any, after all prior-ranking payments, such as preference dividends, have been made. In times of inflation interest rates are raised and the value of fixed-interest securities falls correspondingly, although they have the advantage of providing a fixed income, however great the fall in capital value. Ordinary shares, on the other hand, attract buyers because of the prospect of capital appreciation, the profits from which are not taxed if the shares are held for more than six months. Trustees may now invest up to 50% of their funds in Ordinary shares.

STOCKHOLM, capital of Sweden, on the Baltic Sea. Pop. (1960) 807,600. Situated in beautiful natural surroundings on a series of islands linked by numerous bridges, it is the country's intellectual centre, with museums, libraries, a university and the Nobel Institute. Much of the old town, Staden, was destroyed in a series of fires, but its narrow streets still have many old gabled houses; and the 13th-century St Nicholas Church, the House of the Nobles (17th century) and the Royal Palace (1697—1754) are among the surviving buildings of note. Stockholm produces iron and steel products, beer, silk, tobacco, chemicals, porcelain and leather.

STOKE-ON-TRENT, a city and county borough in Staffordshire, England. Pop. (1961) 265,506. It is a railway centre, famous for its porcelain and earthenware manufactures. The city consists of Arnold Bennett's 'five towns' of Stoke, Burslem, Hanley, Longton and Tunstall which, with Fenton, were united in 1910.

STONEHENGE, a prehistoric structure of upright stones on Salisbury Plain, Wiltshire, England. There are numerous theories seeking to explain its origin which probably dates back to about 1845 B.C. (Illustrated opposite.)

STRADIVARI (Stradivarius), Antonio (*c.* 1644—1737), Italian violin-maker. An expert craftsman, he produced over 1100 violins of various types which have never been surpassed in tone; he was one of a family of violin-makers, working at Cremona.

Stonehenge (aerial view from the southeast)

STRAITS SETTLEMENTS, a former British colony on the Malay peninsula, comprising Singapore, Malacca, Penang and Labuan (a small island off North Borneo); it was dissolved in 1946.

STRASBOURG, capital of Alsace and of the Bas-Rhin department, eastern France, on the Ill and Rhine Rivers. Pop. (1962) 233,549. An old city with medieval streets of carved timbered houses, it has a fine Gothic cathedral with a famous astronomical clock, and the Château des Rohans, now a museum. A communications and industrial centre, it manufactures heavy steel equipment, automobiles, chemicals, metal and leather goods, tobacco, paper and *pâté de foie-gras*. Occupied by Germany from 1870—1918 and from 1940—44, it is now the seat of the Council of Europe.

STRATFORD-ON-AVON, a town in Warwickshire, England. Pop. (1961) 76,847. The birthplace of William Shakespeare, it is a tourist centre, with a memorial library and the Royal Shakespeare Theatre.

STRAUSS, Johann (1825—99), Austrian composer and conductor, one of a family of composers of light music. He composed dance music and operettas which gained unusual popularity. His waltzes include *The Beautiful Blue Danube*, *Artist's Life*, *Tales from the Vienna Woods* and the *Emperor Waltz*. His most successful operetta was *Die Fledermaus.*

STRAUSS, Richard (1864—1949), German composer. A leader of the Romantic school, he composed operas *(Elektra, Salome, Ariadne auf Naxos)* and the musical comedy *Der Rosenkavalier*, tone poems *(Don Juan, Don Quixote, Till Eulenspiegel)* and songs.

STRAVINSKY, Igor (1882—), Russian composer and pianist. He composed ballets *(The Fire Bird, Le Sacre du printemps, Petrushka)*, operas, *The Symphony of Psalms*, chamber music and a piano concerto. In his later work Stravinsky has attempted to exclude all emotional expression from his music. He went to live in the U.S.A. in 1937, and there wrote his first full-length opera, *The Rake's Progress.*

STREAMLINING, a method of designing vehicles in order to lessen the resistance of the medium (air, water) through which they are travelling. Of value only at high speeds, its ideal shape is that of a raindrop.

STREPTOMYCIN, an antibiotic substance made from a fungus-like organism growing in the soil. It is effective in the treatment of tuberculosis, urinary infections, diphtheria, pneumonia and meningitis. Selman A. Waksman discovered it in 1944.

STRIKE, an organised stoppage of work by a group of employees for the purpose of forcing the employer to act in accordance with their wishes. Interference with the conduct of an enterprise is calculated to exert pressure on the employer by causing him financial losses. In Britain the Taff Vale judgment (1906) ruled that trade union funds were liable for damages caused to employers by trade disputes, but this was reversed shortly afterwards by a new Trade Dispute Act. The General Strike (1926) led to a Trade Union Act which outlawed the general strike and restricted sympathetic strikes. After the Second World War trade union leaders tried to curb an outbreak of unofficial strikes, i.e. those not authorised by the unions concerned. The number of working days lost through strikes in a year averaged 2.7 million in 1927—45, 2.0 million in 1946—49, and was 8.4 million in 1957.

STRINDBERG, August (1849—1912), Swedish playwright, novelist, poet and short-story writer. The greatest Swedish dramatist, he wrote about 70 plays, including *The Father*, *Miss Julie*, *Gustavus Vasa* and *Erik XIV*. *The Red Room* and *Married* are among his best novels.

STRONTIUM-90, a radioactive isotope of strontium (see Elements). It is a fission product of nuclear explosions and tends to collect in bones because of its similarity to calcium.

STUART, House of, a royal family of Scotland and England, descended from a Norman baron, Fitzalan, who came to England with William the Conqueror. Walter Fitzalan was appointed by David I (1124—53) to be hereditary Steward of Scotland, and his successors took the name of Steward or Stewart (altered by Mary Queen of Scots to the French spelling, Stuart). The first Stewart King of Scotland was Robert II (1371), whose descendant James VI of Scotland became James I of England in 1603.

STUTTGART, capital of Baden-Württemberg, West Germany, on the Neckar River. Pop. (1960) 637,400. A publishing centre, it produces textiles, machinery, chemicals and engineering products. It has an old castle, a cathedral and a famous library.

SUBMARINE, a naval vessel capable of submerging and proceeding below the surface of the water. Conventional submarines are powered by diesel and electric motors. They are fish-shaped and can fire torpedoes and guided missiles without surfacing. The craft is submerged by letting water into ballast tanks. Nuclear-powered submarines can circumnavigate the earth twice without surfacing. Britain's first atomic submarine, H.M.S. *Dreadnought*, was launched in 1960.

SUDAN, a republic in northeast Africa, on the Red Sea. Pop. (1961) 12,109,000; area 967,501 sq. miles. Consisting of desert in the north and fertile and thick forest in the south, it is traversed by the Nile. The principal products are cotton, gum arabic, groundnuts, sesame and hides and skins. Livestock raising is important. There are deposits of gold, iron, copper, manganese and other minerals. Formerly an Anglo-Egyptian condominium, it became independent in 1956. The capital is Khartoum (pop. 1961 117,685). The largest city is Omdurman (113,551).

SUEZ CANAL, a waterway across the Isthmus of Suez linking the Mediterranean and Red Sea. The total length from Port Said in the north to Suez in the south in 101 miles. At a depth of 33 ft, its minimum width is 197 ft. The average time of passage is 16—20 hours. Opened to traffic in 1869, it was chiefly British-owned and French-administered until nationalised by Egypt in 1956. Subsequent Anglo-French military action to regain control of the Canal was checked by American and U.N. intervention.

SUFFOLK, a county in East Anglia, England, on the North Sea. Pop. (1961) 472,665; area 1482 sq. miles. Consisting mostly of low rolling hills, it is predominantly agricultural. The principal crops are wheat, barley and oats. Livestock raising and dairy farming are important. Agricultural implements are manufactured. The county is divided administratively into East and West Suffolk. The county town is Ipswich.

SUGAR, a group of carbohydrates having a sweet taste, including glucose, fructose, maltose, and the common sucrose to which the term is usually applied. Sucrose occurs in sugar-cane, sugar-beet, sugar maple and sorghum. It is a white, crystalline solid very soluble in water and has 1800 calories per pound, which makes it an important source of energy as it is readily digested and used by the body.

SULLIVAN, Sir Arthur (1842—1900), English composer. An organist and choirmaster, he composed incidental music, an opera, a cantata and oratorios. He is famed for his collaboration with W. S. Gilbert in the writing of comic operas. His works include *Onward! Christian Soldiers* and *The Lost Chord.*

SULPHA DRUGS (Sulphonamides), synthetic drugs for the treatment of general bacterial infections. First introduced in 1936, some of their uses have been taken over by antibiotics. They are effective against pneumonia, venereal diseases, boils, carbuncles, dysentery, cerebrospinal meningitis and wound infections. Different sulphonamides are required for particular types of infections. Their clinical use was discovered by Gerhard Domagk in 1932.

SULPHUR, see Elements.

SUMATRA, an island in Indonesia. Pop. (1961) 15,700,000; area 161,612 sq. miles. Mountainous in the west with a hot moist climate, it produces coffee, rubber, sugar and rice. There are deposits of gold, petroleum, tin and coal. The principal cities are Palembang and Padang.

SUN, the central body in the solar system and the nearest star. It is about 93,000,000 miles away from the earth. Its surface temperature is about 6000°c. and its energy (light, heat and other radiation) is produced by the transmutation of hydrogen into helium in a nuclear chain-reaction (see Atom). The sun's diameter is 865,400 miles and it rotates once in about 27½ days. There are large spots on its surface which increase in size and number every 11 years.

SUN YAT-SEN (1867—1925), Chinese revolutionary. After practising as a physician he decided in 1892 to devote himself to freeing China from the Manchu emperors. He founded the first of many revolutionary organisations and spent his next 20 years in unsuccessful plots and in travelling in Japan, the U.S.A. and London (where he was kidnapped by Chinese Legation staff). In 1911 a *coup d'état* was successful; the emperor was deposed and a republic set up, and Sun Yat-sen was president for 45 days, after which he gave way to a military leader, Yüan Shih-kai. Yüan, however, disappointed his hopes by turning dictator; civil war broke out and Sun was defeated and went into exile. After the Russian Revolution, Sun turned to the Bolsheviks for help, and they sent him Borodin. He reorganised the Kuomintang and was again elected President, but this time of only a small area of southern China around Canton.

In 1925, already in an advanced stage of cancer, he went to Peking to try to reach an accommodation with the northern leaders, but died the same year, three years before the unification of most of China under Chiang Kai-shek. His widow, Mme Sun, one of the Soong sisters, became strongly Communist; her sister married Chiang Kai-shek.

SUNDERLAND, a city and county borough in Co. Durham, England, on the North Sea at the mouth of the Wear River. Pop. (1961) 189,629. It is a seaport, and a shipbuilding and coal-exporting centre. Manufactures include engineering products, textiles, rope, paper, glass, wire and chain cables.

SURINAM (Dutch Guiana), Netherlands colony on the north coast of South America. Pop. (1962) 330,000 (including 33,000 Bush Negroes and 5000 aboriginal Indians); area 55,143 sq. miles. It consists of a coastal plain and unexplored mountains and jungles in the interior. Rice, sugar and coffee are grown. There are valuable deposits of bauxite and gold. The capital is Paramaribo (pop. 118,000).

SURREALISM, a term used from 1922 for art which mirrors the subconscious mind. Surrealist pictures may consist of incongruous objects grouped together ('a sewing-machine and an umbrella on an operating table'); the depiction with photographic accuracy of, for example, a deliquescent watch (one of Dali's favourite subjects) against some absurd background; or an abstract painting with an irrelevant title, such as Paul Klee's *Twittering Machine*.

SURREY, an inland county in southeast England bordering on the Thames. Pop. (1961) 1,733,036; area 722 sq. miles. Much of the northeastern area is in Greater London. Grains, potatoes, vegetables and fruit are grown. Sheep raising and dairy farming are important. There are large residential areas. The county town is Guildford.

SUSSEX, a county in southern England, on the English Channel. Pop. (1961) 1,075,893; area 1457 sq. miles. The South Downs cross the southern part; the north and central portions are wooded, with extensive pasture lands. Livestock raising is important. Sugarbeet, cereals, hops, fruit and flowers are raised. The county is divided administratively into East and West Sussex. The county town is Lewes.

SWANSEA, a city and county borough in Glamorganshire, Wales, at the mouth of the Tawe River. Pop. (1961) 166,740 A metallurgical centre, its industries consist of tin-plating, copper smelting and refining, and zinc and nickel works. It is a port and distributing centre for oil, with storage facilities. Fuel oil and chemicals are also manufactured. The Mumbles is a residential suburb and seaside resort.

SWAZILAND, a British protectorate and enclave in the Republic of South Africa. Pop. (1960) 260,000; area 6704 sq. miles. Mountainous in the west, the land slopes downwards to the low veld on the eastern border. The principal crops are cotton, tobacco, maize, sugar, bananas, timber, pineapples, rice, tomatoes, groundnuts, beans, sweet potatoes and citrus fruit. Livestock raising is important. One of the largest asbestos mines in the world provides most of Swaziland's exports; there are also deposits of tin, barytes and coal. The capital is Mbabane.

SWEDEN, a kingdom in northwest Europe, on the Baltic Sea. Pop. (1960)

7,471,345; area 173,426 sq. miles. It consists of mountains in the north sloping down to a central lowland with many lakes and then to rocky plains with numerous forests. The principal crops are hay, sugar-beet, potatoes and cereals. Lumbering, fishing, livestock breeding and dairy farming are important. There are deposits of coal, iron, silver, lead, copper, zinc, manganese and gold. The leading industries are iron and steel production, engineering, machinery, metal goods, wood and paper, dairy products, textiles and chemicals.

Swedish history begins in 829 when Erik Edmundsson became ruler of the country. In the 10th century Sweden became Christianised. In 1397 the country was joined to Denmark and Norway. Gustavus Vasa established Sweden's independence in 1523 and laid the foundation of the modern state. In 1611 Gustavus Adolphus became king. He concluded peace with Russia, Poland and Denmark and perfected his country's administrative system. In the 17th century Sweden was the leading country in northern Europe. In 1700 Sweden was defeated in a war with Russia, Poland and Denmark, and lost territory. After the Napoleonic wars, Sweden and Norway were joined together under the new dynasty of Marshal Bernadotte of France, who became King Charles XIV. In 1905 the two nations separated. Sweden was neutral in both World Wars. The capital is Stockholm (pop. 807,909). Other large cities are Göteborg (400,814) and Malmö (225,660).

SWEDENBORG, Emanuel (1689—1772), Swedish philosopher, scientist and mystic. He made a number of important contributions to science — especially in the field of engineering and mining — and devoted the last 25 years of his life to religious studies. His followers founded a Church of the New Jerusalem, based on his teachings, claiming to be a development of Christianity.

SWIFT, Jonathan (1667—1745), Anglo-Irish satirical writer. His greatest work is his satire on mankind, *Gulliver's Travels*. He also wrote *The Battle of the Books* and *A Tale of a Tub*. Swift was dean of St Patrick's Cathedral in Dublin.

SWINBURNE, Algernon Charles (1837—1909), English poet. His best poems, of adventure, love and nationalism, are to be found chiefly in his *Atalanta in Calydon*, *Poems and Ballads* (1866) and *Songs before Sunrise*, inspired by Mazzini. In 1879 he went to live with Theodore Watts-Dunton at Putney, and thereafter wrote little of merit.

SWITHIN, St (*c.* 800—862), Bishop of Winchester. According to legend the translation of his remains (July 15, 971) was interrupted by a violent rainstorm, hence the superstition regarding rain on that day, which is not supported by meteorological records.

SWITZERLAND, a federated republic in central Europe. Pop. (1960) 5,298,000; area 15,944 sq. miles. Consisting mostly of a mountainous plateau enclosed by the Jura mountains in the northwest and the Alps in the south, it has many large lakes. The principal crops are cereals, potatoes, sugar-beet, vegetables, tobacco, fruit and grapes. Livestock breeding and dairy farming are important. Lumbering and the mining of salt, iron, manganese and aluminium are leading occupations. The principal industries are electrical engineering, textiles, chemicals, clocks and watches, beer and footwear. Switzerland is visited by at least two million tourists a year. French, German, Italian and Romansch are spoken.

Switzerland consists of 22 sovereign cantons.

Called Helvetia by the Romans, it was in ancient times a federation of fiefs of the Holy Roman Empire. In 1291 the cantons of Uri, Schwyz and Lower Unterwalden formed a defensive league whose scope was gradually increased so that in 1513 it consisted of 13 cantons. In 1648 Switzerland became independent of the Holy Roman Empire. From 1798—1803 it was occupied by French troops under the name of the Helvetic Republic. Napoleon restored its federal status in 1803. The Congress of Vienna in 1815 recognised the country's perpetual neutrality. In 1845 the Catholic cantons seceded and formed a separate union which lasted two years. The constitution of 1848 laid the foundation for Switzerland's political unity as a federated state. Switzerland was neutral in both World Wars. Geneva is the seat of the International Red Cross and the International Labour Organisation, and was the headquarters of the League of Nations. The capital is Berne (pop. 1961 166,100). Other important cities are Zürich (439,600), Basle (205,800) and Geneva (179,400).

SYDNEY, the largest city in Australia and the capital of New South Wales, on Port Jackson Bay. Pop. (1961) 2,181,211. Sydney has one of the finest harbours in the world, spanned by the Sydney Harbour Bridge (1932), carrying four lines of railway, six lanes of road, and two footpaths. The single span is 1650 ft. It is a commercial and industrial centre producing clothing, metals, machinery, transport equipment and foodstuffs. The city has a long seaboard, with such resorts as Bondi Beach.

SYNDICALISM, a semi-anarchist revolutionary labour movement aiming at the ownership and control of all industry by the workers through international federations of trade unions grouped by function and not by geography, and replacing state governments. These aims would be achieved not by political means but 'direct action' — by general strikes and violence. The movement had some influence in Europe, Argentina and Mexico before 1914, but lost ground to Communism, to which it is strongly opposed as being too authoritarian.

SYR DARYA, see River.

SYRACUSE, a city in central New York state, U.S.A. on Onondaga Lake. Pop. (1960) 216,038. It is a communications, educational and industrial centre. Industries include metal goods, engineering products, chemicals, electrical appliances and foodstuffs.

SYRIA, a republic in southwest Asia, on the Mediterranean. Pop. (1962) 5,500,000; area 72,234 sq. miles. It consists of a narrow coastal plain, western mountains, a dry rocky interior plateau and the valley of the Euphrates, which flows across it to Iraq in a southeasterly direction. Predominantly agricultural, it produces cereals, cotton, rice, sugar-beet, chickpeas, lentils, grapes and olives. Livestock breeding is important. The leading industries are foodstuffs, soap, cement, tanning, tobacco, textiles, clothing, brassware and glass articles. It is crossed by an oil pipeline from Iraq. Inhabited by the ancient Phoenicians, it was successively overrun by most of the old empires of the east. From 64 B.C. until A.D. 636 it was under Roman and Byzantine domination. It was ravaged by the Mongols in 1260 and laid waste in 1516 when it passed from the Egyptians to the Ottoman Turks, who ruled it until 1917. After the First World War it became a French mandated territory. In 1946 its proclamation as an independent republic was followed by several military *coups d'état*. Syrian forces participated in the invasion of Palestine in 1948, but suffered reverses. From 1958—61 Syria was dominated by Egypt in the United Arab Republic. The capital is Damascus (pop. 1960, 491,398). Other leading cities are Aleppo (483,083), Homs (157,754) and Hama (112,677).

SZCZECIN (Stettin), a city in Poland, on the Oder River. Pop. (1960) 269,000. It is a port and an industrial centre manufacturing metallurgical products, machinery and textiles. Until 1945 it was part of Germany.

SZECHWAN, a province in south central China. Pop. (1953) 62,303,999; area 144,996 sq. miles. A tableland enclosed by mountains and drained by the Yangtze, it produces cereals, sugar, tea, cotton and silk. There are deposits of coal, iron, petroleum and salt. The capital is Chengtu.

TABRIZ, a city in northwest Iran, on the Talheh River. Pop. (1956) 290,195. Situated 4400 ft above sea-level, it is surrounded by high mountains on three sides. It is a trade centre for dried fruits, rugs, leather, tea and textiles. It was at one time the capital of Persia, and has a famous Blue Mosque.

TADZHIKISTAN, a constituent republic of the U.S.S.R. in central Asia, on the Chinese and Afghanistan borders. Pop. (1962) 2,188,000; area 55,545 sq. miles. Much of the country consists of high mountain ranges, including the Pamirs, with deep valleys and semi-desert steppes in the north and west; it contains the tallest peak (Mt Communism, formerly Mt Stalin) in the U.S.S.R. Cereals, cotton, fruit and flowers are grown. Livestock breeding is important. There are deposits of gold, petroleum and coal. The capital is Dushanbe (formerly Stalinabad; pop. 260,000). The Tadzhiks speak a Persian dialect.

TAGUS, see River.

TAHITI, an island in French Polynesia, south central Pacific Ocean. Pop. (1956) 44,710; area 402 sq. miles. The most important of the Society Islands, it is mountainous with a tropical climate. Copra, pearls, mother-of-pearl and fish are the principal products. The chief town is Papeete.

TAIWAN, see Formosa.

TALLEYRAND-PÉRIGORD, Charles Maurice de (1754—1838), French statesman and diplomat. After helping in Napoleon's *coup d'état* of 1790 Talleyrand was appointed Minister of Foreign Affairs. In 1807 he began to intrigue against Napoleon who dismissed him in 1809. He represented France at the Congress of Vienna with great skill and took part in the restoration of the Bourbons, becoming (1815) once again Minister of Foreign Affairs under Louis XVIII, and ambassador to London under Louis Philippe.

TALLINN (Reval), capital of the Estonian S.S.R., on the Gulf of Finland, U.S.S.R. Pop. (1962) 305,000. It is a seaport, having shipyards and a manufacturing centre for metal goods and textiles. Tallinn was founded in 1219 and acquired from Sweden by Russia in 1710.

TAMERLANE (Timur-i-Lenk, 'Timur the Lame', Marlowe's Tamburlaine; 1336—1405), a Mongol conqueror, born in what is now Tadzhikistan, in 1369 made himself Sultan of Samarkand. Claiming, probably falsely, to be a descendant of Genghis Khan, he set out to rebuild a Mongol empire. Acting with the utmost ruthlessness, looting and killing on the grand scale, this future patron of arts and literature succeeded in conquering Turkestan, Mesopotamia, southern Russia and Armenia. He sacked Moscow, Baghdad, Damascus and Delhi, defeated the Golden Horde, captured the Ottoman Turk Sultan Bajazet at Ankara and received the submission of Egypt. He was on his way to conquer China when he died. His empire fell apart under his Timurid successors.

TAMPA, a city in Florida, U.S.A., on the Gulf of Mexico. Pop. (1960) 274,970. It is a communications, financial, commercial and industrial centre of West Florida. The leading industries are cigars, citrus fruit and vegetable canning. It is a port for shipping phosphates, and a popular winter resort, with a university.

TAMPERE, a city in southwest Finland. Pop. (1961) 128,898. It is an industrial centre situated near rapids providing hydro-electric power, and there are extensive textile mills. Manufactures include metal goods, hosiery, paper and pulp, leather and locomotives.

TANANARIVE, capital of the Malagasy Republic. Pop. (1960) 210,000. A commercial and communications centre, it has meat-preserving factories. It is the former capital of the Hova kingdom.

TANGIER, a city and port of Morocco, on the Straits of Gibraltar. Pop. (1960) 180,000. A commercial centre, it was an international zone from 1923—56.

American Howitzer tank

TANK, military, a self-propelled armoured vehicle having caterpillar traction and equipped with machine-guns and cannon. It is the basic element in a mechanised combat force, important for its mobility and fire and striking power. In combination with air units and attacking infantry, it is a powerful offensive. weapon. Tanks were first used by the British in France in 1916. The Centurion, developed by the British after the Second World War, weighs 50 tons.

TANTALUM, see Elements.

TANZANIA, The United Republic of, a republic in east Africa, and a member of the British Commonwealth. Formerly the republic of Tanganyika and the island state of Zanzibar, the republic was formed in 1964. Pop. 9,708,000; area 363,708 sq. miles. Predominantly agricultural, it produces sisal, cotton, coffee, cloves, coconuts, oil seeds, nuts, tropical fruit and tea. Livestock breeding is important. There are deposits of diamonds, gold, lead and mica. The capital is Dar es-Salaam (pop. 1957 128,732).

TAOISM, a Chinese religious philosophy which advocates a life of submission to the natural order of things, and rejects all forms of violence and compulsion. The basic work on Taoism is the *Tao Te Ching* and its leading exponent was the philosopher Lao-Tsze (6th century B.C.).

TAPESTRY, a form of patterned weaving either by hand or machine, using wool, silk or linen. This is woven on a loom which usually consists of a vertical frame, with heavy uprights holding a horizontal roller top and bottom on which the warps are stretched. There are many different types and weaving is a skilled and ancient art. Tapestry seems to have begun in Syria, but the earliest existing examples come from Egyptian tombs of around 1450 B.C.

TARANTO, a city and port in Italy, on the Ionian Sea. Pop. (1961) 191,515. It is a commercial and industrial centre, and has a naval base. Fishing for oysters and mussels is the chief occupation. The tarantula spider is found there.

TARTARS (properly Tatars), a name which has changed its meaning in the course of history. Originally the Mongols were called Tartars and Tartary was Turkestan. The Tartars of the U.S.S.R. are mainly non-Mongol, Mohammedan peoples of Turkish origin, divided into the Kazan Tartars on the Volga in the Tartar A.S.S.R., and the Krim Tartars of the Crimea.

TASHKENT, capital of the Uzbek S.S.R. on the Syr Darya, U.S.S.R. Pop. (1962) 1,002,000. It is the largest city and the economic and cultural centre of Soviet Central Asia. The leading manufactures are textiles, agricultural machinery, tobacco, leather, silk, steel, chemicals, foodstuffs, and sawmill products. Although it has a long history, Tashkent is now a fine modern city, with parks, wide avenues, a university and technical institutes.

TASMANIA, the smallest state of the Commonwealth of Australia. Pop. (1916) 350,332; area 26,215 sq. miles. It is an island consisting of a plateau with fertile valleys. The principal crops are hops, apples, grain, hay, peas and turnips. Livestock breeding and lumbering are important. Wool, butter, cheese and fish are leading products. There are deposits of zinc, copper, tungsten, lead, tin, gold and silver. Manufactures include metals, paper, woollen goods, timber, chemicals and foodstuffs. Discovered in 1642 by Abel Tasman, who called it Van Diemen's Land, it became a British settlement in 1803. The capital is Hobart (pop. 109,200, with suburbs).

TAWNEY, Richard Henry (1880—1962), English economist and educationist. Professor of economic history at the University of London, he also served as president (1928—44) of the Workers Educational Association. He was the author of numerous books on sociology and economics, including *The Acquisitive Society*, in which he became the first critic of the Affluent Society, and *Religion and the Rise of Capitalism.*

TAXATION, the compulsory payment made by individuals and organisations for the support of government activities according to existing laws. The funds thus collected may be spent as the authorities see fit, with no individual service or benefit to the taxpayer. Taxes are either direct, e.g. income tax, rates, licences, death duties, or indirect, e.g. customs duties, excise, government monopolies, and purchase tax. A more important distinction is that between taxation which must be paid, e.g. income tax, and that which can be avoided, i.e. by not buying the goods taxed.

TCHAIKOVSKY, Peter Ilyich (1840—93), Russian composer. Gifted with a talent for melody and orchestration, he composed symphonies *(Fourth, Fifth, Pathétique)*, concertos, ballets *(Nutcracker Suite, The Sleeping Beauty, Swan Lake)*, orchestral works (overture to *Romeo and Juliet*; *Francesca da Rimini*; *Marche Slave*), and operas *(Eugène Onegin, Queen of Spades)*. His *First Piano Concerto* and *Violin Concerto* are also popular favourites.

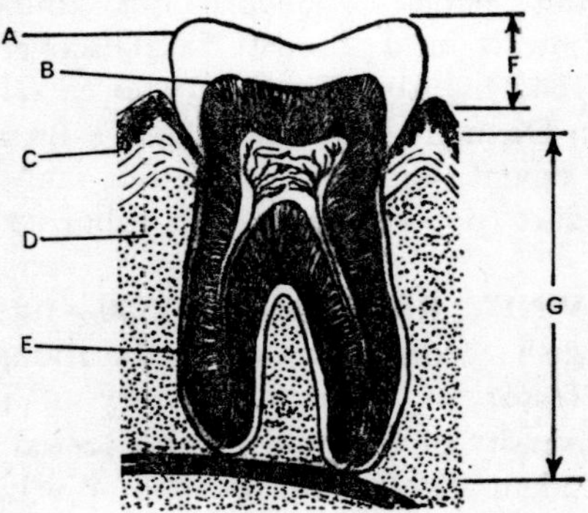

Human tooth (molar)
A. Enamel B. Dentine or ivory C. Gum D. Jawbone E. Cement F. Crown G. Root

TEETH, hard, calcified structures in the mouth for chewing food; they also serve as speech organs and improve the appearance. Man has a temporary set of 20 teeth in childhood, which are replaced by a permanent set of 32, of which 28 are formed by the age of 15. The principal parts of a tooth are the hard outer enamel, the less hard dentine beneath it, and the inner pulp, consisting of a mass of tissue, blood-vessels and nerves. The full complement of each side of each jaw, from front to back, is two incisors, one canine, two bicuspids and three molars, the last and smallest of which is known as the wisdom tooth.

TEHRAN, capital of Iran, on the southern slopes of the Elburz Mountains. Pop. (1956) 1,513,164. A commercial and industrial centre, it manufactures glass, brasswork, chemicals, textiles, tobacco products and foodstuffs. There are beautiful palaces, museums and a university in the city, which has been modernised since 1925.

TEL AVIV-JAFFA, a dual city and port in Israel, on the Mediterranean. Pop. (1961) 386,612. The largest city in the country and its cultural and economic centre, it has diverse industries. Jaffa's archaeological remains date back to prehistoric times. Tel-Aviv was founded by Zionists in 1909.

Telegraph-sending instrument

TELEGRAPH, a device for sending signals by wire over long distances. A single wire, plus the earth to complete the circuit, is used for making and breaking an electric current. Pressing a knob to close the circuit activates an electromagnet in the receiving instrument which produces a click. The period between clicks is a dot when short, and a dash when long. The Morse code utilises dots and dashes to form combinations representing the letters of the alphabet, numbers and special signals.

TELEMETRY, measurement at a distance. It is a system for recording and transmitting data collected in the upper atmosphere and outer space by means of radio apparatus, usually powered by solar batteries.

TELEPATHY, see Extra-Sensory Perception.

TELEPHONE, a device for transmitting sound by wire over a distance. Sound-wave vibrations directed into the mouthpiece compress carbon granules directly behind a diaphragm. The granules, actuated by an electric current, regulate its flow as their density is varied by the degree of compression. The receiver contains an electro-magnet which exerts pressure on a diaphragm in accordance with the pattern of vibrations sent by the device in the mouthpiece. The vibrations set up are heard as sound waves.

TELESCOPE an optical instrument to provide an enlarged image of a distant

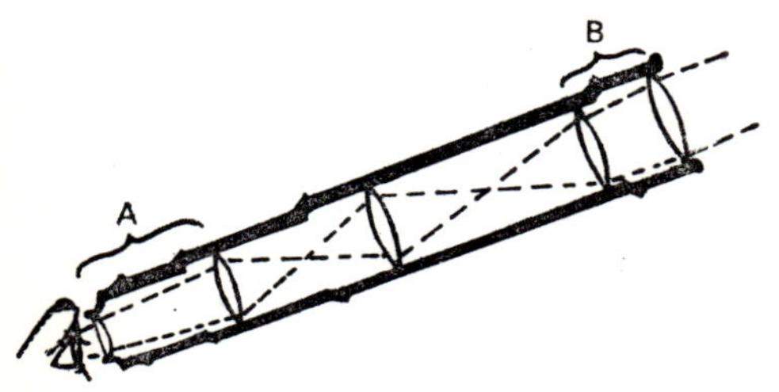

Simple telescope
A. Eyepiece lenses B. Objective lenses

object. A refracting telescope brings the object nearer at the far end of a tube by means of a lens and then magnifies it by means of an eyepiece. In a reflecting telescope, the light from the object is concentrated on a large concave mirror which reflects it to a magnifying eye piece or an instrument (camera, spectrograph, interferometer, etc.). A reflecting telescope is not limited as to size. The largest one, at the Mt Palomar observatory in California, has a 200-inch reflector and can photograph galaxies two thousand million light-years away.

TELETYPE (Teletypewriter), a device for typewriting at a distance on a telephone or telegraph circuit. Messages typewritten on a central keyboard are reproduced by receiving equipment in any number of places.

TELEVISION, a device for transmitting and receiving images by radio. An electronic beam scans a photographic image on a screen consisting of numerous light-sensitive cells and activates in them a current proportional to the quantity of light received. The receiving instrument reconstructs the original light pattern. It was first demonstrated by J. L. Baird in London in 1926. The B.B.C television service began in 1926. The first transatlantic picture was sent by the Telstar communications satellite in 1962.

TEMPERA, a method of painting in which egg yolk replaces oil in binding the pigments. The technique was known in the East long before oil painting. It produces a quick-drying, hard, matt surface.

TEMPLARS, see Knights Templars.

TEN COMMANDMENTS, see Decalogue.

TENNESSEE, a south central state of U.S.A. Pop. (1960) 3,567,089; area 42,244 sq. miles. From east to west it consists of mountains, foothills and lowlands. The principal crops are maize, cotton, tobacco and hay. Livestock breeding is important. Main minerals are coal, zinc and phosphate rock, copper, mica and building stone. Industries include iron and steel products, chemicals and knitted goods. First settled in 1757, it became a state in 1796. It was a member of the Confederacy from 1861—65. The capital is Nashville (pop. 170,874). Other large cities are Memphis (497,525), Chattanooga (130,009) and Knoxville (111,827).

TENNESSEE VALLEY AUTHORITY (T.V.A.), the federal corporation created in 1933 to control an imaginative scheme conceived by David Lilienthal and backed by President Roosevelt to rehabilitate the Tennessee Valley where, in an area about the size of England, some three million people lived in poverty on land ruined by deforestation, unskilled cultivation and consequent soil erosion. The area covered parts of Tennessee, Alabama, Kentucky, North Carolina and Georgia. A number of dams and lakes were created, floods controlled, navigability improved, hydro-electric power and irrigation water provided, fertiliser factories set up, improved methods of soil conservation taught and the land reafforested. Subsidiary benefits were the control of malaria and the provision of tourist attractions, including national parks. The scheme was a great success, but traditional American opposition to federal interference in state affairs has prevented similar schemes from being introduced elsewhere.

TENNYSON, Alfred, 1st Baron (1809—92), English poet and Poet Laureate from 1850—92. As early as 1827, in collaboration with his brother, he published his first volume of poetry. From 1828—31 he studied at Trinity College, Cambridge. Tennyson lived a quiet and secluded life on the Isle of Wight and later in Sussex. His *Poems* (1833) contained *The Lotus Eaters* and *The Lady of Shalott*. *In Memoriam* is a poem of religious despair, written on the death of his friend Arthur Hallam; *Maud* contains some beautiful lyrics but is not successful as a whole; the *Idylls of the King* were affected by the spirit of the age in which he lived, and were therefore immensely popular. Tennyson had an unerring feeling for the sound of words (as, for example, in *Ulysses*) and complete mastery of a wide variety of metres.

TERRY, Dame Ellen (1848—1928), English actress. She excelled in numerous Shakespearean roles and in plays by George Bernard Shaw, a close friend. Her letters to Shaw have been published.

TEUTONES, a Germanic tribe which, in the years 109—105 B.C., inflicted three defeats on the Romans and terrorised Gaul, but which was nearly annihilated by Gaius Marius in a battle (102 B.C.) near the modern site of Aix. They were only one of many German tribes, but for some unknown reason their name became synonymous with 'German'; its etymological connection with *Deutsch* is very doubtful.

TEUTONIC KNIGHTS, a military and religious order founded (1190) at Acre in Palestine by German Crusaders. The influence of the Knights declined after their defeat at Tannenberg (1410) at the hands of the Poles and Lithuanians. The order was suppressed by Napoleon but later revived in Austria.

TEXAS, a south central state of U.S.A., on the Gulf of Mexico and Mexican border. Pop. (1960) 9,579,677; area 267,339 sq. miles. Beyond a 50-mile-wide coastal strip there is a prairie belt with forests. The central portion consists of the Great Plains, with an arid plateau in the northwest and mountains in the southwest. The principal crops are

Aircraft carriers were developed for use during the Second World War. These vast, floating flight decks can transport a large number of fighting aircraft to any part of the world.

Photo: United States Information Service

The 45,000 ton luxury liner *Canberra*, the most modern liner afloat today.

Photo: P & O — Orient Lines

Nuclear power has now come to the world of ships. The American Polaris nuclear-powered submarine can remain underwater for two-month periods. Approximating a small battleship in size, it is capable of fast underwater speeds.

Photo: United States Information Service

The Olympic Games (q.v.) held every fourth summer are preceded by the Winter Olympics. Ski jumping from a special ramp over distances of around 90 metres is one exciting event.

Photo: Associated Press

Giant Slalom, fast and very skilful speed skiing down an obstacle-strewn mountainside.

Photo: Keystone Press

cotton, pecans, sorghum, grain, sweet potatoes, potatoes, citrus fruit, peaches and vegetables. There is extensive livestock raising. Texas is a leading state in the production of petroleum, natural gas and helium. There are deposits of lignite, cement, sulphur and building stone. Fishing and lumbering are important occupations. The main industries are oil refining, foodstuffs, chemicals, machinery, sawmill products, printing and publishing, transport equipment, clothing and textiles. The diversity of climate makes it an ideal region for holiday resorts. Explored by Spaniards early in the 16th century, it was first settled by them at the end of the 17th century. Texas was part of Mexico when the latter country won its independence from Spain in 1821. American settlers in Texas resented Mexican restrictive measures and declared their independence in 1836. In 1845 the Texans' request to become a U.S. state was granted. A boundary dispute with Mexico a year later was the immediate cause of the U.S.-Mexican war. Texas supported the Confederacy during the Civil War. The capital is Austin (pop. 186,545). The largest cities are Houston (938,219), Dallas (679,684), San Antonio (587,718) and Fort Worth (346,268).

THACKERAY, William Makepeace (1811—63), English novelist. The son of an East India Company official, he attended Trinity College, Cambridge, but did not prove to be an industrious student. In 1833 he lost the fortune he had inherited from his father and was forced to find the means of making a livelihood. In 1842 Thackeray joined the staff of *Punch* and rose to prominence with the publication of *Vanity Fair* (1847—8). His other best-known works are *Pendennis* (1850), *Henry Esmond* (1852), *The Newcomes* (1855). *The Four Georges*, a series of historical lectures, was also a success. His panoramas of English society of his time show keen observation and wit, with particular attention to snobbery and hypocrisy and great gifts of characterisation.

THAILAND, a kingdom in southeast Asia, on the Bay of Bengal and the South China Sea. Pop. (1960) 22,718,000; area 198,456 sq. miles. Mountainous in the north, it consists of a central alluvial plain and a plateau in the east. There are dense forests in the north and south. The principal crop is rice. Maize, rubber, tobacco, cotton, sugar-cane, groundnuts and sesame are raised. Livestock breeding, teak and bamboo are important. Tin and tungsten are mined and there are deposits of manganese, iron, rubies and sapphires. The leading industries are foodstuffs, tobacco and chemicals. Until 1932 Thailand (then known as Siam) was an absolute monarchy. The capital is Bangkok (pop. 1960 2,300,000).

THAMES, see River.

THEATRE, see Drama.

THEBES, the Greek name for the ancient capital of Egypt under the 11th Dynasty (2050—1850 B.C.) and the 18th—20th Dynasties (1580—1080), on the Nile. The largest collection of ancient Egyptian remains are in this area, now partly occupied by the towns of Luxor, Karnak, Medinet Habu and Dei el-Bahri. East of the Nile are the two temples of Amon at Luxor and Karnak, once joined by an avenue of sphinxes; and on the west bank are numerous temples, the Ramasseum of Rameses II and the two Colossi of Thebes, of Amenhotep III, the northerly one being also called by the Greeks the 'vocal Memnon' because it sang at sunrise — presumably an effect of wind in the masonry. (Illustrated overleaf.)

THEMISTOCLES (*c.* **514—449** B.C.), Athenian soldier and statesman, who led the fleet of Athens to victory over the Persians in the naval battle of Salamis (480).

THEODOSIUS THE GREAT (*c.* **346—95**), Roman Emperor. Starting his career as a soldier, he became Emperor of the East in 379 and sole ruler of the Empire in 394. He successfully resisted an invasion by the Goths.

Ruins at Thebes. The Necropolis

THEOLOGY, the study of the existence and nature of God and man's relationship to him. The word has subsequently come to denote a particular set of beliefs such as the Christian theology, or Jewish theology.

THEOSOPHY, a religious movement which teaches that fundamental truth may be attained through a mystical union with God. A Theosophical Society, based on the mystical teachings of the oriental religions such as *Karma* and reincarnation, was founded in 1875 by Mme Blavatsky; she was succeeded by Mrs Annie Besant.

THERMODYNAMICS, the branch of physics that studies the relationship of heat to work and to other forms of energy. There are three fundamental laws of thermodynamics. The first states that when work is converted into heat, or vice versa, the quantity of heat is equivalent to the quantity of work. The second law states that heat naturally flows from a hotter to a cooler body; it cannot naturally flow in the reverse direction. Hence no heat-engine (e.g. a steam engine) can make full use of the heat-source from which it is driven, even in ideal conditions. In nature the tendency is for all forms of energy to be dissipated in heat and, since heat is the energy of motion and vibration in all directions of the atoms and molecules which constitute a material body, this is a tendency towards disorder. The measure of the degree of this disorder is called entropy, which may also be defined as the measure of the energy of a closed system which is wasted and becomes unavailable for conversion into mechanical work. The total entropy of any such system must either remain constant or increase; it cannot decrease. Hence the natural tendency of the Universe is towards total disorder of the particles in it.

The third law states that absolute zero temperature cannot be attained, but that all matter tends to become perfectly ordered as it approaches absolute zero. The lowest temperature theoretically attainable is about -273°c. Low-temperature physics investigates the properties of matter at such temperatures.

THERMOMETER, a device for measuring temperature by means of a scale of values. The most common type consists of a glass tube containing mercury or alcohol which expands or contracts as the temperature rises or falls. The scales are graduated in degrees which mark the rise and fall of the liquid. The freezing point of water on the Fahrenheit scale is 32°, corresponding to 0° Centigrade. Water boils at 212°F. (100°c).

THERMONUCLEAR BOMB, see Hydrogen Bomb.

THESSALONIKI (Salonica), a city in northeastern Greece, on the Aegean Sea. Pop. (1961) 377,026. It is a communications and commercial centre, and an important port. Its manufactures include tobacco, textiles, chemicals, foodstuffs, metalwork and leather. Its silk products are particularly fine.

THIRTEEN STATES, the original states constituting the U.S.A. They were Connecticut, Delaware, Georgia, Maryland, Massachusetts, New Hampshire, New Jersey, New York, North Carolina, South Carolina, Pennsylvania, Rhode Island and Virginia.

THIRTY YEARS WAR (1618—48), a conflict originally between Protestants and Catholics but which subsequently engulfed all Europe. The war began with the Protestant Bohemian and German resistance to the accession of Emperor Ferdinand II. At first the forces of the emperor were victorious in putting down the opposition, but Denmark, and later Sweden, under Gustavus Adolphus, came to the aid of the Protestants and inflicted defeat upon the imperial troops. By 1635 the war had lost all semblance of a religious conflict and the troops engaged were mostly mercenaries. It became a battle between France and her ally Sweden against the Hapsburgs of Austria and Spain. Peace was finally negotiated at Westphalia, but it left a devastated Germany, and the Holy Roman Empire was reduced to a minor factor in European politics France gained Alsace.

THOMAS À BECKET, see Becket, Thomas à.

THOMAS À KEMPIS (*c.* 1380—1471), a German monk, member of the Augustinian order and author of the devotional work *The Imitation of Christ.*

THOMAS AQUINAS, St, see Aquinas, Thomas.

THOREAU, Henry David (1817—62), American writer, naturalist and philosopher. Forsaking civilisation, he lived the life of a recluse in the American woods. His experiences are described in his book, *Walden, or Life in the Woods* (1854).

THORIUM, see Elements.

THORNDIKE, Dame Sybil (1882—), English actress. She has played Shakespearean roles and managed a number of theatres. Married to the English actor Sir Lewis Casson, her famous parts include those of Joan of Arc in Shaw's *Saint Joan,* Lady Macbeth, and Hecuba and Medea in plays translated from Euripides.

THRACE, an ancient region in southeast Europe, now divided between Greece, Turkey and Bulgaria. It was never a political unit.

THUCYDIDES (*c.* 460—400 B.C.), Greek historian, author of a history of the Peloponnesian War, in which he himself fought. A feature of the work is the inclusion of long speeches attributed to the protagonists, the most famous of which is the funeral oration over the Athenian dead delivered by Pericles in 430. These help to create the atmosphere of a theatrical drama.

TIBER, see River.

TIBET, an autonomous region in western China. Pop. *c.* 4,000,000; area 469,143 sq. miles. With the Kunlun Mountains to the north and the Himalaya to the south, it is the highest country in the world, no part being less than about 10,000 ft above sea-level. Barley, tea, vegetables and fruit are grown. Livestock raising is important. Tibet, the centre of Lamaism (q.v.), has been under Chinese domination since 1950. The capital is Lhasa.

TIEN SHAN, a huge mountain system in central Asia extending for 1500 miles from the Pamirs near Tashkent to the western borders of the Gobi Desert. They lie partly in Russian Kirghizia and partly in Chinese Sinkiang.

TIENTSIN, a city of Hopei, eastern China, on the Pei-Ho. Pop. (1953) 2,693,831. A rail and water communications centre, it is a commercial and industrial city producing metallurgical and engineering products, chemicals, textiles and foodstuffs. As the entrance to the harbour silts up rapidly, an outport was constructed in 1952 at Tangku.

TIGRIS, see River.

TIMOR, a mountainous island in the Malay archipelago divided between Indonesia in the west and Portugal in the east. Area 14,660 sq. miles. Indonesian Timor (pop. 450,000; area 7328 sq. miles) exports sandalwood, copra, ponies, cattle and hides; the capital and chief port is Kupang. The chief products of Portuguese Timor (pop. 1960 517,079; area 7332 sq. miles) are coffee, rubber and copra. The capital is Dili.

TIN, see Elements.

TINTORETTO (Jacopo Robusti; 1518—94), Italian painter. Working at Venice with a large body of assistants, and taking Titian and Michelangelo as his models he painted huge canvases with well-grouped scenes, excelling in his treatment of light and shade, perspective and effects of depth. He painted an enormous *Paradise* for the Doge's restored palace, and decorated the whole of the Scuola di S. Rocco (his best work). *The Origin of the Milky Way* is in the National Gallery, London.

TITIAN (Tiziano Vecelli; *c.* 1487—1576), Italian painter. He was a gifted portraitist and master of colour. His works also include frescoes, religious and mythological pictures, and altarpieces. He is famous for his *Assumption of the Virgin*, *The Holy Family*, *Bacchus and Ariadne* (National Gallery, London), *The Rape of Europa* and *The Man with a Glove*. He became a personal friend of the Emperor Charles v, whose portrait he painted. Another famous portrait is that of his daughter Lavinia (Vienna). Vienna and Madrid are particularly rich in examples of his work.

TITO (Josip Broz; 1892—   ), Yugoslav military and political leader. Born in Croatia, he was taken prisoner by the Russians during the First World War, and served in the Soviet army (1917—21). He led the Yugoslav resistance against the German occupation forces during the Second World War. Tito became Prime Minister of the Yugoslav government in 1945, and was elected President of the Federal People's Republic in 1953. He was re-elected in 1954, 1958 and 1963.

TOBACCO, a plant of the genus *Nicotiana*, the dried leaves of which are used for smoking, chewing and sniffing. The waste products are ground and used as sheepwash, insecticides and fumigants. See Smoking.

TOBAGO, an island in the West Indies, administered with Trinidad since 1878. Pop. (1960) 33,200; area 116 sq. miles. The principal products are copra, cocoa, tobacco, livestock, vegetables, coconut oil and fibre. The chief town is Scarborough.

TOGO, a republic in West Africa. Pop. (1961) 1,440,000; area 21,200 sq. miles. It consists of savannah-covered plateaux in the north and forests in the south. The principal crops are cocoa, cotton, coffee, palm products, groundnuts, manioc and copra. There are rich deposits of bauxite and phosphates. A German territory before 1914, it was divided between France and Britain after the First World War. The British area was incorporated in Ghana in 1957 and the larger French area became independent in 1960. The capital is Lomé.

TOKYO, capital of Japan, on Honshu. Pop. (1962) 10,003,055. A seaport on the Pacific Ocean, it is a cultural, communications, commercial and industrial centre. The city is intersected by a number of rivers and canals. Tokyo has numerous parks, palaces, government buildings, universities, libraries, Buddhist temples, shrines and art galleries. It is a publishing centre. Its factories produce textiles, metal goods, electrical equipment, machinery, foodstuffs and chemicals.

TOLEDO, a city and port in northwest Ohio, at the mouth of the Maumee River, on Lake Erie. Pop. (1960) 318,003. It has extensive railway yards and is a leading shipping centre for bituminous coal. There are large oil refineries, and manufactures of glass, automobiles, chemicals, metal products, machinery, leather goods and foodstuffs.

TOLSTOY, Count Leo (1822—1910), Russian novelist. The son of a well-to-do landowning family, he served in the Russian army during the Crimean war; the futility and muddle of war was to become one of the themes of *War and Peace*, which describes Napoleon's invasion of Russia. After an uneasy period in aristocratic and literary circles at St Petersburg, Tolstoy retired to Yasnaya Polyana, in Tula, to manage his huge estates with all the zest for innovation and liberal attitude to peasants and the institution of serfdom shown by Levin in *Anna Karenina*, starting, for example, a school for peasant children. It was after his marriage in 1862 that he wrote these two great masterpieces of world literature. In 1879 Tolstoy had a spiritual experience (described in *A Confession*) which caused him to turn to religion, but his unorthodox approach brought about his excommunication from the Russian Church. His liberal, even revolutionary, ideas led to his home becoming a place of pilgrimage for intellectuals from all over the world, but also to clashes with society and in his own family. Finally, he ran away from his home, at the age of 82, and died a few weeks later.

TOMSK, a city in the R.S.F.S.R. in west Siberia, on the Tom River, U.S.S.R. Pop. (1962) 275,000. It is on the Trans-Siberian railway. Engineering products and chemicals are manufactured. The first Siberian university was opened here in 1888.

TONGA (Friendly Islands), a British-protected kingdom in the south central Pacific. Pop. (1961) 65,620; area 269 sq. miles (150 islands). The chief products are copra and bananas. The capital is Nukualofa. Queen Salote has ruled it since 1918.

TORONTO, a city in Canada, capital of Ontario province, at the mouth of the Humber River on Lake Ontario. Pop.

(1961) 1,824,481. The port has a large harbour, handling trade with U.S. ports. The second largest city in Canada, and the most important industrially, it manufactures agricultural machinery and other engineering products, textiles, chemicals and tyres; printing and publishing, and meatpacking, are other activities. The city has Parliament buildings, a university, Roman Catholic and Anglican cathedrals and many fine parks. It was founded by the French in 1749.

TORRICELLI, Evangelista (1608—47), Italian physicist and philosopher. He discovered the principle of the modern barometer and made important improvements in telescopes and microscopes.

TORT (French, 'wrong', 'harm'), a civil or private wrong. The law of Tort deals with wrongs inflicted by one individual against another which do not arise from a contract (q.v.). Torts include trespass on land, assault and battery, nuisances, injury through negligence, defamation, etc.

TOSCANINI, Arturo (1867—1957), Italian conductor, director of La Scala, Milan (1898—1907, 1921—31), conductor of the Metropolitan Opera (1908—15), and founder (1937) of the National Broadcasting Company Symphony Orchestra. His memory for the details of a score, based on prolonged and repeated study, was quite phenomenal, and his interpretations of a wide range of composers were outstanding.

TOTALITARIANISM, a dictatorial regime characterised by the domination of a single political party identical with the government. A small group controls the party which rules the state. There is a secret police which destroys all opposition and executes governmental policy. The state controls every aspect of national life and employs mass-communication media and the school system to entrench itself.

Totem Poles
A. New Zealand B. Canada

TOTEMISM, a system common among primitive societies whereby tribal clans are distinguished by totems (guardian animals). Each group venerates one or more totems which are thought to exercise a spiritual power over their particular tribe.

TOULON, a city in France, on the Mediterranean. Pop. (1962) 172,586. It is a naval base and commercial port. Industries include shipbuilding, wine and armaments. Fishing is important.

TOULOUSE, a city in southwest France, on the Garonne River. Pop. (1962) 330,570. It is a cultural, commercial, industrial and communications centre, with an important market for agricultural products. Manufactures include chemicals, clothing, aircraft engines and engineering products. The Church of St Sernin (11th century) contains the tomb of St Thomas Aquinas, and the university dates from the 13th century.

TOURÉ, Sékou (1923—), Guinea statesman. He has always been particularly interested in African trade unionism and in 1957 started a Pan-African trade union movement (L'UGTAN). After meeting Houphouët-Boigny in Paris in 1948, he formed the Guinea branch of the Rassemblement Démocratique Africain (R.D.A.). He broke with the French Communist party in 1952 and in 1956 was elected to the French National Assembly. His position as virtual President of Guinea from 1958 was confirmed in the election of January 1961. Although not a Communist, he thinks that some features of Marxism can usefully be applied in Africa.

TOWER OF LONDON, ancient palace and prison in London. On the site of older fortifications, William the Conqueror began the building of the White Tower in 1078, and subsequent kings down to Edward I made additions. The Tower served first as a royal residence, later as a prison, and then as an armoury and museum.

TRADE UNION, a voluntary organisation of workers for the purpose of improving their economic status and conditions of work. There are 'horizontal' or craft unions for members possessing the same special skill; 'vertical' unions consisting of workers in the same industry; and general unions covering several occupations and industries. The different types may form federations, and there are also national federations, such as the British Trades Union Congress (with an affiliated membership of over eight million), and the federation formed in the U.S.A. in 1955 by the merging of the Congress of Industrial Organisations and the American Federation of Labor. There are two international federations, the (Communist) World Federation of Trade Unions (1945), and the International Confederation of Free Trade Unions (1949). A union's chief function is collective bargaining with employers on pay and conditions of work. The closed shop is a practice in which employers undertake not to employ non-union labour. The political levy is a contribution collected from trade union members for payment into Labour or other political party funds. In Britain from 1913—27, and again from 1946, members could contract out of this payment; in the intervening period they had to contract in. A shop steward is a representative of his fellow workers who bargains with their employer over conditions of work; this institution is strongest in electrical and engineering industries, where there are complex trade practices and piece rates.

TRADES UNION CONGRESS (T.U.C.), a voluntary association of most of the trade unions in Great Britain. Formed in 1868, it is now governed by a 32-member General Council. The T.U.C. was one of the founders of the British Labour Party in the 1890s. The T.U.C. is affiliated with the International Confederation of Free Trade Unions and is a member of the International Labour Organisation of the U.N.

TRAFALGAR, Battle of (Oct. 21, 1805), a naval battle fought off Cape Trafalgar (south of Cadiz) between the British fleet of 27 ships under Nelson and the combined French and Spanish fleets of 33 ships under Villeneuve and Gravina. Though Nelson was killed, the British won an overwhelming victory, 20 enemy ships being sunk or captured.

TRAGEDY, a form of drama which elicits emotions of apprehension or pity in the spectators and gives them a sense of having seen powerful forces at work or a great personage destroyed because of some defect in his character.

TRANSCENDENTALISM, the philosophical theory propounded by Kant that ultimate reality lies outside the realm of experience and may be attained only by *a priori* reasoning.

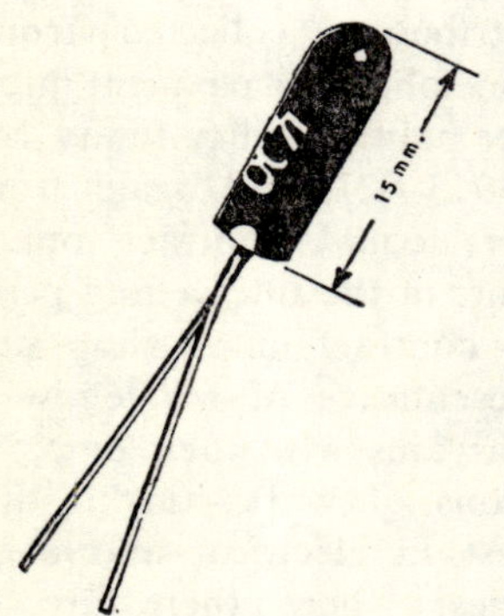

Transistor 'valve'

TRANSISTOR, an electronic device consisting chiefly of a tiny piece of germanium or silicon (semi-conducting metal) to which are connected wires imparting to it the functions of a radio valve. It is compact, requires no time to warm up, and runs on a flashlight battery. The transistor was invented in 1948 by American scientists.

TRANSUBSTANTIATION, a term which denotes the doctrine held by the Roman Catholic and Eastern Orthodox churches to the effect that at the rite of Eucharist the bread and wine are literally transformed into the flesh and blood of Jesus Christ.

TRANSVAAL, a province of the Republic of South Africa. Pop. (1960) 6,273,477 (including 1,468,305 Whites); area 110,450 sq. miles. Consisting of a plateau in the west, it is traversed by mountains followed by lowlands in the east. Livestock raising is the leading pursuit. Grains, cotton and potatoes are grown. Minerals include gold, coal, copper, asbestos and platinum. The province manufactures metal and engineering products, foodstuffs, building materials, tobacco, clothing and transport equipment. Colonised by Boers in 1831, it became independent in 1852 and adopted the name of the South African Republic. Annexed by Britain in 1877, it subsequently went to war and achieved a measure of self-government. The discovery of gold led to a great influx of Uitlanders (foreigners, i.e. British) and war with Britain again resulted in 1899. From 1902—10 it was a British colony. The capital is Pretoria, the administrative capital of the republic. Johannesburg is the chief city.

TRANSYLVANIA, a former province of Rumania. Pop. (1940) 3,420,859; area 22,300 sq. miles. Enclosed by the Carpathian Mountains, it has mineral resources, fertile soil, lumber and heavy industries including oil refineries. It was Hungarian until 1918.

TREATY PORTS, ports on the coast of China (until 1946) and Japan (until 1899) which were opened to foreign trade by a treaty. These ports had zones for foreign residents which enjoyed extra-territorial rights. China at one time had 69 such ports. Tientsin, Tsingtao, Shanghai, Foochow and Amoy were famous Treaty Ports.

TREE, a woody, perennial seed plant with a single trunk extending for some distance above the ground. There are two types — gymnosperms which bear seeds exposed on the surfaces of scales clustered in cones (conifers) and angiosperms, or those bearing flowers (usually inconspicuous). For quick classification it is convenient to divide trees into those with needles (conifers, producing softwoods); those with leaves divided into leaflets (e.g. horse-chestnut, ash, elder, walnut); and the rest. These last again subdivide into those with leaves opposite on the twig (e.g. sycamore) and those with leaves alternate on the twig. The latter are subdivided into evergreens (e.g. holly) and deciduous. The deciduous consist of trees with lobed leaves (e.g. oak, plane) and those with entire or toothed leaves (beech, hazel, lime, wild apple, elm, sweet chestnut, etc.).

TRENT, COUNCIL OF (1545—63), an ecclesiastical council held at Trent (Trento) in Tyrol which condemned the doctrines expounded by the leaders of the Reformation but introduced reforms in the Roman Church. Pope Pius IV confirmed the decrees of the council in 1564. See Counter-Reformation.

TRIESTE, a city and port in northeast Italy, on the Adriatic Sea. Pop. (1961) 273,390. It is a commercial and industrial centre, with shipyards and oil refineries. Trieste was the capital of a Free Territory constituted in 1947 and divided between Italy and Yugoslavia in 1954, the latter receiving the smaller portion.

TRINIDAD, an island in the West Indies, forming with Tobago an independent state within the British Commonwealth. Pop. (1960) 828,000 (with Tobago); area 1864 sq. miles. The principal crops are sugar-cane, cocoa, coconuts, citrus fruit and tonca beans. There are large deposits of oil and asphalt; oil refining is the leading industry. Tourism is a valuable source of revenue. The capital is Port of Spain. Trinidad was discovered by Columbus in 1498 and remained Spanish until the British took it in 1797. It became independent in 1962.

TRINITY, the term used by Christians to designate the threefold character (Father, Son and Holy Ghost) of the Godhead. The early Christian Fathers disputed about the nature of and relationship between the Father (God), the Son (Logos, Christ) and Holy Ghost (Holy Spirit). The Holy Ghost was variously held to be a power of divine origin permeating the universe, God reasoning, God in another form, emanating from God, of like nature, of the same substance. Jesus was the Logos in the form of a man, or God creating. Finally at the Council of Nicaea (325) Athanasius found the orthodox formula, that the one Godhead is a Trinity of the same substance, three Persons of like nature. The Arian heresy subordinated the Son and Holy Ghost to the Father as created beings.

TRIPLE ENTENTE, an unwritten agreement between Great Britain, Russia and France at the end of the 19th century aimed at curbing the power of the Triple Alliance (Germany, Italy, Austria).

TRIPOLI, joint capital (with Benghazi) of Libya, on the Mediterranean. Pop. (1962) 184,000. A commercial centre with minor industries, it has Roman ruins.

TRISTAN DA CUNHA, a group of British islands in the Atlantic Ocean, west of the Cape of Good Hope. Area 38 sq. miles. The entire population of 200 persons was evacuated to England in 1961 because of a volcanic eruption, but nearly all of them returned in 1963.

TROJAN WAR, a war, fought *c.* 1200 B.C. and celebrated in Homer's *Iliad*, by the Greeks under Agamemnon against the Trojans in an effort to recover Helen, wife of Menelaus, King of Sparta, who had been abducted by Paris, the son of the King of Troy, Priam.

TROLLOPE, Anthony (1815—82), English novelist. Employed by the Post Office until 1867, he was a prolific author, writing over 50 novels. His most famous works are those which entertainingly describe the characters and events of ecclesiastical society in the fictitious county of Barsetshire, e.g. *The Warden*, *Barchester Towers* (1857).

TROTSKY, Leon (Lev Bronstein; 1879—1940), Russian revolutionary. He collaborated with Lenin in the Bolshevik October Revolution in 1917 and served as commissar of war until 1919. After the death of Lenin in 1924 Trotsky lost the fight for party control to Stalin, was dismissed from the party and exiled (1929) from Russia. He settled in Mexico, where he was assassinated. He believed that revolutionary progress in Russia (Socialism in one country) should be subordinated to the demands of international revolution, and that Stalin, by concentrating on economic development at home, would create a bureaucratic state with a purely nationalistic outlook.

TROY, the ancient city of Ilium located on the site of Hissarlik, Turkey. Troy was excavated (1871—90) by Schliemann, who discovered nine superimposed cities, going back to *c.* 3000 B.C. Archaeologists hold that 'Troy VII' was the city described by Homer in the *Iliad* and destroyed in the Trojan War (q.v.).

TRUMAN, Harry S. (1884—), American statesman. Elected (1944) Vice-President, he became President of the United States upon the death of Franklin Roosevelt (April 1945). It fell to him to authorise the use of the atomic bomb against Japan. In the 1948 elections he won a surprising victory and served a second term. He recalled Gen. MacArthur (1951) for his repeated criticism of U.S. policy.

TRUST, a legal arrangement providing for the administration of property owned by one person for the benefit of another. The person or institution holding the title to the property which the creator of the trust or donor has designated for the beneficiary is called a trustee.

TSINAN, capital of Shantung province, east China, on the Hwang Ho. Pop. (1960) 680,000. It is a commercial and industrial centre manufacturing metal products, textiles, foodstuffs and glass.

TSINGTAO, a city and port in Shantung province, east China, on the Yellow Sea. Pop. (1960) 917,000. A major commercial port, it is a silk-manufacturing centre. It was a German and Japanese possession before reverting to China in 1922.

TUBERCULOSIS, an infectious disease which in man most often attacks the lungs (pulmonary or respiratory tuberculosis, phthisis, consumption) although it may also infect other parts of the body. Caused by a bacillus, it is characterised by the formation of a tubercle or nodule around the infected spot. Many persons have the disease in an inactive form. Koch discovered the bacillus in 1882; the tuberculin test for the presence of the disease in cattle or man was then invented, and the value of pasteurised milk discovered; the BCG vaccine was introduced in 1924, and from 1944 streptomycin, PAS and other drugs, together with the use of X-rays in early diagnosis, sharply diminished the dangers of this once dreaded disease.

TUBMAN, William (1895—), 18th President of Liberia. The son of the Speaker of the Liberian House of Representatives, a lawyer, and a Senator from 1928, he was elected President in 1943.

TUCSON, a city in southeast Arizona, U.S.A., on the Santa Cruz River. Pop. (1960) 212,892. A road and rail junction 2400 ft above sea-level, it is an educational, marketing and industrial centre, and a winter resort. There is a four-day rodeo each year.

TUCUMÁN, a city in northwest Argentina, on the Sali River. Pop. (1953) 244,628. It is an educational centre in the Sierra Aconquija foothills. Manufactures include sugar, sawmill products and alcohol. Argentina's declaration of independence was drafted here in 1816.

TULSA, a city in northeast Oklahoma, U.S.A., on the Arkansas River. Pop. (1960) 261,685. It is a rich agricultural and oil-producing region, and a communications centre. Tulsa is the headquarters of all the large oil companies. A wholesale and retail distributing centre, it manufactures oilfield equipment, steel, aircraft and chemicals.

TUNGSTEN, see Elements.

TUNIS, capital of Tunisia, on the Mediterranean. Pop. (1960) 695,000. It is a seaport and important trade and industrial centre, manufacturing textiles, pottery and leather. The ruins of ancient Carthage lie to the northeast.

TUNISIA, a republic in North Africa, on the Mediterranean. Pop. (1961) 4,168,000. Mountainous in the north, with fertile valleys, it consists of a central tableland, a coastal lowland and the desert region of the Sahara, containing oases in the south. The principal crops are citrus fruit, grapes, cereals, olives and dates. Livestock and fishing are important. Phosphates, iron, lead, zinc and silver are mined. There are small textile and ceramic industries. A French protectorate from 1881, Tunisia became independent in 1956. The capital is Tunis. An oil pipeline has been built from the rich new oilfields of the Edjéleh area, in the Sahara, to La Skhrira, near Gabes.

TURGENEV, Ivan (1818—83), Russian novelist and short-story writer. He advocated the abolition of serfdom in Russia and was caustic in his criticism of the social scene. His most famous novel is *Fathers and Sons* (1862). He spent much of his later life in France.

TURIN, a city in northern Italy, on the Po River. Pop. (1961) 1,019,230. It is a commercial and industrial centre with many historic buildings and an old university. Manufactures include automobiles, chemicals, textiles and foodstuffs. It was for a short time the capital of the kingdom of Sardinia, and later of Italy.

TURKEY, a republic bridging southwest Asia and southeast Europe. Pop. (1960) 27,802,224; area 301,381 sq. miles. Turkey in Europe (area 9250 sq. miles) is mostly highland; Turkey in Asia (Anatolia; area 292,131 sq. miles) is a vast plateau enclosed by the Pontic Mountains in the north and the Taurus in the south; Mt Ararat (16,946 ft) is in the east. The principal products are cotton, tobacco, cereals, grapes, figs, citrus, silk, olives and olive oil, sugar-beet, flax, skins, hides, furs, sugar and opium. Livestock raising is important. There are deposits of coal, chrome, copper, sulphur, antimony and manganese. Leading industries are textiles, cement, paper, glass, tobacco, ceramics, iron and steel. Turkey abolished the Ottoman caliphate and became a republic in 1924.

In 1307 Osman founded the Ottoman empire after defeating the Seljuk Turks. The Ottoman sultans gradually gained control of the entire Near East and the Balkans, capturing Constantinople in 1453. The reign of Suleiman II (The Magnificent, 1520—66) was the high point of Ottoman power. The defeat of the Turkish fleet at Lepanto in 1571 and of the army besieging Vienna in 1683 marked the beginning of Turkey's decline. Russia moved into the Balkans and in the 19th century Turkey lost Bulgaria, Rumania and Serbia. A revolt in 1909 by the Young Turks established a constitutional régime. In a war with Italy (1911—12) and in the Balkan Wars (1912—13), Turkey suffered more defeats. Allied to Germany in the First World War, Turkey lost her entire Near Eastern empire. Under the post-war leadership of Mustafa Kemal, Turkey introduced numerous reforms, threw off its official Moslem tradition and embarked on the road to becoming a modern country. Turkey was neutral in the Second World War. The capital is Ankara (pop. 646,151). Other important cities are Istanbul (1,459,528), Izmir (370,923) and Adana (230,024).

TURKMENISTAN, a constituent republic of the U.S.S.R., in Central Asia, on the Caspian Sea. Pop. (1962) 1,683,603 sq. miles. Consisting of large desert areas, it is mountainous in the south and southeast. It is predominantly agricultural, producing cotton, wheat, silk, fruit and vegetables. Stock raising, chiefly sheep, is important. There are deposits of oil, sulphur, salt, ozocerite, magnesium and coal. The principal industries are chemicals, textiles, agricultural implements, glass and cement. There are oil refineries. The capital is Ashkhabad (pop. 197,000).

TURKU (Åbo), a city in southwest Finland, on the Gulf of Bothnia. Pop. (1961) 138,380. A Baltic port, it has shipyards and sawmills and manufactures metal products, textiles and foodstuffs. It has Finnish and Swedish universities. During periods of Swedish and Russian rule it was the capital of Finland.

TURNER, Joseph Mallord William (1775—1851), English painter. His earlier landscapes were the result of sketching tours around Britain and Europe. He had a rare sense of colour and experimented brilliantly with effects of light and atmosphere. He left 19,000 of his water-colours, drawings and oil paintings to the nation, including *Dido Building Carthage*, *The Fighting Téméraire*, and *Rain, Steam, and Speed.*

TUSCANY, a region in central Italy, on the Mediterranean. Pop. (1961) 3,267,374; area 8876 sq. miles. Most of the country is hilly; it produces cereals, olive oil and wine, and there are deposits of copper, lead, mercury and marble. Textiles, glass and porcelain are manufactured. Corresponding to ancient Etruria, it formed a duchy which was annexed to Sardinia in 1860 and became part of Italy in 1861. The capital is Florence (pop. 438,138).

TUSSAUD, Marie (1760—1850), Swiss modeller of wax figures. After escaping from France during the Revolution, she established a museum in London in 1802.

TUTANKHAMEN (*c.* 1350 B.C.), Egyptian Pharaoh whose tomb was discovered in 1922 in the Valley of the Kings, west of the Nile at Thebes, by Howard Carter. As it was the only tomb which had not been previously plundered, it contained a wealth of treasure, such as the gold-plated royal throne, now in Cairo Museum.

TWAIN, Mark (1835—1910), pseudonym of Samuel Langhorne Clemens, American writer, lecturer and humorist. His two most famous works are *Tom Sawyer* (1876) and *Huckleberry Finn* (1884), which bring to life the Mississippi frontier civilisation that he knew as a child.

TWO SICILIES, KINGDOM OF THE, the united kingdom of Southern Italy (called the Kingdom of Naples) and Sicily. It was conquered in 1861 by Victor Emmanuel and incorporated into a united Italy.

TYLER, Wat (d. 1381), the instigator of the Peasants' Revolt during the reign of Richard II. Tyler led some 100,000 men in a march on London, whereupon Richard promised to abolish villeinage; Tyler was treacherously stabbed by the Lord Mayor, Sir William Walworth, and the promises were not kept.

TYNDALE, William (*c.* 1490—1536), English reformer. He translated into English the New Testament and, with Miles Coverdale, the Pentateuch. He was arrested and, convicted of heresy, was sentenced to death at the stake.

TYPEWRITER, a machine in which movable types are made to print letters on paper by means of keys struck on a keyboard. After early primitive experiments, a practical typewriter was made in 1867 by the Remington Armoury, Milwaukee. The first portable typewriter was made in 1912. Later developments were the electrically operated typewriter with automatic carriage return, almost noiseless and permitting high speeds, and Plan-a-type, a noiseless portable which types a kind of shorthand, used in verbatim reporting.

TYPOGRAPHY, setting and arranging type for the purpose of printing on paper. There are more than a thousand styles of type. Proper spacing of the words and the positioning of the printed matter on the page are essential elements of a craft in which the art of illustration and decoration play an important role.

TYROL, a region in the Alps divided between Austria and Italy. There are numerous forests and some of the highest peaks of the Alps are to be found here. Livestock grazing, dairy farming and the mining of salt, zinc, lead and sulphur are the principal occupations in the Austrian portion (capital, Innsbruck). The Tyrolese peasants put up a heroic resistance in 1809 to overwhelming French and Bavarian forces, but their revolt was crushed. The southern portion, which contained a large German-speaking population, was awarded to Italy after the First World War, and was named Alto Adige, capital Bolzano.

UGANDA, an independent state in East Africa, and a member of the British Commonwealth. Pop. (1960) 6,538,175; area 93,981 sq. miles, including 13,680 sq. miles of swamp and water, consisting of parts of Lakes Victoria, Albert and Edward, and other lakes. Uganda is bisected by the Nile. Mt Elgon is on the

Kenya border, and the Ruwenzori range on the west. Cotton, coffee, tea, tobacco, maize, groundnuts, sisal and sugar are grown. Livestock raising, lumbering and fishing are important. There are deposits of copper, cobalt, tin, gold and beryl. Under British influence from 1890, the protectorate became independent in 1962. The capital is Kampala.

UKRAINE, a constituent republic of the U.S.S.R. in eastern Europe, on the Black Sea. Pop. (1962) 43,527,000; area 232,046 sq. miles. Consisting mostly of extremely fertile 'black earth', it is rimmed by the Carpathian Mountains in the west. The principal crops are cereals, sunflowers, cotton, flax, hemp, tobacco, sugar-beet, soya beans, hops, potatoes, fruit, rice, tea and vegetables. Livestock breeding and vineyards are important. The Donbas is one of the chief coalfields of Europe; there are also deposits of iron, bauxite, manganese, salt and phosphorites. Important industrially, especially for metal refining, it produces machinery, iron and steel, textiles, transport equipment, chemicals, sugar, gypsum, alabaster and timber. The area of the republic was increased between 1939 and 1945 by the annexation of portions of Poland and Rumania (Ruthenia and parts of Bessarabia). The capital is Kiev (pop. 1,208,000). Other leading cities are Kharkov (990,000) and Odessa (704,000).

ULSTER, see Northern Ireland.

ULTRA-VIOLET RAYS, electromagnetic rays with a greater frequency and shorter wavelength than those of visible light. They cannot penetrate ordinary window glass, thick clothing, or dusty or smoky atmosphere. Their action produces vitamin D in the skin and kills germs. Ultra-violet radiation induces fluorescence (q.v.) in certain materials, producing visible light. The chief source, apart from the sun, is electric discharges, as in the mercury-vapour lamp.

ULYSSES, see Odysseus.

UNCONSCIOUS, that aspect of mental function not subject to conscious control and awareness. It is based on instinctual drives and emotion, seeking only what affords the mind and body pleasure. Permeated by a logic all its own, it fails to differentiate sharply between objects and events. It is capable of storing away countless memories, can reason and solve problems, and plays a decisive role in directing an individual's thoughts and actions. See Psychoanalysis.

UNDSET, Sigrid (1882—1949), Norwegian novelist. Concerned with the need for faith, her writing shows deep understanding of the feminine mind and the environment of the Middle Ages. Her greatest work was *Kristin Lavransdatter*. She received the Nobel Prize for literature in 1928. She became a Roman Catholic in 1924.

UNEMPLOYMENT, the condition of being without work despite the ability and desire to be gainfully employed. In a free economy it is controlled strictly by economic forces. It comes into being when the labour force exceeds the demand for workers as a result of technological progress, seasonal cyclical changes in economic activity, or the natural immobility that keeps employable persons in one area.

UNESCO (U.N. Educational, Scientific and Cultural Organisation) was formed in 1946 to promote collaboration among the nations through education, science and culture, and to further universal respect for the human rights and fundamental freedoms affirmed by the U.N.

Charter. It aims to improve and extend education, and especially education for living in a world community; it promotes international meetings of scientists; and it tries to improve the quality of the world's press by the dissemination of information, research and advice.

UNICEF (U.N. Children's Fund), established in 1946 under the Economic and Social Council, deals with child health, nutrition and welfare programmes. It is financed by voluntary contributions by governments and donations by the public.

UNION OF SOVIET SOCIALIST REPUBLICS, a federated state comprising 15 constituent republics extending across eastern Europe and Asia to the Pacific Ocean. Pop. (1963) 223,000,000; area 8,708,070 sq. miles. The most populous and largest is the Russian Federated S.S.R., after which come (in size of populations) the Ukraine, Kazakhstan, Belorussia, Uzbekistan, Georgia, Azerbaijan, Lithuania, Moldavia, Latvia, Kirgizia, Tadzhikistan, Armenia, Turkmenistan and Estonia (qq.v.). There is a large variety of nationalities, three-quarters of them being Slavs. All phases of the economy are controlled by the state which plans how each branch is to function and develop. The state, which is dominated by the Communist Party, also exercises firm control over every other aspect of national life. Formerly a predominantly agricultural country, it has developed a diversified industry. The U.S.S.R. is the world's largest producer of barley, rye, wheat, sugar-beet, potatoes, flax and hemp; other leading crops are cotton, sunflowers, silk, grapes, rice, citrus and tea. The bulk of the arable land is in Europe, West Siberia and Kazakhstan. Livestock has only in recent years fully recovered from the mass slaughtering that followed the collectivisation campaign of 1928. The country has the largest forest resources in the world, mostly conifers, but four-fifths of them are in relatively inaccessible parts of Asia, and most of the current felling is in Europe. The total fisheries catch is equal to that of the U.S.A. and second only to Japan's. The main oilfield is the Volga-Ural (sometimes called 'Second Baku'), which in recent years has outstripped the older fields of Baku. Coal is equally plentiful in Europe and Asia, the main single coalfield being in the Donbas. The other chief minerals are iron, copper, lead, zinc, chrome, nickel, manganese, mercury, asbestos, potash and phosphate and, among precious metals and stones, gold, platinum and diamonds, the last said to be as plentiful as in South Africa. The chief economic feature of the Soviet régime, to some extent due to the Second World War and strategic reasons in the atomic era, is the formation of huge new industrial areas, in the Urals, the Kuzbas (western Siberia), Karaganda (Kazakhstan), Komsomolsk (Far East), in the vicinity of Irkutsk (central Siberia) and at Rustavi (Georgia). The products of industry are such as are found in any great industrialised country.

In 1918 the Russian Soviet Federated S.S.R. was set up and, in the wake of the civil war which ensued, federated with other Soviet republics to form the nucleus of a union in 1922. In 1941 the Soviet Union was invaded by German troops who devastated a large part of European Russia. After the war the U.S.S.R. emerged as a leading world power. The establishment of close control over East Germany and the Communist republics of eastern Europe added to its strength and influence. The capital is Moscow (pop. 6,296,000). Other large cities are Leningrad (3,498,000) and Kiev (1,208,000). There are 22 other cities with a population exceeding half a million persons.

UNITED ARAB REPUBLIC, the official name of Egypt since, in February 1958, President Kuwatly of Syria and President Nasser of Egypt proclaimed the union of their countries; they were joined later by the kingdom of Yemen in another union, called the United Arab States. In 1961 Syria seceded from both unions.

UNITED KINGDOM, the official name for the kingdom which includes England, Scotland, Wales and Northern Ireland.

UNITED NATIONS, an association of states for the maintenance of peace and international co-operation. Its seat is in New York, U.S. The principal organs of the U.N. are the General Assembly, consisting of all members, each having a single vote; the Security Council, which consists of five permanent members with veto power — U.S.A., U.K., U.S.S.R., France and Nationalist China (i.e. Formosa) — and six elected members, and is responsible for maintaining international peace and security; the Economic and Social Council, consisting of 18 members elected by the General Assembly, which reports to the Assembly on economic, social, cultural, educational and health matters; the International Court of Justice, consisting of 15 judges elected by the Assembly and the Security Council, which settles international disputes; the Trusteeship Council, which protects peoples in trusteeship territories; and the Secretariat, consisting of the secretary-general and his staff. The U.N. has a number of 'specialised agencies' dealing with such matters as labour, food and agriculture, civil aviation, fiscal affairs and health. The U.N. has taken action on the Palestine issue, Korea, Indonesia, India and Pakistan, and the Congo, where it maintains a military force. U.N. forces also participated in the Korean War, and policed sensitive areas on the Israel-Egyptian border.

UNITED STATES OF AMERICA a federal republic in North America. Pop. (1960) 179,323,175; area 3,608,787 sq. miles. From east to west the main features are the northeast-southwest-trending Appalachian Mountains, the Central Plains, and the Rocky Mountains which, with three other ranges to the west of them, form the Cordillera. The Great Lakes mark the country's north central boundary, and the Mississippi-Missouri system traverses it from north to south and flows into the Gulf of Mexico. The climate is mostly of the continental type, with extremes of temperature, but in the south it is sub-tropical. The principal crops in order of value are maize (in the 'corn belt' of Iowa, Illinois and Nebraska), hay, wheat (central and western plains), cotton (southern states), tobacco (in the east), oats, soya beans and barley. The Pacific coast specialises in fruit and vines, the Cordillera in irrigated crops, the western plains in ranching. Dairy farming is a feature in the Great Lakes region and New England, where there is also market gardening. Half the farmland is under pasture. Soil erosion and drought are serious problems in the western plains. A third of the country is forested, the commercial timber being mostly softwoods. Fisheries are important, the total catch being second only to Japan's. The U.S.A. produces half the world's petroleum, mainly in Texas, Oklahoma, California and Louisiana, where natural gas is found with it. Coal is plentiful — anthracite in Pennsylvania, bituminous on the western slopes of the Appalachians. Iron ore is mined around Lake Superior and other minerals include copper, silver, lead, zinc and gold. Heavy industry is chiefly concentrated in a belt from Chicago east to New York. Many of the major industries are grouped round the sources of their raw materials, e.g. chemical industries

A Russian athlete clears the bar during the high jump competition in the 1964 Olympics.
Photo: Associated Press

Swimming events also feature in the Olympics. The semi-final of the men's 200 metre butterfly stroke race.
Photo: Associated Press

Steeplechasing, horseracing over jumps, is popular in many countries. In Britain, the most important 'chase, which closes the steeplechasing season each March, is the Grand National.
Photo: Central Press Ltd

In the United States, pony trotting is a form of racing which is growing in popularity.
Photo: U. S. Trotting Association

The ancient Japanese art of ju-jitsu, a method of offence or defence without weapons in personal encounter, is now a widely practised sport in the Western world. Modern troops are taught ju-jitsu. *Photo: Central Press Ltd*

Wrestling (q.v.) is an enormously popular spectator sport, in which two opponents strive to throw each other to the ground by use of prescribed holds. *Photo: Granada TV*

and oil refining in the oilfield areas, textiles in the southern states, fruit canning on the Pacific coast, where also are aircraft manufacture and shipbuilding. The chief exports are industrial machinery, motor vehicles, grain, chemicals, aircraft, electrical machinery and iron and steel. A country built by immigrants, it became a political entity in 1776 when the 13 original American colonies declared their independence of Great Britain. English, French and Spanish settlers colonised various parts of the country in the 17th century, and by the 18th the British dominated the eastern coastal regions, the French the interior, and the Spanish the southwest. The struggle against Britain had its source in the desire of the colonists to free themselves of taxes which they thought unjust since they were not imposed by their own representatives. In 1783 the War of Independence ended in an American victory. George Washington, the leader of the revolutionary armies, was elected the country's first president. At the beginning of the 19th century the U.S. purchased from France a large strip of land in the central portion known as Louisiana, and from Spain the Florida peninsula. From 1812—14 the U.S. fought another war with Britain over the impressment of American seamen; it ended indecisively. By mid-century the U.S. was in possession of the west coast and the southwest after a war with Mexico and the annexation of the Republic of Texas at the request of its citizens. The question of slavery, which was the economic basis of the South's plantation system, led to the secession of the 11 southern states from the Union which President Abraham Lincoln had pledged to preserve, and set off a Civil War lasting from 1861—65. The Federal Government — the northern states — emerged victorious because of its superior industrial machinery and greater manpower reserves; slavery was abolished. A period of industrial development and the settlement of the west followed in the wake of the Civil War. Large numbers of immigrants built new homes the length and breadth of the country. In 1898, war with Spain gave the U.S. Puerto Rico and temporary control of Cuba and the Philippines. The Hawaiian Islands were annexed at the same time. In 1903 the Panama Canal was completed, opening new vistas for American commerce and power. In 1917 the U.S. entered the First World War on the side of the Allies. A post-war boom ended in the depression of 1929, from which the country was slowly extricated by the efforts of the Democratic government of Franklin Roosevelt. At first neutral in the Second World War, the U.S. aided the Allies in various ways until the Japanese attack on Pearl Harbor in December 1941 made the country a full partner of the anti-Axis forces. The U.S.A. built up a mighty military machine and came out of the war as the most powerful country in the world. American aid to Europe helped to restore the shattered economies of a number of countries. The capital is Washington, D.C. (pop. 763,956). The largest cities are New York (7,781,984), Chicago (3,550,404), Los Angeles (2,479,015), Philadelphia (2,002,512) and Detroit (1,670,144).

UNIVERSITY, an institution for the final stages of higher education, giving three- to five-year courses in the humanities and sciences, and affording facilities for post-graduate research. In the U.K. and the Commonwealth the first degree is the bachelor's, with or without honours; at Oxford and Cambridge the B.A. is the first degree in all subjects, the Oxford B.Sc., etc., being a higher degree awarded for research. A thesis or further examination is required for a mastership, except at Oxford and Cambridge, and a doctorate is awarded for independent research work amounting to a contribution to knowledge. In Scottish universities there is no degree lower than the mastership, and in most European and South American countries the doctorate is the only degree. A university college does not itself grant degrees but is affiliated to a university which grants external degrees. The oldest European university is Salerno (9th century); Al-Azhar (Cairo) was founded in 970. Universities of international fame and a long history include the Sorbonne (Paris), Bologna, Heidelberg, Göttingen, Leyden, Grenoble, Yale, Harvard, St Andrew's (Scotland, 1411), Trinity College, Dublin (1591) and Uppsala (Sweden).

UPANISHADS, a number of philosophical treatises which form the concluding part of the Vedas, the holy scriptures of the Hindus. They are written not as directives, but as discourses, and as such have had a great influence on Indian philosophy.

UPPER VOLTA (Voltaic Republic), a republic in West Africa. Pop. (1961) 3,635,000; area 105,839 sq. miles. The principal crops are millet, sorghum, maize, rice, yams and cotton. Livestock raising is important. Formerly French territory, it became independent in 1960. The capital is Ouagadougou.

UPPSALA, a city in Sweden, on the Fyris River. Pop. (1961) 77,518. The seat of a famous old university and cathedral, it was an ancient capital of Scandinavia. The city is a publishing centre and manufactures chemicals, machinery and iron products.

URAL MOUNTAINS, a low mountain chain in the R.S.F.S.R. separating Europe from Asia, 2,050 miles long. The highest peak is Narodnaya (5,889 ft). Containing rich mineral deposits, the region is a leading industrial centre.

URANIUM, see Elements.

URSULA, St, a legendary English princess who, accompanied by 11,000 virgins, set out on a pilgrimage but was massacred, together with her entourage, by the Huns near Cologne, in the 3rd, or perhaps the 5th century.

URUGUAY, a republic in South America, on the South Atlantic Ocean. Pop. (1962) 2,800,000; area 72,153 sq. miles. Mountainous in the north, it is mostly tableland affording good grazing. The principal crops are wheat, maize, linseed, rice, fruit and groundnuts. Livestock raising is the predominant occupation. Industries include sugar refineries and textile mills. Wool, sheepskins and hides are exported. Uruguay became independent of Spain in 1825. The capital is Montevideo (pop. 1962 900,000).

UTAH, a western state of the U.S.A. Pop. (1960) 890,627; area 84,916 sq. miles. Consisting of lowlands containing deserts in the west, it is traversed from north to south by the Wasatch Mountains in the central portion, with an offshoot, the Uinta Mountains, to the east. Great Salt Lake (area 2000 sq. miles) is in the north centre. The principal crops are wheat, oats, potatoes, hay, lucerne and sugar-beet. There are deposits of gold, silver, uranium, vanadium, copper, coal, petroleum, lead, salt, iron and phosphates, and an important steel industry. Settled mostly by Mormons in 1847, it became a state in 1896. The capital is Salt Lake City (pop. 189,454).

U THANT (1909—), Burmese statesman. After teaching from 1928—47, he became Director of Press Services and adviser to the Prime Minister, U Nu, and from 1957—61 permanent representative to the U.N. On the death of Hammarskjöld he was appointed acting Secretary-General to the U.N., and given the substantive appointment a year later. He has written a *History of Post-War Burma* (1961).

UTOPIA, the name of an imaginary island in the political romance by Sir Thomas More. It represented the ideal form of social and political life. In subsequent usage, Utopia has come to denote an impracticable or impossible ideal.

UTRECHT, a city in the Netherlands, on the Old Rhine River. Pop. (1960) 254,186. A communications, commercial and industrial centre, it manufactures tobacco, chemicals, textiles, foodstuffs and metallurgical products. A bishopric from 695, it became an important religious and political capital in the Middle Ages. The university dates from the 17th century.

UZBEKISTAN, a constituent republic of the U.S.S.R., in Central Asia, on the Aral Sea. Pop. (1962) 8,986,000; area 159,170 sq. miles. It is mountainous with semi-desert plains. It is a leading cotton producer and also raises grain, fruit, silk and rice. Livestock raising and fishing are important. There are deposits of coal, oil, copper, building materials and ozocerite. The leading industries are agricultural machinery, chemicals, paper, textiles, and iron and steel works. The capital is Tashkent (pop. 1,002,000). Other leading cities are Samarkand (215,000) and Andizhan (145,000).

VACCINATION, inoculation with a vaccine for the purpose of producing immunity against a disease. A vaccine is a preparation of dead or weakened bacteria which stimulates the formation of antibodies against a particular disease by inducing it in an extremely mild form.

VALENCIA, a city and port in eastern Spain, on the Turia River, near the Mediterranean. Pop. (1960) 571,452. The centre of a rich agricultural region, it exports citrus fruit, rice, melons, silk and olive oil. Gloves, silk, tobacco and pottery are manufactured. The city was the capital of a Moorish kingdom and temporary capital of the government during the 1936—39 Civil War. It has an old university (1500), a silk exchange (15th century) and a much restored 13th-century cathedral.

VALENCY, the combining power of an atom; it can also be regarded as the number of hydrogen atoms which an atom will combine with or replace, e.g. the valency of oxygen in water (H_2O) is 2. It is determined by the number of electrons (q.v.) in the outermost shell, which cannot exceed the full complement of eight. Elements (e.g. neon) whose atoms have full complements (closed shell) are called inert gases, because they have no valency. An atom which is one short, or which has only one electron in the outside orbit, has a valency of 1; an atom which is short of two or has only two, has a valency of 2, etc. These will more readily give up the odd electrons, receive the electrons required for a full complement, or share electrons with other atoms, and are said to be chemically reactive.

VALENTINE, St (d. *c.* 270), Christian martyr whose feast is celebrated on February 14. The custom of sending valentines is, however, derived from a pagan practice but through association has become connected with the feast of St Valentine.

VALLADOLID, a city in Spain. Pop. (1961) 151,807. It is a railway junction and has several old buildings, including a university and a cathedral. Pottery, gold and silver work, and foodstuffs are manufactured. It is a trade centre.

VALPARAISO, a city and port in Chile, on the Pacific. Pop. (1960) 259,241. A commercial and industrial centre, it is the leading seaport on the Pacific coast of South America. Industries include textiles, silk, railway rolling-stock and locomotives, and chemicals, cement, footwear and foodstuffs.

VANDALS, a Germanic tribe which ravaged Gaul, Spain and North Africa in the 5th century. In 455 they sacked Rome itself and wantonly destroyed the cultural treasures of that city.

VAN DYCK, Sir Anthony (1599—1641), Flemish painter and etcher. The court painter of Charles I of England, where he spent most of his time from 1632, he painted portraits and religious works *(Crucifixion, St Augustine in Ecstasy).*

VANADIUM, see Elements.

VANCOUVER, a city and port in British Columbia, southwest Canada, on the Pacific. Pop. (1961) 790,165. It is a communications, commercial and industrial centre, with an active export trade. The leading industries are fishing, shipbuilding, railway shops, sawmills, foodstuffs, steel and chemicals.

VANCOUVER ISLAND, the largest island off the west coast of North America, belonging to British Columbia, Canada. Pop. (1956) 361,952; area 12,408 sq. miles. It is mountainous, and has valuable forests. Fishing, fruit-growing and dairy farming are important. There are deposits of coal, copper, gold, silver and iron.

VASCO DA GAMA, see Gama, Vasco da.

VATICAN CITY, area of papal sovereignty in the northwest section of Rome. Pop. 1000; area 108 acres. It contains the Vatican and Lateran palaces, gardens, the Church of St Peter, the Sistine and Pauline chapels, a vast library and picture galleries. It is the administrative centre of the Roman Catholic Church and has all the machinery of an independent state. With the Pope's summer palace at Castel Gandolfo, it is all that remains of the Papal States which up to 1861 included much of central Italy. Their possession was confirmed by the Lateran Concordat with Mussolini.

VAUGHAN WILLIAMS, Ralph (1872—1958), English composer. Strongly influenced by English folk music, he wrote nine symphonies (including the 'London' and 'Pastoral'); choral and orchestral works *(Five Tudor Portraits)*; ballet music *(Job)*; and operas *(Hugh the Drover, Riders to the Sea).*

VEDAS, the Hindu sacred books, written in Sanskrit *c.* 1500—200 B.C. The earliest is the *Rig-veda,* composed by priests about the time of the Aryan invasion of northwest India. It contains hymns to the elementary forces of nature (Indra, the god of rain, Surya, the Sun, etc.). The other books are mainly spells, incantations and sacrificial liturgies. The Upanishads (q.v.) were written much later, and represent a reaction towards a more philosophical view of religion.

VEGA, Lope de (1562—1635), Spanish dramatic poet. He wrote lyric poetry and tales and over a thousand plays.

VELÁSQUEZ, Diego Rodríguez de Silva y (1599—1660), Spanish painter. An objective artist, he painted portraits *(The Maids of Honour)*, religious paintings *(Adoration of the Magi)*, mythological subjects (the *Rokeby Venus*), and genre and historical paintings *(Water Carrier of Seville, Surrender of Breda)*.

VENEREAL DISEASES, contagious diseases usually spread through sexual contact. They comprise syphilis, gonorrhoea and chancroid (soft chancre). It is essential to seek early treatment from a qualified doctor; it is equally essential to continue that treatment until the doctor is satisfied that the condition has been cured. One of the major problems in venereal clinics among the less sophisticated communities is the patient who stops attending the clinic when the outward symptoms have disappeared; this is one of the main causes of the serious effects which can, but need not, arise from these diseases, sometimes after as much as 20 years. The other main cause is self-treatment with publicised drugs.

VENEZUELA, a republic on the north coast of South America, on the Caribbean Sea. Pop. (1960) 7,000,000; area 352,143 sq. miles. Generally mountainous, it consists of plains along the Orinoco River in the east central portion. It is a leading producer of petroleum. The principal crops are coffee, cocoa, sugar-cane, cereals, tobacco and cotton. There are rich forest reserves. Minerals include gold, iron, phosphates, manganese, sulphur and diamonds. There are textile mills and cement factories. Venezuela became independent in 1830 after seceding from the Republic of Colombia. The capital is Caracas (pop. 1959 711,673). The second largest city is Maracaibo (345,141) and the third largest is Barquisimeto (153,916).

VENICE, a maritime city in northern Italy, on the Adriatic Sea. Pop. (1961) 336,184. Constructed on a number of islands in a shallow lagoon, it is intersected by 177 canals. The city is noted for its palaces, churches, museums, bridges, guild-halls and other examples of architectural magnificence. It has outstanding art treasures. Venice is a commercial and industrial centre producing glass, jewellery, art work, textiles, ships and steel. Ruled by the doges from the 9th century, it was a powerful republic extending its rule to Lombardy and as far as Greece and the Aegean islands. Until the 15th century, Venice was a great commercial state, becoming also a Renaissance centre of the arts and music. In the 18th century its decline was complete. In 1797 Venice was occupied by Napoleon and later by Austria. In 1866 it became part of Italy.

VERACRUZ, a city and port in Mexico, on the Gulf of Mexico. Pop. (1960) 144,232. Founded in 1519, it is Mexico's most important seaport. It has good communications and is a commercial centre with some industry. There is a university.

VERDI, Giuseppe (1813—1901), Italian operatic composer. He wrote after 1850 some of the finest Italian grand opera, including *Rigoletto*, *Il Trovatore*, *La Traviata*, *La Forza del Destino*, *Don Carlos*, *Aida*, *Otello* and *Falstaff*. He composed the masterly *Falstaff* in his 80th year. Of his other work the *Requiem Mass* and the *Four Sacred Pieces* are outstanding.

VEREENIGING, Treaty of (1902), the peace treaty which concluded the Boer War. It established British authority over the two Boer Republics of the Transvaal and Orange Free State, but granted amnesty to those who had fought against Great Britain and provided for a British indemnity of £3,000,000.

VERLAINE, Paul (1844—96), French poet. One of the first Symbolists, he wrote musical poetry skilfully evoking moods. His works include *Romances sans paroles*, *Jadis et Naguère* and *Sagesse*.

VERMEER, Jan (1632—75), Dutch painter. He was born at Delft, where he seems to have worked, but little is known of his life and few of his works have survived. These few, however, are gems of lovingly detailed tranquil interiors *(The Painter in his Studio)*, landscape *(View of Delft)* and portraits *(Girl with Turban)*.

VERMONT, a northeastern state of U.S.A. Pop. (1960) 389,881; area 9,609 sq. miles. Generally hilly, it is predominantly agricultural. The chief crops are hay, oats, maize, potatoes, maple-syrup, apples and vegetables. Dairy farming and lumbering are important. There are deposits of copper, silver, granite, marble and asbestos. First settled in 1724, it was an independent republic from 1777—91, when it became a state. The capital is Montpelier (pop. 8,782). The largest city is Burlington (35,531).

VERNE, Jules (1828—1905), French novelist. Keenly aware of the trend of technological developments, he wrote scientific romances. His works include *Twenty Thousand Leagues Under the Sea*, *Round the World in Eighty Days* and *Journey to the Centre of the Earth.*

VERONA, a city in northeastern Italy, on the Adige River. Pop. (1961) 221,138. It is a communications, commercial and industrial centre. Textiles, pianos, paper and foodstuffs are manufactured. It has numerous Roman and other historical remains, including marble palaces, statues and tombs, in addition to the famous amphitheatre.

VERONESE, Paolo (Paolo Cagliari; 1528—88), Italian painter. He painted lavish pictures of religious and historical subjects against a Venetian background with contemporary figures (sometimes portraits of famous people); he grouped these with imagination, using novel methods to obtain his effects. Among his greatest canvases are *Marriage at Cana* (Louvre) and *The Family of Darius before Alexander* (National Gallery, London); most of his works are in Venice.

VERONICA, St, according to Christian tradition, was a woman of Jerusalem who took pity on Jesus as he was bearing his cross to Calvary. She used her own handkerchief to wipe the sweat from his face, and the cloth miraculously retained the impression of Christ's countenance. This handkerchief was exhibited in St Peter's, Rome, in 1933.

VERSAILLES, a town in France, near Paris. Pop. (1962) 95,149. The seat of

French kings for more than a century, it contains a famous palace built for Louis XIV. The treaties ending the American War of Independence and the First World War were signed in the palace and the German Empire was proclaimed there in 1871.

VERTEBRATES, animals with a backbone and well developed internal skeleton, a symmetrical body consisting of a head, trunk, and tail region, and a differentiated nervous system. They breathe through lungs, gills or both, possess a closed circulatory system for blood pumped by the heart, and have no more than four limbs. Fish, amphibians, reptiles, birds and mammals are included. They are more properly called Chordates.

VERWOERD, Hendrik Frensch (1901—), South African Nationalist politician. Born in Amsterdam and brought to South Africa as an infant, he was educated at Stellenbosch, Hamburg, Leipzig and Berlin universities, gaining a D.Phil. He was Professor of Applied Psychology (1927) and of Sociology (1933) at Stellenbosch, before becoming in 1937 the editor of the militant *Die Transvaaler*. He was strongly influenced by Nazi ideas, being anti-Semitic, opposing the entry of German refugees into South Africa during the Nazi regime, and never ceasing to agitate against South Africa's participation in the Second World War. Elected Senator in 1948 and appointed Minister of Native Affairs in 1950, he succeeded Strijdom as Prime Minister in 1958. The architect of *apartheid*, he led the campaigns to make South Africa a republic and to leave the Commonwealth. He survived an assassination attempt in 1960.

VESPUCCI, Amerigo (1451—1512), Italian navigator. Employed in commercial houses, he claimed to have made four voyages to the New World. His name (Amerigo) was used by the map-maker Waldseemüller (1507) to denote the new continent. The documents he produced to support his claims contained bearings and distances which were obviously inaccurate, and are generally thought to have been forgeries.

VESUVIUS, a volcanic mountain in southern Italy, overlooking the Bay of Naples. The only active volcano in Europe, it is 3984 ft high. Its eruption in A.D. 79 destroyed Pompeii and Herculaneum. Since then, eruptions in 203, 472, 512, 1631, 1906, 1929 and 1944 have caused considerable damage.

VICHY, a town in south central France, on the Allier River. Pop. (1954) 30,403. It has hot mineral springs supplying drinking water. Vichy was the seat of Marshal Pétain's government from 1940—44 under German occupation.

VICTORIA (1819—1901), Queen of Great Britain and Ireland, and empress of India. She succeeded her uncle William IV to the throne in 1837. In 1840 she married her cousin, Prince Albert of Saxe-Coburg-Gotha. Their happy marriage resulted in nine children. Prince Albert was able to restrain her tendencies to feminine caprice and gave her valuable advice on matters of state. After his death in 1861 she retired into a seclusion so deep as to offend public opinion, but later regained her popularity and was venerated as the epitome of the Victorian virtues. She dismissed Palmerston (1851) and was out of sympathy with the Liberal Gladstone; Melbourne was her favourite minister, but he died in 1848. Disraeli, in spite of his democratic sympathies, gave her great pleasure when he proclaimed her Empress of India; she loved royal pageantry, and the enthusiasm shown at her Golden and Diamond Jubilees (1887 and 1897) did much to lighten the burden of her long widowhood.

VICTORIA, a state of the Australian Commonwealth. Pop. (1961) 2,930,244; area 87,884 sq. miles. In the southeastern portion it is mountainous, with plains in the northwest. The principal crops are cereals, apples and grapes. Livestock breeding is important and the state exports wool, meat, hides and skins and dairy products. There are deposits of gold and coal. Hardware, sugar, textiles, automobiles, agricultural machinery and furniture are manufactured. Until it became a separate colony in 1851, Victoria was part of New South Wales. The capital is Melbourne (pop. 1,907,366).

VICTORIA, capital of Hong Kong (q.v.). Pop. (1960) 1,000,000. A trading centre, it has large textile industries and manufactures iron and steel.

VIENNA, capital of Austria, on the Danube. Pop. (1960) 1,669,546. Once the headquarters of the Hapsburg Austro-Hungarian Empire, and the economic, political and cultural centre of central Europe, Vienna became a sad city of memories after 1918, the capital of a landlocked, mainly mountainous, rump state. The *Anschluss* with Nazi Germany and the Allied occupation, which lasted until 1955, further removed the traces of its former ethos. But the art and other treasures have survived, and the damage to buildings was less serious than it might have been, as it was caused by street fighting and artillery, and not by air bombardment. Most of the old landmarks thus still stand — the Hofburg Imperial Palace (now a museum), the Schönbrunn Palace on the outskirts, St Stephen's Church, the *Rathaus*, the university, the Natural History Museum, and the huge park (the Prater), where after the war scarcely a tree remained. The Opera House was burnt to the ground, but has been rebuilt. Fortunately its geographical position, which made it great, still gives Vienna continuing economic importance. Industries include iron and steel, machinery, chemicals, textiles, paper, rolling stock and gold and silver goods.

VIET-NAM, a region in southeast Asia, divided into two hostile states. South Viet-Nam (pop. 1960 14,100,000; area 66,300 sq. miles), hilly in the north, is predominantly agricultural, producing rice, rubber, tea, coffee, quinine, tobacco, cinnamon, timber, silk, sugar-cane, groundnuts, copra, pigs and poultry. Fishing is important; chemicals, foodstuffs and tobacco are manufactured. The capital is the city and port of Saigon-Cholon (pop. 1958 1,799,175). North Viet-Nam (pop. 1960 15,903,000, area 59,934 sq. miles), mostly mountainous, produces rice, maize, vegetables, tea, coffee, timber and cotton. Fishing is important; there are deposits of coal, manganese, iron, zinc, tin, tungsten, antimony, bauxite and phosphates. Cement, textiles, machine tools, sawmill products and foodstuffs are manufactured. The capital is Hanoi (pop. 1960 643,000). Constituted by the French from the countries of Tonkin, Annam, and Cochin-China in 1946, the Republic of Viet-Nam became independent in 1954.

VIKINGS (Norsemen), the seafaring Scandinavians of the 8th to 10th centuries who, in their long, clinker-built ships with high prow and stern, voyaged to the Mediterranean, where they founded a kingdom in Sicily; to Russia, where Rurik founded the kingdom of Novgorod; to the British Isles, where they were known as 'Danes'; to Normandy, where they were the forebears of

William the Conqueror; to Iceland, Greenland and, according to tradition, North America. Archaeological finds show that they were great craftsmen who quickly mastered and imitated the skills of the countries that they invaded.

Viking longboat

VIRGIL (Vergil; 70—19 B.C.), Roman poet. His first major work, the *Eclogues*, pastoral poems based on Theocritus, brought him to the notice of that famous patron of the arts, Maecenas, and through him to that of Octavian (Augustus). His next work, the *Georgics*, deals with various aspects of farming (bee-keeping, the cultivation of the vine and olive, etc.) but is in essence a song of praise of the Italian countryside. The *Aeneid*, his masterpiece, is a national epic, describing the wanderings of Aeneas after the fall of Troy, his arrival in Carthage where he fell in love with Queen Dido and his desertion of Dido in order to fulfil his destiny by the foundation of Rome. This poem is a celebration of the glories of Roman history, remarkable on many counts but in particular because its hero, Aeneas, is not the embodiment of all the virtues, as might have been expected, but an intensely human being, and because the darker side of war is honestly faced. Virgil's other remarkable achievement was to render the rather intractable Latin language sufficiently ductile for use in a Homeric epic.

VIRGIN ISLANDS, a group of islands in the West Indies between Puerto Rico and the Leeward Islands, divided between the U.K. and the U.S.A. The British group (pop. (1961) 7,338; area 67 sq. miles) lies to the north and comprises 36 islands, of which 11 are uninhabited. The largest is Tortola. Livestock, fish, fruit and vegetables are the chief products. The capital is Road Town. The U.S. group (pop. 1960 32,099; area 133 sq. miles) comprises 50 islands, of which St Thomas, St Croix and St John are the largest. Chief products are rum, bay rum, vegetables and fish, and cattle are raised. There is a tourist trade. The islands were bought from Denmark in 1917. The capital is Charlotte Amalie.

VIRGINIA, an east central state of U.S.A., on the Atlantic. Pop. (1960) 3,966,949; area 40,815 sq. miles. Low-lying in the east coastal region, the surface becomes increasingly high to the west. The principal crops are grains, potatoes, sweet potatoes, cotton, tobacco, groundnuts and apples. Livestock raising and fishing are important. There are deposits of coal, lead, zinc, manganese and silver. The leading industries are tobacco products, textiles and shipbuilding. The scene of the first permanent English settlement in North America (Jamestown, 1607), Virginia played an important role in the early history of the American colonies and of the U.S. It was a member of the Confederacy. The capital is Richmond (pop. 219,958). Other leading cities are Norfolk (304,869), Portsmouth (114,773) and Newport News (113,662).

VIRUS, a substance or organism too small to be seen in an ordinary microscope or caught in the finest filter, but which can be photographed by electron microscope and which, in some forms, can cause disease. The virus diseases in man include the common cold, influenza, measles, mumps, chicken pox, smallpox, poliomyelitis, virus pneumonia, yellow fever and rabies. In plants, viruses produce tobacco mosaic disease in tomatoes and a host of other conditions familiar to the gardener.

The nature of viruses has still to be determined. They were once thought to be extremely small bacteria; later it appeared that they were non-living nucleo-proteins which stimulate the living cell to produce other similar nucleo-proteins, thus representing an intermediate stage between the living and the non-living. Whatever they are, they are found in the cells of plants and animals, where they are parasitic in the sense that only there can they multiply; they are highly specific, i.e. a particular kind of virus is found only in certain tissues of certain species; they are immune to antibiotics, though some viruses inhibit the multiplication of others, and vaccination to forestall the disease is sometimes possible. A feature of virus diseases is that one attack usually gives immunity for life, except for the common cold and influenza.

VISIGOTH, see Goth.

VISTULA, see River.

VITAMINS, organic substances necessary for the proper functioning of the body. An essential part of the diet, they are classified as in the table below. Normal mixed diet produces all the vitamins needed by the body, and the taking of extra vitamins in the form of pills is unnecessary, although usually harmless; an excess of vitamin D may cause damage.

VLADIVOSTOK, a city and port in Asiatic R.S.F.S.R., on the Sea of Japan, U.S.S.R. Pop. (1962) 325,000. The eastern terminus of the Trans-Siberian Railway, it is an industrial centre with oil refineries, and a naval base.

Vitamin	*Function*	*Sources*
A	Growth, healthy skin and mucous membranes; prevents certain eye diseases	Dairy products, liver, fish-liver oils, eggs, leafy yellow vegetables
B-complex		
B_1	Normal appetite; good digestion; metabolism of carbohydrates; growth of young; healthy nervous system; prevents beri-beri	Whole grains, yeast, eggs, liver, meat, beans, peas, lentils and groundnuts
B_2	Lack causes skin lesions and damage to cornea and conjunctiva of eye	Milk, cheese, eggs, whole grains, liver, kidney and lean meat
Nicotinic acid	Prevents pellagra; aids digestion and stimulates appetite; lack harms digestive and central nervous system	Milk, cheese, eggs, whole grains, liver, kidney and lean meat
C	Prevents scurvy; lack causes soreness of gums, loosening of teeth, soreness of joints and tendency to bleeding	Citrus fruit, tomatoes, raw cabbage and potato skins.
D	Prevents rickets; lack causes bones to become soft and teeth to decay	Fish-liver oils, herring, sardine, egg-yolk, liver; ultra-violet rays produce this vitamin in the skin
E	Fertility	Whole grains, eggs, lettuce and leafy vegetables, vegetable oils
K	Blood clotting	Whole-grain cereals, spinach, kale, cabbage.

VOLGA, see River.

VOLGOGRAD, formerly Stalingrad, a city in the R.S.F.S.R., on the Volga River, U.S.S.R. Pop. (1962) 649,000. A commercial and industrial centre, it is situated near rich grain lands and coal deposits. There are oil refineries and steel and engineering products are manufactured. The siege and defence of the city in 1942 against German attack was a turning point in the Second World War.

VOLTA, Alessandro, Count (1745—1827), Italian physicist. He conducted numerous investigations into the nature of electricity and invented the first electric battery (voltaic cell). The practical unit of electrical potential difference, the volt, is named after him.

VOLTAIRE (François-Marie Arouet; 1694—1778), French writer and philosopher. A champion of religious and intellectual freedom, he was often in conflict with the Church and the French court. He attacked the Jesuits and disliked dogma, but he was not an atheist (If God did not exist it would be necessary to invent him). He fought for freedom of speech (I disapprove of what you say, but I will defend to the death your right to say it). In his best work, *Candide*, he attacked Leibniz through Dr Pangloss, who keeps on saying 'all is for the best in the best of all possible worlds' in the face of mounting evidence very much to the contrary. The greatness of Voltaire lies primarily in his stimulation of speculation in others through his incisive and ironic exploration of most realms of thought, rather than in the intrinsic merits of his own books. He spent much of his life abroad, at the court of Frederick the Great, in England, and near Geneva.

VONDEL, Joost van den (1587—1679), Dutch poet. He wrote satirical, religious, lyric and patriotic poems and more than 30 plays *(Jeptha, Lucifer)*, and translated Greek and Latin classics.

WAGNER, Richard (1813—83), German composer. Born at Leipzig, he consorted with Marxists at Dresden and after the 1848 revolution fled to Switzerland for nine years; eventually he was allowed to return and, having won the favour of Ludwig II of Bavaria, to build a national theatre at Bayreuth. His character, life, and views on almost any subject, including music, were deplorable by liberal standards. His operas are at times ludicrously humourless in the Teutonic tradition, but contain some superb music.

Wagner was a revolutionary composer, reacting against the conventions of Italian opera and ambitious to replace it by founding a German school of opera; in spite of his great achievements he was unsuccessful in this, for he had no successors. Becoming his own librettist, he took Scandinavian and other mythologies as his plot sources and invented the *leit-motiv* ('leading theme', a phrase of music attached to a person, emotion or object) to produce a closely knit, highly evocative musical drama of great subtlety. The *Ring Cycle (The Rhinegold, The Valkyrie, Siegfried* and *The Twilight of the Gods)* was his main work, into which he put his feelings on politics, religion and morals. *Tristan and Isolde* was a sensuous expression of hopeless longing for the unattainable, *Parsifal* a mystical evocation of Christianity. *The Mastersingers* is unique, a broad, human comedy, Wagner's only comic opera, but perfect and thus a stumbling-block to the extremer critics of the Anti-Wagner school. Earlier works were *The Flying Dutchman*, *Tannhäuser* and *Lohengrin*, all on the theme of redemption through spiritual love.

WALES, A Principality of Great Britain, part of the U.K., on the Irish Sea. Pop. (1961) 2,196,943; area 7388 sq. miles (excluding Monmouthshire). It is mountainous, bordered on three sides by narrow coastal plains. The Cambrian Mountains (Snowdon 3560 ft), extending from north to south in an arc, are the source of the Severn River which flows southeast into the Bristol Channel. Coal and iron mining in the south are the leading occupations, and there are deposits of copper and zinc. The principal manufactures are steel and steel products, building materials, textiles and tinware. Livestock raising, dairy farming and fishing are important. Wheat, barley, oats and root crops are raised.

The early inhabitants were a mixture of predominantly Celtic peoples. In A.D. 78 the Romans occupied Wales. Cardigan settled there and founded a dynasty, and St David's missionaries converted the rest of Wales in the 7th century. Anglo-Saxon conquerors cut the Welsh off from their kinsmen in Cumberland and Cornwall. Norman penetration, which began in 1072, aroused some resistance. During the reign of Henry I, Wales was reduced to nominal homage to the British Crown. Because the Welsh princes supported the barons, Edward I conquered Wales in 1276—84. To pacify the Welsh, he made his son the Prince of Wales in 1301. There were several small rebellions, culminating in the unsuccessful revolt of Owen Glendower against Henry IV in 1403. Welshmen played a prominent part in the Wars of the Roses on both sides, finally supporting the Earl of Richmond, whose son, Henry VII, descended from an old Welsh family, became King of England and in 1485 reorganised Wales, placing the country under English law. In 1536 the Act of Union joined Wales to England. In the Civil War the Welsh were mainly royalist in sympathy. The Evangelical movement of the 18th century introduced the Nonconformity which is still characteristic of Wales. The Welsh continue to preserve their nationality and their language. The capital is Cardiff (pop. 256,270). Another leading city is Swansea (166,740).

WALLACE, Alfred Russel (1823—1913), British naturalist. After considerable scientific work in South America and the Malay archipelago, he developed a theory of natural selection independently of Charles Darwin. His works include *The Geographical Distribution of Animals* and *Travels on the Amazon.*

WALLACE, Sir William (*c.* 1270—1305), Scottish patriot. Leader of the insurgents against Edward I of England, he won several victories against the English but was captured through Scottish treachery and executed.

WALLENSTEIN, Albrecht von (1583—1634), Bohemian soldier. The outstanding general of the Imperialist forces during the Thirty Years War, he fell victim to political intrigue and was assassinated.

WALPOLE, Sir Robert (1676—1745), English statesman. He served over 40 years as a Whig member of parliament and was, in the modern sense, Prime Minister from 1721—42. His fiscal policy brought England financial prosperity.

WALSALL, a town and county borough in Staffordshire, central England. Pop. (1961) 117,836. It is an industrial centre producing steel tubes, iron and brass goods and leather.

WALTHAMSTOW, a municipal borough, Essex, England. Pop. (1961) 108,788. An industrial and residential suburb of London, it manufactures furniture, plastics and clothing.

WALTON, Izaak (1593—1683), English author. He is known for his work on the delights of fishing as described in *The Compleat Angler, or the Contemplative Man's Recreation* (1653).

WAR, the settlement of national differences by the use of force. The immediate causes of war have been the appearance of a ruler seeking power, the development of political, economic, and social institutions which make aggression worth while, the invention of new tactics, strategy, or weapons which assure an easy victory, economic and political unrest of considerable proportions, and blunders in foreign policy.

WAR OF 1812 (1812—15), a war between the United States and Great Britain. Causes of the war were British support of Indian tribes on the western frontier; the threat to American trade and commerce by British and French blockade; and the rise to power of the War Hawks, a group of young American politicians who mistrusted Britain and advocated American control of Canada. In 1812 the British won the majority of battles, though the Americans countered with successes the following year. In 1814 a triple invasion of America was planned by Britain and, though one force succeeded in burning Washington, the other two were defeated (Battles of Lake Champlain and New Orleans). The war was regarded by the United States as being a second War of Independence.

WARBECK, Perkin (1474—99), pretender to the English Crown. Claiming to be Richard, Duke of York, he gained a following but was defeated in 1497.

WARS OF THE ROSES, see Roses, Wars of the.

WARSAW, capital of Poland, on the Vistula River. Pop. (1961) 1,171,000. It is a communications and industrial centre, producing textiles, chemicals, iron and steel, transport equipment and engineering products. Warsaw became the capital of the Polish kingdom in 1609. It was subsequently occupied by Swedes, Russians, Prussians and Napoleon. Warsaw suffered considerably from Russian rule in the 19th century. In 1939—45 it was almost totally destroyed by the Germans but has since been rebuilt.

WARWICK, Richard Neville, Earl of (1428—71), English military and political leader, known to history as the Kingmaker. He was the head of the House of York during the Wars of the Roses but, as the result of a conflict (1469) with Edward IV, he allied himself with the Lancastrians. He was defeated at Barnet and killed by Edward's forces in 1471.

WARWICKSHIRE, a midland county of England. Pop. (1961) 2,023,289; area 976 sq. miles. Generally lowland, it has deposits of coal, iron, gypsum, manganese and limestone. Grains, fruit, beans, potatoes, turnips, clover and hay are the principal crops. Livestock is raised. Manufactures include iron and steel products, automobiles, jewellery and textiles. The county town is Warwick. Birmingham is the largest city, and Coventry is another industrial centre.

WASH, The, a bay on the east coast of England, between Lincolnshire and Norfolk, on the North Sea. It is 22 miles long and 15 miles wide. Part of it has been reclaimed.

WASHINGTON, a northwestern state of U.S.A., on the Pacific Ocean and the Canadian border. Pop. (1960) 2,853,214; area 68,192 sq. miles. East of the Cascade Mountains, which traverse it from north to south, is a treeless plain, and to the west are lower mountains and a valley. It is a leading timber-producing state and has important fisheries. The principal crop is apples, followed by hops and field peas. Cereals, potatoes, and fruit are raised extensively. Livestock raising is important. There are deposits of coal, lead, zinc, gold, silver, copper, uranium and mercury. The leading industries are foodstuffs and aircraft. First settled in 1811, it was part of Oregon until it became a territory in 1853, and in 1889 a state. The capital is Olympia (pop. 18,057). The largest cities are Seattle (557,087), Spokane (181,608) and Tacoma (147,979).

WASHINGTON, D.C., the national capital of the U.S., on the Potomac River, co-extensive with the District of Columbia. Pop. (1960) 746,958. All branches of the U.S. Government — executive, legislative and judicial — are centred in Washington. The President's offices and residence are in the White House. Congress meets in the Capitol, which dominates the city and determines its layout. There are buildings housing the various departments of government. Washington is also a cultural and educational centre with libraries, museums and universities. The seat of government since 1800, it is a planned city. A British force captured it in the War of 1812 and set fire to a number of government buildings, including the Capitol and the White House.

WASHINGTON, George (1732—99), American statesman, born in Virginia. As Commander-in-Chief in the American War of Independence he received the surrender of Gates at Saratoga (1777) and of Cornwallis at Yorktown (1781). After the war he became the first President of the Republic (1789). He was elected for a second term but refused to stand a third time.

WATER, a liquid resulting from the chemical combination of oxygen and hydrogen. It is colourless, odourless, tasteless, and essential to life, comprising about seven-eighths of a mammal's body. There is no form of life without it. Covering more than five-sevenths of the earth's surface, it also occurs on soil and rocks and in the atmosphere in the form of vapour. Below 32°F, water becomes a solid (ice) and above 212°F it turns into a gas (steam).

WATER-COLOUR, an essentially English technique of painting with pigments ground with water-soluble gums or honey. When diluted with water, these produce a transparent stain, applied in washes to white or tinted paper, the white paper being left untouched to give the highlights. This method is also used in painting miniatures on ivory. Water-colour had a great vogue in the 18th and early 19th centuries for open-air painting of landscape and famous buildings, Cozens, Cotman, Girtin, Turner and Bonington being among the leading practitioners. In water-colours colour is subsidiary to an outline drawn with pen or pencil.

WATERFALL, a precipitous drop in a watercourse. The following are famous waterfalls:

Name	*Location*	*River*	*Height in ft*
Angel	Venezuela	Tributary of Caroni	3300
Gavarnie	Pyrenees, S.W. France	Gave de Pau	1385
Kaieteur	British Guiana	Potaro	741
Kukenaam	Guiana—Venezuela	Ouquenán	2100
Niagara	New York—Ontario	Niagara	167
Ribbon Falls	California	Creek into Yosemite	1612
Sutherland	New Zealand	Arthur	1904
Takakkow	British Columbia	Tributary of Yoho	1200
Victoria	Rhodesia	Zambesi	343
Widow's Tears	California	Tributary of Merced	1170

WATERLOO, Battle of (June 18, 1815), the final and decisive battle of the Napoleonic Wars. The allies (Britain, Belgium, Holland and Prussia) under the leadership of the Duke of Wellington and Marshal Blücher held fast against the onslaughts of the French, and in a counter-attack swept the French from the field.

WATSON, John Broadus (1878—), American psychologist. He founded the behaviourist school of psychology. See Behaviourism.

WATT, James (1736—1819), Scottish inventor. He conceived the idea of separating the condenser of a steam-engine from the cylinder, thus devising an efficient machine useful in industry. In 1775 he joined Matthew Boulton in partnership at the Soho Engineering Works, Birmingham.

WATTEAU, Antoine (1684—1721), French (Flemish) painter. He invented the *fête galante* pictures for which he is famous, in which elegant figures are depicted against a pastoral background. His draughtsmanship was superb, and beneath the superficial frivolity of the subject lie many delicate touches of expression and gesture. His masterpiece is *The Embarkation for the Island of Cythera*, which won him membership of the French Academy.

WATTS, George Frederick (1817—1904), English painter and sculptor. He painted portraits and symbolical pictures. His work includes *Hope*, *King Alfred*, *St George and the Dragon*, *Love and Death*, *Love and Life* and, in sculpture, *Physical Energy*, part of a monument to Cecil Rhodes, of which there is a copy in Kensington Gardens.

WAVELL, Archibald, 1st Earl (1883—1950), British soldier. He saw action in the Boer War and on the Indian frontier before he took part in the First World War, in which he lost an eye. In 1939 he was made commander-in-chief of the British forces in the Middle East and nearly drove the Italians out of North Africa, but the arrival of German reinforcements caused a retreat. He then became supreme commander of British and Dutch forces in southwest Asia for a short time after the entry of Japan into the war; thereafter he was Viceroy of India from 1943—47.

WEALD, The, a triangular area in southeast England between the North and South Downs, comprising part of Sussex, Surrey, Kent and Hampshire. The original forest began to be denuded even before Roman times to provide fuel for the local iron industry. The area is now devoted mainly to orchard and pasture.

WEBB, Sidney, 1st Baron Passfield (1859—1947) and Beatrice (1858—1943), English Socialists and writers on economics and sociology. Married in 1892, they formed a magnificent complementary team. Early members of the Fabian Society, they were instrumental in founding the London School of Economics and *The New Statesman.* Together they wrote a *History of Trade Unionism*, *English Local Government* (10 vols.) and, after a visit to Russia, *Soviet Communism: A New Civilization?* (1935). Sidney Webb was President of the Board of Trade (1924) with reluctance, and, as Lord Passfield, Secretary of State for the Commonwealth and later for the Colonies (1929—31).

WEBER, Carl Maria von (1786—1826), German composer and operatic conductor. His operas include *Der Freischütz*, *Euryanthe* and *Oberon*, the last two handicapped by poor *libretti.* He missed greatness through lack of drive. Of his other works the most noteworthy are the two Clarinet Concertos, the *Konzertstück* for piano and orchestra and *Invitation to the Dance*.

WEBSTER, Daniel (1782—1852), American statesman and orator. Serving as senator (1827—41, 1845—50) and Secretary of State (1841—43, 1850—52), at the threat of secession over the slavery issue in 1830 he finished a speech with the famous words: 'Liberty and Union, now and for ever, one and inseparable'.

WEBSTER, Noah (1758—1843), American lexicographer. He was the author of the *American Dictionary of the English Language* (1828) and *The American Spelling Book*, known as 'Webster's blue-back speller'.

WEDGWOOD, Josiah (1730—95), English potter. Appointed potter to the Queen in 1763, he was especially noted for his reproductions of antique Greek vases and pieces made from designs by Flaxman, in basaltes, jasper and stoneware.

WEIGHTS AND MEASURES, the commonest weights and measures and their metric equivalents are given below:

	Linear measure	
12 inches	= 1 foot	= 0.305 metre
3 feet	= 1 yard	= 0.914 metre
1760 yards	= 1 mile	= 1.609 kilometres
6 feet	= 1 fathom	
6080 feet	= 1 nautical mile	
	Square measure	
144 sq. inches	= 1 sq. foot	= 9.290 sq. decimetres
9 sq. feet	= 1 sq. yard	= 0.836 sq. metres
4840 sq. yards	= 1 acre	= 0.405 hectares
640 acres	= 1 sq. mile	= 2.589 sq. kilometres
	Cubic measure	
1728 cu. inches	= 1 cu. foot	= 0.028 cu. metre
27 cu. feet	= 1 cu. yard	= 0.765 cu. metre
	Liquid measure	
20 ounces	= 1 pint	= 0.568 litre
2 pints	= 1 quart	= 1.136 litres
4 quarts	= 1 gallon	= 4.546 litres
	Weights — avoirdupois	
1 dram	= 27.34 grains	= 1.77 grams
16 drams	= 1 ounce	= 28.35 grams
16 ounces	= 1 pound	= 0.454 kilogram
14 pounds	= 1 stone	= 6.350 kilograms
2000 pounds	= 1 short ton	= 0.907 metric ton
2240 pounds	= 1 long ton	= 1.016 metric ton
	Troy and apothecaries'	
	1 grain = 0,065 gram	
	1 ounce = 31.104 grams	

WEINGARTNER, Felix (1863—1942), Austrian conductor and composer. He conducted in Berlin, Munich, Vienna, etc. His best-known operatic composition is *Sakuntala.* He also composed six symphonies and chamber music.

Basketball (q.v.), the only major sport of wholly U.S. origin, is a very fast ball game which has an enormous following throughout America. The photograph shows a point about to be scored.

Photo: United States Information Service

Cricket (q.v.) the English national summer sport. The batsman, standing before the wicket, has just hit the ball delivered by the bowler.

Photo: Central Press Ltd

American Football (q.v.), was developed from Rugby Football (q.v.). After evading a tackler the runner continues his sprint down the field. *Photo: United States Information Service*

The old Persian game of Polo (q.v.) is one of the few team sports in which mounted ponies are used. *Photo: India House*

Association Football (q.v.), with millions of supporters throughout Europe, has been played in England since the Middle Ages. *Photo: P. A. Reuter*

WELDING, the joining together of two or more pieces of metal (usually the same or similar metals) by applying intense heat to the surfaces to be joined so that they flow into each other. The high temperature is produced either by electricity or gas.

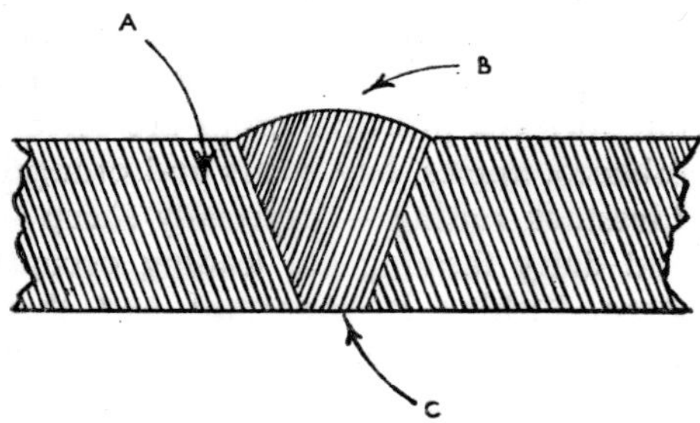

Principle of metal-welding
A. Metal basis B. Weld metal vee C. Fusion to root essential

WELENSKY, Sir Roy (1907—), Rhodesian politician. He joined the Northern Rhodesian Railways in 1924, entered the Legislative Council in 1938 and was appointed to the Executive Council in 1940. In 1941 he founded the Northern Rhodesian Labour party. In the Federation of Rhodesia and Nyasaland he held the posts of Minister of Transport (1953), and Prime Minister from 1956 until the Federation broke up.

WELLAND SHIP CANAL, a waterway in Ontario, Canada, linking the lakes Ontario and Erie. It has three sets of locks and is 27 miles long, 310 ft wide at the top and 30 ft deep. It bypasses the Niagara Falls.

WELLINGTON, capital of New Zealand, on North Island. Pop. (1961) 150,537. A major seaport, it is a commercial centre with manufactures of textiles, engineering products and iron ware.

WELLINGTON, Arthur Wellesley, 1st Duke of (1769—1852), famous British soldier. After having served with distinction in India, he was appointed (1808) commander of the forces which fought against Napoleon in the Peninsular War (q.v.). He was ambassador to Paris when Napoleon escaped from Elba, and led the Allies at the Battle of Waterloo. He served as Prime Minister from 1828—30 and as Foreign Secretary from 1834—35, but without the same success.

WELLS, Herbert George (1866—1946), English novelist. A prolific author, he wrote early science fiction *(The Time Machine, The War of the Worlds)*, novels based on his own early life *(Kipps, History of Mr Polly)*, on the First World War (*Mr Britling Sees it Through*, 1916), short stories *(The Country of the Blind)* and the sweeping, radical *Outline of History* which so annoyed Belloc. Some of his books were filmed, e.g. *The Shape of Things to Come*. He professed to scorn the art of the novelist, using his books to put over the mass of ideas seething in his head on all sorts of subjects; but he was in fact a skilled novelist and short-story writer.

WERFEL, Franz (1890—1945), Austrian poet, playwright and novelist. He left Europe and fled from the Nazis to the United States in 1940. The best-known of his many books are *The Forty Days of Musa Dagh* (1933) and *The Song of Bernadette* (1941).

WESKER, Arnold (1930—), British playwright. Born in London of Jewish parents, after varied employment he wrote a number of plays on social and political themes, with backgrounds supplied by his personal experiences in making a living (*The Kitchen*, *Chips with Everything*, *Chicken Soup with Barley*, *Roots* and *I'm Talking about Jerusalem*). He was active in the Campaign for Nuclear Disarmament, and from 1961 has given much of his time to Centre 42, a movement to encourage an interest in the arts among the workers.

WESLEY, John (1703—91), English clergyman and founder of Methodism. Educated at Oxford, he served as a missionary in Georgia (1735—38), but a chance meeting with Moravian missionaries wrought a spiritual change in his life. He thereafter devoted himself to preaching and organising Methodist societies and classes among the poor.

WEST INDIES, groups of islands extending east and southeast from Florida, U.S.A., and Yucatan, Mexico, to eastern Venezuela. Pop. 16,500,000; area 91,152 sq. miles. They separate the Gulf of Mexico and the Caribbean Sea from the Atlantic Ocean.

WEST IRIAN, a unit of the Indonesian Republic. Pop. (1962) 700,000; area 115,861 sq. miles. It comprises the western two-thirds of the island of New Guinea, and until 1963 was known as Netherlands New Guinea. There are high mountains running east-west and rising to 15,120 ft, and some very large swamps. Oil has replaced copra as the chief export, and rich deposits of cobalt and nickel were discovered in 1956. The capital is Kota Baru (formerly Hollandia).

WEST VIRGINIA, a middle Atlantic state of U.S.A. Pop. (1960) 1,860,421; area 24,181 sq. miles. It is generally mountainous, with large coal reserves. The principal crops are cereals, potatoes, apples, peaches and tobacco. Livestock and lumbering are important. There are deposits of oil, natural gas, lime, salt and building stone. The leading industries are metals and chemicals. West Virginia was formed in 1862 by the inhabitants of the western portion of Virginia after the state had seceded from the Union. It became a state in 1863. The capital is Charleston (pop. 85,796).

WESTERN AUSTRALIA, the largest state of the Australian Commonwealth. Pop. (1961) 736,624; area 975,920 sq. miles. Mountainous in the northwest and southwest, it has large deserts in the interior. The principal crops are cereals, tobacco, apples, hay, pears and oranges. Livestock raising — especially sheep — and dairy farming are leading occupations. Fishing is important and there are timber reserves. The principal minerals are gold, coal, silver, asbestos, lead and manganese. Manufactures include metals, textiles, clothing, rubber and leather goods, foodstuffs, paper and chemicals. The capital is Perth (pop. 419,755, with suburbs and the port of Fremantle).

WESTERN EUROPEAN UNION (W.E.U.), an organisation formed in 1955 by Britain, France, the Benelux countries, West Germany and Italy, when the Allied occupation of Germany ended and West Germany entered N.A.T.O., for collaboration in social and cultural matters and in controlling arms production.

WESTMINSTER, a city and metropolitan borough of London, on the Thames. Pop. (1961) 85,233. It contains the Houses of Parliament, Westminster Abbey, St James's and Buckingham Palace, the Tate Gallery, the Admiralty, War Office, Treasury, Foreign Office and New Scotland Yard.

WESTMINSTER ABBEY, collegiate church in Westminster, London. Built by Edward the Confessor on the site of an ancient church and abbey, it was rebuilt by Henry III and Edward I.

Subsequent additions were made up to the 18th century. From the time of William I it has been the traditional site of coronations, and it contains not only the royal burial vaults but innumerable memorials to the celebrated men of English history.

WESTMORLAND, a county in north-west England, on the Irish Sea. Pop. (1961) 67,222; area 789 sq. miles. It is mountainous and part of the Lake District. Livestock breeding and dairy farming are important. Oats are grown. There are deposits of gypsum, granite, slate, limestone, and lead. Woollen goods, paper and explosives are manufactured. The county town is Appleby.

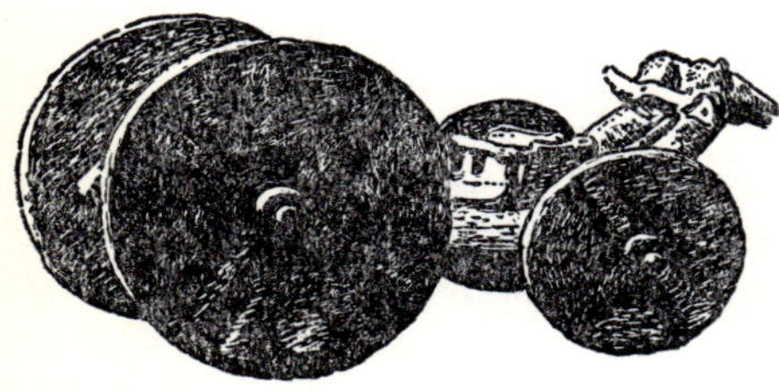

Early solid wheel

WHEEL, a circular frame or solid disc rotating on an axis. Because rolling friction is less than sliding friction, less force is required to move a load on wheels. A wheel firmly attached to an axle is a form of lever since force applied to its rim is multiplied by the radius.

WHIG, in English history the name of the party which opposed the Tories. A word of uncertain origin, it was at first the abbreviated name of the Whiggamore Covenanters (the Scottish Presbyterians), but came to be applied in 1679 to supporters of the bill to exclude the Catholic Duke of York from the succession, and of the 1688 revolution. The Whigs were in power from 1714—60, led by landowning aristocracy but drawing their strength from the middle classes and nonconformists. They stood for religious toleration and reform, and after the passing of the Reform Act of 1832 became known as Liberals.

WHISTLER, James McNeill (1834—1903), American-born painter. Born in Massachusetts, he attended West Point Military Academy, went to live in Paris in 1855 and in 1859 in London. His style was a reaction against the contemporary predilection for pictures in which the subject was dominant; when Ruskin described his *Nocturne in Black and Gold* as 'flinging a pot of paint in the public's face', Whistler sued him, winning a farthing damages — the first of many quarrels. He was influenced by Japanese art, then just coming to be known in Europe. His etchings of London, Venice and Amsterdam were admired even by those who disliked his 'Symphonies' and 'Nocturnes', as were his water-colours. His most widely known portraits are *Thomas Carlyle* and *The Artist's Mother.*

WHITE HOUSE, the official residence at Washington, D.C., of the President of the United States. Designed in 1792, it was destroyed by the British in 1814, but rebuilt according to the original plans.

WHITE SLAVERY, the international traffic in women and children for the purpose of selling them for sexual purposes. It has been stamped out by nearly all governments, with the aid of international agencies, but it still survives in Arabia.

WHITMAN, Walt (1819—92), American poet. A very controversial figure during his lifetime, he is now regarded by scholars and critics as being one of the most original of American major poets.

His best-known works are *Leaves of Grass* and *Democratic Vistas*.

WHITTIER, John Greenleaf (1807—92), American poet, known as the 'Quaker Poet'. A journalist by profession, he espoused the cause of abolition and wrote a number of prose and poetry works attacking slavery. His best-known volumes are *Voices of Freedom* (1846), *Songs of Labor* (1850) and *National Lyrics* (1865).

WIESBADEN, capital of Hessen, West Germany, at the foot of the Taunus Mountains. Pop. (1960) 254,117. It is a wine trading centre and famous for its hot springs. Industries include chemicals, cement, pharmaceuticals and surgical instruments.

WIGHT, Isle of, an island of Britain in the English Channel. Pop. (1961) 95,479; area 147 sq. miles. Separated from southern England by the Solent and Spithead, it is part of Hampshire. Oats, barley, wool, flour and sand are exported. The chief town is Newport.

WILDE, Oscar (1854—1900), Irish author and dramatist. Leader of the aesthetic movement, he was a witty and brilliant writer. His best-known works include the novel *The Picture of Dorian Gray* (1891) and the plays, *A Woman of No Importance* (1894) and *The Importance of Being Earnest* (1899). His imprisonment (1895—97) for homosexual offences resulted in the *Ballad of Reading Gaol* and *De Profundis*.

WILLIAM THE CONQUEROR (1027—87), King of England from 1066—87. As the Duke of Normandy, he appears to have received a promise of succession to the English throne by Edward the Confessor. However, upon the death of the latter (1066) Harold, Earl of Wessex, proclaimed himself king. In the same year William invaded England, killed Harold (Battle of Hastings) and was crowned king. He proceeded to introduce continental feudalism in England, but took care that the central government retained the actual ruling powers.

WILLIAM II (Rufus; *c.* 1056—1100), King of England from 1087—1100. He succeeded his father, William the Conqueror, in England, while his elder brother became Duke of Normandy. The two fought awhile and then joined in alliance against a younger brother. William's extortions brought him into trouble with his barons and with the Church; he spent his last few years ln wars in France. He was killed while hunting in the New Forest.

WILLIAM III (1650—1702), King of England from 1689—1702. Son of William II of Orange. He married (1677) Mary, elder daughter of the future James II of England. In 1688 William and his wife were invited to share the English throne in place of the Roman Catholic monarch James. William was responsible for the organisation of the Grand Alliance against France (1690) which fought the War of the English Succession. William defeated James II, who had landed in Ireland with French assistance, at the Battle of the Boyne. The war ended in the compromise and temporary peace of Ryswick (1697). William took little interest in English domestic affairs and was not popular.

WILLIAM IV (1765—1837), King of England from 1830—37. He succeeded his brother George IV in 1830 and in 1832, by threatening to create new peers, was able to get the Reform Bill passed. Upon his death in 1837, his niece Victoria came to the throne.

WILLIAM I (1797—1888), Emperor of Germany (1871—88) and King of Prussia (1861—88). He is regarded as the father of modern Germany as he succeeded in unifying the country under his rule, under Bismarck's tutelage.

WILLIAM II (1859—1941), Emperor of Germany and King of Prussia from 1888—1918; he was a grandson of Queen Victoria. An impulsive and headstrong ruler, he believed in his divine right to reign and forced Bismarck to resign in 1890. In an attempt to build up a strong Germany he organised the Triple Alliance which then drew Germany into the First World War. He was forced to abdicate in 1918 and fled to spend the rest of his life in Holland.

WILLIAM OF ORANGE (The Silent; 1533—84), Prince of Orange. After unfruitful attempts to curb Philip II's suppression of the Protestants in Holland, he led an open revolt against the Duke of Alba's rule which ultimately resulted in the establishment of the Republic of the United Provinces by the Treaty of Utrecht (1579). He was assassinated by a Roman Catholic fanatic.

WILLIAMS, William Carlos (1883—), American writer and poet. His original and subtle verse includes *Spring and All*, *The Wedge* (1945) and *Paterson* (1946). He has also written novels.

WILSON, Harold (1916—), British Socialist politician. An economist, he held a variety of government offices during 1945—50, when he became President of the Board of Trade. He was leader of the opposition (1963—64 and became Prime Minister in October 1964.

WILSON, Woodrow (1856—1924), American statesman. Elected President of the United States in 1913, he served till 1921. He tried desperately to keep America out of the European conflict, but was finally compelled to ask Congress for a declaration of war. After the First World War the last of his Fourteen Points, which called for a general association of nations, became the cornerstone of the League of Nations, but his programme was rejected in America. Wilson started on a tour of the country in order to gain popular support, but was stricken with paralysis in 1919 and withdrew from active political life.

WILTSHIRE, an inland county in southwest England. Pop. (1961) 422,753; area 1345 sq. miles. Hilly in the north, it is predominantly agricultural. Livestock raising and dairy farming are the leading occupations. There are railway and locomotive works; carpets and broadcloths are also manufactured. Salisbury Plain in the south is used for military training purposes. The county town is Salisbury. Stonehenge and Avebury are famous prehistoric monuments.

WIND, a horizontal movement of air specified by direction and velocity, the latter being measured by anemometer. Winds blow from areas of high atmospheric pressure to low-pressure areas. The earth's rotation deflects winds to the right in the Northern Hemisphere and to the left in the Southern Hemisphere. The distribution of land and water areas also determines the direction and velocity of winds.

WINDSOR, a city in southern Ontario, Canada, on the Detroit River. Pop. (1961) 193,365. It is a communications, commercial and industrial centre. It has oil refineries and is a leading automobile manufacturing city. Chemicals, machinery and foodstuffs are also produced.

WINDWARD ISLANDS, West Indian islands off the north coast of South America. The British group, consisting of Grenada, St Vincent, the Grenadines, St Lucia and Dominica (pop. 290,000; area 826 sq. miles), produces cocoa, nutmegs, coconuts, citrus fruits, bananas, cotton, sugar and vegetables. The Netherlands group consists of St Martin, St Eustatius and Saba (pop. 3692; area 26 sq. miles), and is administered as part of the Netherlands Antilles (q.v.).

WINE, an alcoholic beverage produced by the fermentation of the juice of grapes. The alcoholic content varies from 8—20% by volume. The distinctive character of the many varieties of wine depends on the species of grapes and their locality and method of cultivation. Wines are fortified by the addition of brandy before fermentation.

WINNIPEG, capital of Manitoba, south central Canada, at the junction of the Assiniboine and Red rivers. Pop. (1961) 475,989. It is a commercial and industrial centre with grain, livestock and fur markets. Winnipeg lies at the gateway to a large fishing and hunting region. Its diversified industries include foodstuffs, mining equipment, clothing, iron and steel, and chemicals. It has a university.

WINTER SPORTS, a form of holiday recreation once restricted to countries such as Switzerland and Austria, but now provided in every country where deep snow lies and ice forms for worthwhile and fairly predictable periods. The main sport is ski-ing, and the provision of ski-lifts has made it possible for the beginner to make far more progress in a short holiday than was once the case, while the institution of dry ski-schools has enabled him to start better prepared, and the hiring out of most kinds of ski-ing equipment has removed another obstacle. After learning how to stop and turn on the nursery slopes, the learner will probably want to take part in a novices' race, and then in a slalom, a fast and tortuous downhill race on a course marked by narrowly spaced pairs of flags. Ski-jumping is only for the expert; the skier leaves the platform at about 50 m.p.h. and drops about 150 ft down, and 150 ft outwards, on to a steep slope. A distance of as much as 300 ft has been covered. Ski-joring is, strictly speaking, being towed by unmounted horses, but the term is loosely applied to towing by mounted horses or by vehicle. The bobsleigh takes a team of two to five persons, sitting, of whom the front member steers by wheel or ropes, and the rear member uses a brake. In tobogganing (lugeing), one person lies face down on a sledge and uses his spiked boots to brake. Speeds of 90 m.p.h. have been reached on the Cresta Run at St Moritz, Switzerland, where the winding course drops 514 ft in three-quarters of a mile, with a slope of 1 : 2.8 in one place. Curling is a Scottish game of bowls played on an ice rink with 35-lb stones, which have handles, the player assisting the slowing stone by 'sooping' — sweeping away with a broom at the ice in front of it. Skating includes racing, figure-skating and dancing, all possible also on an indoor rink, as is ice hockey, the characteristically Canadian sport in which a rubber disc (puck) is used instead of a hockey ball.

WISCONSIN, a north central state of U.S.A., on Lakes Superior and Michigan. Pop. (1960) 3,951,777; area 56,154 sq. miles. Mostly a plain, it is the country's leading producer of dairy products. The principal crops are grains, potatoes, cranberries, vegetables and tobacco. Livestock raising is an important occupation. Timber, iron, lead, zinc and building stone are produced. The chief manufactures are automobiles, machinery, furniture, paper, beer and canned foods. First settled in 1670, it was part of New France until 1763, when it became British. It became a state in 1848. The capital is Madison (pop. 126,607). The largest city is Milwaukee (741,324).

WITCHCRAFT, the practice of magic by persons who are believed to have sold their souls to evil forces. It has been associated with various religions. It flourishes mainly among people with little understanding of natural phenomena, during periods of psycho-social stress.

WITTENBERG, a city in East Germany, on the Elbe River. Pop. (1960) 48,100. Known as the 'Cradle of the Reformation', it is the city in which Martin Luther taught and is buried. It has many relics of his life and work, including the door on which he nailed his 95 theses against indulgences in 1517.

WOLSEY, Thomas (*c.* 1471—1530), English cardinal and statesman. He had great political influence during the reign of Henry VIII, but when he was unable to secure a divorce for Henry from Catherine of Aragon, he fell from favour. On suspicion that he had recommended to the Pope that Henry should be excommunicated if he married Anne Boleyn, he was arrested, and died of dysentery on his way to the Tower of London.

WOLVERHAMPTON, a city and county borough in Staffordshire, England. Pop. (1961) 150,385. Situated near iron and coal mines, it is a leading industrial centre. Industries include machinery, tools, steel products, chemicals, electrical appliances, plastics and rubber goods. The church of St Peter was constructed in the 13th and 14th centuries.

WOMEN'S SUFFRAGE, the right of women to vote. The National Union of Women's Suffrage Societies was founded in Great Britain in 1897. British women were given the right to vote in municipal elections in 1907. In 1918, women over 30 were granted the franchise. Age discrimination was finally removed in 1928. See Franchise; Feminism.

WOOD, Grant (1892—1942), informally trained American painter, well known for the skill with which he related human subjects to architectural backgrounds.

WOOLF, Virginia (1882—1941), English essayist and novelist. Together with her husband, Leonard Woolf, she founded (1917) the Hogarth Press. Her best-known works include *To the Lighthouse* (1927), *Orlando* (1928), *The Waves* (1931) and *The Years* (1937).

WOOMERA, a base for testing guided missiles in South Australia, 272 miles northwest of Adelaide. Nuclear weapons are also tested there.

WORCESTERSHIRE, a Midland county, England. Pop. (1961) 568,642; area 699 sq. miles. The principal crops are hops and fruit. Livestock raising is important. Coal is mined. There are porcelain manufactures. The county town is Worcester.

WORDSWORTH, William (1770—1850), English poet. Born in Cumberland, he went to school at Hawkshead in the Lake District. In 1790—92 he paid visits to France, where the Girondins won him over to warm support of the French Revolution in its early stages. The later atrocities produced a deep disillusion described in the *Prelude*, of which the sub-title, *The Growth of a Poet's Mind*, sets the theme. His first important work was *Lyrical Ballads*, a joint volume of poems which he published with Coleridge; it was designed as a protest against the stately traditional poetic diction, and its extreme simplicity of language and subject-matter produced results that were sometimes moving and sometimes banal. This training in writing poetry in everyday English had a lasting effect on his work. It was in the *Preface* to this book that he defined poetry as taking its origin from emotion recollected in tranquillity. In 1779 Wordsworth went to live with his sister Dorothy at Grasmere in the Lake District, where he was joined by the other Lake Poets, Coleridge and Southey, and in 1802 married his cousin Mary, Dorothy continuing to live with them in amity. There followed some of Wordsworth's best sonnets, a form in which he excelled, on liberty, independence, London and other subjects, the outstanding *Ode on Intimations of Immortality* and the rather dull *Excursion*. After 1815 Wordsworth's poetic powers began to fail, as he was aware, and he wrote little of importance; in 1843 he succeeded Southey as Poet Laureate.

WORLD HEALTH ORGANISATION (W.H.O.), formed in 1948 by the U.N. to co-ordinate international health work.

WORLD WAR, First (1914—18), a war which began as a local conflict between Austria-Hungary and Serbia but which eventually involved most of the world. Following the assassination in Sarajevo of Archduke Ferdinand of Austria by a Bosnian nationalist, Austria declared war (July 28, 1914) on Serbia. Russia began immediate mobilisation against Austria, and Germany in turn declared war on Russia (August 1). As France was bound by treaty to Russia, Germany invaded France and Belgium in order to free herself from the threat on the west. The German invasion of Belgium brought Britain into the war on August 14, and a British Expeditionary Force landed in France on August 16. Japan declared war on Germany and Turkey allied herself with the Central Powers in the same year. The German offensive in France was brought to a standstill (October) and both sides settled down to trench warfare along a line stretching from Switzerland to the English Channel which was not significantly changed until the closing stages of the war, despite the German use of poison gas (from April 22, 1915) and the British use of tanks (from September 15), and futile, costly offensives such as the Battle of the Somme (July 1916). In the east the Germans dealt the invading Russian army a devastating blow at Tannenberg (August 26—30, 1914) and invaded Russian Poland in the following spring. British imperial forces tried to relieve the pressure by the diversion of the Dardanelles campaign, but this ended in failure (April-December, 1915). Italy joined the Allies in May, and was decisively defeated by the Austrians at Caporetto in October of the following year. On February 1, 1917, the Germans took the fatal step of opening unrestricted submarine warfare, which brought the U.S.A. into the war in April; the first American troops landing in France on June 26. Their entry was balanced by the disappearance of Russia from the war after the October Revolution. Germany made a final effort to break through on the Western Front in March 1918, but Allied counter-attacks in August brought the war to an end with the abdication of the Kaiser and the Armistice of November 11, 1918.

As to naval operations, after the Battle of Jutland (May 31, 1916) the German fleet remained in port, the men mutinying in October 1918. German submarines sank 16,000,000 tons of Allied and neutral shipping, and the convoy system and other anti-submarine measures were introduced only just in time to prevent complete disaster in 1917.

Air forces were in their infancy at the beginning of the war, but by its end all the main features of future air warfare had been developed, day bombing, night bombing, anti-submarine attack and aircraft carriers; but it was all on a very small scale compared with the Second World War.

By the end of the war the total number of persons killed (including Russian) was 8,000,000, of whom nearly an eighth were British. Lord Kitchener's campaign brought 3,000,000 volunteers to the British armed forces before conscription was introduced in 1916. The number of killed in Commonwealth forces was: India (British and Indian) 73,000; Canada 75,000; Australia and New Zealand 79,000; South Africa 9000 and the Colonies 52,000. The cost to the Allies in money was £40,000 million, of which £13,578 million was contributed by the British Empire. The political results included the reconstitution of Poland as an independent state, the setting up of the new states of Czechoslovakia and Yugoslavia, and the separation of Hungary and Austria.

WORLD WAR, Second (1939—45), a war started by Hitler to acquire *Lebensraum* (living space) for Germany and to recapture the German colonies lost in the First World War. The war was started by the German invasion of Poland on September 1; Britain and France, who were pledged to defend Poland, declared war on Germany two days later, and British troops landed in France on September 11. Germany invaded Denmark and Norway in April, and a small British expedition to help Norway achieved nothing and was withdrawn. The war in Western Europe, after a period of uneasy quiet known as 'the Phoney War', opened on May 10 with the German invasion of Holland, Belgium and France, which made swift progress on a narrow front by the use of panzer divisions backed by Stuka dive-bombers against a French army completely demoralised by the failure of the Maginot line of fortifications. On May 10 Churchill became Prime Minister, and at the end of that month British ships evacuated 335,490 troops from Dunkirk. Mussolini declared war on June 10 hoping, but in vain, to share some of the spoils won by his pupil. France finally capitulated on June 25, the southern half of the country being left unoccupied under the aged Pétain assisted by Laval. Britain was left to carry on alone for 12 months under intensive air attack from August 15, mainly directed against London. In December Wavell began to drive the Italians out of Cyrenaica; German reinforcements arrived and Rommel's Afrika Korps staged a counter-attack at the end of March. In April British troops freed Abyssinia and Germany overran Yugoslavia and Greece. Hitler then invaded Russia on June 22, 1941, reaching Kiev in September and Stalingrad a year later. On December 7, 1941, the Japanese surprise attack on Pearl Harbor brought the U.S.A. actively into the war. In the next few months Japan occupied Malaya, the Philippines, Burma, the Netherland East Indies, Hong Kong and New Guinea.

In the summer and autumn of 1942 the first large-scale air raid on Germany (a thousand-bomber raid on Cologne), the U.S. fleet action off Midway Island, and Montgomery's offensive at El Alamein, marked the turning of the tide, reinforced by Allied landings in North

Africa in November and the beginning of the German retreat from Russia in January 1943. By July North Africa was cleared of the enemy, the occupation of Sicily had led to Mussolini's fall, and the Allied invasion of Italy began. A new phase of the war opened with the Allied landings in Normandy on D-day, June 6, 1944, six days before the first V.1 flying bomb fell on London, followed by landings in the south of France. Paris was liberated in August and Allied forces entered Germany in September, in which month the V.2 rocket attack on London began. On October 25 the U.S. naval victory at Leyte Gulf ended Japanese sea-power. Cologne, Vienna and Berlin fell in the spring of 1945, and U.S. and Russian forces met face to face in Germany on April 27. A few days later Hitler committed suicide and the war with Germany ended on May 8. Atomic bombs were dropped on Hiroshima and Nagasaki, and Japan capitulated on August 14.

In the British Commonwealth forces 544,000 were killed, of which 398,000 came from the British Isles. The U.S.A. lost 292,000 killed, and the Germans some 2¾ million. British air raid casualties among civilians totalled 60,595 (compared with 1413 in the First World War); atomic bombs killed 71,379 at Hiroshima and 35,000 at Nagasaki, out of a total of Japanese homeland civilian casualties from air-raids of 330,000. Britain spent one-quarter of its total national wealth on the war, and liquidated all its foreign overseas investments. The political results of the war included the emergence of the U.S.A. and the U.S.S.R. as by far the most powerful states in the world.

WREN, Sir Christopher (1632—1723), English architect. He designed many public buildings in London after the Great Fire of 1666, including St Paul's Cathedral, additions to Hampton Court Palace, much of Greenwich Observatory and Chelsea Hospital and 52 churches.

WRESTLING, a sport in which there are many styles. The most widespread in Britain is Catch-as-catch-can (Lancashire or Free style), in which the wrestlers start apart and then try to throw one another by various grips or trips, and continue to struggle on the mat to win a fall by forcing both the opponent's shoulders against the ground. In the Cumberland and Westmorland style, also popular in Scotland, the contestants first of all spend much time locking themselves together in a tight hold, with the left arm below and the right arm above the opponent's shoulder. Throws are by footwork only and there is no struggling on the ground; the wrestler whose clasp is broken loses. In West Country or Cornish style the wrestlers wear strong jackets, to which holds must be restricted; there is no mat fighting. On the Continent the Graeco-Roman style is more popular; in this the men start apart, holds must be above the waist, tripping is not allowed, and there is no ground fighting. The U.S.A. introduced professional all-in wrestling, sometimes in mud; it is a spectacle, not a sport, in which the participants groan as if in extreme agony. Judo, a simplifed form of the Sino-Japanese Ju-jitsu, demands a thorough knowledge of anatomy, of how to fall, of the nerve centres through which an opponent can be paralysed, and of holds which give him the choice of yielding or having a bone broken. As a sport, strict rules are required to keep it under control; even stricter rules are needed in Karate, a form so dangerous that moves are merely indicated, not made.

WRIGHT, Frank Lloyd (1869—1959), American architect. He displayed great originality, giving consideration to the kind of materials, the function of the building, and the nature of the climate and the surroundings. Wright integrated diverse building techniques and revolutionised the use of glass. He built the Imperial Hotel in Tokyo, and many private houses.

WRIGHT, Orville (1871—1948) and Wilbur (1867—1912), American inventors and aeronautical pioneers. After experimenting with kites and gliders, they were the first men to fly in a motor-driven heavier-than-air machine. In December 1903 Wilbur flew their aircraft for a distance of 852 ft in 59 seconds.

WROCLAW (Breslau), a city in southwest Poland, on the Oder River. Pop. (1961) 443,000. A commercial and industrial centre, it manufactures textiles, machinery, ships, foodstuffs and porcelain.

WUHAN, see Hankow.

WYCLIFFE, John (*c.* 1324—84), English religious reformer. As a popular preacher he attacked the higher clergy, and when the Pope attempted to suppress him, he renounced papal authority. Together with Nicholas of Hereford, he made the first complete translation of the Bible into English (*c.* 1382). His teachings later had a great influence on Huss and Luther. See Lollards.

WYOMING, a western state of U.S.A. Pop. (1960) 330,066; area 97,914 sq. miles. Mountainous, with the Rockies in the west, it consists of a plateau and rolling plains in the east. The principal crops, cultivated mostly by irrigation, are lucerne, sugar-beet, potatoes and cereals. Cattle and sheep raising is important. There are fisheries and large herds of elk. Minerals consist of oil, natural gas, uranium, coal and iron. Yellowstone National Park is a favourite tourist attraction. The capital and largest city is Cheyenne (pop. 43,505).

XERXES I (*c.* 519—465 B.C.), King of Persia. Son of Darius Hystaspes, he embarked on the conquest of Greece (481) with a huge army, was briefly held by 300 Spartans at Thermopylae, and went on to burn Athens and drive the Greek forces back to the Isthmus of Corinth. He was defeated in the naval battle of Salamis (480), and fled, leaving Mardonius to be put to rout on land by combined Greek forces at the Battle of Plataea (479). Xerxes was assassinated.

X-RAYS (Röntgen Rays), an electromagnetic radiation with a wave-length 1/1,000th to 1/10,000th that of visible light, which penetrates all matter to varying degrees, depending on its density. They are produced when electrons pass through matter. Because they affect photographic film in the same way as light does, they are of value in photographing internal organs of the body, which cast shadows of varying density on the film behind the object.

YANGTZE, see River.

YAROSLAVL, a city in the R.S.F.S.R., on the Volga River, U.S.S.R. Pop. (1962) 443,000. A communications centre, it manufactures motor vehicles, synthetic rubber, chemicals, machinery and textiles. Founded in the 11th century, it is the oldest city on the Volga.

YEAST, microscopic single-celled fungus plants which multiply extremely rapidly by budding. They secrete enzymes which convert sugars into alcohol and carbon dioxide. For this reason they are important in the manufacture of wines, beer and industrial alcohol. They are also used in baking bread which the liberation of carbon dioxide causes to rise. Yeasts are used commercially as a source of proteins and vitamins.

YEATS, William Butler (1865—1939), Irish poet and dramatist. He immersed himself in Irish mythology (the 'Celtic Twilight'), the occult (with Mme Blavatsky and his second wife, who was a medium) and Japanese No-plays, and fell under the influence of Ezra Pound and an immensely wide and varied circle of literary friends. With age came a growing acceptance of the realities of life, such as the Irish revolution and the everyday poverty of Ireland; he even became a Senator (1922—28). Much of his poetry ranks among the best of the century; his verse plays were rather less successful. With Lady Gregory and J. M. Synge he founded the Abbey Theatre movement in Dublin. He was awarded the Nobel Prize for literature in 1923.

YEMEN, a republic in southwest Arabia, on the Red Sea. Pop. (1960) 5,300,000; area 75,920 sq. miles. It is in general mountainous, with a semi-desert coastal region. The principal products are cereals, pearls, gum, resins and coffee. Stock raising is important. The capital is San'a. In 1958 it was federated with the United Arab Republic; in September 1962 the Imam was deposed and thereafter there was civil war between the republicans backed by Egypt and the Imam's party backed by Saudi Arabia. The U.N. intervened in 1963.

YENISEI, see River.

YEOMEN OF THE GUARD, a military corps established by Henry VII in 1485 as a personal bodyguard for the king. Commonly referred to as 'Beefeaters', they now number about a hundred men, employed on ceremonial occasions and as Wardens at the Tower of London.

YEREVAN (Erivan), the capital of the Armenian S.S.R. in the U.S.S.R. Pop. (1962) 583,000. In the centre of a rich agricultural region, the city uses the abundant hydro-electric power locally available to produce synthetic rubber, machinery, textiles and chemicals.

YOKOHAMA, a city and port in Honshu, Japan, on Tokyo Bay. Pop.

(1960) 1,375,100. A financial, commercial and industrial centre, it is a major exporting city. The leading industries are shipbuilding, metal, petroleum products, machinery, chemicals, automobiles and foodstuffs. The city was nearly completely destroyed by an earthquake in 1923. More than half of it suffered serious damage in the Second World War.

YORK, a city and county borough in Yorkshire, England, at the junction of the Ouse and Foss rivers. Pop. (1961) 104,468. It is a trading and industrial centre producing railway rolling-stock, foundry products, machinery, glass, chocolates and leather goods. Formerly surrounded by walls, parts of which still stand, York has an ancient cathedral and historic churches.

YORKSHIRE, the largest county in England, on the North Sea. Pop. (1961) 4,722,661; area 6081 sq. miles. It is hilly in parts, with moors in the northeast and northwest. Administratively it is divided into the three Ridings. The East (pop. 527,051; area 1172 sq. miles) and North Ridings (pop. 554,382; area 2128 sq. miles) are sheep-grazing regions with farms, cultivating grain, sugar-beet, potatoes and turnips, and the North Riding has a thriving iron-ore and heavy industry. The West Riding (pop. 3,641,228; area 2780 sq. miles) is more highly industrialised, with coal-mines, textiles, steel and steel products, and engineering goods. The county town is York. Leeds, Hull, Middlesbrough, Bradford and Sheffield are other leading cities.

YOUNG PRETENDER (1720—88), or Charles Edward Stuart (Bonnie Prince Charlie), was the son of the Old Pretender (q.v.). He landed at Moidart in the Western Highlands in 1745, but the second Jacobite rebellion (see Jacobites) ended in the defeat at Culloden. Prince Charles was helped by Flora Macdonald and others to escape to France in disguise. He tried in vain to enlist Spanish and Prussian support for his cause. Like his father, he died in Rome.

YOUNGHUSBAND, Sir Francis Edward (1863—1942), British soldier, diplomat and explorer. After exploring Manchuria, he served in India and in Tibet, and negotiated a treaty with Tibet in 1904.

YTTERBIUM, see Elements.

YTTRIUM, see Elements.

YUCATAN, a state in southeast Mexico, in the Yucatan peninsula, bordering on the Gulf of Mexico. Pop. (1960) 614,049; area 23,926 sq. miles. Dry and hilly, it is tropical in the south, with valuable forests. Cereals, sisal and cotton are cultivated. Most of the inhabitants are descendants of the ancient Maya people whose ruined cities and temples can still be seen.

YUGOSLAVIA, federated people's republic in southeast Europe, on the Adriatic Sea. Pop. (1961) 18,549,291; area 98,386 sq. miles. Yugoslavia consists of the six republics of Serbia, Croatia, Slovenia, Montenegro, Bosnia and Herzegovina and Macedonia. It has rugged coastal ranges, and fertile plains and valleys in the north and southeast. Primarily agricultural, it produces grain, tobacco, hemp, potatoes and sunflowers. Livestock breeding is a leading pursuit. Lumbering and fishing are also important. There are considerable minerals, including coal, iron, copper, gold, lead, bauxite, manganese, petroleum, chrome, antimony and cement. The leading industries are iron and steel, cement, chemicals and textiles. The kingdom of

Yugoslavia was formed in 1919 and, in 1921, Alexander I of Serbia was crowned King, but was assassinated in 1934. Axis troops who invaded the country in 1941 were opposed by the guerrilla army under the leadership of Josip Broz (Tito). After the defeat of Germany the Federal People's Republic of Yugoslavia was established. The capital is Belgrade (pop. 1961 585,234). Other leading cities are Zagreb (430,802), and Sarajevo (143,117).

YUKON, see River.

YUNNAN, a province in southern China, on the Burmese border. Pop. (1953) 17,472,737; area 162,342 sq. miles. It is in general mountainous and traversed by rivers. The principal crop is rice, followed by other grains, beans, tobacco, tea and silk. Cattle breeding is important. There are deposits of coal, marble and salt, and most of the important metals. Yunnan has been independent for several periods in its chequered history, and was the principal centre of the great Mohammedan rebellion of 1856—72. The capital is Kunming.

Z

ZAGREB, capital of Croatia, Yugoslavia, on the Sava River. Pop. (1961) 430,802. It is a cultural, commercial and industrial centre, manufacturing machinery, textiles, chemicals, paper and asbestos. Under Hungarian rule until 1918, it was known as Agram.

ZAMBEZI, see River.

ZAMBIA, a self-governing state within the British Commonwealth, formerly the British protectorate of Northern Rhodesia in the Federation of Rhodesia and Nyasaland. It achieved independence in 1964. Pop. (1963) 3,545,000, including 74,000 Europeans and 11,200 Asians and Coloureds; area 288,120 sq. miles. The Zambesi forms the boundary with (Southern) Rhodesia. Agriculture is of little account, the chief crops being maize, tobacco and groundnuts. The wealth of the country is concentrated in the copper mines, and to a much lesser extent in the lead and zinc mines of Broken Hill. The copper comes from one narrow strip on the Congolese Katanga border, known as the Copperbelt, and it provides 90% of the total value of exports. Industry is mostly based on the mines. The Victoria Falls attract tourists to Livingstone. The capital is Lusaka; there are several large townships in the Copperbelt.

ZAMENHOF, Lazarus Ludwig (1859—1917), Russian oculist and philologist. He invented the artificial language of Esperanto for the purpose of promoting international understanding.

ZAPOROZHE, a city in the Ukraine, U.S.S.R., on the Dnieper River. Pop. (1962) 490,000. Near the Dnieper dam are large deposits of coal and iron. A major industrial centre, it produces iron and steel, steel alloys, aluminium, ball-bearings, machine tools, tractors, machinery and chemicals.

ZARAGOZA (Saragossa), a city in northeastern Spain, on the Ebro River. Pop. (1961) 326,316. It is a trading centre, having textile and paper mills, iron foundries and breweries. A Moorish city from 777—1118, it was captured by Alfonso I of Aragon, who made it his capital. It has two imposing churches serving as cathedrals, and also a university.

ZEALAND (Sjaellan), the largest and most important Danish island, between the Kattegat and the Baltic Sea. Pop. 1,251,661; area 2840 sq. miles. It is level and fertile. The main town is Copenhagen.

ZEN BUDDHISM, a sect which came into existence in China about the 6th century, but flourished chiefly in Japan after the 13th century, where it was adopted by the Samurai. The aim is to establish contact with the inner workings of our own being as directly as possible without the intervention of anything external. Thus there is in Zen no god, no scripture and no dogma. The student is taught by shock tactics to act spontaneously without thinking and, through the meaningless conundrums that are a Zen feature, to recognise the uselessness of mere words to describe the ultimate realities. Zen Buddhism was a salutary reaction against the Japanese addiction to logical disputation, and it is perhaps for similar reasons that its introduction into Europe by Dr D. T. Suzuki has had such success.

ZEPPELIN, Count Ferdinand von (1838—1917), German inventor. He designed a rigid airship used for a short time from 1910 for a passenger service. Zeppelins were used to bomb Britain during the First World War, but proved very vulnerable. Two Zeppelins operated a transatlantic passenger service after the war, which was discontinued when the *Hindenburg* was burnt out in 1937.

ZEUS (Roman Jupiter), the chief of the Greek gods after he had overthrown his father Kronos. He was originally an Indo-European god of the sky (Sanskrit, Dyaus). His consort was Hera, who bore him Ares and Hephaestus. His numerous amours with mortal women produced Dionysus, Apollo, Artemis and Hermes. He was also the father of the Muses and the Graces. He dwelt with the other gods on Mt Olympus in Thessaly. He alone was allowed to use the thunderbolt.

ZHDANOV (Mariupol), a city in the Ukraine, U.S.S.R. on the Sea of Azov. Pop. (1962) 321,000. It is a major port, and manufactures iron and steel and chemicals.

ZHDANOV, Andrei (1896—1948), Russian political and military leader. He planned the 1939—40 military campaign against Finland, and directed the defence of Leningrad (1941—43). He was the organiser of the Cominform, the successor to the Comintern.

ZINC, see Elements.

ZIONISM, a Jewish nationalist movement organised on a political basis in 1897 for the purpose of re-establishing Palestine as the homeland of the Jewish people. The founding of the state of Israel in 1948 resulted from its efforts.

ZIRCONIUM, see Elements.

ZODIAC, an imaginary belt of the sky lying on each side of the sun's path in its annual movement. It includes the paths of the moon and of all the planets, except Pluto. The zodiac is divided into 12 sections, each consisting of a distinct constellation, which the sun traverses in one year. It is a convenient way of showing the positions of heavenly bodies.

ZOLA, Emile (1840—1902), French novelist. He started his career as a Romantic, but later came under the influence of the Naturalists and became one of their leaders. He established his reputation with the publication of *Thérèse Raquin* (1867) and his subsequent novels enjoyed an equally phenomenal success. In 1898 he began a campaign in defence of Dreyfus with the polemical article *J'accuse,* for which he was exiled.

ZOOLOGY, the branch of biology (q.v.) dealing with the animal kingdom. It includes the classification, structure, distribution, physiology, mental life, group behaviour, ecology, ethnology and life histories of all living creatures, with the exception of man. See Invertebrates; Mammals; Vertebrates.

ZOROASTER (Zarathustra; *c.* **660—583 B.C.),** a Persian prophet who taught a type of monotheism and preached that the world was governed by two forces namely good and evil. Zoroastrianism was all but destroyed by the Moslem conquest, though it is still extant among the Parsees of India, who were converted by refugees fleeing from the Moslems. The sacred scriptures are contained in the *Avesta.* The religion is also sometimes called Mazdaism, although this is properly the name of the pre-Zoroaster traditional religion. See Manichaeism.

ZULULAND, a former African kingdom, now a province in Natal, in the Republic of South Africa, on the Indian Ocean. Pop. 398,000; area 10,427 sq. miles. The principal crops are sugar-cane and cotton. It was annexed by the British in 1887.

ZURICH, a city in northern Switzerland, on the Limmat River by Lake Zurich. Pop. (1960) 433,400. The financial, cultural and educational centre of the country, it manufactures textiles, paper, machinery, electrical goods and foodstuffs. It contains many historical churches, one of which dates from the 9th century, and the 17th-century *Rathaus.*

ZWINGLI, Ulrich (1484—1531), Swiss religious reformer and one of the founders of the Reformed Church. Through his efforts the Reformation became firmly established in Zurich, where he served as pastor, but he had less influence than Calvin on Swiss Protestantism.